TheResourceful Reader SIXTH EDITION

Suzanne Strobeck Webb
Texas Woman's University

Lou Ann Thompson
Texas Woman's University

THOMSON
™
WADSWORTH

Australia ▪ Canada ▪ Mexico ▪ Singapore ▪ Spain ▪ United Kingdom ▪ United States

The Resourceful Reader
Sixth Edition

Suzanne Strobeck Webb and Lou Ann Thompson

Publisher: *Michael Rosenberg*
Acquisitions Editor: *Dickson Musslewhite*
Development Editor: *Karen Smith*
Production Editor: *Eunice Yeates-Fogle*
Director of Marketing: *Lisa Kimball*
Executive Marketing Manager: *Carrie Brandon*
Marketing Manager: *Katrina Byrd*

Senior Print Buyer: *Mary Beth Hennebury*
Compositor: *Thompson Type*
Project Manager: *Anne Seitz*
Photo Manager: *Sheri Blaney*
Cover Photograph: *Juliana Sohn for +hp Brand Campaign*
Cover Designer: *Brian Salisbury*
Printer: *Maple-Vail Printers*

ISBN: 0-8384-0779-X

Library of Congress Control Number: 2003107226

Preface

The Resourceful Reader, Sixth Edition, has been designed expressly to accompany the *Harbrace Handbooks*, both **Hodges' Harbrace Handbook, Fifteenth Edition,** and **The Writer's Harbrace Handbook, Second Edition.** This unique design provides a harmonious interaction between handbooks and reader and, as a result, offers the instructor unprecedented efficiency in teaching. The book, of course, can be used independently of either handbook. This sixth edition has been extensively revised to bring it more in line with current writing theory.

    Sixty-one reading selections, more than half of which are new, focus on contemporary, sometimes controversial subjects while acknowledging the importance of classic concerns, addressed by such well-known authors as Maya Angelou, Richard Rodriguez, Martin Luther King Jr., Bruce Catton, Desmond Morris, Virginia Woolf, and Henry David Thoreau. The authors of both classic and contemporary essays have strikingly different personalities and voices, and write on different subjects, with various purposes, and for various audiences—but all use the particular development strategy being studied in that chapter and often combine strategies.

    The selections are arranged in chapters according to the development strategies outlined in *Hodges'* 15e/*Writer's* 2e—namely, **example, narration, description, process, cause and effect, comparison and contrast, classification and division, definition,** and **argument.** An additional chapter presents a collection of classic essays and images.

    While the **general introduction** continues to stress the interaction between reading and writing and focuses on active, critical reading as well as on the writing process, it has been thoroughly revised and expanded to reflect more current writing theory, asking students to consider the rhetorical situation and to focus on meaning, purpose, audience, and rhetorical strategy as well as on language, grammar, and style. It has nearly tripled in length and now addresses matters of purpose, audience, and occasion in detail, discusses strategies for analyzing images as well as texts, and describes the various methods of development. It provides basic information on finding and exploring a topic, limiting and focusing a subject, developing ideas, planning, drafting, revising, and editing.

    Specific rhetorical issues concerned with audience, purpose, and organization are a significant component of each **chapter introduction.** These introductions define and explain the method of development exemplified by the reading and image selections, offer advice for using the method of development, and provide an annotated student essay (seven of which are new) illustrating the method of development. Noteworthy features of the student essay are identified in the margin, and a subsequent commentary discusses the writer's strategies and choices. Although possible improvements to the student essays are sometimes noted, the emphasis in the commentaries is always positive, stressing the student's achievement. Each chapter introduction concludes with a checklist, summarizing the chapter's points into helpful step-by-step guidelines students can use to revise their own writing.

The Resourceful Reader now includes a **visual rhetoric component.** Chapters 1–9 each include two images that exemplify the rhetorical mode under examination. Questions accompany each set of images, which help students examine visuals rhetorically, just as they read texts rhetorically. Four classic images complete the selections for Chapter 10, "For Further Reading: Classic Essays and Images." The images are not offered merely as gratuitous supplements, but are intended to be an integral part of the discussion of rhetoric.

Throughout, *The Resourceful Reader* aims to demonstrate for students that "the rules"—presented concisely in a handbook—are not arbitrary but are simply principles that good writers apply in writing purposeful compositions. Each professionally written piece is introduced by a note that places the essay in a context, usually social, cultural, or biographical. Each piece is also followed by a strong pedagogical apparatus that includes two sets of questions keyed to the handbooks. References to the handbooks help students understand how the authors applied the handbook principles to their writing. Throughout, the questions in *The Resourceful Reader* emphasize choice: students are continually asked to put themselves in the writer's place and evaluate the writer's opinions. These questions, even the grammatical ones, have been rethought to shift the focus to the rhetorical aspects of the writing process.

- **"Rhetorical Considerations"** direct attention to the choices writers make given the rhetorical context—the audience, purpose, and occasion as well as the rhetorical strategy. These questions focus on concerns treated in *Hodges'* 31–42/*Writer's* 1–15.
- **"Language and Style"** frame matters of grammar and punctuation as rhetorical choices authors have made to reach their audiences and achieve their purposes. These questions alert readers to the ways in which grammar, sentence effectiveness, and diction are rhetorical. Answering them can help develop awareness about the choices writers make—choices that are sometimes conscious, but are often unconscious. These questions focus on concerns treated in *Hodges'* 1–7 and 19–30/*Writer's* 16–30.
- We have also enhanced the **"Writing Suggestions"** provided for each reading, which prompt students to consider the rhetorical situation in their own writing. These writing assignments are always related to the reading but are designed to afford students considerable freedom of choice.

The Resourceful Reader acknowledges that even the best of writers are not exempt from occasional infelicity, a pronoun reference that could be clearer, a modifier that squints a little. We have turned such lapses into pedagogical advantage by asking students to consider the writers' choices and the effectiveness of those choices. In each instance, the student is referred to the appropriate section of the handbooks.

For the convenience of those who wish to compare essays that approach similar subjects with different rhetorical strategies, we have classified them in **"Contents Arranged by Subject,"** which follows the regular table of contents. The regular table of contents includes a brief annotation following each essay's title to give a glimpse of its content. An index makes basic rhetorical concepts, authors, and titles easy to find. As a further aid to the busy instructor, an Instructor's Manual is available (ISBN: 0-8837-7095-4).

Acknowledgments

Numerous people have rendered invaluable help and advice in the preparation of *The Resourceful Reader*, Sixth Edition, for which we are very grateful. Dr. Deb Martin and Christa Downer of Texas Woman's University provided help with the student essays. Thanks also are due to Dr. Sandi S. Reynolds for preparing the Instructor's Manual and Heather Jensen for preparing the index. Continuing thanks go to Roy Fowler and Keisha Jackson for the student essays we have retained from the fifth edition. We also thank Alice Green, Marta Salazar, Veronica Ashida, Timothy Davis, Joaquin Campos, Tanisha Carter, and DeVon Freeman for the seven new student essays. Continuing thanks also go to those who have been particularly helpful and supportive with earlier editions: Kimberly Allison, Tom Broadbent, Marilyn Keef, Bob Miller, and Larry Mapp.

We particularly wish to thank our reviewers for their helpful advice in this extensive revision:

Valerie M. Balester, *Texas A&M University*
Dana Siciliano di Rende, *Riverside Community College*
Rose Mary I. Foncree, *Belhaven College*
L. M. Grow, *Broward Community College, Central Campus*
Ron Israel, *San Diego Mesa College*
Christopher L. Litten, *Florida Hospital College of Health Sciences*
Magnolia Miller-Hampton, *Hinds Community College, Utica Campus*
David Mulry, *Odessa College*
Gary Sligh, *Lake-Sumter Community College*
Angie VanArnam, *Grand Valley State University and Grand Rapids Community College*

At Wadsworth, our thanks go to publisher, Michael Rosenberg; acquisitions editor, Dickson Musslewhite; development editor, Karen R. Smith; production editor, Eunice Yeates-Fogle; director of marketing, Lisa Kimball; executive marketing manager, Carrie Brandon; and photo manager, Sheri Blaney, all of whom have made valuable suggestions and provided other kinds of help.

On a more personal note, we would like to thank R. J. Webb for taking care of things while we worked, and our animals for warming our feet and purring in our ears: Nanni, Cletus, Lisa, and Bodhi; Attila, Chloe, Houdini, and Ralphie.

Suzanne Strobeck Webb
Lou Ann Thompson

Contents

Chapter 4 Process   159

Chapter 7 Classification and Division 295

Chapter 8 **Definition**   339

Contents Arranged by Subject

Culture and Society

Disability

Global Concerns

History and Politics

Humor and Satire

Identity

Language and Writing

Law

Race and Ethnicity

Reform and Revolution

Religion, Spirituality, and Philosophy

Science and Technology

War and Conflict

Reading to Write, Writing to Be Read

Imagine you are digging on an archaeological site and one day you unearth a pot, intricately patterned, variously colored, miraculously whole after centuries of burial. As you hold the pot in your hand, your mind moves from admiration of the object to speculation about how, and by whom, it was created—an awareness that the pot is an artifact, something made by human hands and human intellect. Chances are, however, that it was not made on the first try. Not only did the potter probably have to make hundreds of pots to acquire the skill to produce those graceful lines, but also he or she undoubtedly shaped and reshaped the clay to get that very pot just right. Yet all you have is the pot. The earlier versions are gone, absorbed long ago into the final lovely thing you hold in your hand, and no record of the potter's labor to create it survives.

Like the pot, the selections in this book, both essays and images, are artifacts, things created by human intellect. The writers and image makers, like the potter, began with little more than their own hands and minds and experience. As readers, we see their finished creations, complete and as close to perfect as they could make them—scarcely a seam anywhere, scarcely a lump or lopsidedness. Faced with a finished essay—a text—readers seldom think much about the process (slow, rarely straightforward, often downright messy) that produced it, seldom are aware of how the writer may have labored to discover what was worth saying, then struggled to get the right words into phrases, clauses, sentences, paragraphs that would enable the reader to re-create, from black marks on a page, the ideas that were in the writer's mind. Images are texts, too, and communicate meaning by ordering marks on a page, on a screen, or on film. The artist struggled with balance and proportion, tones of light and dark, color, the right focus, and the right framing to create the image that would convey to the viewer what the artist had in mind. Like anything made with skill and effort, the images and the essays look easy and natural—just as their creators intended.

But as you read the essays and examine the images, you can reconstruct (though not perfectly) the process their creators went through, and in doing so learn much about writing well. This kind of reading requires the investment of time, effort, and attention, but it is an investment that will return a large profit because reading and writing go together: reading improves your writing, and writing makes you a better reader. When you tackle a text as an active, involved reader, you go through much of the same process that you go through to create one, only in reverse. Beginning with the finished product, you take it apart to see how another writer or image maker met challenges similar to those you face when you write. As you analyze the many kinds of choices these authors made, you increase your understanding of the options available to you. Reading can be a rehearsal for writing. *The Resourceful Reader,* designed to be used along with the fifteenth edition of *Hodges' Harbrace Handbook* or the second edition of *The Writer's Harbrace Handbook,* provides the materials for that rehearsal. You, of course, must supply the effort.

Reading to Write

To get the most from any text, you should read it at least twice, the first time for a general idea of what the writer is saying, the second time—and perhaps more times—to see how the writer has gone about saying it, to examine all the means the writer used to make the text work.

Active Reading

As you reread the text, do so actively, pencil in hand to jot down notes in the margin or mark important ideas. *Preview* the text by first looking through to note headings, if any, to check the length, and to get a general idea of what will be involved when you read it. Read through the text rapidly for the *gist* of what the text tells you—the general impression you get on your first time through. Write that down in the margin or near the title of the text. On your next reading, *annotate* the text. Mark important information, note definitions of terms, and identify the main points the author makes. When you have finished that pass through the text, you are ready to *summarize* each of the main points in the essay and state the author's position. Finally, *respond* to the text in writing: what is your position? Do you agree with the author? Why or why not? Is the presentation convincing? Is any important point omitted?

The Rhetorical Situation

An awareness of the rhetorical situation—the author's *purpose, audience,* and *exigence*—will help you understand many of the decisions the writer made while writing. (See *Hodges'* 32a/*Writer's* 1e for more information.)

Purpose

Perhaps the most basic consideration is *purpose*—what the writer intends to accomplish. Is the author's aim to inform the reader, focusing on the topic as objectively as possible, as Jacqueline Berke does in "The Qualities of Good

Writing" (Chapter 7)? Or is the purpose to persuade, to sway the reader to take some action or adopt some point of view the writer considers desirable? For instance, Randall Kennedy argues eloquently in "You Can't Judge a Crook by His Color" (Chapter 9) that "taking race into account at all means engaging in discrimination." (406) And sometimes writers are not so much concerned to inform or persuade a reader as to express themselves—that is, to explore and share their own personal feelings and responses, as John Hockenberry does in his moving "The Hockenberry File" (Chapter 2). But the question of purpose is not a simple one. As you read, bear in mind that in any effective piece of writing one purpose or another is likely to be dominant, but other purposes are sure to be present to some degree. Although Hockenberry's primary aim is to provide information, his essay certainly contains expressive elements and unquestionably aims to persuade us of something, too. And Kennedy's essay, though chiefly persuasive, is also informative.

Audience

Whatever the writer's purpose, to achieve it successfully the writer must have a clear sense of *audience*. Indeed, purpose and audience can scarcely be separated, since all writing is presumably meant to be read by someone (even if only the writer, as with a diary or a grocery list). You can learn a great deal about writing effectively for your own audiences by considering how other writers have written for theirs. Occasionally you will find that the writer explicitly names the intended audience, but more often you will have to infer from clues what kind of audience the writer had in mind. (One possible clue is external: if what you are reading has been published in, for example, a magazine—as some of the reprinted essays in this book originally were—ask yourself what kind of audience that magazine is aimed at.) Consider the tone of the essay, for tone reflects the writer's attitude toward the audience as well as toward the subject. Does the writer seem to assume that the audience will be sympathetic? Interested? Indifferent? Hostile? Consider, too, the writer's assumptions about the reader's knowledge. Does the writer either take pains to define specialized words or to confine the vocabulary to words most general readers would be likely to understand? A piece written for specialists will assume considerable knowledge on the part of the reader and is likely to use a specialized vocabulary. (Although none of the essays in this book were written for highly specialized audiences, you can see a sample of such writing online at www.harbrace.com.)

Exigence

The third element of the rhetorical situation—*exigence*—refers to the circumstances that occasioned the writing, a specific need to write at a certain time or under particular conditions. Exigence combines with purpose and audience to form the context for the writing. For instance, at the time John Hockenberry wrote his essay on Kosovo, the shootings at Columbine High School had torn the nation's attention away from the refugees' plight. Those circumstances contribute to Hockenberry's purpose of getting the United States to pay attention once again, and that purpose relates to his audience—the

American people as well as the readers of *We* magazine, a journal that focuses on issues related to disabilities.

Thesis

With the context clearly in mind, you will be ready to focus more specifically on other elements of the essay. Look for the *thesis*—the central or controlling idea, the main point the writer is making. Being able to pick out and evaluate the thesis of a piece of writing is the very essence of active reading. Often the thesis is stated, but if it is not, it will be implicit in what the writer has to say about the subject. Even in a piece of writing that is mainly descriptive, there will be some focus or reason for describing, some dominant impression the writer means to create in the reader's mind; the details will not be randomly chosen. Similarly, in a narrative some attitude toward the events will be suggested—if not explicitly, then implicitly through the writer's choice of events, details, and language appropriate to his or her view. (See *Hodges'* 32c/*Writer's* 2b for more information.)

Images

Visual literacy involves first looking at an image and seeing exactly and completely what that image depicts and, second, making meaning from what was seen. To do that, you must ask yourself several questions:

- What is in the image? What is its content? That is, are there people, animals, plants, landscapes, buildings, etc.? What kinds and how many of those things does the image portray? In what relationship to each other?
- What is the focus of the image? Among all of the items that may be included in an image, which one seems to be the central or most important figure? Identify and describe it. If the focus is people, describe what is happening, how many people there are, what they are doing, how they look—their dress, the expressions on their faces, and so on. If the focus is an object, what is it, what is it made of, what does it look like?
- What is the setting of the image? Is it indoors or outdoors? What objects, such as furniture or plants, are included? Describe them.
- What is my response to the content of the image? Is my response in any way influenced by the composition of the image? If so, how?

Once you have answered those questions, you will be better able to understand the meaning the artist or photographer was trying to convey. To do that, ask yourself the same kinds of questions you would ask yourself about a verbal text—what is the purpose, who is the audience, what is the exigence?

Methods of Development

One of the most practical things you can do as a reader trying to become a better writer is to pay attention to how other writers and image makers use the various *methods of development* (around which the first nine chapters of this book are organized): (1) example, (2) narration, (3) description, (4) process, (5) cause and effect, (6) comparison and contrast, (7) classification and division, (8) definition, and (9) argument. These are not hollow forms into which writers or photographers pour sentences or images to make texts; they are fundamental *thinking* strategies, basic ways human beings make sense of the world and communicate that sense to one another. Terms such as *narration* and *classification* may sound forbidding and technical, but if you run through the list of strategies again and consider the kinds of common questions each strategy answers, you will see how natural these methods are:

- *Example*—What are some instances?
- *Narration*—What happened (or is happening)?
- *Description*—How does it look, feel, taste, smell, or sound?
- *Process*—How does this work? How is this done?
- *Cause and effect*—Why did this happen? What will be the result?
- *Comparison and contrast*—What is it like? How is it different?
- *Classification and division*—What kinds are there? What are its parts?
- *Definition*—What is it? What does it mean?
- *Argument*—What should be done? What should we believe?

Understanding and practicing these strategies will do more than teach you how to organize essays. You will use them every day, not only in all of your college courses but also in virtually every part of your life beyond the campus. (See *Hodges'* 32e/*Writer's* 2e for more information.)

Analyze the Text

Consider a text's introduction, conclusion, and title. Is the title appropriate? How does it serve (and reveal) the writer's or image maker's purposes? Does it help to establish the tone of the text? (See *Hodges'* 33b/*Writer's* 3b for more information.) If the text is written, does the introduction arouse your interest and get you oriented in the essay by suggesting what it is about? Would you have introduced the essay differently? Why? Does the conclusion bring the essay to a satisfying close?

Analyze the text for logic and for unity and coherence. Has the writer avoided logical fallacies? (See *Hodges'* 35f/*Writer's* 7i for more information.) Are there digressions or irrelevancies? What kinds of signposts does the writer provide to help readers follow the thought from paragraph to paragraph and sentence to sentence? Are the ideas presented in the most effective order? Is each idea adequately developed? Try to see how the writer's concern about these issues has contributed to making the essay effective. If you find weaknesses (no writer is perfect), ask yourself how the writer might have done better. (See *Hodges'* 32b/*Writer's* 2a and 3c for more information.)

Consider the essay at the level of the sentence and the word, with an eye to what you can learn for your own use as a writer. How are sentences constructed to avoid monotony, to achieve the exact emphasis desired, to convey precisely the relationships among ideas? Is anything unclear—for instance, the reference of a pronoun or the relation of a modifier to what it modifies? Are there awkward constructions or inappropriate choices of words or figurative language to distract or confuse the reader? Can you think of better choices the writer could have made? Conversely, where the writer has said something more effectively than you think you would have said it yourself, see if you can explain the difference. (See *Hodges'* 1–7/*Writer's* 16–22 (Grammar), *Hodges'* 18–22/*Writer's* 28–30 (Diction), and *Hodges'* 23–30/*Writer's* 23–27 (Effective Sentences) for more information.)

The writer's choices regarding punctuation and mechanics are also worth studying. Even though punctuation and mechanics are governed to a considerable extent by convention, there are more choices to be made than you may realize—including, of course, the choice to be "correct," to avoid violating the conventions in ways that would distract the reader and undermine your credibility, thereby interfering with communication. Ask questions as you read: Why has the writer chosen to set off a particular parenthetical expression with dashes instead of parentheses or commas when either of these alternatives would have been acceptable? Why has the writer put that word in italics when regular type would also have been correct? Why did the writer choose a semicolon between two clauses instead of a period, or instead of a comma and a coordinating conjunction? Why is a colon better here than a semicolon? Why is this hyphen necessary? (See *Hodges'* 12–17, or *Writer's* 27–35 for more information.)

As you consider all the choices, large and small, that other writers have made, you are continually reconstructing the processes they went through and, in a very real sense, rehearsing for your own writing. Let's now focus on what happens when you write for other readers.

Writing to Be Read

As you have seen, writing is never done in a vacuum. When you write, you are always in a specific situation that involves an *audience,* a known or perhaps hypothetical reader, whose background and interests you must consider; a *purpose* for writing, something you mean to accomplish; and a *subject,* something you will write about. Often your writing situation will clearly dictate your subject; for instance, essay examinations in college courses often specify a topic, and letters and reports written on the job usually deal with subjects that are either assigned or obvious.

When the subject is given, your purpose may seem obvious, too, but you will usually find it worthwhile to consider your purpose a little more carefully: it may not be as simple as you think. Consider the essay examination again. If the question is, "Explain the difference between the budget deficit and the national debt," your purpose seems clear enough: *to explain.* And explain you must, of course, if you want to receive credit. But consider: your instructor *knows* the difference between the budget deficit and the national debt, so your main purpose is to *convince* the instructor, by your explanation, that you have mastered certain basic concepts. Similarly, much business writing is devoted primarily to giving information, but if those writers were not just as much concerned with persuasive aims—giving a favorable impression and winning customers—as with conveying information, business letters might read like this: "Dear Client: The widgets cost $5.00. Yours truly."

Finding and Exploring a Topic

In a college writing course, you may sometimes be entirely free to choose your own subject. If so, you can write an interesting paper on almost any subject you care about. Think about your personal knowledge, interests, and beliefs. What have you read lately? Do you know an interesting character? Has some particular place made a special impression on you? What do you do when you're not in school? Do you work? Do you have a specific interest such as photography or playing in a band? What ambitions do you have for yourself? What are your convictions? What makes you angry? You can find subjects in any of these questions for papers that will interest other people.

Journaling and Freewriting

Or you may want to take advantage of some common strategies for finding a subject. You may want to keep a journal (*Hodges'* 32b/*Writer's* 2a(1a))—a *personal notebook* in which you explore how you feel about what is going on in your life, a *writing journal* in which you keep a record of ideas for future writings and in which you explore those ideas, or a *reading journal* in which you respond to the reading you are doing, perhaps commenting on it, arguing with it, or relating it to your own experiences. Perhaps you will find that *freewriting* will help you find a good topic. (See *Hodges'* 32b/*Writer's* 2a for more information.) Writing for ten minutes or so without stopping and without worrying about what you are saying or how you are saying it often turns up ideas you were unaware you had.

Listing, Clustering, and Questioning

(See *Hodges'* 32b/*Writer's* 2a for more information.) Other approaches to finding a good topic include *listing, clustering,* and *questioning. Listing* is sometimes called *brainstorming.* The point of this informal process is to collect as many ideas as you can in such a way that you can see them at a glance without having to comb through long passages of writing. As in freewriting, ideas may pop up in no particular order and you need not worry about spelling, word choice, or grammar while your ideas are flowing. Just jot them down as fast as you can.

Clustering is a similar technique, in which you place your ideas in a kind of map that shows the relationships among them. To begin, write your general topic in the middle of the page and draw a circle around it. As you think about that topic, sprinkle the ideas that occur to you around the page and circle each of them so that they form nodes around the main circle; then, draw lines to connect each of them to the central circle. Each of these nodes will probably sprout its own collection of ideas that you can circle, and you will soon have a page with circles surrounding circles and interconnecting in a variety of ways.

Questioning involves two structured techniques: *journalist's questions* and Kenneth Burke's *pentad*. With journalist's questions, you ask yourself the following about your topic—Who? What? When? Where? Why? How? These simple questions can help you discover something to say about any topic. For instance, if you were collecting ideas for an essay on a recent crime, you might ask the following questions:

- Who was the criminal? The victim?
- What happened? Think about the sequence of events.
- When did it happen? Was it daytime or evening, winter or summer, this year or a decade ago?
- Where did it happen? What city and state, and where in that location? In a rural area? At a resort? In an alley, beside a pool, behind a barn?
- Why did it happen? What did the criminal or the victim do to precipitate the crime?
- How did it happen? Did the criminal use a gun? Act alone? Plan it carefully? Do it on impulse?

When you use Burke's pentad, you examine the relationships among five elements common to all events—act, actor, scene, agency, and purpose. This technique can reveal more subtle details about your topic. For instance, the same crime examined with the pentad might generate the following questions:

- *Act/actor*—What happened and who did it?
- *Act/scene*—What happened and under what conditions of time and place?
- *Act/agency*—What happened and how was it accomplished?
- *Act/purpose*—What happened and why did all the elements come together to make it happen?
- *Actor/scene*—Who did it and under what conditions of time and place?
- *Actor/agency*—Who did it and how was it accomplished?
- *Actor/purpose*—Who did it and why did all the elements come together to make it happen?
- *Scene/agency*—Under what conditions of time and place did it happen and how was it accomplished?

- *Scene/purpose*—Under what conditions of time and place did it happen and why did all the elements come together to make it happen?
- *Agency/purpose*—How was it accomplished and why did all the elements come together to make it happen?

Limiting and Focusing Your Topic

Limiting

It is more likely, however, that your freedom to choose will be limited in some way. Outside a composition classroom, you will rarely be free to choose a subject drawn from your own experience. For instance, your geology professor may give you complete freedom to write on any aspect of geology that interests you, but you are expected to write a paper demonstrating your mastery of some part of the subject matter of the course. Geologists are interested in mountains, but a paper about the elation you experienced when you successfully completed a difficult ascent of Mount St. Helens, despite the fact that the mountain is an active volcano, will not do. In such a situation, instead of relying on personal experience, look for an interesting subject in your textbook, in your lecture notes, or in the subject catalog in the library; talk to other students or to your professor.

Focusing

Whatever your subject, your writing task will be easier and your finished composition more effective if you take some time to explore your subject and get it sharply in focus before you begin drafting. Visual artists are accustomed to limiting and focusing a subject—to putting boundaries around it, perhaps reducing its scope—to make it manageable and, as with the subject of a photograph, are skilled at deciding on the particular angle from which they wish to view it, what they will highlight, and what they will eliminate as extraneous. When you write, you must also determine the boundaries and scope of what you write and decide what person, object, or concept you will focus on. (See *Hodges'* 32b/*Writer's* 2a for more information.)

Thesis Statements

Constructing a clear, specific thesis statement can help you decide whether you have limited and focused your subject sufficiently and will also help you stay on track as you draft the essay. (See *Hodges'* 32c/*Writer's* 2b for more information.) Writers rarely pluck thesis statements out of thin air. They develop them bit by bit as they limit and focus their subject, establish their purpose, and identify their audiences. This will lead to a controlling idea—a thesis—that will direct your first draft. A thesis is usually a single sentence that states your main idea. For instance, Bruce Catton states his thesis in "Grant and Lee" as follows:

> [Grant and Lee] were two strong men, these oddly different generals, and they represented the strengths of two conflicting currents that, through them, had come into final collision. (256)

Like all good thesis statements, Catton's tells us what he is writing about (two Civil War generals) and why (they are representative of the conflict). It suggests that by showing how these men are different (the method of comparison and contrast) he will illuminate some reasons for the conflict (his approach or purpose). But Catton probably did not come to this thesis statement right away. For most writers such a thesis would be the result of continual revision and refinement of their essay. As you refine your ideas in subsequent drafts, your thesis statement, too, may change.

Developing Ideas

If you have carefully considered your subject and purpose, chances are that the appropriate method of development will follow naturally. For instance, suppose exploring possible subjects for a history term paper led you to focus on famous battles in American military history. You would naturally develop your paper differently depending upon which battles and which aspects of those battles you wanted to use to sharpen your focus.

- *Narration*—What happened in the battles?
- *Process*—How did Grant (or Lee) win (or lose) the battles?
- *Cause and effect*—What events and conditions led to these confrontations?
- *Description*—What kind of battles were they? What did the battlefields look like?
- *Definition*—What distinguishes a *battle* from a *skirmish*? Were these encounters *battles*? Why or why not?
- *Classification and division*—How can I classify the different kinds of fighting that occurred in the Civil War? What are the qualities of a pitched battle or of a naval encounter?
- *Example*—What are some examples of important battles?
- *Comparison and contrast*—How are certain battles in the Civil War the same as some battles that occurred in the Spanish-American War but different from most of those that occurred in the Revolutionary War?

As we've noted, these development strategies are ways in which our minds naturally work. Your task as a writer involves not merely choosing appropriate development strategies, but also employing them effectively. Reading and, above all, practice—writing—are the ways to learn.

Planning

Often, especially for a long paper, you may find it helpful to write down some kind of plan, an informal or even formal outline of your main ideas in what seems the most effective order, to guide you as you write (see *Hodges'* 32d/*Writer's* 2c for more information). The most common kinds of plans are *lists, outlines,* and a *classical arrangement.*

Lists

A *list* is the simplest kind of plan. All that's involved is to jot down your the-sis followed by the main points you plan to cover and then indicate the gen-eral order in which you want to arrange them. A simple list for a paper describing a place you know well might look something like this:

> Thesis: Elk River Falls was a natural and unspoiled playground.
>
> what and where is it?
>
> getting there
>
> the waterfall
>
> the big pool
>
> the rocks

In a list like this, you may find that some of your points overlap. For in-stance, it may not be possible to describe the big pool without describing the rocks. You may not need to cover all of the points, or you may need to add others as you draft. A simple list such as this is easy to modify.

Outlines

You may sometimes need to develop a plan with more detail; a teacher may require it or perhaps you need to submit your plan for approval. And you don't always have to create your outline before you begin to draft. One of the most important uses of an outline is to discover what you may need to do to revise your work. An *informal* or *topic outline* (see *Hodges'* 32d/*Writer's* 2c(2) for more information) for the same subject might contain the follow-ing items:

> I. Introduction
>   A. What Elk River Falls is
>   B. Where Elk River Falls is
> II. Getting there
>   A. Driving directions
>   B. Parking at the trail head
>   C. Following the path to the Falls
> III. The recreation spot
>   A. The waterfall
>   1. Height and width
>   2. How it is made
>   3. What it looks like
>   B. The big pool
>   1. Diameter
>   2. Depth—cold water
>   3. The rock ledges around the bowl
>   a. Formed by basalt
>   b. Make good seats

C. The rocks
   1. What they are made of
   2. What they look like
   3. How they got that way
IV. Conclusion
   A. How the Falls has changed
   B. Why I prefer the memory

Sometimes you may need to state each item in a sentence rather than a phrase. Such an outline might begin as follows:

I. Elk River Falls was a natural and unspoiled playground.
   A. Elk River Falls flows into a natural basalt basin.
   B. Elk River Falls is near the town of Elk River, Idaho.

Classical Arrangement

Another way to organize your writing is to follow a *classical arrangement.* This pattern includes the following:

- an *introduction*—the place to get your readers' attention and state your thesis;
- the *background information*—a description of the subject or a detailing of the *issues, facts,* or *circumstances* that are involved;
- the *discussion*—the information that supports your thesis;
- a *refutation* of opposing views—countering objections and alternate viewpoints;
- a *conclusion*—the place to summarize or highlight significant points, suggest fruitful subjects for further study or a plan of action to follow.

This pattern is particularly useful for persuasive writing. Any plan you develop, however, whether it is a simple list or a sentence outline, is not written in stone; you can change it if you need to, and you probably will.

Drafting

When you begin drafting your essay, try writing quickly, without much concern for matters such as spelling, punctuation, and usage, which you can revise later. Many writers find that this approach is the most productive. The point is to get your ideas to flow as freely as you can, while keeping your purpose and audience in mind. Incidentally, no law says that you must begin at the beginning and slog straight through to the end in spite of any difficulties you may encounter on the way. Some writers find that writing chunks or blocks of an essay without worrying about the order makes their ideas flow more freely; then they put the chunks together, reshaping and connecting them as necessary.

Writer's Block

If you run out of steam in one part of your essay, try moving to another part you feel more comfortable with. Some writers find that when they're stuck, it may help to turn back to what they've already written and look for ways to improve it by correcting errors, finding more exact words, restructuring sentences, or making paragraphs more coherent. (This is revision, but you don't have to wait until you have a complete draft to engage in it. You are, in fact, revising all the time, even while you are planning.) The value of this procedure is that it keeps you engaged with the essay while your unconscious mind has a chance to work on the problem that stopped you. However, you may find that sometimes the best remedy is simply to take a break and think about something entirely different for a while—perhaps take a walk or cook dinner—to give your mental batteries an opportunity to recharge, and then come back fresh to the draft. Researchers on creativity have found that breakthroughs commonly occur when the individual has first struggled hard to solve a problem and then temporarily turned away from it to think of something else. Experiment and find a method that works for you. You aren't exactly like anyone else; your writing process won't be exactly like anyone else's, either.

Revising

This may be the most important step in the writing process. The actual parts of the word *revision* mean "seeing again." Revision gives you the opportunity to see your writing again—as though you have not seen it before. To make yourself ready to do that, set your completed draft aside for a time (if possible a few days, but at least overnight). When you come back to it, try to see it as though someone else had written it. Reading it aloud may help—or having someone else read it to you. Go over your draft several times, first looking to see if you have included all of the information you need, and then checking to see that you have presented that information with the meaning you intended. Make another pass through your writing to assess how well you have accomplished your purpose and whether you have addressed your audience effectively. Is your thesis clearly stated? Have you developed ideas clearly and logically? Have you arranged them effectively? Have you taken account of unity and coherence? Do you have a strong introduction and conclusion? What, if anything, is irrelevant?

If you find that you haven't really addressed the audience you intended or if you find that your purpose has shifted somewhat, go back and rewrite to make sure that all the parts fit together as you intend. You may wind up scrapping some sentences or even paragraphs that you like very much, but if they don't contribute to your rhetorical situation, you should get rid of them, no matter how much you like them. (You may find this easier to do if you shift them to a new document that you call something like "Outtakes.") Similarly, if you find material that is unrelated to your central idea, be ruthless in cutting it out. Is there a place where your reader could have difficulty seeing how an idea is related to the ones before it? Rewrite to make the connections clear. Do you need to provide more details to help your readers understand your point, or do you have a surplus? Add or subtract details as necessary. (See *Hodges'* 33a/*Writer's* 3a–e for more information.)

Introductions and Conclusions

Introductions and conclusions are important for your writing's success. They set your essay up for your readers and tell them when they can stop.

Introductions Your job in your first paragraph or two is twofold. Your opening paragraphs tell your readers what you are writing about and reveal the point you are making. Your introduction must also capture your readers' interest so that they will want to keep reading. Announcing your subject and your point may be as simple as stating your thesis, or it may be as sophisticated as using details to lead up to a sentence that delivers your point with a punch. There are a number of ways to catch your readers' interest. (See *Hodges'* 33b/*Writer's* 3b(1) for more information.) For instance, you can begin with a thought-provoking statement, an anecdote, or a question. Sometimes an unusual fact or statistic will draw readers in, or an appropriate quotation or illustration will make readers want to find out more. Some topics benefit from presenting general information about the subject or from explaining why you chose it.

Conclusions A good conclusion satisfies your readers. It also makes it clear to them that you have developed your idea and made your point. Conclusions take many forms, but some of the most effective ones rephrase the thesis or summarize the main points you have made. They can also direct your readers' attention to larger issues or call for action or a change in attitude. Some essays conclude by presenting a particularly dramatic image. Or you may find that simply restating your introduction is most effective. Whatever method you choose, your intention should be to give your readers closure, a sense of resolution, finality, or decisiveness.

Paragraph Development

Make sure that your paragraphs are not only unified and coherent, but also well-developed. A unified paragraph sticks to its point, which is often stated as a topic sentence. It will also probably include some restriction of that topic sentence and at least one or two illustrative details.

> I think I would have found it dismaying if my middle school had offered a class that taught us about the wiles of Marcie and Tracie: if adults studied their folkways, maybe they were more important than I thought, or hoped. For me, the best antidote to the caste system of middle school was the premonition that adults did not usually play by the same rigid and peculiar rules—and that someday, somewhere, I would find a whole different mattering map, a whole crowd of people who read the same books I did and wouldn't shun me if I didn't have a particular brand of shoes. When I went to college, I found it, and I have never really looked back.
> —MARGARET TALBOT, "Girls Just Want to Be Mean" (242)

This is a common kind of *general to specific ordering* of details. It can also be reversed to present the specific details first and then come to a general statement. In that kind of paragraph, you could begin with a couple of illustrations and then state a generalization about them.

Paragraphs can also be arranged in other orders—*chronological, spatial, emphatic, question-answer,* and *problem-solution.*

Chronological order places the details in a paragraph in the sequence in which they occurred.

> My first victim was a woman—white, well dressed, probably in her early twenties. I came upon her late one evening on a deserted street in Hyde Park, a relatively affluent neighborhood in an otherwise mean, impoverished section of Chicago. As I swung onto the avenue behind her, there seemed to be a discreet, uninflammatory distance between us. Not so. She cast back a worried glance. To her, the youngish black man—a broad six feet two inches with a beard and billowing hair, both hands shoved into the pockets of a bulky military jacket—seemed menacingly close. After a few more quick glimpses, she picked up her pace and was soon running in earnest. Within seconds she disappeared into a cross street.
>
> —BRENT STAPLES, "Just Walk on By" (27)

Spatial order moves from a specific point of reference to another point that is near or far, right or left, up or down, and so on.

> Finally, we reach the marketplace of South Extension, where jean and T-shirt shops are interspersed with stores selling traditional saris and gold jewelry. Even before we mount the dingy marble steps to Nalli's Saree Shop, our hearts are racing. The uniformed doormen open the glass doors with a flourish. At the threshold, a cacophonous opera of voices inside replaces the sounds of the Delhi street behind us. The doormen nod their turbaned heads—the last civilized gesture before we enter.
>
> —SMITA MADAN PAUL AND KIRAN DESAI, "Sari Story" (140)

Emphatic order—order of importance—arranges details in a hierarchy of most to least important or the reverse.

> Not everyone who endures a traumatic experience is scarred by it; the human psyche has a tremendous capacity for recovery and even growth. Recovering from a traumatic experience requires that the painful emotions be thoroughly processed. Trauma feelings can not be repressed or forgotten. If they are not dealt with directly, the distressing feelings and troubling events replay over and over in the course of a lifetime, creating a condition known as post-traumatic stress disorder.
>
> —ELLEN MCGRATH, "Recovering from Trauma" (317)

Question-answer paragraphs pose a question that subsequent sentences answer.

> Would the addresses and stickers affect the rate at which the letters would be mailed? Kemmelmeier wondered. Without the flag stickers, both sets of

letters were mailed at the same rate, about 75 percent of the time. With the stickers, however, the rates changed: Almost all the Christian letters were forwarded, but only half of the Muslim letters were mailed. "The flag is seen as a sacred object," Kemmelmeier says. "And it made people think about what it means to be a good American."

> —MARGO MONTEITH AND JEFFREY WINTERS, "Why We Hate" (221)

Problem-solution paragraphs are organized similarly—the first sentence states a problem that the rest of the paragraph solves.

> This conditioning [not to show anger] can also keep us from learning how to deal with conflict constructively, and as we get older, we may find ourselves in a tug-of-war between what we think we're supposed to do with our anger (hide it) and what we'd really like to do (lash out). For those of us who love to "let 'er rip" when we're upset, it's important to note that a full-on rage, if expressed regularly, can increase blood pressure and heart rate, both of which may put us a greater risk for heart attacks and stroke. But bottling up your feelings "can lead to an unforeseen explosion of emotion, often at something unrelated to the initial cause of the anger," Dr. Shapiro Rok says. "Anger is healthy, normal, and sometimes necessary to our survival." What's key is channeling your energy into a more positive response. So the next time you're so mad that you think your blood is going to boil, try one of these six healthier alternatives to losing control. . . .
>
> —ANAMARY PELAYO, "Hot Tempered?" (171)

Finally, look for what you have not said. What have you left out that your readers might expect to find? What is omitted that might make your paper more effective? Seeing what is not on the page is one of the most difficult tasks a writer faces, and at this point it is often helpful to get feedback from others.

Editing

Once you are reasonably satisfied with the overall shape and content of the essay, turn to the smaller elements (see *Hodges'* 33f/*Writer's* 3f for more information). (It is more efficient to look at large things first: solving larger problems often eliminates many smaller problems, too.) Read your paper over again, specifically considering your *tone*. Do you convey to your readers the proper attitude for your purpose? What kinds of changes will make your sentences more effective? Are some of your sentences overly long? Consider breaking them up. Similarly, if you have some short, choppy sentences, combine them (see *Hodges'* 23–24/*Writer's* 23–24). Do you tend to write the same kind of sentence over and over? Vary your sentence structure (see *Hodges'* 30/*Writer's* 27). Look for ways to make the emphasis in your sentences more appropriate (see *Hodges'* 29/*Writer's* 26) and to make the sentences themselves more effective by using parallel constructions (see *Hodges'* 26/*Writer's* 25).

    Check *grammar and punctuation*. Have you written any sentence fragments or comma splices (see *Hodges'* 2–3/*Writer's* 18–19)? Are there any misplaced or dangling modifiers (see *Hodges'* 25/*Writer's* 20)? Is the form of the verb (see *Hodges'* 1/*Writer's* 22) in every sentence appropriate for the tone and the style? Is the tense consistent? Does each verb agree with its subject? Each pronoun with its antecedent (see *Hodges'* 6/*Writer's* 21)? Are there any unintentional shifts in grammatical structure?

Consider your *diction*. Is every word necessary (see *Hodges'* 21/*Writer's* 30)? Have you left out any necessary words? Have you chosen the appropriate vocabulary for your rhetorical situation? Have you used technical vocabulary that you have not defined (see *Hodges'* 19/*Writer's* 28)? Can any words be replaced with more appropriate or exact ones (see *Hodges'* 19–20/*Writer's* 28–29)? Look for problems with grammar, punctuation, mechanics, and spelling, and make whatever changes are needed.

Proofreading and Final Copy

When you have done your best, or the time comes when you must stop, put your essay into acceptable *manuscript form* (see *Hodges'* 8/*Writer's* 6) and *proofread* carefully. Except in special circumstances, such as when writing an in-class essay or taking an examination (see *Hodges'* 34/*Writer's* 4), make a clean copy, following your instructor's guidelines. Even if you are writing in class, reserve time to make sure that your insertions and deletions are clear and that your paper is as neat as you can make it. Proofread everything you write.

CHAPTER 1

Example

You probably use many examples every day in ordinary conversation. For instance, a friend asks you to explain what you mean and you use an example to clarify your meaning. Or you want to tell someone how to improve his or her performance and you use an example. Using examples is one of the simplest but most effective ways to get an idea across clearly and forcefully, whether you are talking or writing. You can provide a single striking example or a series of examples to help explain a concept or bolster an argument. In fact, a whole essay can be built with examples, as the readings in this chapter demonstrate.

Understanding Examples

What are examples and what do they do? Examples support generalizations. They develop an idea by clarifying it, explaining it, or illustrating it. They help to analyze ideas and processes, identify causes, and show effects. Examples keep readers interested, help to persuade them and answer their questions about a topic.

Examples come in many forms; stories, facts, statistics, and descriptions are the most common. An example may be as short as a word or a few sentences. For instance, look at the following brief *allusion* (reference to a well-known figure), which exemplifies (gives an example of) a point:

> As Robin Hood and Baby Face Nelson show us, you don't always get what you pay for. Sometimes you get what others paid for. When a whole society begins to operate on that principle, that society is in trouble.
>
> —T. Breitfeld

Or a single example might extend to several pages. For instance (note that this phrase means "for example"), "High School Confidential" in this chapter relies on an extended example of how the editor of a high school paper struggled to reveal unsanitary conditions in his school. The essay employs other rhetorical strategies—including narration and description—to clarify and support this example.

Using Examples

Audience

Where will you find examples? That depends in part upon your audience and your purpose. In "Just Walk on By" Brent Staples draws his readers in with an example from his own experience, one that reveals the "vast, unnerving gulf [that] lay between nighttime pedestrians—particularly women—and me." Staples writes:

> My first victim was a woman—white, well dressed, probably in her early twenties. I came upon her late one evening on a deserted street in Hyde Park, a relatively affluent neighborhood in an otherwise mean, impoverished section of Chicago. As I swung onto the avenue behind her, there seemed to be a discreet, uninflammatory distance between us. Not so. She cast back a worried glance. To her, the youngish black man—a broad six feet two inches with a beard and billowing hair, both hands shoved into the pockets of a bulky military jacket—seemed menacingly close. After a few more quick glimpses, she picked up her pace and was soon running in earnest. Within seconds she disappeared into a cross street. (27)

Purpose

In using this example Staples serves both his purpose and his audience. As a black man writing for a mostly white female readership (the essay was first published in *Ms.* magazine), Staples aims to break the tension with his audience by illustrating how public fears of black men create dangerous situations by altering "public space in ugly ways." To accomplish that purpose he tells his readers stories about his own experiences and shows us what he has learned to do to change his situation and assure his own safety.

Selection

When you search for examples to support your generalizations, ask yourself how you know the generalization is true. The evidence that led you to that conclusion is an example—or several examples. Think of stories that explain your idea, facts that support it, statistics that clarify it. Make a list of all the examples you can think of about your topic.

When you look over your list, you will probably notice that some of your examples are more appropriate for your audience and your purpose than others. When you choose an example to illustrate a point, make sure it is relevant to that point. As Brian Doherty remarks in "John Ashcroft's Power Grab," the "stories we choose to tell . . . are, well, telling" (55). Make sure yours tell the tales you want your readers to know. For instance, all of Sue Halpern's examples in "Recipe for Change" show either the problem—urban decay—or the solution she finds. In "The Hidden Life of SUVs" Jack Hitt relies on short, focused examples to suggest reasons for the rapidly growing appeal of sport utility vehicles. In addition to anecdotes (brief stories), facts, and statistics, Julia Cass employs testimonials to accomplish her purpose in "The Moses Factor":

> I used to say, "Man, this is hard. I can't do this," says Jessie Sims, a 16-year-old. "When I finally stopped saying, 'I can't do it,' I started doing it." Another 16-year-old, Sylvester Davis, agrees. "I use what Mr. Moses does in my other subjects," he says. "Like I'm taking Spanish. Those verbs scare me. I think of what Mr. Moses says: 'Look at it. Apply what you already know.'" (51)

How do you know whether your examples will be appropriate for your readers? Some writers imagine a typical reader standing before them and then try to explain their point using various examples. When writers sense that an example will offend or, at best, fail to engage the reader, they choose a better one. In "The Moses Factor" Cass's examples speak to the readers of *Mother Jones* magazine—adult liberals—not to the 14-year-olds the essay discusses and not to educational conservatives who believe in teaching solely by the textbook. And, obviously, one would not expect to engage an audience of college freshmen on the value of thrift by drawing upon examples of social security recipients. Such an example wouldn't seem relevant to the readers, even though it might be representative of the value of thrift.

Number

Generally speaking, you will need to use more than a single example to develop most generalizations, but how will you know if you have used enough? There is no easy rule; perhaps the best advice is to put yourself in your reader's shoes again and ask yourself whether, from the reader's point of view, your points are as clear as they need to be. An essay discussing the horrors of college registration might benefit from two or three well-chosen examples but become tedious with more. On the other hand, an essay defining terrorism might require many examples to convey the complexity of that subject. The decision depends on your subject and purpose and, as always, the needs of your audience. In this chapter, Jack Hitt's essay on SUVs requires numerous brief examples. In "High School Confidential," however, Lara Kate Cohen illustrates her extended example by combining short examples detailing how a young person made a difference.

A single striking example often makes an effective beginning for an essay, quickly capturing the reader's interest while preparing the way for the writer's main idea, or thesis. Brent Staples begins "Just Walk on By" with a memorable anecdote that establishes his main point—the public fears black men. Once that idea has been stated, Staples presents a number of other examples to develop it.

Images

Occasionally, you may find that there is a photograph, chart, graph, map, or drawing that will enhance your readers' understanding of what you are writing about. Visual images sometimes explain better than words do. Photographs can give a sense of place as well as show readers exactly what you are writing about. Charts and graphs often summarize the information you are presenting and so help a reader understand the point you are making. Where geographic information is important, maps may be good examples, and drawings can highlight specific points you want to stress. The photograph and advertisement in this chapter exemplify the concept of "diversity," but how successful they are in conveying their message to a broad enough audience is up to the viewer to decide. See *Hodges'* 8/*Writers'* 6 for more information.

Organization

Choosing examples is only part of the battle; you must also arrange them effectively. Once you have made sure that the examples you are using are clearly related to your thesis and serve your rhetorical purpose, you can turn your attention to how you will present them. Any of several organizing principles might be appropriate: time, space, complexity, or importance. (See *Hodges'* 32d/*Writer's* 2c for more information.) After introducing her subject, Cohen arranges her examples in chronological (time) order to tell the story of Matthew Chayes's battle with the New York public schools. Sue Halpern puts her most important example last, where she describes Deborah Horne's elation at being approved for instant credit. Jack Hitt and Julia Cass are attentive to the complexity of their subjects when they arrange their examples.

Usually, you will want to present your generalization first, as Cohen does, before you illustrate it with examples. But it is also effective to present examples and then draw the generalization from them. Staples successfully uses this technique in the introduction to his essay. Sometimes you will want to give each example a paragraph of its own; at other times you may find that it works well to group several related examples in a single paragraph (see *Hodges'* 31c/*Writer's* 2d for more information). Of course, an extended example may require several or even many paragraphs. And to announce to your readers that an example will follow, you will often want to use such phrases as *for example, for instance, to illustrate*, and *a case in point*.

A danger in using examples is that they may be so engrossing that you lose sight of the point you are trying to make. Keep your purpose and your point in mind and make sure your readers do, too. Direct them back to your generalization from time to time. Another danger is that, just as too few examples can make an essay weak, too many can overload it. Be selective (even ruthless) in choosing which examples you will use. Keep only the best.

Student Essay

In the following essay, student Alice Green uses examples to explain how other people react to her being blind.

Chick with the Stick

Introduction

Context

On Mondays, Wednesdays, and Fridays between my 9 and 11 o'clock classes, I sit on the same wooden bench just outside the student commons area. The same people pass by day after day. Even though I can't see them, I know they are there. Some students walk a wide circle around me, actually going out of their way to avoid contact. And then there are the ones who get quiet as they pass by. I suppose they are uncomfortable with my blindness, afraid they will say or do the wrong thing.

Implied thesis with multiple short examples

Or they may be afraid that my condition is contagious, like tuberculosis or the measles. It could be that they don't especially like looking at me. My eyes are disfigured. Both pupils are covered in a milky film. Because I don't use my eyes to see, some of the muscles in my face have weakened. The eye sockets have sunk. Although I cannot feel it, I am told that my eyes jitter from side to side. People sometimes suggest I wear dark glasses. I ask them incredulously, "Glasses for someone who can't see?" That seems pointless!

Appeal to emotion

On the opposite extreme are the people who act like I am not there at all. They ignore me but will come up to my dog to pet him and feed him scraps of bagels with cream cheese or whatever else they have left in their book bags. They'll talk to him and say, "What a pretty dog; you must be smart." I get so sick of being overshadowed by a dog.

Effective transition

Sometimes Jolly, my dog, serves as a good icebreaker though, an easy way for guys, or anybody new, to come up and chat. But if, after ten minutes, the conversation still keeps coming back to questions about the dog, I get bored and have to excuse myself. Once when that happened, I lied and said that I was late for my driving test. The truth is, training Jolly requires constant work. He's not even that smart. Dogs are subject to unfair stereotypes, just as people are.

Not everybody walks around me when I'm sitting on the bench. Some students who have met me in a class make it a point to say "hello." When they first get up the nerve to speak, they sometimes talk so loudly that I have to remind them I am blind, not deaf. The wisecrack gets us both laughing and relieves some of the tension. At least they are engaging me

Positive example

and that's a good thing.

Extended example

Another problem I have when talking to people who haven't had much experience being around me is that they want me to "look" at them. People with sight find the lack of eye contact extremely uncomfortable and even interpret it as rude and socially unacceptable. It's a no-brainer but I have to say it anyway: people with blindness find it nearly impossible to make eye contact. I try to fake it sometimes but more often my efforts turn out to be comical. There I am nodding and gesturing to an open

continued

space while the person I am talking to is facing another way. Passers-by probably think I am talking to myself.

I love talking about all kinds of topics although most people who talk to me are interested in what it is like to be blind. It's not my favorite subject but if a discussion can help clear up a few misconceptions, I'll talk. Almost any contact is welcomed because I am lonely. Even though I am finishing a bachelor's degree in environmental science and working at the university ten hours a week, I don't have very many friends. It has been a hard adjustment coming from a school specifically for the blind to a small-town university where there are not many blind people.

Another appeal to emotion

The residential school was great. I went there for six months to learn how to be blind. We learned practical skills like how to tag clothes using an identification system. In the morning when dressing I can avoid mismatching plaids with stripes and feel confident my clothes match. We learned Braille and how to use assistive devices on the computer. For the newly blind, learning how to take care of basic hygiene is important. We learned to habitually clean under our fingernails. We also practiced crossing busy streets and getting around town using the city bus system and learned techniques for how to maintain a checkbook and make purchases.

Description establishes her own credibility

All of these skills are important but that is not what I loved about the school. I had the best social life. People there, both blind and sighted, seemed to be comfortable around me. The sense of community is not the same here. Being the only blind person in a group makes a big difference. This past summer is a good example.

Last summer I belonged to a community group that took on trail building as a summer project. Each evening for two or three hours our group of volunteers would meet at the nature center's trail head and work on portions of the trail. In some places we needed to build completely new sections. There were about 25 of us, mostly women of the garden club variety, a few retired folks, and a handful of other college students. I put in a fair amount of time and effort but not as much as some of the others. Repairing the trail was hard at first. It cut through some rough terrain with big rocks and thick bramble. To complicate matters, Jolly was not used to the sights and smells of the great outdoors. His distracted state got me into trouble on several occasions. The rocks and prickly brush proved difficult to navigate and, to be honest, I don't know how much I actually contributed to the project, but it was fun being outdoors and the work experience helped me land a job at the interpretive center.

Use of details

As the summer wore on, Jolly settled down and I got better too, but there were other volunteers there who were much more dedicated. I mention this because at the end of the project we had an awards reception.

Preliminary thesis

By the time most of the awards had been passed out and I had yet to receive one, I had a sinking feeling I was going to be put on the proverbial "courageous blind girl overcomes obstacles" pedestal. And sure enough, it happened. Expecting it did not make my baptism as a flesh-and-blood saint any easier. First, receiving the top volunteer award ahead of others who truly deserved it was embarrassing. And second, my role in life is not to give the more "fortunate ones" a reason to feel more fortunate. That is to say, I don't want to be your living reminder of how lucky you have it. I simply want to be accepted for who I am.

Extended appeal to her own credibility

Instead of speaking my mind, I received the trophy sheepishly and lied about how much the experience had meant to me. They wouldn't get it anyway. I'm not sure I completely do, either. Understanding my blind identity hasn't been easy.

I lost my sight gradually and was reluctant to take on the trappings of "the blind" . . . the dark glasses, the dog, and the rest. Like middle-aged people who fight the necessity of bifocals, I resisted the cane. Carrying it meant I really was blind. Besides, flashing a white cane makes it hard to pass as a seeing person, even for a little while. And passing, even for a few minutes, is my opportunity to be treated as normal.

Thesis
.

When nondisabled people look at "the disabled" they see wheelchairs and dark glasses. They see helmets and hearing aids and white canes. With a few exceptions, they don't pick up on how we are individual people; instead they notice the tools we use. And those tools to the general public equal a disturbing difference. But the tools are only the first step. The second step is the behavior that is expected, given a certain set of tools. I have a dog and a cane; I am blind and therefore expected to act a certain way. Whatever that way is, it is not me. To counter that "blind girl" image I tell people to call me the "chick with the stick." It's not a cane; it's a stick in the same way any person might use a stick. That is all it is.

Conclusion echoes thesis

Two years ago I had to get the smallest toe on my right foot amputated. It was gangrenous and the doctors left me no choice. Later, I became so depressed. Then after almost an entire summer of lying around feeling sorry for myself, I realized people are able to live without toes. While my health is compromised from diabetes, I am definitely alive. So when you see me sitting on that bench between classes, even if you don't have time to stop, give the chick with the stick a shout.

Commentary

In her introduction, Green establishes the context for her essay and presents several brief examples. Her introduction appeals to the reader's sensitivity as she cites instances of how people react to her.

Green'sorganization is more complex than it may initially seem. First she gives examples of various kinds of reactions sighted people have to her blindness. She then follows with a discussion of what it was like to go to school with other blind students, where she was simply considered normal. As the essay moves along, she takes up her experience of being the only blind person in a volunteer group and the group's overreaction to her participation. Finally, she explains her experience with another disability, the amputation of one of her toes.

Each paragraph addresses a different reaction she has had to deal with, arrayed in order of increasing importance. Green begins with simple avoidance behavior—people thinking she doesn't know they're present because she is blind. She then moves on to another way that sighted people act around her, which is paying attention to her dog but ignoring her. She contrasts that sense of isolation with her sense of easy inclusion at the school she attended to "learn how to be blind." From this follows her experience of being a "courageous blind girl" for doing something that blind people are not expected to be able to do, build and repair trails. Next, she discusses the props and behavior that people expect from her as a blind person, which rob her of her identity to the nondisabled. She sums up by reclaiming her identity, further educating her audience.

✦ CHECKLIST FOR WRITING ESSAYS DEVELOPED BY EXAMPLE

- Is your *thesis* clearly stated or implied? (*Hodges'* 32c/*Writer's* 2b)
- Do you have a *generalization* that identifies your focus? Is it too broad?
- Can you state your *purpose* in a single sentence? (*Hodges'* 32a/*Writer's* 1e)
- What kinds of *readers* are you writing for and are your examples appropriate for that audience? (*Hodges'* 32a/*Writer's* 1e)
- Do you have enough *examples?* Do you have too many? Are they all relevant to your purpose and focus? Are they representative of your subject and your audience?
- Have you *organized* your examples effectively?
- Could a *visual example* help your readers to understand your point better?

◆

Just Walk on By: A Black Man Ponders His Power to Alter Public Space

Brent Staples

Born in 1951 in Chester, Pennsylvania, Brent Staples holds a bachelor's degree from Widener University and a Ph.D. in psychology from the University of Chicago, where he was a Danforth Fellow. Currently a member of the editorial board of the *New York Times,* Staples began his work for the *Times* as the first assistant metropolitan editor in 1985. "Just Walk on By" first appeared in *Ms.* magazine in 1986.

My first victim was a woman—white, well dressed, probably in her early 1 twenties. I came upon her late one evening on a deserted street in Hyde Park, a relatively affluent neighborhood in an otherwise mean, impoverished section of Chicago. As I swung onto the avenue behind her, there seemed to be a discreet, uninflammatory distance between us. Not so. She cast back a worried glance. To her, the youngish black man—a broad six feet two inches with a beard and billowing hair, both hands shoved into the pockets of a bulky military jacket—seemed menacingly close. After a few more quick glimpses, she picked up her pace and was soon running in earnest. Within seconds she disappeared into a cross street.

That was more than a decade ago. I was twenty-two years old, a gradu- 2 ate student newly arrived at the University of Chicago. It was in the echo of that terrified woman's footfalls that I first began to know the unwieldy inheritance I'd come into—the ability to alter public space in ugly ways. It was clear that she thought herself the quarry of a mugger, a rapist, or worse. Suffering a bout of insomnia, however, I was stalking sleep, not defenseless wayfarers. As a softy who is scarcely able to take a knife to a raw chicken—let alone hold it to a person's throat—I was surprised, embarrassed, and dismayed all at once. Her flight made me feel like an accomplice in tyranny. It also made it clear that I was indistinguishable from the muggers who occasionally seeped into the area from the surrounding ghetto. That first encounter, and those that followed, signified that a vast, unnerving gulf lay between nighttime pedestrians—particularly women—and me. And I soon gathered that being perceived as dangerous is a hazard in itself. I only needed to turn a corner into a dicey situation, or crowd some frightened, armed person in a foyer somewhere, or make an errant move after being pulled over by a policeman. Where fear and weapons meet—and they often do in urban America—there is always the possibility of death.

In that first year, my first away from my hometown, I was to become 3 thoroughly familiar with the language of fear. At dark, shadowy intersections in Chicago, I could cross in front of a car stopped at a traffic light and elicit the *thunk, thunk, thunk* of the driver—black, white, male, or female—hammering down the door locks. On less traveled streets after dark, I grew accustomed to but never comfortable with people who crossed to the other side of the street rather than pass me. Then there were the standard unpleasantries with police, doormen, bouncers, cab drivers, and others whose business it is to screen out troublesome individuals *before* there is any nastiness.

4   I moved to New York nearly two years ago and I have remained an avid night walker. In central Manhattan, the near-constant crowd cover minimizes tense one-on-one street encounters. Elsewhere—visiting friends in SoHo,[1] where sidewalks are narrow and tightly spaced buildings shut out the sky—things can get very taut indeed.

5   Black men have a firm place in New York mugging literature. Norman Podhoretz[2] in his famed (or infamous) 1963 essay, "My Negro Problem—And Ours," recalls growing up in terror of black males; they "were tougher than we were, more ruthless," he writes—and as an adult on the Upper West Side of Manhattan, he continues, he cannot constrain his nervousness when he meets black men on certain streets. Similarly, a decade later, the essayist and novelist Edward Hoagland extols a New York where once "Negro bitterness bore down mainly on other Negroes." Where some see mere panhandlers, Hoagland sees "a mugger who is clearly screwing up his nerve to do more than just *ask* for money." But Hoagland has "the New Yorker's quick-hunch posture for broken-field maneuvering," and the bad guy swerves away.

6   I often witness that "hunch posture," from women after dark on the warrenlike streets of Brooklyn where I live. They seem to set their faces on neutral and, with their purse straps strung across their chests bandolier style, they forge ahead as though bracing themselves against being tackled. I understand, of course, that the danger they perceive is not a hallucination. Women are particularly vulnerable to street violence, and young black males are drastically overrepresented among perpetrators of that violence. Yet these truths are no solace against the kind of alienation that comes of being ever the suspect, against being set apart, a fearsome entity with whom pedestrians avoid making eye contact.

7   It is not altogether clear to me how I reached the ripe old age of twenty-two without being conscious of the lethality nighttime pedestrians attributed to me. Perhaps it was because in Chester, Pennsylvania, the small, angry industrial town where I came of age in the 1960s, I was scarcely noticeable against a backdrop of gang warfare, street knifings, and murders. I grew up one of the good boys, had perhaps a half-dozen fist fights. In retrospect, my shyness of combat has clear sources.

8   Many things to into the making of a young thug. One of those things is the consummation of the male romance with the power to intimidate. An infant discovers that random flailings send the baby bottle flying out of the

---

[1] A district of lower Manhattan known for its art galleries.

[2] A well-known literacy critic and editor of *Commentary* magazine.

crib and crashing to the floor. Delighted, the joyful babe repeats those motions again and again, seeking to duplicate the feat. Just so, I recall the points at which some of my boyhood friends were finally seduced by the perception of themselves as tough guys. When a mark cowered and surrendered his money without resistance, myth and reality merged—and paid off. It is, after all, only manly to embrace the power to frighten and intimidate. We, as men, are not supposed to give an inch of our lane on the highway; we are to seize the fighter's edge in work and in play and even in love; we are to be valiant in the face of hostile forces.

Unfortunately, poor and powerless young men seem to take all this non-   9
sense literally. As a boy, I saw countless tough guys locked away; I have since buried several, too. They were babies, really—a teenage cousin, a brother of twenty-two, a childhood friend in his mid-twenties—all gone down in episodes of bravado played out in the streets. I came to doubt the virtues of intimidation early on. I chose, perhaps even unconsciously, to remain a shadow—timid, but a survivor.

The fearsomeness mistakenly attributed to me in public places often has   10
a perilous flavor. The most frightening of these confusions occurred in the late 1970s and early 1980s when I worked as a journalist in Chicago. One day, rushing into the office of a magazine I was writing for with a deadline story in hand, I was mistaken for a burglar. The office manager called security and, with an ad hoc posse, pursued me through the labyrinthine halls, nearly to my editor's door. I had no way of proving who I was. I could only move briskly toward the company of someone who knew me.

Another time I was on assignment for a local paper and killing time be-   11
fore an interview. I entered a jewelry store on the city's affluent Near North Side. The proprietor excused herself and returned with an enormous red Doberman pinscher straining at the end of a leash. She stood, the dog extended toward me, silent to my questions, her eyes bulging nearly out of her head. I took a cursory look around, nodded, and bade her good night. Relatively speaking, however, I never feared as badly as another black male journalist. He went to nearby Waukegan, Illinois, a couple of summers ago to work on a story about a murderer who was born there. Mistaking the reporter for the killer, police hauled him from his car at gunpoint and but for his press credentials would probably have tried to book him. Such episodes are not uncommon. Black men trade tales like this all the time.

In "My Negro Problem—And Ours," Podhoretz writes that the hatred he   12
feels for blacks makes itself known to him through a variety of avenues—one being his discomfort with that "special brand of paranoid touchiness" to which he says blacks are prone. No doubt he is speaking here of black men. In time, I learned to smother the rage I felt at so often being taken for a criminal. Not to be so would surely have led to madness—via that special "paranoid touchiness" that so annoyed Podhoretz at the time he wrote the essay.

I began to take precautions to make myself less threatening. I move   13
about with care, particularly late in the evening. I give a wide berth to nervous people on subway platforms during the wee hours, particularly when I have exchanged business clothes for jeans. If I happen to be entering a

building behind some people who appear skittish, I may walk by, letting them clear the lobby before I return, so as not to seem to be following them. I have been calm and extremely congenial on those rare occasions when I've been pulled over by the police.

14   And on late-evening constitutionals along streets less traveled by, I employ what has proved to be an excellent tension-reducing measure: I whistle melodies from Beethoven and Vivaldi and the more popular classical composers. Even steely New Yorkers hunching toward nighttime destinations seem to relax, and occasionally they even join in the tune. Virtually everybody seems to sense that a mugger wouldn't be warbling bright, sunny selections from Vivaldi's *Four Seasons*. It is my equivalent of the cowbell that hikers wear when they know they are in bear country.

Rhetorical Considerations

1. What advantage does Staples gain by introducing his essay with an example of how one woman saw him as a threat? How does this example help him establish his main idea? (*Hodges'* 33b/*Writer's* 3b)
2. Where is the main idea of paragraph 2 found? How do the examples that begin the paragraph prepare the reader for the main idea? (*Hodges'* 31a/*Writer's* 3c)
3. How does Staples achieve coherence in paragraph 13? Mark and label all the devices he uses. (*Hodges'* 31b/*Writer's* 3c–d)
4. What clues do the vocabulary and the details of "Just Walk on By" provide about Staples's intended audience? Describe the audience. (*Hodges'* 32a/*Writer's* 1e)
5. Does Staples ever state his purpose for writing "Just Walk on By"? If so, where? If not, what do you think his purpose is? (*Hodges'* 32a/*Writer's* 1b–c)
6. Comment on the tone of this essay. What evidence do you find for your assessment of the tone Staples takes? (*Hodges'* 33a/*Writer's* 3a)

Language and Style

1. Look up the following words in your dictionary: affluent (paragraph 1); *quarry* and *dicey* (paragraph 2); *bandolier* (paragraph 6); *perilous* and *posse* (paragraph 10); *skittish* (paragraph 13); *warbling* (paragraph 14). (*Hodges'* 19e/*Writer's* 28e)
2. How does Staples use the word *victim* in the first paragraph? Explain why he refers to the woman as a *victim*. (*Hodges'* 20a/*Writer's* 29a)
3. In the first sentence of paragraph 14, Staples uses the clause, "what has proved to be an excellent tension-reducing measure: I whistle melodies from Beethoven and Vivaldi and the more popular classical composers." How does this clause function grammatically? As exactly as you can, explain how this clause advances Staples's main idea. (*Hodges'* 1g/*Writer's* 17b)
4. In the first sentence of paragraph 6, what advantage does Staples gain from using *warrenlike* to modify *streets*? (*Hodges'* 20b/*Writer's* 29b)
5. In the final clause of the third sentence of paragraph 10, Staples uses the passive voice. Would the active voice have been a better choice? Explain your answer. (*Hodges'* 7c/*Writer's* 22c)

Writing Suggestions

1. Write an essay in which you use examples to describe how someone judged you unfairly and how you responded to the judgment.
2. Write an essay using examples to illustrate how you once had to alter your public behavior for reasons beyond your control. For instance, people often modify their public behavior because of the expectations of their families, because of peer pressure, or because of standards imposed by an institution such as a school or the military.

♦

HIGH SCHOOL CONFIDENTIAL

Lara Kate Cohen

This essay was published in *Brill's Content* magazine, which focused on media and other cultural phenomena and was controversial because it was both owned and published by its editor, Stephen Brill. The publication's interest was in reporting those stories not covered by the mainstream press. Not surprisingly, this essay examines first amendment issues at a basic level.

1 Of the extracurricular options at Francis Lewis High School—a typically overcrowded Queens, New York, facility—the student newspaper is hardly considered the coolest. "It's just not," says *The Patriot*'s 18-year-old editor, Matthew Chayes, a string bean of a kid with big ears and a buzz cut. "I would play football, but I would probably get killed." Instead, Chayes tackled the principal. Last November, despite a campaign by the school's administration to censor the story, *The Patriot* printed Chayes's 3,000-word exposé of the unsanitary and unlawful conditions in the school's lavatories. Chayes's crusade, which was covered by *The New York Times* and ABC's New York affiliate, became a model of public service journalism and an unlikely case study in First Amendment protection.

2 A gray monolith in the shadow of the Long Island Expressway, Francis Lewis High School was designed, in 1958, to house about 2,000 students. But as New York City's student population exploded in the eighties and nineties—and as funding to build new schools evaporated—the halls became more crowded and now overflow, the Board of Education says, with roughly 3,600 teenagers. On the outdoor basketball court, rickety trailers serve as makeshift classrooms; students must lug their winter coats from class to class because many of the already-scarce lockers were bolted after drugs or firearms were found inside. A former principal of the school told *The New York Times* in 1995, when 3,200 students were enrolled, that he felt like a "chief surgeon" in an army hospital. "It's triage," he said.

3 The students, however, were bothered most by the bathrooms. Senior Jessica Santaromita, 18, says, "They were so dirty, I just wouldn't use them." Although New York City building codes mandate that schools provide one toilet for every 35 students and one sink for every 75—and although Francis Lewis contains 14 lavatories for student use—the school closed all but two bathrooms in the fall, offering a total of four sinks, four urinals, and eight toilets for the entire student body. The current principal, Catherine Kalina, whose office is equipped with a private rest room, says, "The bathrooms have to be supervised. There wasn't enough staff available to monitor them safely, so I had to close them off."

The Patriot's Matthew Chayes wasn't sympathetic. "The toilets and the 4 sinks were always clogged," says Chayes, who joined the paper as a sophomore in 1998. "The floors were gross." In early October, he mobilized his staff—and braced for a confrontation with Kalina, 49, who, with an assistant principal, must approve the quarterly newspaper's every story idea and manuscript before publication. Too often, Chayes says, journalistic quality isn't one of her criteria. Kalina, who has been principal since 1998, says, "I think every [*Patriot*] piece should have a good and sound purpose. Being right is not always as important as kids might think." Last spring, for instance, Kalina halted Chayes's investigation of a student website, rife with racial epithets, called the "Most Hated Franny Lew Teachers," which Kalina says "wasn't the kind of thing that should be reported on. . . . The website was in violation of [school board] regulations."

According to Mark Goodman, executive director of the Student Press 5 Law Center—an organization in Arlington, Virginia, that monitors freedom of the press in academia—most public schools consider Kalina's prior-review process antiquated and only a few practice it nationally. Prior review "inevitably leads to censorship," Goodman says, adding, "it is bad journalism, and it's a bad way to teach students the skills of journalism." Kalina says, "Responsible journalism in a high school implies not being mean-spirited. . . . Critical pieces belong on the editorial page."

School newspapers are rarely run entirely by students—usually a faculty 6 adviser, acting as both an educator and an ombudsman, watches over the publication. *The Patriot's* paid adviser during the website and bathroom stories was a retired history teacher named Robert Harris who worked with the editors part time. According to Chayes and others on the *Patriot* staff, Kalina overrode many of Harris's and the assistant principal's decisions and blocked stories that even she acknowledged were well reported. Harris didn't return calls for comment, but Kalina doesn't dispute this, adding that she takes no pleasure in acting as a censor. "I would love one less thing to do," she says. But a Francis Lewis teacher who spoke on the condition of anonymity says, "She likes to be the queen—she has to be in control of everything."

As for Chayes, one of his history teachers has described him as a "mis- 7 guided genius." He scored a perfect 800 on the writing section of the Scholastic Aptitude Test, for instance, but has struggled in math and science courses. He often stays awake all night reading *The Wall Street Journal* and *The New Yorker* and drafting letters to *The New York Times* about the evils of Big Tobacco, two of which the paper has printed. Although Chayes's mother, a secretary, and his father, a salesman, are both Democrats, he considers himself a budding Libertarian.

Last October, without telling Kalina, Chayes deployed *Patriot* photogra- 8 phers to the Francis Lewis lavatories to document the trash-filled urinals and clogged toilets. Chayes then began reporting—phoning the city's board of health and education to investigate hygienic standards and a urologist to determine the medical ramifications of resisting the need to urinate. "It wasn't just a one-way conversation," says Dr. Simon Barkagan. "He already knew the physiology of the bladder."

9   The final draft of the story, set to run in the fall issue, included graphic, clinical descriptions of the bathrooms. An assistant principal was quoted as saying, "I'm ashamed to be part of the problem." Chayes submitted the article to Kalina, who recalls that after reading it, she feared the faculty's response and decided the "tone" had to change. The Francis Lewis teacher who spoke anonymously adds, however, that "the teachers here, if anything, were strongly in favor of the article."

10   Chayes was summoned to the principal's office for a two-hour meeting, in which, Kalina says, she insisted that Chayes remove the "disparaging remarks made" about the school and the "indication that people weren't doing their job." Chayes refused, saying, he recalls, "It's not right to have the person the article is critical of reviewing that article."

11   While the story sat, unchanged, on Kalina's desk, Chayes sent a copy to the Student Press Law Center, which declared it to be thoroughly and fairly reported and free of libel and slander. Encouraged, Chayes investigated publishing and distributing the article independently. He and a classmate began a fund-raising campaign on campus, asking students to donate lunchroom change to help raise the $400 print-shop costs. The school administration immediately forbade the campaign as a violation, Chayes says, of "school policy." Says Kalina, "If [a certain] procedure isn't followed, money can't be collected on school grounds."

12   Chayes wouldn't back down. He wrote a letter to Kalina that said, "The lawyers [of the Student Press Law Center] declared this article fair, unbiased and accurate. . . . We will not change the focus, content or anything else." Chayes added, "If you do not change your mind, the bathroom item will appear in another medium." Fearing negative publicity, Kalina opened four additional bathrooms. And though she insists she never said, as Chayes originally wrote, that students should "bring [their] own toilet paper" from home—Chayes changed the quote to "bring [their] own tissues"—she agreed to publish his article.

13   But Chayes still wasn't satisfied. He knew that future *Patriot* articles would face the same censorship—such as a piece he had assigned about the administration's failure to explain the absence and subsequent replacement of a physics teacher. Chayes expressed his frustration with Kalina to the editor of the student newspaper at Stuyvesant High School, a New York City public school for the academically gifted that does not practice prior review. An editor from *The New York Times* who helps the Stuyvesant students produce the paper read Chayes's letter and was intrigued by the bathroom saga's First Amendment implications. He assigned the story to a *Times* reporter; the January 7 article noted that "New York City's most outspoken Revolutionary War hero [for whom the school is named]. . . . would be outraged." Producers at New York's ABC affiliate read the *Times* article and, shortly after it appeared, sent a reporter and a cameraman onto the campus to profile Chayes and Kalina, who defended their positions on the air.

14   Ever since, Chayes says, Kalina and the Francis Lewis administration have inappropriately monitored him and *The Patriot*. Kalina disagrees, say-

ing, "Matthew's one of my kids, and I'm in this business for the kids." However, Chayes notes, when *Brill's Content* phoned the school (unsolicited by Chayes) to investigate the story and seek comment, assistant principal Jeffrey Scherr called Chayes's parents several times. Says Scherr sarcastically, 15 "Matthew and I are tight."

As the school year draws to a close, *The Patriot* continues to chase controversial stories, such as an outbreak of neo-Nazi graffiti on campus. But Kalina still believes in reviewing articles prior to publication, and interviews with several Francis Lewis students give no indication that Chayes or *The Patriot* enjoys a newfound prominence. Student Jessica Santaromita says most students still don't read the paper and have no idea why their bathrooms now sparkle. That's fine with Chayes. He's looking forward to graduating this month and studying liberal arts at a college—as of early April, he hadn't decided which—"where the administration doesn't make your life hell."

Rhetorical Considerations

1. How does the introductory paragraph establish the character of Matthew Chayes? Why is this important for the essay? (*Hodges'* 33b/*Writer's* 3b)
2. Examine Cohen's use of direct quotations. What sources does she quote? Why are these appropriate and/or effective? (*Hodges'* 31c/*Writer's* 2d)
3. Find any evidence of the author's opinion regarding her subject. (*Hodges'* 35c/*Writer's* 7c)
4. Look up the exact wording of the First Amendment. Are you surprised by what you find? How does this essay relate to the issue of the First Amendment?
5. Does Cohen use concrete details effectively? How does her use of detail contribute to the essay's purpose? (*Hodges'* 31c/*Writer's* 2d)

Language and Style

1. Look up the following words in your dictionary: *monolith* and *triage* (paragraph 2); *epithets* (paragraph 4); *Libertarian* (paragraph 7); *saga* (paragraph 13). (*Hodges'* 19e/*Writer's* 28e)
2. What is the difference between *libel* and *slander* (paragraph 11)? (*Hodges'* 19e/*Writer's* 28e)
3. In the third sentence of the second paragraph, Cohen joins two clauses with a semicolon. Is this punctuation used correctly? What other methods could have been used to join these two clauses? How does the combination of the clauses with a semicolon affect the sentence rhetorically? (*Hodges'* 14 and 24/*Writer's* 31 and 24)
4. The last sentence of paragraph 6 starts with a coordinating conjunction. Why might Cohen have used this transition? Why might she have decided to separate this clause as a complete sentence? (*Hodges'* 24/*Writer's* 24)

Writing Suggestions

1. Write an essay about a problem you perceive on your campus or in your local community, citing specific examples of how this problem affects those directly involved.
2. Write an essay in which you cite examples that support the need for a certain degree of censorship.

RECIPE FOR CHANGE

Sue Halpern

Sue Halpern has been a writer and editor for many publications and is a regular columnist for *Mother Jones* magazine, where this essay first appeared. Her articles have appeared in *Granta, Antaeus,* the *New York Times* magazine, *Audubon, Sierra, Traveler,* the *New York Review of Books,* and many other publications. She is the author of *Migrations to Solitude* (1992) and *Four Wings and a Prayer: Caught in the Mystery of the Monarch Butterflies* (2001). She has taught at Columbia University, Bard College, Bryn Mawr College, and the New York State Writers' Institute. She has received both a Guggenheim award and an Echoing Green Nonfiction Fellowship. She lives with her husband, Bill McKibben, and their daughter, Sophie, in the Adirondack mountains of New York state, where she is a founder and trustee of The Town of Johnsburg Library.

1   Thirty-two people—in their 30s for the most part, male and female, Hispanic, African American, West Indian—are jammed into a basement classroom at the Urban Horizons Center for Culinary Arts discussing snails.

2   "People actually like to eat them," a young man says, his voice one part awe to two parts revulsion. He casts his eyes around the small room, looking for a response. More than one student nods his head or screws up her face. Most remain impassive.

3   It is the first day of class and almost no one knows anyone. Nearly half the group hasn't dropped out yet, as they will by the end of the six-month program, and the ones who will remain haven't yet become the colleagues they will by graduation.

4   "I've always wanted to try snake," a woman in the front ventures, to moderate groans. The cinder-block walls of the room are covered with pictures of broccoli and peppers, and a poster of corn.

5   "What about rat?" Tony Lee, the instructor, asks, waving a reprint of a *New Yorker* article about Chinese cuisine that they've been reading. The class protests. This is the South Bronx, where rats are not a delicacy. Which is why, in a way, Urban Horizons is here at all.

6   "I had never set foot in the Bronx till 1988," recalls Nancy Biberman, a former legal-aid lawyer who is the founder and president of the Women's Housing and Economic Development Corporation (WHEDCO), which runs the culinary-arts program. Back then, in the late 1980s, the South Bronx was synonymous with urban decay. Biberman's job was to build apartments for poor people, to repopulate the neighborhood.

7   The problem was, she says, "the place was rotten to the core. There was no infrastructure. Just putting up housing wasn't going to work. There

wasn't anything here. No stores, no schools, nothing." After intense negoti-ations, the City of New York let Biberman devote a corner of several new buildings she was putting up to what she conceived of as a "horizontal set-tlement house"—an after-school program in one, a daycare center in an-other, a physician's office in a third.

8   Still, she realized, even this was not enough to re-create a neighborhood from scratch. Biberman needed something bigger: a bigger vision, a bigger space. She found it in 1991, a few blocks away in the South Bronx. It was the aged, shuttered Morrisania Hospital, left to rot for 20 years until it was waist-deep in trash and home to drug dealers and squatters. It was Nancy Biberman's particular gift, however, not to see the building this way at all. Instead, she could see it as it is today, transformed by $23 million in public and private funds: 132 apartments, pilasters down the hall and wainscoting along the walls, arched windows opened to the sun, vaulted ceilings. She could see nearly 100 kids in Head Start, and a basement given over to a health clinic, a fitness center, rooms of job developers and job seekers, com-puter software classes, ESL, and family daycare certification training, and the culinary-arts center on the first floor, a state-of-the-art professional kitchen filled with people eager to get off welfare and stake a claim in the land of the middle class.

9   "I'm all for shelter, but it's just not enough," Biberman says, walking through the building, pointing out the before-and-after pictures in the lobby, the sconces, the tile work on the floor. "Bring beauty and dignity into people's lives—that's transformative. If it wasn't so damned beautiful, it wouldn't have half the impact."

10   Downstairs, in the gleaming kitchen, things of beauty are made every day and sent out the door. Miniature crab cakes with chili-lime aioli, penne pasta with herb pesto, spiced samosas, gravlax florets, Linzer torte, Cuban sandwiches. In addition to running the culinary-arts training program, Urban Horizons operates a high-end catering company that counts Gold-man Sachs, Columbia University, Christie's East Auction House, and the Carlyle Hotel among its clients. Supervised by professional instructors, culi-nary students at Urban Horizons—roughly half of whom are on public assis-tance—staff the business, learning to bake focaccia and cure salmon and wield a paring knife while filling the orders that come in every day and are posted on the wall board near the garde-manger station. The Urban Hori-zons Cafe, which opened recently in the Parkchester section of the Bronx, is also a regular, if more down-home, outlet. Trays of Jamaican jerk chicken wings and carrot cake and coconut rice and peas regularly leave Morrisania for Parkchester, where the only other dining-out options are a diner and fast-food franchises like Burger King; whatever doesn't sell is donated to food pantries and soup kitchens.

11   "The food company is a social venture that has a double bottom line," Biberman explains. "It's training people for good jobs—not as McDonald's hamburger flippers but in upscale restaurants and catering companies and corporate kitchens." At the same time, she adds, the catering business brings in money to cover the costs of the on-the-job training. Although the com-

pany isn't turning a profit yet, the goal, in time, is for it to help fund much of the culinary-arts school—the ultimate self-help program.

Deborah Horne, a Class of 2000 graduate of the Center for Culinary Arts, 12 is standing behind the counter at the Urban Horizons Cafe when Biberman and I show up for lunch (grilled chicken Caesar salad, tuna wrap, Equal Exchange coffee, Rice Krispy treats). Horne, who is in her 40s, chanced upon the cooking school a couple of years ago. At the time, she was on public assistance after a leg injury kept her at home, unable to work. But that was after federal welfare-reform legislation in 1996, which required people on public assistance to work in order to continue receiving aid, and New York's decision the following year to require welfare recipients to put in at least 14 hours every week at city-approved work sites. Horne was sent to WHEDCO to do "whatever," but there wasn't whatever to do. Instead, she saw the flyer for the cooking program and asked to be considered for that. Three interviews later, she was in—though she had to fight to get the city to approve the Center for Culinary Arts as her work-fare assignment.

"When I stepped in there it was like a church," she recalls. "Everyone 13 was smiling. A free cooking program? I told myself, 'This cannot be true.' I don't have that kind of luck. And it was so beautiful. I couldn't believe welfare had sent me there. Everywhere else they sent me was a dungeon. But this, this was a castle."

There was a month of classes, 20 hours of which were devoted to knives, 14 and an hour in the gym every day, building up stamina. There were four months in the kitchen, rotating through eight stations, working with chefs who had been trained at the best cooking schools in the world and who had a whole constellation of starred restaurants on their resumes. Then there was a month in Manhattan at Flick International, a private catering service, and after that, graduation. "This is the first time in my life that I have a certificate that says I completed something," says Horne, who left high school in the 11th grade.

If the measure of employment training is how many of its graduates get 15 jobs, then Urban Horizons is doing pretty well. Roughly 90 percent of its students graduate to jobs, most of them in the most up-to-the-minute kitchens in New York, jobs the majority of them still hold after two years. And then there are the ones who don't leave, Deborah Horne among them. She was hired as a teaching assistant at Urban Horizons and then, when the cafe was about to open, as one of the managers there.

When Nancy Biberman started WHEDCO in 1991, the organization had 16 two employees and a $75,000 budget. A decade later it employs 120 people with a budget of $8 million from a patchwork of state, federal, and corporate sources. The employees, for the most part, are people who live in the neighborhood. The former hospital is no longer a rat-infested building on a forsaken, crime-ridden block. A brand-new magnet school recently opened down the street, dozens of shops are now unshuttered and open for business, and people stroll casually down clean and unthreatening streets.

"The point is to raise incomes so businesses will want to move in here," 17 Biberman says, pointing out that it takes more than warm bodies to encourage restaurants and dentists and florists and dry cleaners to venture into a new place. That is the real lesson of WHEDCO and its ancillary programs—that communities grow and flourish where people have beauty and comfort and standing in their lives.

18   At our table in the cafe, Horne gets up suddenly and gets her purse from behind the counter. "I can do a lot more than I could two years ago," she says, rifling through it. I think she's talking about her mastery of puff pastry or the way she sears a duck. She pulls out an envelope and waves it in my direction. Maybe it's a letter of recommendation, something about her saffron paella, her chicken potpie.

19   Horne lays the envelope on the table and encourages me to look inside. The return address says J.C. Penney. "The other day I went to Penney's and they gave me instant credit. I couldn't believe it. Me." She removes a red card and shows it around. Her first charge card. "I am proud to pay my bills," she says.

Rhetorical Considerations

1. Halpern opens the essay with an anecdote. Is this an effective opening? Why or why not? (*Hodges'* 33b/*Writer's* 3b)
2. Halpern focuses on one extended illustration of a project which appears to be successful. What other examples does she include in her essay? (*Hodges'* 31c/*Writer's* 2d)
3. Examine specific details Halpern uses in her essay and consider how they contribute to your reading of the essay. (*Hodges'* 31c/*Writer's* 2d)
4. Why does Halpern use direct quotations? Do her quotations represent an adequate sample of the community she is writing about? (*Hodges'* 31c/*Writer's* 2d)
5. Do you see any evidence of the author's opinion in this essay? (*Hodges'* 35c/*Writer's* 7c)
6. How effective is Halpern's conclusion? (*Hodges'* 33b/*Writer's* 3b)

Language and Style

1. Look up the following words in your dictionary: *revulsion* and *impassive* (paragraph 2); *infrastructure* (paragraph 7); *squatters, pilasters,* and *wainscoting* (paragraph 8); *sconces* (paragraph 9); *garde-manger* (paragraph 10); *sears* (paragraph 18). (*Hodges'* 19e/*Writer's* 28e)
2. Find examples of metaphor or other figurative language in the essay. (*Hodges'* 20b/*Writer's* 29b)
3. Comment on the sentence variety in paragraph 2. (*Hodges'* 30/*Writer's* 27)
4. In the first sentence of paragraph 10, why is *are* used instead of *is*? (*Hodges'* 6a/*Writer's* 22e)
5. What is the subject of the first sentence of paragraph 15? (*Hodges'* 1b/*Writer's* 16a)

Writing Suggestions

1. Write an essay about a particular cuisine you enjoy. Give examples of dishes and describe them in detail.
2. Write an essay in which you propose a project in your own community that is similar to the one depicted in this essay.

◆

THE HIDDEN LIFE OF SUVs

Jack Hitt

Jack Hitt is a writer for *GQ* magazine and a contributing editor for Public Radio International and WBEZ's *This American Life*. His book, *Off the Road: A Modern-Day Walk Down the Pilgrim's Route into Spain*, was published by Simon and Schuster in 1994.

1   What's in a name? What do you make of a passenger vehicle called a Bronco? Or one dubbed a Cherokee? How about a Wrangler? Are they just chrome-plated expressions of sublimated testosterone flooding the highways? Check out the herd that grazes the average car lot these days: Blazer, Tracker, Yukon, Navigator, Tahoe, Range Rover, Explorer, Mountaineer, Denali, Expedition, Discovery, Bravada. Besides signaling that we're not Civic or Gallant, they indicate there's something else going on here.

2   These are, of course, all names of sport utility vehicles, the miracle that has resurrected Motown. Think back to the dark days of the previous decade when the Japanese auto industry had nearly buried Detroit. In 1981, only a relative handful of four-wheel-drives traveled the road, and the phrase "sport utility vehicle" hadn't entered the language. Today, they number more than 14 million, and that figure is growing fast. If you include pickups and vans, then quasi trucks now constitute about half of all the vehicles sold in America. Half. They're rapidly displacing cars on the highways of our new unbraking economy.

3   Go to any car lot and jawbone with a salesman, and you'll find that big is once again better. Any savvy dealer (clutching his copy of Zig Ziglar's *Ziglar on Selling*) will try to talk you up to one of the latest behemoths, which have bloated to such Brobdingnagian dimensions as to have entered the realm of the absurd.

4   Ford, in fact, has unveiled a new monster, the Excursion, due to hit the showrooms before the millennium. With a corporate straight face, its literature touts as selling points that the Excursion is "less than 7 feet tall . . . and less than 20 feet long" and is "more fuel efficient . . . than two average full-size sedans."

5   These Big Berthas have even spawned new vocabulary words. The biggest of the big, for instance, can no longer fit comfortably in a standard-size garage or the average parking space. So salesmen will often sell you on one of the "smaller" SUVs by praising its "garageability."

6   What, then, explains the inexorable advance of these giant SUVs into our lives? Why do we want cars that are, in fact, highclearance trucks with four-wheel drive, an optional winch, and what amounts to a cowcatcher?

The answer, in part, lies in the vehicles themselves. Cars are not fickle   7
fashions. They are the most expensive and visible purchases in an economy
drenched in matters of status and tricked out with hidden meanings.

Some people will tell you that the shift from car to truck can be explained   8
simply: We Americans are getting, um, bigger in the beam. We aren't comfortable in those Camrys, so we trade up to a vehicle we can sit in without
feeling scrunched. Here's a new buzzword for Ziglar disciples: fatassability.

But I think the key is found not so much in their size or expense (al-   9
though both keep ballooning) but in those ersatz Western names. The other
day, I saw an acquaintance of mine in a boxy steed called a Durango. Say it
out loud for me: "Durango." Can you get the syllables off your tongue without irony? In the post-"Seinfeld" era, can anyone say *Durango* without giving it an Elaine Benes enunciation at every syllable? Doo-RANG-Go.

The true irony comes from the fact that this thoroughly market-   10
researched word no longer has any core meaning. No one comprehends its
denotation (Colorado town) but only its vague connotations (rugged individualism, mastery over the wilderness, cowboy endurance). The word does
not pin down meaning so much as conjure up images.

These names are only the end product of the intense buyer-profiling   11
that the car companies and the marketing firms continuously carry out. By
the time they make it to the lot, these cars are streamlined Frankensteinian
concoctions of our private anxieties and desires. We consumers don't so
much shop for one of these SUVs as they shop for us.

A typical focus-group study might be one like the "cluster analysis" con-   12
ducted by college students for Washington, D.C.–area car dealers in 1994
and reported in *Marketing Tools*. The analysts coordinated numerous data-
bases, mail surveys, and census information to profile the typical "Bill and
Barb-Blazers," whose consumer apprehensions can shift from block to block,
but can be pinpointed down to the four-digit appendix on the old zip code.

Each Bill and Barb then got tagged as "Young Suburbia" or "Blue-Collar   13
Nursery" or "Urban Gentry." Translation, respectively: "college-educated, up-
wardly mobile white" or "middle-class, small-town" or "educated black" people. The students next identified what images spoke to the underlying appeal
of an SUV for each group (prestige, child space, weekend leisure). Then they
developed targeted ads to run in the media most favored by each group: the
Wall Street Journal, National Geographic, Black Entertainment Television.

Many of the ads they developed were directed at women. For example,   14
the one meant for upscale homeowners depicted a "woman architect standing next to her four-door [Blazer] at a Washington-area construction site"
and "conveyed her professional leadership in a city with one of the highest
rates of labor force participation for women."

Sport utility vehicles are quickly becoming women's cars. In fact, cur-   15
rent statistics show that 40 percent of all SUV sales are to women, and the
proportion is growing. (More men, on the other hand, are buying bigger,
tougher pickup trucks.) But one wonders what's going on in the mind of
that female architect or that soccer mom, high above the world in her

soundproof, tinted-glass SUV, chatting on her cellular phone as she steers her mobile fortress down the street.

16   When GMC decided to launch the Denali (an SUV named for the Alaskan mountain), the auto-trade papers discussed the subtleties of that outdoorsy name: Even though most buyers "will never venture into territory any less trampled than the local country club parking lot," wrote *Ward's Auto World*, "the important goal of the Denali marketing hype is to plant the image in customers' minds that they can conquer rugged terrain. The metaphor of Alaska is particularly apt because SUVs, especially the larger of the species, depend on the myth that we have new frontiers yet to pave. Perhaps we're trying to tame a different kind of wilderness. Indeed, in an age of gated communities . . . the SUV is the perfect transportation shelter to protect us from fears both real and imagined."

17   In one focus group, female drivers confessed they hesitated even to exit the interstate "because they are afraid of what they are going to find on some surface streets."

18   G. Clotaire Rapaille, a French medical anthropologist and student of the consumer mind, practices a more advanced marketing technique called "archetype research." In one session he has consumers lie on the floor and lulls them into a relaxed alpha state with soothing music. Then he asks them to free-associate from images of different vehicle designs and write stories about what they hoped the design would become. Overwhelmingly, Rapaille told the *Wall Street Journal*, his participants had the same reaction: "It's a jungle out there. It's Mad Max. People want to kill me, rape me. Give me a big thing like a tank."

19   More and more, SUV's give us that tank-like security, and part of the feeling derives from their literal altitude. Down there is the old working class, the new peasants who haven't figured out how to snatch a six-figure income out of our roaring economy—the little people who don't own a single Fidelity fund. There's a brutal Darwinian selection at work: They huddle down in their wretched Escorts and their Metros—not merely because they are poor but because they deserve to be.

20   These are the new savages: people who drive cars. They scrape and fetch about in their tiny compacts, scuttling along on surface streets. But above it all, in their gleaming, skyscraping vehicles, is the new high society—the ambitious, the exurban pioneers, the downtown frontiersmen.

21   It's been said that the most distinctive feature of the American character is that we continually define ourselves as pilgrims facing a new frontier. In their darkest hearts, the members of the new-money bourgeoisie have convinced themselves that we live in an unforgiving wilderness of marauders and brutes. The hidden meaning of our new conveyances can be found right on the surface. Once upon a time, Trailblazers, Explorers, and Trackers tamed the Wild West. Now, through the sorcery of focus groups, the bull-market gentry have brought the Pathfinders and Mountaineers back into their lives in the belief that they need to conquer the savage land one more time.

Rhetorical Considerations

1. What is Hitt's primary purpose? Is he against SUVs? (*Hodges'* 32a/*Writer's* 1e)
2. What kinds of examples does Hitt use to support his thesis? (*Hodges'* 31c/*Writer's* 2d)
3. What authorities does Hitt cite? Are these the appropriate authorities for this topic? (*Hodges'* 38a/*Writer's* 9a)
4. Is beginning the essay with a series of questions effective? Does Hitt answer those questions? (*Hodges'* 33b/*Writer's* 3b)
5. At what point does Hitt's essay go beyond the subject of vehicles and address more serious issues of economic class? (*Hodges'* 36a/*Writer's* 7a)

Language and Style

1. Look up the following words in your dictionary: *behemoths* and *Brobdingnagian* (paragraph 3); *inexorable* (paragraph 6). (*Hodges'* 19e/*Writer's* 28e)
2. What is accomplished by Hitt's use of language in phrases like *herd that grazes* (paragraph 1) and *boxy steed* (paragraph 9) in enhancing his thesis? (*Hodges'* 20b/*Writer's* 29b)
3. What is the relative pronoun in the last sentence of paragraph 3? What is its antecedent? (*Hodges'* 6b/*Writer's* 21d)
4. What part of speech is *jawbone* in paragraph 3? What is effective about Hitt's use of the word in this way? (*Hodges'* 20b/*Writer's* 29b)

Writing Suggestions

1. Write an essay in which you look at the names of some other product and consider what qualities manufacturers and advertisers emphasize with these names.
2. Explain how the car you drive does or does not accurately reflect your personality and lifestyle.

◆

THE MOSES FACTOR

Julia Cass

Long-time staff reporter for the *Philadelphia Inquirer,* Julia Cass was part
of the large investigative team that reported the notorious Three Mile
Island story in 1979. She is also the co-author of *Black in Selma: The Uncommon Life of J. L. Chestnut, Jr.* (1990) and writes freelance articles for a
number of publications. This essay was first published in *Mother Jones*
magazine.

1   The students enter the classroom noisily and take their places in groups of
five or six at a series of beat-up tables. Some open the clear plastic folders
containing their work and look over what they did in yesterday's class.
Others rummage through their backpacks and talk with their neighbors.

2   Bob Moses stands at the front of the spare white room, taping sheets of
newsprint to a flip chart. With his wire-rim glasses, gray goatee, and serene
composure, he looks like a cross between a college professor and a yogi. Even
in a roomful of 25 ninth-graders, Moses has the calm, self-contained manner of an Eastern mystic.

3   "Okay, listen up," he says. "Enter your data, then get the means and dis-
placements." Moses designed this lesson, called the wingspan exercise, to
teach key concepts about algebra and statistics. First, students measure one
another's outstretched arms from fingertip to fingertip; then they calculate
the mean for their group and the "displacement" of each person's wingspan
from the mean.

4   The students settle down to work. Along two walls, big windows offer a
glimpse of the sagging houses and vacant lots that border the school. Lanier
High is located on Martin Luther King Jr. Drive in Jackson, Mississippi, and
like so many other streets named for the Civil Rights leader in black communities across America, it speaks more of defeat than of dreams. Lanier
was the first African American high school in Jackson, and it remains virtually all black, with two whites in its student body of 911. Some 83 percent
come from families with incomes below the poverty line. Most read and do
math below their grade level. A third fail to graduate. Only a handful go on
to attend four-year colleges.

5   Moses goes from table to table, helping students with their algebra problems. The children were not yet born when their teacher first came to Mississippi in 1961, and few realize that the man checking their math was one
of the most venerated leaders of the Civil Rights movement, considered by
some to be the equal of King. As a "field secretary" with the Student Non-
Violent Coordinating Committee (SNCC), Moses organized sharecroppers,

domestics, and others at the bottom of society to fight for their right to vote—an effort that sparked a violent backlash from whites accustomed to unchallenged rule. In the face of beatings and arrests, Moses became legendary for his humility and calm commitment. In 1964, he orchestrated Freedom Summer, the ambitious project that drew nearly 1,000 volunteers to the state and focused the national spotlight on Mississippi when the Klan murdered three Civil Rights workers.

"Moses pioneered an alternative style of leadership from the princely church leader that King epitomized," says Civil Rights historian Taylor Branch, author of *Parting the Waters*. "He was the thoughtful, self-effacing loner. He is really the father of grassroots organizing—not the Moses summoning his people on the mountaintop as King did, but, ironically, the anti-Moses, going door-to-door, listening to people, letting them lead." 6

Now, nearly four decades after he left the state, Moses is back in Mississippi to work on what he sees as a second revolution: math literacy. Teaching algebra to descendants of sharecroppers doesn't involve the same danger as Civil Rights organizing. Indeed, Moses has received many official honors—including the designation of a Bob Moses Day—from the state that once branded him an "outside agitator." His new work is quieter but, he contends, potentially more radical. 7

"The absence of math literacy in urban and rural communities is as urgent an issue today as the lack of registered voters was 40 years ago," he says during a break between classes. "And I believe solving the problem requires the same kind of community organizing that changed the South then. If we can succeed in bringing all children to a level of math literacy so they can participate in today's economy, that would be a revolution." 8

Every Monday morning, Moses, now 67, leaves his home in Cambridge, Massachusetts, at 5:30 and takes a flight through Cincinnati to Jackson—a seven-hour trip. He spends the next four days teaching ninth-grade algebra and geometry at Lanier. On Friday evenings, he makes the reverse trip to Cambridge. 9

Moses believes that mastering algebra, preferably by the eighth grade, is the modern-day equivalent of the right to vote because it represents a dividing line between having—or not having—a chance in life. "In the 1960s, we opened up political access," he says. "The most important social problem affecting people of color today is economic access, and this depends crucially on math and science literacy, because the American economy is now based on knowledge and technology, not labor." 10

It's easy to see why Moses considers higher math to be the key to economic equality. A study by the Department of Education shows that high school students who take rigorous math and science courses are more than twice as likely to go to college as those who don't. But the same study reveals that many minority and low-income students are steered away from such courses or attend schools that don't offer advanced math. As a result, many lack the skills they need to find decent work. 11

Moses began his new movement, the Algebra Project, when he was helping his own children with math 20 years ago. The nonprofit organization 12 and its affiliates, based in Cambridge and Jackson, now have 22 full-time employees and an annual budget of $2.5 million. It currently reaches 10,000 students in 13 states, the majority at middle schools in the South.

13   Moses has developed a special curriculum to make algebra more accessible to students, and his organization trains local teachers in his method. But what makes the Algebra Project unique among education-reform movements is its emphasis on grassroots organizing. Just as Moses did during the Civil Rights movement, project leaders work and live in the communities they're trying to change. Every school that offers the Algebra Project holds regular meetings to organize parents, students, teachers, and community leaders around math literacy the way Moses organized sharecroppers around the vote. "In the 1960s, people said sharecroppers weren't interested in voting until they stood up and demanded the franchise," he says. "Today the kids themselves are the only people who can dispel the idea that they don't want to learn."

14   Such a bottom-up approach is unusual among education reformers, who typically focus on hiring more teachers or boosting test scores. "Bob is in the trenches, building a culture around math that draws kids into his program," says Uri Treisman, a University of Texas math professor who is a national leader in efforts to improve the math performance of minority students. "It's an inspired notion—and it works."

15   Moses draws students into learning algebra by starting with a simple physical event, like measuring wing-spans. Rather than simply asking children to manipulate mysterious symbols, he gives them a concrete experience to help them understand the concepts of math. The students then talk about the experience, isolate the features that are mathematical, and work with them.

16   In his classroom at Lanier, students have finished calculating the displacement of wingspans in their groups. Moses then asks them to write down what they did and why—not just in numbers but in sentences. "Students need to learn to understand what the problems are about," he explains. As they work, Moses and Wilma Morris, a former Tougaloo College math professor who teaches the class with him, go from table to table asking questions. "Now what's the next step? What did you do? Where is your mean?" Porchia Jefferson has written a whole paragraph. "Mr. Moses, is this right?" she asks brightly. He reads her work and asks, "What is a displacement? What are we getting at here?" When he moves on to a different table, the girl sitting next to Porchia asks what he told her. "He said I wrote what I did but not what was meant," she says and starts over.

17   "Can I do this?" Ahmed Dortsch asks, coming up to Moses and showing him his calculations. Moses asks a few questions, and Ahmed goes back to his table. "I think I got it," he says, and shows another boy what he learned. "He breaks it down for you to understand," Ahmed says of Moses. "Other teachers struggle with you, but he'll find your problem and get straight to it."

18   Other students put their heads on the table, stare into space, talk, crack jokes, slip over to other tables. Moses and Morris hone in on them. "Did

you get your mean, Courtney?" "Shawn, have you done your calculations? You need to get started."

"I need a job," one boy comments.   19

"You have a job—to train your mind," Moses responds.   20

Moses remains calm during these interactions. He does not raise his   21 voice or express frustration, even when he sends a student to the principal's office for disrupting class. He answers questions deliberately, his eyes seeming to focus inward for answers, and he rarely smiles or laughs. Moses sees his students as inheritors of "the legacy handed down through the history of this country around the education of black people." He calls this legacy "sharecropper education"—a limited education for people assigned manual work. Sharecropper education is not confined to the South, but also permeates inner-city schools in the North.

"If you think of sharecropper schooling, you went through it, but your   22 options were you were going to chop and pick cotton or do domestic work," Moses says. "Your education wasn't tied to opportunity. The connection between education and a change for the better in your own life wasn't made."

Despite the Colin Powells and Condoleeza Rices, he adds, that link still   23 is not clear among many poor African Americans because they do not see anyone they know whose success is tied to education. "The big question we need to address in this country today is, How do we shift the culture in our inner cities and develop these expectations and beliefs for these kids?"

Before he was a Civil Rights worker, Moses was a math teacher. Raised   24 in a Harlem housing project, he attended Stuyvesant High School, which specialized in math and science, then Hamilton College in upstate New York, where he majored in philosophy and logic. He had received a master's degree in philosophy from Harvard University and was teaching math at Horace Mann, a private school in the Bronx, when the student sit-in movement drew him to the South. As one of the few black students in white institutions, Moses had learned to avoid confrontation and repress his feelings of humiliation. "I felt a great release when I began doing something to take on prejudice and racism," he recalls.

The Mississippi that Moses entered in 1961 was a closed society, with   25 apartheid enforced by the law and the Klan. Within a few months of his arrival, Moses was beaten up by the sheriff's cousin when he accompanied two local blacks to the courthouse in a county where not a single black was registered to vote, and a local leader was shot and killed. People were afraid to challenge the status quo. "They were frozen," Moses recalls. What broke the ice, he found, were small workshops where sharecroppers and domestics talked about practical issues that bothered them, brainstormed about what to do, and took steps to do it.

"Bob never set us down and said, 'This is what you should do, or this is   26 how you should do it,'" says L.C. Dorsey, a former sharecropper who attended the meetings. "He kept putting the questions out: 'Why do you think that is? What do you think we ought to do about that?' He'd listen to what you said and force you to think about it. That was his genius. He could hold his own ideas in abeyance and wait for you to finally develop the picture."

27   His refusal to lead in the traditional sense created a powerful organization—but it also maddened people desperate for guidance and caused SNCC
meetings to drag on into the night. Freedom Summer registered 75,000
blacks and elected representatives to oppose the state's all-white delegation
at the Democratic National Convention. But the victory came at a heavy
price. Four people were killed and 80 were beaten that summer, the party refused to seat the black delegates, and the model integration among SNCC
organizers fell apart in bitter arguments over race and black consciousness.
Within a year, Moses left SNCC and the South.

28   "He was finely attuned to the implications of what they were doing,"
says Branch, the Civil Rights historian. "Would people be hurt? Was he leading them down a primrose path? His sensitivity could be seen as a weakness. King was more like General Sherman when his people were killed, and
you need this toughness to keep going. It tore Moses apart." Moses, who
dislikes talking about his feelings, sums up that period in his life by saying
only, "It wasn't a happy time."

29   In 1968, when his draft board refused to grant him conscientious objec-
tor status, Moses left the country. He and his wife, Janet, a Civil Rights
worker who now is a pediatrician, lived in Tanzania, where three of their
four children were born and Moses taught math at a school where nobody
knew his past. "I lived a life as just another person," he says. "That helped
me get grounded again and helped our family be just a family."

30   What would become the Algebra Project began after Moses moved to
Cambridge in 1976 and began work on a Ph.D. in the philosophy of math
at Harvard. Freed from financial burdens by a MacArthur "genius grant," he
was "fishing around for a kind of movement"—and he found one that combined the two previous chapters of his life. Upset that his oldest daughter
Maisha's middle school did not offer algebra, he asked the teacher to let her
sit with him in a corner of the classroom and do more advanced math. The
teacher asked if he would take a few other students too. Recognizing that
many children were falling behind, Moses drew on the organizing skills he
had honed in Mississippi to bring parents together. Within a few years, the
school was offering algebra to all eighth-graders.

31   But Moses didn't stop with his daughter's school, expanding the project
to other states. In the classroom, he noticed that some children had difficulty moving from an arithmetic understanding of numbers to an algebraic
one. One student in particular kept getting the wrong answer because he
didn't pay attention to whether the numbers were positive or negative. "He
had only one question, the arithmetic question of 'how much?' I had to add
another question you need for algebra: 'which way?'" From this insight,
Moses developed the Algebra Project curriculum.

32   To add "which way" to "how much," Moses takes students on trips that
make the concepts real for them—the subway in Cambridge or a tour of
Civil Rights landmarks in Mississippi. "On the subway, the first decision you
are faced with is inbound or outbound," he says. "Then you get into how
many stops." The students draw a trip line with any stop as the benchmark,
which is assigned the coordinate zero. The stops to the left are assigned a

negative value, to the right, a positive, so any trip represents a number of stops (how many?) in either direction (which way?).

This method of teaching math produces "aha!" moments even for some 33 of the more experienced teachers trained in the Algebra Project. "When I went to the training, I began to understand math concepts I had only memorized, to be honest with you," says Lynn Moss, a former sixth-grade teacher at Brinkley Middle School in Jackson. "More than that, I learned an instructional practice—starting with an experience—that is so much more meaningful."

The innovative curriculum may excite students and teachers, but Moses 34 knows that it's not enough, by itself, to turn schools around. For this, the Algebra Project relies on community organizing to try to produce a demand from the "target population" of students and parents for more math and better education. "People will not follow other people's agenda," Moses says. "Goals have to be internalized." He considers the "most strategic part" of his approach to be the Young People's Project, which mobilizes teenagers to run math camps and workshops for younger students. Some 70 students in Cambridge and Jackson tutor math on a regular basis, with another 40 helping in the summer camps.

The youth project is led by Moses' daughter Maisha, now 31, and son 35 Omo, 30. During the week, Moses lives with Maisha and Omo in their ranch-style home on the outskirts of Jackson, and students involved in the project often meet here. Moses considers these teen-agers his real success stories, and whenever he speaks in public about the Algebra Project, he brings some of them with him to demonstrate math exercises. Just as the Civil Rights movement required African Americans to challenge not only the white power structure, but their own fears, the students who accompany Moses must push themselves to learn something well enough to stand up in public and explain it. "I used to say, 'Man, this is hard. I can't do this,'" says Jessie Sims, a 16-year-old. "When I finally stopped saying, 'I can't do it,' I started doing it." Another 16-year-old, Sylvester Davis, agrees. "I use what Mr. Moses does in my other subjects," he says. "Like I'm taking Spanish. Those verbs scare me. I think of what Mr. Moses says: 'Look at it. Apply what you already know.'"

One thing Moses didn't expect when he began the Algebra Project was 36 that it would bring him back to Mississippi. He first returned to Jackson in 1989 after the release of *Mississippi Burning*, a movie about the murder of three Civil Rights workers during Freedom Summer. Distressed that the heroes in the movie are FBI agents, Moses and others met to discuss how to respond. At the gathering, he convinced Dave Dennis, another veteran of the movement, that math literacy is the contemporary Civil Rights issue.

Dennis, who'd become a lawyer in Louisiana, agreed to join Moses in 37 bringing the Algebra Project to schools in the South. Moses began teaching classes at Jackson's Brinkley Middle School in 1996, and the following year he came to Lanier. At first, Moses says, his interest in returning to Mississippi was primarily strategic. "Because of the history, Mississippi is a theater where we can lift our program out of the 'let's teach math better' box and take it to the country as a Civil Rights issue." But when he began driving down the roads he had traveled decades earlier, the history became more personal. He made contact with the doctor who had stitched up his head after one beating and another doctor who had treated a fellow SNCC worker when he was shot. "I began to feel that this was a good place for me," he says.

38   Almost every week, Moses drives an hour and a half to the town of Mc-Comb to visit C.C. Bryant, the local NAACP leader who put him up when he first came to Mississippi in 1961. Bryant, now 85, still lives in the little yellow house where Moses stayed, though today it is located on C.C. Bryant Drive. Entering through the back door, Moses finds Bryant and his wife watching television. As they talk politics and exchange banter, Moses visibly relaxes, even breaking into laughter. His host knows the reason for the change. "When he comes here," Bryant explains, "he's comin' home."

39   When Moses isn't in Mississippi, he's often on the road, training teachers in his method, speaking at conferences on education reform, visiting university math departments, and lobbying to put math literacy higher on the national agenda. His book about the Algebra Project, *Radical Equations*, was published last year. He's equally driven in his spare time, maintaining a vegetarian diet, meditating regularly, and swimming 1,500 yards each day. He is known for following his principles even in minor matters. "You won't find Bob in a tuxedo even at a fancy fundraiser," says Harvard psychiatry professor Alvin Poussaint, a friend since childhood. "He sees this as a way the upper classes pull rank on the lower classes."

40   Poussaint, who serves on the Algebra Project board, says the organization once lost a research grant because Moses insisted community people be involved in designing the research to be funded.

41   The available evidence indicates that the Algebra Project works. An evaluation of four schools across the country conducted by researchers at Lesley University in Cambridge found that graduates of the program enroll in upper-level courses at a much higher rate than their peers, making it more likely that they will go on to college. Standardized-test scores improve at schools where at least half of all students learn math from Algebra Project–trained teachers. At Lanier, enrollment in geometry and advanced algebra has gone up substantially since Moses arrived, and his students surpass their peers on standardized tests. The school has now expanded the program to include all ninth-graders.

42   But despite the progress, the Algebra Project faces serious obstacles. Even with the special curriculum created by Moses, getting students to pay attention remains a problem. Enlisting parents and community leaders in the education of their children is also slow going. When Moses called a special meeting for parents at Lanier one evening, just 18 showed up. Clustered in one corner of the school's cavernous auditorium, the tiny group seemed to symbolize just how far Moses remains from his goal.

43   Everyone gives Moses high marks for his commitment, but some suggest that his methods and personality may not always be the most effective. One advanced math teacher at Lanier faults him for letting his students use calculators too much and not requiring them to do more math drills.

Other criticisms mirror those made against Moses in the 1960s. His in- 44
sistence on including everybody in meetings—and requiring meetings for
just about everything—can exhaust even the most faithful. "The more inclusive you are, the less efficient," says Stewart Guernsey, a lawyer who helps
raise money for the project. Poussaint notes that "some people wish Moses
would be more forceful." His speeches at fundraisers are often less than rousing and he dislikes socializing with wealthy donors, making it harder for
the project to raise money.

Moses responds to such criticism by doing exactly what he's been do- 45
ing for 40 years—listening to people no one else listens to, asking probing
questions in the hope that they will figure out what's wrong and take it
upon themselves to improve their lives. One afternoon, a student he
had suspended comes in with his mother to see him after school. "Mothers
seem to be the one place where there's a real connection," Moses explains.
As the three of them sit at a table in the empty classroom, the boy
looks subdued. Moses explores in a tone of inquiry, not judgment, why
the boy wasn't paying attention. If you couldn't see what I was doing,
why didn't you move? he asks. Why do I have to keep after you? What are
your plans after high school? Do you have a backup plan if the NBA doesn't
work out?

After that, Moses spends an hour patiently going over, step by step, the 46
wingspan exercise.

Rhetorical Considerations

1. Is Cass's introduction effective? Why or why not? (*Hodges'* 33b/*Writer's* 3b)
2. Why do some educators object to Moses's methods? Why does Cass mention these objections? Might there be other reasons his colleagues would object to his methods? (*Hodges'* 32a/*Writer's* 1b)
3. What have been the effects, short- and long-term, of Moses's project?
4. How does algebra relate to other subjects, according to Moses and this essay?
5. The essay ends with an example. Is this an effective ending? Why or why not? (*Hodges'* 33b/*Writer's* 3b)

Language and Style

1. Look up the following words in your dictionary: *yogi* (paragraph 2); *self-effacing* (paragraph 6); *franchise* (paragraph 13); *repress* (paragraph 24); *apartheid* (paragraph 25); *abeyance* (paragraph 26). (*Hodges'* 19e/*Writer's* 28e)
2. Which descriptive words suggest Moses is an "alternative" teacher? (*Hodges'* 20/*Writer's* 29)
3. What part of speech is *arithmetic* in paragraph 31? (*Hodges'* 1a)
4. Comment on the sentence variety in paragraph 4. (*Hodges'* 30/*Writer's* 27)
5. Is the colon used correctly in the first sentence of paragraph 7? What other punctuation marks could have been used? (*Hodges'* 17d/*Writer's* 35d)

Writing Suggestions

1. Write an essay about a teacher who has influenced you (positively or negatively), giving examples of that teacher's behavior and the effects it has had
   on you.
2. Bob Moses believes that "math literacy" is an important factor in combating
   poverty and racism. Write an essay to junior high school students explaining
   to them the importance of math literacy.

◆

John Ashcroft's Power Grab

Brian Doherty

Brian Doherty is an associate editor for *Reason,* a monthly political magazine, where this essay was first published. He began as a reporter for
Reason and later worked as assistant editor for four years. His work has
also appeared in the *Washington Post,* the *Los Angeles Times, Mother Jones,
Spin, National Review,* the *Weekly Standard,* the *San Francisco Chronicle,*
and other publications. He earned a Warren Brooks Fellowship in Environmental Journalism at the Competitive Enterprise Institute in 1999.
He received his BA in journalism from the University of Florida. Doherty also writes under the pseudonym "Eugen von-Bohm Bawerk" for
Wired Ventures' *Suck.com* and runs Cherry Smash Records out of his
apartment. He is currently writing a book on the history of the American libertarian movement.

When U.S. Attorney General John Ashcroft was eight years old, his father, 1
J. Robert Ashcroft, took the boy up in a Piper Cub airplane. Then Dad blessed
young John with a special treat.

"John, I'd like you to fly this plane for a while," he said. 2

"I was one awestruck kid," Ashcroft remembers lovingly at the very be- 3
ginning of his 1998 memoir, *On My Honor: The Beliefs That Shape My Life.*
But he was also a lost one: "What do I do?" he shouted to his pa.

"Just grab the stick and push it straight forward." 4

Which of course sent the plane into a terrifying "bombing-raid dive to- 5
ward a farm . . . I lost all sense of time or place as fear gripped my insides."

Turned out it was all just a practical joke. Dad saved them in the nick 6
of time—and, recounts John, "had a good chuckle" at the expense of his
naive son.

Was young John mistrustful of his trickster father after such an intense 7
prank? In his autobiography, Ashcroft chooses the high road, completely re-
casting what might seem a particularly mean bit of joshing as a deliberate
attempt to teach him a valuable lesson. The lesson, Ashcroft writes, is that
"actions have consequences. . . . In a positive sense, I learned that wherever
I was, if I put my hand to something, I could make a difference."

Uh, yeah. The boy in the famous joke, digging through the pile of ma- 8
nure looking for the pony, has nothing on our nation's top cop. The most
obvious response to Ashcroft's version of this story is, *What the hell is wrong
with this guy?* While it's certainly the type of thing a boy is apt to remember,
what would possess a man writing a memoir—meant largely to honor dear
old dad—to start his book with this particular anecdote?

The stories we choose to tell on ourselves are, well, telling. Given its 9
place of pride in his book, Ashcroft's father tricking him seems to be his

55

most beloved, or at least most vibrant, childhood memory. Ashcroft, one can infer, believes in something like Tough Love. (Indeed, treating juvenile crooks as adults has been a pet theme through his entire political career.) And if the attorney general, the "nation's top cop," is the symbolic disciplinarian and parental figure for American society, then we're all Ashcroft's kids now—which could mean some harrowing times ahead.

10   Yet Ashcroft is a far more complicated father figure than most of his enemies grant. They see him in one role only: the stern disciplinarian driven by an unshakable belief that God and he are as one, a man so prudish he can't tolerate unclothed statuary. But the American father-figure template includes many different roles, and Ashcroft has filled more than a few during his public life. At times, he's come across as an obsessive, driven, and ultimately self-destructive tyrant given to fits of rage (think Robert Duvall in *The Great Santini*). Other times, he's an overly earnest goody-two-shoes quick with an uplifting Bible verse (think *The Simpsons'* Ned Flanders). And sometimes, he comes across as a sleepy-brained, bumbling doofus falling into trouble (think *Blondie's* Dagwood Bumstead).

11   Especially given the immense power he's holding in post-9/11 America, it's worth contemplating the varied facets of John Ashcroft—and their flaws. He's a religious man at loggerheads with the dominant culture; a politician who has mostly been (despite surface appearances) a failure; and an attorney general who may be turning into something worse than his enemies anticipated—though perhaps not in the way they assumed.

True Believer

12 In December, *The Weekly Standard,* as staunch a friend as Ashcroft has in the media, did a laudatory cover story on "General Ashcroft," praising the fightin' spirit that 9/11 brought out in the former senator from Missouri. Indeed, Ashcroft is a man at war not simply with Muslim extremists, but with secular America. Central to any consideration of him is his religion, which was also one of the reasons, rightly or wrongly, that he was hated and feared by the left long before 9/11. Born in 1942, Ashcroft grew up the dutiful child of a roving Assemblies of God minister who later settled down to run various Bible colleges in Missouri. Grandpa was an Assemblies holy man as well.

13   The Assemblies of God is the largest Pentecostalist denomination in America, with 2.3 million members in the United States and 30 million worldwide. It was the first centralized religious institution to emerge from the radically decentralized Pentecostal movement that began to sweep America in the first decade of the 20th century. Pentecostals believe that every child of God should be his own minister, imbued directly with the Holy Spirit and the gift of speaking in tongues. Ashcroft is thus that most derided figure on the American religious landscape, the Holy Roller—an actual, serious one. (The notorious Jim Bakker and Jimmy Swaggart, icons of ridiculous religiosity, were both Assemblies preachers.)

14   Besides speaking in tongues, the Assemblies practice such peculiarities as faith healing. In short, it's the sort of religion that scares cosmopolitan

secularists witless. In biblical style, Ashcroft has had himself anointed in oil (Crisco, if that's all that's on hand) upon ascending to political office. He once vowed that were he ever to become president, he would publicly kneel and pray for divine guidance while being sworn in. That's the sort of statement that makes centrist liberals, hardcore lefties, and the odd atheistic right-winger fear Ashcroft as much as he fears God. And the attorney general follows other Assemblies dictates that further place him outside the American mainstream: He's staunchly opposed on religious grounds to drinking, gambling, and even dancing.

Yet he is, in his own straight-laced and traditional way, a radical cul-   15
tural rebel. Despite his outsider status and the opprobrium it generates, he won't give in. Like a caring though peculiar dad advising against peer-group conformity, he stands against the crowd and is publicly (and by all accounts privately) true to the values of a serious religious conservative with one-and-only-one wife (Janet, a law professor with whom he's collaborated on legal textbooks) and three kids.

He's also hopelessly corny, creating waves of contemptuous mirth all   16
across the Internet, where clips of him singing one of his self-composed gospel songs abound. While a member of the Senate, he and three colleagues formed a vocal quartet, the Singing Senators, to record and perform patriotic and devotional ditties. The group even trekked to that capital of American cornpone hokum, Branson—tellingly located in Ashcroft's home state—to croon with the Oak Ridge Boys.

Ashcroft's squeaky-clean Christian image is built on more than personal   17
habits. People have reported that while being interviewed for jobs by Ashcroft, they were asked if they had ever committed adultery. (One applicant reports being asked if he were gay, a story Ashcroft denies.) He was the first senator to publicly call upon President Clinton to resign over his affair with that woman, Monica Lewinsky. As Missouri governor, he vetoed a Sunday liquor sales bill, signed into law the first Missouri restrictions on underage smoking, restricted rentals of violent movies to minors, and cracked down on casual drug use (even as one of his top aides was exposed by a squealing college buddy as a pothead and coke-sniffer and quietly resigned). As federal attorney general, he has revived the sort of porn prosecutions that languished in the Bill Clinton-Janet Reno era.

Still, Ashcroft is not some backwoods, Holy Roller hick. He is part of a   18
generation of Pentecostals who have engaged the larger world rather than staying within their own separatist institutions. Hence, Ashcroft attended college at Yale and law school at the University of Chicago. "Ashcroft," notes Edith Blumhofer, a historian at Wheaton College who has written several books on the Assemblies, "was brought up in what was in some ways a conservative Assemblies of God home. His father was very pietist and devoted to prayer. Yet Ashcroft was not told to go to Yale and fight the battle—he went there simply as a student, with no agenda to convert the place." For a devout member of the Assemblies, says Blumhofer, Ashcroft was exceptional in combining the secular and the religious.

The religious historian Grant Wacker once described Pentecostals as   19
having a "jut-jawed stress on personal autonomy," and Ashcroft is the first

Assemblies worshipper to be elected either governor or senator. In that context, Ashcroft's political career can be read as an experiment in the assimilation of a peculiarly independent religious tradition into the mainstream.

20   The experiment can only be described as an awkward semi-success so
far. Certainly, John Ashcroft is the attorney general of the United States—a
position of considerable power and influence. But by following the dictates
of his faith and upbringing, he has crafted a public image that media so-
phisticates on both coasts see as charmingly goofy at best and dangerously
retrograde at worst. Though many Americans agree with him (at least generally) about such matters as God, family, and abortion, Ashcroft has surely
noticed that it just isn't OK to the opinion makers to be who he is.

21   One reason the very Pentecostal Ashcroft has been able to make the
headway he has in national politics is because, despite his demonization as
a zealot, he's always been more Ned Flanders than Cotton Mather. He's
never fought back at his critics with fire and brimstone. Instead, he's more
likely to appear in friendly surroundings, such as Orange County, California's famous Crystal Cathedral, and quip, "I always thought that if I was accused of being a strong Christian there was enough evidence to convict me."

22   As he shifted his political ambitions from Missouri, where serious Pen-
tecostalism is less outré than elsewhere, to the national stage, Ashcroft has
insisted again and again that "it's against my religion to impose religion on
people." At least once, though, while speaking to the Christian magazine
Charisma, he let slip that "I think all we should legislate is morality."

23   Yet it's safe to say that Ashcroft is a gentler kind of modern religious
man, a compassionate conservative before it was cool. As senator he worked
to allow religious groups to administer federal aid of various sorts. He made
new flextime requirements one of his major concerns—so parents can attend Little League games (as, he notes glumly in his memoirs, his traveling
preacher father didn't) and take care of scraped knees.

24   It's worth noting about Assemblies members that, as historian
Blumhofer says, "When they look at the world, the divine is quite immanent to them." Practices such as morning prayer meetings in the office are
as natural as breathing to Ashcroft, even if they are anathema to a large segment of the populace he is supposed to serve. His strong and oft-expressed
religiosity makes for an awkward relationship between Ashcroft the cop and
the beat he walks.

Born to Lose

25   Take a quick look at his résumé, and you'd conclude that John Ashcroft has
had a stunningly successful political career. A deeper read, however, suggests something more complicated, a pattern of embarrassing defeats and
hollow victories.

26   After graduating from Yale in 1964 and the University of Chicago Law
School three years later, Ashcroft taught law at Southwest Missouri State
University—a position of such vital national importance that he used it to
get an occupational deferment during the Vietnam War. His political career

began poorly with two defeats, the first in a GOP primary while running for Congress in 1972. His respectable 45 percent showing in the primary brought him to the attention of Republican Gov. Kit Bond, who appointed Ashcroft to a midterm vacancy for state auditor. But Ashcroft lost the job when he actually had to face the voters in '74.

It was all uphill from there—at least in Missouri, and at least on paper. 27 In 1975 he was appointed to assistant attorney general of the state. In 1976, he squeaked through a tight election and became Missouri's attorney general. He went on to serve eight years in that post, followed by eight years as governor and then six as U.S. senator.

But Ashcroft's political tenure in Missouri seems more comic-gothic 28 than inspiring or statesmanlike. Events just didn't give him many occasions to rise to. Instead, we see Ashcroft signing the papers to disincorporate the city of Times Beach, victim of a notorious dioxin scare; urging tourists to avoid his state lest they interfere with an ongoing FBI manhunt for neo-Nazis; petulantly refusing for a time to return a commemorative silver dinner set to its rightful owner, the *U.S.S. Missouri*; commuting a death sentence because the condemned man's attorney told the jury, "Why sully your hands with this piece of flotsam?"; being sued on behalf of a fetus whose lawyers claimed was illegitimately imprisoned inside a ne'er-do-well mom; legalizing rape due to a clerical error; begging constantly for federal aid as his hapless state was battered by floods and crop failures; and unsuccessfully bowing and scraping on *Donahue* to General Motors execs in the hopes that they would site new auto plants in his state. Colorful, sad, besieged place, Ashcroft's Missouri.

Ashcroft did win something important during his Missouri days, 29 though: a couple of powerful national enemies in the civil rights and women's lobbies. Eventually they would help make his confirmation process for U.S. attorney general so grueling (and so amusing to read about). Accusations of racism have stalked Ashcroft from his days as Missouri's attorney general, when he fought a court-imposed school integration plan—not out of any racist intention, he insisted, but because it placed an unfair tax burden on the people of Missouri.

If his opposition to the school plan issued from his principles, it's less 30 clear what motivated him to block Bill Clinton's appointment of the black Missouri Supreme Court Judge Ronnie White to a federal judgeship. Ashcroft advanced inchoate feelings that White just might be too "activist" and got the entire GOP to go along with him by spreading misleading accounts of White's being soft on capital punishment. In reality, Judge White had voted to uphold death penalty convictions 41 out of 59 times, and almost always voted with the panel majority. So at the very least, there was rank demagoguery behind Ashcroft's campaign against the judge. Speaking at the anti-race-mixing Bob Jones University and giving an interview to the Confederate fan magazine *Southern Partisan*—which he praised for trying to convince Americans that the Confederates were not "giving their lives, subscribing their sacred fortunes and their honor to some perverted agenda"—didn't help Ashcroft's reputation with the civil rights cognoscenti either.

31   In attempting to deflect accusations of racism, Ashcroft's goofy, hapless Dagwood Bumstead persona comes to the fore. He assures readers of his memoir that his father possessed "the foresight to prevent his son's prejudices at an early age" by playing him Mahalia Jackson records and making him read the left-wing black novelist Richard Wright (while not, Ashcroft assures us, "subscrib[ing] to everything Wright advocated"). A further sign of the Ashcroft family's progressive stance on race is that his parents let black guests rake leaves in the backyard—just as they would any other visitor.

32   The women's movement has had it in for Ashcroft since he came up with a startling antitrust innovation in the late '70s. As Missouri's attorney general, he sued the National Organization for Women because they were leading a boycott of the state over its failure to pass the Equal Rights Amendment. The boycott, Ashcroft argued, was a "restraint of trade." Get it? The judge didn't either. Ashcroft lost.

33   His steadfast rhetorical objection to abortion (except to save the life of the mother) and some restrictions on it he either passed or advocated in Missouri (he wanted to completely ban *second* abortions, for instance) have also made him a women's movement pariah.

34   Yet even his enemies typically grant that there's a certain kind of basic personal integrity that we can expect from Ashcroft. He is unlikely to screw the interns, accept bribes, gamble, or, God forbid, dance. Of course, that is the least important kind of integrity to expect from a politician.

35   When it comes to a more substantive integrity—devotion to core political principles—there aren't very many important ideas that Ashcroft is solid on. He is more likely to adopt specific proposals in an ad hoc, disconnected way. He was for trade sanctions against Sudan because they don't respect religious freedom; yet he later plumped (rightly) to end the Cuban boycott (after earlier supporting it). He was foursquare against national standards for education but insists on them for drug and suicide laws.

36   Ultimately, Ashcroft's appeal to conservatives seems to be rooted more in his persona and his religiosity than actual conservative legislative achievements. And that appeal has proven pretty thin outside Missouri. Although he won with 64 percent of the vote in his second gubernatorial race and swept every county in his first Senate race, Ashcroft was a nobody on the national stage until Bush tapped him for attorney general. Dating back to the first Reagan administration, Ashcroft had been a perpetual name floating up as someone who *just might* be named attorney general in a Republican administration. Similarly, he was a prominent might-have-been vice presidential candidate for Bob Dole in '96. He ran hard for president through most of '97 and '98 in that "just looking" way, rousing much excitement among the likes of Pat Robertson. But he eventually acknowledged in January 1999 that the support wasn't there.

37   It hadn't been there earlier in the decade, either, when Ashcroft made a spectacularly weak run for chairman of the Republican National Committee. He'd been term-limited out of the Missouri state house in '93 and was cooling his heels before he could run for Senate in '94. Despite having far and away the most prominent political experience of any of the candidates

for chairman, Ashcroft came in third on the first ballot, behind Haley Barbour (then just a former Reagan aide) and current Secretary of Energy Spencer Abraham (then just a former Dan Quayle aide). He was so despondent at his loss that he avoided the traditional stand-on-the-dais-together unity display.

Later, even his home state let him down. In 2000, Ashcroft famously 38 suffered what is surely one of the most humiliating political defeats in American history. Not only did he fail to get re-elected to the Senate—something 80 percent of incumbents pull off—but he lost to a dead man, Democratic Gov. Mel Carnahan. What made the loss all the more dramatic was the long-time rivalry between Ashcroft and Carnahan, who had been lieutenant governor when Ashcroft was Missouri's chief executive.

Bad blood between them flowed long and deep, from the days when 39 Ashcroft went to court to establish that he didn't cede power to his lieutenant every time he left the state. Ashcroft even pettily ended the practice of paying Carnahan a pro-rated higher salary on days Ashcroft was absent. Their Senate election was bitter and mean: If Carnahan tried to insinuate Ashcroft had a race problem, John's boys would distribute old photos of Carnahan in blackface. The Show Me State, indeed.

Then, less than a month before the election, Carnahan's plane crashed, 40 killing the governor, his eldest son, and a trusted aide. When the person who wins Senate elections in Missouri can't serve, the governor—in this case, Democrat Roger Wilson—appoints someone to the vacancy until the next election. Wilson made it clear that he would choose the grieving widow and mother, Jean Carnahan. In the pollster's argot, the late Mel suddenly had no negatives and Jean's mere ability to stride in public purposefully with the ghosts of husband and son hovering nearby was enough to dig Ashcroft's political grave.

There Ashcroft was, then—a small-account politician of no particular 41 achievement or rigor from a difficult little state, repudiated on the national stage and suffering a uniquely stinging political defeat. Yet Ashcroft gallantly chose not to challenge the election, though he had various procedural tacks he could have taken. In his highly praised concession speech, Ashcroft said that "the will of the people has been expressed with compassion" and that he "hope[s] that the outcome . . . is a matter of comfort to Mrs. Carnahan."

However tough that loss must have been, it must have been even more 42 bruising when, a few months later, the new Sen. Carnahan voted against Ashcroft for attorney general. Mr. Dithers couldn't have humiliated poor, hapless Dagwood any better.

Angry Attorney General

It might have seemed that Ashcroft was politically dead after losing to the 43 late Carnahan. But as he wrote in his memoir, for every crucifixion there's a resurrection. President George W. Bush rolled away the stone by nominating Ashcroft for attorney general, and even the doubting Thomases in the

Senate hearings had to recognize that Ashcroft had arisen. Even then, though, Ashcroft was not a first choice, but a compromise sop to the GOP's religious right wing. His confirmation battle was brutal even by contemporary standards, and a lifetime's worth of political foes portrayed Ashcroft as a freakish chimera of Anita Bryant, Torquemada, and George Lincoln Rockwell. His own performance in the hearings seemed to hurt, not help, his cause. Analysts predicted at the beginning of the hearings that a good 80 of his erstwhile colleagues would support him, but he eventually squeaked through by only four votes, 52–48.

44   As he launched the newest phase of his career, Ashcroft first played the role of the dad with the soft touch, shuffling along, doing whatever it takes to keep the family happy. He seemingly scheduled every day around publicly kissing up to the people who hate him most. He was no racist, by God, so he said he was going to make ending "racial profiling" his major concern. (Post-9/11, of course, profiling is back with a vengeance, and with a new target about whom no one seems upset.) Does Ashcroft's religion think homosexuality is an abomination? Sure, but that wouldn't stop him from meeting with the Log Cabin Republicans. Despite his consistent opposition to racial preferences while a legislator, Ashcroft's Justice Department filed an enthusiastic defense of such programs in the *Adarand* case—a case that Sen. Ashcroft particularly liked to moan about. The staunchly anti-abortion Ashcroft ordered federal marshals to protect abortion doctors, and his DOJ collared the killers of abortionists in France.

45   We cannot presume to know what a politician really thinks, even, or perhaps especially, from listening to what he says. So we must imagine how the long series of defeats and disappointments—and the constant attacks from the country's dominant culture—must have burned in Ashcroft's psyche before 9/11. Ashcroft's immediate response to the attacks was to sink into a dark Orwellian morass of secret detentions, warrantless wiretaps, and eavesdropping on lawyers. Meanwhile, he instructed his charges at the Department of Justice to do whatever was legally possible to ignore and stonewall Freedom of Information Act requests. It's irresistible to wonder if the post-9/11 Ashcroft is a long-suffering, go-along-to-get-along dad who finally snaps, yanks up his trousers tight, and stomps forth, insistent that he just ain't gonna take it anymore. The days of pushing around Big John Ashcroft are over. Round up the Arabs and convene the military tribunals. And no, Mr. Liberal Media, I won't tell you who I've got locked up over here.

46   In prepared statements—not unscripted press conference bluster—Ashcroft famously warned his critics that they are essentially traitors. "Those who scare peace-loving people with phantoms of lost liberty," he inveighed before Congress, "your tactics only aid terrorists." He needed only to add "and comfort" to his statement to charge dissenters worried about infringements on civil liberties with the constitutional definition of treason.

47   The right-wing media are still loyally on his side. *National Review*'s Jonah Goldberg wrote a painful syndicated column excoriating the liberal media for their "canards" about Ashcroft. It centered on the notion that since Ashcroft didn't use the *word* traitor it is completely unfair to characterize

that statement as saying such. "So now Ashcroft is calling people 'traitors'? Go back and read what he actually said," Goldberg instructs of the quote above. "He didn't say anyone who questions the government is wrong, let alone a traitor." Sure—and calling someone a "long-eared, slow, patient, sure-footed domesticated mammal" isn't the same as calling him an ass.

In any case, it is surely no small matter, even during wartime footing,   48
that Ashcroft has ordered the detention of hundreds of people without making public their identities or the charges they face. This is not simply an affront to the detainees, but to all of us. We deserve transparency from our government and justice that acts according to settled and traditional rules—even toward immigrants without full constitutional protections.

To the delight of small-government mavens, Ashcroft once averred, "We   49
are here to make government smaller, not larger. We are here to uphold personal freedom and responsibility, not . . . construct an even bigger Nanny State to micro-manage our lives." Yet he has proven that his conservative side trumps any alleged libertarian leanings, even when the topic is completely unrelated to the war on terrorism.

He's spearheaded the Drug Enforcement Administration in actions   50
against people in states that have passed liberal laws on medical marijuana and assisted suicide. Despite his years in state government talking up the blessings of federalism, Ashcroft has proven he barely meant a word of it.

As the Cato Institute's constitutional expert Roger Pilon puts it, "one   51
can understand that the executive branch's job is to see that the laws be faithfully executed. At the same time we all know that discretion is a key element of the prosecutorial function." The attorney general's supporters try to rescue him from charges of hypocrisy by saying it's his job to enforce the law; but where he chooses to aim his resources is up to him, and his prosecutorial indiscretions mark him as a hypocrite on states' rights.

And elsewhere. Sen. Ashcroft was a firm defender of Internet privacy. Of   52
the Clipper Chip and other surveillance features the government sought to build into computers and communications hardware, he said that "individuals will be outraged when they understand that the administration wants to hand the FBI access to your private communications." But Attorney General Ashcroft has enthusiastically pushed for and embraced USA PATRIOT Act provisions that give increased authority for warrantless Internet taps.

Of course, these ideas have long been in play. They're not Ashcroft's per-   53
sonal new wave of tyranny. As the Electronic Frontier Foundation's Lee Tien, a fan of Ashcroft's senatorial stance toward electronic privacy, says, a lot of it is the hat he's wearing as attorney general in a time of crisis. But he isn't wearing it well. Even in non-terrorism issues, Ashcroft shows a peculiar tone-deafness to First Amendment liberties. His Justice Department is behind the vindictive assault on journalist Vanessa Leggett, who had been jailed for nearly six months for not turning over notes relating to a murder to a grand jury, a civil contempt charge. Ashcroft's DOJ had threatened her with the possibility of a criminal contempt charge for the same thing—potentially adding years in jail to the months she's already languished. Then in January the DOJ went ahead and indicted the accused murderer in

question on federal charges related to the same murder for which he's already been acquitted by the state of Texas—without using Leggett's evidence, and raising disturbing double jeopardy questions. (Leggett still fears being subpoenaed in that case.) If Ashcroft hasn't yet lived up to the worst fears of his foes, he seems more than willing to let civil liberties fall by the wayside if he thinks there's any excuse for it.

Reckless Pilot

54   There were areas, like abortion and civil rights, where his foes feared his personal beliefs would shape his law enforcement. So far, that seems not to be the case. Anywhere his beliefs might lead toward less enforcement of laws, they have had no effect at all. Just as the death-penalty-hating Janet Reno signed many a federal death warrant, Ashcroft will not be making his personal preferences the law of the land.

55   But he is known, as one conservative activist who has worked with DOJ officials under Ashcroft told me, for being "good in a chameleon-like way at representing his constituencies within conservatism." That's the best way to explain the one thing he's done as attorney general that has lived up to liberal fears—and libertarian hopes—about him: In a May 2001 letter to the National Rifle Association, he stated unequivocally that he considers the right to bear arms an individual one.

56   Having stated that, he has shown it in only two rather restrained ways. First, he reduced the time that records of gun background checks are kept from 90 days to one. Second, he extended one procedural courtesy to those mysterious, anonymous, locked-away aliens: He refused to check whether they had made gun purchases, agreeing with FBI lawyers that such an investigation went beyond the statutory purpose of the Brady Bill. As Eric Sterling of the Criminal Justice Policy Center says regarding Ashcroft's rhetoric on Second Amendment rights, "It doesn't clarify any federal policy and it doesn't give guidance to the ATF or FBI. It ends up being a political sop to a very powerful political interest."

57   So his pro-gun statements, as revolutionary as they may seem on the surface, merely maintain the status quo. His admirers are reinforced in their admiration, his enemies are reassured he is everything they hate him for, and the law basically stays the same.

58   For all his flaws and foibles, Attorney General Ashcroft has his hand on the control stick of the Department of Justice. He is a man whose upbringing and beliefs place him at odds with the dominant cultural elite, who dog and question his every move and decision. He's a man who has occupied many offices with little to show for it all except one huge, unique humiliation—after which he has been thrust into a position of great legal power in a time when the country is uniquely ready to roll over to authority. Given his Assemblies of God background and its concomitant sense of the divine in the mundane, it's impossible to think that (though he'd never admit it to a secular press) Ashcroft isn't feeling that it's part of God's providence that he's attorney general during a time of national crisis and panic. That it's an occasion that Ashcroft, the stern and firm father figure, should rise to.

Which may well be reason to worry. Constitutionalists view the attor- 59
ney general's job as representing the people of the United States and their
Constitution. Ashcroft seems to think differently. His policies to date show
it, and so do some telling words. When asked to defend one of his actions
as Missouri's attorney general during his confirmation hearing, he noted,
"When the state is attacked, I think it's important to expect the attorney
general . . . to defend the state." This has been the alarming philosophy behind almost all of his post-9/11 decisions and pronouncements. His power
as attorney general may well be, to him, as reckless and out of control as
that Piper Cub he remembers so strongly from his childhood.

But this time, we're all stuck with him in the pilot's seat.   60

Rhetorical Considerations

1. Examine the introduction and conclusion of the essay. How does one effectively relate to the other? (*Hodges'* 33b/*Writer's* 3b)
2. Does this essay have a thesis sentence? If you can, find an explicit statement
   of thesis. If you can't find one, write one in your own words. (*Hodges'*
   32c/*Writer's* 2b)
3. This is a long essay. How does Doherty organize it effectively to make the
   length more manageable? (*Hodges'* 32d/*Writer's* 2c)
4. Find evidence of the author's opinions regarding his subject. (*Hodges'*
   35c/*Writer's* 7c)
5. What example illustrates Ashcroft at his best? What example illustrates
   Ashcroft at his worst? Are these examples a matter of the author's perceptions
   and bias, or are they objectively portrayed? (*Hodges'* 31c/*Writer's* 2d)

Language and Style

1. Look up the following words in your dictionary: *infer* and *harrowing* (paragraph 9); *loggerheads* (paragraph 11); *laudatory* and *secular* (paragraph 12); *denomination, imbued, derided,* and *icons* (paragraph 13); *opprobrium* (paragraph
   15); *mirth* (paragraph 16); *pietist* (paragraph 18); *zealot* (paragraph 21); *outré*
   (paragraph 22); *immanent* and *anathema* (paragraph 24); *gothic, notorious, petulantly, sully,* and *flotsam* (paragraph 28); *grueling* (paragraph 29); *inchoate* and
   demagoguery (paragraph 30); *deflect* (paragraph 31); *rhetorical* and *pariah* (paragraph 33); *dais* (paragraph 37); *incumbents* (paragraph 38); *argot* (paragraph
   40); *hapless* (paragraph 42); *sop* and *chimera* (paragraph 43); *Orwellian* and
   morass (paragraph 45); *excoriating* (paragraph 47); *mavens* (paragraph 49); *concomitant* (paragraph 58). (*Hodges'* 19c/*Writer's* 28e)
2. Find three uses of figurative language in the essay. (*Hodges'* 20b/*Writer's* 29b)
3. Justify, if you can, the sentence fragment in paragraph 5. (*Hodges'* 2/*Writer's* 18)
4. The last sentence in paragraph 20 is a complex sentence. How would the sentence be affected rhetorically if the order of the two clauses were reversed?
   (*Hodges'* 1e/*Writer's* 17c)
5. Comment on the word order of the second sentence in paragraph 28. Would
   another order have been more effective? (*Hodges'* 29f/*Writer's* 26f)

Writing Suggestions

1. Write an essay in which you describe the professional life of someone you know well.
2. Write an essay in which you take the role of the defender and supporter of Ashcroft and rebut Doherty's characterization of him in this essay.

✦

IMAGES
Example

Diversity has become a popular issue in marketing tactics. The following images all make a point that their products or services are for "everyone." The Texas Woman's University image is featured on the admissions home page of the university's Web site. Texas Woman's University characterizes itself as an institution "primarily for women" since a controversial move in 1994 to admit men into all its programs. The university also has a large percentage of "nontraditional students." It is also interesting to note that the Ford Motor Company advertisement appeared before September 11, 2001.

Texas Woman's University

✦

IMAGES (CONT.)

Example

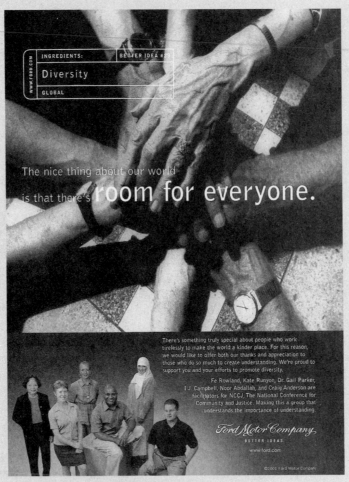

Ford Motor Company

Rhetorical Considerations

1. Look closely at each image. See if you can figure out what the target audience of each image and each individual model is. Can you think of anyone who is not represented in these images? Are you represented? (*Hodges* 32a/*Writer's* 1b–1c)
2. Two of the most common characteristics addressed in diversity approaches are race and ethnicity. These images appear here in black and white. Are the subtleties of skin tones evident? What implications might the models' appearances have on different audiences?
3. Which of the images seems to address the issue of diversity more aggressively? Does either seem to be just giving lip service to the issue?
4. Where do you think the Ford ad might have been placed—in mainstream magazines, like *Time*, or magazines directed toward a particular group? (*Hodges* 32a/*Writer's* 1b and 1e)

Writing Suggestions

1. Write a letter to an advertiser of an ad you have found that does not represent a segment of society, urging the company or organization to include that group more visibly in their marketing.
2. Look at magazine ads and television commercials, focusing on a particular type of product or a particular group of people. Write an essay in which you explain either how the product is being marketed (to whom and why) or how a group of people are either still being excluded from the new diversity movement or are now finally being acknowledged.

CHAPTER 2

Narration

Narration is the telling of a story—a sequence of events setting out facts relevant to a situation, either true or fictional. Narratives may be short, such as jokes, which often tell a story, or they may be long, as are Russian novels. They may be factual, such as newspaper and magazine articles (like many of the selections in this book), laboratory reports (see www.harbrace.com or *Writer's* 14), company financial reports, instructions for using products, government white papers, diaries, and biographies can all contain narrative elements, or they may be fictional, such as are short stories, novels and even plays and some poems. In this chapter, we will discuss factual narratives.

Understanding Narration

All narratives share certain elements:

- a beginning, a middle, and an end;
- one or more characters;
- a setting;
- some kind of action or conflict.

Notice how the following narrative—a simple series of events—contains all of the above elements:

Character — Lisa was worried that she might miss her flight to Chicago, so she — Setting

Action — was driving a little fast. In her — Beginning

rearview mirror she saw flashing lights moving rapidly toward her. — Middle

She pulled over into the right lane and slowed down as the ambulance raced by. — End

Having a beginning, a middle, and an end shows movement and allows the narrator to make a point, in this case the point that Lisa knew she was taking a risk. Your beginning should identify the character or characters (Lisa), reveal the setting (a moving auto), and introduce the action (driving).

The middle shows the conflict and tells, or insinuates, the story (Lisa saw flashing lights and thought she was about to be stopped by the police). The end resolves the conflict and draws the tale to a close (the lights announced an ambulance, not a police car).

Point of View

Successful narratives also have a consistent *point of view.* Point of view refers to the narrator's perspective. When we say that the narrative is told from a *first-person* point of view, we mean that the narrator was a participant in or observer of the events that he or she is reporting. First-person point of view is often deeply subjective (although it need not be), emphasizing the writer's reactions to certain events, as Angelou's and Hockenberry's narratives demonstrate. First-person narratives consistently use first-person pronouns and past tense verbs. When we say that the narrative is told from a *third-person* point of view, we mean that the narrator is reporting events in which he or she was not a participant and that he or she did not observe firsthand. Cecilia Ballí's essay, "Return to Padre," is an example of third-person narrative. Like Ballí's, narratives that take the third-person point of view are usually objective although they may still show the writer's feelings or opinion. They consistently use third-person pronouns and past tense verbs. Other examples of narratives employing third-person point of view are easily found in newspaper reports of recent events or in history books.

Conflict

Narratives often contain conflict and suspense. In fact, all of the writers in this chapter present a conflict as the core of their tales. The conflict may be with oneself or another person, as in the essays by Said, Reynoso, and Ballí; or with society, as with Oron, Angelou, and Hockenberry.

Using Narration

Purpose

Narratives (excluding fictional narratives, which are beyond the scope of this book) may have an expressive, informative, or persuasive purpose or may combine these. (See *Hodges'* 32a/*Writer's* 1e for a full discussion of *purpose.*) When a narrative is primarily expressive, it focuses on the writer's feelings about events; when primarily informative, it focuses on the events themselves; when primarily persuasive, it uses the events to influence the reader's opinion or to move the reader to some course of action. Reynoso's narrative is primarily expressive. Notice here how she focuses on her feelings about her father:

> In the beginning, Papi would protect our innocence and let us hide in our rooms while he did his thing. As I got older, though, my father would sit

me on his lap and ask me to pick whom I'd like to live with when he divorced my mother. I'd mumble and stare at the floor and pray for different
parents. (86)

She tells us about her father's actions—both good and bad—during her
childhood and how they made her feel. She concludes her essay by explaining how she resolved her feelings of conflict before her father died. Said's
essay, in contrast, is primarily informative, although her language and style
do reveal her feelings:

> When a townsman finally showed me an empty place [to live], the fact that
> the walls reached only to the level of my head seemed like a minor incon-
> venience. . . . But my half-erected home forced me away from the solitude I
> found so comfortable and placed me amid the chaos that occurs in the space
> between people. (79)

Assaf Oron gives us considerable detail in order to persuade us of his point:

> we employ the IDF in two types of terror. One type is quite visible: violent acts
> of killing and destruction. . . . But the worse type of terror is the silent one . . .
> of Occupation, of humiliation on a personal and collective basis, of depriva-
> tion and legalized robbery, of alternating exploitation and starvation. (91–92)

Thesis

Your thesis develops out of your purpose: what do you want your readers to
understand when they read your narrative? Frame that desire into a sentence and it will provide the basis for your thesis. For instance, Hockenberry
clearly wants his readers to understand the human cost of war, of having to
abandon "those items which make . . . life safe, possible" (83). His point is
that the world, and the United States especially, needs to pay attention, but
"after two boys opened fire in a Colorado high school . . . America stopped
paying attention" (84).

Audience

As you write narratives, always keep your purpose and your audience clearly
in mind. Hockenberry writes about the Albanian refugees for an audience of
people interested in issues related to disabilities. Writing for *Latina*, Patricia
Reynoso assumes her audience will share a number of cultural values. Cecilia Ballí addresses her Texas audience by referring to Texas history and
using Spanish words and phrases throughout her essay. But sometimes writers have a more complex task when assessing their audience. For instance,
although Assaf Oron addresses his letter to those who, according to him,
blindly and unthinkingly support the war against the Palestinians, his use
of irony reveals that his real audience is probably those who are not committed either way:

> Then came the 1973 war, and for a child of 7 it was the perfect proof that,
> indeed the Arabs want to throw us into the sea, and what a great opportu-
> nity it was for our glorious IDF to teach them a lesson. (89–90)

This strategy is risky if Oron expects to change the minds of the true believ-
ers, but it shows that he has considered his audience carefully. *Tikkun,* where
this piece first appeared, is a magazine published by a Jewish community
that supports peace. Oron's letter would indeed appeal to the majority of its
readers. If you read your audience well, you will be better able to decide
which events are significant and how they can best be arranged to achieve
the effect you want. (See *Hodges'* 32d/*Writer's* 2c for more information.) You
will also be better able to choose the kinds of specific details that will make
the events real for your readers.

You can plan your strategy most effectively if you keep the five journalist's questions in mind—and you can be sure your readers will want to know
the answers to these questions:

- *What* happens (action)?
- *Who* is involved in the events (actors)?
- *When* do the events occur (time)?
- *Where* do they happen (place, which, with time, is often referred to as
  the *setting*)?
- *Why* do the events occur (cause—perhaps the most interesting question)?

These questions can remind you of what your readers want to know.

Organization

Traditional chronological order, which begins with the precipitating event
and ends with its resolution, may seem like the easiest approach to organizing a narrative, but selecting that precipitating event can be difficult and
readers may need background information, which may dilute the impact of
your opening. Maya Angelou solves this problem with a dazzling dramatic
description of the precipitating event, her toothache.

> The angel of the candy counter had found me out at last, and was exacting
> excruciating penance for all the stolen Milky Ways, Mounds, Mr. Goodbars,
> and Hersheys with Almonds. I had two cavities that were rotten to the gums.
> The pain was beyond the baliwick of crushed aspirins or oil of cloves. (94)

Narratives can also begin in the middle or at the end of the story, as
Reynoso's does, and provide "flashbacks" to earlier events (or "flash-forwards"
to later ones). Beginning in the middle (the literary term is *in medias res,*
Latin for "in the middle of things") lends immediacy to the unfolding
events, while beginning at the end is often dramatic and provides a sense of
inevitability. Here are the first three sentences of Reynoso's narrative, which
are echoed in her essay's conclusion:

The sympathetic expression on her face said it all. My father's doctor walked toward me, and I could see in her eyes that the news she was getting ready to give me was terrible. "Your father has lung cancer," she said softly. (85)

Occasionally a narrative recounts events in the order of their importance, as Said's and Hockenberry's do, rather than in the time sequence in which they occurred.

Images

Sometimes pictures tell a story as clearly as words do, and sometimes even more clearly. Consider, for example, the story people constructed around van Eyck's painting of the Amolfinis. The details in the painting led viewers to believe that it depicts a wedding. Those details also suggested to viewers something about the woman's family and their economic status. The Chevy Malibu ad depicts a different story, using both words and images to convey its message. If you choose to include a picture, chart, or graph in your own narrative, make sure that it enhances your presentation of events.

Student Essay

Notice how Roy Fowler, a nontraditional student, provides answers to the traditional journalist's questions as he recounts a frustrating experience.

Roadblocks

Introduction

Context

Point

Setting—where and when

Minor conflict

Last week I arrived ten minutes late for a major anatomy exam. It wasn't my fault. I left my part-time job with plenty of time for driving to campus, parking, and getting to my seat in the classroom, but two trucks—a semi and a dump truck—collided on the interstate and stopped traffic for thirty minutes. It never fails. Why is it, whenever I really need to be somewhere, someone or something is always in my way, just like when I was on that Air Force training exercise in southern Germany.

It was a very cold morning back in January 1990. The snow crunched beneath my feet, and the cold breeze stung my face as I quickly walked back from the breakfast tent to my sleeping tent, where I removed my coat, gloves, scarf, and sweater and lay down on my cot trying to get warm. I only had an hour, and I wanted to soak up as much heat as

---

continued

possible before I had to go outside for the rest of the day. As I drifted between sleep and wakefulness, someone roughly shook me back to consciousness. Had time passed that quickly? Surely my hour wasn't up.

Precipitating event

The captain was shaking me awake to congratulate me on becoming the
father of a little girl. I became fully alert as I realized he was also holding
something back: There were complications; my newborn daughter was in
the intensive care unit in San Antonio, Texas; she might not live.

Background and details

Event

Event

The military has a system for everything, even getting people home for
emergencies. I quickly packed my bags, changed into civilian clothing, and
hurried towards the administration tent to sign out of the unit before leaving for Frankfurt International Airport. But I had to wait nearly an hour until
someone was available to drive me to the division support unit (DSU) that
handled all the Red Cross notifications for emergency leave. There, I completed leave forms and picked up plane tickets—paperwork required for
me to leave Germany. But then, there I was, stuck sitting in another tent,

Event

waiting for another ride. Finally, after lunch, I got into an old army-green
VW bus, top speed 80 kph—about 50 mph. Three hours dragged by as
that old bus lumbered down the autobahn toward Frankfurt. I mentally
cheered as we arrived at the U.S. Air Force side of the airport. I was ready
to fly across the ocean to my gravely ill baby girl. I wasn't ready for the
surprise that waited for me at the personnel office, though.

Event

The last flight back to the States had left at two o'clock. I was so close,
but I was not going home that day. The chaplain, there to give me support, said, "We'll get you out of here tomorrow morning." There was nothing to do but call the hospital in Texas to check on my family. My wife was

Note expressive aim

fine, but my little girl was scheduled for surgery the next morning, surgery
she had only a fifty percent chance of surviving. I spent that evening sitting in the Air Force club, and soon realized that, though drinking myself
to sleep might make the night seem to pass more quickly, it wouldn't
bring me any closer to my wife and little girl in Texas. After all, there were
no flights until the next day.

Events

Early the next day one of the chaplain's drivers gave me a ride to the
other side of the airport for my 10:00 flight. Ticket in hand, I checked in at
the gate and boarded the plane. After everyone settled into their seats, I

Note effect of details

watched the flight attendant close the cabin door, felt the bump of the tug
as it hooked to the plane, and rejoiced as we pushed away from the gate.
We taxied away from the terminal and traveled down the taxiway, feeling
every crack in the asphalt, and lined up for takeoff. Waiting for the plane
to take off, I drifted so deeply into thoughts of home and my baby daughter
that I never felt the plane roar down the runway and leap into the air. I
was startled when ten minutes after the plane was in the air, the pilot announced, "We are having trouble with the landing gear. We can't make it

*First set of com-
plicating events*

Expressive aim

Event details

*Second set of
complicating
events*

Details

*Details here par-
allel details in
paragraph 5*

*Resolution of
travel conflict*

*Resolution of
family conflict*

*Conclusion—
summarizes
major conflict,
puts it in per-
spective, and ties
it to initial
minor conflict*

retract, we do not have enough fuel to fly to the United States with the gear down, and we are too heavy to land back at Frankfurt. We are going to fly out over the ocean, and if we still cannot get the gear to retract, we will have to dump some fuel and return to Frankfurt." One moment my stomach turned with anticipation, and the next it churned with frustration. Four hours later I was back at the Frankfurt terminal and no closer to home.

But I wasn't licked yet, and Delta was not the only American carrier in Frankfurt. I ran to the TWA ticket counter and exchanged my ticket for the 7:00 p.m. flight to London with an early-morning flight from there to the USA. The clock in the airport lounge where I waited slowly ticked away four hours before I stood in front of the departure gate ready to board another plane. The gate attendant announced a delay. There was a problem with the fuel lines. I waited until 10:00 p.m. when it was announced that the repair could not be made and the flight was canceled. There were no flights to the States until the following day. The airline put us up at a small hotel an hour away from the airport.

Day three, six in the morning; I waited for a taxi to the airport to change my ticket yet again. And then I was back at the Delta departure gate waiting to board for the third time. I entered the plane, located my seat, sat down, watched the flight attendant close the door, felt the tug connect to the plane, felt our movement away from the terminal. I was back on the runway waiting for takeoff, just as I had been the day before, but this day, this time, this plane was going to take me home even if I had to fly it myself. Once in the air and dreading an announcement that might cancel my flight home, I settled into my seat with a sigh of relief when I felt the landing gear thump into place and I began to compute my arrival time in Dallas.

Seven hours later the plane landed at DFW airport. At least I was in the United States; I could manage any roadblocks here. Once in the terminal, I called my home unit at Fort Hood to make arrangements to get to San Antonio. As the plane they booked me on taxied toward the Killeen terminal, I saw the turning rotor blades of the waiting army helicopter. I left the plane, ran across the ramp, boarded the helicopter, and, ninety minutes later, landed on the grass in front of the army hospital in San Antonio. My father and father-in-law greeted me and took me to see my wife. And then I went to ICU where my pretty baby girl fought for life. (Six years old now, with wheels, she gives perpetual motion a new definition.)

In this supersonic age it had taken me three days to fly from Germany to the USA. Roadblocks: bureaucracy, scheduling problems, technical difficulties all conspired to delay me in a time of serious family crisis. Traffic jams, dead batteries, traffic lights—they're still hidden behind every corner and occasionally slow me down, but they can never hold me back. I took my family home intact and I aced my anatomy exam.

Commentary

The introduction establishes the context for Fowler's essay; he begins by re-counting a recent event, being late for an exam. His analysis of the source of his frustration provides a rationale for the essay. Then he moves back-ward in time to a specific event in 1990.

From this point on, the essay is organized in a straightforward chronolog-ical order, moving from the background events in Germany through the events that followed. Within this chronological frame Fowler establishes why the events occurred, while making the setting (the military and other bureau-cracies) concrete by offering details about how he continually had to hurry up and then wait. These details, as well as those he includes to tell us about how worried he was about his newborn daughter, contribute to his expressive aim.

Fowler's frustration about not getting to class on time is a conflict that frames the primary conflict between him and the roadblocks that delay him on his journey home from Germany—bureaucracy, scheduling inadequacies, and technical failures. Although how he is late for his exam is briefly described rather than fully developed, this incident lends force to the main conflict.

Fowler makes skillful use of parallelism when he reports the sequence of his actions as he boards each plane. In the first instance, his actions empha-size his worried anticipation; in the second, they almost function as a scale upon which he measures his frustration.

Note, too, how Fowler's reference to roadblocks in his conclusion echoes his introduction. The essay ends snappily, tightly drawing together the two events in a single sentence: "I took my family home intact and I aced my anatomy exam."

✦ CHECKLIST FOR WRITING NARRATIVES

- Can I state the *purpose* for my narrative in a single sentence? (*Hodges'* 32a/*Writer's* 1e)
- Does the *thesis* or the point of my narrative grow out of my purpose? (*Hodges'* 32c/*Writer's* 2b)
- Have I assessed my *audience* correctly? Who do I see as my readers? (*Hodges'* 32a/*Writer's* 1e)
- What kind of *organization* have I used? (*Hodges'* 32d/*Writer's* 2c) If my purpose requires an open-ended story, have I begun at the beginning? Does my narrative begin with a dramatic event in the middle of the sequence of events? If I begin with the end of the sequence, do all of the other events lead up to it?
- Have I maintained a consistent *point of view*? Is it subjective (first-person) or objective (third-person)?
- Does my narrative depict a *conflict*? Have I presented that conflict as clearly and accurately as possible?
- Are the *transitions* between events smooth? (*Hodges'* 31b/*Writer's* 3c)
- Have I used *visuals* to help tell the story? If so, what part of the story does the visual tell? Could it be told better without the visual? Why or why not?

◆

HALF-WALLS BETWEEN US
Maria Said

This essay was first published in *re:generation quarterly,* a publication whose purpose is "to provide commentary, critique, and celebration of the church and contemporary culture," and whose roots are founded in orthodox Christianity. The magazine has received much critical acclaim, including being named one of the "top ten resources for cultural literacy" by *Christianity Today* and earning the *Utne Reader's* Alternative Press Award for spiritual coverage. The essay included here illustrates why this publication has found considerable readership outside the Christian community.

1 For two years, I shared my home with more than 30 children, four freedom fighters, a government bureaucrat, a wife-beater, a Red Cross worker with a taste for liquor, a number of prostitutes, a madman, and all the customers of the tea shop next door. This was not my original intention in moving to the desert, but rather the unexpected circumstance of living in a room with only half-walls.

2 When I decided to work in international development, I imagined living in a small hut of my own, with a palm tree to the side. Instead, when I arrived in town, I found that no housing had been arranged for me. After a few nights sleeping outside on a rope bed, scrounging water from people I didn't know, and living on kilos of bananas, I was anxious for a room of my own. When a townsman finally showed me an empty place, the fact that the walls reached only to the level of my head seemed like a minor inconvenience.

3 On my first visit to Agordat, a small town in Eritrea, a country in the Horn of Africa, I fell in love with its mystery, its quiet, its soft sandy colors. The searing heat created a lethargy and engendered a lifestyle that seemed more like a snapshot than a moving image. At any hour of the day, one could look out onto the street and see a camel in midstep, a child with a finger in his mouth, a local tribesman carrying baskets suspended from the ends of a pole laid across his bony shoulders.

4 Traditionally, the desert calls mystics into its presence, and its vast silence allows them to confront the chaos in their hearts. But my half-erected home forced me away from the solitude I found so comfortable and placed me amid the chaos that occurs in the space between people. The liquid ideas of "community" and "neighbor" I had so often espoused and romanticized metamorphosed into solid matter, sometimes in the form of a crutch under my arm, other times as a thorn dug deep into my skin.

5 There are no secrets in this kind of community. The air itself, filled with the sounds of anger and laughter and the smells of cooking and fires, moved in and out of our homes, bringing messages from one place to another. I soon

learned that the rhythmic clattering meant that a young Muslim woman whose husband had left her was teaching her sewing class in order to pay the bills. The moans and grunts meant that an old man who had lost his mind had woken from his nap. The crying of a woman followed by the singing of older women told me that a new baby had been born. Every week or so, the sound of smacks and screams meant that the one-eyed man next door was hitting his wife. And the smell of coffee from my good friend's home, right on the other side of the wall, told me I would soon receive an invitation to visit.

6   In this kind of community, there is no time-out when one can take a deep breath, reapply the makeup, brush down loose ends. Whatever rough ends exist become rougher. Honestly, I hated this transparency. It forced me to recognize that I was neither as nice nor as neighborly as I had always assumed. I couldn't maintain an image of perfection. I, too, was judged for my actions. In fact, my activities provided the main attraction of many people's days. Often, after a long day teaching 300 students, my roommate and I would want to vent our frustrations, but we knew that in the tea shop next door, a group of teenagers sat glued to the wall, waiting to practice their English-listening skills. Just by being a foreigner, I provided an endless supply of material. The physical nearness of people imposed vigilance on my speech and actions. It is much easier to be a hypocrite when life can be divided into public and private parts. In a community with half-walls, there is little room for pretense.

7   At first I thought I had difficult neighbors. By the end, I counted myself as one of the crowd. After two years of sharing lives with a vast array of characters, I had to admit the similarities between us. I had heard the frustration, irritation, sadness, and jealousy in my voice as well as theirs. I had seen the fighter, the cripple, the prostitute, and the madman in myself. For two years, this proved to be my greatest challenge: to love people through their darkness and, even harder, accept the fact that they knew mine. After all, I was probably the strangest neighbor they ever had.

8   Yet from this communion, times of joy and comfort emerged. One of the women who lived next door became my best friend. When the dust storms came and the lights blew out, she would place her candles on top of the wall so that we could share the light. On nights when she worked late, I passed bowls of American-style food over the wall and listened as she and the tea shop customers tried to identify and swallow the strange meals. Each night, after we dragged our rope beds out of the hot rooms into the small courtyards, we would whisper over the wall and wish blessings for the next day. She called me "sister" and her family knew me as a member.

9   Now, living again in America and encapsulated in my own private ghetto, I sometimes revel in, and other times am repelled by, anonymity. I have to remember that I stand before God in a room with no walls. He calls us to reach out to our neighbors over the half-erected walls, and be seen.

Rhetorical Considerations

1. What is the effect of the first sentence? What is the effect of delaying explanation until the end of the first paragraph? (*Hodges'* 33b/*Writer's* 3b)

2. How specific is the author in terms of the time and place of the events she is narrating? Does she provide all the details necessary for your understanding? Does she provide more than is necessary? If so, what effect does this information have on your reading? (*Hodges'* 31c/*Writer's* 2d)
3. What is Said's point about how people arrange spaces in their lives? (*Hodges'* 32a/*Writer's* 1b)
4. What is Said's ultimate purpose in this essay? Does she have an explicit thesis statement? (*Hodges'* 32a/*Writer's* 1b and 1e)
5. Does the perspective Said now has (back in the United States) allow her some insights she might not have had while living in Agordat? How? What are those insights?

Language and Style

1. Look up the following words in your dictionary: *lethargy* and *engendered* (paragraph 3); *metamorphosed* (paragraph 4); *communion* (paragraph 8); *encapsulated* (paragraph 9). (*Hodges'* 19e/*Writer's* 29e)
2. Find descriptive passages in the essay that are particularly effective. (*Hodges'* 20b/*Writer's* 29c)
3. Evaluate the parallelism in paragraph 1. Why is parallelism effective here? (*Hodges'* 26/*Writer's* 25)
4. Identify all the prepositional phrases in paragraph 4. (*Hodges'* 1f /*Writer's* 17a)

Writing Suggestions

1. Write an essay in which you narrate a time in your life when you lived in stressful conditions.
2. Write an essay about a past experience that was difficult at the time but about which you have newfound feelings or have learned a great deal.

THE HOCKENBERRY FILE

John Hockenberry

John Hockenberry has established a respected reputation in journalism in all media of radio, television, and print. He has won Peabody Awards and an Emmy, and he was the first western broadcast journalist to report directly from Kurdish refugee camps. Born in Dayton, Ohio, and educated at the University of Chicago and University of Oregon, Hockenberry has been paraplegic since a car accident at the age of nineteen. His memoir, *Moving Violations: War Zones, Wheelchairs, and Declarations of Independence* (1995), outlines his experiences as a reporter in a wheelchair. He can be seen on NBCs *Dateline* and he had his own show *Hockenberry* on MSNBC. He lives in New York with his wife and two daughters.

1 A refugee camp has no stairs but in this one, just outside Kukes, Albania, where it had rained the entire night before, stairs might have actually helped in getting through this mud. Rolling carefully to avoid the open toilets, I ventured into the center of the camp to speak with a group of families, carefully thinned of their adult males, huddled behind their tractor wagons draped with clear or occasionally green plastic. These convoys of red tractors full of weeping old women and smiling children have become the emblems of this, the last atrocity in an atrocity-filled century.

2 During my first three days, 25,000 Kosovar refugees had crossed the Albanian border and an even greater number had crossed into Macedonia. People sat together on the ground anywhere they could find a rock or stump. The oldest and most frail were on brown blankets stained with dark puddles of rainwater. A tiny baby was wrapped tightly in a wooden cradle. A feeble old woman in a scarf rocked while gazing back at the mountain peaks she had so recently crossed. She had made it over. In her eyes was the disheartening assumption she would not be making the return trip in this lifetime.

3 Among the little piles of objects arranged at the back of each wagon, the ornately carved cradle stood out. This was the one object that even allowed for the possibility that life was dedicated to something besides crude, pure necessity. Everything else, dented metal pots, rope, drab clothes, random pieces of flatware, plastic forks with metal spoons grabbed by the fistful, was absent of any decoration. All of it had been hastily collected in the rush to leave. Staying warm and dry over miles and weeks in the snow and rain was the only goal. Each family had its heroic inventory of the items within reach at the moment they became too terrified to stay. For these Kosovar-Albanians, now home is no longer within reach.

4 I asked questions about places, dates. Probing to find a system behind this mass exodus, a pattern emerged. Village by village, paramilitary police had come. They marked the doors of each Albanian home and had ordered

the people to leave. Many used colorful language. *Go find your Clinton. He has a home for you.* Or else it came out, *You belong to NATO now.*

Where were the men? There were various stories. "They stayed behind 5 to fight the Serbs," some said. "They fought and died already," said others. Most said only, "They were taken away." Each family had pictures of its men and laid them out for curious journalists to see. People and pictures together like this made eerie gap-toothed family *tableaux* with blurry snapshots where the brothers, fathers and sons should have been.

I knew this place. I had been to places like these before. This hasty hu- 6 manitarian retreat was an old story. The Kosovars were little different from any people uprooted. As in Romania, Somalia, Iraq, Iran and Kurdistan, the adults were the ones terrified and sad, their faces said "refugee." On the other hand, their children seemed to be having the time of their lives. They ran wild. Their faces said that the squalid camp had become in their innocent eyes a place of adventure, the first in their young lives.

This was expressed in chilling contradictions. At the same moment one 7 family was sobbing about the loss of their sons, a young boy, the last son, showed me his arm. On it was written UCK, the acronym of the Kosovo Liberation Army. He marched back and forth in front of his family's tent anxious to go off and fight. "And if you don't come back?" I asked.

"I will go to heaven," was his joyous reply. His family watched vacantly. 8 His mother said to me, "These camps make our children into beggars and soldiers. Unless we go home they will be able to do nothing else."

Disability was something of an abstract concept here. From the height of 9 my wheelchair, which could have made the trip over the mountains more bearable for any pair of refugees, I towered over the people sitting on the ground. My chair looked useful to them. But otherwise it was not important. I did not stand out in any way. It was a welcome relief from the constant staring and the day to day freak-show mentality in America whenever a wheelchair arrives on the scene. The same blessed anonymity I had known before, in feeding camps in Somalia or at a border checkpoint in Iraq crowded with Kurdish refugees. One man who drove me from place to place in a large van had built a wooden ramp for rolling me up and into his vehicle. He had painted it proudly and affixed non-skid strips for my wheels. Osman was his name. He wanted me to call him Señor Ramp. We soon became fast friends although we knew not a syllable of each other's respective languages.

Going to Albania was a return to places I had not seen for many years. 10 In the beginning, as the first horrible reports began to filter out of Kosovo, I went into a closet and pulled out a beat-up aluminum suitcase I had not looked at for a decade. It had been my companion in the Middle East for the years I lived in Jerusalem as a radio correspondent, during the Gulf War, Kurdistan, and Somalia. Every person with a disability has such a case, a bag, a box in which are stored those items which make an independent life safe, possible. Each case contains those items which an individual has tested through experience, each case as different as each independent life.

I opened my case. There were the spare inner tubes, wheelchair tires, 11 hex wrenches, cans of motor oil, catheters, seven bottles of hydrogen peroxide, iodine solution, batteries, flashlights, hammers, files and dozens of small tools for any conceivable wheelchair repair. When I saw that it was ready to go, I knew I was.

12   Unlike any other time in a foreign war zone this time I would be broadcasting live television. The main risk of doing live TV from the middle of a refugee camp in Albania is that America will suddenly stop paying attention. At the end of the twentieth century, war is not a reliable story line for American television viewers anymore. I stayed in Albania for about three weeks. I left after two boys opened fire in a Colorado high school on April 20. America stopped paying attention. The refugee crisis goes on. I still miss my friend, Señor Ramp.

Rhetorical Considerations

1. This essay appeared in *WE* magazine, which focuses on issues related to disabilities. Would it be of interest to a broader audience? (*Hodges'* 32a/*Writer's* 1b and 1d)
2. What is the specific purpose of Hockenberry's narration? (*Hodges'* 32a/*Writer's* 1b and 1d)
3. Find evidence that Hockenberry's disability informs his perspective. (*Hodges'* 38a/*Writer's* 9a)
4. How does this narration place the author in a conflict or create suspense? (*Hodges'* 32e/*Writer's* 2e)
5. How does Hockenberry focus on individual experiences? (*Hodges'* 31c/*Writer's* 2d)

Language and Style

1. Look up the following words in your dictionary: *ornately* (paragraph 3); *tableaux* (paragraph 5); *abstract* (paragraph 9). (*Hodges'* 19e/*Writer's* 28e)
2. Find particularly effective descriptive language in this essay. (*Hodges'* 20b/*Writer's* 29b)
3. What is the subject of the last sentence of paragraph 2? What is the effect of the word order of this sentence? (*Hodges'* 1b/*Writer's* 16a)
4. Why is the plural *were* used in the second sentence of paragraph 11? (*Hodges'* 6a/*Writer's* 22e)

Writing Suggestions

1. Hockenberry describes his case that contains his necessary items for "an independent life." Similarly, the refugees have had to leave their country with only what is necessary. If you were forced to leave your home at short notice, which necessary or irreplaceable things would you carry with you and why?
2. Hockenberry worries that Americans are no longer paying attention to the problems in Albania because our attention has been directed to other, more local problems. Write an essay in which you narrate your observation or experience of an event or situation that you would like others to pay more attention to.

◆

LOVING PAPI

Patricia Reynoso

Patricia Reynoso is a senior beauty editor at *W* magazine in New York City. This essay was first published in *Latina* magazine.

The sympathetic expression on her face said it all. My father's doctor walked 1 toward me, and I could see in her eyes that the news she was getting ready to give me was terrible "Your father has lung cancer," she said softly. I didn't cry. Instead, I stood still, letting the news sink in, as nurses, doctors, and families bustled by me in the crowded, chaotic hospital corridor. The doctor said he had six months to live. Papi was just a few feet away, lying in his bed. He knew nothing. How, I wondered, was I going to tell him this?

As my parents' oldest daughter, I had always accepted the role of trans- 2 lator. My Dominican father's English consisted of, at best, five words. I had helped him prepare for his U.S. citizenship test. I filled out his Medicaid forms. And when a letter from the bank came, I'd sit beside him reading aloud what it said. But on this cold October night eight years ago, I put my foot down. This was one piece of information I couldn't bear to translate. "I'm not telling him," I said to the doctor, who, of course, didn't speak a word of Spanish. "You're just going to have to find a way to do it yourself."

To this day I have no idea how she broke the news to him, but I do know 3 that my father took it astoundingly well. *"¿Qué se va a hacer?"* he asked me rhetorically and in the same breath praised the country where a lowly immigrant senior citizen is worthy of a private consultation and a caring word with a medical professional. Four months later, just hours before he slipped away, he opened his eyes and saw me standing by the hospital room window, tears streaming down my cheeks. He chuckled and put his thumb in his mouth, gesturing that I was being a baby for crying. It was a classic Papi.

In the years since his death, I have realized what a complex man my fa- 4 ther, Rafael Espaillat, was. His famously violent temper, his drinking problem, and his depression often led to the police coming to our house. And yet Papi somehow found it in him to be a wonderful father who lavished his kids with kind words and praise, who never failed to tell us how proud of us he was, and who taught us the value of humility and hard work. It's true—my younger brother and sister and I lived a childhood filled with more drama than the most dramatic novela imaginable. But today when I think of Papi, I don't remember the police at my house; instead I think that in so many other ways, he was a role model for what a parent should be.

Bueno *vs.* Evil

5   Unfortunately, he wasn't exactly a role model for what a husband should be. Papi was 27 years older than my mother. They met in the Dominican Republic, and when they started dating, he was already engaged to another woman. It was a not-so-small detail he failed to reveal to Mami at the time. So when the town's priest told my mother that her *comprometido* was actually engaged to someone else, she was devastated. She fled to another town, hoping to forget him. Papi married and moved to New York City to start a new life, but within a year his wife had left him. He returned to the Dominican Republic heartbroken and went searching for my mother. When he found her, he pleaded for forgiveness. Amazingly, my mother took him back. They married soon after, and once again Papi moved to New York with a new bride in tow.

6   But from the beginning, there was trouble. On their very first night together in their Manhattan apartment, my father shook my mother by the shoulders and warned her not to leave him as his previous wife had.

7   I came into the picture a little over a year later. Growing up, I could never understand how the evil Papi who fought constantly with my mother could so easily transform into the Papi who was sweet and loving to me. All it took was a few beers after coming home from his factory job, and no amount of pleading from my mother could get him to sit and eat dinner. On those nights, he would sit in his chair in the kitchen in his white T-shirt, with his legs crossed in that particular way he had, and he'd just start ranting and raving in Spanish. Often, he liked to show how mad he really was by smashing plates against the wall. I never knew what exactly he was raving about, but familiar subjects included my mother's supposed disrespect for him and, always, money.

8   In the beginning, Papi would protect our innocence and let us hide in our rooms while he did his thing. As I got older, though, my father would sit me on his lap and ask me to pick whom I'd like to live with when he divorced my mother. I'd mumble and stare at the floor and pray for different parents.

9   But then the sun would rise on a weekend morning and so would my father, looking fresh and smelling clean and excited about the day's adventures. Our annual trip to Coney Island was the highlight of our summer, and Papi made it fun from the minute my brother and sister and I walked out of our apartment. He agreed to ride the Cyclone roller coaster with me, but only after making sure I understood how scary it could be. When I nearly fainted after we got off, he hugged me until I could walk steadily again. In between bites of pink cotton candy, Papi would tell us that there was nothing more admirable than working hard, being educated, and staying humble. My mother always stayed at home, and instead of feeling as if my family was incomplete, I felt blessed to have my father all to myself. I soaked up his praise like a thirsty sponge—"*¡Qué bijita tan linda e inteligente tengo yo!*" he'd often say. I could count on these words after a good report card, a pretty school picture, and much later, when I appeared in a magazine, and he showed it to as many people as cared to see it.

The Fighting Ends

The divorce finally happened the summer that I turned 13, and instead 10
of sadness, I felt incredible relief. Relief that the fights would stop, that
my drunken Papi would disappear and that the sweeter Papi I loved would
reappear.

It was painful to see my father in the years after the marriage ended, 11
which were clearly the saddest of his life. He tried living on his own but
could afford only a rented room in someone's home. He had virtually no
space to himself and had to ask permission to make a cup of coffee. Finally,
he decided to return to the Dominican Republic to start anew yet again. He
remarried, and over the next 10 years, Papi vacationed in New York every so
often. Although he lived far away, he would instantly return to his role of
supportive father.

It took me many years to reconcile my father's complexities and to un- 12
derstand that, even though he exposed his kids to things kids should never
see, his kind words and pride managed to squeeze their way through and
make a positive, unforgettable impact. Admittedly, he was a flawed man,
but he did the best he could for me. What more could I ask? Ultimately, I
learned that love can always work its magic.

The call from the hospital came at dawn. It was Papi's doctor, the one 13
who couldn't speak Spanish, urging me to get there quickly because my father was expected to live only a few more hours. I rushed over to find Papi
unconscious. Suddenly, he opened his eyes, and he spotted my crying by
the window. When he teased me about being a baby, I laughed through my
tears. Even on the edge of death, my father was doing what he knew how to
do best: be my Papi.

Rhetorical Considerations

1. How is this essay organized? Is it a chronological narrative? Look at the introduction and conclusion. What is the effect of tying these together? (*Hodges'*
   32d and 33b/*Writer's* 2c and 3b)
2. In what way can Reynoso be said to be ambivalent toward her father?
3. How does Reynoso inform us of her father's flaws without making him unlik-
   able? (*Hodges'* 31c/*Writer's* 2d)
4. How much time has passed between the author's writing of this essay and
   the death of her father? How do you know? Would this time be a significant
   factor in how she views her father? (*Hodges'* 31c/*Writer's* 2d)
5. Find a sentence in the essay that best expresses Reynoso's thesis. (*Hodges'*
   32c/*Writer's* 2b)

Language and Style

1. Why does Reynoso quote her father in Spanish? Why doesn't she provide us
   with a translation? Does this affect your reading of the essay? (*Hodges'*
   19c/*Writer's* 28c)

2. Find words that describe the author's feelings toward her father. (*Hodges'* 20/*Writer's* 29)
3. Examine the sentence variety in paragraph 1. (*Hodges'* 30/*Writer's* 27)
4. Find and justify (if appropriate) the sentence fragment in paragraph 10. (*Hodges'* 2/*Writer's* 18)

Writing Suggestions

1. Write an essay about your relationship with someone who was both a positive and a negative influence in your life.
2. Write an essay in which you recount a difficult experience that has had a profound effect on you.

✦

A Letter to American Jews (and Other Friends of Israel)

Assaf Oron

Assaf Oron is one of some 530 "refuseniks," reservists in the Israeli Defense Forces (IDF) who refuse the order to serve in the West Bank and Gaza Strip (referred to in this piece as "the Territories"). An American Jewish group called "Tikkun" placed in March 2002 a *New York Times* ad supporting the "refuseniks." Overwhelmed by the hostile response from other American Jews, Tikkun leaders asked refuseniks to help by explaining their cause directly. The letter below is an abridged version of the original that was written as an email in March 26, 2002, in response to this request.

Dear People,   Passover Eve, 2002

Yesterday I was informed of an interesting phenomenon: a peace-supporting   1
Jewish organization called Tikkun published an ad in favor of us, the Israeli reservist refuseniks, and was immediately bombarded with hate mails and phones from other American Jews. Even Jews considering themselves supporters of peace have denounced the Tikkun ad. Most of these "civilized" attacks, so I understand, were seemingly aimed at this or that detail of the Tikkun ad. This is nothing new to me. Over the past two months since we came out with our public pledge to refuse, I've heard and read so many specific arguments about specific aspects of our act. The moment you refute them, new specific arguments sprout up like mushrooms. It is clear that there is something very general and non-specific behind all this criticism.

The general theme is the tribal theme. A very very loud voice (and in Is-   2
rael nowadays, it is the only voice that is allowed to be fully heard) keeps shouting that we are in the midst of a war between two tribes: a tribe of human beings, of pure good—the Israelis—and a tribe of sub-human beings, of pure evil—the Palestinians. To those who find this black-and-white picture a bit hard to believe, the same voice shouts that this is a war of life and death. Only one tribe will survive, so even if we are not purely good, we must lay morality and conscience to sleep, shut up and fight to kill—or else, the Palestinians will throw us into the sea.

Does this ring a bell to you? It does to me. As a little child growing up   3
in Israel under Golda Meir and Moshe Dayan, all I heard was that the Arabs are monsters who want to throw us into the sea, they understand only force, and since our wonderful IDF has won the Six Day War they know not to mess with us anymore—or else. And of course, we must keep the Liberated Territories to ourselves, because there's no one to talk with. Then came the 1973 war, and for a child of 7 it was the perfect proof that indeed the Arabs

89

want to throw us into the sea, and what a great opportunity it was for our glorious IDF to teach them a lesson.

4   A few years passed and a funny thing happened: those throw-us-into-the-sea Arabs came to talk with us, and in exchange for all of Sinai they would sign a full peace. The IDF chief of staff shouted that it is a hoax, that we should not believe Saadat. Already a teenager, I went and protested against the withdrawal from Sinai. After all, it was a purely logical issue: the Arabs are not to be trusted, that's what we've learned from day one. Well, lucky for the country, the government and the majority of the people employed a different logic, and the peace with Egypt was not missed.

5   But the throw-us-into-the-sea paradigm immediately found new fields for play. There was an inconvenient reality on the Northern border, and even though the forces on the other side (Palestinians! Phew!) had strictly adhered to a secret cease-fire for about a year, they were Arabs and therefore could not be trusted. So we talked ourselves into invading Lebanon and setting up a friendlier regime there. The mastermind was defense minister Ariel Sharon, and Shimon Peres, then head of opposition, voted together with his party in favor of the invasion. Only later, when it turned sour, and after many refuseniks already sat in jail, would the main opposition turn against the whole affair. For me at 16 it was also a turning point. When I understood that the government had lied to me in order to sell me this war, I turned from "center-rightist" to "leftist". Sadly enough, it has taken me almost 20 more years, in a slow and painful process, to understand how deeply the lies and self-delusion are rooted in our collective perception of reality.

6   Anyway, when Peres withdrew most of our forces from Lebanon in 1985, the Arabs could still not be trusted. And so, to soothe our endless paranoia and suspicion, we created that perpetual source of death and crime ironically known as "the Security Zone." It took many years, a lot of blood and Four Mothers—against almost all politicians, generals, and columnists—to finally pull us out of Lebanon. In the long and hard way, we learned that even the Lebanese are human beings whose rights must be respected.

7   But not the Palestinians. Because the Palestinians are too painfully close, like a rival sibling, we have singled them out for a special treatment. We have perfected our treatment in this strange no man's land created in 1967, and known as the Occupied Territories. There we have created an entirely hallucinatory reality, in which the true humans, members of the Nation of Masters, could move and settle freely and safely, while the sub-humans, the Nation of Slaves, were shoved into the corners, and kept invisible and controlled under our IDF boots.

8   I know. I've been there. I was taught how to do this, back in the mid-1980's. I did and witnessed as a matter of fact, deeds that I'm ashamed to remember to this day. And fortunately for me, I did not have to witness or do anything truly "pornographic," as some friends of mine experienced.

9   Since 1987, this cruel, impossible, unnatural, insulting reality in the Territories has been exploding in our face. But because of our unshakeable belief that the Palestinians are monsters who want to throw us into the sea, we reacted by trying to maintain what we've created at all costs. When a fledgling

and hesitating peace process tried to work its way through this mess, one major factor (perhaps THE factor) that undermined it and voided its meaning was our establishment's endless fear and suspicion of The Other. To resolve this fear and suspicion, we chose the insane route of demanding full control of The Other throughout the process. When The Other felt cheated out of his freedom, violence erupted again, and all our ancient instincts woke up. There they are, we said in relief, now we see their true face again. The Arabs want to throw us into the sea. There's no one to talk with ("no partner", in our beloved ex-PM Barak's words), and they understand only force. And so we responded again with more and more and more force. This time, the effect was that of putting out a fire with a barrel of gasoline. And that's the moment when I said to myself, NO, I'm not playing this game anymore.

But what about the existential threat, you may ask? Well I ask you, have   10 you not eyes? Don't you see our tanks strolling in Palestinian streets every other day? Don't you see our helicopters hovering over their neighborhoods choosing which window to shoot a missile into? What type of existential need are we answering in trampling the Palestinians?

Prevention of terror, I hear you say. Let me use the words of my friend   11 Ishay Rosen-Zvi: *"You are "fighting against terror"? What a joke. The policies of Occupation have turned the Territories into a greenhouse for growing terror!!!"* You know what? When you treat millions of people like sub-humans for so long, some of them will find inhuman strategies to fight back. Isn't that what the Zionists, and other Jewish revolutionaries, argued about a hundred years ago in order to explain the questionable strategies of survival that Jews used in Europe? Didn't our forefathers say, "Let us live like human beings, and see how we'll act just like other human beings"?

So here's the deal. I don't buy the "they want to throw us into the sea"   12 crap. It"s a collective self-delusion of ours. But more importantly, I don't see tribes. I see people, human beings. **I believe that the Palestinians are human beings like us.** What a concept, eh? And before everything else, before EVERYTHING else, we must treat them like human beings without demanding anything in return. And no (to all die-hard Barak fans), throwing them a couple of crumbs in which they can set up pitiful, completely controlled Bantustans in between our settlements and bypass roads, and believing it to be a great act of "generosity", does NOT come close to answering this basic requirement. This requirement is NOT negotiable; moreover, in a perfect demonstration of historical justice, it is a vital requirement for the survival of our own State.

In the meanwhile, I refuse to be a terrorist in my tribe's name. Because   13 that's what it is: not a "war against terror", as our propaganda machine tries to sell. This is a war OF terror, a war in which, in return for Palestinian guerrilla and terror attacks, we employ the IDF in two types of terror. One type is quite visible: violent acts of killing and destruction, those which some people still try to explain away as "surgical acts of defense." But the worse type of terror is the silent one, which has continued unabated since 1967 and through the entire Oslo process. It is the terror of Occupation, of humiliation on a personal and collective basis, of deprivation and legalized robbery, of alternating exploitation and starvation. This is the mass of the iceberg, the terror that is itself a long-term greenhouse for counter-terror. And I simply refuse to be a terrorist and criminal, even if the entire tribe denounces me.

14   This, indeed, is how our establishment has received us so far—denunciation and short prison terms. We are protected from worse by important voices of public support in Israel and abroad (as expressed by ads like the Tikkun ad). The moment the government or IDF staff will think the lights are out, and no one sees or cares—they will find or invent the "legal" clause and throw some of us in for long jail terms.

15   **But that's nothing, because the moment our government will sense a "lights out" situation—such as a huge terror attack—there will be a horrible bloodbath in the Territories, compared to which the last year and a half will be remembered as a happy picnic.**

16   Last week, Jose Saramagu visited the Occupied Territories with a delegation of world famous writers, and compared the reality there to the Nazi concentration camps. This is of course an exaggeration, and Jews worldwide and in Israel fervently denounced Saramagu. The denouncers seem to pay much less attention to what some powerful forces inside Israel are saying, planning and doing.

17   Parties that support the essentially Nazi idea of deporting all Palestinians have been part of our Knesset and our "legitimate" political map since 1984. Recent opinion polls show that 35% of the Jewish public now supports this "solution", as it is sometimes called. Last weekend, General (re.) Effi Eitam, fresh out of the military, received a flattering cover story on Haaretz supplement. He unfolded his chilling ideology, calling to expel those Palestinians who don't want to remain here as our serfs to Jordan and Egypt. And he said this: why should us, the country poorest in land resources, bear the burden of solving the Palestinian problem? Well I don't know about you, but I remember some of the Nazi rhetoric in that dark period before the war, when Jews were expelled from Germany but could find no safe haven anywhere else. When I see a retired IDF general and rising political star use the exact same Nazi rhetoric on Israel's most "liberal" newspaper, without any criticism—I feel hair-raising horror.

18   My friend, Captain (re.) Dan Tamir, decided to refuse to serve in the Territories about a year ago. He realized that in his last reserve duty as an intelligence officer, he laid out the plans to convert a large Palestinian town into a closed ghetto. The vast majority of Palestinians in the Territories now starve in such ghettos. One of the top commanders in the Territories was quoted in *Haaretz* (Jan. 25, 2002) as saying that in order to prepare for potential battles in dense urban neighborhoods, the IDF must learn, if necessary, how the German army "operated" in the Warsaw Ghetto. A week later, the reporter confirmed this quote, stated that this is a widespread opinion in the IDF, and went on to morally defend it. Almost no one in the Jewish world was interested in following up on this story, and it died down. Where were all these holy souls, scolding anyone who dares allude to the Nazi hor-

ror, when a senior IDF officer proudly called, "in order to beat the Palestinians, let's do what the Nazis did"?

I have little hope that the Israeli public will wake up in time to prevent 19 all that's to come. The Israeli public, in its fear and confusion, wants to go to sleep and wake up only "after it is all over". But it won't be over, because while our mind sleeps our muscles tighten the death grip, instead of doing the only sensible thing—which is to let go. Will you guys join the hypocrite mobs singing lullabies to Israel, and pouncing upon the refuseniks, upon Tikkun, upon Saramagu, to shut us up? Or will you finally take responsibility and be the true friends that Israel needs now—even if it means not being "nice" to Israel for a while?

As you sit tonight at the Seder table, please remember the dozen or so 20 refuseniks who spend this Seder in a military jail. More importantly, please remember the thousand or so people, three-quarters Palestinians and one-quarter Israelis, who were here with us a year ago and have been murdered. Most of them could have been here with us, if you and we had acted sooner. We have now acted, done what little we can do. Please think of the many thousands that may be doomed soon, if you continue sitting on the fence.

May you have a happy Holiday of Freedom. Please help us struggle free 21 from fear, racism, hatred and the deaths they produce.

Yours,
Assaf Oron

Afterword

A few hours after the original version of this letter was sent, a suicide bomber exploded in Netanya hotel during a Passover Seder celebration, killing 30 people. Over the next few days, the IDF invaded and re-occupied all West Bank cities. At the Jenin refugee camp, locals decided to fight this time. The ensuing two-week-long battle ended with about 100 dead from both sides, and with the entire center of the camp razed to the ground. During the year following this letter, over two thousand Palestinians and Israelis died from hostilities. Most Palestinians in the West Bank are still (April 2003) confined to ghetto-like enclaves, under ever-worsening conditions. Ex-general Eitam, whose opinions are briefly described in the letter, is now a senior minister in Sharon's cabinet. The original version of the letter, as well as the statement by Cap. (res.) Dan Tamir, can be found on www.seruv.org.il.

Rhetorical Considerations

1. What exactly is Oron narrating? Is he recounting a sequence of events or something else? (*Hodges'* 32a/*Writer's* 1b and 1e)
2. How is this letter organized? Would another method of organization have been more effective? Why or why not? (*Hodges'* 32d/*Writer's* 2c)

3. What is the "tribal theme" (paragraph 2) that Oron denounces, and why, according to him, does it lead to these conflicts?
4. What has caused Oron to change his opinion from the one he held earlier?
5. How does Oron use quotations from other sources? (*Hodges'* 31c/*Writer's* 2d)

Language and Style

1. Look up the following words in your dictionary: *paradigm* (paragraph 5); *perpetual* (paragraph 6); *fledgling* (paragraph 9). (*Hodges'* 19e/*Writer's* 28e)
2. Find references to people, places, events, and organizations that Oron does not define or identify. Why does he not identify them? (*Hodges'* 19c/*Writer's* 28c)
3. What is the effect of the repetition of the phrase "want to throw us into the sea"? (*Hodges'* 29e/*Writer's* 26e)
4. What is the origin of the word refusenik? (*Hodges'* 19e/*Writer's* 28e)
5. Examine the use of transitions in paragraph 5. (*Hodges'* 31/*Writer's* 3)

Writing Suggestions

1. Write an essay in which you trace the development of your opinion about a particular subject.
2. Write an essay about your experience with your own "tribe," defining *tribe* in any way you choose. What has been your experience with membership in a particular community?

MOMMA, THE DENTIST, AND ME

Maya Angelou

Born Marguerite Johnson in St. Louis in 1928, Maya Angelou was raised with her brother, Bailey, in Stamps, Arkansas, by her grandmother, who, with Uncle Willie, operated a country store. After leaving Stamps, she lived in Los Angeles, where she had a dancing career, and in New York, where she became an active worker in the civil rights movement. She has produced a series on Africa for PBS-TV and written three books of poetry as well as four volumes of her autobiography. This selection is from the first of those autobiographical volumes, *I Know Why the Caged Bird Sings* (1969).

The angel of the candy counter had found me out at last, and was exacting 1 excruciating penance for all the stolen Milky Ways, Mounds, Mr. Goodbars and Hersheys with Almonds. I had two cavities that were rotten to the gums. The pain was beyond the bailiwick of crushed aspirins or oil of cloves. Only one thing could help me, so I prayed earnestly that I'd be allowed to sit under the house and have the building collapse on my left jaw. Since there was no Negro dentist in Stamps, nor doctor either, for that matter, Momma had dealt with previous toothaches by pulling them out (a string tied to the tooth with the other end looped over her fist), pain killers and prayer. In this particular instance the medicine had proved ineffective; there wasn't enough enamel left to hook a string on, and the prayers were being ignored because the Balancing Angel was blocking their passage.

I lived a few days and nights in blinding pain, not so much toying with 2 as seriously considering the idea of jumping in the well, and Momma decided I had to be taken to a dentist. The nearest Negro dentist was in Texarkana, twenty-five miles away, and I was certain that I'd be dead long before we reached half the distance. Momma said we'd go to Dr. Lincoln, right in Stamps, and he'd take care of me. She said he owed her a favor.

I knew there were a number of whitefolks in town that owed her favors. 3 Bailey and I had seen the books which showed how she had lent money to Blacks and whites alike during the Depression, and most still owed her. But I couldn't aptly remember seeing Dr. Lincoln's name, nor had I ever heard of a Negro's going to him as a patient. However, Momma said we were going, and put water on the stove for our baths. I had never been to a doctor, so she told me that after the bath (which would make my mouth feel better) I had to put on freshly starched and ironed underclothes from inside out. The ache failed to respond to the bath, and I knew then that the pain was more serious than that which anyone had ever suffered.

4   Before we left the Store, she ordered me to brush my teeth and then wash my mouth with Listerine. The idea of even opening my clamped jaws increased the pain, but upon her explanation that when you go to a doctor you have to clean yourself all over, but most especially the part that's to be examined, I screwed up my courage and unlocked my teeth. The cool air in my mouth and the jarring of my molars dislodged what little remained of my reason. I had frozen to the pain, my family nearly had to tie me down to take the toothbrush away. It was no small effort to get me started on the road to the dentist. Momma spoke to all the passers-by, but didn't stop to chat. She explained over here shoulder that we were going to the doctor and she'd "pass the time of day" on our way home.

5   Until we reached the pond the pain was my world, an aura that haloed me for the three feet around. Crossing the bridge into whitefolks' country, pieces of sanity pushed themselves forward. I had to stop moaning and start walking straight. The white towel, which was drawn under my chin and tied over my head, had to be arranged. If one was dying, it had to be done in style if the dying took place in whitefolks' part of town.

6   On the other side of the bridge the ache seemed to lessen as if a white-breeze blew off the whitefolks and cushioned everything in their neighbor-hood—including my jaw. The gravel road was smoother, the stones smaller and the tree branches hung down around the path and nearly covered us. If the pain didn't diminish then, the familiar yet strange sights hypnotized me into believing that it had.

7   But my head continued to throb with the measured insistence of a bass-drum, and how could a toothache pass the calaboose, hear the songs of the prisoners, their blues and laughter, and not be changed? How could one or two or even a mouthful of angry tooth roots meet a wagonload of powhite-trash children, endure their idiotic snobbery and not feel less important?

8   Behind the building which housed the dentist's office ran a small path used by servants and those tradespeople who catered to the butcher and Stamps' one restaurant. Momma and I followed that lane to the backstairs of Dentist Lincoln's office. The sun was bright and gave the day a hard real-ity as we climbed up the steps to the second floor.

9   Momma knocked on the back door and a young white girl opened it to show surprise at seeing us there. Momma said she wanted to see Dentist Lin-coln and to tell him Annie was there. The girl closed the door firmly. Now the humiliation of hearing Momma describe herself as if she had no last name to the young white girl was equal to the physical pain. It seemed ter-ribly unfair to have a toothache and a headache and have to bear at the same time the heavy burden of Blackness.

10   It was always possible that the teeth would quiet down and maybe drop out of their own accord. Momma said we would wait. We leaned in the harsh sunlight on the shaky railings of the dentist's back porch for over an hour.

11   He opened the door and looked at Momma. "Well, Annie, what can I do for you?"

He didn't see the towel around my jaw or notice my swollen face.   12

Momma said, "Dentist Lincoln. It's my grandbaby here. She got two rot-   13
ten teeth that's giving her a fit."

She waited for him to acknowledge the truth of her statement. He made   14
no comment, orally or facially.

"She had this toothache purt' near four days now, and today I said,   15
'Young lady, you going to the Dentist.'"

"Annie?"   16

"Yes, sir, Dentist Lincoln."   17

He was choosing words the way people hunt for shells. "Annie, you   18
know I don't treat nigra, colored people."

"I know, Dentist Lincoln. But this here is just my little grandbaby, and   19
she ain't gone be no trouble to you. . . ."

"Annie, everybody has a policy. In this world you have to have a policy.   20
Now, my policy is I don't treat colored people."

The sun had baked the oil out of Mamma's skin and melted the Vaseline   21
in her hair. She shone greasily as she leaned out of the dentist's shadow.

"Seem like to me, Dentist Lincoln, you might look after her, she ain't   22
nothing but a little mite. And seems like maybe you owe me a favor or two."

He reddened slightly. "Favor or no favor. The money has all been repaid to   23
you and that's the end of it. Sorry, Annie." He had his hand on the doorknob.
"Sorry." His voice was a bit kinder on the second "Sorry," as if he really was.

Momma said, "I wouldn't press on you like this for myself but I can't take   24
No. Not for my grandbaby. When you come to borrow my money you didn't
have to beg. You asked me, and I lent it. Now, it wasn't my policy. I ain't no
moneylender, but you stood to lose this building and I tried to help you out."

It's been paid, and raising your voice won't make me change my mind.   25
My policy . . ." He let go of the door and stepped nearer Momma. The three
of us were crowded on the small landing. "Annie, my policy is I'd rather
stick my hand in a dog's mouth than in a nigger's."

He had never once looked at me. He turned his back and went through   26
the door into the cool beyond. Momma backed up inside herself for a few
minutes. I forgot everything except her face which was almost a new one to
me. She leaned over and took the doorknob, and in her everyday soft voice
she said, "Sister, go on downstairs. Wait for me. I'll be there directly."

Under the most common of circumstances I knew it did no good to   27
argue with Momma. So I walked down the steep stairs, afraid to look back
and afraid not to do so. I turned as the door slammed, and she was gone.

*Momma walked in that room as if she owned it. She shoved that silly nurse   28
aside with one hand and strode into the dentist's office. He was sitting in his chair,
sharpening his mean instruments and putting extra sting into his medicines. Her
eyes were blazing like live coals and her arms had doubled themselves in length.
He looked up at her just before she caught him by the collar of his white jacket.*

*"Stand up when you see a lady, you contemptuous scoundrel." Her tongue had   29
thinned and the words rolled off well enunciated. Enunciated and sharp like little
claps of thunder.*

30   *The dentist had no choice but to stand at R.O.T.C. attention. His head dropped after a minute and his voice was humble. "Yes, ma'am, Mrs. Henderson."*

31   *"You knave, do you think you acted like a gentleman, speaking to me like that in front of my granddaughter?" She didn't shake him, although she had the power. She simply held him upright.*

32   *"No, ma'am, Mrs. Henderson."*

33   *"No ma'am, Mrs. Henderson, what?" Then she did give him the tiniest of shakes, but because of her strength the action set his head and arms to shaking loose on the ends of his body. He stuttered much worse than Uncle Willie. "No, ma'am, Mrs. Henderson, I'm sorry."*

34   *With just an edge of her disgust showing, Momma slung him back in his den-tist's chair. "Sorry is as sorry does, and you're about the sorriest dentist I ever laid my eyes on." (She could afford to slip into the vernacular because she had such eloquent command of English.)*

35   *"I didn't ask you to apologize in front of Marguerite, because I don't want her to know my power, but I order you, now and herewith. Leave Stamps by sundown."*

36   *"Mrs. Henderson, I can't get my equipment . . ." He was shaking terribly now.*

37   *"Now, that brings me to my second order. You will never again practice den-tistry. Never! When you get settled in your next place, you will be a vegetarian car-ing for dogs with the mange, cats with the cholera and cows with the epizootic. Is that clear?"*

38   *The saliva ran down his chin and his eyes filled with tears. "Yes, ma'am. Thank you for not killing me. Thank you, Mrs. Henderson."*

39   *Momma pulled herself back from being ten feet tall with eight-foot arms and said, "You're welcome for nothing, you varlet, I wouldn't waste a killing on the likes of you."*

40   *On her way out she waved her handkerchief at the nurse and turned her into a crocus sack of chicken feed.*

41   Momma looked tired when she came down the stairs, but who wouldn't be tired if they had gone through what she had. She came close to me and adjusted the towel under my jaw (I had forgotten the toothache; I only knew that she made her hands gentle in order not to awaken the pain). She took my hand. Her voice never changed. "Come on, Sister."

42   I reckoned we were going home where she would concoct a brew to eliminate the pain and maybe give me new teeth too. New teeth that would grow overnight out of my gums. She led me toward the drugstore, which was in the opposite direction from the Store. "I'm taking you to Dentist Baker in Texarkana."

43   I was glad after all that I had bathed and put on Mum and Cashmere Bouquet talcum powder. It was a wonderful surprise. My toothache had quieted to solemn pain, Momma had obliterated the evil white man, and we were going on a trip to Texarkana, just the two of us.

44   On the Greyhound she took an inside seat in the back, and I sat beside her. I was so proud of being her granddaughter and sure that some of her magic must have come down to me. She asked if I was scared. I only shook my head and leaned over on her cool brown upper arm. There was no chance that a dentist, especially a Negro dentist, would dare hurt me then.

Not with Momma there. The trip was uneventful, except that she put her arm around me, which was very unusual for Momma to do.

The dentist showed me the medicine and the needle before he dead- 45 ened my gums, but if he hadn't I wouldn't have worried. Momma stood right behind him. Her arms were folded and she checked on everything he did. The teeth were extracted and she bought me an ice cream cone from the side window of a drug counter. The trip back to Stamps was quiet, except that I had to spit into a very small empty snuff can which she had gotten for me and it was difficult with the bus humping and jerking on our country roads.

At home, I was given a warm salt solution, and when I washed out my 46 mouth I showed Bailey the empty holes, where the clotted blood sat like filling in a pie crust. He said I was quite brave, and that was my cue to reveal our confrontation with the peckerwood dentist and Momma's incredible powers.

I had to admit that I didn't hear the conversation, but what else could 47 she have said than what I said she said? What else done? He agreed with my analysis in a lukewarm way, and I happily (after all, I'd been sick) flounced into the Store. Momma was preparing our evening meal and Uncle Willie leaned on the door sill. She gave her version.

"Dentist Lincoln got right uppity. Said he'd rather put his hand in a dog's 48 mouth. And when I reminded him of the favor, he brushed it off like a piece of lint. Well, I sent Sister downstairs and went inside. I hadn't never been in his office before, but I found the door to where he takes out teeth, and him and the nurse was in there thick as thieves. I just stood there till he caught sight of me." Crash bang the pots on the stove. "He jumped just like he was sitting on a pin. He said, 'Annie, I done tole you, I ain't gonna mess around in no niggah's mouth.' I said, 'Somebody's got to do it then,' and he said, 'Take her to Texarkana to the colored dentist' and then's when I said, 'If you paid me my money I could afford to take her.' He said, 'It's all been paid.' I tole him everything but the interest been paid. He said ''Twasn't no interest.' I said, ''Tis now, I'll take ten dollars as payment in full.' You know, Willie, it wasn't no right thing to do, 'cause I lent that money without thinking about it.

"He tole that little snippity nurse of his'n to give me ten dollars and 49 make me sign a 'paid in full' receipt. She gave it to me and I signed the papers. Even though by rights he was paid up before, I figger, he gonna be that kind of nasty, he gonna have to pay for it."

Momma and her son laughed and laughed over the white man's evil- 50 ness and her retributive sin.

I preferred, much preferred, my version.   51

Rhetorical Considerations

1. How would you describe Angelou's purpose in "Momma, the Dentist, and Me"? Is it mainly to share an experience, to move her reader to indignation, or both? Point to evidence in the essay. (*Hodges'* 32a/*Writer's* 1b and 1e)

2. Comment on the difference in tone between the account of Momma's confrontation with the dentist given in italics and that given at the end of the essay. (*Hodges'* 32a/*Writer's* 1e)
3. Although Angelou narrates the events involved in a trip to two dentists, the account deals with more than just the pain of a toothache. Explain. (*Hodges'* 32c/*Writer's* 2b)
4. What is Angelou's main point? How do you know? (*Hodges'* 32c/*Writer's* 2b)
5. In what kind of order does Angelou relate the event? Why is this organization appropriate? (*Hodges'* 32d/*Writer's* 2c)
6. Identify and account for any changes in the point of view Angelou uses in this essay. (*Hodges'* 32a/*Writer's* 1e)

Language and Style

1. Angelou uses two kinds of vocabulary in this essay. Dictionaries attach labels to words that are not in Edited American English. Use your dictionary to check for labels on the following words: *bailiwick* (paragraph 1); *calaboose* and *powhitetrash* (paragraph 7); *nigger* (paragraph 25); *epizootic* (paragraph 37); *varlet* (paragraph 39); *crocus* (paragraph 40); *peckerwood* (paragraph 46); *snippety* (paragraph 49); *retributive* (paragraph 50). If one of these words is not listed in your dictionary, what do you think that indicates? (*Hodges'* 19e/*Writer's* 28e)
2. Paragraphs 13 through 24 contain a number of expressions that would be grammatically incorrect in most written English. Why are they acceptable here? Are there any other instances in which these expressions might be acceptable in writing? Explain. (*Hodges'* 19c/*Writer's* 28c)
3. This essay contains several similes. Find three and explain why each is appropriate. (*Hodges'* 20b/*Writer's* 29b)
4. The last sentence of paragraph 29 is elliptical; that is, important grammatical elements are implied rather than stated. Supply the omitted parts and comment on the difference in effect. (*Hodges'* 1e/*Writer's* 16d)
5. The first sentence of this essay contains the verb *had found*, the fifth sentence contains the verb *had dealt*, and the first sentence of paragraph 3 contains the verb *had lent*. To what time sequence do these verbs refer? What would be the effect of rewriting each sentence, instead using *found, dealt,* and *lent* respectively? (*Hodges'* 7b/*Writer's* 22b)

Writing Suggestions

1. Write an essay about an event where someone was unthinkingly and unnecessarily cruel.
2. Write an essay in which you give two versions of a single event, each from a different point of view. You might do as Angelou did and write about the event as you wanted it to be and also as it actually was, or you might write about how you could look at a single event in two different ways depending upon external influences.

◆

RETURN TO PADRE
Cecilia Ballí

Cecilia Ballí is working on a doctorate in anthropology at Rice University. Born in Brownsville, Texas, she majored in American studies and Spanish at Stanford University, from which she graduated with honors and distinction in 1998. She has worked as a staff writer for the *San Antonio Express-News* and a contributor for *Texas Monthly*. She is a recipient of the prestigious Paul and Daisy Soros New American Fellows for 2002, which grants fellowships to naturalized citizens or their children for graduate study in the United States. Ballí feels strongly that academic writing need not be inaccessible to the general public, and she continues to pursue projects that combine her interests in anthropology and journalism.

As sixteen-year-old of skinny arms and knobby knees, I stood at the front of 1 a U.S. history class with a big red poster board and a bit of self-righteousness. Our teacher had assigned a research project, and as I roamed the Brownsville library's bookshelves without direction, I had found a tiny treasure: a book about a Mexican man from my own hometown. It was thin and floppy, written by a graduate student in history at the University of Chicago. The subject was Juan Cortina, the man who had rounded up an army and shot several men as he declared war against the violent change of power South Texas experienced when it became part of the United States. In an 1859 proclamation, Cortina decried the arriving Anglos for forming, "with a multitude of lawyers, a secret conclave, with all its ramifications, for the sole purpose of despoiling the Mexicans of their lands and usurping them afterwards." In traditional historical accounts Cortina went down as a border bandit, a "plunderer and murderer." But in 1949, Charles W. Goldfinch offered a different image, one that had lived on in Mexican border ballads, that rendered Cortina a man outraged by the plight of his people. And so, on a cheap slice of cardboard, I drew a balance with all the ugly descriptions on one side and all the pretty ones on the other. The moral of the story was simply that history had more than one telling. To me, this most basic idea was the most profound revelation. I did not fully realize it at the time, but Juan Cortina's story was, in a way, my story too. For my family had been in South Texas at the time of the Cortina uprising and for more than a hundred years before, and in time they also would fight for the land they had lost, though with law books and lawyers instead of guns.

Anyone who remembers seventh-grade Texas history class knows that in 2 textbooks the story of our state begins just far back enough to show how brave men with Anglo surnames had conquered a cruel, empty brushland. They briefly recount that this land had been a Spanish province, then Mexican territory. But there is no mention, for instance, of the great Mexican ranches that already dotted the area when the Anglos arrived or of the ranchers' winter trips to the area's cities, where there were social clubs, colorful silk dresses, romantic violin serenades. An entire way of life, governed by a sophisticated system that rewarded and discriminated based on birth, class, and skin color, slipped into the whiteness of pages, erased and selectively forgotten.

3   It was into that social system that José Nicolás Ballí was born—on the privileged side, to be sure. In 1749, 72 years before Stephen F. Austin would set foot in Texas, the first Ballís had arrived from northern Mexico to the province of Nuevo Santander, what is now the Lower Rio Grande Valley. There they would become a powerful landed dynasty. Ten years later, King Carlos III granted the offshore island, then called Isla de Santiago, to Nicolás Ballí, the grandfather of José Nicolás. But it was the grandson, by then a Roman Catholic priest, who surveyed the property, claimed it as his own in 1800, and put up a ranch there. With the help of a nephew, Juan José Ballí, he raised cattle, horses, and mules and worked to Christianize the area's Karankawa Indians. Eight months after the priest died, in 1829, the newly independent Mexican government finally confirmed title to him and his nephew. By that time Isla de Santiago was already acquiring the name by which it is known today: Padre Island.

4   To Texans and Mexicans alike, Padre Island is a nice getaway for the limited budget, a beach resort close enough for three-day weekends. Here, Winter Texans dine on fresh fish while their relatives up north shiver through December. Here, college students drink a week of their lives away and dance with barely dressed strangers in sticky outdoor clubs. Rich Mexicans pick up tans during Holy Week and cruise late at night in their shiny Jettas. Skinny beauty pageant contestants strut around in high heels and wide smiles in hopes of a crown. But to the Ballís, the island whispers of a proud but sad past. The last family members to claim a piece of it sold out at the close of the Great Depression, expecting to receive royalties from its underground riches. They never saw a cent. The island's very presence was a continuing reminder of their fall from preeminence—until last summer, when a Brownsville jury heard their arguments and vindicated their claims.

5   News of the verdict appeared in dozens of papers nationwide, spread across the pages of the *New York Times,* the Chicago *Tribune,* and *USA Today,* and as far away as Argentina. "Six decades after a New York lawyer bought Padre Island from a Mexican American border family, a jury determined Wednesday that he had swindled the family's impoverished descendants out of $1.1 million in oil and gas royalties," the Associated Press reported. Historians called it "revolutionary," an overdue acknowledgment of a shady time in Texas history during which hardworking people were stripped of their land. My branch of the family was not involved in the Padre Island lawsuit, but distant relatives were, and we celebrated together. "The victory of the Ballí heirs," wrote Gilberto Hinojosa, a dean at the University of the Incarnate Word and a South Texas historian, "confirms a heartfelt sentiment among Mexican Americans that this is their land and they belong here." Once a family whose last name few outside the Valley could pronounce (By-yee), the Ballís became, almost overnight, world-famous.

Yet the victory took centuries of work and lifetimes of hope. It took gen- 6
erations of white-haired matriarchs and patriarchs passing on the story to
their grandchildren, decades of searching for old documents that would
speak the truth. It took marches and massive family meetings and some miracles too. The Ballí family is a family of self-made genealogists, historians,
lawyers. When nobody would acknowledge their roots, the Ballís unearthed
them. When nobody would tell their side of the story, they wrote and pro-
claimed it themselves. When nobody would represent them, they asked to
approach the bench, Your Honor, and they said what they had to say. You
see, the Ballís weren't just born Ballí, they became it. And once they began
to change, there was no turning back.

"I've been telling people I'm gonna move on with my life after this," 7
Pearl Ballí Mancillas mumbled as we waited in the Brownsville federal court-
house for the jury's verdict. She sighed. "But then I ask, 'What is my life?
This is all I've ever known.'"

The history of the Ballí lawsuit really begins in the blurry years after 8
Padre Ballí's death. Just months afterward, his nephew, Juan José, sold the
island, but the story goes, Santiago Morales, the Mexican man who bought
it, may have suffered buyer's remorse. Exactly what was happening on Padre
Island at that time is impossible to know. The Ballís had divided the island
among themselves into two large tracts, north and south. At the same time,
Anglos who arrived from throughout the United States and Europe set foot
on other parts of the island and called it theirs. Among these was John
Singer, the brother of the man who invented the modern sewing machine.
And there was Pat Dunn, the famed Duke of Padre Island, who, the Ballís'
lawyers say, erected guard posts to keep others out, and in 1928, claimed
title to almost the whole island through squatter's rights. The whole time,
various Ballís with island roots and from other landed branches had been
trying to determine what they owned. One of them was Ignacio Ballí Tijerina, whose ancestors had possessed an even larger tract on the mainland
known as La Barreta, where cattle baron Miflin Kenedy later built his ranching empire. "Before the law, we are all equal men," Tijerina wrote in the articulate, typed notes he left behind. "Before society, we are not." Over lunch
at one of the five tables in the Brownsville Cafe, in a white T-shirt with an
imprint of the Ballí coat of arms, his daughter Herminia Ballí Chavana tells
me the story. Her father and his brothers, she says, were approached in 1910
by a Mexican American man who had been sent by an Anglo lawyer to offer
them 25 pesos each for their signatures. His brothers refused the offer and
instead sent Tijerina to the Mexican archives in Reynosa to find out what
their ancestors had owned.

But he was not let in, he wrote in his notes, so he sought special permis- 9
sion from a Matamoros judge some sixty miles away, then made his way
back to Reynosa. The archives were in disarray. "Los americanos," as he called
the Anglos, had already been there—without the extra trip to Matamoros.
They pieced together land ownership through wills and birth and marriage
certificates, bribing the archives' keeper for some of the originals or simply
taking what wasn't theirs. Herminia's voice grows furious as she paraphrases
her father's memoir. "The Anglos would steal the deeds," Herminia says

angrily, her hand shaking violently as she grabs a white paper napkin from the table and stuffs it under an imaginary jacket. Later they would hire locals to pay landowners to sign documents that some of them could not even read, sealing the transfer of their land.

10   As the research of land ownership progressed, speculation abounded and theories surfaced. Some of them seeped into the newspapers, and one of these articles, a 1937 story that appeared in the Brownsville paper, was mailed to a prominent New York lawyer named Frederic Gilbert by a business associate in South Texas. The article reported that a document had been found showing Juan José Ballí's sale of the island in 1830 to Santiago Morales had been rescinded. This suggested that a group of Ballís might still hold title to more than half of the island. In New York, Frederic Gilbert summoned his 24-year-old nephew, Gilbert Kerlin, a sharp young graduate of Harvard Law School, and gave him his first assignment: Go down to Padre Island and buy the Ballís' titles.

11   And so Gilbert Kerlin, who today is 91 years old, stepped into what had become common South Texas practice: Figure out who owns land, round them up, and offer to buy. He was a "baby lawyer" then, as attorneys in the island case described him in court last summer, and he spoke no Spanish. But he was resourceful, so he got help—the best help, in fact, he could find. To track down the Ballís who might still have claims to the island, he hired one of their own, a man named Primitivo Ballí, who was paid $750. Primitivo's daughter Librada, who testified at the trial, would be Kerlin's secretary. And for legal advice, Kerlin knocked on the door of Francis William Seabury, a powerful lawyer well known for his extensive research of South Texas land grants. Originally from Virginia, Seabury had become a prominent Valley politician and served four terms in the Texas Legislature, including one as Speaker. Some spoke English; some did not. Most weren't very educated. But the Ballís who descended from the priest's nephew held claims to the beach that Kerlin's uncle thought might be worth something. At the time, the island was but an empty swath of sand, with only a Coast Guard station and an abandoned fishing shack. Yet underneath lay the slick stuff of Texas riches. Seabury tried to warn Kerlin off. "Developments since you left confirm my original opinion that you would have no reasonable chance of making good title to any part of Padre Island acquired by deed from the supposed heirs of Juan José Ballí," Seabury wrote Kerlin's uncle in a letter dated August 11, 1938. Had the 1830 rescission really occurred? It wasn't entirely clear, Seabury argued. Almost prophetically, he closed with a warning: "Please do not go too fast in this matter. There is a fine chance for you and your associates to get badly stung if you rely on any fact that is not proven by almost conclusive evidence." Undeterred, Gilbert instructed his nephew to press forward.

12   Eventually, 54 Ballís signed eleven deeds. There is disagreement over how much each was paid—suggestions range from nothing to $300—but one thing was clear: It was agreed, by deed, that they would retain a small portion of mineral rights, which was more than the cash-poor family was getting from the empty land anyway. Deeds acquired, Kerlin moved on, cutting deals with other island claimants and battling in the courts to secure as much of the beach as possible. In 1940 he faced off with the State of Texas,

which had sued the Ballís and other island claimants in an attempt to take the acreage by which the property exceeded the 1829 survey dimensions, amounting to roughly two thirds of the island. The state eventually lost its case and was refused a hearing by the U.S. Supreme Court. In 1941 Kerlin sued the powerful King Ranch, which claimed to own a six-thousand-acre strip of the island. Lawyers for the ranch settled that case out of court, granting Kerlin half of the mineral rights to the disputed land.

Kerlin's next challenge was daunting—to bring down Pat Dunn. Forming an unusual coalition through his lawyer Seabury, he banded with other Anglos who were claiming ownership of parts of the island. In 1942, while Kerlin was serving in World War II, they sealed that ownership when *Havre v. Dunn* was settled, then sat down to exchange 135,000 acres of land among themselves. Kerlin walked away with 20,000 acres, plus an additional 1,000 acres of mineral rights. That victory was temporarily jeopardized when, during World War II, the federal government announced that it intended to take the southern quarter of the island to use as a bombing range. The war ended before the government's plan could be put into effect, allowing Kerlin to retain the land. He would strike one last time—in 1978, when he sued the state, which claimed to own 30,000 acres of mudflats in the Laguna Madre that he argued were part of the island. Like his other deals, the resolution of that case exemplified Kerlin's knack for winning. When it was settled, in 1980, the state had lost 27,000 acres to the shrewd New Yorker. 13

The Ballís never heard from Kerlin again, never learned that such monumental lawsuits had been settled. And they never received the small royalty checks that would have justified the sale of their lands. In the early fifties Primitivo Ballí mailed several letters to New York; Kerlin responded to one of them by saying the family's deeds had been worthless. So in 1953, the Ballí who would forever be shunned by his relatives for enabling their loss sent Kerlin a final, respectful request: Could the Ballís have their birth certificates back? 14

The streets of Brownsville are awfully quiet without Johnny. These aren't his times anyway. In 2001 we don't walk into government buildings and make demands; we don't block streets until people listen to what we have to say, as Johnny liked to do. I wonder, in fact, what it would have been like for Johnny to sit still in the courtroom, as his sisters did, and listen to hours of testimony knowing that anyone who made a racket would be thrown out. No, that wasn't his style. Johnny liked to be heard. I met Johnny Ballí when I was eighteen, and I haven't seen him again. I was writing for the Brownsville *Herald* that summer, and he had caught my name in the paper; so one day he walked into the newsroom and, in that imposing way of his, asked everyone at once, "Who is Cecilia Ballí?" They pointed him to my desk, and he walked up in his boots and shook my hand hard. Who was my father, he wanted to know, and did I know the Ballís once owned Padre Island? Ask the residents of Brownsville and they will say they remember Johnny too, the liquor-tax collector at the Gateway International Bridge whose life mission was to let the town know where the Ballís came from. You see, in my times, after Johnny had persuaded the Cameron County Commissioners Court and the Texas Historical Commission to put a statue of the priest on 15 the island, being Ballí was an honor, a title that made people look at us with a little more respect, even if we had nothing to show for it. But in Johnny's time, if he said the Ballís had owned the island, people, including family friends, laughed.

16   Decades had passed since Primitivo Ballí had heard from Gilbert Kerlin, but the Ballís' memory of the New York lawyer, instead of withering, grew thick layers as time passed, like the bark of a tree rooted stubbornly in their back yards. Those who had signed over their deeds remained mum for a generation, shamed about what had happened to them. But as the elders began to grow old, they started telling the story to grandchildren. For a family that had descended from landed gentry to working class, the tale became its members' only heirloom. It lost details as it transcended generations but picked up meaning as other branches of the Ballís claimed it as their own, a moral to be learned about trust and the lot of little people.

17   Johnny was born into this culture, the grandson of one of the 54 Ballís who had signed over their deeds to Kerlin. In the late sixties he began agitating. A charismatic man recognized instantly for his cowboy hat and his commanding presence, he became the family spokesman, setting out to shake the city's conscience. Once, he stomped into a county commissioners' meeting and declared, "As a member of the Ballí family, I am officially claiming possession of Padre Island." "He was quickly arrested," wrote his sister Pearl in a 126-page book, where she pressed her family's plight between two hard, brown covers. The politicians weren't interested at first, but Johnny was able to persuade local businesses like Cowen's Used Cars and the Flamingo Motel to dot the town with "Erect Statue of Padre Ballí on Padre Island!" portable signs. He led family members and supporters on three marches to the beach, in one case blocking the causeway to the island with their cars as they waved the U.S. flag next to the Ballí coat of arms. Finally, in 1983, the bronze arrived at its site at the entrance to the beach and was hoisted out of its wooden crate, with Johnny watching emotionally. Like the good Catholic he was, he repaid the Virgin Mary for the blessing by making a sixty-mile pilgrimage by foot to the Virgin of San Juan del Valle shrine, television cameras trailing. The story is that when he arrived, in the middle of mass, the congregation clapped and wept.

18   Today Johnny sits at home with brain tumors, only sporadically comprehending what goes on around him. But although Johnny's times have passed, the Ballí family as it is today is his legacy. For when others began to believe their story, the Ballís learned that there was power in numbers, in doing things systematically. They began to hold large family reunions. They sold self-published books. They went to the media. They formed organizations and held thoughtfully planned meetings. Those with computers constructed Ballí Web sites, family chat rooms where distant cousins could reconstruct their ancestries, announce family gatherings, and discuss strategy. Ballís began to check in from the various states where many of their parents or grandparents had relocated to do farmwork and realized they were part of a huge family. Estella Ballí Trimble didn't know she had any cousins until her mother, nearing death, told her. So Estella set off to find them. "Can

you imagine living in this world and not knowing you have three thousand relatives?" she asked me once over the phone. "It's like counting the stars."

But the Ballís knew it wasn't enough to say they had lost their land. In   19 the end, legal justice would require evidence, and only a few lines of the family might have the documents needed to prove that they had been wronged. While Johnny was organizing in Brownsville, another island heir, a onetime paralegal named Connie Gonzales who lived in Houston, had begun to do research. It pained her to think that her grandmother had migrated back and forth to Wisconsin to work in a cannery while Padre's new owners had gotten rich. So for years she spent days in the archives of county records throughout South Texas, her husband and children touring the cities they visited while she searched in stuffy rooms for any documents that mentioned the Ballís.

For decades, when family members had talked of what had happened,   20 they had referred to Kerlin only as "the gringo" or "the bolillo," and there were so many Anglo names in the title abstracts that Gonzales scoured. She didn't even know if the man her grandmother had dealt with was still alive. All she could do was jot down every name, then run them by the elders in her family. Gilbert Kerlin, one aunt thought, sounded familiar. Gonzales' hopes soared. She called New York information: The name of the law firm he had worked for still existed. An operator provided the number. She placed two calls, left messages, and waited in suspense.

Two weeks later her phone rang, and a voice at the other end said it was   21 Gilbert Kerlin. "At that point," she recalls vividly, "I asked him point-blank if it had been him. And immediately he said, 'Yeah, but those deeds weren't valid.'" And then he said something else: Did she have a lawyer? Because the burden of proof in a lawsuit would be on the Ballís, and fighting him was going to cost a fortune.

Gonzales pressed forward. With her brother, she had created el Comité   22 Padre José Nicolás Ballí, and they summoned other Ballís through classified ads in the Brownsville *Herald*. At the first meeting, she joined forces with Johnny and Pearl. She continued her archival research, and in 1985—almost magically, it seemed—she found her treasure. In the bowels of the Kleberg County Courthouse, in Kingsville, she found the original eleven deeds the Ballís had signed over to Gilbert Kerlin in 1938. "It was like gold," she remembers. With only enough cash to copy a handful of them, she had to send a niece back for the rest.

Kerlin had a point, though: As much as they had come to despise attor-   23 neys, the Ballís would need one. In 1991 the family hired Brian Scott and Murray Fogler of Houston. But after nearly two years of work, they washed their hands of the case. "I think the excuse was that there wasn't enough production in the oil wells [on the island] for them to pursue it," Gonzales recalls. My branch of the family, which had begun to pursue the La Barreta case on the mainland, faced the same problem. Individual families mustered little payments worth more than a week of groceries—$100 here, $200 there—to pay the expenses of their lawyers, who drove to preliminary hearings throughout South Texas and wined and dined as professionals do. The lawyers quit anyway. For most of them, the case represented a big gamble;

the probability of winning wasn't worth their time and expense, not to mention the difficulty of representing hundreds of people who were spread throughout the country and often couldn't agree with each other. My uncle, a La Barreta heir, received a letter last year from a Dallas law firm that said only, "We regret to inform you that circumstances have developed which hinder our continued effective litigation of the lawsuit." Two hundred twenty-three Ballís were dumped.

24   But in 1994 a young Houston lawyer named Hector Cárdenas, whose grandmother had signed one of the eleven Kerlin deeds, undertook the mission to save the island case. After his own law firm declined to take it, Cárdenas, who was just out of law school, contacted some twenty firms, to no avail. Even Houston's top plaintiffs lawyers turned him down. Then, a lawyer who went to church with his aunt offered the name of Tom McCall, an Abilene native who is now a well-regarded Austin oil and gas lawyer. Meanwhile, Kerlin wasn't the Ballís' only adversary: The clock was ticking. While McCall was reviewing the case, a state district judge dismissed the lawsuit for want of prosecution. The Ballís had just thirty days to reinstate it. McCall agreed to take the case, then filed a motion to reinstate on behalf of Hector Cárdenas' mother and four of her siblings—just one day before the deadline expired.

25   The story of what occurred next has become family legend. In April 1995 McCall showed up in a crowded state district court in Brownsville, where he argued that the case was not dead: He only needed a little time to sign up the rest of the family. Then, to prove his point, he turned to face hundreds of Ballís who were attending the hearing and asked, "Who here is going to join us?" Almost every hand in the audience shot up. By the time the room was cleared that afternoon, McCall had picked up at least a hundred new clients. The Ballí family, after all, would have its day in court.

26   Tom McCall never meant to reverse a family's fortunes, never meant to refuel a South Texas movement to reclaim lands, never meant to help rewrite Texas history from a Mexican American perspective. At first, he just meant to win a lawsuit. He is a 52-year-old lawyer with an office nestled in the hills of West Austin. A quiet man who usually carries a smile, he has a straightforward character that makes him automatically likable. It is reflected in the way he maintains his cool in front of a judge, the way he often paces alone outside the courtroom during long waits instead of visiting with other lawyers at their table. Britton Monts, a Dallas lawyer who is McCall's close friend and has teamed up with him in the courtroom for sixteen years, calls him "a real Don Quixote," a man who believes in the concept of good over evil. Hector Cárdenas regards him as the true lawyer ideal. "Tom, I've got to say, is the closest to the Atticus Finch character in *To Kill a Mockingbird* that I've ever worked with," he says. "That character is why I went to law school." When he reviewed the Ballí case, McCall remembers, he instantly spotted an argument. Given that the history of the island was so muddy, he would have a tough time proving the Ballís had held title in 1938, when the Kerlin deeds were signed. So McCall turned to another legal strategy called estoppel, a way of saying a man will be held to the benefit of his bargain. It would prevent Kerlin from denying the validity of the Ballí deeds if he had previously used them to make other legal claims to the island. Seldom invoked today,

estoppel was used long ago, before a sophisticated title system was developed to facilitate the tracking of property ownership. "We spent, maximum, ten minutes talking about it in law school," Cárdenas says. In McCall's view this was the perfect opportunity to apply it. So he joined up with Monts, then completed the legal team with his twin brother David, whose specialty is land titles, their associate Robert Johnson, and Cárdenas. In Brownsville, Cárdenas had asked Frank Costilla to step in as local counsel.

For five years they built a case. As time passed, the lawyers began to feel 27 they had stepped into something truly bigger than life—something guided, it seemed, by an invisible hand. "It almost felt like fate was moving us along, and I don't mean to sound superstitious," Monts says in retrospect. "There are some cases that feel like they're snakebitten from the start, but this one just felt like it was fated." It seemed like fate, for instance, that Kerlin still had boxes of old letters his uncle had exchanged with Seabury regarding his island transactions, which he turned over to his Houston attorney, M. Steve Smith, when they were subpoenaed by the court. It was in reading those 30,000 pages of letters and documents, over months of trips to Smith's office, that McCall began to suspect that the Ballís had been deliberately cheated from the beginning. He caught statements buried in that correspondence hinting that Kerlin, his uncle, and Seabury had conspired to leave the Ballís and their royalty interests out of *Havre v. Dunn* and the later cases that settled the title to Padre Island. In one letter, Seabury, who had told the court he represented both Kerlin and the Ballís in those cases, identified the former as his "real client." Another letter revealed that Kerlin's uncle had intended to "let the Ballí title, if such it may be called, die in Kerlin." The more McCall studied the documents, the more he was convinced that the carving up of Padre Island after *Havre v. Dunn* was settled was designed to wash the Ballís' claims out of the record. Although the island dealings stand out in Seabury's legal career, those files did not go into the collection of his papers that was donated to the Center for American History library at the University of Texas at Austin but were separated and eventually passed on to Kerlin in New York, who kept them in a filing cabinet. "I'm sure," says Robert Johnson, "Seabury never dreamed that the courts were going to give the Ballís the key to open that locked drawer."

On those allegations, the island trial began in Brownsville on an un- 28 bearably hot afternoon last May. At ninety years of age, Kerlin returned to South Texas by plane, dressed impeccably like the prominent lawyer he had become, flanked by Smith and Brownsville attorney Horacio Barrera (ironically, the descendant of another Ballí branch). Ballís drove in by the carloads, ice chests and family albums in tow, from as far away as Florida and Illinois and California. Retired senior state district judge Pat McDowell arrived from Dallas to try the case, replacing a local judge who had recused himself. The trial had been moved to the federal courthouse, where the courtroom was completely filled with Ballís, with hundreds more waiting in the halls, all of whom could confront at last the man who had been, for years, a faceless villain.

He was instantly spottable at the defense table, frail but erect, his thin- 29 ning silvery hair neatly combed and turned up at the ends. *"Ahí está el viejo"* ("There is the old man"), one gray-haired woman said as she took her tan leather seat. For a few seconds she stared indignantly. Through large, thick glasses, he peered back. He almost evoked pity sitting there that way, his cheeks sagging heavily over the corners of his mouth. The Ballís who had arrived in cotton and rayon and polyester might have been a little less condemning if they had known Gilbert Kerlin better, if they had been aware, for instance, that he is a charitable man who contributes heavily to environmental and preservation causes in New York and even donated land for Andy Bowie Park on Padre Island. But there was no way they could know him—not now anyway, sitting under the high ceilings of a chilly, elegant white courtroom. They had not spoken for decades.

30   One by one, they took the stand—Ballí grantors and their descendants, oil and gas consultants, a title lawyer. Kerlin, ever sharp, testified for eight contentious days. Because of the complexity of the case, jurors were allowed to take notes and slip questions to the judge. In the audience, family members filled their own notebooks with scribblings. While McCall and the rest of the Ballí team used hundreds of letters and documents projected on a huge screen to prove the conspiracy, Kerlin's attorneys stuck by the argument that he had made to Primitivo Ballí long ago and to Connie Gonzales on the telephone: The Ballís' deeds had been no good when they sold them in 1938. Kerlin did not, they argued, enter the *Havre v. Dunn* case relying on the Ballís' deeds, as the family's lawyers contended, but by using titles he acquired later through lawsuits and deeds from several Anglo families. If the Ballís' deeds had been any good, Barrera told the jurors, "They wouldn't be using this fancy term called 'estoppel.'" In fact, if anyone had been cheated, it was Kerlin's late uncle, they said, when he spent $80,000 to acquire and defend these worthless deeds. Kerlin was acting only as an agent for his uncle, and although the Ballís kept harping on how they had slipped into poverty, Barrera added, "Who's poor and who's rich doesn't matter in the courts, because that's the way of life."

31   On the testimony went, for nine weeks. The jurors, attentive for the most part, began to grow nervous about being away from their jobs and slipped another question to the judge: "Once this trial is over, should a juror experience employment difficulties [directly attributable] to his/her jury service in this trial, what would be the avenue of relief?" The family continued to fill the courtroom early every morning, drawing family trees, proudly passing around snapshots of themselves standing in front of the courthouse with their attorneys. Kerlin appeared consistently too, shuffling in with small but steady steps, riding up and down the elevator alone, and reading the *New York Times* quietly. He would not discuss the case because of a gag order, but we had a pleasant chat one day about nothing important. Later that afternoon he gave me his business card with a small smile, ignoring his lawyer's suggestion that we speak through attorneys, and for a moment, I wanted to like him.

32   Then the trial was over and the judge gave the jury 27 questions to answer. (In civil trials in Texas, juries answer questions and judges apply the law based on their answers.) Nowhere was the jury asked to decide whether the Ballís had actually held title to the island when they sold their deeds in 1938. Instead, the charge opened by asking whether Kerlin was "estopped" to deny the validity of the deeds. By making estoppel the basis of his case,

McCall was able to get around the need to prove that the Ballís had a valid title to the island in 1938, which would have been next to impossible to do, given the long passage of time. Instead, he needed to prove only that the Ballís had been cheated. Based on a request from Kerlin's attorneys, the judge tagged on an issue at the end: Were the Ballís guilty of waiting too long to bring this case to court?

When the judge called the jury in for a verdict four days later, on August 2, McCall blinked once, swallowed hard, then rose slowly. In the audience the Ballís filled every inch on the benches; teenagers, fathers, and grandmothers sat on the floor or stood in the back. About a dozen reporters were asked to stand along a side wall to make more room for the family. Before a row of chairs, a string of plaintiffs stood, clutching each other, eyes closed, heads imploring God in silent prayer. Kerlin was missing; he had been forced to leave for New York the day before, his lawyers said, because his wife, who was sick, needed him.

Wasting no time, the judge began to read what the jury had handed him. For the family, the answers that followed rang like sweet church bells. Was Kerlin estopped from denying that the Ballís' deeds were valid? Yes. Did he acquire an interest in those deeds? Yes. Did he fail to comply with his fiduciary duty to the Juan José Ballí grantors and their heirs? Yes. Did Seabury breach his fiduciary duty to the family when *Havre v. Dunn* was settled? Yes. During that settlement, did Kerlin conspire with Seabury to breach Seabury's fiduciary duty to the Ballís? Yes. During that settlement, did Kerlin conspire with Seabury to commit fraud against the Ballís? Yes. During that settlement, did Seabury commit fraud against the Ballís? Yes. Did that breach of fiduciary duty result from malice? Yes. Any way one put it, the Ballís, eleven of twelve jurors concluded, had been wronged—and in a blatant, conspiratorial way. "The documents were there, and that's what I found so amazing," jury foreman Cesar Cisneros, a retired school administrator, said later. "I just felt the evidence was so overwhelming that, as they say, *hasta la pregunta es necia*"—it was a moot question.

Less than an hour after the decision was read, McCall and his team arrived at the family's celebration at the Fort Brown hotel, the same place where U. S. troops under General Zachary Taylor had gathered in 1846 to take South Texas from Mexico. More than one hundred Mexican Americans offered the lawyers a standing ovation when they entered, and someone cried out with deep pride, "*Arriba* Tom McCall!" Cameras flashed. Old women hugged him. But the victory would be tempered by what happened just a few days later. A week after the vindicating verdict, after hearing a string of family members describe their lives in poverty, the all-Hispanic jury refused to award punitive damages. One juror—the only one who did not sign the original decision—told a reporter that the Ballís did not deserve compensation for their economic fate, which was shared by countless other Brownsville families. "If you were poor," the juror said, "you just had to struggle a little harder to get out of that hole, that's all." Another juror said that withholding punitive damages was the only decision all jurors could agree to. The outcome meant that a man whose attorneys said is worth $68 million would have to give back only what he had failed to pay.

36   Assuming that the decision is not overturned on appeal, the Ballís will get $3.3 million in damages for fraud and unpaid royalties, of which their attorneys will receive 40 percent. The jury also concluded that the Ballís should have received mineral rights to 7,500 (plus accretion) of the 20,000 acres Kerlin acquired in settling *Havre v. Dunn*. So they now will be due small but regular oil and gas royalty payments for that property. All of this will be divided among roughly three hundred plaintiffs. Kerlin does not have to file an appeal until a final judgment is entered, but he has already hired Rusty McMains of Corpus Christi, a prominent appellate lawyer.

37   It is ironic that the Ballís ultimately prevailed the American way—by hiring a damn good lawyer—and that their attorneys used a legal doctrine that originated in English common law, the basis of our country's justice system. For it was the same system, sixty years ago, that created the loopholes through which their land had disappeared, and it was another Anglo lawyer who had authored their loss. Inevitably, some will see the case as something else, as the start of the repossessing of South Texas by Mexican Americans, who always have made up the majority of the population. But legal experts agree that most cases are lost causes because of statutes of limitations, lack of documentation, and transfers of land that were legitimate. Still, the Ballí case touched hundreds of people who have heard similar rumblings in their own families, and they have descended upon county courthouses and libraries, unraveling their own histories.

38   I must have been six when my father left Brownsville to attend a Ballí gathering in San Antonio and returned with tiny T-shirts of the Alamo for his three daughters. Like the rest of his siblings, our dad knew little about history and even less about law. I still have that shirt in a drawer back home, small holes where my bony shoulders used to rub. He died sick on a hospital bed, and other than a little bit of pride and lots of love, he couldn't leave us much. He was a cab driver with cancer. He was 41. But he left us a special last name, and there lay the treasure. I guess, with time, I too became Ballí. I became Ballí when, on childhood trips to the island, we pulled up by the priest's statue and admired how our last name looked engraved on a plaque. I became Ballí when, in high school, my twin sister and I penned a family history to show our classmates that ancestry ran much deeper than grandparents. And I became Ballí when, as a college freshman, my first A was on a paper about nineteenth-century relations between Anglos and Mexicans in Brownsville. "Can you believe how blessed we are to have been born into this family?" my sister asked in disbelief when news of the island trial went national. Because we descend from the priest's uncle, ours is the branch that will now pursue the La Barreta case against the John G. and Marie Stella Kenedy Memorial Foundation. I haven't decided whether to join the lawsuit, which is scheduled to go to trial on October 22.

39   The island victory, though, was for all of us to relish. In a way, its story is universal. For it is a story about how some people are washed out of their own histories. It testifies that important men like Seabury and Kerlin, like all other people, are both good and bad. And it offers a glimmer of hope that sometimes—not often, but sometimes—the little man does win. Sitting

in a warm McDonald's in south Houston, Connie Gonzales reminded me how Kerlin had prevailed in so many lawsuits over island ownership—defeating the Kings, the Duke, the state. "And we brought him down!" she exclaimed triumphantly, throwing her head back with a loud, liberating laugh. "Little ranching family brought him down!"

Rhetorical Considerations

1. What is the effect of Ballí's opening her essay with a personal anecdote? (*Hodges'* 33b/*Writer's* 3b)
2. What order does Ballí use for her narrative? Does she ever break away from this pattern? If so, where and to what effect? (*Hodges'* 32d/*Writer's* 2c)
3. How many quotations does Ballí use? What kinds of authorities does she cite? (*Hodges'* 31c/*Writer's* 2d)
4. This essay was first published in *Texas Monthly* magazine. Find evidence of Ballí's awareness of her audience as consisting primarily of readers from Texas. (*Hodges'* 32a/*Writer's* 1b and 1d)
5. How does Ballí personalize this narrative? How does she make it of interest to readers who are not members of the Ballí family? (*Hodges'* 32a/*Writer's* 1e)

Language and Style

1. Look up the following words in your dictionary: *conclave* and *usurping* (paragraph 1); *rescinded* (paragraph 10); *rescission* (paragraph 11); *fiduciary* (paragraph 34). (*Hodges'* 19e/*Writer's* 28e)
2. How many Spanish words and phrases does Ballí use? When does she provide translation? When does she omit translation? Did you have any difficulty with the inclusion of Spanish words? Why or why not? (*Hodges'* 19c/*Writer's* 28c)
3. Find five descriptive words (adverbs or adjectives) in the essay. How does Ballí use descriptive language to convey her thesis more effectively? (*Hodges'* 4/*Writer's* 20)
4. The second sentence of paragraph 1 is a compound-complex sentence. Break it down into its major clauses. What is the effect of combining these elements in one sentence? (*Hodges'* 1e/*Writer's* 16d)
5. What is the subject of the last sentence of paragraph 14? (*Hodges'* 1b/*Writer's* 16a)

Writing Suggestions

1. Write an essay in which you recount a struggle some branch of your own family has encountered.
2. Look at the ethnic diversity of the community of which you are a part. Look, for example, at the names in the telephone directory, the types of restaurants or specialty grocery stores, or the languages represented in the video store. Write an essay in which you explore the cultural background of your community.

✦

IMAGES

Narration

It has long been said that a picture is worth a thousand words. Each of the images here in some way tells a story. Look at the images and see if you can relate a story around each.

Jan van Eyck, *The Arnolfini Portrait*, 1434

Chevy Malibu

Rhetorical Considerations

1. The first image is a painting by fifteenth-century Dutch master Jan van Eyck (ca. 1390–1441). It is commonly called *The Arnolfini Marriage*, and has long been thought to depict or commemorate the wedding of Giovanni di Nicolao Arnolfini and Giovanna Cenami. Why might this interpretation have persisted for so long?

✦

IMAGES (CONT.)

Narration

2. The second image is an advertisement from *Latina* magazine. We selected a Spanish-language advertisement so that many of you would not be distracted by the text and would have to rely on the image itself for meaning. What is being narrated here, and how is the narrative a part of the sales pitch? Can you relate to the narrative? Who would relate to it? (*Hodges'* 32a/*Writer's* 1b–c)
3. The two images were produced over 500 years apart. Do they share any similarities? What are they? What significant differences do you see?

Writing Suggestions

1. Find an image (a magazine ad or a personal photograph, for example) that tells a story. Narrate the events of the story, pointing out particular aspects of the image that reflect the tale.
2. It is now thought that *The Arnolfini Marriage* may not portray a wedding, and that it is the style of the woman's dress that makes her look pregnant. Find an image that seems to tell a story. Narrate the events of a different story the image could plausibly tell, using particular details of the image to support your narrative.

CHAPTER 3

Description

Description uses language to re-create for the reader what is experienced through the senses—sight, sound, taste, touch, and smell. Because it is grounded in the senses, description relies especially on specific, concrete images. (See *Hodges'* 31c/*Writer's* 2d for more information.) This emphasis on concreteness and specificity is what makes description so effective in bringing a story to life or making an argument persuasive. Indeed, description most often occurs in combination with other rhetorical strategies, particularly narration; description can explain and expand a comparison, a process, a definition, an argument, a classification, or any other strategy.

Understanding Description

Whatever your reason for writing, description helps you and your readers share an experience or an impression. It can help you make your feelings tangible for your readers or show them what an object looks like. You use description every day when you talk to friends and family members, and you encounter it daily in newspaper articles, business reports, textbooks, advertising, recreational reading, and even on television.

Description uses sensory details to capture an impression of a person, a place, or an object. These details are *images* gathered by using the five senses of sight, sound, smell, touch, and taste. Most of these images tend to be visual. But images of sound, touch, smell, and taste can have an equally strong impact. These images are important tools for sharing your perceptions of the world and making those perceptions vivid for your readers.

Description also helps you share your awareness of and responsiveness toward your emotional and intellectual life. Whether you feel love or anger, whether you remember, whether you respond to danger or to beauty, you can share all this through description. Through description, you can explain yourself or your ideas, you can amuse or divert your companions, you can change someone else's mind.

Using Description

Purpose

People generally write descriptions for three reasons:

- to inform people about a person, a place, or an object;
- to entertain them with pleasurable images;
- to convince them of a particular point.

These three aims are often combined. For example, Patricia Brady writes about the blobs to inform her audience about the appearance of an interesting life form, but she entertains in the process by using descriptive details and language that give her readers pleasure. Bruce Barcott seeks to persuade his audience that something must be done about reclaiming wild rivers, but he has to inform his readers about the proliferation of large dams before a general audience can understand the implications of his argument. Consequently, his essay is packed with details, some of which carry a powerful impact.

Audience

A good sense of audience is important for description because you will use that sense as your yardstick to measure the number and variety of details to present. The details that will impress a committee of scientists reviewing your grant application are vastly different from those that will appeal to a reader interested in buying a sari or visiting Lincoln, Nebraska. Be aware of who you are writing for and select only the relevant details that will capture their interest.

Organization

Your purpose will govern not only your selection of details but also your arrangement of them. You might arrange your details in various ways:

- *Spatially*—near to far, top to bottom, left to right, larger to smaller, and so forth;
- *Chronologically*—beginning with the earliest and ending with the latest;
- *Emphatically*—in order of importance, working from the most important to the least or vice versa;
- *Categorically*—general to specific, or vice versa.

Whatever pattern you choose, follow through with it; jumping back and forth between different principles or arrangements can blur the impression you are trying to build.

A good way to begin a description is to jot down, either from observation or from recollection, as many details, however tiny or seemingly unimportant, as you can. Then, according to your purpose, you can select the most significant details and arrange them in the most effective pattern for your purpose.

Dominant Impression

The main task in writing successful description is to make sure that all of the details you select will contribute to a single *dominant impression* that fulfills your purpose. To convey a dominant impression, select details that will show your readers the overall sense of what you are describing, the quality you want your readers to respond to, and the atmosphere you are trying to convey. Choose those details according to your purpose and your specific audience. For instance, if you were writing about your grandmother's face, you would need to decide whether you want to show her as she would appear in a harsh light to a stranger or whether you want to allow your feelings for her to soften the portrait. In either case, you would not include details of her dress or the timbre of her voice because they would tell the reader nothing about her face. Nor would you include *every* detail of her face. When describing, select only the best and most relevant details to convey the impression you want to achieve.

A dominant impression can often be stated in a single sentence that includes your perspective on the subject and encapsulates its important elements. That sentence is usually the *thesis* for your description. However, even if your description does not lend itself to a succinct thesis statement, it must have a controlling idea that you convey through the details you select and the focus and organization you choose.

Language and Style

Objective and Subjective Description

Description can be *objective* or *subjective,* or may be a blend of the two. If you are writing to present factual information, you will probably use *objective* description, which relies on sensory data uncolored by your feelings and attitudes. For example, if you were to write, "Pitted with tiny depressions, the skin of the orange exudes a pungent odor when scraped," you would have written an objective description. In contrast to informative writing, *subjective* description emphasizes your personal response to an object rather than the characteristics of the object itself. If you were to write, "The scraped skin of the orange is redolent of lazy summer mornings," you would have written a subjective description. Gallegos's essay, "Singing with All the Saints," combines objective and subjective description to great effect.

Sometimes the difference between objective and subjective description is mainly a matter of the connotations of the words the writer chooses: "The skin under her eyes crinkled into fine networks when she laughed, and delicate traces of powder dusted her soft, smile-creased cheeks" is more subjective than "The skin under her eyes was crossed and recrossed by tiny lines, and her cheeks, which bore traces of powder, had lost their former firm roundness." Notice how words like *crinkled, networks, dusted,* and *smile-creased* contribute to the subjective quality of the first description.

Denotation and Connotation

Much of the impact of description comes from careful attention to words' denotations and connotations and from judicious use of imagery and figurative language. *Denotation* refers to words' specific meaning, their dictionary definition. *Connotation* refers to the words' dictionary definitions as well as the feelings or impressions the words evoke. The following passage from Mary Pipher's *The Middle of Everywhere* is relatively free of connotations: her readers must supply their own.

> Next to the old man in overalls selling sweet corn at the farmers' market, a Vietnamese couple sells long beans, bitter melons, and fresh lemongrass. A Yemeni girl wearing a veil stands next to a football fan in his Big Red jacket. Beside McDonald's is a Vietnamese karaoke bar. Wagey Drug has a sign in the window that says, TARJETAS EN ESPAÑOL SE VENDEN AQUI. On the Fourth of July, Asian lion dancers perform beside Nigerian drummers. (130)

On the other hand, Patricia Brady depends upon the connotations evoked by the words she uses to describe the mysterious blobs:

> A brilliant morning revealed the creatures lying in long, snaky lines at the edge of the water, some rolling back and forth in the wash of the waves, others just lazing there on the beach, shining in the sun. (125)

By characterizing these "creatures" as "lying on the beach," "rolling back and forth" in the waves, "lazing there," and "shining in the sun," Brady implies that, whatever these things are, they are harmless, even endearing. Compare that sentence with the two below:

> A blinding morning exposed the aliens clumped like snakes at the tide line, some swishing back and forth in the wash of the waves, others stranded on the beach with the sun beating down on them.

> A sunny morning showed the blobs washed up in long lines at the edge of the water, some floating in the wash of the waves, others on the sand.

Both sentences describe Brady's scene, but each gives its own feel. "Aliens" has a different connotation than "creatures" or "blobs"; "clumped like snakes" has a different tone than "lying in long, snaky lines" or "washed up in long lines"; "swishing" feels different than "rolling" or "floating"; "stranded on the beach" is dramatically different than "lazing there" or the simple, objective phrase "on the sand." While the denotation of these words are fairly similar, what makes these sentences stand out is the words' differing connotations. Brady's sentence and the first example above are written to present a subjective opinion, while the second example sentence is objective and factual.

Figurative Language and Imagery

Also important for descriptive writing are *figurative language* and *imagery*. Figurative language includes such features as *simile, metaphor,* and *personification.* This passage from Greg Smith's "The Body Farm" uses a simile (a comparison using *like* or *as*) of a gardener to describe a forensic anthropologist:

> Bass' tone is gentle, instructive, as if he were a gardener noting the details of a flower. (138)

Bruce Barcott describes a dry riverbed by using a vivid metaphor (a comparison of two unlike things) to show his audience the environmental damage a dam can wreak:

> Riverbeds and banks may turn into cobblestone streets, large stones cemented in by the ultrafine silt that passes through the dams. (146)

Carefully using figurative language can enhance your reader's understanding of specific points within your description as well as strengthen its overall effect.

Imagery is akin to figurative language, but it represents the world in terms of sight, sound, smell, touch, or taste. This passage from "Sari Story" by Smita Madan Paul and Kiran Desai opens with an olfactory image ("the smell of boiled worms"), then takes up an auditory one ("the din of bustling streets"), before settling in to a rich visual picture of India:

> Long after the smell of boiled worms and the din of bustling streets have left one's memory of India, the colors remain. Color is so infused in every aspect of life that the word *raga* is used for both color and mood. Red connotes love and passion; saffron represents worldly detachment; indigo reflects sorrow or mourning. Combinations can be startling: tangerine and fuchsia, purple and parrot green, chartreuse and crimson. Other shades are so subtle that they seem to correspond to an emotion with no verbal equivalent. (142)

Images

Language can indeed evoke powerful imagery, but images themselves often describe feelings beyond our verbal capacity, as Paul and Desai suggest in the preceding passage. The photographs in this chapter capture some of the human reactions to the September 11, 2001, attacks on the World Trade Center in New York City as perhaps no verbal description could. If you decide to incorporate visuals into your descriptions, be sure they lend themselves to your purpose, audience, and dominant impression. When appropriate, images can help bolster the points you are trying to make.

Student Essay

As you read the following description essay by student Marta Salazar, notice that her purpose is primarily expressive. Notice also the kinds of details she uses to convey her corollary point that encounters with the wilderness can lead to enhanced self-awareness.

Welcome to Wilderness!

Introduction

Thesis

Wilderness has become an important part of our world. Even if we don't visit the wilderness, we find comfort in knowing there are places where natural systems function without human interference and the complex web of life continues uninterrupted. For those of us who do visit the wilderness, a sense of renewal, spiritual refreshment, self-reliance, and simplicity are our rewards. I went to the Boundary Waters to experience that kind of renewal and found solace for the past and hope for the future.

Objective description

Subjective description

The Boundary Waters Canoe Area Wilderness is located on Minnesota's northern border. It is a remote and pristine area comprised of hundreds of lakes, ancient canoe routes, clean air, abundant wildlife, and a silence so profound that, when standing on top of a rock, I was stunned to hear my own heart beat. In the first few days of my week-long paddling trip, I became lulled by the sights and sounds of nature: the paddle dipping rhythmically into the water, the slap of a beaver tail, the eerie echoing call of a loon, tall pines whispering in the wind, a northern sun setting on a glassy green lake.

Objective description

Subjective description

Subjective description

Visual images

With hundreds of lakes covering the trail map, I was amazed to find that each lake has its own unique characteristics. Lakes distinguish themselves by their size and shape, by the land that surrounds them, and by the unique characteristics of their water. Lake Alton, for example, is large, deep, and entirely spring fed. Its water is crystal clear and cold. After paddling down long Lake Kelso, an old lake geologically, I was treated to the beautiful floating bogs of the Kelso River. These mysterious bogs are treasures of unusual insects and rare plant life. The shallow and muddy bottom casts a rust color through the water and gives the lake and adjoining river their distinct hue. Several lakes and a long portage past Kelso, the trail leads to Lake Zenith, remarkable in its spacious oval shape and high, imposing banks. Shimmering white birch trees surround Hug Lake. There the leaves catch the morning sun's first glint, throwing a matrix of light onto the water's rippling surface. Northern pines of varying heights dominate some lakes while other lakes sport a colorful combination of aspen, virgin white pine, and dark-green cedar.

Blended image

By far the most curious landform I discovered came just before entering Lake Lujenida from the South. In plain view there sits a large, imposing boulder perched under three smaller rocks, situated squarely on top of a small, bald island. Legend has it that Vikings built the strange structure as a geographical marker. Others believe it is a natural occurrence, a vestige of the last ice age.

Auditory image

Locals here don't wear watches. They say the days move to the ancient rhythms of the sun, moon, wind, and rain. The weather my last night out told me to hunker down and pray. That night I lay in my tent listening to the wind tug at the tent pegs and cause the cathedral-sized trees surrounding me to creak and groan. Until the night of the storm, sunny skies and clear moonlit nights left me oblivious of nature's more dangerous

Visual image

side. The darkness of this night seemed strange: no moonshine to hedge against the pitch-blackness. Soon the cave-like darkness was interrupted.

Tactile and auditory image combined

A deafening crack, a bright white flash, and then, seconds following, a thunderous boom made my teeth vibrate. Nothing but the thin nylon of my tent separated me from the worst thunderstorm imaginable.

Tactile image

Lightning bolts gave way to torrential rain, more lightning, and longer and even louder thunder. As the soggy tent pitched and swayed against the wind, I cursed the day I thought of coming here and swore, if I were to live, never to tempt fate again. But, once the storm finally cleared, the winds calmed, and day dawned upon a clear blue sky, I had a revelation.

Preparation for conclusion

I came to the Boundary Waters seeking peace and relaxation and left knowing, intimately, the awesome and sometimes terrible power of nature. Without the storm, I would have left with a different impression of the Boundary Waters, perhaps simply recalling it as a nice place to visit. Because of the storm, I am reminded of just how fragile life is and how good it feels to be alive. I left the wilderness with a new understanding of those

Restatement of thesis

times in life that I simply endured and of those demands for endurance that will inevitably come.

Commentary

In the first paragraph, Salazar clearly states the thesis that will guide her description: "For those of us who do visit the wilderness, a sense of renewal, spiritual refreshment, self-reliance, and simplicity are our rewards." She restates this thesis more specifically in the final sentence: "I left the wilderness with a new understanding of those times in life that I simply endured and of those demands for endurance that will inevitably come." The two statements act to frame the essay. In between are passages of objective and subjective description, and visual, auditory, and tactile images. The description of the storm explains Salazar's sense of self-understanding and establishes a context for her appreciation of the natural beauty of the Boundary Waters. Salazar narrows the reader's view from the panoramic perspective of the introductory paragraph to the very minute focus on the leaves shining in the sun.

Throughout the essay, she emphasizes sensory details that show the reader exactly what she experiences—the sun on the water, the roar of the wind, the wetness of the tent. In addition to her effective use of visual and auditory images, Salazar takes advantage of rarely used tactile images that lend immediacy and richness to the picture she paints.

Her movement through the essay is not only chronological—from the beginning of her journey to the end—but also linear—from lake to river to lake. To accompany her description of the beauty of the place, she also includes a perception of the rhythms of nature and the frailty of humankind in the face of nature's awesome power.

In her conclusion, Salazar recalls her reason for visiting the Boundary Waters ("seeking peace and relaxation") and then explains the significance of the storm before she ends by stating how the experience changed her.

◆ CHECKLIST FOR WRITING ESSAYS DEVELOPED BY DESCRIPTION

- Have you identified your *purpose*? Is it to inform, entertain, or persuade? (*Hodges'* 32a/*Writer's* 1e)
- Do you have a clear sense of who your *audience* is? Are the details and language you have chosen appropriate for those readers? Have you used an organizational pattern these readers will find effective?
- Can you state the *dominant impression* of your essay in a single sentence? What quality or atmosphere are you concentrating on? Do the details you have selected support that impression?
- Do you have a *thesis*? (*Hodges'* 32c/*Writer's* 2c) Can you state it in a single sentence? If you do not have a thesis, do all of your details add up to a controlling idea?
- What kinds of details have you used? Are *objective* details phrased in neutral, *denotative* language? Do you express *subjective* details using *connotative* words and phrases to convey a clear sense of your perception? (*Hodges'* 20a/*Writer's* 29a)
- Have you included details that appeal to the senses (*images*)?
- How have you *organized* your description? Can you explain why the viewpoint you have used is appropriate or effective?
- If you have used *visuals*, what specifically do they bring to the description?

♦

THE BLOBS

Patricia Brady

Patricia Brady writes speeches and op-ed pieces, produces multimedia presentations (including most recently a history of African-American activism in Boston), and cohosts a local affairs television program. She lives in Gloucester, Massachusetts.

It was a time to remember, the time the blobs came to Gloucester. The paper 1 ran a front-page story headlined "The Blobs," describing local shores "carpeted with mysterious masses." A picture of a big hand showed something like a crystalline caterpillar creeping across the palm.

Gloucester is an old sea town on the north shore of Massachusetts. It 2 was explored by Champlain, settled by Puritans, fished out of by generations of seafarers. But the blobs were a new experience for Gloucester, according to the *Gloucester Daily Times*. As one fisherman said, no one had ever seen anything like them.

They'd come silently upon the waves. Little jellylike creatures the size 3 of your fingertip—some of them quite independent, others curiously stuck together in chains six inches long, or six feet, or maybe even sixteen feet. Clear as spring water, each little blob, with a thread of bluish purple winding deep within. What were they, everyone wanted to know. "Squid eggs," declared some. "Alien spawn," asserted others. Might they be poisonous? Dangerous? There were reports of boat engine intakes being clogged by them. People thought of birds flying into the engines of jet planes and wondered what toll the blobs might take. Harvard had been contacted, ditto the New England Aquarium, the National Marine Fisheries Service, Northeastern University. The top minds of a nation were homing in on the blobs of Gloucester.

Meanwhile, locals headed for the beach to experience the blobs person- 4 ally. A brilliant morning revealed the creatures lying in long, snaky lines at the edge of the water, some rolling back and forth in the wash of the waves, others just lazing there on the beach, shining in the sun. And so many of them. Indeed, as the paper had reported, you could not walk along the water's edge without stepping on dozens of them.

But people at the beach were not stepping on the blobs. They were walk- 5 ing near them, touching them with the toes of their shoes, poking them gently, leaning down to peer at them. Some (the bolder) picked up a sampling to study it more closely; they stood still with heads bowed over open palms, like people reading their own fortunes. Strangers talked to one another, shaking their heads, testifying to the mysteriousness of it all.

6   No one knew what the blobs were, but one thing was certain: Everyone liked them. Couldn't help it. They were simultaneously cute and strange, like babies from outer space. Familiar in a way but refusing to divulge their name, at once individuals and masses, very little and (those hooked together) pretty big, maybe plants but could be animals: The blobs tapped into a deep human curiosity that is indistinguishable from delight. They made the humans smile, the blobs did. Shake their heads and smile.

7   Those little blobs had a powerful effect, it cannot be denied. They puzzled the people on the beach, charmed them, tickled them, seduced them, lured them sweetly out of their personal selves and into the mystery surrounding them. If anything offers hope amid the dark complexities of our history-laden times, it is the enduring connection between us and the natural world, the way it calls to us and the way we answer it, the way we go on answering it, as helpless against its appeal, as unthinking, as weak in the knees as lovers. Enthralled by the blobs, the people on the beach in Gloucester lifted their gaze from the glistening sand and stared out across the blue-and-white sea with the waves collapsing so delicately and gave themselves over, for a moment, to the larger reality that sang to them.

8   A week or two later, the blobs were gone, washed back into the sea. They resurfaced briefly in the local paper, when the experts revealed them to be advanced invertebrates. It turned out that our little half-teaspoons of jelly had muscles, nerves, pharynxes that were notably large, and hearts that had long fascinated science with their ability to pump in both directions. Some had green blood! People were naturally pleased to learn all of this, and pleased, too, to discover that the scientific name of the blobs was *Thalia,* which is also the name of the muse of comic poetry.

9   The blobs had struck a lot of us as both comical and poetic, so light they seemed, and so finely put together. The word *thalia* means blooming, which felt just as right, for the blobs had certainly bloomed upon our beaches— bloomed and faded, and disappeared like the blossoms of spring and the generations that had stood and wondered on the beach before us. It all fit. Except the common name, the name we were supposed to call the blobs, which is *salps.*

10   *Salps?* No. No one in Gloucester is ever going to call the blobs *salps.* It's just not a name that covers the experience of encountering them on the beach, lying and lolling and rolling in the surf, clean and bright and friendly as bubbles, and shining like the first day of creation. When the blobs returned for a visit this fall, a fisherman who spotted them called the *Times* and said, "Those frog eggs are back." You could tell he was pleased.

Rhetorical Considerations

1. Is Brady's essay written primarily to express, inform, or persuade? (*Hodges'* 32a/*Writer's* 1b and 1d)
2. How early in the essay do you realize that the blobs are nonthreatening?
3. Are Brady's images mostly visual? What other senses does she involve? (*Hodges'* 32e/*Writer's* 2e)

4. What is accomplished by including descriptions of the townspeople's reactions? (*Hodges'* 31c/*Writer's* 2d)
5. What is accomplished by including the scientific information? (*Hodges'* 31c/*Writer's* 2d)

Language and Style

1. Find descriptive words that suggest the blobs are not dangerous. Can you find any words that are threatening? (*Hodges'* 20/*Writer's* 28)
2. How can blobs be "poetic" (paragraph 9)? Does the metaphor Brady uses in this paragraph help to explain this quality? (*Hodges'* 20/*Writer's* 28)
3. What image is conjured up with the word *blob*? (*Hodges'* 20/*Writer's* 28)
4. Comment on the use of sentence fragments in paragraph 6. Are they justifiable? (*Hodges'* 2/*Writer's* 18)
5. In the fourth sentence of paragraph 6, why is *that* used instead of *which*? (*Hodges'* 19/*Writer's* 28)

Writing Suggestions

1. Write an essay in which you describe something mysterious.
2. Write an essay in which you describe something very common, but try to describe it using exotic or mysterious details.

EXCERPT FROM THE MIDDLE OF EVERYWHERE

Mary Pipher

Mary Pipher earned her PhD in psychology from the University of Nebraska and holds a BA in cultural anthropology from the University of California at Berkeley. Her books include *Reviving Ophelia: Saving the Selves of Adolescent Girls* (1994), *The Shelter of Each Other: Rebuilding Our Families* (1996), *Another Country: Navigating the Emotional Terrain of Our Elders* (1999), and *The Middle of Everywhere: The World's Refugees Come to Our Town* (2002), from which this essay is excerpted.

I AM FROM

I am from Avis and Frank, Agnes and Fred,
Glessie May and Mark.
From the Ozark Mountains and the high plains of
Eastern Colorado,
From mountain snowmelt and lazy southern
creeks filled with water moccasins.
I am from oatmeal eaters, gizzard eaters, haggis
and raccoon eaters.
I'm from craziness, darkness, sensuality, and
humor.
From intense do-gooders struggling through
ranch winters in the 1920s.
I'm from "If you can't say anything nice about
someone don't say anything" and "Pretty is as pretty
does" and "Shit-mucklety brown" and "Damn it all
to hell."
I'm from no-dancing-or-drinking Methodists, but
cards were okay except on Sunday, and from tent-
meeting Holy Rollers,
From farmers, soldiers, bootleggers, and
teachers.
I'm from Schwinn girl's bike, 1950 Mercury two-
door, and West Side Story.
I'm from coyotes, baby field mice, chlorinous
swimming pools,
Milky Way and harvest moon over Nebraska
cornfields.
I'm from muddy Platte and Republican, from
cottonwood and mulberry, tumbleweed and
switchgrass from Willa Cather, Walt Whitman, and

Janis Joplin,
   My own sweet dance unfolding against a cast of
women in aprons and barefoot men in overalls.

As a girl in Beaver City, I played the globe game. Sitting outside in the thick 1
yellow weeds, or at the kitchen table while my father made bean soup, I
would shut my eyes, put my finger on the globe, and spin it. Then I would
open my eyes and imagine what it was like in whatever spot my finger was
touching. What were the streets like, the sounds, the colors, the smells?
What were the people doing there right now?

   I felt isolated in Beaver City, far away from any real action. We were a 2
small town of white Protestants surrounded by cow pastures and wheat
fields. I had no contact with people who were different from me. Native
Americans had a rich legacy in Nebraska, but I knew nothing of them, not
even the names of the tribes who lived in my area. I had never seen a black
person or a Latino. Until I read *The Diary of Anne Frank,* I had never heard of
Jewish people.

   Adults talked mostly about crops, pie, and rainfall. I couldn't wait to 3
grow up and move someplace exotic and faraway, and living where I did,
every place appeared faraway and exotic. When I read Tolstoy's book on the
little pilgrim who walked all over the world, I vowed to become that pilgrim
and to spend my life seeing everything and talking to everyone.

   As a young adult, I escaped for a while. I lived in San Francisco, Mexico, 4
London, and Madrid. But much to my surprise, I missed the wheat fields,
the thunderstorms, and the meadowlarks. I returned to Nebraska in my mid-
twenties, married, raised a family, worked as a psychologist, and ate a lot of
pie. I've been happy in Nebraska, but until recently I thought I had to
choose between loving a particular rural place and experiencing all the beautiful diversity of the world.

   Before the Europeans arrived, Nebraska was home to many Indian tribes. 5
The Omaha, the Ponca, the Pawnee, and the Nemaha lived in the east, the
Lakota Sioux in the west. In the late 1800s immigrants from Europe pushed
out the Native Americans. Wave after wave of new pioneers broke over Nebraska and we became a state of Scots, Irish, British, Czechs, Swedes, and
Danes. For a while, we had so many Germans that many schools held classes
in German. But after World War I, when nativist sentiments swept our state,
our unicameral made instruction in German illegal.

   Mexican workers came to build the railroads and to work on farms and 6
in meatpacking. African Americans came to farm and to work in our cities.
Nebraska's first free black person, Sally Bayne, moved to Omaha in 1854,
and an all-black colony was formed at Overton in Dawes County in 1885.
Malcolm X was born in Omaha in 1925.

   Even though people of color have a rich history in our state and, of 7
course, the Native Americans were here first, our state's identity the last 150
years has been mainly European. Until recently, a mixed marriage meant a
Catholic married to a Methodist. After World War II, so many Latvians came
here that we became the official site of the Latvian government in exile. Our

jokes were yawners about farmers or Lutherans—"What did the farmer say after he won a million dollars in the lottery?" "Thank God I have enough money to farm a few more years." Or, "Wherever four Lutherans are gathered there is always a fifth."

8   However, in the last fifteen years something surprising has happened. It began with the boat people, mostly Vietnamese and Cambodians, coming in after the Vietnam War. In the 1980s Lincoln began having a few Asian markets, a Vietnamese Catholic church, a Buddhist temple, and English Language Learners (ELL) classes. Around the same time, Mexican migrant workers, who had long done seasonal work in our area, bought houses and settled down. Refugees from the wars in Central America trickled in.

9   The real change occurred in the 1990s. Because Lincoln had almost no unemployment and a relatively low cost of living, we were selected by the U.S. Office of Refugee Resettlement as a preferred community for newly arrived refugees. Now we are one of the top-twenty cities in America for new arrivals from abroad. Our nonwhite population has grown 128 percent since 1990. We are beginning to look like East Harlem.

10   Suddenly, our supermarkets and schools are bursting with refugees from Russia, Serbia, Croatia, Bosnia, Hungary, and Ethiopia. Our Kurdish, Sudanese, and Somali populations are rapidly increasing. Even as I write this, refugees from Afghanistan, Liberia, and Sierra Leone are coming into our community. Some are educated and from Westernized places. Increasingly, we have poor and uneducated refugees. We have children from fifty different nationalities who speak thirty-two different languages in our public schools.

11   Our obituary column shows who came here early in the 1990s. It is filled with Hrdvys, Andersens, Walenshenksys, and Muellers. But the births column, which reflects recent immigration patterns, has many Ali, Nguyen, and Martinez babies. By midcentury, less than half our population will be non-Latino white. We are becoming a brown state in a brown nation.

12   Lincoln has often been described by disgruntled locals and insensitive outsiders as the middle of nowhere, but now it can truthfully be called the middle of everywhere. We are a city of juxtapositions. Next to the old man in overalls selling sweet corn at the farmers' market, a Vietnamese couple sells long beans, bitter melons, and fresh lemongrass. A Yemeni girl wearing a veil stands next to a football fan in his Big Red Jacket. Beside McDonald's is a Vietnamese karaoke bar. Wagey Drug has a sign in the window that says, TARJETAS EN ESPAÑOL SE VENDEN AQUI. On the Fourth of July, Asian lion dancers perform beside Nigerian drummers. Driving down Twenty-seventh Street, among the signs for the Good Neighbor Center, Long John Silver's, Fat Pat's Pizza, Snowflakes, and Jiffy Lube, I see signs for Mohammed's Barber Shop, Jai Jai's Hair Salon, Kim Ngo's jewelry, Pho's Vietnamese Café, and Nguyen's Tae-Kwon Do.

13   We celebrate many holidays—Tet, Cinco de Mayo, Rosh Hashanah, and Ramadan. At our jazz concerts, Vietnamese families share benches with Kurdish and Somali families. When my neighbor plays a pickup basketball game in the park, he plays with Bosnian, Iranian, Nigerian, and Latino players. I am reminded of the *New Yorker* cartoon which pictured a restaurant with a

sign reading, RANCHO IL WOK DE PARIS, FEATURING TEX-MEX, ITALIAN, ASIAN, AND FRENCH CUISINES.

Women in veils exchange information with Mexican grandmothers in 14 long black dresses. Laotian fathers smoke beside Romanian and Serbian dads. By now, every conceivable kind of grocery store exists in our city. And the ethnic shelves in our IGA grocery stores keep expanding. The produce sections carry jicama and cilantro. Shoppers can buy pitas, tortillas, egg rolls, wraps, and breads from all over the world. My most recent cab driver was a Nigerian school administrator who fled his country because he was in a pro-democracy group. S. J. Perelman's description of Bangkok—"It seemed to combine the Hannibal, Missouri, of Mark Twain's childhood with Beverly Hills, the Low Countries, and Chinatown"—could now apply to Lincoln.

Rhetorical Considerations

1. What is the descriptive effect of the opening lines in italics? (*Hodges'* 33b/ *Writer's* 3b)
2. Why does Pipher describe the history of Nebraska's cultural makeup? (*Hodges'* 31c/*Writer's* 2d)
3. Does Pipher reveal a judgment about whether the changes in Nebraska's culture have had a positive or negative effect? If so, what is that judgment?
4. What are the negative effects of the cultural changes in Nebraska?
5. What kinds of details does Pipher use? How do they help to describe the changes she focuses on in this essay? (*Hodges'* 31c/*Writer's* 2d)

Language and Style

1. Look up the following words in your dictionary: *unicameral* (paragraph 5); *disgruntled* and *juxtapositions* (paragraph 12). (*Hodges'* 19e/*Writer's* 28e)
2. What is the difference between an *immigrant* and a *refugee?* (*Hodges'* 19e/ *Writer's* 28e)
3. Is the pronoun case correct in the third sentence of paragraph 2? Why or why not? (*Hodges'* 5/*Writer's* 21)
4. What is the subject of the last sentence of paragraph 11? (*Hodges'* 1b and 1d/ *Writer's* 16a)

Writing Suggestions

1. Write an essay in which you describe the cultural or ethnic diversity in your own community.
2. Keep a record for a period of a week of anything you do, purchase, eat, or otherwise experience that is a result of increased cultural diversity in America. Then write an essay describing the effect immigration has on American life.

SINGING WITH ALL THE SAINTS

Aaron McCarroll Gallegos

Aaron McCarroll Gallegos is a freelance writer who lives in Toronto. Formerly an editor for *Sojourner* magazine, he is working on a book on Latino youth and alternatives to gang violence.

1   By the time my wife and I arrived for morning worship at St. John Coltrane African Orthodox Church, waves of intense sound were already flowing from the Divisadero Street storefront. Located in San Francisco's Western Addition district, between the gritty Tenderloin and groovy Haight-Asbury neighborhoods, St. John's has a powerful witness the local community can't ignore. Even the most jaded pedestrians were poking their heads in the door to see what all the racket was about.

2   In spite of the church's huge reputation, the sanctuary is only the size of your average living room, and it feels even smaller because of the radiant Byzantine-style icons that cover the walls: Jesus the Alpha and Omega, Mary the Mother of God, the Tree of Life, and, above the altar, the icon that testifies to the uniqueness of this congregation—a noble image of the church's patron saint, jazz musician John Coltrane, complete with golden halo and holy fire streaming from his saxophone.

3   While some might find it odd that a church would so honor a jazz musician, this diverse gathering of church members, music lovers, tourists, and the spiritually curious didn't seem to mind. Throughout several hours of worship, the brilliantly colored church pulsated with Coltrane's music, led by a drumly-beating, sax-playing team of clergy. Shouts of "Hallelujah!" "Amen!" and "Praise God!" punctuated chants and melodies from Coltrane's masterwork, *A Love Supreme.*

4   Some recent accounts in the press about this church have missed the point, mistakenly concluding that the church worships Coltrane himself. In fact, its theology is quite traditional. What makes this church wildly different—and somewhat controversial—is its use of the music and words of a jazz musician to express devotion to God. But something else is going on at St. John's as well. I believe their unique form of worship raises important issues about the changing nature of modern American religion, especially mainstream Christianity, as we enter the twenty-first century.

5   John Coltrane is certainly not the most likely candidate for Christian sainthood. He wasn't a conventional Christian, nor was he a conventional musician. Until his death in 1967, "Trane," an endless seeker, pursued an eclectic spiritual path influenced by Christianity, Islam, Hinduism, the Kabbalah, astrology, and Einstein's theory of relativity. He expressed this spiritual search in his music, and he invited his listeners along on the pilgrimage.

132

Coltrane had a strong Christian upbringing in the North Carolina home 6
of his minister grandfather, but music—not religion—was his life's passion.
He took up the clarinet and saxophone in high school, then moved to Philadelphia in search of work, Coltrane practiced hard, often silently fingering
his sax late into the night in the boardinghouse room he shared with his
cousin Mary.

After a short stint in the navy, Coltrane became deeply involved with 7
the postwar jazz scene, backing some of the era's top performers, including
Dizzy Gillespie, Johnny Hodges, and Miles Davis. But jazz wasn't the only
thing consuming Trane. Like Charlie Parker, one of his idols, he got hooked
on both heroin and alcohol. While opinions vary as to how severely
Coltrane's addictions affected his music, he did get fired from several gigs,
including his most prominent one, with trumpeter Davis.

In 1957 Coltrane overcame his addictions, and, like many others who 8
conquer their personal demons, found his way to a greater spiritual depth.
"I experienced, by the grace of God," he later wrote, "a spiritual awakening
which was to lead me to a richer, fuller, more productive life. At that time,
in gratitude, I humbly asked to be given the means and privilege to make
others happy through music." Coltrane produced an amazing amount of
work in the 10 years he had left to live. By the time he died of liver cancer
in 1967 at age 40, he had taken the saxophone, and jazz itself, to new places,
raising the art of improvisation to a level that few if any have equaled.

Coltrane's hallowed status at St. John's is largely the work of the 9
church's founder and bishop, Franzo Wayne King. King founded the church
in 1971 as the One Mind Temple Evolutionary Transitional Body of Christ.
In 1982 the church joined the African Orthodox Church, a small denomination started by African Americans who had been drawn to aspects of
Greek, Russian, and Coptic Orthodox liturgy. Appointed the church's
bishop, King dropped its old name and chose Coltrane as its patron saint.
As a young man, King—not unlike Coltrane—had fled the religion of his
Pentecostal parents for the jazz clubs. Seeing Coltrane play in 1965 was the
"sound baptism" that started King on a "very serious and earnest journey to
seek out God." At St. John's, he hoped to lead others to the transformative
spiritual experience he had encountered in Coltrane's music.

St. John's attracts a diverse group of seekers: disaffected Gen-Xers, afflu- 10
ent African-American businesspeople, dreadlocked hippies, aging beats.
Even those who are familiar with Coltrane's music may not be prepared for
the positive vibrations of "St. John, the sound Baptist," as the church calls
him. On the Sunday I attended, the tiny chapel was nearly full when the
service began, but within minutes people started slipping out. The din of
saxophones, drums, congas, bass, and percussion quickly overwhelmed the
uninitiated. A trumpet inches from the back of my head screeched and
honked the artist's avant-garde music throughout the service. But the worship style, flowing out of the Pentecostal and black church traditions, is as
fervent and powerful as you'll find anywhere.

Many Christians have criticized St. John's for granting sainthood to a 11
jazz musician and former addict; but given Coltrane's spiritual impact on

African-American community and beyond, the decision isn't so strange. In many ways, mainstream Christianity's refusal to consider canonizing exceptional people like Coltrane parallels the dominant Western culture's assertion that the only truly "classical" music is by Beethoven, Mozart, and other white Europeans. Yet the music of Duke Ellington, Miles Davis, Billie Holiday, Bob Marley, and, yes, John Coltrane is equally "classic"—or more so, some would argue.

12   On another level, the service at St. John's challenges mainstream assumptions about worship itself. While people around the world spend hours, if not days, celebrating their spiritual traditions, North American churchgoers often get irritable if services last more than an hour. At St. John's, the hours of worship filled with unsettling sounds are a challenge to mainstream churches that have conformed in many ways to the dominant paradigms of Western society: consumerism instead of personal sacrifice, entertainment instead of prophecy, the individual instead of community.

13   In the coming decades, as the center of Christianity moves from Europe and North America to Africa, Asia, and Latin America, other cultural expressions of worship are destined to become more influential. St. John's is an indication of that trend. Indeed, the cultural reshaping of spiritual expression has been going on as long as humans have gathered for religious worship. Still, many find it hard to equate worship with "ugly" music which is how some would describe much of Coltrane's later work. Can art that challenges our sense of aesthetics be said to inspire us? Or can only the art we consider beautiful and attractive lift our hearts and souls toward the divine?

14   Coltrane's later work is, in fact, beautiful, at least for many who have delved into it. Some Coltrane critics have called it "anti-jazz," but others would disagree. In his recent biography, *John Coltrane: His Life and Music* (University of Michigan, 1998), Lewis Porter, professor of jazz theory at Rutgers University, explores one of Coltrane's most obtuse works, "Venus," recorded in 1966 with drummer Rashied Ali. Porter concludes that "Venus" is an exceedingly complex study of chord contortions based on systematic, almost mathematical, musical theory.

15   But what Coltrane was doing went far beyond technical virtuosity. After recording *A Love Supreme* in 1964 (a work he said had come to him as a vision from God), Coltrane stated that 90 percent of his playing was actually prayer. "I know there are bad forces, forces that bring suffering to others and misery to the world," he once said, "but I want to be the opposite force, I want to be the force which is truly for good." By all accounts a humble and gentle man, Coltrane no doubt would have been uncomfortable being called a saint. But he surely would have been happy to hear his music moving people toward a deeper relationship with the divine.

Rhetorical Considerations

1. Is this essay intended primarily for description, or does it have another purpose? (*Hodges'* 32a/*Writer's* 1b and 1e)

2. In describing the St. John Coltrane African Orthodox Church, does Gallegos draw comparisons with other churches? Why or why not? (*Hodges'* 32c/ *Writer's* 2e)
3. What kinds of concrete details does Gallegos use? How do these details make the essay more effective? (*Hodges'* 31c/*Writer's* 2d)
4. Which of the senses does Gallegos primarily draw on for his description? (*Hodges'* 31c/*Writer's* 2d)
5. Is this description mostly objective or subjective? Find evidence in the essay that supports your answer. (*Hodges'* 35c/*Writer's* 7c)

Language and Style

1. Why is the Haight-Ashbury neighborhood described as "groovy" (paragraph 1)? (*Hodges'* 19c/*Writer's* 28c)
2. Find words in the essay that you would expect to find in a description of a church. Are there any words that you would not expect to find in such a description? (*Hodges'* 20/*Writer's* 29)
3. Look up the following words in your dictionary: *Byzantine* and *icon* (paragraph 2); *hallowed* (paragraph 9). (*Hodges'* 19e/*Writer's* 28e)
4. Find examples of Gallegos's use of active verbs in paragraph 3. (*Hodges'* 1c/*Writer's* 16b)
5. Why is the plural *their* used in the last sentence of paragraph 4? (*Hodges'* 6b/*Writer's* 21d)

Writing Suggestions

1. Write an essay in which you describe an unusual event or place.
2. Write an essay describing your first visit to a memorable place.

◆

THE BODY FARM

Greg Smith

This essay was originally published in *The Oxford American,* a quarterly magazine founded in 1992 in Oxford, Mississippi, and currently published by the popular novelist John Grisham. Billing itself as "The Southern Magazine of Good Writing," the periodical offers articles on a variety of historical, cultural, and political topics with a southern focus.

1   Just outside Knoxville, Tennessee, a university-issue white Ford pickup truck cuts diagonally across the nearly empty parking lot behind the University Medical Center and pulls to a stop in front of a chain-link gate. A car door opens, and out bounds Dr. William Bass, a burly man, solid and fit for his 71 years. He has close-cropped gray hair, oversized glasses, gray tweed jacket, white button-down shirt. On the ring that holds the keys to his truck, house, and office are the keys to the University of Tennessee Anthropology Research Facility, known to the locals by a more familiar name: the Body Farm.

2   Cars pull into other spots in the lot. Doctors, nurses, and medical students walk briskly to morning classes without so much as a glance toward the fence that rings the Farm. It's two fences, really: The outside fence is chain-link, six feet high, with $2,000 worth of fresh razor wire tangled along its top. That fence is backed by a wooden "modesty" fence similar to one that might separate your backyard from your neighbor's—except that this barrier hides three acres unlike any others in the world.

3   Bass, a forensic anthropologist by training, began his career in the classroom, but over time began to help police departments across the United States identify bodies. He learned a lot from examining bodies at crime scenes, and setting up an outdoor laboratory where he could conduct experiments on human bodies left to weather the elements was a natural extension of his work. Eventually he'd be able to tell law enforcement agencies more about the bodies they discovered. Thus, in 1971, the Body Farm was born.

4   The gates swing open, and we walk into a clearing the size of a backyard, ringed by thick underbrush and a stand of vine-covered trees. Crossing the threshold snaps the senses to a state of full awareness; it's like passing through an invisible wall that keeps two worlds apart. The smell is noticeable, but it's more stale than wretched. I see an old mailbox, a few cardboard boxes, a couple of old rusting cars, a ladder, and some shovels leaning up against the fence. And the dead bodies. About a dozen are in plain view, stretched out on the ground. Most are covered by thick black plastic tarps or white cotton bedsheets. Each body wears two bright orange plastic tags, strapped to arm and ankle. Next to each body is a small metal sign that, like

the orange tags, identifies the body by code. "WM 43 2/97" translates as "white male, 43 years old, the second body placed at the Farm in 1997." Names and personal histories are kept in a locked file cabinet in Bass' office.

Many people stipulate in their wills that their bodies be donated to sci- 5 ence. Few of them are likely to have in mind Bass' field of study, a little-discussed area of forensic science. The bodies are first used by forensic science students; eventually, the bones are turned over to the anthropology department for further study. In this way, the Body Farm makes scientific sense, just like the organ donor checkoff on your driver's license. It's the intersection of science and emotion that's a bit hard to get around.

The human body goes through a number of changes when it dies. Sci- 6 entists have a pretty good handle on what happens within the first few hours: The heart stops, the brain ceases functioning, fluids leak out, stiffness sets in, and so on. At this point, a trained professional can make a pretty good guess about how long a person has been dead. It's in the days and weeks beyond death that forensic scientists still struggle to understand the process of human decay. That's where the bugs come in.

"One of the best ways of telling how long a body has been dead, up until 7 about two and a half weeks, is to look at the insects," says Bass. "The blowflies arrive first, stay for a while, then lay their eggs, which hatch into maggots. The maggots then metamorphose from the worm to the fly stage, and the process starts all over again. This cycle usually takes 18 to 21 days." A trained eye can look at the bugs in a body and tell how long a person's been dead by the stage of metamorphosis.

Most of the bodies on the Farm at the time of my visit were in advanced 8 stages of decay: skin transformed into a leathery sheath, bones exposed. But it's the recent arrivals, skin still pink and ripe, that give you pause.

As you might imagine, says Bass, "not everyone wants to do this." In 9 fact, Bass doesn't want to do it much longer himself. He soon plans to retire from his teaching post and from his work with the FBI and local law enforcement. Until then, he has a pool of graduate students who are eager to tap his forensic knowledge. His method is simple, Bass explains: Give each of the students one skeleton per week and have them tell him "who the person was—gender, age, everything." The bones never lie.

Once a year, Bass holds a memorial service for the people who donated 10 their bodies to the Farm. This year I'm invited to attend. A cardboard box containing the remains of a randomly selected skeleton is laid on a large conference table in an anthropology department classroom. A simple white linen cloth covers the box. The gathering is small, just a few students and professors. Also present are James McSween and his son. McSween donated his wife's body to the Farm, something they discussed before she died. He has come here to find connection and comfort with the decision he made.

After the service is over, Bass huddles with the McSweens in a corner. 11 His tone is that of a pastor after a Sunday service—calm, reassuring. He gestures toward the door, and father and son make their way down narrow halls and stairways to the skeleton-storage room in the basement. I follow at a respectful distance. There, several long tables and desks compete for space with rows of floor-to-ceiling shelving. On the shelves are some 2,000 cardboard boxes just like the one from the memorial service.

12   The three men work their way around a table and stop before a wall of boxes. Bass searches the labels. "Here she is," he says, and pulls down one of the boxes. He carefully removes the lid, reaches inside, and lifts out the skull. A small number is written on its base. The number matches the label on the box. Bass' tone is gentle, instructive, as if he were a gardener noting the details of a flower.

13   "Oh, I see she had open-heart surgery," he says, and lifts out the rib cage. The bones are taupe and smooth; three strands of bright silver wire join the two halves. "And this one," he continues. "It looks like she nicked this leg bone at some point." The son stands rigid, a look of confusion clouding his face. McSween is no longer listening to Bass' impromptu lecture. He tentatively puts his hand in the box and withdraws an arm bone. He turns it slowly in his hand. A subtle wave of emotion seems to wash over him. He replaces the bone. Bass pauses, then puts his hand gently on McSween's shoulder. "You can come visit her anytime you'd like." He replaces the lid, then the box.

14   Bass never dreams about his work or his guests at the Farm, but he has thought a lot about God and the nature of our being. "The thing that makes us different from most animals," he says, "is that we have a soul; what makes us human is the spirit." But this man, who understands the scientific process of death and dying, also has personal knowledge of death's emotional toll.

15   "I will have to admit that with the death of my second wife," he says softly, "I have seriously wondered whether there really is a God. She was a very, very nice lady. She died of lung cancer. Never smoked a day in her life. We did everything science could do and did not have what it took to overcome what happened. I am religious. I do go to church. But if you ask me, am I 100 percent sure there's a God, I would have to say I don't know." He looks down at his hands, rubs them together twice, then lays them flat on the desk in front of him.

16   The traditional trappings of death don't appeal to him. "I don't like mourning," he says. "I don't like funerals." He won't be cremated; the idea doesn't fit well with a life that's been devoted to anthropology, which raises a question: Is there a place waiting for him at the Farm? "You know, it's funny," he says. "I talked it over with my first wife, and we decided that I'd go to the Farm after I died. But she died first. And so I discussed it with my second wife, who was against it. But then she died unexpectedly as well. So now I'm remarried, just a year now, and I haven't broached the idea with her." He ponders the thought in the manner of a man who has already made up his mind. "I have to be honest," he says. "I'm leaning toward it."

Rhetorical Considerations

1. How does Smith make such a gruesome subject appealing to his audience? (*Hodges'* 32a/*Writer's* 1b and 1e)

2. What emotions allow people to overcome their usual revulsion at the Body Farm?
3. How does Smith describe Dr. Bass? Why might he pay so much attention to this description and to the details of Dr. Bass's personal life? (*Hodges'* 31c/ *Writer's* 2d)
4. Why does Smith bring up the subject of religion and God? (*Hodges'* 32a/ *Writer's* 1b and 1e)
5. How does Smith describe the various sensory elements of the Body Farm? (*Hodges'* 31c/*Writer's* 2d)

Language and Style

1. Look up the following words in your dictionary: *forensic* (paragraph 3); *metamorphose* (paragraph 7); *impromptu* (paragraph 13). (*Hodges'* 19e/*Writer's* 28e)
2. Find effective examples of sentence variety in the essay. (*Hodges'* 30/*Writer's* 27)
3. Smith compares Dr. Bass to a pastor in paragraph 11 and a gardener in paragraph 12. What effect does this comparison have on your perception of Dr. Bass? (*Hodges'* 32e/*Writer's* 2e)
4. What is the subject of the last sentence of paragraph 1? (*Hodges'* 1b and 1d/*Writer's* 16a)
5. Comment on the order of the phrases in the last sentence of paragraph 1. (*Hodges'* 1f and 29f/*Writer's* 17a and 26f)

Writing Suggestions

1. Write an essay in which you describe something that most people would find repulsive or frightening.
2. Write an essay in which you describe your job to someone who finds the job boring, gross, or otherwise unappealing.

SARI STORY

Smita Madan Paul and Kiran Desai

Smita Madan Paul, a freelance videojournalist and writer based in New Delhi, India, has written for a number of newspapers and currently works for Video News International (VNI), a New York Times company. Kiran Desai's first novel, *Hullabaloo in the Guava Orchard* (1998), received much critical acclaim. She is the daughter of novelist Anita Desai. This essay first appeared in the magazine *Civilization*, published by the Library of Congress.

1   An opaque, humid fog blankets New Delhi, making the streets seem particularly grimy. Our driver navigates the motorized rickshaw through a crowd of exhaust-spewing cars, trucks, and other auto-rickshaws, conceding right-of-way to the roaming cows that view us and the surrounding scene with an enviable moony detachment.

2   Finally, we reach the marketplace of South Extension, where jean and T-shirt shops are interspersed with stores selling traditional saris and gold jewelry. Even before we mount the dingy marble steps to Nalli's Saree Shop, our hearts are racing. The uniformed doormen open the glass doors with a flourish. At the threshold, a cacophonous opera of voices inside replaces the sounds of the Delhi street behind us. The doormen nod their turbaned heads—the last civilized gesture before we enter.

3   Inside, women are lined up three-deep along the counter; overhead, shop clerks unfurl yards of one of India's most ancient treasures: silk. With a satisfying whack, men snap out the cloth, releasing a scent of rice starch as the fabric wafts onto the counter. Before there is a chance to admire one sari, another is revealed the same way.

4   Sari buying is a contact sport—if you're not careful, you'll be elbowed hopelessly out of reach of the counters. You grab one beautiful sari only to reel in a competing buyer. And be wary of the brides-to-be, identified by the henna patterns on their hands: Out to buy their wedding trousseaus, they are the most aggressive. We throw ourselves into the fray and a few hours later emerge victorious, if a little bruised, woven treasures in tow.

5   The sari, the mainstay of India's weaving tradition, is an evolutionary triumph. This most simple of garments is the oldest continuously worn dress in history, dating back to the second century B.C. Invasions have come and gone, empires have risen and crumbled, yet nothing has changed the popularity of the sari. And, while factories have expedited much of the process, many handlooms are still used, weaving the same patterns and employing the same dye processes developed centuries ago. Saris are now made

of cotton, silk, rayon, or polyester, but they are still six- to nine-yard lengths of uncut cloth, folded and tied around the body. India's textile industry has survived to the present day because of its willingness to adopt new influences while holding onto the old.

Now, however, there is a new kind of threat: the changing aesthetic 6 sense of the new generation, formed in the global economy. Ironies abound in that economy at a time when Indian silk is fodder for couture-show runways and elite boutiques, when New York socialites and British sensualists have come to fetishize the fabric, when high-end designers make personal pilgrimages to India in search of material for purses, skirts, and shirts. China and Italy continue to outrank India in silk exports to the United States, but while China's and Italy's numbers dropped last year by 6 percent, India's figure ballooned by 22 percent. In the urban centers of India, however, it is blue jeans, T-shirts, and baseball caps that mark a glamorous wardrobe.

The sari is a good reminder that there has always been a global economy. 7 The world has always coveted Indian fabrics, from the Pharaohs and ancient Greeks to Anna Sui and Goldie Hawn. In the 13th century, Marco Polo said, "embroidery is here [in India] produced with more delicacy than anywhere in the world." In India's handloom-woven-silk industry alone, there are more than ten million embroiderers, weavers, spinners, and dyers—more than the entire population of many countries. During the Raj, however, the British tried to crush the handloom-weaving tradition, making the subcontinent dependent on cheaply made English cloth. Mahatma Gandhi turned this against the British, using the spinning wheel as an icon of independence: From 1941 to 1947, the spinning wheel graced India's flag.

We journeyed across India to visit some of the people responsible for 8 producing this homespun beauty. The tropical countryside of Orissa, about 800 miles east of Delhi, possesses a meditative calm, a relief from the nervy capital city. The landscape is a patchwork of red scrub, rice fields, lush lotus ponds, and palm tree jungles. We passed little villages and the wide Mahanandi River as it winds its way to the Bay of Bengal. The white-sand strip along the coast matches the white spires of Puri's 12th-century Jagannath Temple and is punctuated by the dark ruins of the ninth-century Surya Temple in Konarak. For centuries, when ships from the Far East arrived to pick up Orissan silk for the royal families of Indonesia and Thailand, crews used the temple spires as landmarks. While Jagannath's prominence in the Hindu faith—and its large temple complex—attracts crowds of pilgrims, the Surya Temple, no longer sacred and set in a quiet forest, is known for its sculptures. Some of the 13th-century carvings—depicting everything for love to war—are so risqué that visitors rear back and fall off the temple steps. The government has recently considered putting up railings.

Coastal Orissa is one of the centers of *ikat* fabric. *Ikat* refers to a tech- 9 nique that involves resist-dyeing the thread: Warp and weft threads are divided into bundles and tied with dye-resistant material—cotton yarn or strips of leaf or plastic. Once the resist material is removed from the dyed threads, the pieces are then aligned according to a pattern. The patterns, involving complex calculations, are often retained in the minds of the weaving masters until they are taught to their children. In Nuapatna, designs have trickled down eight generations.

10   In a cluster of tiny red-colored mud houses grouped around a stone temple, the entire population of Nuapatna seems to be involved in the production of *ikat* saris. Little children run between the mud houses clasping bundles of raw silk. Women hang freshly dyed yarn between the temple arches, and dyers can be spotted by their permanently colored hands. From every dark interior, bits of bright silk gleam. Weavers work on ramshackle wooden looms with only a bald light bulb for light, while objects we might consider refuse are used as weights to produce just the right amount of tension for the yarn. Yet the work is executed with incredible precision.

11   Long after the smell of boiled worms and the din of bustling streets have let one's memory of India, the colors remain. Color is so infused in every aspect of life that the word *raga* is used for both color and mood. Red connotes love and passion; saffron represents worldly detachment; indigo reflects sorrow or mourning. Combinations can be startling: tangerine and fuchsia, purple and parrot green, chartreuse and crimson. Other shades are so subtle that they seem to correspond to an emotion with no verbal equivalent.

12   Paid only about 400 rubles (about ten dollars) for a sari that may take two weeks to complete, many of these weavers cannot afford to buy the saris they spend their days making. Nor can they afford the raw materials, which are given to them by a government cooperative, which in turn gets the silk from the lush tropical state of Kanartaka, about 1,200 miles south of New Delhi.

13   After flying into Kanartaka's bustling commercial capital, Bangalore, we drove the road to Mysore, where carts, trucks, and bicycles—bearing everything from coconuts to kerosene—dodge each other going to market.

14   As we approached the outskirts of Mysore, renowned for sandalwood and jasmine as well as for silk, we saw farmers cycling to the Government Cocoon Market in Ramnagar, balancing giant sacks of cocoons on their heads. At the marketplace, the cocoons are tossed in the air and sorted by size, fluffiness, elongation, and shade of yellow, and then argued and bartered over. Proprietors of reeling factories turn them into thread, which is then sold to weavers.

15   According to K. Ravindranath, India's assistant director of sericulture, the real threat to Indian silk comes not from The Gap, but from China. The demand for silk has outstripped domestic supply—about 5,000 metric tons were imported from China last year, where the thread is cheaper and thinner. But there is an audible, as well as visible, difference between Indian and Chinese silks, he says: "Suppose two Chinese women dressed in silk come rushing through a doorway. It doesn't make any sound at all. But when two Indian women come crashing together, it gives that fantastic sound of silk." That sound, he explains, comes from the thicker threads and higher starch content in Indian silk.

16   In Ramnagar's reeling factories, the cocoons are boiled, killing the worms and softening the silk, which is then spun into one long thread. The end of the thread is then attached to a reeling machine that winds it onto a

spool. On another machine, thread from ten spools is twisted into a diamond shape to produce a skein of thread bought by weavers. The clatter of machinery and the rotting smell of boiled worms fill the streets of this suburb, which is predominantly Muslim and poorer than most Hindi areas.

A little further down the road in Mysore, the silk manufacturers are 17 known for a high-thread-count georgette, inspired by 1940s French chiffon. But there are many kinds of silk: There is coarse tussar silk, made from wild, uncultivated cocoons. There is heavy, rustling silk, and silk so fine it is called "woven water." And, because the Jain community is opposed to harming any other creature, "freedom" silk is woven from cocoons after the worms have escaped.

At the Central Silk Technological Research Institute in the northern city 18 of Varanasi, scientists are out to improve Indian silk in every way possible. Om Karnath at the Eco-Testing Research Institute proudly shows off his gadgets for testing stiffness, absorption, crimping, drapery, cohesion, rubbing-fastness, air permeability, tearing strength, and crease recovery. All of this elaborate technology lies idle, however, rendered useless by another of India's anachronistic ironies: The electricity has gone out again.

Sitting on the holy Ganges River, Varanasi, a sacred city for Hindus, 19 Muslims, Buddhists, and Jains, is also a center for classical dance, music, and, of course, weaving—a tradition here since the first century A.D. We arrived just after the Muslim festival of Id; leftover streamers and tinsel decorations crisscrossed the ceiling of the home workshop of Ansar Ahmed, a textile designer we visited. He explains that the depiction of animals and people was forbidden during the Mughal period (from the early-16th to the mid-18th centuries), inspiring floral brocades that made the city famous. During the 1890s, some weavers brought back wallpaper samples from England to create new designs.

These days, Muslim weavers also make the maroon cloth used for Ti- 20 betan robes and the rich brocades that frame Buddhist religious paintings. Perhaps the most famous Varanasi saris are the *kincabs,* or "little dreams." These wedding brocades, embroidered with gold, are prized among Hindu brides, who often make pilgrimages to buy one. Should a family fall on hard times, the sari is burned and the gold recovered.

Ahmed shows us his designs, worked out on graph paper. They will be 21 transferred to punch cards and fed into semi-mechanized Jacquard looms. His skills are a "gift by nature, learnt through God," he says. But sometimes the designs come from less-than-divine inspiration. When disco fever hit India, irregular saris were labeled "disco" saris—the jagged foul-ups resembled the dance craze—and put on the market. Nowadays, weavers are inspired by the latest blockbusters in Bollywood, as the Bombay film industry is known.

But even in Bollywood, films feature women wearing baseball caps and 22 playing basketball—fashion cues picked up since the advent of satellite television about six years ago. With a population of close to one billion, it will take more than a little black box to alter the most fundamental wardrobe item for the majority of India's women. Jeans and a T-shirt may be India's latest trend, but shopping for Levi's hardly compares with the parade of sounds, smells, characters, and a scenery that accompany the pursuit of a sari.

Rhetorical Considerations

1. What is the purpose of this essay? Does the essay have a thesis beyond that of description? (*Hodges'* 32a/*Writer's* 1b–c)
2. How many different places do Paul and Desai describe? Characterize each place in your own words. (*Hodges'* 31c/*Writer's* 2d)
3. Why is the history and process of silk making relevant to this essay? (*Hodges'* 32e/*Writer's* 2e)
4. Most of the description in the essay is visual. Find as many examples as you can of other sensory descriptions (taste, smell, sound, or touch). (*Hodges'* 31c/*Writer's* 2d)
5. According to Paul and Desai, what are the greatest threats to sari making in India?

Language and Style

1. Look up the following words in your dictionary: *opaque* and *moony* (paragraph 1); *cacophonous* (paragraph 2); *trousseaus* (paragraph 4); *fodder* and *fetishize* (paragraph 6); *icon* (paragraph 7); *risqué* (paragraph 8); *warp* and *weft* (paragraph 9); *sericulture* (paragraph 15); *anachronistic* (paragraph 18); *Jacquard* (paragraph 21). (*Hodges'* 19e/*Writer's* 28e)
2. Is *further* used correctly in paragraph 16? Why or why not? (*Hodges'* 20a/*Writer's* 29a)
3. What is the main clause of the second sentence of paragraph 2? Would the sentence change rhetorically if the order of the main clause and subordinate clause were reversed? Why or why not? (*Hodges'* 1e/*Writer's* 16d)
4. Is the dash used correctly in the first sentence of paragraph 4? What other punctuation marks could be used instead? Would different punctuation produce a better effect?

Writing Suggestions

1. Write an essay describing your favorite outfit in detail.
2. Write an essay in which you describe a fashion that has passed out of popularity. Write the essay for a younger generation that does not recall the fashion.

✦

BEYOND THE VALLEY OF THE DAMMED

Bruce Barcott

Seattle writer Bruce Barcott is the author of *The Measure of a Mountain: Beauty and Terror on Mount Rainier* (1997), co-author of *Mount Rainier: A Climbing Guide* (1999), and editor of *Northwest Passages: A Literary Anthology of the Pacific Northwest from Coyote Tales to Roadside Attractions* (1994). "Beyond the Valley of the Dammed" was first published in 1999 in *Outside* magazine, which focuses on outdoors travel and environmental matters.

By God but we built some dams! We backed up the Kennebec in Maine and 1 the Neuse in North Carolina and a hundred creeks and streams that once ran free. We stopped the Colorado with the Hoover, high as 35 houses, and because it pleased us we kept damming and diverting the river until it no longer reached the sea. We dammed our way out of the Great Depression with the Columbia's Grand Coulee, a dam so immense you had to borrow another fellow's mind because yours alone wasn't big enough to wrap around it. Then we cleaved the Missouri with a bigger one still, the Fort Peck Dam, a jaw dropper so outsized they put it on the cover of the first issue of *Life*. We turned the Tennessee, the Columbia, and the Snake from continental arteries into still bathtubs. We dammed the Clearwater, the Boise, the Santiam, the Deschutes, the Skagit, the Willamette, and the McKenzie. We dammed Crystal River and Muddy Creek, the Little River and the Rio Grande. We dammed the Minnewawa and the Minnesota, and we dammed the Kalamazoo. We dammed the Swift and we dammed the Dead.

One day we looked up and saw 75,000 dams impounding more than 2 half a million miles of river. We looked down and saw rivers scrubbed free of salmon and sturgeon and shad. Cold rivers ran warm, warm rivers ran cold, and fertile muddy banks turned barren.

And that's when we stopped talking about dams as instruments of holy 3 progress and started talking about blowing them out of the water.

Surrounded by a small crowd, Secretary of the Interior Bruce Babbitt stood 4 atop McPherrin Dam, on Butte Creek, not far from Chico, California, in the hundred-degree heat of the Sacramento Valley. The constituencies represented—farmers, wildlife conservationists, state fish and game officials, irrigation managers—had been wrangling over every drop of water in this naturally arid basin for most of a century. On this day, however, amity reigned.

With CNN cameras rolling, "Babbitt hoisted a sledgehammer above his 5 head and—with evident glee," as one reporter later noted—brought this tool of destruction down upon the dam. Golf claps all around.

6   The secretary's hammer strike in July 1998 marked the beginning of the end for that ugly concrete plug and three other Butte Creek irrigation dams. All were coming out to encourage the return of spring-run chinook salmon, blocked from their natural spawning grounds for more than 75 years. Babbitt then flew to Medford, Oregon, and took a swing at 30-year-old Jackson Street Dam on Bear Creek. Last year alone, Babbitt cracked the concrete at four dams on Wisconsin's Menominee River and two dams on Elwha River in Washington state; at Quaker Neck Dam on North Carolina's Neuse River; and at 160-year-old Edwards Dam on the Kennebec in Maine.

7   By any reckoning, this was a weird inversion of the natural order. Interior secretaries are supposed to christen dams, not smash them. Sixty years ago, President Franklin D. Roosevelt and his interior secretary, Harold Ickes, toured the West to dedicate four of the largest dams in the history of civilization. Since 1994, Babbitt, who knows his history, has been following in their footsteps, but this secretary is preaching the gospel of dam-going-away. "America overshot the mark in our dam-building frenzy," he told the Ecological Society of America. "The public is now learning that we have paid a steadily accumulating price for these projects. We did not build them for religious purposes and they do not consecrate our values. Dams do, in fact, outlive their function. When they do, some should go."

8   Many dams continue, of course, to be invaluable pollution-free power plants. Hydroelectric dams provide 10 percent of the nation's electricity (and half of our renewable energy). In the Northwest, dams account for 75 percent of the region's power and bestow the lowest electrical rates in the nation. In the past the public was encouraged to believe that hydropower was almost free; but as Babbitt has been pointing out, the real costs can be enormous.

9   What we know now that we didn't know in 1938 is that a river isn't a water pipe. Dam a river and it will drop most of the sediment it carries into a still reservoir, trapping ecologically valuable debris such as branches, wood particles, and gravel. The sediment may be mixed with more and more pollutants—toxic chemicals leaching from abandoned mines, for example, or naturally occurring but dangerous heavy metals. Once the water passes through the dam it continues to scour, but it can't replace what it removes with material from upstream. A dammed river is sometimes called a "hungry" river, one that eats its bed and banks. Riverbeds and banks may turn into cobblestone streets, large stones cemented in by the ultrafine silt that passes through the dams. Biologists call this "armoring."

10   Naturally cold rivers may run warm after the sun heats water trapped in the reservoir; naturally warm rivers may run cold if their downstream flow is drawn from the bottom of deep reservoirs. Fish adapted to cold water won't survive in warm water, and vice versa.

11   As the toll on wild rivers became more glaringly evident in recent decades, opposition to dams started to go mainstream. By the 1990s, conservation groups, fishing organizations, and other river lovers began to call for actions that had once been supported only by environmental extremists and radical groups like Earth First!. Driven by changing economics, environmental law, and most of all the specter of vanishing fish, government

policy makers began echoing the conservationists. And then Bruce Babbitt, perhaps sensing the inevitable tide of history, began to support decommissioning as well.

So far, only small dams have been removed. Babbitt may chip away at 12 all the little dams he wants, but when it comes to ripping major federal hydropower projects out of Western rivers, that's when the politics get national and nasty. Twenty-two years ago, when President Jimmy Carter suggested pulling the plug on several grand dam projects, Western senators and representatives politically crucified him. Although dam opponents have much stronger scientific and economic arguments on their side in 1999, the coming dam battles are apt to be just as nasty.

Consider the Snake River, where a major confrontation looms over four 13 federal hydropower dams near the Washington-Idaho state line. When I asked Babbitt about the Snake last fall, he almost seemed to be itching for his hammer. "The escalating debate over dams is going to focus in the coming months on the Snake River," he declared. "We're now face to face with this question: Do the people of this country place more value on Snake River salmon or on those four dams? The scientific studies are making it clear that you can't have both."

Brave talk—but only a couple of weeks later, after a bruising budget skir- 14 mish with congressional dam proponents who accused him of planning to tear down dams across the Northwest, Babbitt sounded like a man who had just learned a sobering lesson in the treacherous politics of dams. The chastened interior secretary assured the public that "I have never advocated, and do not advocate, the removal of dams on the main stem of the Columbia-Snake river system."

Showdown on the Snake

Lewiston, Idaho, sits at the confluence of the Snake and Clearwater Rivers. 15 It's a quiet place of 33,000 solid citizens, laid out like a lot of towns these days: One main road leads into the dying downtown core, the other to a thriving strip of Wal-Marts, gas stations, and fast-food greaseries. When Lewis (hence the name) and Clark floated through here in 1805, they complained about the river rapids—"Several of them verry bad," the spelling-challenged Clark scrawled in his journal. Further downriver, where the Snake meets the Columbia, the explorers were amazed to see the local Indians catching and drying incredible numbers of coho salmon headed upriver to spawn.

The river still flows, though it's been dammed into a lake for nearly 150 16 miles. Between 1962 and 1975, four federal hydroelectric projects were built on the river by the Army Corps of Engineers: Ice Harbor Dam, Lower Monumental Dam, Little Goose Dam, and Lower Granite Dam. The dams added to the regional power supply, but more crucially, they turned the Snake from a whitewater roller-coaster into a navigable waterway. The surrounding wheat farmers could now ship their grain on barges to Portland, Oregon, at half the cost of overland transport, and other industries also grew to depend on this cheap highway to the sea.

17   Like all dams, however, they were hell on the river and its fish—the chinook, coho, sockeye, and steelhead. True, some salmon species still run up the river to spawn, but by the early 1990s the fish count had dwindled from 5 million to less than 20,000. The Snake River coho have completely disappeared, and the sockeye are nearing extinction.

18   In and around Lewiston, the two conflicting interests—livelihoods that depend on the dams on the one side, the fate of the fish on the other—mean that just about everyone is either a friend of the dams or a breacher. The Snake is the dam-breaching movement's first major test case, but it is also the place where dam defenders plan to make their stand. Most important, depending in part on the results of a study due later this year, the lower Snake could become the place where the government orders the first decommissioning of several big dams.

19   In the forefront of those who hope this happens is Charlie Ray, an oxymoron of a good ol' boy environmentalist whose booming Tennessee-bred baritone and sandy hair lend him the aspect of Nashville Network host. Ray makes his living as head of salmon and steelhead programs for Idaho Rivers United, a conservationist group that has been raising a fuss about free-flowing rivers since 1991. At heart he's not a tree hugger, but a steelhead junkie: "You hook a steelhead, man, you got 10,000 years of survival instinct on the end of that line."

20   Despite Ray's bluff good cheer, it's not easy being a breacher in Lewiston. Wheat farming still drives a big part of the local economy, and the pro-dam forces predict that breaching would lead to financial ruin. Lining up behind the dam defenders are Lewiston's twin pillars of industry: the Potlatch Corporation and the Port of Lewiston. Potlatch, one of the country's largest paper producers, operates its flagship pulp and paper mill in Lewiston, employing 2,300 people. Potlatch executives will tell you the company wants the dams mainly to protect the town's economy, but local environmentalists say the mill would find it more difficult to discharge warm effluent into a free-flowing, shallow river.

21   Potlatch provides Charlie Ray with a worthy foil in company spokesman Frank Carroll, who was hired after spending 17 years working the media for the U.S. Forest Service. Frankie and Charlie have been known to scrap. At an anti-breaching rally in Lewiston last September, Carroll stood off-camera watching Ray being interviewed by a local TV reporter. Fed up with hearing Ray's spin, Carroll started shouting "Bullshit, Charlie, that's bullshit!" while the video rolled. Ray's nothing more than a "paid operative," Carroll says. Ray's reaction: "Yeah, like Frankie's not."

22   "A lot of people are trying to trivialize the social and economic issues," Carroll says, "trying to tell us the lives people have here don't count, that we'll open up a big bait shop and put everyone to work hooking worms. We resent that. Right now, there's a blanket of prosperity that lies across this whole region, and that prosperity is due to the river in its current state—to its transportation."

23   Ever since the dams started going up along the Snake River, biologists and engineers have been trying to revive the rapidly declining salmon runs. Their

schemes include fish ladders, hatcheries, and a bizarre program in which young smolts are captured and shipped downriver to the sea in barges. By the late 1980s, it was clear that nothing was working; the fish runs continued to plummet. In 1990, the Shoshone-Bannock Indians, who traditionally fished the Snake's sockeye run, successfully petitioned the National Marine Fisheries Service to list the fish as endangered. Every salmon species in the Snake River is now officially threatened or endangered, which means the agencies that control the river must deal with all kinds of costly regulations.

In 1995, under pressure from the federal courts, the National Marine 24 Fisheries Service and the Army Corps of Engineers (which continues to operate the dams) agreed to launch a four-year study of the four lower Snake River dams. In tandem with the Fisheries Service, the Corps made a bombshell announcement. The study would consider three options: maintain the status quo, turbocharge the fish-barging operation, or initiate a "permanent natural river drawdown"—breaching. The study's final report is due in December, but whatever its conclusions, that initial statement marked a dramatic shift. Suddenly, an action that had always seemed unthinkable was an officially sanctioned possibility.

Two separate scientific studies concluded that breaching presented the 25 best hope for saving the river. In 1997 the *Idaho Statesman,* the state's largest newspaper, published a three-part series arguing that breaching the four dams would net local taxpayers and the region's economy $183 million a year. The dams, the paper concluded, "are holding Idaho's economy hostage."

"That series was seismic," says Reed Burkholder, a Boise-based breach- 26 ing advocate. Charlie Ray agrees. "We've won the scientific argument," he says. "And we've won the economic argument. We're spending more to drive the fish to extinction than it would cost to revive them."

In fact, the economic argument is far from won. The *Statesman*'s num- 27 bers are not unimpeachable. The key to their prediction, a projected $248 million annual boost in recreation and fishing, assumes that the salmon runs will return to pre-1960s levels. Fisheries experts say that could take up to 24 years, if it happens at all. The $34 million lost at the Port of Lewiston each year, however, would be certain and immediate.

The Northwest can do without the power of the four lower Snake River 28 dams: They account for only about 4 percent of the region's electricity supply. The dams aren't built for flood control, and contrary to a widely held belief, they provide only a small amount of irrigation water to the region's farmers. What the issue comes down to, then, is the Port of Lewiston. You take the dams out, says port manager Dave Doeringsfeld, "and transportation costs go up 200 to 300 percent."

To breach or to blow?

The pro-dam lobbyists know they possess a powerful, not-so-secret weapon: 29 Senator Slade Gorton, the Washington Republican who holds the commanding post of chairman of the Subcommittee on Interior Appropriations. Gorton has built his political base by advertising himself as the foe of liberal

Seattle environmentalists, and with his hands on Interior's purse strings, he can back up the role with real clout. As determined as Bruce Babbitt is to bring down a big dam, Slade Gorton may be more determined to stop him.

30   During last October's federal budget negotiations, Gorton offered to allocate $22 million for removing two modest dams in the Elwha River on the Olympic Peninsula, a salmon-restoration project dear to the hearts of dam-breaching advocates. But Gorton agreed to fund the Elwha breaching if— and only if—the budget included language forbidding federal officials from unilaterally ordering the dismantling of any dam, including those in the Columbia River Basin. Babbitt and others balked at Gorton's proposal. As a result, the 1999 budget includes zero dollars for removal of the Elwha dams.

31   Gorton's Elwha maneuver may have been hardball politics for its own sake, but it was also a clear warning: If the Army Corps and the National Marine Fisheries Service recommend breaching on the Snake in their study later this year, there will be hell to pay.

32   Meanwhile, here's a hypothetical question: If you're going to breach, how do you actually do it? How do you take those behemoths out? It depends on the dam, of course, but the answer on the Snake is shockingly simple.

33   "You leave the dam there," Charlie Ray says. We're standing downstream from Lower Granite Dam, 35 million pounds of steel encased in concrete. Lower Granite isn't a classic ghastly curtain like Hoover Dam; it resembles nothing so much as an enormous half-sunk harmonica. Ray points to a berm of granite boulders butting up against the concrete structure's northern end. "Take out the earthen portion and let the river flow around the dam. This is not high-tech stuff. This is front-end loaders and dump trucks."

34   It turns out that Charlie is only a few adjectives short of the truth. All you do need are loaders and dump trucks—really, really big ones, says Steve Tatro of the Army Corps of Engineers. Tatro has the touchy job of devising the best way to breach his agency's own dams. First, he says, you'd draw down the reservoir, using the spillways and the lower turbine passages as drains. Then you'd bypass the concrete and steel entirely and excavate the dam's earthen portion. Depending on the dam, that could mean excavating as much as 8 million cubic yards of material.

35   Tatro's just-the-facts manner can't disguise the reality that there is something deeply cathartic about the act he's describing. Most environmental restoration happens at the speed of nature. Which is to say, damnably slow. Breaching a dam—or better yet, blowing a dam—offers a rare moment of immediate gratification.

The Glen Canyon story

36 From the Mesopotamian canals to Hoover Dam, it took the human mind about 10,000 years to figure out how to stop a river. It has taken only 60 years to accomplish the all-too-obvious environmental destruction.

37   Until the 1930s, most dam projects were matters of trial and (often) error, but beginning with Hoover Dam in 1931, dam builders began erect-

ing titanic riverstoppers that approached an absolute degree of reliability and safety. In *Cadillac Desert,* a 1986 book on Western water issues, author Marc Reisner notes that from 1928 to 1956, "the most fateful transformation that has ever been visited on any landscape, anywhere, was wrought." Thanks to the U.S. Bureau of Reclamation, the Tennessee Valley Authority, and the Army Corps, dams lit a million houses, turned deserts into wheat fields, and later powered the factories that built the planes and ships that beat Hitler and the Japanese. Dams became monuments to democracy and enlightenment during times of bad luck and hunger and war.

Thirty years later, author Edward Abbey became the first dissenting 38 voice to be widely heard. In *Desert Solitaire* and *The Monkey Wrench Gang,* Abbey envisioned a counterforce of wilderness freaks wiring bombs to the Colorado River's Glen Canyon Dam, which he saw as the ultimate symbol of humanity's destruction of the American West. Kaboom! Wildness returns to the Colorado.

Among environmentalists, the Glen Canyon Dam has become an al- 39 most mythic symbol of riparian destruction. All the symptoms of dam kill are there. The natural heavy metals that the Colorado River used to disperse into the Gulf of California now collect behind the dam in Lake Powell. And the lake is filling up: Sediment has reduced the volume of the lake from its original 27 million acre-feet to 23 million. One million acre-feet of water are lost to evaporation every year—enough, environmentalists note, to revive the dying upper reaches of the Gulf of California. The natural river ran warm and muddy, and flushed its channel with floods; the dammed version runs cool, clear, and even. Trout thrive in the Colorado. This is like giraffes thriving on tundra.

Another reason for the dam's symbolic power can be traced to its his- 40 tory. Four decades ago, David Brower, then executive director of the Sierra Club, agreed to a compromise that haunts him to this day: Conservationists would not oppose Glen Canyon and 11 other projects if plans for the proposed Echo Park and Split Mountain dams, in Utah and Colorado, were abandoned. In 1963, the place Wallace Stegner once called "the most serenely beautiful of all the canyons of the Colorado" began disappearing beneath Lake Powell. Brower led the successful fight to block other dams in the Grand Canyon area, but he remained bitter about the compromise. "Glen Canyon died in 1963," he later wrote, "and I was partly responsible for its needless death."

In 1981 Earth First! inaugurated its prankster career by unfurling an 41 enormous black plastic "crack" down the face of Glen Canyon Dam. In 1996 the Sierra Club rekindled the issue by calling for the draining of Lake Powell. With the support of Earth Island Institute (which Brower now chairs) and other environmental groups, the proposal got a hearing before a subcommittee of the House Committee on Resources in September 1997. Congress has taken no further action, but a growing number of responsible voices now echo the monkey-wrenchers' arguments. Even longtime Bureau of Reclamation supporter Barry Goldwater admitted, before his death last year, that he considered Glen Canyon Dam a mistake.

42   Defenders of the dam ask what we would really gain from a breach. The dam-based ecosystem has attracted peregrine falcons, bald eagles, carp, and catfish. Lake Powell brings in $400 million a year from tourists enjoying houseboats, powerboats, and personal watercraft—a local economy that couldn't be replaced by the thinner wallets of rafters and hikers.

43   "It would be completely foolhardy and ridiculous to deactivate that dam," says Floyd Dominy during a phone conversation from his home in Boyce, Virginia. Dominy, now 89 years old and retired since 1969, was the legendary Bureau of Reclamation commissioner who oversaw construction of the dam in the early 1960s. "You want to lose all that pollution-free energy? You want to destroy a world-renowned tourist attraction—Lake Powell—that draws more than 3 million people a year?"

44   It goes against the American grain: the notion that knocking something down and returning it to nature might be progress just as surely as replacing wildness with asphalt and steel. But 30 years of environmental law, punctuated by the crash of the salmon industry, has shifted power from the dam builders to the conservationists.

45   The most fateful change may be a little-noticed 1986 revision in a federal law. Since the 1930s, the Federal Energy Regulatory Commission has issued 30- to 50-year operating licenses to the nation's 2,600 or so privately owned hydroelectric dams. According to the revised law, however, FERC must consider not only power generation, but also fish and wildlife, energy conservation, and recreational uses before issuing license renewals. In November 1997, for the first time in its history, FERC refused a license against the will of a dam owner, ordering the Edwards Manufacturing Company to rip the 160-year-old Edwards Dam out of Maine's Kennebec River. More than 220 FERC hydropower licenses will expire over the next 10 years.

46   If there is one moment that captures the turning momentum in the dam wars, it might be the dinner Richard Ingebretsen shared with the builder of Glen Canyon Dam, Floyd Dominy himself. During the last go-go dam years, from 1959 to 1969, this dam-building bureaucrat was more powerful than any Western senator or governor. Ingebretsen is a Salt Lake City physician, a Mormon Republican, and a self-described radical environmentalist. Four years ago, he founded the Glen Canyon Institute to lobby for the restoration of Glen Canyon. Ingebretsen first met Dominy when the former commissioner came to Salt Lake City in 1995 to debate David Brower over the issue of breaching Glen Canyon Dam. To his surprise, Ingebretsen found that he liked the man. "I really respect him for his views," he says.

47   Their dinner took place in Washington, D.C., in early 1997. At one point Dominy asked Ingebretsen how serious the movement to drain Lake Powell really was. Very serious, Ingebretsen replied. "Of course I'm opposed to putting the dam in mothballs," Dominy said. "But I heard what Brower wants to do." (Brower had suggested that Glen Canyon could be breached by coring out some old water bypass tunnels that had been filled in years ago.) "Look," Dominy continued, "those tunnels are jammed with 300 feet of reinforced concrete. You'll never drill that out."

48   With that, Dominy pulled out a napkin and started sketching a breach. "You want to drain Lake Powell?" he asked. "What you need to do is drill

new bypass tunnels. Go through the soft sandstone around and beneath the dam and line the tunnels with waterproof plates. It would be an expensive, difficult engineering feat. Nothing like this has ever been done before, but I've done a lot of thinking about it, and it will work. You can drain it."

The astonished Ingebretsen asked Dominy to sign and date the napkin. 49 "Nobody will believe this," he said. Dominy signed.

Of course, it will take more than a souvenir napkin to return the na- 50 tion's great rivers to their full wildness and health. Too much of our economic infrastructure depends on those 75,000 dams for anyone to believe that large numbers of river blockers, no matter how obsolete, will succumb to the blow of Bruce Babbitt's hammer anytime soon. For one thing, Babbitt himself is hardly in a position to be the savior of the rivers. Swept up in the troubles of a lame-duck administration and his own nagging legal problems (last spring Attorney General Janet Reno appointed an independent counsel to look into his role in an alleged Indian casino-campaign finance imbroglio), this interior secretary is not likely to fulfill his dream of bringing down a really big dam. But a like-minded successor just might. It will take a president committed and powerful enough to sway both Congress and the public, but it could come to pass.

Maybe Glen Canyon Dam and the four Snake River dams won't come 51 out in my lifetime, but others will. And as more rivers return to life, we'll take a new census of emancipated streams: We freed the Neuse, the Kennebec, the Allier, the Rogue, the Elwha, and even the Tuolumne. We freed the White Salmon and the Souradabscook, the Ocklawaha and the Genesee. They will be untidy and unpredictable, they will flood and recede, they will do what they were meant to do: run wild to the sea.

Rhetorical Considerations

1. What is Barcott's thesis? Is it simply that we have overbuilt dams in this country? (*Hodges'* 32c/*Writer's* 2b)
2. How does Barcott use anecdotes? How does he use other kinds of examples? (*Hodges'* 31c/*Writer's* 2d)
3. Find a descriptive passage in the essay that strikes you as particularly effective. What features make this passage appealing to you? (*Hodges'* 32c/*Writer's* 2e)
4. How does Barcott organize his essay? Would another method of organization have been as effective? Why or why not? (*Hodges'* 32d/*Writer's* 2c)
5. What point is Barcott making when he describes Richard Ingebretsen as a "Salt Lake City physician, a Mormon Republican" (paragraph 46)?

Language and Style

1. Look up the following words in your dictionary: *constituencies* and *amity* (paragraph 4); *consecrate* (paragraph 7); *chastened* (paragraph 14); *oxymoron* (paragraph 19); *effluent* (paragraph 20); *smolts* (paragraph 23); *seismic* (paragraph 26); *behemoths* (paragraph 32); *berm* (paragraph 33); *cathartic* (paragraph 35); *riparian* (paragraph 39). (*Hodges'* 19e/*Writer's* 28e)

2. Find Barcott's use of religious language. What effect does this have on the reader? (*Hodges'* 19/*Writer's* 28)
3. How does Barcott use language to keep his essay from being a dry historical piece? (*Hodges'* 20/*Writer's* 29)
4. Why are there no commas separating the list in the second sentence of paragraph 2? (*Hodges'* 12/*Writer's* 31)
5. Justify the sentence fragment in paragraph 5. (*Hodges'* 2/*Writer's* 18)
6. Why is there a comma after *Oregon* in the last sentence of paragraph 16? (*Hodges'* 12/*Writer's* 31)

Writing Suggestions

1. Write an essay in which you describe the negative consequences of a change that has recently been imposed on your environment (a change in degree requirements, or the closing of a particular park or business, for example).
2. Find out if there is a dam in your area. Then research its history and purpose, and write an essay in which you describe its effects on the local community.

✦

IMAGES

Description

The images here, of course, are just two of the many riveting images that depict what the first moments were like when the World Trade Center towers collapsed after the terrorist attacks on September 11, 2001, in New York City.

Lorenzo Ciniglio, People run for their lives as one of the Twin Towers collapses, September 11, 2001

✦

IMAGES (CONT.)

Description

Jennifer Brown, A NYPD officer is treated at a triage center following the collapse of both World Trade Center towers, September 11, 2001

Rhetorical Considerations

1. What details in each image convey the urgency of the moment? How many people are in each photograph? What is each person doing?
2. How would you characterize the tone of each photograph? Do they all evoke the same emotion in you? Explain.
3. Though both images contain more than one individual, does either of the images seem to focus on only one person? If so, does that photograph create a different response for you? Explain.
4. Do you have a more emotionally intense response to any one of the images? Explain which one and why.

Writing Suggestions

1. Find a group of images that were taken at a disaster site, and write an essay in which you use these images to describe the incident either from the victims' perspective or from the bystanders' perspective.
2. Write an essay describing a vivid event in your life, and find two images that illustrate its effect on you.

CHAPTER 4

Process

As you might suppose, process is closely related to narration. Like narration, process analysis is usually organized chronologically, according to time. Unlike narration, which relates a single series of events, process analysis explains a series of steps that can be repeated—for instance, the steps involved in changing a spark plug on your car, installing a new software program, tapping trees for maple syrup, or treating an orangutan's cardiac problems.

Understanding Process Analysis

Process explanations are of two kinds:

- directions that tell a reader how to perform some task;
- information about how something works.

In both of these, the writer describes a sequence of steps, generally in chronological order, with one step leading to the next. They differ, however, according to who performs the action. A *directive process explanation* is intended for readers who will work through the sequence of steps themselves. An *informative process explanation* is intended for readers who want to know what the steps are that someone else used to accomplish a task or set of tasks. A directive process analysis is primarily instructional; an informative process analysis is primarily explanatory. A directive process analysis addresses readers using *you*; an informative process analysis uses *I, he, she,* or *they.*

Effective process analyses can be developed in a variety of ways. One method is to take advantage of analogies to explain how something works. For instance, the biological processes of our bodies are often explained by making analogies to the way mechanical objects work: our brains to the functioning of computers, our hearts to pumps, our lungs to bellows, our kidneys to filters, and so on. Occasionally, a writer may explain a process by using an extended analogy, carrying the likeness out for several paragraphs or even the entire essay.

Another method is to present directions as brief narratives. Anamary Pelayo uses this method of development in "Hot Tempered?" to show readers how each step of anger management might play out. In other kinds of directions, such as recipes or assembly instructions, the sequence is especially important. If results can vary, that information is also important so that readers do not interpret such variations as evidence of having made a mistake in following the directions. (And of course, if there is anything dangerous about the process you are describing, you need to make sure your readers know about the risks involved.) Directive process explanations are frequently accompanied by diagrams, drawings, or photographs showing the various steps. Indeed, most process analyses, whether directive or informative, can benefit from the inclusion of well-chosen images. A writer will also sometimes catalogue a set of negative instructions, such as those on how to deal with other people's anger that appeared in a sidebar to Pelayo's article: "Don't take it personally," "Don't assume he or she means every word," and so on.

Using Process Analysis

Purpose

When you write a process document, whether it is an informative analysis or a set of directions, you want to have a clear sense of your purpose. People write about processes for a variety of reasons. The most common kind of process writing is, of course, directive, showing the reader step by step how to do something, such as cook a meal, install a thermostat, and so on. The purpose for writing directions is both to explain what must happen and to teach how to accomplish the necessary steps. Leonard Felder shows us how to "improve your health, reduce stress, and increase your daily energy and sense of awe at the wonders of the universe" in "Developing a Mindful Way of Eating" (166); in "Click! The Housewife's Moment of Truth," Jane O'Reilly offers six steps toward freedom while arguing persuasively for women to stop allowing themselves to be made second-class citizens.

When you want to explain something, such as how castles were built or how to take an ape's electrocardiogram, your purpose is to inform your readers about some interesting aspect of the world, to help them understand something magical about the everyday. Some of the most interesting examples of this kind of writing can be found in books like *Cathedral* (1973), *Pyramid* (1975), or *Castle* (1977) by David Macaulay. Stone by stone, with words and with images, Macaulay leads his readers through the construction of these magnificent structures. His readers are, indeed, informed, but are also intrigued, entertained, and even awed. On a smaller scale, Margery Guest's "Sugaring" reveals the mysteries of maple sugar production, Michael Kernan leads his audience through the fascinating world of "Zoo Medicine," and Garrison Keillor entertains as he advises his readers how to write a letter. Opportunities to explain a process are before you all the time, whenever you are asked to solve a problem, describe a rule or regulation, or even to write a lab report for your biology class.

When you're thinking about your purpose, it's important that you also think about your thesis. To fully understand why you want to explain a process, you probably need to be able to state clearly the general aim of your process analysis and its significance. Look at the thesis statements for two essays in this chapter. Leonard Felder notes that people today "eat with so much anxiety that their bodies can't possibly digest and process what is being shoveled down" (166), and shows his readers ways to overcome that problem. Garrison Keillor's lesson on letter writing concludes with a statement about the significance of written correspondence: "You can't pick up a phone and call the future and tell them about our times. You have to pick up a piece of paper" (176). Like Keillor's, essays may have more than one purpose. The obvious purpose of Keillor's lesson is to encourage shy people to write letters, but he has an additional one. Writing letters means that people use paper, a fact that is sure to please the company (International Paper) that commissioned his essay. Clearly, that would never become part of his thesis statement, but it points out the reasons for thinking beyond an author's explicit purpose.

Audience

Because your audience is closely related to your purpose, you need to consider carefully what your readers are likely to already know. You probably wouldn't give directions on how to tie shoelaces to an adult, but you might catalogue the steps involved in applying for a mortgage. The key question to consider is what kind and amount of background information your readers are likely to have. Anamary Pelayo assesses what her readers—Latinas—are likely to know about anger and how to manage it for a healthful life:

> We Latinas are taught at an early age to hold in our anger, not to mention our rage. How many times was I told as a child that *niñas buenas no gritan?* Some of us are discouraged from raising our voices to *los viejitos* and even—God forbid—men. Research has shown that Latinas are more likely than other women to use the silent treatment—especially toward the opposite sex—to express anger. (170)

Knowing the variety and extent of background information your readers are likely to have can help you decide how detailed your analysis should be. Sometimes you may need to break the process down into a number of very specific steps; other times, you may be able to compress a large number of steps into a few essential ones. Your understanding of what your readers already know will be your best guide for presenting your information effectively.

One word of advice: *explain* everything, even those things you think are obvious. The story may be apocryphal, but technical writers talk about how a company was sued because the directions that accompanied an electric lawnmower did not include the warning that it was not to be picked up and used as a hedge clipper. You will usually be safe if you assume your readers know less than you think. Define any terms that may be specialized and clarify anything that might confuse your readers or cause them to misunderstand your point.

Organization

A clear sense of audience will affect the way you organize your process analysis. If your readers are knowledgeable about the subject, you can plunge into the process with minimal attention to background information. If not, you will have to enlarge your scope to provide whatever information your readers will need to negotiate the steps of the process successfully or to understand what is involved in the way something is done. Thus, you need to determine a clear beginning and end for your process analysis.

Arrange your information in the most effective way for your audience and purpose. If you are writing a simple set of directions, you will probably find that a chronological order is most effective. If your topic is more complex, you may find that an emphatic order is most effective, taking up the most important (or least important) element first and building from there. In any case, make sure that you have arranged the steps in the proper order and have not omitted any steps that are necessary to completing the process. As you determine what steps to include, make sure that if you have substeps for one stage, you have them for all stages, and that each step has enough pertinent details to enable your readers to understand what needs to be done. You may find that an outline listing the various steps is a useful guide to help you make sure that you distribute the steps evenly and arrange them in the proper order. It can also be helpful to number the steps in a set of directions.

Transitional words and phrases (see *Hodges'* 31b/*Writer's* 3d for more information) are essential to keeping your audience on track as they read through a process analysis. Words such as *first, second, before, after, next,* and the like will help your readers follow your logic. Special care with verb tenses (see *Hodges'* 7b/*Writer's* 22b for more information) is also part of the key to success, since making time relationships clear in a process analysis is crucial for the reader.

Images

Readers also benefit from diagrams, charts, maps, photographs, and other visual aids that can make a process more concrete and thus clearer and more efficient. As you prepare your process analysis, consider whether typographical features—such as boldface and italics, or underlined and highlighted text—would enhance your readers' understanding. Add an image to your process analysis if it will help elucidate the steps, not further complicate them. Look at the images included in this chapter. Would a textual description of each process depicted help clarify the steps, or do the images alone most accurately and succinctly explain what is going on?

Student Essay

In the following student essay, Veronica Ashida gives directions for making shapes out of folded paper, the Japanese art of origami. Notice how she combines explanation with instructions, describing each move before telling the reader exactly what to do. Notice, too, how she uses verb tenses and transitional expressions signaling time to keep the sequence of steps clear.

Paper Mountains, Paper Valleys

Introduction

Purpose and thesis

Although historians dispute the origins of the ancient art of paper folding, believing the Chinese, Koreans, or Japanese could have invented it, the art is generally attributed to the Japanese. In fact, paper folding derives its name, *origami,* from the Japanese words *oru* (to fold) and *kami* (paper). To become a paper-folder, an origami artist, all you need is paper, an imagination, and a good set of instructions; once you master a few of the common folds, the fun and creative potential of origami is limitless.

Necessary supplies

Begin with several sheets of origami paper, which can be found at most art-and-craft stores. The paper is usually cut into six-inch squares, and each square is white on one side and a bright, beautiful color on the opposite side, making your model, a finished origami figure, an eye-pleaser. Although master folders are known to use many different objects, such as cardboard or sheet metal, when they do use paper, it must be strong and crease well. In addition to thin, strong paper that creases well, you will need origami instructions.

Background information

Today, origami diagrams are easy to find. In fact, since the 1950s, the world's grandmaster of origami, Yoshizawa Akira, has published several books that depict thousands of origami models. Also, master Yoshizawa developed the standard set of origami diagram symbols used across the globe in modern origami instruction. You can easily find origami instructions in bookstores and your local library. In addition, you can access multiple Internet Web pages dedicated to the ancient art.

In Japanese culture, it is through oral tradition that many mothers pass down to their daughters the artistry of origami. My mother provided me with the below instructions on how to fold the classic swan. She taught me how to fold, and her mother taught her. With my instructions, you, too, will learn how to fold the swan and will, I hope, begin a pleasant journey into the history and art of paper folding.

Instructions— note use of transitions

Most origami models start with one of four common bases: kite base, fish base, bird base, or frog base. To create the classic swan figure, begin

continued

First step

with the kite base. First, place a sheet of origami paper in front of you on a flat surface with the color side facing up. Fold the paper in half, diagonally, and make a well-defined crease. You are making a "valley" fold, a basic fold that is formed by bringing the paper toward yourself. The opposite fold is a "mountain" fold, in which you fold the paper away from yourself. After creasing on the diagonal, open the square back up and turn it over so that the white side is now facing up. Next, bring the two corners

Second step

(right and left sides) parallel to the center line and crease each side. Make sure the sides meet perfectly, being careful that they don't overlap and that no space shows through. You have created the kite base!

Third step

Next, turn the base over, repeat folding the right and left corners toward the center line, and crease again. Now you are ready to define the

Decisions

swan's body. How long do you want the neck to be? The length of the neck depends on where you decide to crease the narrow section of the kite base. To make the neck, fold the narrow section back toward the

Fourth step

wide part of the kite base. After you have made the neck, you must now choose the size of the swan's head. By folding the tip of the narrow section back toward yourself, you will create the head, and, therefore, the point at which you locate the crease will establish its size. After the swan's body has been defined, fold the figure in half along an imaginary

Fifth step

center line, using a mountain fold (remember this means folding away from yourself, or folding the sides of the figure under). The last step is to

Final step

pull the swan's neck up until it is at a 90° angle, and then pull its head out so it looks forward. Squeeze the base of its neck to ensure that it will stay erect. Congratulations—you have made a classic swan model!

Origami is not only an extremely accessible art (most everyone can find paper to fold) that is aesthetically pleasing, but it also has been proven to be beneficial in many fields such as education, mathematics,

Conclusion— revisits and expands thesis

psychology, and engineering. Once considered a child's activity, the ancient art now enjoys an international acclaim for its technical and artistic merits. Now that you are a paper-folder, the more time that you spend learning the patience of following the sequential steps of a diagram, the better prepared you will become at creating your own original origami models. Happy folding!

Commentary

Veronica Ashida begins her process essay with a bit of background information and a nod to the convention of listing the necessary equipment. Her equipment list includes not only a description of the proper kind of paper, but also the instructions for folding and where the reader can find such instructions. She then acknowledges that her instructions were provided by her mother. The next two paragraphs describe the folding process.

Ashida assumes that her audience knows little about origami, though the art is becoming more widespread. Accordingly, she begins with simple directions for a relatively simple figure. The directions quickly become more difficult, however, as the process continues. Nevertheless, Ashida describes the moves well and is careful to describe each step involved in folding a swan. After she has described each fold and the adjustments necessary to make the swan sit up, she concludes by commenting on the various uses of origami. With one exception, this process essay is clear and direct, providing all the information the rank novice needs to begin.

◆ CHECKLIST FOR WRITING PROCESS ANALYSES

- Can you state your *purpose* (*Hodges'* 32a/*Writer's* 1e) for analyzing this process? Do you intend to show readers how to do something or show how something works?
- Is there a *thesis*? (*Hodges'* 32c/*Writer's* 2b) Can you state it in a single sentence? Have you done so?
- Have you assessed what your *audience* is likely to know about the topic? Have you used a level of detail appropriate for your readers' level of expertise?
- Is your *organization* chronological or emphatic? Have you used the best method for your topic? Have you followed that method consistently?
- Have you provided *transitional words and phrases* to keep your readers oriented correctly? (*Hodges'* 31b/*Writer's* 3d)
- What *visual aids* have you offered your readers? Would features such as boldface or italic type call attention to important steps? Would diagrams or charts help your readers better understand?
- Does your *conclusion* (*Hodges'* 33b/*Writer's* 3b) help your readers to feel that they can reproduce the steps in the process correctly? What purpose does your conclusion serve?

DEVELOPING A MINDFUL WAY OF EATING

Leonard Felder

Leonard Felder is originally from Detroit, Michigan, and graduated from Kenyon College in Ohio. He was the Director of Research for Doubleday and Company in New York before moving to Los Angeles to complete his PhD in psychology. He is now a psychologist in private practice in Los Angeles. Dr. Felder is a popular speaker nationwide on the subject of spirituality and personal growth. He has appeared on the *Oprah Winfrey Show,* NBC News, CNN, the *CBS Early Show, AM Canada,* and in many radio interviews. His books include *Making Peace with Your Parents* (1983), *A Fresh Start* (1987), *When a Loved One Is Ill* (1990), *Does Someone at Work Treat You Badly?* (1993), *Making Peace with Yourself* (1996), and, most recently, *Seven Prayers That Can Change Your Life* (2001).

1 Many years ago when I lived in New York, I used to eat occasionally at Brownie's Health Food Restaurant on Fifth Avenue. One day I observed a very famous health writer at the next table gobbling down his food and arguing with his wife. Several years later I read in the newspaper that this health guru had died of a heart attack. I wondered if his anxious eating style was in any way related to his heart trouble. Certainly there are many causes of heart ailments and health problems, but watching such a brilliant man eat with so little awareness of the stressful way he was gobbling down his meal made me a lot more cautious about the way I take food into my body.

2 As a psychologist, I've observed that we live in a time when men and women are obsessed with counting calories and cholesterol, yet they eat with so much anxiety that their bodies can't possibly digest and process what is being shoveled down. Medical research tells us that even the most well-educated, health-conscious individual is likely to get indigestion, health problems, and poor absorption of nutrients when most meals are gulped down while your mind is beset by worries, oppressively long "to do" lists, and a constant feeling of running behind schedule. In the words of Rabbi Zalman Schachter-Shalomi, "We live in a world that wants us to be on commodity time—always rushing and producing. To be a Jew is to rebel against commodity time and find a connection to holy moments and timelessness."

3 One of the most effective ways to liberate yourself and your loved ones from the hectic pace of modern life is to explore the wisdom of saying a prayer or taking a moment to center before each meal. If you want to improve your health, reduce stress, and increase your daily energy and sense of awe at the wonders of the universe, here are a few insights from Jewish spiritual teachings that can make a huge difference. I have found as a thera-

pist and in my own life, that these much-overlooked ideas about meal-time words of connection have been extremely helpful for many of my counseling clients, my family members, and myself. The next time you sit down to a breakfast, lunch, or dinner, consider the following:

I. Stepping Out of Commodity Time

Instead of racing into the meal mindlessly, Jewish insights into meal-time   4
prayers give you a chance to step out of the stressful emotions and find a peaceful connection at least three times a day. Could there be an improvement in your emotional well-being, your digestion, and your sense of mental clarity if you stopped briefly before each meal to rise above the tensions of the day? What if you took a moment to let go of the rushing and instead reconnected with a sense of holiness or inner peace? According to the nineteenth-century scholar Solomon Ganzfried, the hand-washing prayer before meals (*"Netilat yadayim*—lifting up the hands or actions") is said not because our hands are dirty, but because we need to remember several times a day to raise up our energies for a higher purpose.

If you have never tried it before, or if you have never truly said this   5
prayer with heartfelt intention, take a moment before your next meal to use this prayer to lift your soul out of commodity time and into a sense of freedom and renewal. Say out loud or silently, *"Baruch Atah Adonai Eloheinu melekh ha-olam, asheyr kid'shanu b'mitzvotav vitzivanu al netilat yadayim,"* which can be liberally translated, "Blessed are You, Eternal One, pulsing Source of all that exists in the world, Who guides us on ways to become holy, and Who inspires us to lift up our hands and raise up our actions to be of service." See for yourself if this blessing helps you to eat more slowly and with an appreciation that this food is nourishing you for doing good in your corner of the world.

II. Locating the Source

Most Jews today either say nothing before a meal or they say *"Hamotzi*   6
lechem min ha-aretz (Who brings forth bread from the earth)." What gets left out for many people is the key step in the prayer before meals—to stop and become mindful of the sensual, earthy process of where the food comes from and how we are part of an amazing circle of life.

Many of us were never taught in our families or Hebrew schools of the   7
key step of figuring out which prayer to say over the food in front of you, depending on what's in the food. Is it fruit from a tree? Does it grow directly from the earth? Is it a grain like barley, oats, rye, spelt, or rice? Is it bread? Is it fruit from the vine? Is it a mixture from a complex source? Taking a moment to consider what you are eating, where it comes from, who helped plant it, harvest it, transport it, prepare it, serve it—these are all steps recommended by our tradition so that we are mindful of the connected web of life that surrounds and nourishes us. Instead of being stressed-out and alone in your thoughts, you can then reconnect with the amazing process of

ongoing creation that allows us to be nourished and supported by sunlight, soil, farming, distribution, and humans who provide service.

8   In addition, most Jews haven't been taught that the fascinating, all-encompassing prayer you can say at any meal is not "*hamotzi lechem* (the prayer for bread)" but rather, "*Baruch Atah Adonai Eloheinu Melech ha-olam, sheh-hakol nih-hiyeh bid-varo,*" which can be translated, "Blessed is the Eternal Source, ruling force of the universe, through Whose expression everything comes to be." What a remarkable idea—that there is an energy Source in the universe which is forever expressing Itself in nature, in our bodies, and in our activities. If you take these ancient words to heart, you might see yourself at each meal as a remarkable element in a continually flowing process of creative expression. This change of perspective can snap you out of your hurried mind and into your sense of curiosity and awe at the wonders of the universe.

III. Giving Thanks

9 Instead of approaching the meal from a perspective of deprivation, desperation, and ravenous appetite, our tradition reminds us to recognize that we are extremely fortunate, nourished, and connected to sources of support. In this way, when you take your first bite you can take it with a relaxed sense of adding to your fullness, and not with a sense of needing to rush or overeat. Can you imagine how many health problems, diet problems, and mood problems could be improved if we took in nourishment from a more peaceful and optimistic outlook? Instead of our bodies having to work double-time to sift out the nutrients from food that is wolfed down anxiously, what if we gave our bodies an easier time of it?

10   Yet many of us grew up at family dinner tables where there was either tension or disconnection, or the parents and children were so busy they rarely, if ever, had time to sit together and have a peaceful meal. A creative way to overcome some of these tensions or unhealthy meal-time habits we learned growing up is to take a moment at each meal to offer thanks for the fullness of creation, the beauty of nature, the holiness of life, or the joy of being around people you care about. Bringing our Jewish spiritual teachings into our family meals encourages us to start our meals by asking each family member to take a moment to comment on any small or large things for which we feel grateful.

11   For example, I recently counseled a busy two-career couple who said they wanted their three young children to grow up with a stronger sense of spirituality and centeredness. I asked them if they would try taking a moment before every family meal for a few weeks to let each child and adult thank God or the universe for something that meant a lot to that person, something that brings joy or connection to the meal.

12   The couple told me four weeks later, "Our kids resisted the first night, but when they saw we really cared and we wanted to know what they were thankful for; they began to enjoy this meal-time ritual. All of our three children seem to relish having a turn to speak up and announce something for

which they are grateful. These blessings before each family meal have changed the tone of our dinners from what used to be complaints and power struggles to some wonderful conversations of what's going right in each of our different, busy lives. Our family time does feel a lot more spiritual and centered as a result."

Is it any wonder?   13

Rhetorical Considerations

1. Find evidence in the essay of Felder's perception of who his audience is. (*Hodges'* 32a/*Writer's* 1b and 1e)
2. Is Felder's profession as a psychologist relevant to this essay? What other elements of Felder's life make him an appropriate authority on this subject? (*Hodges'* 38a/*Writer's* 9a)
3. What is the basis of organization of the essay's three parts that describe the process of eating in a "mindful" manner? (*Hodges'* 32d/*Writer's* 2c)
4. What variety of examples does Felder include? (*Hodges'* 31c/*Writer's* 2d)
5. What is accomplished by the anecdotes Felder uses to begin and end his essay? (*Hodges'* 33b/*Writer's* 3b)

Language and Style

1. Why does Felder include translations of the Hebrew prayers he incorporates into his essay? Why does he also provide them in the original Hebrew? (*Hodges'* 19c/*Writer's* 28c)
2. Find descriptive words in the essay that relate to the idea of mindfulness. (*Hodges'* 20/*Writer's* 29)
3. What is the subject of the last sentence of paragraph 2? (*Hodges'* 1b and 1d/*Writer's* 16a)
4. Is the pronoun case correct in the third sentence of paragraph 3? Why or why not? (*Hodges'* 5/*Writer's* 21)
5. Is the pronoun number correct in the second sentence of paragraph 12? Why or why not? (*Hodges'* 6b/*Writer's* 21d)

Writing Suggestions

1. Choose another activity that most people rush through, often to their detriment. Write an essay urging people to engage in that activity more mindfully.
2. Practice mindful eating for a week. Write an essay in which you offer your own advice regarding the process.

♦

HOT TEMPERED?

Anamary Pelayo

Anamary Pelayo was the senior research and travel editor at *Fitness* magazine in New York City, and is now senior lifestyle editor of *Latina* magazine, where this essay was first published.

1   I recently did something I'd never done before. It happened one morning when *mi novio* and I pulled up to a drive-through window after getting a late start on a road trip. I ordered a bagel and coffee, but the cashier at the window said breakfast was no longer being served. I freaked. I told her it was 10:30 in the morning, and did she really think I was ready for a hamburger? She apologized, and I scowled.

2   A short while later, part of me was still upset (I was starving), but I was also ashamed of the way I'd lost my temper. After all, the poor woman was just doing her job. Somehow my disappointment over a lack of breakfast had turned into full-fledged anger.

3   Unfortunately, my public display of rage—toward someone I didn't even know—hardly makes me unique. "Anger manifests itself with a stranger because you feel you can indulge the feeling without threatening someone you care about," says Ester Shapiro Rok, Ph.D., an associate professor of clinical psychology and Latino studies at the University of Massachusetts at Boston. "It's a clue that something else had upset you and the feelings were brewing." It's true. Between work deadlines and planning my wedding, many things had gone wrong for me that week, and I was beginning to feel perpetually pissed.

4   "Much of the way we respond to anger is through behavior that we begin developing during childhood," says Dr. Shapiro Rok. We Latinas in particular are taught at an early age to hold in our anger, not to mention our rage. How many times was I told as a child that *niñas buenas no gritan?* Some of us are discouraged from raising our voices to *los viejitos* and even— God forbid—men. Research has shown that Latinas are more likely than other women to use the silent treatment—especially toward the opposite sex—to express anger. "Even when they were open with their anger with each other, we found many women of Hispanic descent being less direct with men," says Sally Stabb, Ph.D., an associate professor of psychology at Texas Woman's University in Denton and cofounder of the Women's Anger Project, a study of women and anger.

5   But then again, we're also raised with the glamorized stereotype of Latinas as hot-tempered women (think Rita Moreno's Anita in *West Side Story*). "The image of the Latina spitfire is a woman who is passionate," says Ang-

harad Valdivia, Ph.D., a research associate professor of communications and Latina-Latino studies at the University of Illinois at Urbana-Champaign. "She is usually exotic, very loud, and hypersexual, since the anger and sexuality go hand in hand."

No wonder we may feel confused. "On the one hand, we're taught to 6 suppress our feelings in order to put others' needs first; on the other, our culture encourages expression and passion," Dr. Shapiro Rok says, "contradictions that make it difficult to know where to draw the line."

This conditioning can also keep us from learning how to deal with con- 7 flict constructively, and as we get older, we may find ourselves in a tug-of-war between what we think we're supposed to do with our anger (hide it) and what we'd really like to do (lash out). For those of us who love to "let 'er rip" when we're upset, it's important to note that a full-on rage, if expressed regularly, can increase blood pressure and heart rate, both of which may put us at greater risk for heart attacks and stroke. But bottling up your feelings "can lead to an unforeseen explosion of emotion, often at something unrelated to the initial cause of the anger," Dr. Shapiro Rok says. "Anger is healthy, normal, and sometimes necessary to our survival." What's key is channeling your energy into a more positive response. So the next time you're so mad that you think your blood is going to boil, try one of these six healthier alternative to losing control.

Tell it, don't demand it. There is a big difference between being assertive— 8 which means expressing your feelings directly and honestly without stomping on those of other people—and being aggressive. "The latter shows disrespect for others and can involve degrading or humiliating someone," says psychologist Ana Nogales, Ph.D. To be assertive, speak in the first person to avoid sounding accusatory ("I feel that my feelings are being disregarded," for example, rather than "You're not listening to me!"). Avoid using words such as "always" and "never." ("I'd feel better if you listened to me" is more effective than "You never listen to me" or "You always ignore me.")

Give yourself a time-out. Experts agree that suppressing your anger 9 temporarily can help it air itself out, so to speak, but be careful not to let it sit for too long. Allow yourself—and perhaps someone else—enough time to cool off. Then take responsibility for your actions, suggests Dr. Nogales. "By acknowledging a problem and your reaction to it, you'll be better able to control your response next time," she says.

Try to change the way you visualize a situation. This is easier said than 10 done, but it is possible. If you're late for an interview and you're stuck in traffic, for example, say to yourself, This is frustrating, but it's not the worst thing that could happen, and getting mad is not going to get me there any sooner. If fact, there's a greater likelihood that you'll make a bad impression if you arrive frazzled and frowning. As difficult as it may be in tough situations, put a smile on your face when trying to make a good first impression. "Smiling makes us more positive, and research shows that people are more attracted to others who are in a good mood," says Dr. Nogales.

11 **Add a dash of humor.** "Bringing humor into an angry situation can defuse rage and help you get a more balanced perspective," says Dr. Shapiro Rok. For example, imagine yourself driving on the traffic-free street to that interview, thinking of funny ways that you could have made a bad impression. What if you had worn a different shoe on each foot, or if last night's hair *tinte* had gone away and you now had pink hair? It's not about disregarding or minimizing your problems; it's about finding a more constructive way to deal with them. A word of caution: Avoid making sarcastic comments to others, since such talk is often anger disguised as humor, warns Dr. Shapiro Rok. "Sarcasm can be another way to express angry feelings inappropriately, and if it's directed at someone, it's likely to offend," she says.

12 **Change the scene—or imagine a different one.** Sometimes it's not one person or thing that infuriates you; it's an environment, such as that weekly status meeting at work during which a colleague gets credit for your hard work. In cases like this, it may not be feasible (or necessary) to avoid the situation altogether by ditching the meeting or quitting your job, but you can create a buffer zone for yourself. Schedule a lunch date with an amiga after the meeting when you know you'll need to unwind, or go shopping—anything that will get you into a different environment and take your mind off the situation.

13 **Borrow an ear.** "When you're angry, talking to someone you trust can help you see things from a fresh point of view," says Dr. Nogales. A friend may also have good suggestions for how to deal with your anger effectively. "Sometimes we're so busy being mad that it's hard to face the underlying problem," adds Dr. Shapiro Rok. Once you're armed with an objective viewpoint, go to a beach or a park to ponder your thoughts. "Nature is a great healer," says Dr. Nogales. "Answers are easier to see when you're inspired by the simplicity of life."

Rhetorical Considerations

1. Find evidence of Pelayo's awareness of her audience. Who does she presume her audience to be? (*Hodges'* 32a/*Writer's* 1b and 1d)
2. In your own words, precisely explain the thesis of Pelayo's essay. (*Hodges'* 32c/*Writer's* 2b)
3. Why is much of Pelayo's essay concerned with expressing anger towards men? (*Hodges'* 32a/*Writer's* 1b and 1d)
4. What authorities does Pelayo cite in her essay? Are all the authorities used appropriately? Why or why not? (*Hodges'* 38a/*Writer's* 9a)
5. What negative effects is someone who expresses anger likely to experience?

Language and Style

1. Pelayo includes several expressions in Spanish, but she does not offer translations of any of them. Why not? See if you can figure out what the words mean from their context, then look them up in an online Spanish to English dictionary. (*Hodges'* 19c/*Writer's* 28c)
2. What does *hypersexual* mean (paragraph 5)? List five other words that are created by using the *hyper-* prefix. (*Hodges'* 19/*Writer's* 28)
3. Is the fourth sentence in the first paragraph a sentence fragment? Why or why not? (*Hodges'* 2/*Writer's* 18)
4. Comment on the sentence variety of paragraph 2. (*Hodges'* 30/*Writer's* 27)
5. Is the semicolon used correctly in the first sentence of paragraph 12? Why or why not? (*Hodges'* 14/*Writer's* 32)

Writing Suggestions

1. Write your own process paper about how to control a negative or potentially harmful emotion.
2. Write an essay about your own experiences with anger.

♦

HOW TO WRITE A PERSONAL LETTER

Garrison Keillor

Writer and broadcaster Garrison Keillor was born in Anoka, Minnesota, in 1942. A graduate of the University of Minnesota, Keillor published his first story in 1969 in the *New Yorker.* Keillor is best known as the host of the popular National Public Radio program *Prairie Home Companion,* which aired between 1974 and 1987, when Keillor left the program to write. Keillor has also published *Happy to Be Here* (1982), *Lake Wobegon Days* (1985), and *Leaving Home: A Collection of Lake Wobegon Stories* (1987). "How to Write a Personal Letter," which Keillor wrote as an advertisement for the International Paper Company, offers humorous and insightful advice to help shy people make their mark upon the world.

1   We shy persons need to write a letter now and then, or else we'll dry up and blow away. It's true. And I speak as one who loves to reach for the phone, dial the number, and talk. I say, "Big Bopper here—what's shakin,' babes?" The telephone is to shyness what Hawaii is to February, it's a way out of the woods, *and yet:* a letter is better.

2   Such as sweet gift—a piece of handmade writing, in an envelope that is not a bill, sitting in our friend's path when she trudges home from a long day spent among yahoos and savages, a day our words will help repair. They don't need to be immortal, just sincere. She can read them twice and again tomorrow: *You're someone I care about, Corinne, and think of often and every time I do you make me smile.*

3   We need to write, otherwise nobody will know who we are. They will have only a vague impression of us as A Nice Person, because frankly, we don't shine at conversation, we lack the confidence to thrust our faces forward and say, "Hi, I'm Heather Hooten, let me tell you about my week." Mostly we say "Uh-huh" and "Oh really." People smile and look over our shoulder, looking for someone else to talk to.

4   So a shy person sits down and writes a letter. To be known by another person—to meet and talk freely on the page—to be close despite distance. To escape from anonymity and be our own sweet selves and express the music of our souls.

5   Same thing that moves a giant rock start to sing his heart out in front of 123,000 people moves us to take ballpoint in hand and write a few lines to our dear Aunt Eleanor. *We want to be known.* We want her to know that we have fallen in love, that we quit our job, and we're moving to New York, and we want to say a few things that might not get said in casual conversation: *thank you for what you've meant to me, I am very happy right now.*

The first step in writing letters is to get over the guilt of *not* writing. You 6
don't "owe" anybody a letter. Letters are a gift. The burning shame you feel
when you see unanswered mail makes it harder to pick up a pen and makes
for a cheerless letter when you finally do. *I feel bad about not writing, but I've
been so busy,* etc. Skip this. Few Letters are obligatory and they are *Thanks for
the wonderful gift* and *I am terribly sorry to hear about George's death* and *Yes,
you're welcome to stay with us next month,* and not many more than that.
Write those promptly if you want to keep your friends. Don't worry about
the others, except love letters, of course. When your true love writes *Dear
Light of My Life, Joy of My Heart, O Lovely Pulsating Core of My Sensate Life,*
some response is called for.

Some of the best letters are tossed off in a burst of inspiration, so keep 7
your writing stuff in one place where you can sit down for a few minutes
and *Dear Roy, I am in the middle of an essay for International Paper but thought
I'd drop you a line. Hi to your sweetie too* dash off a note to a pal. Envelopes,
stamps, address book, everything in a drawer so you can write fast when the
pen is hot.

A blank 8" × 11" sheet can look as big as Montana if the pen's not so 8
hot—try a smaller page and write boldly. Or use a note card with a piece of
fine art on the front; if your letter ain't good, at least they get the Matisse.
Get a pen that makes a sensuous line, get a comfortable typewriter, a
friendly word processor—whichever feels easy to the hand.

Sit for a few minutes with the blank sheet in front of you, and meditate 9
on the person you will write to, let your friend come to mind until you can
almost see her or him in the room with you. Remember the last time you
saw each other and how your friend looked and what you said and what
perhaps was unsaid between you, and when your friend becomes real to
you, start to write.

Write the salutation—*Dear You*—and take a deep breath and plunge in. 10
A simple declarative sentence will do, followed by another and another and
another. Tell us what you're doing and tell it like you were talking to us.
Don't think about grammar, don't think about lit'ry style, don't try to write
dramatically, just give us your news. Where did you go, who did you see,
what did they say, what do you think?

If you don't know where to begin, start with the present moment: *I'm* 11
*sitting at the kitchen table on a rainy Saturday morning. Everyone is gone and the
house is quiet.* Let your simple description of the present moment lead to
something else, let the letter drift gently along.

The toughest letter to crank out is one that is meant to impress, as we 12
all know from writing job applications; if it's hard work to slip off a letter to
a friend, maybe you're trying too hard to be terrific. A letter is only a report
to someone who already likes you for reasons other than your brilliance.
Take it easy.

Don't worry about form. It's not a term paper. When you come to the 13
end of one episode, just start a new paragraph. You can go from a few lines
about the sad state of rock'n roll to the fight with your mother to your fond

memories of Mexico to your cat's urinary tract infection to a few thoughts on personal indebtedness to the kitchen sink and what's in it. The more you write, the easier it gets, and when you have a True True Friend to write to, a *compadre*, a soul sibling, then it's like driving a car down a country road, you just get behind the keyboard and press on the gas.

14   Don't tear up the page and start over when you write a bad line—try to write your way out of it. Make mistakes and plunge on. Let the letter cook along and then let yourself be bold. Outrage, confusion, love—whatever is in your mind, let it find a way to the page. Writing is a means of discovery, always, and when you come to the end and write *Yours ever* or *Hugs and Kisses*, you'll know something you didn't when you wrote *Dear Pal*.

15   Probably your friend will put your letter away, and it'll be read again a few years from now—and it will improve with age. And forty years from now, your friend's grandkids will dig it out of the attic and read it, a sweet and precious relic of the ancient Eighties that gives them a sudden clear glimpse of you and her and the world we old-timers knew. You will then have created an object of art. Your simple lines about where you went, who you saw, what they said, will speak to those children and they will feel in their hearts the humanity of our times.

16   You can't pick up a phone and call the future and tell them about our times. You have to pick up a piece of paper.

Rhetorical Considerations

1. Keillor wrote this essay as an advertisement for the International Paper Company. Use evidence in the essay to comment on Keillor's assumptions about his audience. (*Hodges'* 32a/*Writer's* 1b and 1d)
2. Would you say Keillor's purpose in writing this essay is mainly to express his feelings about writing, to inform the reader, or to persuade the reader? Can you find evidence of aims other than the one you chose as primary? Explain. (*Hodges'* 32a/*Writer's* 1b and 1d)
3. Could a reader use this essay as a guide for writing a personal letter? Why or why not? (*Hodges'* 32a/*Writer's* 1b)
4. Explain what Keillor accomplishes in his introduction. Where does he establish a context for the essay? (*Hodges'* 33b/*Writer's* 3b)
5. Keillor's conclusion accomplishes more than simply telling how to end a personal letter. Explain what else it accomplishes and how it does so. (*Hodges'* 33b/*Writer's* 3b)
6. Comment on the use of humor in this essay. (*Hodges'* 33a/*Writer's* 3a)

Language and Style

1. Keillor uses the word *ain't* (paragraph 8), which is referred to in the *American Heritage Dictionary* as "nonstandard" and "beyond rehabilitation." What justification can you find for his using this word? (*Hodges'* 19c/*Writer's* 28c)
2. Paragraph 8 begins with a simile. Explain why the comparison is humorous. (*Hodges'* 20b/*Writer's* 29b)

3. List and define three synonyms for *write* that Keillor uses. Then write sentences using each of these synonyms. (*Hodges'* 19f/*Writer's* 28f)
4. Notice that most of the verbs in Keillor's essay are in the present tense. What does he accomplish by using the present tense throughout the essay? Try converting the verbs in one paragraph to the past tense. In what ways does the past tense change the effect of the essay? (*Hodges'* 7b/*Writer's* 22b)
5. The first sentence of paragraph 7 begins with a passive construction. Try to rewrite the sentence using the active voice. What difficulties do you encounter? (*Hodges'* 7c/*Writer's* 22c)
6. Justify Keillor's use of a sentence fragment at the end of paragraph 7. (*Hodges'* 2/*Writer's* 18)

Writing Suggestions

1. Take Keillor's advice as you write a personal letter.
2. Using Keillor's essay as a loose model, write an essay explaining how to accomplish some common but unpleasant daily task that requires mainly mental effort, such as paying bills, planning menus, or scheduling appointments.

◆

SUGARING

Margery Guest

Margery Guest is a columnist and travel writer who was born in Detroit, Michigan, and now resides in Grand Rapids. She came to writing about twenty years ago and has published her work in regional and national magazines such as *Reader's Digest* and *Travel & Leisure*. She has a BA in English from Western Michigan University.

1   When I was a kid growing up in Michigan, Dad made pancakes every Sunday. "Golden blacks!" he'd holler out as a way of calling us to the table. The pancakes were rarely black, but he liked them on the dark side, and he always encouraged us to like what he liked. Some Sundays he made buckwheat pancakes and, in that case, "Buckwheats!" was the call to action.

2   We behaved like hungry prospectors at a mining camp during these pancake feasts even though we'd just come from doing nothing more industrious than watching cartoons and playing Lincoln Logs in our pajamas. On the table would be stacks of fluffy pancakes, enough for all five of us to have as many as we wanted, and always a pitcher of hot maple syrup. At the end of the table, there'd be a bottle of this other stuff. It had a red label and the *fifth* ingredient listed on it was maple syrup. It was never heated because Dad was trying to make a point. Too indulgent to simply *not offer* this alternative, he was expressing how utterly incomprehensible it was to him that anyone could actually prefer it. It was my favorite.

3   Part of becoming an adult is learning how good *real* spaghetti, *real* macaroni and cheese, and *real* maple syrup are compared to the stuff we liked as kids. I grew up late, came to real maple syrup late. Because I'd been such a stubborn kid, refusing to even taste the real stuff, I had a lot of catching up to do. My knowledge of maple syrup involved a sizable gap: I knew it began with a maple tree and somehow wound up poured from a colorful tin container onto my pancakes. But how did it get from the tree to my table?

Mother Nature is in Charge

4   Over 80 percent of the world's maple syrup production comes from the province of Quebec, with the largest export market being the States. Ten percent more is produced in Ontario and the remaining 10 percent in our country. Of that 10 percent, Vermont, New York, Wisconsin, Ohio, and my home state of Michigan are all large contributors. However, Vermont is the place with the reputation, the mystique, the tall tales, the state that produces a half million gallons in an average year, and the one of the few states

that actually *grades* its syrup. To fully experience "sugaring," I knew I had to visit Vermont.

I began my quest at Shaker Maple Farm, owned by Steve and Leah 5 Willsey. It's in Starksboro, Vermont, up in the Green Mountains. Vermont natives refer to sugaring time as the "fifth season"—mud season. The maple syrup season can last from three to six weeks, but no one can rush it, push it, delay it, or alter it in any way. The maple syrup farmer is at the mercy of Mother Nature. He or she knows this and has the utmost respect for it. As it has always been since before recorded history and will always be, Mother Nature runs this operation.

Because the process depends so much on nature's whim, it hasn't 6 changed much in hundreds of years. When spring comes and temperatures begin to rise above freezing during the day, the maple trees (*Acer saccharum*) begin to unfreeze from the outside in. The "sap-flow mechanism" remains a mystery to even educated scientists, but remember phloem and xylem from eighth grade science?: It works something like that. The sap begins to run up and down the inside of the tree to nourish the buds. Meanwhile, carbon dioxide gas is forming inside the tree and needs to escape. Any opening will begin to leak sap. As the temperature drops during the day, the sap stops running and begins again on the next day of thawing temperatures.

When the sap begins to run, or shortly beforehand, it's time to tap the 7 trees. With an old-fashioned brace and bit drill (or a gas-powered one for modern operations) a hole is made 7/16 of an inch in diameter and two or three inches deep into the trunk of the tree. This tap is actually a wound in the tree. Then a "tap," "spout," or "spile" is placed inside the hole and tapped in with a hammer, just until it's sitting nicely in the tree and sap starts to run out like from a faucet. A tree with a diameter of ten to eighteen inches can have one tap; nineteen to twenty-four inches, two taps; and so on. Too many taps will take too much sap from the tree and thus harm it. Steve Willsey hugs the tree to determine how many taps he'll use. If his fingers don't touch, it gets two taps. If they touch, only one. Then, for the trees around the farmhouse, he hooks a bucket onto the spile, covers it with a lid, and moves on.

Instead of buckets, most modern operations (including Steve's) use plas- 8 tic tubing strung elaborately around the hillsides to carry the sap by force of gravity right into the sugarhouse. Some (either purists or gluttons for punishment) still do it the old-fashioned way, attaching buckets by hand, checking them daily and making the rounds, sometimes with horse-drawn drays, to gather the sap.

When the sap comes out of the tree it's clear. That's because it's about 9 two percent sap and 98 percent water. When enough sap is gathered into the sugarhouse it's time for boiling. It will take forty gallons of boiled sap to produce one gallon of syrup.

The sugarhouse is usually a small, wooden cabin. An enormous wood 10 "arch" (stove) called an evaporator takes up most of the room inside and when boiling begins, will demand constant stoking. Pallets of lumber are stacked outside to feed a roaring fire huge enough to thrill Sam McGee.

11   On top of the evaporator are large partitioned stainless pans with boiling sap reaching several different stages on its way to becoming syrup. When the temperature of the sap hits 219 degrees, it's syrup. The density of the syrup must be checked with a hydrometer to make sure it's exactly right. Too soon and bacteria survives, with its attendant risk of fermentation; too late and it's overboiled and begins to crystallize.

12   Boiling is an exciting social event. Some Vermonters say it serves to wake people up after the long cold winter. Neighbors gather when they see steam rising from the sugarhouse and know they'll be welcomed. The phone rings constantly with the question, "You boiling tonight?"

Hazardous Duty

13   Although everyone at Shaker Maple Farm assured me there was absolutely no danger, they couldn't fool me. Think about it: you're in a tiny *wooden* building with an enormous *raging* fire inside and sparks flying around the opening of a huge furnace. A crowd of men heaves logs through the open doors of this furnace, while several large dogs wander around. (Their purpose still escapes me except that *everyone* in Vermont owns a large dog.) Once in a while, someone revs up a huge tractor and backs it noisily into the sugarhouse to dump a pallet full of wood. The men holler and lift, lift and holler, until the tractor is freed of the pallet. On top of the evaporator is a 16-foot-long by six-foot wide pan filled with hundreds of gallons of frothing, hot sticky liquid, threatening to bubble over at any moment. Extra people mill about, chatting, laughing, eating, drinking, and generally getting in the way.

14   This whole operation is done in steam so thick you often can't see the face of the person next to you. And it's not done in the morning when everyone is fresh and alert—oh no. It's done at night, often after a full day's work. Why have we never seen this headline: "Thirty-five Die in Latest Maple Syrup Mishap?" Leah Willsey assured me there was nothing to worry about. Well, there was that one time her hair caught on fire. "What did you do?" I asked, horrified. "I put it out," she said. Vermonters are a calm lot.

15   There is controversy about how the making of maple syrup began in America. Its origins have been lost because they go so far back. Instead, we have an abundance of theories. Some think French explorers or missionaries taught the native Iroquois, Micmac, Huron, Ojibway, and Abenaki Indians to boil sap. Others insist it was the other way around. Still others prefer the squirrel theory: the common squirrel was often seen biting into maple trees, then returning later to savor the sugar crust that had dried at the wound. All humans did was watch the squirrel and improve on the method a bit.

Know Your Terms

16   If you go to Vermont, or any sugaring state, you do not want to appear a bumpkin. I've put together a brief lexicon from my experience in Vermont to prevent this from happening:

- *Maple sugaring*—the process of turning sap into syrup

- *Sugarbush*—the maple grove
- *Sugarhouse*—the wooden building where all this alchemy takes place
- *Running*—during thaws, the time when sap is coursing through the trees
- *Tapping*—pounding taps into trees
- *Boiling*—the process of reducing the water content of the sap and thickening it to syrup
- *Run*—one start and stop of the entire syrup-making process (a good year might have twenty-five separate runs)
- *Ayup*—a northern New England term meaning, *that's correct;* same as yes in all other states. (e.g., *"Are you boiling?" "Ayup."*)

Having witnessed this process first-hand, and learned what is involved, 17
I would never begrudge the price of real maple syrup. Making maple syrup may be the most labor-intensive job a person could have, particularly for those who do it the old-fashioned way with buckets and horses. Most producers have other jobs, so sugaring is an exhausting labor of love. It's terrifically hard work, but it keeps them close to their families, close to their neighbors, close to the basics of life. It keeps them tough. Perhaps it contributes to the stoical, laid-back attitude I noticed among Vermonters. *Mother Nature will either cooperate this year or she won't.* Don't get uptight over what you can't control.

I'm all through making golden blacks for my kids and look forward to 18
making them for my grandkids. But I'm going to make one change: I won't even put that other stuff on the table. I'll be tough, like those Vermonters. I'll serve only real maple syrup and if any of my hypothetical grandkids have the nerve to ask, *Is this all we've got?"* I'll just stare 'em down and answer, *ayup.*

Rhetorical Considerations

1. Is Guest's primary purpose in writing this essay expressive, informative, or persuasive? (*Hodges'* 32a/*Writer's* 1e)
2. Find evidence in this essay of Guest's awareness of her audience. (*Hodges'* 32a/*Writer's* 1b and 1e)
3. Is Guest's essay designed to instruct her readers so that they can follow the process described? (*Hodges'* 32a/*Writer's* 1b)
4. What purpose does the introduction serve in establishing a context for the essay? (*Hodges'* 33b/*Writer's* 3b)
5. In addition to describing the process of sugaring, what attitude about the process does this essay develop? (*Hodges'* 35c/*Writer's* 7c)
6. Comment on the use of humor in Guest's essay. (*Hodges'* 33a/*Writer's* 3a)

Language and Style

1. Look up synonyms for *bumpkin* (paragraph 16). (*Hodges'* 19e/*Writer's* 28e)
2. What is a *hydrometer* (paragraph 11)? What do the roots of the word mean? (*Hodges'* 19e/*Writer's* 28e)

3. Explain how the word *stuff* in paragraph 2 prepares the reader for the tone of the essay. (*Hodges'* 19c/*Writer's* 28c)
4. Find words that lend an informal tone to Guest's essay. (*Hodges'* 19c/*Writer's* 28c)
5. Guest uses several contractions throughout her essay. Identify these contractions and comment on their appropriateness for this essay and their effect on tone. (*Hodges'* 19c/*Writer's* 28c)
6. Does the last sentence of paragraph 4 contain a split infinitive? If so, can its use be justified? (*Hodges'* 25/*Writer's* 20)

Writing Suggestions

1. Using Guest's essay as a loose model, write an essay in which you examine two ways of doing something (the traditional way and the modern way, or your way and someone else's way, for example).
2. Write an essay in which you describe how learning about a process made you appreciate something more.

ZOO MEDICINE

Michael Kernan

Since graduating with a BA from Harvard in 1949, Michael Kernan has
had a varied and distinguished career in journalism. He wrote for the
Washington Post for over twenty years, and since 1994 has penned the
regular column, "Around the Mall and Beyond," for *Smithsonian Magazine*. Kernan has also published two novels, *The Violet Dots* (1978) and
The Lost Diaries of Frans Hals (1994), as well as articles in *Life, Reader's
Digest, National Geographic, Traveler,* and other magazines.

Question: How do you give a 448-pound gorilla an EKG? 1
Answer: With a lot of help. 2

It takes ten people to lift a sedated hulk named Mopie onto the operat- 3
ing table at the National Zoological Park hospital. Actually, the 24-year-old
silver-back is getting much more than an electrocardiogram. For over an
hour he will be put through some of the most sophisticated heart tests we
have, including an exam with a transesophageal ultrasonic scope, part of a
Doppler echocardiograph machine.

The scope is a silvery L-shaped tube, hardly a foot long, and it costs 4
$48,000. It is hand-built, with 64 crystals that can be fired in phased se-
quence to vibrate and thus send sound waves into the heart; the waves that
bounce back are digitally reconstructed into a video image. Inserted into
the esophagus next to the heart, the instrument provides an extraordinary
picture of that organ, its valves, the aorta and everything else, as it pumps
away. What we have here is a charming switch: the latest developments in
human medicine being used to benefit animals.

"Cardiovascular disease is a significant problem in orangutans and go- 5
rillas, especially male gorillas," Dr. Richard Cambre, head of the Zoo's Department of Animal Health, tells me "We've done all nine of our orangutans
and now are working on the nine gorillas with echocardiograms, blood pressure exams and blood workups for cholesterol and lipid levels."

Though zoo animals live longer than wild ones as a rule—35 years is the 6
average age for gorillas; the record is 54—they tend to develop heart trouble. No one knows just why. Is it hypertension? Arteriosclerosis? And why
the high cholesterol? Though the Zoo provides the apes with a diet that is
as close as possible to what they would eat in the wild, are the apes missing
some trace item, some leaf or plant that they find in the lowlands of Zaire
and Cameroon?

"These exams will give us baseline stats," Cambre says, "so we can fol- 7
low them in later years. One thing: we don't have heart data on gorillas

while they're awake. We might be able to train orangutans to accept a blood pressure cuff, but gorillas, I don't know."

8   They are not ideal patients. When Dr. Lucy Spelman, associate veterinarian at the Zoo, approached Mopie earlier this morning with the dart gun that would anesthetize him, Cambre recalls, "he figured out what was going on before she had a chance to fire the dart, though he'd never seen this particular type of equipment before. He knew what was going to happen to him." So Mopie produced from the source a gigantic handful of fresh gorilla manure and hurled it at Dr. Spelman, spattering her from hair to heels.

9   Undaunted, she is in the operating room working away on Mopie with the rest of the doctors when I arrive. She has wiped the stuff off her glasses but is otherwise concentrating on what she has come here to do. All in a day's work. The place has a pungent smell, somewhat like a bad case of halitosis. The vets tell me this is the normal scent of a gorilla when he's scared.

10   The dart, fired from an air pistol, goes into the leg muscles and puts a gorilla down in 15 minutes or so. After that he is kept under anesthesia with isoflurane gas, inhaled through a tube.

11   Now Mopie lies there with his silverhaired knees splayed and his giant paws curled like a sleeping child's fingers. A transducer clipped to his tongue tracks his blood oxygen saturation and pulse rate. His eyes are slightly open. The doctors bustle around him in their surgical masks and gloves, taking notes, checking the video monitors, moving probes about on his vast chest.

12   When I ask how she got into doing this, Dr. Spelman says simply that she always wanted to be a zoo vet. She was in private practice but prefers the variety of experience in a zoo. In one day she may help with a cardiac workup on a gorilla, do a root canal on a Sumatran tiger, take blood from a sea lion.

13   As Mopie's heart thumps away in living color on the Doppler machine, a frighteningly accomplished trunkful of electronics costing six figures and loaned by Hewlett-Packard as a friendly gesture, I talk to Dr. Steven Goldstein, one of three Washington cardiologists who have given up this Sunday and volunteered to help. I ask if Mopie's heart rate of 123 beats per minute, duly recorded on the monitor, is very bad.

14   "It would be bad for a human but might be not so bad for an ape. This may be mild for him." Goldstein does, however, see what appears to be a problem in the main pumping chamber, the left ventricle. Normal human ventricles eject 60 to 70 percent of the blood in a given contraction. In orangutans, the efficiency is down to 55 to 65 percent. Mopie's is as low as 35 percent.

15   "I think it's abnormal, but I've only seen 10 or 11 great apes," says Goldstein, who has been volunteering at the Zoo since September 1995. "He's the second gorilla that I've seen with this condition. His father died at 37 of a heart problem, but then his father was born in the wild. Apes do live artificially long in captivity.

16   The beauty of the Doppler machine, National Zoo primates curator Lisa Stevens tells me, is that you can literally watch and videotape the heart at work. A conventional heart x-ray might be obscured by the ribs and, besides,

is two-dimensional and static. When the ultrasonic scope is inserted, you can see everything in motion, even the aortic valve opening and closing.

Stevens came to the National Zoological Park straight from Michigan 17 State, 18 years ago. "I thought I'd do this for a few years, but then I realized that this was it. I started with cats, then bears, seals and sea lions. You become specialized eventually, but most people are very versatile. You work with all the animals, from elephants to fish. And you appreciate and respect them all."

Dr. Cambre, who came here two years ago after 15 years at the Denver 18 Zoo, says that being a zoo veterinarian gets into your blood. "Animal personalities are fascinating. We have Ph.D. curators here and a keeper staff that's mostly college educated. We depend on them to report unusual behavioral patterns for individual animals to us. Sometimes these are early warning signs of illness. It takes a team effort to figure out what's going on." Without an owner to tell them what an animal's problem is, Zoo people have to rely on their own close observations. Is an animal eating well? Defecating normally? Moody? Under stress?

On another of my visits to the Zoo, Azy, a large male orangutan, spot- 19 ted Cambre as we strolled past. Azy rushed back and forth in his cage, pushing a huge barrel before him in an impressive display of power. "It's a lot of bluster," Cambre said. "He's trying to intimidate me. He knows who I am. He knows who's going to win if I get my dart gun. So he's bluffing. Of course, if I was stupid enough to wander into his cage, he'd kill me. They're forgiving up to a point. But they don't like us, because if they're sick we've got to dart 'em."

After the heart exam, as Mopie lies on his back, half covered by a blan- 20 ket and breathing peacefully, Dr. Spelman cleans the gorilla's wicked-looking teeth with dental tools. Yes, even apes are prone to cavities and gum disease.

Now Mopie is being unplugged from the monitors and transferred to an 21 x-ray table for a complete set of pictures. Even moving him from one table to another takes a half-dozen people hauling on the heavy canvas netting he's lying on.

"We'll take him off anesthesia when he's back in a cage," explains 22 Stevens. "He'll recover pretty fast. He'll be groggy for the rest of the day, but awake and eating. He might be a little cross. He's into that role of being the big dominant male. Mopie can be sullen, but he has his light moments. By tomorrow he'll be back to normal."

The team struggles through narrow doorways with Mopie and deposits 23 him in a van for the trip back to the ape house. There they tug and push him though barred passageways to a cage, where the anesthesia tube is removed. Immediately he begins to clear his throat, sounding exactly like my father in the morning. In a minute he starts to move, and the staff leaves to give the same round of tests to another gorilla.

I hear some serious screams and the pounding of bare feet as a large fe- 24 male named Mesou flees down a runway. Following her, holding a long dart gun, comes the intrepid Dr. Spelman in clean coveralls, her brown hair pulled back in a ponytail. She moves with deliberation, intent and calm.

25   The CO_2 gun pops. "There," she says. "That was a good one." Mesou sits down with a philosophic grunt.

Rhetorical Considerations

1. What is the primary purpose of Kernan's essay? (*Hodges'* 32a/*Writer's* 1b and 1e)
2. Is Kernan's essay mainly expressive, informative, or persuasive? (*Hodges'* 32a/*Writer's* 1b)
3. Would the reader be able to follow this process? Why or why not? (*Hodges'* 32e/*Writer's* 2e)
4. Find examples of comparison and contrast in this essay. (*Hodges'* 32e/*Writer's* 2e)
5. How does Kernan make the animals seem more "human"? Why might he do this?
6. Does Kernan use adequate examples? (*Hodges'* 31c/*Writer's* 2d)

Language and Style

1. What is accomplished by including a number of technical terms in the essay? Does the reader need to know them in order to understand the essay? (*Hodges'* 19c/*Writer's* 28c)
2. Find words that emphasize the difficulty of the process described. (*Hodges'* 20/*Writer's* 28)
3. Look up the following words in your dictionary: *halitosis* (paragraph 9); *curator* (paragraph 16). (*Hodges'* 19e/*Writer's* 28e)
4. Justify the use of a fragment in the answer to the opening question. (*Hodges'* 2/*Writer's* 18)
5. Comment on the agreement in the relative clause in paragraph 13. (*Hodges'* 6/*Writer's* 21d and 22e)

Writing Suggestions

1. Describe a process that requires the participation and cooperation of a team of people.
2. Write an essay in which you explain to someone how to take a child to the zoo for the first time.

CLICK! The Housewife's Moment of Truth

Jane O'Reilly

Jane O'Reilly, a freelance writer on the subject of women and politics, has been a contributing editor to *Ms.* magazine and *New York Magazine* and a contributor to *Time* magazine. She won her first major notice with her humorous essays in *Ms.* She is also the author of *The Girl I Left Behind* (1980) and *No Turning Back: Two Nuns' Battle with the Vatican over Women's Right to Choose* (1990). This essay was first published in *Ms.* in 1972 and is considered a classic.

Last June, 40 people were lying on a floor in Aspen, Colorado, floating free 1 and uneasy on the indoor/outdoor carpet, eyes closed, being led through a cathartic workshop.

We closed our eyes and cleared our minds. Infinitely slowly, we began 2 to evolve into the animal that most expressed our own ideas of ourselves— of our sensual selves. Minutes passed and we became aware of the other animals around us. At last we opened our eyes and those animals that felt like it did whatever seemed natural. Most of the women twittered or purred. Most of the men growled, or attempted to wag tails. I was a cat, black, with a lovely long tail, sitting under a red geranium in a sunny window. We formed groups in our part of the conference-room forest, and told each other what we had become.

"I was a snake," said a beautiful young woman, a professional designer. 3 "As I was moving through the grass, enjoying my slithering, curving progress, I realized I had no fangs. No bite. I couldn't even hiss. My only protection was that I could change color in reaction to the people that passed by. I started to go through my garden and I saw that there were panthers draped over all the lawn furniture. I went into my house, and there were panthers everywhere, filling every chair, curled up in groups in all the rooms. They were eating, rather elegantly, and no one paid any attention to me, even when I asked if they wanted anything more to eat. I was interested, but I was different, and finally I withdrew."

The women in the group looked at her, looked at each other, and . . . 4 click! A moment of truth. The shock of recognition. Instant sisterhood. "You became a housewife," we said, excited, together, turning to the men to see if they understood. "She is describing a housewife. Do you know that?"

"Hmm, yes, well, uh . . ." they said, sensitized for the morning, but eager 5 to recount their own stories of becoming spotted leopards in green forests, of turning to griffins with human heads who know and see all. The next time, or perhaps the time after that, they will recognize the click! of recognition, that parenthesis of truth around a little thing that completes the

187

puzzle of reality in women's minds—the moment that brings a gleam to our eyes and means the revolution has begun.

6   Those clicks are coming faster and faster. American women are angry. Not redneck-angry from screaming because we are so frustrated and unfulfilled-angry, but clicking-things-into-place-angry, because we have suddenly and shockingly perceived the basic disorder in what has been believed to be the natural order of things.

7   In Houston, Texas, a friend of mine stood and watched her husband step over a pile of toys on the stairs, put there to be carried up. "Why can't you get this stuff put away?" he mumbled. Click! "You have two hands," she said, turning away.

8   Last summer I got a letter, from a man who wrote: "I do not agree with your last article, and I am cancelling my wife's subscription." The next day I got a letter from his wife saying, "*I* am not cancelling *my* subscription." Click!

9   On Fire Island my weekend hostess and I had just finished cooking breakfast, lunch, and washing dishes for both. A male guest came wandering into the kitchen just as the last dish was being put away and said, "How about something to eat?" He sat down, expectantly, and started to read the paper. Click!

10   A woman I know in St. Louis, who had begun to enjoy a little success writing a grain company's newsletter, came home to tell her husband about lunch in the executive dining room. She had planned a funny little anecdote about the deeply humorous pomposity of executives, when she noticed her husband rocking with laughter. "Ho ho, my little wife in an executive dining room." Click!

11   Attitudes are expressed in semantic equations that simply turn out to be two languages: one for men and another for women. One morning a friend of mine told her husband she would like to hire a baby sitter so she could get back to her painting. "Maybe when you start to make money from your pictures, then we could think about it," said her husband. My friend didn't stop to argue the inherent fallacy in his point—how could she make money if no one was willing to free her for work? She suggested that, instead of hiring someone, he could help with the housework a little more. "Well, I don't know, honey," he said, "I guess sharing the housework is all right if the wife is really contributing something, brings in a salary. . . ." For a terrible minute my friend thought she would kill her husband, right there at breakfast, in front of the children. For ten years, she had been hanging wallpaper, making curtains and refinishing floors so that they could afford the mortgage on their apartment. She had planned the money-saving menus so they could afford the little dinners for prospective clients. She had crossed town to save money on clothes so the family could have a new hi-fi. All the little advances in station—the vacations, the theater tickets, the new car—had been made possible by her crafty, endless, worried manipulation of the household expenses. "I was under the impression," she said, "that I *was* contributing something. Evidently my life's blood is simply a non-deductible expense."

In an office, a political columnist, male, was waiting to see the editor- 12
in-chief. Leaning against the doorway, the columnist turned to the first
woman he saw and said, "Listen, call Barry Brown and tell him I'll be late."
Click! It wasn't because she happened to be an editor herself that she refused to make the call.

In the end, we are all housewives, the natural people to turn to when 13
there is something unpleasant, inconvenient, or inconclusive to be done. It
will not do for women who have jobs to pretend that society's ills will be
cured if all women are gainfully employed. In Russia, 70 percent of the doctors and 20 percent of the construction workers are women, but women still
do all the housework. Some revolution. As the Russian women's saying goes,
it simply freed us to do twice the work.

It will not do for women who are mostly housewives to say that 14
Women's Liberation is fine for women who work, but has no relevance for
them. Equal pay for equal work is only part of the argument—usually described as "the part I'll go along with."

We are all housewives. We would prefer to be persons. That is the part 15
they don't go along with.

"That broad . . ." begins a male guest who Hasn't Thought. 16

"Woman," corrects the hostess, smiling meaningfully over her coffeepot. 17

"Oh, no," groans the guest. "Don't tell me you believe in this Women's 18
Lib stuff!"

"Yes," says the hostess. 19

"Well, I'll go along with some of it, equal pay for equal work, that seems 20
fair enough," he concedes. Uneasy now, he waits for the male hoots of
laughter, for the flutter of wives rushing to sit by their husbands at the mer-
est breath of the subject of Women's Liberation. But that was three or four
years ago. Too many moments have clicked in the minds of too many
women since then. This year the women in the room have not moved to
their husbands' sides; they have . . . solidified. A gelid quality settles over
the room. The guest struggles on.

"You can't tell me Women's Lib means I have to wash the dishes, does it?" 21

"Yes." 22

They tell us we are being petty. The future improvement of civilization 23
could not depend on who washes the dishes. Could it? Yes. The liberated
society—with men, women, and children living as whole human beings,
not halves divided by sex roles—depends on the steadfast search for new solutions to just such apparently trivial problems, on new answers to tired old
questions. Such questions as:

Denise works as a waitress from 6 A.M. to 3 P.M. Her husband is a cab- 24
driver, who moonlights on weekends as a doorman. They have four children. When her husband comes home at night, he asks: *"What's for dinner?"*

In moments of suburban strife, Fred often asks his wife, "Why haven't 25
you mended my shirt and lubricated the car? *What else have you go to do but
sit around the house all day?"*

How dare he ask such a question? What sort of bizarre social arrange- 26
ment is post-industrial-revolution marriage? What kind of relationship

involves two people sharing their lives without knowing, or apparently caring, what the other does all day?

27   According to insurance companies, it would cost Fred $8,000 to $9,000 a year to replace Alice's services if she died. Alice, being an average ideal suburban housewife, works 99.6 hours a week—always feeling there is too much to be done and always guilty because it is never quite finished. Besides, her work doesn't seem important. After all, Fred is paid for dong whatever it is he does. Abstract statistics make no impact on Alice. "My situation is different," she says. Of course it is. All situations are different. But sooner or later she will experience—in a blinding click!—a moment of truth. She will remember that she once had other interests, vague hopes, great plans. She will decide that the work in the house is less important than reordering the work so she can consider her own life.

28   The problem is, what does she do then?

29   The first thing we all do is argue. We present our case: It is unfair that we should bear the whole responsibility for the constant schema of household management.

30   We may get agreement, but we will never get cooperation or permission. Rebuttals may begin at the lowest level: "It is a woman's job to wash dishes." Men at a higher stage of enlightenment may argue, "Why do we need a washing machine? I wash my socks and we send everything out." They simply cannot understand that we are the ones who must gather and list and plan even for the laundry we send out. It is, quite simply, *on our minds*. And *not* on theirs. Evenings of explanation and understanding will still end with, "Honey, do I have any clean shorts for tomorrow?" Most women will decide that it is not worth making an issue out of shorts.

31   In fact, underwear is as good a place to begin as anywhere. Last summer I carried the underwear downstairs, put it in the hamper, sorted it, washed and dried it, folded it, carried it upstairs, and put it away. One day, I decided that as an act of extreme courage I would not carry the laundry upstairs. I put it on the couch in the room with the television set. The family moved it to one side of the couch so they could sit down. I left it there. I put more on the couch. They piled it up. They began to dress off the couch. I began to avoid the television room. At last, guilty and angry, my nerve failed and I carried the laundry upstairs. No one noticed. Out of that experience, I formulated a few rules which I intend to follow as soon as I finish the painful process of thinking about the assumptions that make them necessary.

32   (1) *Decide what housework needs to be done. Then cut the list in half.* It is no longer necessary to prove ourselves by being in motion all day and all night. Beds must be made and food cooked, but it is unfair to demand that the family share the work if your standards include cooking like Julia Child and bouncing dimes on the bedspread. Beware of useless and self-defeating standards. It is preposterous and not unusual for a woman to feel her house must look as though no one lived there. Who's looking? Who cares?

33   (2) *Decide what you will and will not do.* Keep firmly in mind the notion of personal maintenance as an individual responsibility. If children cannot put away their clothes and therefore cannot find them and have to go to school

looking like ragpickers—well, presumably they will learn from experience. Their appearance does not make *you* a bad person. (If you can acknowledge and act on that fact, you are becoming liberated.) If you spend four or five hours a day driving your children places, ask yourself why. Are they cripples? Are there no safe streets they can walk along? Why? Seizing responsibility from children has been women's way to compensate for their own lack of responsibility for themselves, and it has resulted in two generations of non-adults.

(3) *Make a plan and present it as final.* There will, of course, be democratic 34 argument, but it is only fair to state your purpose. Not that anyone will pay attention. They will laugh nervously and expect life to go on as usual. Do not be distracted by sophisticated arguments, such as, "Well, let's take the relative value of our days." Yes. Let's. A wife who figures out that his important business meeting is no different from her P.T.A. committee meeting may opt for equal hours and quit her own work at five o'clock.

Another diversionary remark is: "But honey, this isn't a business agree- 35 ment. This is a home. It is a question of helping each other reach fulfill-ment." In my home, when I am working against a deadline, I sit in front of a typewriter and shout, "More tea!" The whole family hustles in with more tea. I call out, "Go to bed." "Get some lamb chops." It is an emergency situation and they all spring to, helping me fulfill myself. But *I* am still in charge of remembering to get the lamb chops. It is a problem that may not be solved in my lifetime.

Almost equally difficult is deciding who does what. Men will always opt 36 for things that get finished and stay that way—putting up screens, but not planning menus. Some find washing dishes a peaceful, meditative experi-ence. It has to be worked out. The important thing is to get the argument away from philosophy and onto assigned chores.

(4) *Think revolutionary thoughts.* The nineteenth century ended 72 years 37 ago, but we are still trying to arrange our households according to that "idea" image of family life. Think of something new. I know a man and woman who decided to stop eating dinner. She had been rushing around putting children to bed, and then laying on a candlelit dinner with three kinds of food on the plate for her husband. They liked chatting at dinner. He helped clean up. They never finished before ten. But one night they discovered that both were dreaming of long cozy evenings reading by the fire. So they have skipped the ritual feast—and replaced it with sandwiches. They get up earlier and have family talks at breakfast. Who knows what daring innovations may follow? He may demand an end to success based on overtime. Both may demand less homework so the children can assume some responsibilities.

(5) *Never give in.* Empty one dishwasher, and it leads to a lifetime of emp- 38 tying dishwashers. Remember that nothing will ever get done by anyone else if you do it. If you are the only person who worries about it, perhaps it isn't worth worrying about. If it is very important to you that you not live in a sty, then you must persuade everyone else that what is important to you counts.

It is very hard not to give in. One evening recently two men came to 39 our house for the weekend. "When shall we eat?" they asked, beaming.

"Whenever you want," I said, bravely. "I'm not cooking. I'm working tonight." They cooked, while I held myself in my chair by an incredible effort of will, the words blurring before my determined eyes. The next day, I expiated my guilt by going the whole route, including homemade bread. "Ah!" they said. "How wonderful! You are a real woman, And working, too."

40   (6) *Do not feel guilty.* I have never met a woman who did not feel guilty. We can post signs in our hearts and on our walls saying: "It is not wrong to inconvenience my family—it is making us all responsible, ego-strong adults." But when a man we are attached to goes out with a button off his coat, we—not he—feel feckless. The only near-cure is to have something more interesting to think about. Even if "something to do" means going back to easy courses in school—back to the point where we abdicated for marriage—it is a beginning, and we are older now and will learn rapidly, because at least we know we want things some other way.

41   I cannot imagine anything more difficult than incurring the kind of domestic trauma I describe. It requires the conscious loss of the role we have been taught, and its replacement by a true identity. And what if we succeed? What if we become liberated women who recognize that our guilt is reinforced by the marketplace, which would have us attach our identity to furniture polish and confine our deepest anxieties to color coordinating our toilet paper and our washing machines? What if we overcome our creeping sense of something unnatural when our husbands approach "our" stoves? What if we don't allow ourselves to be treated as people with nothing better to do than wait for repairmen and gynecologists? What if we finally learn that we are not defined by our children and our husbands, but by ourselves? Then we will be able to control our own lives, able to step out into the New Tomorrow. But the sad and solemn truth is that we may have to step out alone.

42   The more we try, and argue, and change, the more we will realize that the male ego will be the last ting in this world to change. And the *last* place it will change is at home.

43   Some women pride themselves on the intransigence of their men. I have always taken pride in the liberated attitudes of mine. And yet, last weekend, when I buckled my seatbelt in the car, he growled: "You don't have to do that with *me* driving." My God! We were back to Start; he was threatened by my safety measure. How do we argue with feelings like that? With the constant demands to bolster and boost egos grown fat and fragile, with the blocks and jealousies and petty meannesses that drain off our energies? Too often the only way to find ourselves is to leave.

44   Men's resistance is more subtle than simply leaving the dishes unwashed. A woman I know was married for seventeen years to a man who threatened to smash her sculpture whenever they fought. He complained about the cost of her tools, he laughed at her work in public. When she finally left, she was dazed to discover that the critics found her work excellent.

45   I have a friend in Cleveland who left high school to marry. She raised two children and worked nights in her husband's office. When she went back to college, it happened mysteriously that they had an exhausting fight the night before every exam. When she still got high marks, he took credit for encouraging her.

No, the question of housework is not a trivial matter to be worked out 46 the day before we go on to greater things. Men do not want equality at home. A strong woman is a threat, someone to be jealous of. Most of all, she is an inconvenience, and she can be replaced. They like things as they are. It's pleasanter.

I had never realized how seductive the role of master is until the other 47 day. I was watering a plant, and the water began to run on the floor. I stood where I was and moaned about the puddle until the live-in babysitter dropped what she was dong and brought me the rag it would have been easier for me to get. She, at least, was not saying, "Don't worry darling, let me take care of it." But my excuse was . . . I have more important things to think about than housework.

Rhetorical Considerations

1. How is O'Reilly's essay organized? Would another organizational pattern have been as or even more effective? Why or why not? (*Hodges'* 32d/*Writer's* 2c)
2. How does it affect the essay for O'Reilly to concede, "It is a problem that may not be solved in my lifetime" (paragraph 35)? (*Hodges'* 33b/*Writer's* 3b)
3. Find evidence in the essay that this piece was written more than 30 years ago.
4. What does O'Reilly mean when she writes that "we are all housewives" (paragraphs 13 and 15)?
5. Why is it important that O'Reilly include herself among her examples? (*Hodges'* 31c and 35e/*Writer's* 2d and 7h)

Language and Style

1. Look up the following words in your dictionary: *cathartic* (paragraph 1); *semantic, inherent,* and *fallacy* (paragraph 11); *gelid* (paragraph 20); *schema* (paragraph 29); *rebuttals* (paragraph 30); *feckless* and *abdicated* (paragraph 40). (*Hodges'* 19e/*Writer's* 28e)
2. Why is there a comma after *Colorado* in paragraph 1? (*Hodges'* 12/*Writer's* 31)
3. Why does O'Reilly say the women "twittered" and "purred," whereas the men "growled" (paragraph 2)? (*Hodges'* 20/*Writer's* 20)
4. Why is the quotation in the last sentence of paragraph 24 italicized? (*Hodges'* 10/*Writer's* 38)
5. What is the rhetorical effect of the questions in paragraph 41? (*Hodges'* 30/*Writer's* 27)

Writing Suggestions

1. Write a contemporary version of O'Reilly's essay.
2. Write a process essay from a male perspective about household equality or about sharing household chores.

✦

IMAGES

Process

Included here is a photograph demonstrating how human (and canine) work-ers are lowered from a building during a rappelling drill. It is a photograph that relies solely on the image itself to convey the complexity of a process. Also included is a diagram illustrating one of the methods by which uranium changes into a form that has fewer "heavy" atoms (Uranium^{238}) and more "middle-weight atoms" (Uranium^{235}), which is the isotope required for nu-clear reactions. This diagram uses labels to help explain a chemical process.

Eric Parsons, Jenny, a search and rescue dog, is lowered during a rappelling drill

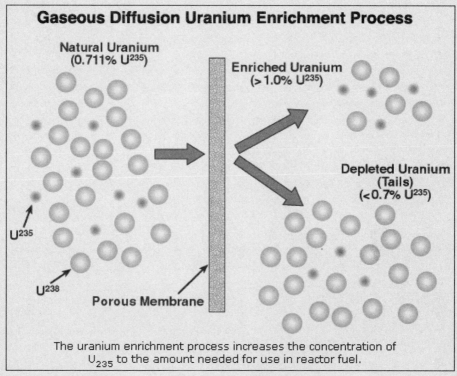

NRC, Gaseous diffusion uranium enrichment process

Rhetorical Considerations

1. What feelings are evoked by the photograph of the rescue dog that might not be evoked by a mere textual description of the process?
2. Is there any aspect of the process depicted in this photo that could benefit from textual description? If so, what?
3. Who might be the intended audience for this photo? How can you tell?
4. The diagram of the uranium enrichment process was found on the Web site for the U.S. Nuclear Regulatory Commission, a government agency. Can you discern from the diagram who the intended audience of this Web site might be?
5. Does this diagram explain the process clearly to you, or does it need text beyond the labels provided to clarify the image? Why or why not?

Writing Suggestions

1. Write a process essay in which you supplement the text with images of any kind (photographs, charts, or drawings, for example).
2. Find another image that illustrates a process. Write an essay in which you explain what the image demonstrates.

CHAPTER 5

Cause and Effect

Cause and effect are complementary terms: *cause* refers to what makes things happen (reasons); *effect* refers to what happens (results). A cause presupposes one or more effects; an effect has one or more causes. Cause-and-effect essays may focus on exploring either causes or effects or may analyze a causal chain, in which an effect becomes the cause of an effect that in turn also is a cause, and so on. In this chapter, for example, Margo Monteith and Jeffrey Winters's "Why We Hate" discuss effects, while John M. Williams's "And Here's the Pitch" explores a causal chain.

Understanding Cause and Effect Analysis

Causal relationships are rarely simple. Any given effect is likely to have several causes, some more immediate than others, and of course each of those causes may have produced a variety of effects besides the one under consideration. Consider all of the following statements:

- I'm cold because it's winter.
- I'm cold because it's only 30 degrees Fahrenheit.
- I'm cold because I left my coat on the bus.
- I'm cold because a friend was talking to me on the bus and made me forget my coat.
- I'm cold because I live in Bemidji, Minnesota, rather than near the equator.
- I'm cold because heat is being exchanged between my body and the atmosphere in accordance with the second law of thermodynamics.
- I'm cold because the metabolic processes of human beings do not produce enough heat to keep them warm in Bemidji.
- I'm cold because I don't have fur.

All of these causes can be true simultaneously. And note that every one of them has effects besides making me cold. Even leaving my coat on the bus has other effects: I'll have to go to the bus company's lost-and-found room (a nuisance that will cause me to miss doing something else), and if the coat hasn't been turned in I'll have to buy another one (which in turn will cause me to forgo something else I could have bought with that money). Yet this example, my shivering in Bemidji, is a very simple one (which, by the way, demonstrates narration and process in addition to cause and effect) . Imagine, then, how long a possible list might be for something really complicated, such as the causes of crime.

So writers must guard against oversimplifying. Discovering the immediate cause of an event may be easy, but other, more remote causes may be more important. The firing on Fort Sumter is often seen as the immediate cause of the Civil War. But of course the issue of slavery was a far more basic cause, and slavery was in turn causally related to economic factors such as Northern control of banking and Southern control of cotton supplies for the Northern fabric mills, as well as to political factors such as the Southern championship of states' rights and the Northern commitment to federalism. All of these factors contributed to the conflict, though some more immediately and more visibly than others.

Clearly, events are more complex than they may seem on the surface, but this complexity is not the only difficulty writers face in cause-and-effect analysis. Vested interests sometimes deliberately obscure causal relationships for their own benefit. For instance, when the Warren Commission investigated the cause of President John F. Kennedy's assassination, one of the obstacles it met was that certain government agencies tried to blame each other to avoid being blamed themselves.

Finally, in assigning causes to effects, writers must be not only objective but also rational. It can be all too easy to ignore evidence that points to a cause a writer does not wish to consider. And even the most fair-minded writer can still fall into those logical traps to which we are all vulnerable, called *fallacies,* discussed below. (See *Hodges'* 35f/*Writer's* 7i for more information.)

Using Cause and Effect Analysis

When you write using cause and effect analysis, you need to consider your subject, your purpose and audience, your organization, your language and style, and your presentation of images, just as you do with other modes of development. All of these will affect the way you present the relationships you discover in your analysis.

Subject

When you write a causal analysis, you will need to carefully consider your choice of subject. As we have discussed, determining causes and effects can be extremely tricky, and you can find yourself in deep water if you do not sharply focus your topic. For a short paper, you cannot expect to do more than discuss one immediate and one remote cause (or effect). A topic based on your personal experience and observation will be among the most manageable. Topics discussing current events may also prove useful if you are careful to limit your scope. Geopolitical issues such as the economy or the environment require extensive research and are generally too large to handle except in a long paper or a book.

Look at the topics the writers in this chapter chose and consider how they limited their scope and focus to make them manageable. Jack E. White tackles the huge and prickly topic of racism in "Growing Up in Black and White," but he manages it in a relatively short essay by restricting the scope to his own family and the focus to his young daughter. John M. Williams explores the causes for the new visibility of disabled people in advertising but does not focus on a general discussion of disability issues. In "Right Here, Write Now," Susan K. Perry focuses solely on the health benefits of journal writing. Margo Monteith and Jeffrey Winters concentrate on the more immediate causes for xenophobia in their exploration of why people hate others, and Walt Mueller in "What's So Bad about Bullies?" restricts his discussion of behavioral issues regarding school-age children to the causes and effects of bullying. In "Girls Just Want to Be Mean," Margaret Talbot confines her discussion to "relationship aggression" in teenage girls. All of these writers have done some research, and all have deliberately focused their topics to make them manageable.

As you explore your subject, it may be helpful to know that logicians classify causes according to how important they are for producing an effect or how near in time or probability they are:

- *Primary cause*—the most important cause; may be the necessary cause or the sufficient cause, but need not be;
  - A *necessary* cause cannot produce an effect by itself, but it must be present if the effect is to occur.

    The engine of a car must be running for the car to move under its own power, but the crankshaft and the wheels must also turn (and other events must occur) to produce that effect. Just running the engine is not enough.

  - A *sufficient* cause can produce an effect by itself and does not require a contributory cause (see below). A sufficient cause may also be a necessary cause. There are relatively few sufficient causes.

    The fertilization of an egg by a sperm produces pregnancy. That is all it takes. This cause is also necessary because the effect (pregnancy) cannot occur without it.

- *Contributory cause*—the most common type of cause; cannot produce an effect by itself, and a particular effect might occur without the presence of a contributory cause;

    Reading is an important skill for learning, but other factors also contribute to learning, such as intelligence, opportunity, and so on. Furthermore, a person may learn even if he or she cannot read.

- *Immediate cause*—the cause closest in time to the effect;
- *Remote cause*—a cause at some distance in time from the effect or one that is less likely.

A similar kind of scheme can be used to classify effects:

- *Primary effect*—the most important result;
- *Secondary effect*—other results that derived from the primary and contributory cause(s);
- *Immediate effect*—the effect closest in time to the cause;
- *Remote effect*—the effect that manifested considerably later.

When causes and effects occur in a linked series, with the effect produced by a cause becoming the cause for another effect and so on, they are said to form a *causal chain.* For instance, you get a paycheck from your job that provides money, the money pays your rent, the rent provides shelter, the shelter keeps you safe so you can work, and so on.

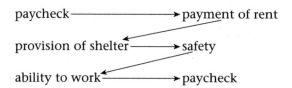

paycheck ————————→ payment of rent

provision of shelter ———→ safety

ability to work ←——————→ paycheck

Causal chains demonstrate how complex causal relationships can be.

The most common logical fallacies in causal analysis are assuming that because *x* happened before *y* that *x* is the cause of *y*, also referred to as *post hoc, ergo propter hoc*, and the *hasty generalization*. (See *Hodges'* 35f/*Writer's* 7i for more information.) *Post hoc, ergo propter hoc* is Latin for "After this, therefore because of this." For instance, a person who went to bed with wet hair and woke up with the flu might conclude that going to bed with wet hair caused him or her to be sick, not understanding that the cause of the flu is a virus. A *hasty generalization* is a conclusion drawn from too little evidence. For instance, if a person were to stand in the middle of a prairie and look around in all directions, he or she might conclude that mountains could not exist, but that would be to theorize without enough information.

To avoid fallacies and to make sure that you understand the correct relationships between events, you should maintain a healthy skepticism and remember that causes are almost always complex. Keeping that in mind, look at each situation to discover what events (or results) are likely to follow. Then look at each event to discover what probably made it happen. If you are careful and thorough, you should be able to avoid these common fallacies.

Purpose

Although cause-and-effect essays occasionally have a mainly expressive aim, emphasizing the writer's personal responses, usually they are intended to be informative or persuasive. An *informative* essay objectively focuses on causal relationships, simply as facts the reader will find useful or interesting. A *per-*

suasive essay explores causal relationships in order to sway the reader to the writer's point of view or to move the reader to some kind of action—for instance, to correct a particular condition that has undesirable effects. (See *Hodges'* 32a/*Writer's* 1e(1) for more information.)

Your thesis will stem from your purpose. A good thesis statement for a cause-and-effect analysis should include three elements:

- What your subject is and how you have limited it;
- Why you are analyzing it;
- What you think the pertinent causes and/or effects are.

Look at the thesis statement Jack E. White uses: "How had she [his three-year-old daughter] got that potentially soul-destroying idea ['Mommy, I want to be white'] and, even more important, what should we do about it?" (211). The essay that follows answers those questions and informs us, as well as White and his wife, of some important concerns in child-rearing. Monteith and Winters use two sentences for their thesis statement: "Despite our better nature, it seems, fear of foreigners or other strange-seeming people comes out when we are under stress. That fear, known as xenophobia, seems almost hardwired into the human psyche" (220). John M. Williams, Walt Mueller, and Margaret Talbot work with a single controlling idea in their essays. Williams focuses on the causes of the increasing visibility of disabled people in television commercials; Mueller discusses the harmful effects of bullying; and Talbot shows us how "Girls Just Want to Be Mean." All of these articles intend to inform us about specific issues, and some of them are also persuasive—particularly White's and Mueller's.

Audience

Considering the audience for your cause-and-effect analysis is not significantly different from considering it for any other mode of development. To reach your readers, you need to assess what they are like—whether they are young or old, whether they are specialists in the field you are examining, what their level of education probably is, and so on. When you have done that, you will know how much background information, if any, they will need in order to understand your points and perhaps act upon them. The primary difference between cause-and-effect analyses and essays using other methods of development is that you will probably need to consider more carefully than usual what your readers will expect you to say. For example, religion was very important to the original audience for Mueller's essay about bullying, and in his essay he discusses the importance of "Godly guidance and direction" (228), both for the bullied and for those who bully. If the topic of bullying were discussed in a sociological journal, on the other hand, Mueller's explicit references to God would not be appropriate, although more generalized references such as "guidance from one's religious faith" might be.

Organization

The focus you select for your causal analysis will in large part determine your organization. Generally speaking, cause-and-effect essays are organized chronologically or emphatically. If your causal analysis focuses on a discussion of immediate versus remote causes, you will probably want to select a chronological organization. That does not mean that you must keep to the strict time sequence you would follow for a process analysis; it does mean, however, that you should pay attention to which causes were more recent, perhaps precipitating, and which occurred earlier—perhaps even underlying the whole chain of events. If, however, you are mainly concerned with a primary cause, or even a necessary or sufficient cause, you will be more concerned with importance than with sequence and so you would probably choose an emphatic organization. For that, you would select the most or least important cause and then work up or down the scale of contributory causes.

Language and Style

Using qualifying words and phrases will help you avoid appearing dogmatic about the causes and effects you are discussing. There is a considerable difference between saying "Slavery was the inevitable cause of the Civil War" and "Slavery was one of the more important causes of the Civil War." The latter acknowledges that there were other causes that also contributed to igniting the conflict. Words such as *probably, may,* and *might* can help to tone down what might seem too assertive a stance.

If your purpose is to inform, you also want to keep your tone as objective as possible since you are striving for a neutral impression. That means keeping value words to a minimum—words such as *obviously, clearly,* or even *most important.* If, on the other hand, your purpose is to persuade, you will want to use such words. After all, you can hardly expect someone else to take a stance you yourself will not acknowledge. Always consider whether your tone is appropriate for your purpose and your audience.

Transitional words are especially useful in cause-and-effect essays. They help keep your reader on track, and focused throughout your argument. Some transitional words and phrases are *as a result, accordingly, because, brings about, consequently, hence, however, therefore,* and *thus.* Use them to help your reader see how you have reached your conclusions and how an effect follows from a cause (or vice versa).

Images

Images can be important for causal analysis. For example, consider the description of the causal chain on page 200. How helpful for your understanding of a causal chain was the diagram that accompanies it? Charts and graphs can help readers understand the data that you use to isolate causes and determine effects. They can also express their own causal relationships. Consider the advertisements in this chapter. Notice how effective the map in the GlobalWarmingAlert.org ad is for illustrating possible effects of global warming. Does the eDiets.com ad use visuals as effectively?

Student Essay

In the following essay, student Timothy Davis develops his analysis of causes and effects into an effective argument. Note especially how Davis addresses both the immediate and the remote causes of trade imbalances.

World Trade or World Charade?

Introduction

Context

Thesis

First cause-and-effect relationship

Specific example

Second cause-and-effect relationship

History books tell of the exotic Silk Road, a trade route from a thousand years ago, originating in eastern China and stretching all the way to Europe. More recently, financial pages tout the Magnificent Mile, a fiscally vibrant street of high-end retail shops and businesses along Chicago's lake front. These examples make one thing abundantly clear: trade is and historically has been a vital force in the world. The exchange of goods brings cultures together and stimulates economies. Today, world trade is a source of unprecedented wealth. Yet, even in our own country, this increased prosperity produces an increasing and unparalleled gap between the rich and the poor. This essay explores some of the causes of trade imbalances in the new world economy and explains their often devastating effects.

Corporate executives and financial speculators, those raking in the largest profits in the new world economy, are the most able to take big risks with investors' money, and they do, often at the expense of the average investor. Notorious, high-stakes gambling by Enron, for example, caused the company to go bankrupt. Besides the employees, the biggest losers were the average investors who were not as able to recuperate from such large-scale losses. Because there is no governing body large enough and powerful enough to force these corporations to act ethically and fairly with money that does not necessarily belong to them, their practices go unchecked. Average citizens, the millions who invest monthly for retirement purposes, stand to lose the most.

Agricultural subsidies, money offered by rich countries to protect their farmers during commodity fluctuations, artificially deflate prices and cause surpluses that eventually saturate world markets. These price supports are probably a good idea for stabilizing local or even regional markets but do not take into consideration the vast number of capital-poor countries that cannot afford to pay farmers when prices are low. Poor

continued

countries comprised of small farms cannot compete with the low prices and end up deeper in poverty as farmers harvest crops for pennies a pound.

Third cause-and-effect relationship

Similar to the effects of price supports, powerful multinational corporations use their monopolistic buying power to set low prices for the farmers in developing nations while maintaining obscenely high retail prices in other markets. Coffee is a classic example. Farmers in Mexico, Chile, and Peru are currently receiving five cents a pound for their coffee beans while, at the consumer end of things, Americans are now used to paying

Specific example

up to three dollars a cup for their favorite mocha latté.

Employment practices that work against mid-range and low-level wage earners are hurting the world's majority of workers. Unscrupulous employers looking to cut costs or turn a profit look first at labor costs. The result is that workers in the "new economy" have less job security than ever before. They are less likely to have union protection and are more vulnerable than ever to layoffs and plant closing. A new class of workers

Fourth cause-and-effect relationship

in America, dubbed the "working poor," face substandard working conditions, no paid vacations, no health insurance, and few benefits. Many are forced to work two and even three part-time jobs just to make ends meet. At the same time, corporate executive officers in multinational businesses secure record profits with large severance packages as safety nets. The gap between the "haves" and the "have-nots" is widening.

As described here, imbalances in money and power are resulting in the exploitation of the masses for the profit of the few. Yet, global trade

Conclusion echoes thesis

has the potential to be a positive force, one that brings countries and cultures together, raising the standard of living for millions living in poverty. It's time to recognize current trade practice as the charade it is and demand a more just system.

Commentary

Davis's essay is both an analysis of causes and effects and an argument calling for action. Davis begins by providing a context for the points he will make and quickly follows with a thesis that reveals his purpose. He then addresses four main cause-and-effect relationships: between unregulated use of investments and unethical use of investors' funds; between price supports and farm failures; between exploitation of third-world workers and excessive profits; and between unscrupulous labor practices and worker exploitation. Davis's conclusion then comments upon the potential long-term effects of such practices and calls upon the reader to act to prevent such abuses from continuing.

Davis analyzes causes and effects for a persuasive purpose—he wants something done to keep large predatory companies and organizations from profiting at the expense of the ordinary worker. To illustrate his points and to make the problem more immediate for the general reader, Davis makes use of specific and detailed examples. He points out that the problem exists both in this country and abroad. Since he is trying to persuade his audience, he uses words such as "obscenely high," "unscrupulous employers," and "charade" rather than an objective tone. His final paragraph returns to his thesis, that "imbalances in money and power are resulting in the exploitation of the masses for the profit of the few."

◆ CHECKLIST FOR WRITING CAUSE-AND-EFFECT ANALYSES

- What *subject* are you analyzing? Have you identified a basis for your analysis? If you analyze causes, have you identified effects? If you discuss effects, have you pointed out causes? (*Hodges'* 32e(4)/*Writer's* 2e(4))
- Can you identify *immediate causes* and *remote causes*? *Primary causes* and *contributory causes*?
- Is your *purpose* to persuade? To inform? To entertain? A blend? Can you state your specific purpose in a single sentence? (*Hodges'* 32a/*Writer's* 2a)
- Have you stated a *thesis* and focused your analysis around that statement? (*Hodges'* 32c/*Writer's* 2b)
- Have you checked your essay to be sure you have not fallen into any *logical fallacies*? (*Hodges'* 35f/*Writer's* 7i)
- Have you presented your causes/effects in a particular *order*? What is it, and why is it appropriate for your *purpose* and *audience*? (*Hodges'* 31b/*Writer's* 3c(3))
- Have you resolved any potential conflicts of interpretation?
- Do *transitional words and qualifiers* link the different parts of the essay? (*Hodges'* 31b/*Writer's* 3d)
- What is the purpose of your *conclusion*? (*Hodges'* 33b(2)/*Writer's* 3b(2))
- Have you used *images* to help clarify your analysis? (*Hodges'* 8b–c/*Writer's* 6a–b)

♦

AND HERE'S THE PITCH

John M. Williams

John M. Williams publishes *Assistive Technology News* and writes a bi-weekly assistive technology column for *Business Week Online.*

This essay was originally published in 1999 in *WE* magazine, a publication about disability issues.

1 There is a quiet, politically correct revolution taking place on our TV screens. It is led by more than 100 high-profile corporations eager to tap a new market and willing to cough up around $150 million in creative and developmental costs with major ad agencies to do so, according to *Advertising Age,* the industry's publication of record. Some are doing it to soften their hard-core image as greedy corporate monoliths. Others are aiming to attract new customers. They all recognize that the time is right to buck the ad industry's long-held tendency to show only "perfect" people on TV commercials.

2 What's up in ad land? Agencies are using people with a wide range of disabilities in TV spots, plugging everything from Internet search engines to Oreos. The emotionally charged commercials feature shopping, eating, using assistive technology in the workplace, traveling, playing, skiing, driving, drinking soft drinks, eating snacks, teaching, learning and doing the full range of activities that traditional ads have used. The commercials are running during prime time and top-rated sports events in major markets. They are getting high marks from industry insiders, consumers and advocates in the disability movement for the indelible, positive images of ability they portray and their contribution to the progress of mainstreaming.

3 The ads arrive on a breath of fresh air that is filling the sails of an industry so vast ($79.3 billion a year in the U.S. in 1998 and growing at an 8.3% clip each year, with $1.92 billion a year in Internet advertising alone, according to a recent report from PricewaterhouseCoopers) that it takes quite a breeze to get it moving on a new course. With a few notable exceptions—the classic DuPont spot of over a decade ago that featured double amputee Bill Demby on the basketball court stands out—agencies and marketing experts have stayed close to the shoreline on the issue of showing people with disabilities. This reflects their adherence to the received wisdom that only the image of the ideal, as determined by demographic studies, now outdated, could move product. "Madison Avenue has always been scared of alienating the largest population in the country and so has always been behind the social times," admits Thomas Learner, a 15-year veteran of the industry. "We were creative in our messages, but we believed our audience was the same—white, able-bodied and perfect. I was Wall Street accounts during an era when we did not show a black person in an ad. When we did, we

sanitized them. To show a disabled person using products went against the mainstream Madison Avenue's paternalistic view."

The social and economic crosscurrents propelling this change are 4 known to the vanguard of the disability community, but are still news to marketing experts. One important motive is the dire need for corporations to discover new markets, and the recognition that the 54 million Americans with disabilities have never been targeted in campaigns as rigorous and sophisticated as those used to reach smaller minority groups based on ethnicity or gender. The ads, which follow the paradigmatic shift from cause to customer marketing as pioneered by business strategy expert Jeannette Harvey, show that corporate America is waking up to the power of people with disabilities as consumers and borrowers. A second force is the rapid rise to social acceptability, and higher visibility, of celebrities, athletes and business leaders with disabilities. Cynics say that this is coupled with the need to clean up corporate images and present an aspect that is more caring and human. The fourth element is the movement toward reality and the use of actual people with experiences closer to our own in an effort to shake up the typical uptopian expectations of what an ad will show and hold up the mirror to who we are.

The multimillion-dollar campaigns that massive corporations launch— 5 as a rule of thumb, ad budgets equal between 3% and 10% of annual sales, and the world's leading advertiser, Procter & Gamble, spends over $5 billion annually—are moving rapidly into these waters. Just ask David Matthews, senior manager in charge of affirmative action at Nabisco, a food giant based in Parsippany, New Jersey, with $8 billion in sales, that is running a terrific new spot featuring a hard-of-hearing kid enjoying Oreos. He notes, "I think society's attitude toward people with disabilities has changed. The ADA has had impact in this field. We see more people with disabilities in the mainstream, and because we do, they are no longer the invisible consumers." Ann Smith, a company spokesperson, says, "We use people with disabilities in our Oreo ads because the message has impact. A commercial showing a deaf child signing to his mother communicates the power of the moment."

One of the real success stories has been a great spot for Internet search 6 engine Snap.com, launched earlier this year to combat the wacky, bold commercials of rival Yahoo. To make users feel better and smarter than Yahoo-types, Snap.com turned to the concept of people helping people. A talented NBC scriptwriter named Mark Bennett, whose experience with an autistic relative gave him a window into the world of disability, created a touching ad in which a deaf boy boards a school bus in the morning and sits alone, under the watchful eye of a classmate who rushes to the computer that evening to learn how to sign so that on the ride the next morning they can communicate. One decision was a snap: Casting insisted that an actual deaf child star in the ad. As Bertina Ciccerelli, an NBC exec, says, "We took the high road. We wanted realism in the ad, and we achieved it." After the ad ran during NBC's prime time at the breaks in *Dateline* and *Providence,* Snap.com was deluged with thousands of positive responses from the hard-of-hearing community.

7   By the year 2000, the spending power of people with disabilities will reach the trillion-dollar mark. That's enough to catch the interest of auto-motive giant GM, where the disability angle is the frontier in a demographic landscape that has been mapped, sliced and diced so finely when it comes to minorities that it is a wonder there was this large a chunk left. Ken Tre-genza, employment relations administrator at General Motors, Detroit, says, "Using people with disabilities in ads is becoming part of our institutional-ized thinking at GM and of course we see it at other companies. We now recognize there is a market out there for accessible vans and other products. We recognize them as consumers." Keeping up the pace, Saturn, Ford and Chrysler have also turned to ads featuring people with disabilities.

8   Beyond Nabisco, Microsoft and the Big Three, ads have either appeared or are in the works at IBM, McDonald's, AT&T, Bell Atlantic, Pacific Bell, Chevron, Campbell's, Target, Gatorade, Nike, VISA, General Mills, Wal-Mart, K-Mart, Coca Cola, Pepsi, Disney, Hallmark, DuPont, JC Penney, Sears, Bank of America, The Gap, Charles Schwab, Starbucks, NationsBank and Unum. Ad industry insiders, including sources at NW Ayers, J. Walter Thompson and BBDO, three of the major agencies, project that the current ads are only the tip of the iceberg.

9   Change of this magnitude usually comes from the top. Getting the CEO's commitment to use people with disabilities counts for winning more than half the battle, particularly in a tradition-bound field such as advertis-ing where the rank and file have to be kicked and dragged into giving up their familiar fare. Charles Schwab's name is on the door, and he happens to have a disability (dyslexia), so it is not surprising that the brokerage's ads, including one very powerful spot currently running that features a blind in-vestor, are disability friendly. Another force is the focus groups composed either of people with disabilities or those who work with them. Eventually, their responses make it to the small screen. "We must develop ads that in-clude disabled people in the mainstream of the community's perception of the abilities a disabled person has," says Tregenza. "Our ads cannot be so narrow that they only appeal to disabled consumers. The able-bodied popu-lation must be able to identify with the product being promoted, too."

10   The ratings are already coming in, and the scores are high. McDonald's, one of the first companies to show people signing in their ads, reports a marked increase in business from the blind, hard-of-hearing and wheelchair-using public. K-Mart and Wal-Mart have reported similar increases in their stores. It also shows in their hiring. McDonald's note that more than 70 per-cent of their restaurant managers report hiring a disabled worker. "We value our customers and workers with disabilities. We have gained from using people with disabilities in our ads, and we are better and stronger for doing so," says Rogercarole Rogers of McDonald's. Microsoft, GM, Boeing, Wal-Mart, K-Mart, IBM are inundated with resumes from people with disabilities applying for jobs. At IBM, Paul Luther, a specialist in assistive technology based in Austin, Texas, says, "When we advertise people with disabilities using our products, we sell more of those products."

One of the most dramatic instances of the direct lift given to brand 11
awareness by an ad featuring people with disabilities came from a spot for
U.S. Robotics featuring the great astrophysicist Stephen Hawking. According
to Michael Diedrich of the boutique advertising firm Leap Frog, when U.S.
Robotics conducted the "pre-post" study to measure impact, it showed that
over the course of just four months after the ads appeared, brand awareness
leaped from 36 percent to 48 percent, an increase that Diedrich calls "significant." In the all-important category of recall, the jump from 52 percent to 67
percent was considered by Diedrich to be (excuse the pun) astronomical. The
positive effect on brand awareness was directly traced to a similar dramatic
increase in advertising awareness, which jumped from 19 percent to 39 percent. Diedrich, who created the campaign, was ecstatic. "Talk about a break-
through! These are tremendous gains, particularly in light of the loud 'noise'
in the modem category of late. In short, the results are phenomenal."

The community's response to using the ads is enormous and positive. 12
Companies receive hundreds and sometimes thousands of favorable letters
from people with disabilities, and their parents, relatives and friends after
an ad is shown. Smith says, "People tell us in their letters they remember
our ads with disabled people in them because it shows a special bond between the people in the ads. Their responses are what we are looking for."
When DuPont debuted the Bill Demby basketball spots in 1987, the thousands of letters they received in the first week prompted the company to
pull the rest of its other commercials for an entire season.

Just about the only downside to the trend is grumbling from those in 13
the disability community who find the images too glossy and upbeat. The
executive director of a well-known national service organization in the Midwest, speaking on condition of anonymity, complains, "There is a problem
showing the positive images of disabled people on TV. In raising money, we
appeal to the paternalism of the giver. If that paternalism is not there, we
have more trouble raising money to find cures." But the United Way, beset
by a bout of bad publicity amid charges of corruption five years ago, made a
comeback with a series of TV ads that depict the people with disabilities
who have been the beneficiaries of their funding. Audience studies showed
a marked increase in the reputation of United Way for doing so, according
to Mario Pellegrini, who writes and directs the ads for Vital Productions.
They run as public service announcements during broadcasts of NFL games
as well as in movie theaters.

The darker side to the phenomenon is the latent fear of reprisal from a 14
minority group that, so far, has not been known for its consumer activism.
In the boardrooms of major American companies, memories of the ethnic
boycots of the '60s die hard. While most disability advocacy groups focus
their attention on government, the prospect of pickets in wheelchairs,
backed by family and friends, is daunting. A bitter foretaste of how this
could happen was experienced a decade ago when country and western
singer Mel Tellis, who stutters, was used in a humorous ad campaign by
Petrofina promoting oil and gas products. The backlash from disability

organizations was fast and furious, and the ads were pulled within a week, in part because of the picketing and boycots. That kind of painfully negative spin is yet another reason to keep the new ad campaigns disability-friendly. As they say on Madison Avenue, where disability is hot, we'll run it up the flagpole and see who salutes.

Rhetorical Considerations

1. This essay was published in a magazine about disabilities. Would it require any changes to be published for a more general audience? Why or why not? (*Hodges'* 32a/*Writer's* 1e)
2. To what extent does this essay focus on causes and effects? (*Hodges'* 32e/*Writer's* 2e)
3. Does the author reveal any bias toward the subject he discusses? Explain. (*Hodges'* 35c/*Writer's* 7c)
4. Does the author use adequate examples? Are they well selected?
5. Is Williams's comparison of the depiction of the disabled in advertising to that of ethnic minorities appropriate? Why or why not? (*Hodges'* 32e/*Writer's* 2e)

Language and Style

1. How many acronyms can you find in this essay? Does Williams identify all of them? Why or why not? (*Hodges'* 11e/*Writer's* 39e)
2. How many different disabilities does Williams refer to specifically? How does he refer to them? Does he use language you are accustomed to? Is his language "politically correct"? (*Hodges'* 19c/*Writer's* 28c)
3. Look up the following words in your dictionary: *monoliths* (paragraph 1); *paradigmatic* (paragraph 4); *beneficiaries* (paragraph 13); *boycotts* (paragraph 14). (*Hodges'* 19e/*Writer's* 28e)
4. Find all the pronouns in the third sentence of paragraph 6. Are they in the correct case and number? (*Hodges'* 5 and 6b/*Writer's* 21d)
5. Identify the subject and the predicate in the first sentence of paragraph 9. (*Hodges'* 1b/*Writer's* 16a)

Writing Suggestions

1. Watch television over a period of a few days and observe the commercials shown during a specific time (after school, during sports events, etc.). Describe how well the commercials reflect their intended audience. Do they show the viewers as they are or as they want to be?
2. Write an essay in which you discuss the effect on you of increased visibility in the popular culture of a particular group (having a specific disability, religion, ethnicity, sexual orientation, etc.).

♦

GROWING UP IN BLACK AND WHITE

Jack E. White

Jack White, author of the "Dividing Line" column and national correspondent for *Time* magazine, is the first African-American journalist to
rise to the high-ranking positions of nation editor for *Time* and senior
producer for domestic news for ABC News' *World News Tonight,* as well as
the first to become a columnist for a national newsweekly. His articles
have appeared in the *Columbia Journalism Review,* the *Progressive, Ebony
Magazine,* and *Our World News,* an online version of a forthcoming black-
controlled national newspaper. Among his numerous journalism awards
are the National Association of Black Journalists' First Place for Magazines, the Griot Award from the New York Association of Black Journalists, and the Unity Award from Lincoln University for commentary.

A native of North Carolina, White attended Swarthmore College
and in 1976–1977 was a Nieman Fellow at Harvard University with a
concentration on African affairs and American ethnic politics. He is
married and the father of three sons and a daughter.

"Mommy, I want to be white." 1

Imagine my wife's anguish and alarm when our beautiful brown- 2
skinned three-year-old daughter made that declaration. We thought we were
doing everything right to develop her self-esteem and positive racial identity. We overloaded her toy box with black dolls. We carefully monitored
the racial content of TV shows and videos, ruling out *Song of the South* and
Dumbo, two classic Disney movies marred by demeaning black stereotypes.
But we saw no harm in *Pinocchio* which seemed as racially benign as *Sesame
Street* or *Barney* and a good deal more engaging. Yet now our daughter was
saying she wanted to be white, to be like the puppet who becomes a real
boy in the movie. How had she got that potentially soul-destroying idea
and, even more important, what should we do about it?

That episode was an unsettling reminder of the unique burden that 3
haunts black parents in America: helping their children come to terms with
being black in a country where the message too often seems to be that being
white is better. Developing a healthy self-image would be difficult enough
for black children with all the real-life reminders that blacks and whites are
still treated differently. But it is made even harder by the seductive racial
bias in TV, movies and children's books, which seem to link everything
beautiful and alluring with whiteness while often treating blacks as after-
thoughts. Growing up in this all-pervading world of whiteness can be psychologically exhausting for black children just as they begin to figure out
who they are. As a four-year-old boy told his father after spending another

day in the overwhelmingly white environment of his Connecticut daycare facility, "Dad, I'm tired of being black."

4   In theory it should now be easier for children to develop a healthy sense of black pride than it was during segregation. In 1947 psychologists Kenneth and Mamie Clark conducted a famous experiment that demonstrated just how much black children had internalized the hatred that society directed at their race. They asked 253 black children to choose between four dolls, two black and two white. The result: two-thirds of the children preferred white dolls.

5   The conventional wisdom had been that black self-hatred was a by-product of discrimination that would wither away as society became more tolerant. Despite the civil rights movement of the 1960s, the black-is-beautiful movement of the '70s, the proliferation of black characters on television shows during the '80s and the renascent black nationalist movement of the '90s, the pro-white message has not lost its power. In 1985 psychologist Darlene Powell-Hopson updated the Clarks' experiment using black and white Cabbage Patch dolls and got a virtually identical result: 65% of the black children preferred white dolls. "Black is dirty," one youngster explained. Powell-Hopson thinks the result would be the same if the test were repeated today.

6   Black mental-health workers say the trouble is that virtually all the progress the U.S. has made toward racial fairness has been in one direction. To be accepted by whites, blacks have to become more like them, while many whites have not changed their attitudes at all. Study after study has shown that the majority of whites, for all the commitment to equality they espouse, still consider blacks to be inferior, undesirable and dangerous. "Even though race relations have changed for the better, people maintain those old stereotypes," says Powell-Hopson. "The same racial dynamics occur in an integrated environment as occurred in segregation; it's just more covert."

7   Psychiatrists say children as young as two can pick up these damaging messages, often from subtle signals of black inferiority unwittingly embedded in children's books, toys and TV programs designed for the white mainstream. There are many more positive images about black people in the media than there used to be, but there's still a lot that says that white is more beautiful and powerful than black, that white is good and black is bad, says James P. Comer, a Yale University psychiatrist who collaborated with fellow black psychiatrist Alvin F. Poussaint on *Raising Black Children* (Plume).

8   The bigotry is not usually as blatant as in Roald Dahl's *Charlie and the Chocolate Factory*. When the book was published in 1964, the *New York Times* called it a "richly inventive and humorous tale." Blacks didn't see anything funny about having the factory staffed by "Oompaoompas," pygmy workers imported in shipping cartons from the jungle where they had been living in the trees.

9   Today white-controlled companies are doing a better job of erasing racially loaded texts from children's books and movies. But those messages still get through, in part because they are at times so subtle even a specialist like Powell-Hopson misses them. She recently bought a book about a cat for

her six-year-old daughter, who has a love of felines. Only when Powell-Hopson got home did she discover that the beautiful white cat in the story turns black when it starts behaving badly. Moreover, when the products are not objectionable, they are sometimes promoted in ways that unintentionally drive home the theme of black inferiority. Powell-Hopson cites a TV ad for dolls that displayed a black version in the background behind the white model "as though it were a second-class citizen."

Sadly, black self-hatred can also begin at home. Even today, says Powell- 10
Hopson, "many of us perpetuate negative messages, showing preference for lighter complexions, saying nappy hair is bad and straight hair is good, calling other black people 'niggers,' that sort of thing." This danger can be greater than the one posed by TV and the other media because children learn so much by simple imitation of the adults they are closest to. Once implanted in a toddler's mind, teachers and psychologists say, such misconceptions can blossom into a full-blown racial identity crisis during adolescence, affecting everything from performance in the classroom to a youngster's susceptibility to crime and drug abuse. But they can be neutralized if parents react properly.

In their book, Comer and Poussaint emphasize a calm and straightfor- 11
ward approach. They point out that even black children from affluent homes in integrated neighborhoods need reassurance about racial issues because from their earliest days they sense that their lives are "viewed cheaply by white society." If, for example, a black little girl says she wishes she had straight blond hair, they advise parents to point out "in a relaxed and unemotional manner . . . that she is black and that most black people have nice curly black hair, and that most white people have straight hair, brown, blond, black. At this age what you convey in your voice and manner will either make it O.K. or make it a problem."

Powell-Hopson, who along with her psychologist husband Derek, has 12
written *Different and Wonderful: Raising Black Children in a Race-Conscious Society* (Fireside), takes a more aggressive approach, urging black parents in effect to inoculate their children against negative messages at an early age. For example, the authors suggest that African-American parents whose children display a preference for white dolls or action figures should encourage them to play with a black one by "dressing it in the best clothes, or having it sit next to you, or doing anything you can think of to make your child sense that you prefer that doll." After that, the Hopsons say, the child can be offered a chance to play with the toy, on the condition that "you promise to take the very best care of it. You know it is my favorite." By doing so, the Hopsons claim, "most children will jump at a chance to hold the toy even for a second."

White children are no less vulnerable to racial messages. Their reactions 13
can range from a false sense of superiority over blacks to an identification with sports superstars like Michael Jordan so complete that they want to become black. But if white parents look for guidance from popular child-care manuals, they won't find any. "I haven't included it because I don't feel like an expert in that area," says T. Berry Brazelton, author of *Infants and Mothers*

and other child-care books. "I think it's a very, very serious issue that this country hasn't faced up to." Unless it does, the U.S. runs the risk of rearing another generation of white children crippled by the belief that they are better than blacks and black children who agree.

14   As for my daughter, we're concerned but confident. As Comer says, "In the long run what children learn from their parents is more powerful than anything they get from any other source." When my little girl expressed the wish to be white, my wife put aside her anguish and smilingly replied that she is bright and black and beautiful, a very special child. We'll keep telling her that until we're sure she loves herself as much as we love her.

Rhetorical Considerations

1. White establishes the context for "Growing Up in Black and White" in paragraph 1. What event occasioned the essay and what were the circumstances surrounding that event? (*Hodges'* 32a/*Writer's* 1e)
2. What is White's main point and where does he state it? How is information about the relative numbers of positive black and white images related to the main idea? How is information about approaches to parenting related to the main idea? (*Hodges'* 32c/*Writer's* 2b)
3. Pointing to specific evidence in the essay, comment on White's purpose in "Growing Up in Black and White." To what extent can the essay be said to be expressive, informative, or persuasive? (*Hodges'* 32a/*Writer's* 1e)
4. White indicates a number of causes, both immediate and remote, that contribute to the negative image of blackness that many African Americans internalize. What are three of these causes? Which does White identify as immediate and which as remote? (*Hodges'* 32e/*Writer's* 2e)
5. For what kind of audience would you say White is writing? Does anything in the essay reveal or suggest the intended audience? Be specific. Might any particular group or groups find the essay offensive? If so, which, and why? (*Hodges'* 32a/*Writer's* 1e)
6. What devices does White use to achieve coherence in paragraph 6? Paragraph 12? (*Hodges'* 31b/*Writer's* 3c–d and 4)

Language and Style

1. Look up *O.K.* (paragraph 11) in at least three different dictionaries (such as *Webster's Collegiate Dictionary*, the *American Heritage Dictionary*, or the *Random House Dictionary*). What does each give as the word's origin? Do any of the dictionaries comment on usage? If so, which ones, and what do they say? (*Hodges'* 19e/*Writer's* 28e)
2. In this essay White uses three different terms to refer to black people. Identify each of these terms and justify its use in its context. Is this usage racist? Why or why not? (*Hodges'* 19c/*Writer's* 28c)
3. What is the grammatical function of the infinitive phrase *To be accepted by whites* in the second sentence of paragraph 6? Of *embedded* in the first sentence of paragraph 7? (*Hodges'* 1f/*Writer's* 17a)

4. In the second sentence of paragraph 7, the subject and the verb appear not to agree. Is there in fact a problem? If so, what is it? If not, why not? (*Hodges'* 6a/*Writer's* 22e)
5. How many separate simple sentences can you derive from the third sentence of paragraph 11? Has White gained anything by combining all these ideas in a single sentence? If so, what? If not, why not? (*Hodges'* 1e/*Writer's* 16d)

Writing Suggestions

1. Write an essay in which you identify at least two influences in society that positively or negatively affected your own upbringing.
2. White describes how subtle elements in our society conspire to foster an unhealthy self-image in African-American children. Write an essay in which you identify, describe, and explain the effect of such an element or combination of elements in your own life or in that of a person you know well. (An emphasis on being thin or on keeping a stiff upper lip could be examples of such elements.)

♦

RIGHT HERE, WRITE NOW

Susan K. Perry

Susan K. Perry, Ph.D., is the author of *Writing in Flow: Keys to Enhanced Creativity* (1999) and a number of books on parenting. This essay was first published in *Psychology Today*.

1 Babette Williams always knew she'd write her life story someday. But her life kept getting in the way. She sold real estate and bred show horses, married four times and raised three daughters. At 71, Williams finally started writing short stories and a memoir, interspersing her works with animal tales and wry vignettes about married life. She has a natural flair for clear writing. "I'm having a blast," she says.

2 Williams isn't alone. Many people want to write, and the funny secret is, anyone can write. We all have the ability. But people often put off setting pen to paper because it can seem just too intimidating. Writing takes time and work, and it's often hard to find hours for writing in a normal, busy schedule.

3 The rewards are so great, however, that you should not wait until you retire to express yourself. Writing provides a host of emotional and physical benefits that can enrich your life. And it is never too late—or too early—to begin.

4 It's long been known that writing can have a huge effect on one's sense of well-being. Writing has certainly helped me. When I knew my youngest son would be leaving for college, I began an empty nest journal. By recording and reflecting on my emotional state, I was better able to cope with the actual event when it occurred. People who write fiction convert their life experiences, no matter how painful, into stories that can help the writers make sense of them.

5 Writing is also a good way to leave behind a more accurate record of your life. A student of mine recently told me the poignant reason she felt an urge to write about her life now, not later. When her mother died, she ransacked the house seeking some kind of message, something in writing that would offer her one last bit of connection. There was nothing.

6 Often writing can help provide a purpose in difficult experiences. The process allows you to reach out and share those experiences with others. For example, the parents of Lo Detrich were devastated when Lo was diagnosed with cystic fibrosis as an infant. By the time she was 15, however, her parents had learned so much about the illness that they wrote a book, *The Spirit of Lo*. The parents hoped that people dealing with the same types of issues could benefit from the shared experiences.

Writing about important life matters may even make it easier for you to 7 access your memories. Kitty Klein, Ph.D., a researcher at North Carolina State University, led a study demonstrating that writing frees up working memory. She reports in the *Journal of Experimental Psychology* that people who were asked to write expressively about stressful events experience significant gains in their working memories when compared with subjects who were told to write about trivial events.

Researchers once believed that the main benefits of writing were purely 8 psychological. But there is new evidence of the health value of forming coherent stories out of the chaotic elements of your personal history. In the *Journal of Clinical Psychology,* James Pennebaker, Ph.D., and Janet Seagal, Ph.D., of the University of Texas at Austin, report that people who write about personal details are healthier than those who don't.

In one of their studies, Pennebaker and Seagal asked groups of students 9 to write about an assigned topic for 15 minutes on four consecutive days. Later in the year, the students were asked about their health: the students who had written about emotional topics had far fewer doctors' visits. "Having a narrative is similar to completing a job, allowing one to essentially forget the event," Pennebaker concludes. Once you take your most pressing memories and put them into story format, "the mind doesn't have to work as hard to bring meaning to them."

Other physiological benefits have been documented. Researchers led by 10 Joshua M. Smyth, Ph.D., studied 112 patients suffering from either asthma or rheumatoid arthritis and who wrote in a journal every day. In 1999 Smyth and his colleagues reported in the *Journal of the American Medical Association* that writing about stressful life experiences had a beneficial effect on symptoms.

Go With The Flow

One way to increase these health benefits is to learn how to write more flu- 11 idly and with less angst and frustration. When you're engaged with what you're doing, the rest of the world recedes. The poet David St. John describes this experience: "When I'm working, I don't know how much time has elapsed. It really is becoming part of some pulse, other than yourself."

This altered state is known as flow. Psychologist Mihaly M. Csikszent- 12 mihalyi, Ph.D., of the Peter Drucker School of Management at Claremont Graduate University has studied the phenomenon for more than two decades and has even written several books on the subject. In one of his earliest studies, Csikszentmihalyi provided teens with beepers and diaries to record how engaged they felt in a variety of activities. Some individuals, he found, are good at learning to tap into flow regardless of what they're doing. With practice you may learn to control your ability to enter such a frame of mind.

And if you write more often, you may raise the odds of producing a mas- 13 terpiece. Research by psychologist Dean Simonton, Ph.D., shows that the more works an artist produces over a lifetime, the more likely it is that great works are created.

14 Of course, not everyone can turn out a book every year. Many people struggle half a lifetime to finish a single short story. Why do some people have a hard time writing? Figuring out how to put your thoughts into written words may be one constraint, but you might also be concerned with other fears. What if someone gets upset with you for writing this? What if you don't know enough about this subject?

The Write Ritual

15 Such constraints and fears may add up to what is called writer's block. It can happen to anyone, but successful writers have learned not to panic. Here are some suggestions that may help you reframe your nonwriting periods and figure out what you need to do before you continue writing:

- Set reasonable goals. Giving yourself a daunting task, such as "I will write the story of my life and appear on *Oprah*," is antithetical to the writing process. It is better to trivialize the task and realize that no single writing session really matters.
- Increase your knowledge of your subject. Search the Internet or go to the library to look for more details you can add to your story.
- Take risks. When Suzanne Greenberg, an assistant professor at California State University at Long Beach, researched risk-taking in creative writing, she found that many people are afraid of the repercussions of saying something honest. "It's an emotional stretch to really look at life and see all its gray areas," she says. Remember: Even though writing can sometimes feel risky, you're not really risking anything in the writing. Take a chance.
- Visualize your ideal reader. Don't picture an old boyfriend saying, "Who'd want to read that stuff?" Instead, imagine a writing buddy or a good friend who appreciates the efforts you make and never puts you down.
- Find a ritual or routine to help you through the process. Sometimes the hardest part of writing is deciding if it's worth the effort this time. But if you simply follow a pattern, it becomes automatic. As mystery author Sue Grafton explains, "I think part of the issue is presenting yourself for the task. So I show up at my desk at 9 o'clock every morning. I think your internal process needs to be geared to the fact that you will show up for work at a certain time every day."
- Remain focused on what's important and filter out irrelevant things. "The feeling that people have of being overwhelmed is verifiable in the lab," says Ronald Kellogg, Ph.D., of the University of Missouri at Rolla and author of *The Psychology of Writing* and *Cognitive Psychology*. To eliminate the confusion, Kellogg recommends outlining and prioritizing your ideas.
- Organize your thoughts. If you find yourself struggling to get words down, you might try an informal organizing device such as clustering, where you splatter information about your topic on a large sheet of paper.

- Change something about what you're doing. If you're stuck, try to write something else, perhaps in a different genre. Or find an anecdote that makes you laugh. Putting this down on paper may revive your interest in the subject.

So go ahead, you have nothing to lose and a happier, healthier life to gain. 16

Rhetorical Considerations

1. Perry uses many examples. What kinds of examples does she include and why is the variety important? (*Hodges'* 32e/*Writer's* 2e)
2. In paragraph 2 Perry maintains that "anyone can write." How do you interpret this statement? (*Hodges'* 35d/*Writer's* 7h)
3. Does Perry focus on any particular kind of writing? If so, what kind? If not, what different kinds does she mention? (*Hodges'* 31c/*Writer's* 2d)
4. What stumbling blocks does Perry perceive the reader might encounter in trying to write about traumatic or emotional events? (*Hodges'* 31c/*Writer's* 2d)
5. What is the purpose of the final section of the essay? (*Hodges'* 33b/*Writer's* 3b)

Language and Style

1. Look up the following words in your dictionary: *interspersing* (paragraph 1); *poignant* (paragraph 5); *angst* (paragraph 11); *antithetical* (paragraph 15). (*Hodges'* 19e/*Writer's* 28e)
2. Find examples of casual language. What effect do these words have on your reading of the essay? (*Hodges'* 19c/*Writer's* 28c)
3. What is the effect of using the contraction *It's* in paragraph 4? (*Hodges'* 19c/*Writer's* 28c)
4. Find three transitions between paragraphs. (*Hodges'* 31d/*Writer's* 3d)
5. What is the subject of the second sentence in paragraph 15? (*Hodges'* 1b/*Writer's* 16a)

Writing Suggestions

1. Write a cause-and-effect essay about how you engaged in some activity (reading, writing, overeating, or exercise, for instance) to make it through a difficult period in your life. Would you use that method again, and would you recommend it to others? Why or why not?
2. Write an essay in which you propose that your reader engage in a regular activity in order to improve psychologically and/or physiologically.

WHY WE HATE

Margo Monteith and Jeffrey Winters

Margo Monteith earned her PhD from the University of Wisconsin, Madison, and is an associate professor of psychology at the University of Kentucky. Her research focuses on the area of stereotyping and prejudice. Jeffrey Winters is a New York-based science writer.

1   Balbir Singh Sodhi was shot to death on September 15 in Mesa, Arizona. His killer claimed to be exacting revenge for the terrorist attacks of September 11. Upon his arrest, the murderer shouted, "I stand for America all the way." Though Sodhi wore a turban and could trace his ancestry to South Asia, he shared neither ethnicity nor religion with the suicide hijackers. Sodhi—who was killed at the gas station where he worked—died just for being different in a nation gripped with fear.

2   For Arab and Muslim Americans, the months after the terrorist attacks have been trying. They have been harassed at work and their property has been vandalized. An Arab San Francisco shop owner recalled with anger that his five-year-old daughter was taunted by name-callers. Classmates would yell "terrorist" as she walked by.

3   Public leaders from President George W. Bush on down have called for tolerance. But the Center for American-Islamic Relations in Washington, D.C., has tallied some 1,700 incidents of abuse against Muslims in the five months following September 11. Despite our better nature, it seems, fear of foreigners or other strange-seeming people comes out when we are under stress. That fear, known as xenophobia, seems almost hardwired into the human psyche.

4   Researchers are discovering the extent to which xenophobia can be easily—even arbitrarily—turned on. In just hours, we can be conditioned to fear or discriminate against those who differ from ourselves by characteristics as superficial as eye color. Even ideas we believe are just common sense can have deep xenophobic underpinnings. Research conducted this winter at Harvard reveals that even among people who claim to have no bias, the more strongly one supports the ethnic profiling of Arabs at airport-security checkpoints, the more hidden prejudice one has against Muslims.

5   But other research shows that when it comes to whom we fear and how we react, we do have a choice. We can, it seems, choose not to give in to our xenophobic tendencies.

The Melting Pot

6   America prides itself on being a melting pot of cultures, but how we react to newcomers is often at odds with that self-image. A few years ago, psychol-

ogist Markus Kemmelmeier, Ph.D., now at the University of Nevada at Reno, stuck stamped letters under the windshield wipers of parked cars in a suburb of Detroit. Half were addressed to a fictitious Christian organization, half to a made-up Muslim group. Of all the letters, half had little stickers of the American flag.

Would the addresses and stickers affect the rate at which the letters 7 would be mailed? Kemmelmeier wondered. Without the flag stickers, both sets of letters were mailed at the same rate, about 75 percent of the time. With the stickers, however, the rates changed: Almost all the Christian letters were forwarded, but only half of the Muslim letters were mailed. "The flag is seen as a sacred object," Kemmelmeier says. "And it made people think about what it means to be a good American."

In short, the Muslims didn't make the cut. 8

Not mailing a letter seems like a small slight. Yet in the last century, 9 there have been shocking examples of xenophobia in our own backyard. Perhaps the most famous in American history was the fear of the Japanese during World War II. This particular wave of hysteria led to the rise of slurs and bigoted depictions in the media, and more alarmingly, the mass internment of 120,000 people of Japanese ancestry beginning in 1942. The internments have become a national embarrassment: Most of the Japanese held were American citizens, and there is little evidence that the imprisonments had any real strategic impact.

Today the targets of xenophobia—derived from the Greek word for 10 *stranger*—aren't the Japanese. Instead, they are Muslim immigrants. Or Mexicans. Or Chinese. Or whichever group we have come to fear.

Just how arbitrary are these xenophobic feelings? Two famous public- 11 school experiments show how easy it is to turn one "group" against another. In the late 1960s, California high school history teacher Ron Jones recruited students to participate in an exclusive new cultural program called "the Wave." Within weeks, these students were separating themselves from others and aggressively intimidating critics. Eventually, Jones confronted the students with the reality that they were unwitting participants in an experiment demonstrating the power of nationalist movements.

A few years later, a teacher in Iowa discovered how quickly group dis- 12 tinctions are made. The teacher, Jane Elliott, divided her class into two groups—those with blue eyes and those with brown or green eyes. The brown-eyed group received privileges and treats, while the blue-eyed students were denied rewards and told they were inferior. Within hours, the once-harmonious classroom became two camps, full of mutual fear and resentment. Yet, what is especially shocking is that the students were only in the third grade.

Social Identity

The drive to completely and quickly divide the world into "us" and "them" is 13 so powerful that it must surely come from some deep-seated need. The exact identity of that need, however, has been subject to debate. In the 1970s, the late Henri Tajfel, Ph.D., of the University of Bristol in England, and John Turner, Ph.D., now of the Australian National University, devised a theory to explain the psychology behind a range of prejudices and biases, not just xenophobia. Their theory was based, in part, on the desire to think highly of oneself. One way to lift your self-esteem is to be part of a distinctive group, like a winning team; another is to play up the qualities of your own group and denigrate the attributes of others so that you feel your group is better.

14   Tajfel and Turner called their insight "social identity theory," which has proved valuable for understanding how prejudices develop. Given even the slenderest of criteria, we naturally split people into two groups—an "in-group" and an "out-group." The categories can be of geopolitical importance—nationality, religion, race, language—or they can be as seemingly inconsequential as handedness, hair color or even height.

15   Once the division is made, the inferences and projections begin to occur. For one, we tend to think more highly of people in the in-group than those in the out-group, a belief based only on group identity. Also, a person tends to feel that others in the in-group are similar to one's self in ways that—although stereotypical—may have little to do with the original criteria used to split the groups. Someone with glasses may believe that other people who wear glasses are more voracious readers—even more intelligent—than those who don't, in spite of the fact that all he really knows is that they don't see very well. On the other hand, people in the out-group are believed to be less distinct and less complex than are cohorts in the in-group.

16   Although Tajfel and Turner found that identity and categorization were the root cause of social bias, other researchers have tried to find evolutionary explanations for discrimination. After all, in the distant past, people who shared cultural similarities were found to be more genetically related than those who did not. Therefore, favoring the in-group was a way of helping perpetuate one's genes. Evolutionary explanations seem appealing, since they rely on the simplest biological urges to drive complicated behavior. But this fact also makes them hard to prove. Ironically, there is ample evidence backing up the "softer" science behind social identity theory.

Hidden Bias

17 Not many of us will admit to having strong racist or xenophobic biases. Even in cases where bias becomes public debate—such as the profiling of Arab Muslims at airport-security screenings—proponents of prejudice claim that they are merely promoting common sense. That reluctance to admit to bias makes the issue tricky to study.

18   To get around this problem, psychologists Anthony Greenwald, Ph.D., of the University of Washington in Seattle, and Mahzarin Banaji, Ph.D., of Harvard, developed the Implicit Association Test. The IAT is a simple test that measures reaction time: The subject sees various words or images projected on a screen, then classifies the images into one of two groups by pressing buttons. The words and images need not be racial or ethnic in nature—one group of researchers tested attitudes toward presidential candidates. The string of

images is interspersed with words having either pleasant or unpleasant connotations, then the participant must group the words and images in various ways—Democrats are placed with unpleasant words, for instance.

The differences in reaction time are small but telling. Again and again, 19 researchers found that subjects readily tie in-group images with pleasant words and out-group images with unpleasant words. One study compares such groups as whites and blacks, Jews and Christians, and young people and old people. And researchers found that if you identify yourself in one group, it's easier to pair images of that group with pleasant words—and easier to pair the opposite group with unpleasant imagery. This reveals the underlying biases and enables us to study how quickly they can form.

Really though, we need to know very little about a person to discrimi- 20 nate against him. One of the authors of this story, psychologist Margo Monteith, Ph.D., performed an IAT experiment comparing attitudes toward two sets of made-up names; one set was supposedly "American," the other from the fictitious country of Marisat. Even though the subjects knew nothing about Marisat, they showed a consistent bias against it.

While this type of research may seem out in left field, other work may 21 have more "real-world" applications. The Southern Poverty Law Center runs a Web version of the IAT that measures biases based on race, age and gender. Its survey has, for instance, found that respondents are far more likely to associate European faces, rather than Asian faces, with so-called American images. The implication being that Asians are seen as less "American" than Caucasians.

Similarly, Harvard's Banaji has studied the attitudes of people who favor 22 the racial profiling of Arab Muslims to deter terrorism, and her results run contrary to the belief that such profiling is not driven by xenophobic fears. "We show that those who endorse racial profiling also score high on both explicit and implicit measures of prejudice toward Arab Muslims," Banaji says. "Endorsement of profiling is an indicator of level of prejudice."

Beyond Xenophobia

If categorization and bias come so easily, are people doomed to xenophobia 23 and racism? It's pretty clear that we are susceptible to prejudice and that there is an unconscious desire to divide the world into "us" and "them." Fortunately, however, new research also shows that prejudices are fluid and that when we become conscious of our biases we can take active—and successful—steps to combat them.

Researchers have long known that when observing racially mixed 24 groups, people are more likely to confuse the identity of two black individuals or two white ones, rather than a white with a black. But Leda Cosmides, Ph.D., and John Tooby, Ph.D., of the Center for Evolutionary Psychology at the University of California at Santa Barbara, and anthropologist Robert Kurzban, Ph.D., of the University of California at Los Angeles, wanted to test whether this was innate or whether it was just an artifact of how society groups individuals by race.

25   To do this, Cosmides and her colleagues made a video of two racially integrated basketball teams locked in conversation, then they showed it to study participants. As reported in the *Proceedings of the National Academy of Sciences,* the researchers discovered that subjects were more likely to confuse two players on the same team, regardless of race, rather than two players of the same race on opposite teams.

26   Cosmides says that this points to one way of attacking racism and xenophobia: changing the way society imposes group labels. American society divides people by race and by ethnicity; that's how lines of prejudice form. But simple steps, such as integrating the basketball teams, can reset mental divisions, rendering race and ethnicity less important.

27   This finding supports earlier research by psychologists Samuel Gaertner, Ph.D., of the University of Delaware in Newark, and John Dovidio, Ph.D., of Colgate University in Hamilton, New York. Gaertner and Dovidio have studied how bias changes when members of racially mixed groups must cooperate to accomplish shared goals. In situations where team members had to work together, bias could be reduced by significant amounts.

28   Monteith has also found that people who are concerned about their prejudices have the power to correct them. In experiments, she told subjects that they had performed poorly on tests that measured belief in stereotypes. She discovered that the worse a subject felt about her performance, the better she scored on subsequent tests. The guilt behind learning about their own prejudices made the subjects try harder not to be biased.

29   This suggests that the guilt of mistaking individuals for their group stereotype—such as falsely believing an Arab is a terrorist—can lead to the breakdown of the belief in that stereotype. Unfortunately, such stereotypes are reinforced so often that they can become ingrained. It is difficult to escape conventional wisdom and treat all people as individuals, rather than members of a group. But that seems to be the best way to avoid the trap of dividing the world in two—and discriminating against one part of humanity.

Rhetorical Considerations

1. Why do the authors focus more on the plight of Muslims? Are they the only victims of xenophobia? (*Hodges'* 32a/*Writer's* 1e)
2. What is the significance of the historical examples cited in the essay? (*Hodges'* 31c/*Writer's* 2d)
3. The authors cite a variety of studies done on the causes and effects of xenophobia. What varieties are represented in terms of who conducted the study, where it was conducted, and what the focus population was? (*Hodges'* 32e/*Writer's* 2e)
4. Name three causes of xenophobia that the authors cite. (*Hodges'* 32e/*Writer's* 2e)
5. Is there any way of overcoming the kind of prejudice described in this essay? How? What do the authors accomplish by mentioning this possibility? (*Hodges'* 32e/*Writer's* 2e)

Language and Style

1. Look up the origins of the following words: *xenophobia* and *psyche* (paragraph 3); *hysteria* (paragraph 9). (*Hodges'* 19e/*Writer's* 28e)
2. What is the difference between an *immigrant* and an *emigrant*? (*Hodges'* 19e/*Writer's* 28e)
3. Justify (if possible) the sentence fragments in paragraph 10. (*Hodges'* 2c/ *Writer's* 18c)
4. Rewrite the fourth sentence of paragraph 15 to eliminate sexist language. (*Hodges'* 19d/*Writer's* 28d)

Writing Suggestions

1. Write about a time you felt uncomfortable because you were different from most of the people in a particular situation. The difference can be any factor: your age, your gender, your ethnic group, your religion, or some aspect of your physical makeup, for example.
2. Write an essay in which you examine one of your own prejudices, its origins, and how you might combat it.

♦

What's So Bad about Bullies?

Walt Mueller

Walt Mueller is president and founder of the Center for Parent/Youth Understanding, a Bible-based nonprofit organization that serves churches, schools, and community organizations around the world. Mueller is the author of *Understanding Today's Youth Culture* (1994).

1   Kelly Yeoman's dad described his bubbly 13-year-old daughter as a "charming little angel who would do anything for anybody." She was. Kelly played the tambourine in the local Salvation Army band to raise money for the poor. She spent lots of time visiting with elderly residents at a local nursing center. But Ivan and Julie Yeoman's bright-eyed and selfless daughter wasn't treated by her peers with the same respect she afforded others.

2   For three years Kelly put up with insults and taunts hurled at her by schoolmates. They teased her about her weight, calling her "fatty" and "smelly." At school, they dumped salt on her lunch and threw her clothes in the garbage. During gym class they made fun of what she looked like in her exercise clothes. At home, they would stand outside Kelly's house yelling strings of insults.

3   In October of 1997, Kelly's tormentors surrounded her house on several consecutive nights. Along with their insults they threw stones. After that came eggs and butter, the ingredients for cake. Eventually, the little girl who rarely talked about the constant harassment finally said to her parents, "Mom and Dad, it's nothing to do with you but I can't stand it anymore." That night, she ingested a fatal overdose of painkillers.

4   In Kelly's home country of England, they call such behavior "bullying." It's become so common that an Anti-Bullying Campaign has been launched to help parents help kids who are either bullying or being bullied. The campaign's hot line receives over 16,000 calls a year. In England, they take the problem of bullying seriously. Perhaps it's time we take bullying a bit more seriously here in North America.

5   The now all-too-familiar names of Eric Harris and Dylan Klebold have been linked to bullying. Just hours after the Littleton school shootings were first reported, a profile of the type of kids who would commit such an act began to formulate in my head. That profile included a picture of young men left feeling powerless, detached, and alone. In my mind I envisioned a number of contributing factors. But based on what I've seen and heard so many times before, I imagined the perpetrators at Columbine had boiled

over after being squashed so frequently that they had decided to exact revenge by doing some squashing themselves.

I was shocked but not surprised by what happened in Littleton. In conversations with numerous people since, I've talked about the role that bullying may have played in sending two kids on a path of destruction. While their violent behavior was wrong and inexcusable, it's not difficult to see why Harris and Klebold would get to the point of deciding to do what they did. 6

Shortly after Columbine, *Washington Post* reporters Lorraine Adams and Dale Russakoff investigated reports that Harris, Klebold, and others were sent further and further to the fringe of their local peer society by a "jockocracy"—a group of Columbine athletes—that allegedly enjoyed favored status and played by their own set of rules. The two were constantly harassed, pushed up against lockers, and intimidated in a variety of ways. On one occasion, a carload of athletes threw a bottle at them while the pair was standing outside the school with a friend. Klebold reportedly told the friend, "Don't worry, man. It happens all the time." Adams and Russakoff conclude that "some parents and students believe a school wide indulgence of certain jocks—their criminal convictions, physical abuse, sexual and racial bullying—intensified the killers' feelings of powerlessness and galvanized their fantasies of revenge." Without a doubt, the same thing is happening to "outcasts" in schools across North America. 7

Over the past few months, I've been asked on numerous occasions to address the Littleton shootings in light of my knowledge of today's teenagers and their rapidly changing culture. Every time I mention the role bullying may have played, someone follows up by saying, "We were bullied as kids, but we never chose to kill people because of it." While that may be true, the cultural context of "the bullied" has changed so much over the years that there are more and more kids like Kelly Yeoman, Eric Harris, and Dylan Klebold who get buried under the pressure, see no way out, and choose to respond by inflicting violence on themselves and/or others. 8

What is it about today's changing cultural context that makes a growing number of rejected and bullied kids resort to such extreme responses? There are a number of factors which work alone or in combination. 9

First, more and more kids face the confusing years of adolescent change and confusion alone. The seen and unseen changes that take place during the shift from childhood to adulthood are difficult to deal with. Living through the teen years in the context of loving and supportive home relationships serves as a buffer when peers tend to be at their meanest. The connections of a loving home enable a young person to process difficult peer relationships and respond positively. When the home serves as a buffer and support base, kids can be bullied and still come out better for it. But if they are forced to go it alone due to parental absence and/or neglect, they risk becoming bitter, angry, and even vengeful. 10

Second, the loss of our culture's corporately shared moral compass leaves kids to be blown about by the winds of personal preference and feeling rather than Godly truth. The results can be seen in our attitudes and 11 behaviors. Bullying used to be wrong—now we cheer for grown men who get paid millions of dollars to bully on athletic playing fields and courts. And what about the bullied? Rather than deciding to respond to bullying by examining God's truth to discover God's will for handling adversity, the supreme guide for making decisions becomes individual preference based on personal feelings. Consequently, there's nothing "wrong" with fighting fire with fire. The bullied now bully back.

12   Third, today's world of adolescent music and media fills the void left in the wake of parental silence and moral confusion by offering kids plenty of guidance and direction on how to handle interpersonal conflict. Video games train kids to fight and kill. Some kids exact revenge by venting their rage in the video fantasy world. A few, take their fantasies off the screen and live them out in the real world. The increasingly popular world of televised professional wrestling fills young hearts and minds with uncivility as they view broadcasts where behemoths rumble in arenas packed with people rooting for the bad guy to win. Stone Cold Steve Austin, perhaps the wrestling world's most beloved star, elicits cheers when he recites his motto—Austin 3:16—"I just whooped your ass!" Musical artists like Marilyn Manson, himself an outcast who was bullied in school, appeal to the bullied and call them to fight back through hate and fascist uprisings. The list goes on. This steady media diet and all its messages are soaked up by impressionable young sponges who, through no fault of their own, have no source of Godly guidance and direction. For the powerless, music and media is a source of guidance, answers, and direction that leads them to the power that has for so long been so elusive.

13   And fourth, when the church does not reach out to the bullies and bullied, God's message of hope, peace, grace, power, and reconciliation can't be heard. If God's Good News and order for life are never presented as an option, it won't be an option. Kids are left to search for something else to fill the void. Sadly, the void only grows and a growing number of kids resort to angry, hopeless, and immoral responses that may leave themselves and others hurting all the more.

14   Parents, educators, and youth workers need to proactively respond to bullying. First, it's important for us all to understand that the way kids mistreat other kids should be aggressively addressed because no matter how you look at it, bullying of any type is wrong. We must lovingly challenge those who throw rocks, bottles, butter, or insults at kids like Yeoman, Harris, and Klebold. Second, we've got to come alongside kids like Kelly, Eric, and Dylan and love them through the difficult times so that life is more attractive than the option of self-inflicted death or revenge. And finally, we must counter the prevailing winds of the culture by providing our kids with the gifts of a loving home that's a refuge, the knowledge of God's design for responding to adversity and persecution, and a daily model of God's truth.

15   Jesus said, "There is a saying, 'Love your friends and hate your enemies.' But I say: Love your enemies! Pray for those who persecute you!" (Matthew 5:43 & 44). With God's help, we'll see young hearts bent on hopelessness and vengeance transformed into hearts filled with hope and love.

Rhetorical Considerations

1. How effective is the opening anecdote in this essay? Why? (*Hodges'* 33b/*Writer's* 3b)
2. Mueller's essay is very clearly organized. In your own words, what are the four major causes for violent responses to bullying? (*Hodges'* 32e/*Writer's* 2e)
3. How much of Mueller's essay is informed by his religious principles? How much of it could be considered secular? (*Hodges'* 35c/*Writer's* 7c)
4. Which of the following more accurately sums up the primary focus of the essay: what causes bullying or what causes victims of bullying to react violently? Why might the author have chosen one topic over the other? (*Hodges'* 32b/*Writer's* 2a)

Language and Style

1. What does Mueller mean when he says he was "shocked but not surprised" by the events at Columbine High School (paragraph 6)? (*Hodges'* 20a/*Writer's* 29a)
2. How is the word *corporately* used in the first sentence of paragraph 11? (*Hodges'* 19e/*Writer's* 28e)
3. Find three metaphors in the essay. (*Hodges'* 20b/*Writer's* 29b)
4. Is the second sentence in paragraph 1 a sentence fragment? Why or why not? If it is, can it be justified? (*Hodges'* 2/*Writer's* 18)
5. Does the verb agree in number with its subject in the last sentence of paragraph 9? (*Hodges'* 6a/*Writer's* 22e)

Writing Suggestions

1. Write your own account of bullying based on your personal observations at school, work, or elsewhere. Try to attribute the causes of bullying to specific factors.
2. In a similar vein, look at the effects of bullying, drawing from your own personal experiences and observations.

GIRLS JUST WANT TO BE MEAN

Margaret Talbot

Margaret Talbot is a contributing editor at *The New Republic,* and a contributor to the *New York Times* and the *Atlantic Monthly,* in which this essay was first published. She is the co-editor of *Relative Freedoms: Women and Leisure* (1988) and editor of *Gender, Power and Culture* (2002).

1 Today is Apologies Day in Rosalind Wiseman's class—so, naturally, when class lets out, the girls are crying. Not all 12 of them, but a good half. They stand around in the corridor, snuffling quietly but persistently, interrogating one another. "Why didn't you apologize to me?" one girl demands. "Are you stressed right now?" says another. "I am so stressed." Inside the classroom, which is at the National Cathedral School, a private girls' school in Washington, Wiseman is locked in conversation with one of the sixth graders who has stayed behind to discuss why her newly popular best friend is now scorning her.

2 "You've got to let her go through this," Wiseman instructs. "You can't make someone be your best friend. And it's gonna be hard for her too, because if she doesn't do what they want her to do, the popular girls are gonna chuck her out, and they're gonna spread rumors about her or tell people stuff she told them." The girl's ponytail bobs as she nods and thanks Wiseman, but her expression is baleful.

3 Wiseman's class is about gossip and cliques and ostracism and just plain meanness among girls. But perhaps the simplest way to describe its goals would be to say that it tries to make middle-school girls be nice to one another. This is a far trickier project than you might imagine, and Apologies Day is a case in point. The girls whom Wiseman variously calls the Alpha Girls, the R.M.G.'s (Really Mean Girls) or the Queen Bees are the ones who are supposed to own up to having back-stabbed or dumped a friend, but they are also the most resistant to the exercise and the most self-justifying. The girls who are their habitual victims or hangers-on—the Wannabes and Messengers in Wiseman's lingo—are always apologizing anyway.

4 But Wiseman, who runs a nonprofit organization called the Empower Program, is a cheerfully unyielding presence. And in the end, her students usually do what she wants: they take out their gel pens or their glittery feather-topped pens and write something, fold it over and over again into origami and then hide behind their hair when it's read aloud. Often as not, it contains a hidden or a not-so-hidden barb. To wit: "I used to be best friends with two girls. We weren't popular, we weren't that pretty, but we had fun together. When we came to this school, we were placed in different classes. I stopped being friends with them and left them to be popular. They

despise me now, and I'm sorry for what I did. I haven't apologized because I don't really want to be friends any longer and am afraid if I apologize, then that's how it will result. We are now in completely different leagues." Or: "Dear B. I'm sorry for excluding you and ignoring you. Also, I have said a bunch of bad things about you. I have also run away from you just because I didn't like you. A." Then there are the apologies that rehash the original offense in a way sure to embarrass the offended party all over again, as in: "I'm sorry I told everybody you had an American Girl doll. It really burned your reputation." Or: "Dear 'Friend,' I'm sorry that I talked about you behind your back. I once even compared your forehead/face to a minefield (only 2 1 person though.) I'm really sorry I said these things even though I might still believe them."

Wiseman, who is 32 and hip and girlish herself, has taught this class at 5 many different schools, and it is fair to say that although she loves girls, she does not cling to sentimental notions about them. She is a feminist, but not the sort likely to ascribe greater inherent compassion to women or girls as a group than to men or boys. More her style is the analysis of the feminist historian Elizabeth Fox-Genovese, who has observed that "those who have experienced dismissal by the junior-high-school girls' clique could hardly, with a straight face, claim generosity and nurture as a natural attribute of women." Together, Wiseman and I once watched the movie "Heathers," the 1989 black comedy about a triad of vicious Queen Bees who get their come-uppance, and she found it "pretty true to life." The line uttered by Winona Ryder as Veronica, the disaffected non-Heather of the group, struck her as particularly apt: "I don't really like my friends. It's just like they're people I work with and our job is being popular."

Wiseman's reaction to the crying girls is accordingly complex. "I hate to 6 make girls cry," she says. "I really do hate it when their faces get all splotchy, and everyone in gym class or whatever knows they've been crying." At the same time, she notes: "The tears are a funny thing. Because it's not usually the victims who cry; it's the aggressors, the girls who have something to apologize for. And sometimes, yes, it's relief on their part, but it's also somewhat manipulative, because if they've done something crappy, the person they've done it to can't get that mad at them if they're crying. Plus, a lot of the time they're using the apology to dump on somebody all over again."

Is dumping on a friend really such a serious problem? Do mean girls 7 wield that much power? Wiseman thinks so. In May, Crown will publish her book-length analysis of girl-on-girl nastiness, "Queen Bees and Wannabes: Helping Your Daughter Survive Cliques, Gossip, Boyfriends and other Realities of Adolescence." And her seminars, which she teaches in schools around the country, are ambitious attempts to tame what some psychologists are now calling "relational aggression"—by which they mean the constellation of "Heathers"-like manipulations and exclusions and gossip-mongering that most of us remember from middle school and through which girls, more often than boys, tend to channel their hostilities.

"My life is full of these ridiculous little slips of paper," says Wiseman, 8 pointing to the basket of apologies and questions at her feet. "I have read thousands of these slips of paper. And 95 percent of them are the same. 'Why are these girls being mean to me?' 'Why am I being excluded?' 'I don't want to be part of this popular group anymore. I don't like what they're doing.' There are lots of girls out there who are getting this incredible lesson that they are not inherently worthy, and from someone—a friend, another girl—who was so intimately bonded with them. To a large extent, their definitions of intimacy are going to be based on the stuff they're going through in sixth and seventh grade. And that stuff isn't pretty."

9   This focus on the cruelty of girls is, of course, something new. For years, psychologists who studied aggression among schoolchildren looked only at its physical and overt manifestations and concluded that girls were less aggressive than boys. That consensus began to change in the early 90's, after a team of researchers led by a Finnish professor named Kaj Bjorkqvist started interviewing 11- and 12-year-old girls about their behavior toward one another. The team's conclusion was that girls were, in fact, just as aggressive as boys, though in a different way. They were not as likely to engage in physical fights, for example, but their superior social intelligence enabled them to wage complicated battles with other girls aimed at damaging relationships or reputations—leaving nasty messages by cellphone or spreading scurrilous rumors by e-mail, making friends with one girl as revenge against another, gossiping about someone just loudly enough to be overheard. Turning the notion of women's greater empathy on its head, Bjorkqvist focused on the destructive uses to which such emotional attunement could be put. "Girls can better understand how other girls feel," as he puts it, "so they know better how to harm them."

10   Researchers following in Bjorkqvist's footsteps noted that up to the age of 4 girls tend to be aggressive at the same rates and in the same ways as boys—grabbing toys, pushing, hitting. Later on, however, social expectations force their hostilities underground, where their assaults on one another are more indirect, less physical and less visible to adults. Secrets they share in one context, for example, can sometimes be used against them in another. As Marion Underwood, a professor of psychology at the University of Texas at Dallas, puts it: "Girls very much value intimacy, which makes them excellent friends and terrible enemies. They share so much information when they are friends that they never run out of ammunition if they turn on one another."

11   In the last few years, a group of young psychologists, including Underwood and Nicki Crick at the University of Minnesota, has pushed this work much further, observing girls in "naturalistic" settings, exploring the psychological foundations for nastiness and asking adults to take relational aggression—especially in the sixth and seventh grades, when it tends to be worst—as seriously as they do more familiar forms of bullying. While some of these researchers have emphasized bonding as a motivation, others have seen something closer to a hunger for power, even a Darwinian drive. One Australian researcher, Laurence Owens, found that the 15-year-old girls he interviewed about their girl-pack predation were bestirred primarily by its entertainment value. The girls treated their own lives like the soaps, hoard-

ing drama, constantly rehashing trivia. Owens's studies contain some of the more vivid anecdotes in the earnest academic literature on relational aggression. His subjects tell him about ingenious tactics like leaving the following message on a girl's answering machine—"Hello, it's me. Have you gotten your pregnancy test back yet?"—knowing that her parents will be the first to hear it. They talk about standing in "huddles" and giving other girls "deaths"—stares of withering condescension—and of calling one another "dyke," "slut" and "fat" and of enlisting boys to do their dirty work.

Relational aggression is finding its chroniclers among more popular 12 writers, too. In addition to Wiseman's book, this spring will bring Rachel Simmons's "Odd Girl Out: The Hidden Culture of Aggression in Girls," Emily White's "Fast Girls: Teenage Tribes and the Myth of the Slut" and Phyllis Chesler's "Woman's Inhumanity to Woman."

In her book, the 27-year-old Simmons offers a plaintive definition of rela- 13 tional aggression: "Unlike boys, who tend to bully acquaintances or strangers, girls frequently attack within tightly knit friendship networks, making aggression harder to identify and intensifying the damage to the victims. Within the hidden culture of aggression, girls fight with body language and relationships instead of fists and knives. In this world, friendship is a weapon, and the sting of a shout pales in comparison to a day of someone's silence. There is no gesture more devastating than the back turning away." Now, Simmons insists, is the time to pull up the rock and really look at this seething underside of American girlhood. "Beneath a facade of female intimacy," she writes, "lies a terrain traveled in secret, marked with anguish and nourished by silence."

Not so much silence, anymore, actually. For many school principals and 14 counselors across the country, relational aggression is becoming a certified social problem and the need to curb it an accepted mandate. A small industry of interveners has grown up to meet the demand. In Austin, Tex., an organization called GENaustin now sends counselors into schools to teach a course on relational aggression called Girls as Friends, Girls as Foes. In Erie, Pa., the Ophelia Project offers a similar curriculum, taught by high-school-aged mentors, that explores "how girls hurt each other" and how they can stop. A private Catholic school in Akron, Ohio, and a public-school district near Portland, Ore., have introduced programs aimed at rooting out girl meanness. And Wiseman and her Empower Program colleagues have taught their Owning Up class at 60 schools. "We are currently looking at relational aggression like domestic violence 20 years ago," says Holly Nishimura, the assistant director of the Ophelia Project. "Though it's not on the same scale, we believe that with relational aggression, the trajectory of awareness, knowledge and demand for change will follow the same track."

Whether this new hypervigilance about a phenomenon that has existed 15 for as long as most of us can remember will actually do anything to squelch it is, of course, another question. Should adults be paying as much attention to this stuff as kids do or will we just get hopelessly tangled up in it ourselves? Are we approaching frothy adolescent bitchery with undue gravity or just giving it its due in girls' lives? On the one hand, it is kind of satisfying to think that girls might be, after their own fashion, as aggressive as boys. It's an idea that offers some relief from the specter of the meek and mopey, "silenced" and self-loathing girl the popular psychology of girlhood has given us in recent years. But it is also true that the new attention to girls as relational aggressors may well take us into a different intellectual cul-de-sac, where it becomes too easy to assume that girls do not use their fists (some do), that all girls are covert in their cruelties, that all girls care deeply about the ways of the clique—and that what they do in their "relational" lives takes precedence over all other aspects of their emerging selves.

16   After her class at the National Cathedral School, Wiseman and I chat for a while in her car. She has to turn down the India Arie CD that's blaring on her stereo so we can hear each other. The girl she had stayed to talk with after class is still on her mind, partly because she represents the social type for whom Wiseman seems to feel the profoundest sympathy: the girl left behind by a newly popular, newly dismissive friend. "See, at a certain point it becomes cool to be boy crazy," she explains. "That happens in sixth grade, and it gives you so much social status, particularly in an all-girls school, if you can go up and talk to boys.

17   "But often, an Alpha Girl has an old friend, the best-friend-forever elementary-school friend, who is left behind because she's not boy crazy yet," Wiseman goes on, pressing the accelerator with her red snakeskin boot. "And what she can't figure out is: why does my old friend want to be better friends with a girl who talks behind her back and is mean to her than with me, who is a good friend and who wouldn't do that?"

18   The subtlety of the maneuvers still amazes Wiseman, though she has seen them time and again. "What happens," she goes on, "is that the newly popular girl—let's call her Darcy—is hanging out with Molly and some other Alpha Girls in the back courtyard, and the old friend, let's call her Kristin, comes up to them. And what's going to happen is Molly's going to throw her arms around Darcy and talk about things that Kristin doesn't know anything about and be totally physically affectionate with Darcy so that she looks like the shining jewel. And Kristin is, like, I don't exist. She doesn't want to be friends with the new version of Darcy—she wants the old one back, but it's too late for that."

19   So to whom, I ask Wiseman, does Kristin turn in her loneliness? Wiseman heaves a sigh as though she's sorry to be the one to tell me an obvious but unpleasant truth. "The other girls can be like sharks—it's like blood in the water, and they see it and they go, 'Now I can be closer to Kristin because she's being dumped by Darcy.' When I say stuff like this, I know I sound horrible, I know it. But it's what they do."

20   Hanging out with Wiseman, you get used to this kind of disquisition on the craftiness of middle-school girls, but I'll admit that when my mind balks at something she has told me, when I can't quite believe girls have thought up some scheme or another, I devise little tests for her—I ask her to pick out seventh-grade Queen Bees in a crowd outside a school or to predict what the girls in the class will say about someone who isn't there that day or to guess which boys a preening group of girls is preening for. I have yet to catch her out.

Once, Wiseman mentions a girl she knows whose clique of seven is gov- 21
erned by actual, enumerated rules and suggests I talk with this girl to get a
sense of what reformers like her are up against. Jessica Travis, explains Wiseman, shaking her head in aggravated bemusement at the mere thought of
her, is a junior at a suburban Maryland high school and a member of the
Girls' Advisory Board that is part of Wiseman's organization. She is also, it
occurs to me when I meet her, a curious but not atypical social type—an
amalgam of old-style Queen Bee-ism and new-style girl's empowerment,
brimming over with righteous self-esteem and cheerful cattiness. Tall and
strapping, with long russet hair and blue eye shadow, she's like a Powerpuff
Girl come to life.

When I ask Jessica to explain the rules her clique lives by, she doesn't 22
hesitate. "O.K.," she says happily. "No 1: clothes. You cannot wear jeans any
day but Friday, and you cannot wear a ponytail or sneakers more than once
a week. Monday is fancy day—like black pants or maybe you bust out with
a skirt. You want to remind people how cute you are in case they forgot over
the weekend. O.K., 2: parties. Of course, we sit down together and discuss
which ones we're going to go to, because there's no point in getting all
dressed up for a party that's going to be lame. No getting smacked at a party,
because how would it look for the rest of us if you're drunk and acting like a
total fool? And if you do hook up with somebody at the party, please try to
limit it to one. Otherwise you look like a slut and that reflects badly on all
of us. Kids are not that smart; they're not going to make the distinctions between us. And the rules apply to all of us—you can't be like, 'Oh, I'm having my period; I'm wearing jeans all week.'"

She pauses for a millisecond. "Like, we had a lot of problems with this 23
one girl. She came to school on a Monday in jeans. So I asked her, 'Why you
wearing jeans today?' She said, 'Because I felt like it.' 'Because you felt like
it? Did you forget it was a Monday?' 'No.' She says she just doesn't like the
confinement. She doesn't want to do this anymore. She's the rebel of the
group, and we had to suspend her a couple of times; she wasn't allowed to
sit with us at lunch. On that first Monday, she didn't even try; she didn't
even catch my eye—she knew better. But eventually she came back to us,
and she was, like, 'I know, I deserved it.'"

Each member of Jessica's group is allowed to invite an outside person to 24
sit at their table in the lunch room several times a month, but they have to
meet at the lockers to O.K. it with the other members first, and they cannot
exceed their limit. "We don't want other people at our table more than a
couple of times a week because we want to bond, and the bonding is endless," Jessica says. "Besides, let's say you want to tell your girls about some
total fool thing you did, like locking your hair in the car door. I mean, my
God, you're not going to tell some stranger that."

For all their policing of their borders, they are fiercely loyal to those who 25
stay within them. If a boy treats one of them badly, they all snub him. And
Jessica offers another example: "One day, another friend came to school in
this skirt from Express—ugliest skirt I've ever seen—red and brown plaid,
O.K.? But she felt really fabulous. She was like, Isn't this skirt cute? And she's

my friend, so of course I'm like, Damn straight, sister! Lookin' good! But then, this other girl who was in the group for a while comes up and she says to her: 'Oh, my God, you look so stupid! You look like a giant argyle sock!' I was like, 'What is wrong with you?'"

26 Jessica gets good grades, belongs to the B'nai B'rith Youth Organization and would like, for no particular reason, to go to Temple University. She plays polo and figure-skates, has a standing appointment for a once-a-month massage and "cried from the beginning of 'Pearl Harbor' till I got home that night." She lives alone with her 52-year-old mother, who was until January a consultant for Oracle. She is lively and loquacious and she has, as she puts it, "the highest self-esteem in the world." Maybe that's why she finds it so easy to issue dictums like: "You cannot go out with an underclassman. You just cannot—end of story." I keep thinking, when I listen to Jessica talk about her clique, that she must be doing some kind of self-conscious parody. But I'm fairly sure she's not.

27 On a bleary December afternoon, I attend one of Wiseman's after-school classes in the Maryland suburbs. A public middle school called William H. Farquhar has requested the services of the Empower Program. Soon after joining the class, I ask the students about a practice Wiseman has told me about that I find a little hard to fathom or even to believe. She had mentioned it in passing—"You know how the girls use three-way calling"—and when I professed puzzlement, explained: "O.K., so Alison and Kathy call up Mary, but only Kathy talks and Alison is just lurking there quietly so Mary doesn't know she's on the line. And Kathy says to Mary, 'So what do you think of Alison?' And of course there's some reason at the moment why Mary doesn't like Alison, and she says, Oh, my God, all these nasty things about Alison—you know, 'I can't believe how she throws herself at guys, she thinks she's all that, blah, blah, blah.' And Alison hears all this."

28 Not for the first time with Wiseman, I came up with one of my lame comparisons with adult life: "But under normal circumstances, repeating nasty gossip about one friend to another is not actually going to get you that far with your friends."

29 "Yeah, but in Girl World, that's currency," Wiseman responded. "It's like: Ooh, I have a dollar and now I'm more powerful and I can use this if I want to. I can further myself in the social hierarchy and bond with the girl being gossiped about by setting up the conference call so she can know about it, by telling her about the gossip and then delivering the proof."

30 In the classroom at Farquhar, eight girls are sitting in a circle, eating chips and drinking sodas. All of them have heard about the class and chosen to come. There's Jordi Kauffman, who is wearing glasses, a fleece vest and sneakers and who displays considerable scorn for socially ambitious girls acting "all slutty in tight clothes or all snotty." Jordi is an honor student whose mother is a teacher and whose father is the P.T.A. president. She's the only one in the class with a moderately sarcastic take on the culture of American girlhood. "You're in a bad mood one day, and you say you feel fat," she remarks, "and adults are like, 'Oh-oh, she's got poor self-esteem, she's depressed, get her help!'"

Next to Jordi is her friend Jackie, who is winsome and giggly and very 31
pretty. Jackie seems more genuinely troubled by the loss of a onetime friend
who has been twisting herself into an Alpha Girl. She will later tell us that
when she wrote a heartfelt e-mail message to this former friend, asking her
why she was "locking her out," the girl's response was to print it out and
show it around at school.

On the other side of the room are Lauren and Daniela, who've got boys 32
on the brain, big time. They happily identify with Wiseman's negative portrayal of "Fruit-Cup Girl," one who feigns helplessness—in Wiseman's example, by pretending to need a guy to open her pull-top can of fruit
cocktail—to attract male attention. There's Courtney, who will later say,
when asked to write a letter to herself about how she's doing socially, that
she can't, because she "never says anything to myself about myself." And
there's Kimberly, who will write such a letter professing admiration for her
own "natural beauty."

They have all heard of the kind of three-way call Wiseman had told me 33
about; all but two have done it or had it done to them. I ask if they found
the experience useful. "Not always," Jordi says, "because sometimes there's
something you want to hear but you don't hear. You want to hear, 'Oh, she's
such a good person' or whatever, but instead you hear, 'Oh, my God, she's
such a bitch.'"

I ask if boys ever put together three-way calls like that. "Nah," Jackie 34
says. "I don't think they're smart enough."

Once the class gets going, the discussion turns, as it often does, to 35
Jackie's former friend, the one who's been clawing her way into the Alpha
Girl clique. In a strange twist, this girl has, as Daniela puts it, "given up her
religion" and brought a witch's spell book to school.

"That's weird," Wiseman says, "because usually what happens is that 36
the girls who are attracted to that are more outside-the-box types—you
know, the depressed girls with the black fingernails who are always writing
poetry—because it gives them some amount of power. The girl you're describing sounds unconfident; maybe she's looking for something that makes
her seem mysterious and powerful. If you have enough social status, you
can be a little bit different. And that's where she's trying to go with this—
like, I am so in the box that I'm defining a new box."

Jackie interjects, blushing, with another memory of her lost friend. "I 37
used to tell her everything," she laments, "and now she just blackmails me
with my secrets."

"Sounds like she's a Banker," Wiseman says. "That means that she col- 38
lects information and uses it later to her advantage."

"Nobody really likes her," chimes in Jordi. "She's like a shadow of her 39
new best friend, a total Wannabe. Her new crowd's probably gonna be like,
'Take her back, pulleeze!'"

"What really hurts," Jackie persists, "is that it's like you can't just drop a 40
friend. You have to dump on them, too."

"Yeah, it's true," Jordi agrees matter-of-factly. "You have to make them 41
really miserable before you leave."

42   After class, when I concede that Wiseman was right about the three-way calling, she laughs. "Haven't I told you girls are crafty?" she asks. "Haven't I told you girls are evil?"

43   It may be that the people most likely to see such machinations clearly are the former masters of them. Wiseman's anthropological mapping of middle-school society—the way she notices and describes the intricate rituals of exclusion and humiliation as if they were a Balinese cockfight—seems to come naturally to her because she remembers more vividly than many people do what it was like to be an adolescent insider or, as she puts it, "a pearls-and-tennis-skirt-wearing awful little snotty girl."

44   It was different for me. When I was in junior high in the 70's—a girl who was neither a picked-on girl nor an Alpha Girl, just someone in the vast more-or-less dorky middle at my big California public school—the mean girls were like celebrities whose exploits my friends and I followed with interest but no savvy. I sort of figured that their caste was conferred at birth when they landed in Laurelwood—the local hillside housing development peopled by dentists and plastic surgeons—and were given names like Marcie and Tracie. I always noticed their pretty clothes and haircuts and the smell of their green-apple gum and cherry Lip Smackers and their absences from school for glamorous afflictions like tennis elbow or skiing-related sunburns. The real Queen Bees never spoke to you at all, but the Wannabes would sometimes insult you as a passport to popularity. There was a girl named Janine, for instance, who used to preface every offensive remark with the phrase "No offense," as in "No offense, but you look like a woofing dog." Sometimes it got her the nod from the Girl World authorities and sometimes it didn't, and I could never figure out why or why not.

45   Which is all to say that to an outsider, the Girl World's hard-core social wars are fairly distant and opaque, and to somebody like Wiseman, they are not. As a seventh grader at a private school in Washington, she hooked up with "a very powerful, very scary group of girls who were very fun to be with but who could turn on you like a dime." She became an Alpha Girl, but she soon found it alienating. "You know you have these moments where you're like, 'I hate this person I've become; I'm about to vomit on myself'? Because I was really a piece of work. I was really snotty."

46   When I ask Wiseman to give me an example of something wicked that she did, she says: "Whoa, I'm in such denial about this. But O.K., here's one. When I was in eighth grade, I spread around a lie about my best friend, Melissa. I told all the girls we knew that she had gotten together, made out or whatever, with this much older guy at a family party at our house. I must have been jealous—she was pretty and getting all this attention from guys. And so I made up something that made her sound slutty. She confronted me about it, and I totally denied it."

47   Wiseman escaped Girl World only when she headed off to California for college and made friends with "people who didn't care what neighborhood I came from or what my parents did for a living." After majoring in political science, she moved back to Washington, where she helped start an

organization that taught self-defense to women and girls. "I was working with girls and listening to them, and again and again, before it was stories about boys, it was stories about girls and what they'd done to them. I'd say talk to me about how you're controlling each other, and I wrote this curriculum on cliques and popularity. That's how it all got started."

Wiseman's aim was to teach classes that would, by analyzing the social hierarchy of school, help liberate girls from it. Girls would learn to "take responsibility for how they treat each other," as Wiseman's handbook for the course puts it, "and to develop strategies to interrupt the cycle of gossip, exclusivity and reputations." Instructors would not let comments like "we have groups but we all get along" stand; they would deconstruct them, using analytic tools familiar from the sociology of privilege and from academic discourse on racism. "Most often, the 'popular' students make these comments while the students who are not as high in the social hierarchy disagree. The comments by the popular students reveal how those who have privilege are so accustomed to their power that they don't recognize when they are dominating and silencing others." Teachers would "guide students to the realization that most girls don't maliciously compete or exclude each other, but within their social context, girls perceive that they must compete with each other for status and power, thus maintaining the status system that binds them all." 48

The theory was sober and sociological, but in the hands of Wiseman, the classes were dishy and confessional, enlivened by role-playing that got the girls giggling and by Wiseman's knowing references to Bebe jackets, Boardwalk Fries and 'N Sync. It was a combination that soon put Wiseman's services in high demand, especially at some of the tonier private schools in the Washington area. 49

"I was just enthralled by her," says Camilla Vitullo, who as a headmistress at the National Cathedral School in 1994 was among the first to hire Wiseman. "And the girls gobbled up everything she had to say." (Vitullo, who is now at the Spence School in Manhattan, plans to bring Wiseman there.) Soon Wiseman's Empower Program, which also teaches courses on subjects like date rape, was getting big grants from the Liz Claiborne Foundation and attracting the attention of Oprah Winfrey, who had Wiseman on her show last spring. 50

Wiseman has been willing to immerse herself in Girl World, and it has paid off. (Out of professional necessity, she has watched "every movie with Kirsten Dunst or Freddie Prinze Jr." and innumerable shows on the WB network.) But even if it weren't her job, you get the feeling she would still know more about all that than most adults do. She senses immediately, for example, that when the girls in her Farquhar class give her a bottle of lotion as a thank-you present, she is supposed to open it on the spot and pass it around and let everybody slather some on. ("Ooh, is it smelly? Smelly in a good way?") When Wiseman catches sight of you approaching, she knows how to do a little side-to-side wave, with her elbow pressed to her hip, that is disarmingly girlish. She says "totally" and "omigod" and "don't stress" and 51

"chill" a lot and refers to people who are "hotties" or "have it goin' on."
And none of it sounds foolish on her yet, maybe because she still looks a little like a groovy high-schooler with her trim boyish build and her short,
shiny black hair and her wardrobe—picked out by her 17-year-old sister,
Zoe—with its preponderance of boots and turtlenecks and flared jeans.

52   Zoe. Ah, Zoe. Zoe is a bit of a problem for the whole Reform of Girl
World project, a bit of a fly in the ointment. For years, Wiseman has been
working on her, with scant results. Zoe, a beauty who is now a senior at
Georgetown Day School, clearly adores her older sister but also remains
skeptical of her enterprise. "She's always telling me to look inside myself
and be true to myself—things I can't do right now because I'm too shallow
and superficial" is how Zoe, in all her Zoe-ness, sums up their differences.

53   Once I witnessed the two sisters conversing about a party Zoe had given,
at which she was outraged by the appearance of freshman girls—"and not
ugly, dorky ones, either! Pretty ones!"

54   "And what exactly was the problem with that?" Wiseman asked.

55   "If you're gonna be in high school," Zoe replied, with an attempt at patience, "you have to stay in your place. A freshman girl cannot show up at a
junior party; disgusting 14-year-old girls with their boobs in the air cannot
show up at your party going"—her voice turned breathy—"Uh, hi, where's
the beer?"

56   Wiseman wanted to know why Zoe couldn't show a little empathy for
the younger girls.

57   "No matter what you say in your talks and your little motivational
speeches, Ros, you are not going to change how I feel when little girls show
up in their little outfits at my party. I mean, I don't always get mad. Usually
I don't care enough about freshmen to even know their names."

58   Wiseman rolled her eyes.

59   "Why would I know their names? Would I go out of my way to help
freshmen? Should I be saying, 'Hey, I just want you to know that I'm there for
you'? Would that make ya happy, Ros? Maybe in some perfect Montessori-
esque, P.C. world, we'd all get along. But there are certain rules of the school
system that have been set forth from time immemorial or whatever."

60   "This," said Wiseman, "is definitely a source of tension between us."

61   A little over a month after the last class at Farquhar, I go back to the
school to have lunch with Jordi and Jackie. I want to know what they've remembered from the class, how it might have affected their lives. Wiseman
has told me that she will sometimes get e-mail messages from girls at schools
where she has taught complaining of recidivism: "Help, you have to come
back! We're all being mean again"—that kind of thing.

62   The lunchroom at Farquhar is low-ceilinged, crowded and loud and
smells like frying food and damp sweaters. The two teachers on duty are
communicating through walkie-talkies. I join Jordi in line, where she selects
for her lunch a small plate of fried potato discs and nothing to drink. Lunch
lasts from 11:28 to 11:55, and Jordi always sits at the same table with Jackie
(who bounds in late today, holding the little bag of popcorn that is her
lunch) and several other girls.

I ask Jackie what she remembers best about Wiseman's class, and she 63 smiles fondly and says it was the "in and out of the box thing—who's cool and who's not and why."

I ask Jordi if she thought she would use a technique Wiseman had rec- 64 ommended for confronting a friend who had weaseled out of plans with her in favor of a more popular girl's invitation. Wiseman had suggested sit- ting the old friend down alone at some later date, "affirming" the friend- ship and telling her clearly what she wanted from her. Jordi had loved it when the class acted out the scene, everybody hooting and booing at the behavior of the diva-girl as she dissed her social inferiors in a showdown at the food court. But now, she tells me that she found the exercise "kind of corny." She explains: "Not many people at my school would do it that way. We'd be more likely just to battle it out on the Internet when we got home." (Most of her friends feverishly instant-message after school each afternoon.) Both girls agree that the class was fun, though, and had taught them a lot about popularity.

Which, unfortunately, wasn't exactly the point. Wiseman told me once 65 that one hazard of her trade is that girls will occasionally go home and tell their moms that they were in a class where they learned how to be popular. "I think they're smarter than that, and they must just be telling their moms that," she said. "But they're such concrete thinkers at this age that some could get confused."

I think Wiseman's right—most girls do understand what she's getting 66 at. But it is also true that in paying such close attention to the cliques, in taking Queen Bees so very seriously, the relational-aggression movement seems to grant them a legitimacy and a stature they did not have when they ruled a world that was beneath adult radar.

Nowadays, adults, particularly in the upper middle classes, are less 67 laissez-faire about children's social lives. They are more vigilant, more likely to have read books about surviving the popularity wars of middle school or dealing with cliques, more likely to have heard a talk or gone to a workshop on those topics. Not long ago, I found myself at a lecture by the best-selling author Michael Thompson on "Understanding the Social Lives of our Chil- dren." It was held inside the National Cathedral on a chilly Tuesday evening in January, and there were hundreds of people in attendance—attractive late-40's mothers in cashmere turtlenecks and interesting scarves and ex- pensive haircuts, and graying but fit fathers—all taking notes and lining up to ask eager, anxious questions about how best to ensure their children's so- cial happiness. "As long as education is mandatory," Thompson said from the pulpit, "we have a huge obligation to make it socially safe," and heads nodded all around me. He made a list of "the top three reasons for a fourth- grade girl to be popular," and parents in my pew wrote it down in hand- some little leather notebooks or on the inside cover of Thompson's latest book, "Best Friends, Worst Enemies." A red-haired woman with a fervent, tremulous voice and an elegant navy blue suit said that she worried our chil- dren were socially handicapped by "a lack of opportunities for unstructured cooperative play" and mentioned that she had her 2-year-old in a science class. A serious-looking woman took the microphone to say that she was troubled by the fact that her daughter liked a girl "who is mean and controlling and once wrote the word murder on the bathroom mirror—and this is in a private school!"

68   I would never counsel blithe ignorance on such matters—some children are truly miserable at school for social reasons, truly persecuted and friendless and in need of adult help. But sometimes we do seem in danger of micromanaging children's social lives, peering a little too closely. Priding ourselves on honesty in our relationships, as baby-boomer parents often do, we expect to know everything about our children's friendships, to be hip to their social travails in a way our own parents, we thought, were not. But maybe this attention to the details can backfire, giving children the impression that the transient social anxieties and allegiances of middle school are weightier and more immutable than they really are. And if that is the result, it seems particularly unfortunate for girls, who are already more mired in the minutiae of relationships than boys are, who may already lack, as Christopher Lasch once put it, "any sense of an impersonal order that exists independently of their wishes and anxieties" and of the "vicissitudes of relationships."

69   I think I would have found it dismaying if my middle school had offered a class that taught us about the wiles of Marcie and Tracie: if adults studied their folkways, maybe they were more important than I thought, or hoped. For me, the best antidote to the caste system of middle school was the premonition that adults did not usually play by the same rigid and peculiar rules—and that someday, somewhere, I would find a whole different mattering map, a whole crowd of people who read the same books I did and wouldn't shun me if I didn't have a particular brand of shoes. When I went to college, I found it, and I have never really looked back.

70   And the Queen Bees? Well, some grow out of their girly sense of entitlement on their own, surely; some channel it in more productive directions. Martha Stewart must have been a Q.B. Same with Madonna. At least one of the Q.B.'s from my youth—albeit the nicest and smartest one—has become a pediatrician on the faculty of a prominent medical school, I noticed when I looked her up the other day. And some Queen Bees have people who love them—dare I say it?—just as they are, a truth that would have astounded me in my own school days but that seems perfectly natural now.

71   On a Sunday afternoon, I have lunch with Jessica Travis and her mother, Robin, who turns out to be an outgoing, transplanted New Yorker—"born in Brighton Beach, raised in Sheepshead Bay." Over white pizza, pasta, cannoli and Diet Cokes, I ask Robin what Jessica was like as a child.

72   "I was fabulous," Jessica says.

73   "She was," her mother agrees. "She was blond, extremely happy, endlessly curious and always the leader of the pack. She didn't sleep because she didn't want to miss anything. She was just a bright, shiny kid. She's still a bright, shiny kid."

74   After Jessica takes a call on her pumpkin-colored cellphone, we talk for a while about Jessica's room, which they both describe as magnificent. "I

have lived in apartments smaller than her majesty's two-bedroom suite," Robin snorts. "Not many single parents can do for their children what I have done for this one. This is a child who asked for a pony and got two. I tell her this is the top of the food chain. The only place you can go from here is the royal family."

I ask if anything about Jessica's clique bothers her. She says no—because 75 what she calls "Jess's band of merry men" doesn't "define itself by its opponents. They're not a threat to anyone. Besides, it's not like they're an A-list clique."

"Uh, Mom," Jessica corrects. "We are definitely an A-list clique. We are 76 totally A-list. You are giving out incorrect information."

"Soooorry," Robin says. "I'd fire myself, but there's no one else lining 77 up for the job of being your mom."

Jessica spends a little time bringing her mother and me up to date on 78 the elaborate social structure at her high school. The cheerleaders' clique, it seems, is not the same as the pom-pom girls' clique, though both are A-list. All sports cliques are A-list, in fact, except—of course"—the swimmers. There is a separate A-list clique for cute preppy girls who "could play sports but don't." There is "the white people who pretend to be black clique" and the drama clique, which would be "C list," except that, as Jessica puts it, "they're not even on the list."

"So what you are saying is that your high school is littered with all these 79 groups that have their own separate physical and mental space?" Robin says, shaking her head in wonderment.

When they think about it, Jessica and her mom agree that the business 80 with the rules—what you can wear on a given day of the week and all that— comes from Jessica's fondness for structure. As a child, her mom says she made up games with "such elaborate rules I'd be lost halfway through her explanation of them." Besides, there was a good deal of upheaval in her early life. Robin left her "goofy artist husband" when Jessica was 3, and after that they moved a lot. And when Robin went to work for Oracle, she "was traveling all the time, getting home late. When I was on the road, I'd call her every night at 8 and say: 'Sweet Dreams. I love you. Good Night.'"

"Always in that order," Jessica says. "Always at 8. I don't like a lot of 81 change."

Toward the end of our lunch, Jessica's mother—who says she herself was 82 more a nerd than a Queen Bee in school—returns to the subject of cliques. She wants, it seems, to put something to rest. "You know I realize there are people who stay with the same friends, the same kind of people, all their life, who never look beyond that," she says. "I wouldn't want that for my daughter. I want my daughter to be one of those people who lives in the world. I know she's got these kind of narrow rules in her personal life right now. But I still think, I really believe, that she will be a bigger person, a person who spends her life in the world." Jessica's mother smiles. Then she gives her daughter's hair an urgent little tug, as if it were the rip cord of a parachute and Jessica were about to float away from her.

Rhetorical Considerations

1. What is the primary purpose of this essay: informative, persuasive, or expressive? Explain your answer. (*Hodges'* 32a/*Writer's* 1e)
2. What age group of girls does Wiseman offer these classes to? Why that age? (*Hodges'* 32b/*Writer's* 2a)
3. According to the essay, how do girls' aggressions differ from those of boys?
4. The essay offers two major adult perspectives of the girls discussed. What are these two perspectives? How do they differ? Why is it useful for the reader to have both perspectives? (*Hodges'* 32e/*Writer's* 2e)
5. When did serious studies begin regarding girls' aggressive behavior? How have these studies influenced or changed our views of girls? (*Hodges'* 32b/*Writer's* 2a)
6. Do you see evidence in this essay of any of the factors Walt Mueller mentions as causes for bullying problems? If so, what are they? (*Hodges'* 32e/*Writer's* 2e)
7. Do these classes produce the consequences (the effects) Wiseman hopes for? Why or why not? (*Hodges'* 32e/*Writer's* 2e)

Language and Style

1. Look up the following words in your dictionary: *baleful* (paragraph 2); *ostracism* (paragraph 3); *scurrilous* (paragraph 9); *trajectory* (paragraph 14); *disquisition* and *preening* (paragraph 20); *amalgam* (paragraph 21); *loquacious* (paragraph 26); *winsome* (paragraph 31); *recidivism* (paragraph 61); *laissez-faire* (paragraph 67). (*Hodges'* 19e/*Writer's* 28e)
2. What is a "Darwinian drive" (paragraph 11)? (*Hodges'* 19e/*Writer's* 28e)
3. Explain the apparent shift in tense in the last sentence of paragraph 1. (*Hodges'* 27a/*Writer's* 22b)
4. Why are there no commas separating the items in the first sentence of paragraph 3? (*Hodges'* 13/*Writer's* 31g)
5. Explain the use of commas in the seventh sentence of the last paragraph. (*Hodges'* 12/*Writer's* 31)

Writing Suggestions

1. From the perspective offered in the previous essay by Walt Mueller, respond to the ideas described in this essay.
2. Write about your own experiences with cliques in high school or any other level of school, considering the long-term consequences of these experiences.

✦

IMAGES

Cause and Effect

Cause and effect are ploys often used in advertising. Companies try to convince you that using their product or service will make your life better in some way, that it will have a desired effect. Although the two ads here stem from very different sources—one from an online dieting service, the other from an environmental-watch organization—they both employ the rhetorical strategy of cause and effect to elicit a certain response from you, the consumer.

Losing Weight Has Never Been This EASY!

eDiets.com offers you The New Diet Solution

We understand that finding an effective weight loss program is difficult. Even more difficult is finding a program that will work around your schedule and lifestyle. With eDiets.com you will find the convenience you need in a program that not only helps you lose weight, but teaches you how to live a healthier lifestyle.

Online dieting provides an effective program that works around your busy schedule:

• Customized meal plans, complete with recipes and grocery shopping lists
• Customized fitness programs to help you achieve your goal weight
• Access to licensed dietitians, fitness experts, and behavioral specialists
• 24/7 online support offering chat rooms, support groups and virtual meetings

So, What are you waiting for? Log on today and experience the New Diet Solution for yourself at www.ediets.com/PT

eDiets .com

eDiets.com

✦

IMAGES (CONT.)

Cause and Effect

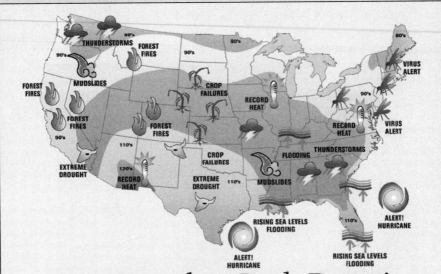

Since President Bush Doesn't Understand Climate Change, Let Us Draw Him a Map.

Global Warming Alert!

Hundreds of the world's top scientists agree -- global warming is not just a possibility -- it is a reality. And the actions by the Bush administration will only exacerbate this already dire situation. Global warming can be slowed. But it will take a radical change in policies by the Bush Administration, which will require a united and loud voice by the American people. You can help. Make your voice heard by clicking on the button below...

TAKE ACTION NOW

GlobalWarmingAlert.org

Rhetorical Considerations

1. What do you observe about the large photograph in the eDiets.com ad? How does the woman look? Is she overweight? How would you describe the expression on her face? What is the man in the background doing? Does this contribute to the effectiveness of the ad? If so, why? If not, why not? (*Hodges'* 31c/*Writer's* 2d)
2. In the GlobalWarmingAlert.org ad, what attracts your attention first? Second? What is the function of the map in the ad? Is the amount of text useful or distracting? (*Hodges'* 32b/*Writer's* 2a)
3. Which of the two ads do you find most effective? Explain your answer.

Writing Suggestions

1. Find a group of ads for a particular type of product or service (such as a weight-loss program, shampoo, or running shoes). Write an essay that analyzes the implications made by the ads in regards to cause and effect.
2. Find an ad that you think is very effective. Examine it carefully for logical fallacies (see p. 200). Can you rewrite the ad so it has no fallacies? Write an essay about your findings and what they imply about advertising in general.

CHAPTER 6

Comparison and Contrast

Should you walk or take the bus? Vote Democratic, Republican, or not vote at all? Major in classics or accounting? Watch the news or a sitcom? Order a pizza or cook? Such decisions—and hosts of others, both trivial and important, that you confront every day—require you to compare and contrast alternatives. You continually consider the similarities and differences of objects, ideas, or possible courses of action in order to understand them better and thus make informed choices and decisions. And since having your audience understand and be able to make intelligent decisions are two of the most important goals of factual writing, comparison and contrast are important in your writing, especially college writing.

Understanding Comparison and Contrast

Comparing, which focuses on similarities, and contrasting, which focuses on differences, may sound like opposites, but in practice the two must be considered together (and so they are often referred to by the single term *comparison,* as we shall do in the following discussion). This is because usually only things that are likely to exhibit both similarities and differences are worth considering in a side-by-side, comparative analysis. Although people often do compare identical things, they rarely write about this sameness at any length, and most readers would not find such a comparison very interesting. There would have to be some significant point for enumerating the similarities of two things that are known to be identical, whether they are identical spoons in a drawer or identical positions on a social issue.

Conversely, why examine the differences between two things known to have *nothing* in common? Examining the merits of the electric shaver versus the "safety" razor can be productive because both are devices for removing hair from skin; exploring whether to shave with a blade or with a banana is not likely to be, shall we say, fruitful (except, perhaps, in the hands of an absurdist such as Steve Martin or Woody Allen). There must be some significant similarity in order for differences to be meaningful.

In short, there must be a *basis for comparison*—the generalization that identifies how the items to be compared are alike. All of the *points of comparison* that you will address develop from that basis. When writing a comparison-and-contrast analysis, always ask yourself, "Have I chosen for comparison things whose similarities and differences are sufficient to make the comparison worthwhile for me and my readers?" The basis for comparison need not be obvious; however, you can *make* it clear. In "The Male God of the Desert" Richard Rodriguez does so in one tightly focused paragraph:

> I am interested that Judaism, Christianity, and Islam are alike religions of the desert. They are brother-faiths, more like one another than any one of them is like an eastern religion—Hinduism, or Buddhism. The religions of the desert are alike monotheistic, alike paternalistic. They are male in popular imagination, because they are male in tradition. (277)

A special kind of comparison called *analogy* does not have an obvious basis for comparison and involves two or more essentially unlike things. Analogy is an extended verbal comparison that depends on showing unexpected likenesses between two dissimilar things, usually one familiar and one unfamiliar. Beth Ann Fennelly makes use of this technique in "Fruits We'll Never Taste, Languages We'll Never Hear," in which she draws an analogy between the extinction of certain agricultural products and of languages. Her purpose is not the analogy itself; she employs this analogy to argue that variety and diversity are necessary in all human endeavors.

Using Comparison and Contrast

Purpose

You must have a purpose for your analysis of likenesses and/or differences. Sometimes the purpose is simply to provide the insight that two things generally viewed as very different (such as rap and traditional poetry) are actually quite similar, or that what may be revealed by the comparison is interesting or important in itself, as is the case with Robin Morgan's "Dispatch from Beijing." But often the purpose is to evaluate: to establish that one thing is better than the other (the PC over the Mac, for example) or that one is more appropriate for certain situations (the Mac may be better for users who are working with high-resolution graphics). Comparison can also be useful for clarifying decisions for oneself, such as, "Should I major in classics or accounting?" When comparison is used for informative purposes, it usually explains similarities or differences, discusses them, or evaluates two or more items by comparing and contrasting them.

When you consider two objects side by side, each emphasizes certain features of the other that would not be as evident if you examined the objects individually. That is why college instructors so often give assignments that are comparative: compare two poems or two characters in a story or play, such as King Lear and Cordelia; compare two biological specimens, such as a ginko leaf and an oak leaf; compare two historic documents, such as the Magna Carta and the Constitution; compare two historic figures, such as Ben Franklin and Thomas Jefferson; or compare the conditions of two geographical areas, such as those in the North and those in the South.

Comparison can also be a powerful persuasive strategy. When used for persuasive purposes, it usually helps readers choose between two or more items by demonstrating how they are alike or different. These demonstrations are generally evaluations, but are sometimes simply explanations. For example, David Morris in "Small is Still Beautiful" explains the relative advantages of small and large enterprises to persuade readers that unchecked growth has not brought the benefits we have expected.

Writers who use comparison to develop their ideas generally have a *thesis* that grows out of the basis for comparison and takes the purpose into account. For instance, Bruce Catton's thesis in "Grant and Lee" that these generals represented "two diametrically opposed elements in American life" (258) grows out of his intent to explain how the outcome of the Civil War determined American culture for decades to come.

Audience

When you think about readers of your comparison-and-contrast essay, you want to be sure that they have the necessary background information to understand the basis of your comparison. You must ask yourself who your reader is and speculate as to whether *that reader* would find the basis for comparison apparent. In "Requiem," Paul Goldberger does not find it necessary to point out the similarities between the planning of the memorials in Oklahoma City and New York City. He must, however, explain the differences—economic, cultural, logistical, and aesthetic—to readers who may not have a full understanding of both cultures. Richard Rodriguez knows that his primarily Hispanic audience (readers of *El Andar* magazine) is Christian, mostly Roman Catholic, as he is. This awareness of his audience helps him to focus on what he needs to include in his essay (more information about the two religions his readers are less likely to be familiar with—Judaism and Islam) and what he can omit (details traditionally taught in Christian religious education).

Organization

A comparison paper can be organized *subject by subject, point by point,* or a combination of the two. A subject-by-subject comparison (also called a *whole-by-whole* or *block comparison*) is divided into two major blocks (usually plus an introduction and a conclusion). The first block considers one of the items (or ideas or courses of action) being compared and examines all its pertinent points; the second block does the same for the other item (or idea or course of action).

A point-by-point (also called *part-by-part*) comparison partitions the subject differently. The points of comparison rather than the things themselves are the main basis of organization. One point or feature is raised at a time, and both things are compared in relation to that point before the next point is raised.

A comparison of typical families in the 1950s with those in the 2000s will help to make the distinction between the two kinds of organization clear. We can use either a subject-by-subject, or block, structure or a point-by-point structure. A general outline of block structure would look something like the one illustrated on the left. For a point-by-point structure, the outline would look like the one on the right.

Subject by Subject	*Point by Point*
I. Fifties families (1st subj.)	I. Mothers' role (point 1)
A. Mothers' role (point 1)	A. Fifties families (1st subj.)
B. Fathers' role (point 2)	B. Millennium families (2nd subj.)
C. Children's role (point 3)	II. Fathers' role (point 2)
II. Millennium families (2nd subj.)	A. Fifties families (1st subj.)
A. Mothers' role (point 1)	B. Millennium families (2nd subj.)
B. Fathers' role (point 2)	III. Children's role (point 3)
C. Children's role (point 3)	A. Fifties families (1st subj.)
	B. Millennium families (2nd subj.)

Each arrangement has its advantages and disadvantages. The subject-by-subject organization has the advantage of helping the reader keep each subject in mind *as a whole.* But if this organization is used in a long, complex comparison that has many points, the reader may have a hard time keeping all the points in mind until it is time to turn from one subject to the other. So the subject-by-subject arrangement is usually best suited to short, simple comparisons involving only a few points. The disadvantage of the point-by-point arrangement has already been implied: the reader tends to lose sight of the whole while focusing on the parts. However, when the parts being examined are numerous, point-by-point is usually the practical choice. You can greatly diminish the drawbacks of either strategy if you include appropriate transitional devices to keep your reader on track and if you supply reminders from time to time to help the reader see how your various points are related.

Subject-by-subject and point-by-point strategies are often combined in the same essay, as they are in Bruce Catton's "Grant and Lee." Catton employs a subject-by-subject approach in revealing the numerous differences between the two great Civil War generals, presenting first a full-length picture of Lee, then one of Grant. But he then shifts to a point-by-point approach for showing their similarities.

Balance is very important when writing comparisons. This does not mean that you are obliged to devote equal space and emphasis to every point or even to each of your subjects; your purpose will determine what should be emphasized. But your reader is certain to be puzzled, and perhaps confused, if you raise points about one subject that you ignore about the other.

Language and Style

Typically, comparisons are developed by using parallel descriptions. Make sure that you take advantage of parallel structures (see *Hodges'* 26e/*Writer's* 25e for more information) to express your points. You should also pay particular attention to the connotations and tone of the language you use so that you do not inadvertently elevate the value of one item of comparison above that of another. Also, as noted above, transitions help your audience keep your thesis in mind while reading either a point-by-point or subject-by-subject comparison.

Images

Sometimes similarities and differences are best discerned visually, in images. Look, for instance, at the two advertisements in this chapter. Each places two images, not necessarily related, side by side to nudge the reader towards a certain impression of the product being marketed. If you use images in your own comparison, be sure to consider how they address your purpose and whether they are appropriate for your audience.

Student Essay

In the following student essay, notice how Keisha Jackson establishes fundamental similarities, a basis for comparison, as well as fundamental differences, a basis for contrast, before she develops each, using a point-by-point approach.

The Real Truth about Cats and Dogs

Introduction

Context

Basis for comparison

Thesis

At least once a week I get an e-mail from a friend listing the undesirable qualities of cats. These examples of "humor" always come from dog people, who insist, in ignorance, that cats are lazy and selfish and have made fools of their owners. As the owner of a dog and two cats, I think I can make a more informed judgment about which makes the better pet. And for me, at least, cats are better than dogs.

Point—cleanliness

First of all, cats are clearly cleaner and easier to take care of than dogs. Rocky, my eight-year-old Golden Lab, has to be washed regularly. Every time it rains Rocky is covered in mud. I have to stop everything I'm doing and clean him up before he gets on my mom's furniture. I can't just leave him outside because he will bark and whine and annoy all the neighbors. Not only do I not have to clean my cats, they wouldn't permit me if I wanted to. They clean themselves several times a day. And they wouldn't go near mud.

Although some might argue that litter boxes are inconvenient, I would much rather clean the litter box once a day than get out of bed in the

continued

Point—
convenience in
maintenance

middle of the night to let the dog out. Cats are self-maintaining when it comes to doing their business. And I don't have to inconvenience myself to feed them either. I leave water and dry food out so they can help themselves. Unlike dogs, cats will pace themselves when it comes to eating. If I left a week's worth of food out for Rocky, he would eat it all at once and then really need to go outside. As a result, I can be gone overnight or even for two nights and my cats will be okay, but Rocky requires maintenance throughout the day.

Point—
affection

Another myth about cats and dogs is that dogs are more affectionate than cats. Of course, cats are not as demonstrative as dogs about showing you how much they love you, but I could do without the slobbering eighty pounds of love that is Rocky. He seems to love me the most when I'm all dressed up to go out. My two cats, Whitney and Mariah, on the other hand, are content to sleep in my lap while I'm reading or watching television. Cats are smart. They know you can have too much of a good thing.

Point—energy

Anyone who thinks cats are lazy and not playful has never seen a cat in the presence of a paper bag. My cats play several times a day. They chase each other around the house and they play with me, but they do not have to rely on anyone else for their amusement. They can turn anything into a toy. My cats love the little plastic rings that come around milk jugs. Sometimes Rocky's tail is the favored toy. But I've seen them play with toys and chase critters that I couldn't see. Rocky has to have a playmate, and that playmate is usually yours truly.

Rocky doesn't care if I'm busy doing something else. And he would play all day if I would only cooperate. Sometimes I think Rocky would chase his tennis ball until he dropped dead. A cat would never do that. They know when to rest.

Conclusion—
restatement of
thesis

Don't get me wrong. I love my dog, but even Rocky—with the cat scratch across his nose—even Rocky would have to agree that cats are superior to dogs.

Commentary

Jackson introduces her essay by telling us what occasion stimulated her thinking on the subject—that is, that she receives regular e-mails from "dog people" maligning cats as lazy and selfish. She then draws her basis for comparison and cites her own authority, as an owner of both a dog and two cats. Then she states her thesis: for her, cats are the superior pets. She devotes the next two paragraphs to explaining how cats are more convenient than dogs. She uses the examples of their cleanliness and the convenience of feeding and maintaining them as her points of comparison. She balances these details with contrasting details that support her thesis that dogs are more trouble.

Jackson then dispels the idea that cats are not affectionate. Again she uses details to describe both dogs and cats so that the reader can clearly see the basis of her preference for cats. The next paragraph argues that cats are not lazy as they are purported to be; Jackson uses the contrasting idea of cats' pacing themselves in terms of physical activity to point out that cats are generally smarter than dogs. This provides an effective transition to a humorous restatement of her thesis.

✦ CHECKLIST FOR WRITING ESSAYS DEVELOPED BY COMPARISON AND CONTRAST

- What is the *basis for your comparison* (or contrast)? What point(s) do these items, ideas, or courses of action have in common? (*Hodges'* 32e(5)/*Writer's* 2e(5))
- Why are you comparing or contrasting these things? Is your *purpose* to evaluate them? To explain their similarities or differences so that your readers can make a decision? (*Hodges'* 32a/*Writer's* 1e)
- Can you state your *thesis* in a single sentence? Does that sentence come in the first or second paragraph? If not, why not? (*Hodges'* 32c/*Writer's* 2b)
- Have you evaluated *what your readers are likely to know* about these things? Is one thing likely to be more familiar than the other? If so, have you made sure your essay is balanced between the two? (*Hodges'* 36b/*Writer's* 7b)
- Have you used a *point-by-point* or *subject-by-subject organization*? Why is the one you have used appropriate for your subject matter?
- Have you used *transitional words and phrases* to guide your readers while they are reading your comparison? (*Hodges'* 31b/*Writer's* 3d)
- Would pictures, charts, graphs, or other *visual aids* be helpful for this comparison? If so, where have you used them? Are they properly labeled? (*Hodges'* 8c/*Writer's* 6b)
- Does your *conclusion* make your readers understand why this comparison is important? What do you want them to do as a result of reading your essay? Is that clear in the conclusion? (*Hodges'* 33b(2)/*Writer's* 3b(2))

◆

GRANT AND LEE: A STUDY IN CONTRASTS

Bruce Catton

Bruce Catton began his career as a journalist and worked for several newspapers, including the *Cleveland Plain Dealer.* His abiding interest in history, however, led to his becoming a noted authority on the Civil War, about which he published more than a dozen books. In 1954 he received both the Pulitzer Prize and the National Book Award for *A Stillness at Appomattox* (1953). Among the others—all good reading for the non-specialist as well as the historian—are *Mr. Lincoln's Army* (1951), *This Hallowed Ground* (1956), *Never Call Retreat* (1965), *Terrible Swift Sword* (1967), and *Gettysburg: The Final Fury* (1974). The essay that follows, "Grant and Lee: A Study in Contrasts," first appeared in a collection of historical essays written by prominent historians, *The American Story* (1956), and has been widely reprinted since. In it Catton compares and contrasts the two greatest Civil War generals in terms of the different traditions they represented.

1   When Ulysses S. Grant and Robert E. Lee met in the parlor of a modest house at Appomattox Court House, Virginia, on April 9, 1865, to work out the terms for the surrender of Lee's Army of Northern Virginia, a great chapter in American life came to a close, and a great new chapter began.

2   These men were bringing the Civil War to its virtual finish. To be sure, other armies had yet to surrender, and for a few days the fugitive Confederate government would struggle desperately and vainly, trying to find some way to go on living now that its chief support was gone. But in effect it was all over when Grant and Lee signed the papers. And the little room where they wrote out the terms was the scene of one of the poignant, dramatic contrasts in American history.

3   They were two strong men, these oddly different generals, and they represented the strengths of two conflicting currents that, through them, had come into final collision.

4   Back of Robert E. Lee was the notion that the old aristocratic concept might somehow survive and be dominant in American life.

5   Lee was tidewater Virginia, and in his background were family, culture, and tradition . . . the age of chivalry transplanted to a New World which was making its own legends and its own myths. He embodied a way of life that had come down through the age of knighthood and the English country squire. America was a land that was beginning all over again, dedicated to nothing much more complicated than the rather hazy belief that all men had equal rights, and should have an equal chance in the world. In such a land Lee stood for the feeling that it was somehow of advantage to human

society to have a pronounced inequality in the social structure. There should be a leisure class, backed by ownership of land; in turn, society itself should be keyed to the land as the chief source of wealth and influence. It would bring forth (according to this ideal) a class of men with a strong sense of obligation to the community; men who lived not to gain advantage for themselves, but to meet the solemn obligations which had been laid on them by the very fact that they were privileged. From them the country would get its leadership; to them it could look for the higher values—of thought, of conduct, of personal deportment—to give it strength and virtue.

Lee embodied the noblest elements of this aristocratic ideal. Through him, the landed nobility justified itself. For four years, the Southern states had fought a desperate war to uphold the ideals for which Lee stood. In the end, it almost seemed as if the Confederacy fought for Lee; as if he himself was the Confederacy . . . the best thing that the way of life for which the Confederacy stood could ever have to offer. He had passed into legend before Appomattox. Thousands of tired, underfed, poorly clothed Confederate soldiers, long-since past the simple enthusiasm of the early days of the struggle, somehow considered Lee the symbol of everything for which they had been willing to die. But they could not quite put this feeling into words. If the Lost Cause, sanctified by so much heroism and so many deaths, had a living justification, its justification was General Lee. 6

Grant, the son of a tanner on the Western frontier, was everything Lee was not. He had come up the hard way, and embodied nothing in particular except the eternal toughness and sinewy fiber of the men who grew up beyond the mountains. He was one of a body of men who owed reverence and obeisance to no one, who were self-reliant to a fault, who cared hardly anything for the past but who had a sharp eye for the future. 7

These frontier men were the precise opposites of the tidewater aristocrats. Back of them, in the great surge that had taken people over the Alleghenies and into the opening Western country, there was a deep, implicit dissatisfaction with a past that had settled into grooves. They stood for democracy, not from any reasoned conclusion about the proper ordering of human society, but simply because they had grown up in the middle of democracy and knew how it worked. Their society might have privileges, but they would be privileges each man had won for himself. Forms and patterns meant nothing. No man was born to anything, except perhaps to a chance to show how far he could rise. Life was competition. 8

Yet along with this feeling had come a deep sense of belonging to a national community. The Westerner who developed a farm, opened a shop or set up in business as a trader, could hope to prosper only as his own community prospered—and his community ran from the Atlantic to the Pacific and from Canada down to Mexico. If the land was settled, with towns and highways and accessible markets, he could better himself. He saw his fate in terms of the nation's own destiny. As its horizons expanded, so did his. He had, in other words, an acute dollars-and-cents stake in the continued growth and development of his country. 9

10   And that, perhaps, is where the contrast between Grant and Lee becomes most striking. The Virginia aristocrat, inevitably, saw himself in relation to his own region. He lived in a static society which could endure almost anything except change. Instinctively, his first loyalty would go to the locality in which that society existed. He would fight to the limit of endurance to defend it, because in defending it he was defending everything that gave his own life its deepest meaning.

11   The Westerner, on the other hand, would fight with an equal tenacity for the broader concept of society. He fought so because everything he lived by was tied to growth, expansion, and a constantly widening horizon. What he lived by would survive or fall with the nation itself. He could not possibly stand by unmoved in the face of an attempt to destroy the Union. He would combat it with everything he had, because he could only see it as an effort to cut the ground out from under his feet.

12   So Grant and Lee were in complete contrast, representing two diametrically opposed elements in American life. Grant was the modern man emerging; beyond him, ready to come on the stage, was the great age of steel and machinery, of crowded cities and a restless, burgeoning vitality. Lee might have ridden down from the old age of chivalry, lance in hand, silken banner fluttering over his head. Each man was the perfect champion of his cause, drawing both his strengths and his weaknesses from the people he led.

13   Yet, it was not all contrast, after all. Different as they were—in background, in personality, in underlying aspiration—these two great soldiers had much in common. Under everything else, they were marvelous fighters. Furthermore, their fighting qualities were really very much alike.

14   Each man had, to begin with, the great virtue of utter tenacity and fidelity. Grant fought his way down the Mississippi Valley in spite of acute personal discouragement and profound military handicaps. Lee hung on in the trenches at Petersburg after hope itself had died. In each man there was an indomitable quality . . . the born fighter's refusal to give up as long as he can still remain on his feet and lift his two fists.

15   Daring and resourcefulness they had, too; the ability to think faster and move faster than the enemy. These were the qualities which gave Lee the dazzling campaigns of Second Manassas and Chancellorsville and won Vicksburg for Grant.

16   Lastly, and perhaps greatest of all, there was the ability, at the end, to turn quickly from war to peace once the fighting was over. Out of the way these two men behaved at Appomattox came the possibility of a peace of reconciliation. It was a possibility not wholly realized in the years to come, but which did, in the end, help the two sections to become one nation again . . . after a war whose bitterness might have seemed to make such a reunion wholly impossible. No part of either man's life became him more than the part he played in their brief meeting in the McLean house at Appomattox. Their behavior there put all succeeding generations of Americans in their debt. Two great Americans Grant and Lee—very different, yet under everything very much alike. Their encounter at Appomattox was one of the great moments of American history.

Rhetorical Considerations

1. Is Catton's purpose in this essay primarily informative, expressive, or persuasive? What evidence can you find to support your answer? Is there evidence of all three purposes? (*Hodges'* 32a/*Writer's* 1e)
2. What kind of audience do the details in the essay lead you to imagine Catton had in mind? In what way(s) are you or are you not a member of that audience? (*Hodges'* 32a/*Writer's* 1e)
3. What advantage does Catton gain by contrasting the two generals before he compares them? What would have been the effect of approaching the subject the opposite way? (*Hodges'* 32d/*Writer's* 2c)
4. Analyze Catton's use of both subject-by-subject (whole-by-whole or block) organization and point-by-point (part-by-part) organization. Where, and for what kind of information, is each pattern used? Might alternative arrangements have been as effective? Why or why not? (*Hodges'* 32e/*Writer's* 2e)
5. Analyze Catton's use of various transitional devices throughout the essay to help readers keep their bearings. In particular, comment on the functions of paragraphs 12 and 13 within the whole essay and on the transition between these two paragraphs. (*Hodges'* 31d/*Writer's* 3d)
6. Explain how the introduction and conclusion frame the essay, providing and reinforcing the basis for Catton's comparison. (*Hodges'* 33b/*Writer's* 3b)

Language and Style

1. Look up the following words in your dictionary: *virtual* and *poignant* (paragraph 2); *aristocratic* (paragraph 4); *chivalry* (paragraph 5); *sanctified* (paragraph 6); *obeisance* (paragraph 7); *static* (paragraph 10); *diametrically* and *burgeoning* (paragraph 12); *aspiration* (paragraph 13); *tenacity* (paragraph 14). (*Hodges'* 18e/*Writer's* 28e)
2. Explain the meaning (both the denotation and the connotations) of *tidewater* in the first sentences of paragraphs 5 and 8. (*Hodges'* 18e/*Writer's* 28e)
3. The next-to-last sentence of the essay is a deliberate fragment. What reason might Catton have had for using it? Had Catton written a complete sentence instead, what would it have been? How would the effect have been different? (*Hodges'* 2c/*Writer's* 18c)
4. Comment on the use of parallel structure in the last sentence of paragraph 5. (*Hodges'* 26/*Writer's* 25)
5. Explain how Catton's inversion of normal sentence order in the first sentence of paragraph 15 contributes to the sentence's effectiveness. (*Hodges'* 29f/*Writer's* 26f)

Writing Suggestions

1. Write an essay comparing and contrasting two professionals you know (for instance, teachers, ministers, or doctors) who represent different professional styles but who are both excellent in their work.
2. Report an imaginary encounter between two historical figures who have something in common, but whose differences are striking enough to make

the meeting interesting to observe. Locate your characters wherever it suits you: at a party, in adjacent airplane seats on a long flight, in the dentist's waiting room, or even in a chance encounter in heaven (or elsewhere, as may be appropriate). A few possibilities include: Babe Ruth and Barry Bonds; General Patton and Colin Powell; Janet Reno and Condoleeza Rice; George Clooney and Cary Grant; Oprah Winfrey and Madonna; Martin Luther King, Jr., and Malcolm X; Hillary Rodham Clinton and Laura Bush.

♦

Dispatch from Beijing

Robin Morgan

Now a feminist writer and activist, Robin Morgan starred in the 1950s television show *I Remember Mama* and had her own radio show *(The Little Robin Morgan Show)* in the 1940s. She recounts her difficult background as a child actor and model in *Saturday's Child: A Memoir* (2001). She has also written poetry and fiction, and her books include *The Demon Lover: On the Sexuality of Terrorism* (1989), *Upstairs in the Garden: Poems Selected and New, 1968–1988* (1990), and *A Hot January: Poems, 1996–1999* (1999).

This essay was published in *Ms.* magazine as a report on the 1995 United Nations Fourth World Conference on Women held in Beijing, China. The conference was fraught with controversy, not the least of which was its taking place in a country with such a notorious human rights record, especially women's rights. The essay's tone is chatty and informal, yet Morgan does not forget her serious purpose.

As you read, look for evidence that Morgan knows her audience's interests and values.

Remember the story about conflicting definitions of an elephant, each by 1 someone describing a different part? Those are the varied reports about the United Nations Fourth World Conference on Women (September 4–15, 1995) and the overlapping NGO (nongovernmental organizations) Forum on Women '95 (August 30–September 8). But most would agree that the Platform for Action emerging from the conference is remarkable—a document that even with its flaws is the strongest official statement on women internationally to date.

This triumph was at least 20 years in the making. Momentum built dur- 2 ing the 1975–85 U.N. Decade for Women (the Mexico City, Copenhagen, and Nairobi women's conferences), and women declined to disperse obediently at the decade's end; instead, we intensified both grassroots organizing efforts and NGO pressure on governments. Furthermore, women broke out of the ghetto and mobilized regarding the U.N. general conferences: the Conference on Environment and Development (Rio de Janeiro, 1992), the World Conference on Human Rights (Vienna, 1993), the International Conference on Population and Development (Cairo, 1994), and the World Summit for Social Development (Copenhagen, 1995) all witnessed the growing presence—and clout—of women. At each of these conferences, a daily Women's Caucus, organized for NGOs by the Women's Environment and Development Organization (WEDO), directed and focused on-site sophisticated lobbying efforts so that government delegations were forced to realize that all issues are "women's issues." Meanwhile, women were painstakingly learning the complex ways of the U.N. and how to make an impact on its policies. Groups went through the process of application for accredited NGO status; activists dragged themselves to the numerous regional preparatory meetings that precede each conference, where the real work of affecting content and agendas takes place and from which the draft document emerges. They learned that by the time that draft actually goes to the conference for which it's intended, it's not likely to be substantively changed, and that the time for lobbying governments with new input is by then past. They also learned to push hard for the inclusion of NGO representatives on government delegations. It was the most organized international effort to date.

3   But first, the forum, since it began first. This report is a mix of facts, analysis, and the generously shared thoughts of old and new friends from around the globe. You probably shouldn't feed it peanuts.

The Forum: Spins, Security, Sisterhood

4 The good news: 30,000 women "rose above it." The bad news: we had to. The plain truth: men would never have tolerated such treatment. Women did—not necessarily something to be proud of.

5   A spin has emerged in forum post-mortems that accentuates the positive to a ludicrously inaccurate degree. It claims that only feminists from northern countries complained about the forum planners or Chinese-government attempts to control thousands of grassroots activists. But there were equal opportunities for outrage: African women charging their Chinese hosts with racist attitudes; South Asian women protesting visa delays/denials; Latin Americans complaining of arbitrary detentions; Middle Easterners appalled at some of the overcrowded, even unsanitary, Huairou living accommodations; Pacific Islander women infuriated at the Chinese press for censoring their hottest issue, French nuclear testing. (China also conducts nuclear tests, remember.)

6   Frankly, it's an act of disrespect to Chinese women—all the non-hand-picked, non-Stepford feminist ones we never got to meet—to pretend that the Chinese government was the dandiest host conceivable and that China's just a developing nation that did its best, gee whiz. China's also a world power, by golly—and judging from all the semi-pornographic billboards promulgating multinational corporate products—its government lusts after the worst the West offers while fearing the best, such as even a pretense of free speech. When Kenya (a developing nation that's *not* a world power) hosted the 1985 Women's Conference and Forum, the Kenyan government, unlike the Chinese, didn't issue warnings to its citizens to be weary of these foreign radicals who might run around naked and be HIV/AIDS positive.

7   See, the Beijing Boys really wanted the Olympics in the year 2000. Losing out because of their human rights record made them cranky, so the U.N. awarded a consolation prize: us. But hordes of political women instead of reams of apolitical athletes were maybe less their compensatory ideal than their worst nightmare. Wistfully pretending that gold medalists, not feminists, were advancing on the Forbidden City, they based the U.N. Confer-

ence next to Beijing's Asian Games Village and staged epic ceremonies, with torch-passing at the National Olympic Sports Center Stadium, fashion shows (huh?), martial arts teams, and battalions of heavily lipsticked children costumed as matadors *(huh?)*, dancing or releasing thousands of stoned doves dizzy from being released for such spectacles. (The acrobats *were* fabulous, and the Chinese Women's Philharmonic impressive, although there are just so many times you can appreciate Beethoven's "Ode to Joy" in one three-day period.)

Red carpets (literally) and interpreters who actually spoke languages 8 other than Mandarin were reserved for the conference. Uneasy with the non-governmental concept, the Chinese government exiled the forum from its planned Beijing site to "scenic" Huairou, more than 90 minutes (in rain, more than two hours) away. NGOs threatened to boycott. But forum officials reassured NGOs of government guarantees: excellent lodging and communications facilities would be built for those staying in Huairou, and buses would shuttle every 20 minutes between Huairou and Beijing.

Fits of mirth. 9

Specially constructed buildings lacked walls and roofs. Only toward the 10 forum's end, after women got blessedly "shrill," did buses appear every half hour—sort of. "Volunteer Guides" were politely unfamiliar with Huairou and with any non-Chinese language. Workshop venues were changed with no notice and the Official Schedule listing the almost 5,000 workshops lacked an index. Honest. Tent-area "paths"—thin concrete squares laid without fixative on bare earth—turned graham-crackery with rain and sank in the surrounding mud. Draconian "security" measures were not exaggerated by the western press; uniformed and plainclothes police, body frisks, room searches, confiscation of literature/videos/signs; "appointed" hotels and "designated" restaurants (quality control or female control?); even a "regulated" protest area: a *playground.*

Why did women endure such treatment? For each other's sake. (This is 11 how they get us.) Here's another montage:

A virtual city of female people. Turbans, caftans, saris, sarongs, kente 12 cloth, blue jeans. Workshops—on micro-credit, caste, women's studies, "comfort" women, solar stoves, refugees, you name it. Round-the-clock networking. Nonstop cultural events. A "once and future pavilion" demystifying men's technology and celebrating women's alternative technologies. First-timers, euphoric at the sheer numbers, finally feeling part of a vast global movement. Veterans delighted that "cultural defense" justifications finally wilted under a unifying assault against purdah, sexual slavery, polygyny.

Special honors go to a triad that emerged in spontaneous leadership: 13 (1) disability NGOs, outraged at crumbly paths, workshop assignments to second-floor, no-elevator venues, and too-steep ramps—"for ski-jumping, not chairs," quipped one Filipina feminist on wheels; they daringly staged the first demonstration outside the "designated protest area," an energetic roll-in. (2) The U.S. Women of Color coalitions—a de facto microcosm of the world's women, but with a shared language, and experience in alliance-building—who found themselves ascendant as coalition facilitators. And

(3) lesbian activists, who exuberantly staged the first march (*far* from the designated playground, kiddo), chanting "Liberté, Egalité, Homosexualité." This set the tone for other breakout demos—a daily defiance teaching the Chinese police how to study their shoe-tips intently.

14   More than 1,000 women united for the Women in Black vigil on violence against women, organized by Asia-Pacific groups. (How I somehow wound up making and carrying the sign reading "Don't Forget the women of Tiananmen Square"—and my experience afterward—is another story. I'd been *trying* to be good. But authoritarian regimes bring out the 1960s in me.)

15   Meanwhile, back in Beijing, the conference suffered from a minor epidemic of "first ladies." Hillary Rodham Clinton deserves praise for facing down the U.S. right wing by going to China and speaking substantively both in Beijing and Huairou. But more than one delegate (names tactfully withheld) conveyed discomfort that the drive toward women holding power directly was subtly undermined by the presence of at least 16 first ladies.

16   Of the (fewer) female heads of state or government, Pakistan's Prime Minister Benazir Bhutto delivered the most virtuoso speech. In this juggling act, she deftly (1) decried fundamentalism, while defending Islam from accusations of misogyny; (2) affirmed the "traditional family as the bedrock of society," while attacking female infanticide as the cause of the current sex imbalance in more than 15 Asian countries; and (3) defended cultural values, while announcing that Pakistan would become a signatory to CEDAW (the U.N. Convention on the Elimination of All Forms of Discrimination Against Women). And her visual subtext! Bhutto's usual elegantly draped head scarf—her chic gesture to the *hijab*—was unsecured over her sleek hair, so that it slipped backward, a millimeter at a time, with each nod of her head. This double message to the mullahs back home magnetized every gaze present. Riveting suspense: *would* she catch it before it slid off completely? At the last possible moment, with the barest riddle of a smile, she'd resettle her chiffon banner—only to have it promptly begin its slippage again.

17   The best "position paper" was the single page signed by Marye Kat and Meike Keldenich (ages 12 and 11), members of the Netherlands delegations: "Most of you promised to [include youth in delegations]. . . . Now, as far as we know, we are again the only ones. If you don't do what you have promised, how can we believe you [will] do what you are promising now at this conference?" These girls have a political future. So does the Netherlands.

18   The general terminology reflected a conceptual shift. Words once risked only by radical feminists have entered the policy mainstream. I can remember being criticized for using "oppression," "liberation," and "power"— as opposed to the less threatening "discrimination" and "equality"; Bhutto's speech included all five of those words. I remember buttons reading "All Women Are Working Women" (for a 1970s welfare rights demonstration), and how we had to explain that shocking concept. Now, there it was, in bold letters, on the front of the U.N. International Labour Office press packet.

19   Which brings us to the Platform for Action itself. The draft document was strong; activist NGO women had helped write it, remember, a five re-

gional prep-cons. But the fundamentalist Christian-Islamist-Vatican coalition, availing itself of U.N. procedure, imposed brackets around text it deemed controversial, so the draft went to Beijing with a substantial third of it caged in so-called Holy Brackets.

The first brackets melted away through negotiated compromise language in closed-session trade-offs between delegates. Then the conservatives dug in. Finally, three forces prevailed, working in tandem through all-night sessions: the European Union; the Scandinavian countries (decried in fundamentalist leaflets as the "Satanic Nordic Group"); and especially the group of '77, the major coalition from the South, skillfully chaired by the Philippines' Senator Leticia Shahani. So 189 countries adopted the final Platform for Action and its shorter preamble, the Beijing Declaration, by consensus. 20

There's too much abstract language, yes: too little on resource allocation, institutional reform, implementation—although more than 90 governments committed to specific actions. The wording is bland on many points, including the right to inheritance. And we failed to retain the phrases "sexual orientations" and "sexual rights." 21

Still. We consolidated, even broadened, gains won previously. Paragraph 96: "The human rights of women include their right to have control over and decide freely and responsibly on matters related to their sexuality, including sexual and reproductive health, free of coercion, discrimination, and violence." Many countries pledged voluntarily to interpret lesbian rights as covered under paragraph 46, which recognizes that women face additional barriers to full equality, such as race, age, ethnicity, culture, disability, because they are indigenous, or "because of other status." Not good enough. But a great stagger forward. 22

The document also criticizes structural adjustment programs; advises cuts in military spending in favor of social spending; urges women's participation at all peace talks and in all decision-making affecting development and environment; confronts violence against women; calls for measuring women's unpaid work; and refers to "the family in its various forms." 23

Bringing It All Back Home

"This document is a contract with the world's women," says our own former congresswoman Bella Abzug, a major voice at both the forum and conference. Unenforceable in a strict legal sense, the plan nonetheless sets precedents, exerts a political force, and can act as a lever. *If* we use it. 24

Since China was the first country in all my travels where I'd been unable to contact nonofficially approved women (feminist independents and dissidents had been sent well out of the Beijing/Huairou area), I left frustrated. On my way home via Hong Kong, I read of a cigarette-lighter factory explosion in Dunde City, Guangdong—a tragedy that had left 60 women working critically injured and more than 20 burned to death. Hong Kong–based unionists had entreated the Chinese government to lift the media ban on such accidents, and had appealed to the conference and 25 forum, desperate to draw attention to conditions that mainland women factory workers face. *Not one word of this tragedy had ever reached us in Beijing or Huairou.* My anger at the government's treatment of international activists refocused, fittingly, to its treatment of Chinese women—20 percent of all female people on earth.

26   But wait. Nearly 60 percent of China's population is under 25, and half (despite the resurgence of female infanticide) is female. There's a growing divorce rate—it's doubled in Beijing over the past four years—and 70 percent of divorces are women-initiated.

27   Since it's women who hold up half the sky, the Chinese government should read the story of Chicken Little.

Rhetorical Considerations

1. Written for *Ms.* magazine, this essay is directed to a particular audience. How can you tell Morgan was aware of her audience's interests and values? (*Hodges'* 32e/*Writer's* 2e)
2. How does Morgan organize her essay? How does the beginning relate to the ending? List all the comparisons Morgan makes in her essay. (*Hodges'* 32d–e and 33b/*Writer's* 2c, 2e, and 3b)
3. Why is it important for Morgan to discuss some of the history of the conference? (*Hodges'* 32e/*Writer's* 2e)
4. What's lamentable about the prevalence of first ladies at the conference? Why doesn't Morgan see the need to explain this? (*Hodges'* 32a/*Writer's* 1e)

Language and Style

1. Look up the following words in your dictionary: *platform* (paragraph 1); *disperse, grassroots,* and *affecting* (paragraph 2); *spin, post-mortems, ludicrously,* and *arbitrary* (paragraph 5); *promulgating* (paragraph 6); *reams, apolitical,* and *wistfully* (paragraph 7); *boycott* (paragraph 8); *mirth* (paragraph 9); *shrill* and *Draconian* (paragraph 10); *montage* (paragraph 11); *virtual, euphoric, purdah,* and *polygyny* (paragraph 12); *triad, coalitions, de facto, microcosm,* and *exuberantly* (paragraph 13); *epidemic* (paragraph 15); *virtuoso, deftly, fundamentalism, misogyny, signatory, hijab,* and *mullahs* (paragraph 16); *tandem* (paragraph 20); *allocation* and *implementation* (paragraph 21); *consolidated, coercion,* and *indigenous* (paragraph 22); *dissidents* (paragraph 25); *resurgence* (paragraph 26). (*Hodges'* 18e/*Writer's* 28e)
2. How would you characterize Morgan's tone? What uses of language contribute to her tone? (*Hodges'* 31d/*Writer's* 3d)
3. Language is an important subject in Morgan's essay. Why? Look particularly at paragraphs 10 and 18.
4. Find the passive constructions in paragraph 8. Rewrite them in the active voice. What difference can you detect in the sentences' effect? (*Hodges'* 29/ *Writer's* 2b)

Writing Suggestions

1. Write an essay in which you describe or narrate an event that is antithetical to where it takes place.
2. Find an issue important to your local community (your campus, town, or workplace, for instance) and write an essay in which you compare different attitudes and responses to the issue.

♦

FRUITS WE'LL NEVER TASTE, LANGUAGES WE'LL NEVER HEAR: The Need for Needless Complexity

Beth Ann Fennelly

Originally from a suburb north of Chicago, Beth Ann Fennelly received her BA from the University of Notre Dame and her MFA in poetry from the University of Arkansas. She taught English in a coal-mining village on the border between Poland and the former Czechoslovakia for a year. The recipient of many awards and fellowships for her writing, Fennelly now teaches at Knox University in Galesburg, Illinois. Her nonfiction and poetry have been widely published (in the *American Scholar*, the *Kenyon Review*, and *TriQuarterly*, to name a few). Her first book of poems, *Open House: Poems*, was published in 2002.

The following essay was originally published in *Michigan Quarterly Review*, and was later reprinted in the *Utne Reader*, a popular magazine for a wider readership. As you read, look for elements that may have a broader appeal than perhaps Fennelly herself had originally anticipated.

1   Imagine cupping an Ansault pear in your palm, polishing its golden-green belly on your shirtsleeve. Imagine raising it to your lips and biting, the crisp snap as a wafer of buttery flesh falls on your tongue. Imagine the juice shooting out—you bend at the waist and scoot your feet back to prevent the drops from falling on your sneakers. . . .

2   Imagine it all you can, for it's all you can do. You'll never eat an Ansault pear. They are extinct, and have been for decades: dead as dodo birds. How could this happen to a pear variety which agriculturist U.P. Hetrick described, in a 1921 report called "The Pears of New York," as "better than any other pear," with a rich sweet flavor, and distinct but delicate perfume"? The dismaying truth is that you can apply that question to thousands of fruits and vegetables. In the last few decades we've lost varieties of almost every crop species. Where American farmers once chose from among 7,000 apple varieties, they now choose from 1,000. Beans, beets, millet, peanuts, peas, sweet potatoes, and rice all have suffered a large reduction in varieties. In fact, over 90 percent of crops that were grown in 1900 are gone.

3   Of course, next to "Save the Whales," a bumper sticker reading "Save the White Wonder Cucumbers" sounds a bit silly. And as long as we haven't lost pears altogether, the loss of a particular variety, no matter how good, isn't cataclysmic. We have a lot of other worries. How many years of sunlight do we have left? Of clean air? Water? But when we lose a variety of pear or cucumber, even one we're not likely to taste, or, in an analogous situation, when we lose a language, even one we're not likely to hear, we're losing a lot more than we think. We're losing millions of bits of genetic

information that could help us solve our big questions, like who we are and what we're doing here on earth.

Farming has always been subject to the manipulations of human desires, but up until the last several decades these manipulations increased crop diversity. Long before Mendel came along, our farmer ancestors were practicing a kind of backyard Darwinism. Early Peruvian farmers, for example, noticed mutations among the colors of their cotton fibers, and by breeding the cotton selectively, they were able to grow different colors to weave vibrant cloth. When farmers moved, they took their seeds with them, and various growing conditions increased crop diversity even further as the varieties reacted to new environments or evolved new defenses for pests or blights. And in this way farmers farmed for about 10,000 years. Even at the beginning of this century, small farms were varied; each grew many crops and sometimes several varieties of a particular crop. If a blight attacked one species of a farmer's corn, it was likely that the farmer, or another farmer nearby, would also have grown a variety of corn that turned out to be resistant.

But as the century wore on, agribusiness was born. Now, giant agricultural agencies develop fruits and vegetables specifically for giant farms, which concentrate on a single variety of a single crop sanctioned for high-yield growth. These new crops aren't self-reliant—many hybrids can't even produce offspring, putting an end to the age-old tradition of gathering seeds from the current harvest for next year's crop. They are dependent upon intensive fertilizers, pesticides, and insecticides. They are grown only if they can withstand mechanical harvesting and the rigors of shipping to distant markets, and these packing considerations shape our diet in startling ways, as anyone who's followed the quest for the square tomato can tell you. Some biotech companies have taken the human manipulations of crops to a profitable—if seemingly unnatural—extreme. Biotech giant Monsanto, maker (and dumper) of hazardous chemicals like PCB, filed for a patent in 1997 for a seed whose germination depends not on being exposed to a rise in temperature or an inch of rainfall, but being exposed to a certain chemical.

So now, according to the International Food Information Council, we have scientists crossing two potatoes to make a new hybrid which will be higher in starch and need less oil for frying, resulting in lower-fat fries. But genetic engineers don't stop with crossing two kinds of potatoes. Genes from a potato could be crossed with a carrot, or a banana, or a daschund, if genetic engineers thought such a crossing would improve the potato's shelf-life. Recently, genetic engineers have crossed the strawberry with a gene from the flounder to make a strawberry resistant to the cold. In this way, millions of years of nature's "decisions"—which crops should fail, which thrive, which qualities parents should pass to their offspring—are reversed almost overnight. The Union of Concerned Scientists is—well—concerned. Poet W. S. Merwin likens our position in history now to the start of the nuclear age—we are rushing to embrace technology that will change us in unalterable, unforeseeable ways.

A problem with miracles is that sometimes they don't last. A miracle yield hybrid's defenses are often based on a single gene, an easy thing for continuously evolving pests to overcome. And meanwhile back at the ranch, there is no more ranch—the small farms that grew the original parent varieties that crossed to make the super vegetable have failed. The parents are extinct. Unless genetic raw material resistant to the pest can be found in some other variety, the hybrid will be lost as well.

8   The first crop to be nearly wiped out due to lack of genetic diversity is the humble spud, which the Europeans brought home with them after "discovering" the New World. King Louis XVI of France saw the potato's potential for feeding the poor and was determined to spread the crop. He knew that publicly endorsing the potato, however, would earn it the commoner's enmity. So Louis grew a bumper crop and had the field guarded all day, but he removed the guards at night so the locals could raid the field. Potatoes were soon growing throughout France and beyond. In Ireland, the potato became the staple crop—by the 1840s a third of the Irish were dependent on it for nourishment. But since all the potatoes grown in Europe were the descendants of that original handful of potatoes brought over from the Andes, the crop had a narrow gene pool. When *Phytophtora infestans* struck in 1845, the potato lacked the resistance to combat it. *The Freeman's Journal* reported on Sept. 11 of that year that a "cholera" had rotted the fields; one farmer announced that he "had been digging potatoes—the finest he had ever seen" on Monday, but when he returned Tuesday he found "the tubers all blasted, and unfit for the use of man or beast." A five-year famine followed that slashed the population of Ireland by 20 percent, killing between one to two million people and forcing one to two million others to emigrate to the U.S. The potato was saved only when resistance to the blight was found in more diversified varieties of the potato still growing in the Andes and Mexico. Had it not been, it's unlikely the potato would be around today as a major crop.

9   While the potato famine might seem like dusty history, the U.S. corn blight proves we're not doing much to stop history from repeating itself. In *Shattering: Food, Politics, and the Loss of Genetic Diversity,* environmentalists Cary Fowler and Pat Mooney describe the 1970s hybrid corn plants as "sitting ducks." As a result of a cost-cutting measure, each of the several hundred varieties of hybrid corn seed had the same type of cytoplasm. That made the entire crop susceptible to any disease that could come along and exploit that uniformity—and, of course, one did. Even today we have several dangerously unstable crops including—gulp—coffee and chocolate. The dangers of genetic uniformity are currently being cited in an altogether new arena—the Genome Project. Now that scientists have engineered vegetable hybrids, what's stopping scientists from crating human hybrids? Could cloning so narrow our gene pool that a single epidemic could destroy us like the potato blight nearly destroyed the potato?

10   Imagine hiking high into the Sierra Nevadas and coming across the Northern Pomos. Imagine being able to converse with them in their language. Imagine clicking your tongue against the back for your teeth to say "sunset," aspirating in your throat to say "waterfall." Imagine learning the idiomatic expression for "hungover" and using it to great effect, comparing it with oth-

ers you know—how the Japanese expression for "hungover" translates as "suffer the two-day dizzies," how Italians say "I'm out of tune," how the Czechs say "there's a monkey swinging in my head," how Arabs don't have any word at all for "hungover." Imagine trading recipes with an elderly Northern Pomo, then walking with his wife through a stand of ponderosa pine, their trunks so thin, because of the high atmosphere, that you could fit your hand around them. You tell her you need to stop talking, for you've developed a sore throat. She questions you about it, then bends down to a small plant and yanks it out of the ground. This yerba del manza will soothe your throat, she tells you, and she gives hints on how to recognize the plant again should your soreness return. Imagine going to bed that night, your throat calmed, your mind blossoming with Northern Pomo words that will fill the cartoon bubbles of your dreams. . . .

Imagine it all you want, but Northern Pomo, spoken for millennia in 11 Northern California, has perished like the Ansault pear; its last speaker, a woman in her eighties, died a few years ago.

Today we have the impression that there's a rough 1:1 correlation be- 12 tween countries and languages; each nation is monolingual. But this has never been the case. In the sixteenth century, for instance, five major languages were spoken in the English King's domain. Our country was especially language rich because each Native American tribe clung fiercely to its tongue as a signifier of cultural difference; Edward G. Gray in *New World Babel* estimates that, when European contact occurred, there were between 1,000 and 2,000 distinct tongues in the Americas, nearly half of which are now extinct. A graphic way to understand this is to peruse the maps in *The Atlas of World Languages* edited by C. Moseley and R. E. Asher. The maps showing pockets of language before the colonizers arrived in America are many-colored, many-patterned quilts; each subsequent map is increasingly bleached, increasingly pattern-free.

Languages don't die because they are in any way inferior or deficient, 13 as has been sometimes supposed in the past. They die because of pressures on minority communities to speak the majority language. Sometimes this pressure is economic, as seen, for example, with the Waimiri-Atroari of Brazil, a tribe of 500 prople in the Brazilian Amazon, whose tongue is listed in the *UNESCO Red Book of Endangered Languages*. The Waimiri-Atroari are mostly monolingual, but they have experienced increasing contact with the Portuguese-speaking majority. The tribe is growing in bilingual members because learning Portuguese widens the Waimiri-Atroari's potential market from 500 members to 160 million. As the proportion of bilingual members of the tribe rises, members of the tribe might begin using Portuguese when speaking to each other; it follows that the motivation for children to learn their native tongue will erode. The language's death will surely follow.

Sometimes the pressure for a minority community to speak the major- 14 ity language is not economic but political, as has been the case with Native American languages in the U.S. since European settlement began. Early U.S. settlers had a romantic notion of language difference as a cause of personality difference. Since some Native American languages were found to lack abstract concepts like *salvation, Lord,* and *redemption,* the settlers presumed the speakers of these languages to be unable to grasp these higher concepts. It seemed to follow that Native Americans' salvation could only be achieved by "liberating" them from their restrictive native tongues. "In the present state of affairs," Albert Gallatin wrote of Native Americans in *Archaeologia Americana* in 1836, "no greater demand need be made on their intellectual faculties, than to teach them the English language; but this so thoroughly, that they may forget their own." In this report on Indian affairs, Reverend Jedediah Morse recommended the suppression of any texts in Native American tongues. There were supporters of America's original languages—Thomas Jefferson, for one, compiled vocabulary lists of Native American words throughout his lifetime. But even today we haven't a national policy of language preservation. In fact, between 1981 and 1990, fifteen states enacted "Official English" laws to guarantee English as the language of the U.S. government. As Alexis de Tocqueville observed in his 1839 *Democracy in America,* "the majority lays down the law about language as about all else."

15   Languages are termed "moribund" if they are spoken only by a small group of older people and not being learned by children. These languages stand in contrast to "safe" languages, as defined by criteria set out in Robins and Uhlenbeck's *Endangered Languages.* A safe language has, at a minimum, "a community of 100,000 speakers" and the "official support of a nation-state." These numbers don't necessarily represent a swelling, robust population—Gaelic, for example, is among the safe languages—but 80 percent of the languages spoken in North America fail to meet even those standards. In Australia, 90 percent of the languages are moribund. As I write this, sixty-seven languages in Africa are being spoken for what may be the last time. The more fortunate of them are being documented by linguists, who spend much of their professional lives rushing to record a language before it dies. When it does, they find themselves in the rather lonely position of linguist Bill Shipley, the last human being on earth who can speak Maidu.

16   In my girlhood I thought that languages were codes that corresponded; each word in English had its exact equivalent in every other language, and language study was the memorization of these codes. Later when I studied my first languages I learned that such codes do not exist; each language is a unique repository of the accumulated thoughts and experiences of a community. What do we learn about a culture by examining its language? The Inuit people live in the northernmost regions of the world, in small, road-less communities on the ice, and lack our modern electronic conveniences. They have no word for boredom. Poet Anne Carson writes of the Yamana of Argentina, a tribe extinct by the beginning of the twentieth century, who had fifteen names for clouds, fifty for different kinds of kin. Among the Ya-mana variations of the verb "to bite" was one that meant "to come surprisingly on a hard substance when eating something soft, e.g., a pearl in a mussel." The Zuni speak reverently of "penaµ taµshana," a "long talk prayer" so potent it can only be recited once every four years. The Delaware Indians have a term of affection, "wulamalessohalian," or "thou who makest me happy." The Papago of the Sonoran Desert say "S-banow" as the superlative of "one whose breath stinks like a coyote."

During this century, eight-seven languages spoken in the Amazon basin 17 have become extinct because their native speakers were scattered or killed. Some of these forest dwellers were both nonviolent (their languages lacked vocabulary words for war and bloodshed) and democratic (they included terms for collective decision making). When these languages died, they took with them not only the specialized knowledge that the tribes had gained from thousands of years of natural healing and conservation, but ways of living we might have done well to study. In the absence of these examples, as John Adams wrote, "we are left to grope in the dark and puzzle ourselves to explain a thousand things which would have appeared very simple if we had . . . the pure light of antiquity."

But even beyond this rather romantic notion of the need for language 18 preservation, there are concrete and empirical losses to science when languages become extinct. There's a wealth of information that can be extracted from languages by the use of statistical techniques, and this information can be used not only by linguists, but by anthropologists, cognitive psychologists, neuroscientists, geneticists, and population biologists, among others. Hypotheses about human migration patterns can be tested by seeing whether words have been assimilated into a language from the languages of nearby populations. Hypotheses about neural structures and processes can be tested by analyzing the phonology and syntax of a language. Hypotheses about the hardware of our brains capable of generating sentences can be tested against the different sentences. What must all infant brains have in common that any child can acquire any language? The more data we have, the closer we can come to answering questions such as this. Furthermore, recent studies indicate that language learning causes cognitive and neural changes in an individual. At a recent conference at the Center for Theories of Language and Learning, Dr. Mark Pagel argued that when a child acquires a disposition to categorize objects through word-learning, some neural connections in the brain are strengthened, while others are weakened or eliminated. Previous learning affects a system's way of categorizing new stimuli, and so Pagel concluded that, although it may be true that all humans "think in the same way," one's native language influences one's perceptions. When we lose linguistic diversity we suffer a consequent loss in the range of ways of experiencing the world.

Yet we needn't constrain ourselves to discussions of hard science, for 19 the issues involved in diversity are more far-reaching. If the language ability, as many theorists hold, is what separates us from animals, it is the central event of human evolution. Each language that dies takes with it everything it might have taught us about this unique aspect of our constitution. If language is a well-engineered biological instinct, as Steven Pinker argues in *The Language Instinct,* each language that dies takes from us another clue to the mystery of what keeps the spider spinning her web or the hen warming the eggs in her nest. The cognitive organization which shapes our language facilities also shapes other mental activities related to language, such as music and mathematics. Each language that dies not only weakens linguistics but all of these related fields—all fields, in fact, that seek to understand the human brain. Each language that dies takes from us a few crucial parts of nature's tale, so much of which (even how and when the universe was created) still eludes us. In fact, each language that dies weakens our most vital challenge—to engage the world in all its complexity and to find meaning there. This is the definition of both art and religion. To lessen the complexity of the world is to lessen our moral struggle.

20   I've written "personal essays" before, and this isn't one of them. I haven't told you very much about myself. I haven't told you if I'm a scientist (I'm not) or a linguist (I'm not). I'm a poet. So the argument could be made (perhaps some of you are making it right now) that I'm not qualified to write this essay. But I'm qualified to make metaphors, and that's what I've tried to do. I read books on crops and languages and I begin to hear them speaking to each other, and soon the desire is born in me to speak of them to you.

21   I've argued for empirical reasons we need diversity on our table and in our ears. But I think one of the most important reasons we need diversity isn't based on grubby need, isn't based on a what-can-nature-do-for-me mentality. I don't want the argument to rest solely on that because plenty of people will think they have all that they need. And in a way they're right. After all, we live in an era of hysterical data. It's exhausting. Let's have enough faith in our own self-interest, if in nothing else, to assume we will never lose the pear or the potato. Let's have enough faith in our own torpidity, if in nothing else, to assume we will never have a unilingual world. So okay, we lose a few varieties of Ethiopian sorghum—varieties once so beloved they were named "Why Bother with Wheat?" and "Milk in my Cheeks." Do we really need forty kinds? Isn't four enough? It's not like only having four friends, or even four varieties of dogs. A seed company streamlining its offerings isn't like a museum streamlining its Van Gogh collection. And if we lose a few obscure languages, maybe that's the price one pays for having fewer translators and English as a "universal business language," saving time, frustration, and money. Why should we be overly concerned if what's lost wasn't useful to us in the first place?

22   Of course, there's an old rejoinder but a good one—our responsibility to the future. In poem No. 1748, Emily Dickinson writes, "If nature will not tell the tale/Jehovah told to her/Can human nature not survive/without a listener?" But nature ceaselessly tries to tell her tale to the patient and attentive, and her tale is still unfolding. Each seemingly interchangeable variety of sorghum contains a distinct link of DNA that reveals part of nature's story. Similarly, each language is a biological phenomenon that reveals millions of bits of genetic information and contains within itself clues that help us understand how our brains are organized. What clues our progeny will need is beyond our power to know. We can't imagine what will be useful, necessary, what will provide a link, prove or disprove a hypothesis. Losing plants, losing languages: it's like losing pieces to a puzzle we'll have to put together in a thousand years, but by then puzzles may look entirely different. We might put them together in the dark, with our toes.

23   Yet beyond the idea of what will be useful to future generations, we, right here, right now, have a need for needless diversity. A world with fewer

fruits and vegetables isn't only a world with an endangered food supply. It's also a world with less flavor, less aroma, less color. We suffer a diminution of choice. As Gregory McNamee writes in "Wendell Berry and the Politics of Agriculture," we're experiencing "an impoverishment of forms, a loss of the necessary complexity that informs an art rightly practiced."[1] And a world with fewer languages isn't only a world with more limited means of communication. It's also a world with fewer stories and folk tales, fewer hagiographies, fewer poems, myths, and recipes, fewer remedies, fewer memories. We possess the accumulated vision and wisdom of fewer cultures. We become like hybrid corn: less diverse, with less accumulated defenses, susceptible to dangers that our "parents" might have battled and overcome, dangers they could have helped us with, were they not in their graves.

What I want to say is this: for twenty-eight years I've been carrying on a 24 love affair with words and the world and I've come to believe that the sheer magnitude of creation blesses us. The gross numbers, the uncountability of it; as if the world were a grand, grand room full of books and though we might read all we can we will never, ever outstrip its riches. A thought both unsettling and comforting. If we are stewards of the world, we are stewards of a charge beyond our comprehension; even now science can tell us less about the number of species we have on earth than about the number of stars in our galaxy. There is something important in the idea of this fecundity, this abundance, this escape hatch for our imaginations. I have read Robert Frost's poem "Design," and I have read Gordon Grice's essay on how the black widow spider kills her prey with ten times the amount of poison she needs, and I'm not one for making teleological arguments, but I can tell you that somehow, despite our savagery, we have been over-provided for, and I believe it is a sign of love.

Poet Wendell Berry urges us to care for "the unseeable animal," even if 25 it means we never see it. So, I would argue, must we care for the untastable vegetable, the unhearable language, which add their link, as we add ours, to nature's still-unfolding tale. They deepen nature's mystery even as they provide clues to help us comprehend that mystery. They enrich us not only because they can serve us, not only because they are useful, but because *they are*. Their existence contributes to the complexity of the world in which *we are*, a world we still strive—thankfully, nobly—to understand.

Rhetorical Considerations

1. Why does Fennelly use subject-by-subject organization? How would her essay be affected if it were reorganized with the point-by-point method? (*Hodges'* 32d/*Writer's* 2c)
2. What is the subject, precisely, of Fennelly's essay? (*Hodges'* 32c/*Writer's* 2b)

---

[1]See *Wendell Berry*, ed. Paul Merchant (Lewiston, ID: Confluence Press, 1991), 90–102.

3. Find evidence in Fennelly's essay of the use of example, narration, description, process, and cause and effect (chapters 1–5). Why do you think we chose to include the essay in this chapter? (*Hodges'* 32e/*Writer's* 2e)
4. How does Fennelly express her ethos in this essay? What sources or authorities does she employ? Are these adequate and appropriately selected? (*Hodges'* 32a/*Writer's* 1e)
5. As the headnote indicates, this essay was originally published in *Michigan Quarterly Review,* an academic journal, but was reprinted in the *Utne Reader,* a popular magazine. What makes this essay appealing to a general reader? Is any of it unappealing to such a reader? Why? (*Hodges'* 32a/*Writer's* 1e)
6. How specifically does Fennelly draw her two different subjects together? (*Hodges'* 32b/*Writer's* 2a)

Language and Style

1. Look up the following words in your dictionary: *cataclysmic* and *analogous* (paragraph 3); *mutations, evolved,* and *blights* (paragraph 4); *hybrid* (paragraph 6); *cytoplasm* (paragraph 9); *aspirating* (paragraph 10); *millennia* (paragraph 11); *monolingual* and *erode* (paragraph 13); *moribund* (paragraph 15); *repository, potent,* and *superlative* (paragraph 16); *extracted, statistical, cognitive, neuroscientists, hypotheses, assimilated, neural, phonology, syntax,* and *stimuli* (paragraph 18); *diminution* and *hagiographies* (paragraph 23); *gross* and *fecundity* (paragraph 24). (*Hodges'* 18e/*Writer's* 28e)
2. Fennelly is a poet as well as a nonfiction writer. Locate three examples of descriptive language you find particularly effective in this essay. (*Hodges'* 20b/*Writer's* 29b)
3. Find examples of scientific or technical language in the essay. Does the use of this language impede your reading or make the essay more effective? Explain. (*Hodges'* 19c/*Writer's* 28c)
4. Fennelly begins paragraphs 1, 2, 10, and 11 with "Imagine." What is effective about this repetition? (*Hodges'* 29e/*Writer's* 26e)
5. Are *who's* in paragraph 5 and *whose* in paragraph 13 used correctly? Why or why not? (*Hodges'* 5/*Writer's* 21)
6. Are the sentence fragments in paragraph 3 justifiable? Why or why not? (*Hodges'* 2/*Writer's* 18)

Writing Suggestions

1. Write an essay in which you speculate how life would be different if a major phenomenon (such as electricity or the Internet) or an item (such as a food product or an animal) disappeared for one day or forever.
2. Have you ever lost something that was valuable to you? Write a personal essay in which you compare your life with the person or thing you lost to your life without it.

◆

THE MALE GOD OF THE DESERT

Richard Rodriguez

Richard Rodriguez is an author and editor whose commentary can frequently be heard on PBS's *MacNeill/Lehrer News Hour*. The son of Mexican immigrants, Rodriguez is a native of San Francisco and attended Stanford University and the University of California at Berkeley, where he earned his PhD in English Renaissance literature. His books include *Hunger of Memory: The Education of Richard Rodriguez: An Autobiography* (1982), *Days of Obligation: An Argument with My Mexican Father* (1992), and *Brown: The Last Discovery of America* (2002).

This essay was one of many by prominent writers responding to the events of September 11, 2001, and was published in *El Andar* magazine, which describes itself as a "Latino magazine for the new millennium."

As you read, consider Rodriguez's ethos. In other words, look for how he establishes himself as part of the community he is analyzing.

Since September 11th, priests and mullahs and rabbis and ministers in the 1 United States have officiated at ceremonies of grief. What no priest or mullah or rabbi or minister confesses is how religion has brought us to this terrible moment.

Instead, it was British Prime Minister Tony Blair (albeit within a war 2 psalm) who rehearsed a commonplace about the history of religion: Men have, through centuries, blasphemed the name of God to justify human atrocity. Blair recalled Christianity's Crusade against Islam amounted to little more than rape and pillage.

In Washington, President Bush has been careful to distinguish Islam 3 from crimes committed in the name of Islam. His tact is commendable and shrewd. European diplomats have repeated Bush's assurance that the West is not engaged in a religious war; is not at war with Islam.

The face of bin Laden floats up from his cyber-cave to incite Muslims to 4 war with the West. Osama bin Laden describes America as a "Jewish-Christian alliance." In Pakistan, in Indonesia, crowds of men cheer the prospect of jihad against the satanic West.

I am interested that Judaism, Christianity, and Islam are alike religions 5 of the desert. They are brother-faiths, more like one another than any one of them is like an eastern religion—Hinduism, or Buddhism. The religions of the desert are alike monotheistic, alike paternalistic. They are male in popular imagination, because they are male in tradition.

All three religions of the desert are revealed religions. God is an activist 6 God; God works in history; God instructs men how He wishes to be worshipped and God makes covenants with men. In the case of Judaism and

Islam, the covenant is cut upon the male organ. Christianity may be a feminine sprig of Judaism, but Christianity definitely found its he-man in St. Paul.

7   At their best, these three theologies instruct humans not to despair in
their lives, in their histories, for "I am with you always."

8   Rescue workers at the site of the World Trade Center spontaneously erect
a cross of tortured steel over the rubble, seeking to hallow a field of desolation. I do not gainsay such an impulse; my own impulse would be the same.
Nor would I pause to question the symbol. The urgent thing is the reminder
that God lives in relationship to men and women.

9   But at their worst, the desert religions have taken innocent lives in the
name of God. Christian anti-Semitism gave rise to the Holocaust. Jewish settlers in the West Bank today enforce an eschatological claim on the land.
Muslims justify murder by calling it jihad.

10   I was driving a friend of mine, a woman of eighty—Jewish—to a funeral
two weeks ago. In response to nothing I had said (perhaps it was that we
were on our way to a funeral) my friend announced her conviction—another commonplace—that the world would, in her opinion, be better off
without religion. "I mean all of them," she said. An angry gesture of her
hand, still a strong hand, wiped them all away.

11   As we drove on in silence, it occurred to me that I interpreted what my
friend had said as something about men, though she had not said men. She
had said "religion."

12   I think that if theology can inure us to the suffering of others it is bad
theology. But perhaps partisan theologians would call mine a gelded theology, for it leaves out righteousness.

13   In latter days, fundamentalist Jerry Falwell sounded very much like an
anti-American imam when he described the terrorist attack on America as
representing God's abandonment, which he attributed to the activities of the
American Civil Liberties Union, to gays, to pro-abortionists, and some others.

14   Before he was overwhelmed by a reflux of patriotism, Falwell was sec-
onded by his rival, Pat Robertson. And, for a moment, amidst all the sorrow,
the rhetoric, the malaise, Americans glimpsed a likeness that unites Jewish
settlers in the West Bank to bearded mobs in Yemen to Christian fundamentalists in Virginia. They are united in their certainty of God's plan and their
own situation within God's plan—a righteous confraternity of hormonal
clarity that accounts for much of the history of misery on our planet.

15   Most Americans are not so certain, though most Americans belong to
one of the three great desert faiths. And most Americans, after September
11th, were willing to conflate, to confuse the political with the religious—
whether at street-corner shrines or in response to the oratory of politicians.
(At my parish church last week, the congregation sang "My Country 'Tis of
Thee" during the Offertory.)

16   President Bush, who describes himself as "a born-again Christian," describes the United States as being on the right side; describes the enemies of
the United States as "on the side of evil."

17   Federal phrasemakers—who decides such things?—initially titled the
American retaliation project as "Infinite Justice." The title was withdrawn as

offensive to "Muslim Americans." It was offensive also to me. Men, however large their hat-sizes, do not wield infinite justice.

America owes its civic organization to pagan Greece and to Enlightenment 18 France. America was founded as an alternative to the sectarian nations of Europe, where wars within religions and among religions saturated the soil with martyrs' blood, infidels' blood. Secular America protects and tolerates persons of every faith. The Constitution of the United States protects the right of each to worship God or Goddess or daemon or Redwood Tree or Nothing At All.

For all our tolerance of separate faiths, we behave as though we are 19 oblivious of the ways our religions overlap and initiate one another in sin as well as in goodness. Many American Christians and Jews were shocked by the blowing up of the Buddha by the Taliban government.

But Northern Europe was full of broken Madonnas (the Protestant Re- 20 formation). My own church, the Roman Catholic Church, made something of a specialty, during the Spanish colonial era, of erecting churches atop Aztec or Inca temples and calling the practice syncretism.

What alone moderates the three religions I call "masculine" have been 21 intuitions of the "feminine" within each. I speak not of men and women but of masculine and feminine impulses. These impulses, furthermore, are responses to the self-same God.

The masculine impulse is to stand, to prophesy, to defend the faith, to 22 convert the infidel or to slay him. Prophesy and its interpretation are masculine, as are schism, holy war, inquisition, reformation, excommunication. The masculine impulse will fight to defend its theology against a variant theology of the same God.

The feminine impulse recognizes itself among all religions. The femi- 23 nine impulse touches bodies, rescues the Samaritan, accomplishes charity, regardless of male permission or orthodoxy.

In my own church, John Paul II has insisted that orthodoxy is male—for- 24 ever. My suspicion, however, is that the age of post-modern Catholicism will be remembered more for the tough, pragmatic humanitarianism of Mother Teresa than for the charismatic, sentimental authoritarianism of the Polish pope, who is credited by his defenders as having, like some ancient Crusader, "defeated" communism. Perhaps our age will be remembered more for the feminine, pan-religious cult of Princess Diana than for either of the above.

The feminine impulse (again, I speak not of men and women) tends 25 toward the mystical, toward listening rather than utterance, toward the imagination of one's neighbor as oneself. Though the admissibility of the mystical tradition into orthodoxy has always been under the jurisprudence of the masculine.

The notion of relinquishing one's will to God—God as lover, bride- 26 groom, revelator—is feminine. Joan of Arc is an example of the feminine mystical impulse attempting to enter into the male cult of action. Joan of Arc was burned at the stake as a heretic.

I find magnificence in the masculine tradition of the great cathedrals 27 and mosques and green deserts and towering Buddhas immemorial; religious universities and their libraries; the human desire to write the summa.

28   But the summa seeks to limit God by defining Him. What I find abhor-rent in religion—admittedly what we have most sought from religion—is certainty, refutation of imagination, churches militant.

29   In many societies, including my own, religion is often and easily dis-missed as something for women, and old women at that. Very well, then, why is it that only women know—another commonplace about religion—that all religions are one, despite the funny hats; that theological differences are minute, as minute as differences in DNA and undetectable by satellite; that contradictions seemingly irreconcilable can be resolved, as in arabesque?

30   Whether one lights a candle at the shrine of Our Lady of Sorrows or at the shrine of an elephantine God, feminine spirituality will acknowledge that the impulse is the same—to plead for the protection of a fragile world.

31   If we survive the coming war of the 12th or the 21st century among the three desert religions, my suspicion is that a deeper reflux awaits us. The masculine principle in religion will be challenged by a feminine spiritual force that is gathering strength behind veils. And that force might best be characterized as something very like what my friend at the funeral ex-pressed: If religion can bring us to this pass, who needs it?

Rhetorical Considerations

1. What marks the occasion of Rodriguez's writing of this essay? In other words, why does he write the essay at this particular time? Is the context personal or of a broader nature? (*Hodges' 32a/Writer's 1e*)
2. This essay originally appeared in *El Andar,* a bilingual Latino magazine. Find evidence that Rodriguez has identified his audience's interests, background, and values. (*Hodges' 32a/Writer's 1e*)
3. What is Rodriguez's thesis? Does it appear explicitly in the essay? Where? (*Hodges' 32c/Writer's 2b*)
4. Find all the comparisons (as opposed to contrasts) Rodriguez draws among the three "desert religions." (*Hodges' 32e/Writer's 2e*)
5. Is this essay organized point by point, subject by subject, or by using a combi-nation of both methods? Is Rodriguez's organizational method the most effec-tive for this subject and this essay? Why or why not? (*Hodges' 32d/Writer's 2c*)
6. Describe Rodriguez's ethos. How does he depict himself in this essay? What is his relationship to his audience? (*Hodges' 32a/Writer's 1e*)

Language and Style

1. Look up the following words in your dictionary: *mullah* (paragraph 1); *psalm, blasphemed, atrocity,* and *pillage* (paragraph 2); *commendable* and *shrewd* (para-graph 3); *jihad* (paragraph 4); *monotheistic* and *paternalistic* (paragraph 5); *covenants* (paragraph 6); *hallow* and *gainsay* (paragraph 8); *eschatological* (para-graph 9); *conviction* and *commonplace* (paragraph 10); *inure, partisan,* and *gelded* (paragraph 12); *fundamentalist* and *imam* (paragraph 13); *reflux, rhetoric, malaise,* and *confraternity* (paragraph 14); *conflate, oratory,* and *Offertory* (para-graph 15); *wield* (paragraph 17); *civic, pagan, sectarian, infidels, secular,* and *dae-*

mon (paragraph 18); *syncretism* (paragraph 20); *schism, inquisition, reformation,* and *excommunication* (paragraph 22); *Samaritan* and *orthodoxy* (paragraph 23); *pragmatic* and *charismatic* (paragraph 24); *mystical, utterance,* and *jurisprudence* (paragraph 25); *relinquishing, revelator,* and *heretic* (paragraph 26); *immemorial* and *summa* (paragraph 27); *abhorrent, refutation,* and *militant* (paragraph 28); *minute* and *arabesque* (paragraph 29); *elephantine* (paragraph 30). (*Hodges'* 18e/*Writer's* 28e)

2. See how many words you can find in the essay that have to do with religion. (*Hodges'* 19/*Writer's* 28)
3. How does Rodriguez's language implicitly reveal his attitudes towards Jerry Falwell, Pat Robertson, and George W. Bush? (*Hodges'* 19a/*Writer's* 28a)
4. What is different about Rodriguez's use of the semicolon in paragraphs 3 and 6? (*Hodges'* 14/*Writer's* 32)
5. What is the rhetorical effect of setting off *Jewish* with dashes in paragraph 10? (*Hodges'* 17e/*Writer's* 35e)

Writing Suggestions

1. Compare the "masculine" and the "feminine" in a culture (a classroom, an organization, or your own family, for instance). Do not simply compare men and women but, like Rodriguez, identify and define the "masculine" and the "feminine" impulses and characteristics of that culture. It might be interesting to choose a culture that includes members of only one gender.
2. Choose someone you are close to who is a member of the opposite sex. Write an essay comparing the two of you in terms of stereotypical masculine and feminine characteristics. Again, if you are female, you may find you have some "masculine" characteristics; by the same token, your male friend may be somewhat "feminine."

◆

REQUIEM

Paul Goldberger

Paul Goldberger is a professor at Yale University and an architecture critic for the *New Yorker*. He has won the Pulitzer Prize and has published articles in many journals, including *Art in America* and *Architectural Digest*.

This essay was published in the *New Yorker* magazine just four months after the terrorist attacks on the World Trade Center in New York City and the Pentagon in Washington, D.C. Though at the time it was estimated it would take a year to eighteen months to clear the wreckage in New York City, speculation was already prevalent as to what would be done to restore the site. Goldberger looks back to a similar experience in Oklahoma City, relaying the process that ultimately led to the dedication of the site to a memorial. His analysis of the significant differences between the two places and events offers some insight into how carefully the decision has to be made and by whom.

1   The debate about how to memorialize the victims of the bombing of the Alfred P. Murrah Federal Building in Oklahoma City—the only event in recent American history that comes remotely close to the terrorist attack on the World Trade Center in lower Manhattan—went on for more than two years. Oklahoma City is a small town compared to New York, with a population of roughly five hundred thousand, and it is relatively homogeneous. There was no pressure to restore the site of the bombed building to commercial use, as there is at the World Trade Center, and yet the Oklahoma City National Memorial, as the park on the site is called, wasn't dedicated until the fifth anniversary of the bombing. The other half of the memorial, an interactive museum and information center, opened recently, nearly six years after the event it was created to commemorate. It is difficult to imagine things being easier, or moving faster, in New York.

2   The main feature of the Oklahoma City memorial is a set of a hundred and sixty-eight chairlike objects, made of bronze and glass, one for each person killed. The chairs are arranged in rows and spread out across the footprint of the Murrah Building. They face a large reflecting pool and an elm tree that escaped damage in a parking lot across the street. The tree became known as the "survivor tree," and it is now surrounded by a stone terrace. Two monumental bronze-panelled walls serve as gateways to the site. One of them is inscribed "9:01" and the other "9:03," marking the minute before the bomb went off on the morning of April 19, 1995, and the minute after. The space between the two gateways represents 9:02.

3   I went to Oklahoma City late this fall, when fires were still smoldering at Ground Zero. Larry Silverstein, who held the lease on the Trade Center towers, was loudly vowing to rebuild the same amount of office space, pos-

sibly in four shorter towers. Since then, Silverstein has quieted down a bit, and concedes that there might be room for various other things on the site. The head of the new state authority charged with rebuilding, John C. White-head, has said that he expects to build a memorial that is the equal of the Lincoln, Jefferson, and Vietnam Veterans Memorials in Washington, D.C., although he didn't indicate what he meant by that. He has also talked about including housing, office towers, and cultural facilities on the site, which is certain to arouse the ire of many families of the victims of the attack, who want it to be treated as hallowed ground.

Oklahoma City faced many of the same issues. In "The Unfinished   4
Bombing: Oklahoma City in American Memory" (Oxford; $30), Edward T. Linenthal writes that "conducting business as usual would defile the site in the eyes of many." Linenthal, who teaches at the University of Wisconsin and has also written about the struggle over the creation of the Holocaust Museum in Washington, sets out a narrative that prefigures many of the events surrounding the World Trade Center catastrophe. Firemen became national icons, fences became spontaneous memorials, covered with pictures, notes, messages, and memorabilia. Some people felt that "a new building would signal defiance of terrorism," Linenthal writes, and others suggested leaving the ruins in place as "an evocative reminder of loss, and of the enduring dangers of violence." The Okalahoma City wreckage became a kind of pilgrimage site, attracting both mourners and voyeurs.

Leaving the ruins of the Murrah Building as a monument in themselves   5
was never much of an option. The governor of Oklahoma, Frank Keating, said that what was left was "an eyesore . . . a symbol of destruction and terror that people here would much rather put behind them." In the end, several nearby buildings that had been seriously damaged were taken down, the street that the Murrah Building faced was closed, and three acres was turned into a memorial district. A building that had been damaged and whose tenant chose not to return was used to house the museum.

Within days after the bombing, public officials in Oklahoma City had   6
been deluged with suggestions for the obvious arches, obelisks, and fountains, as well as a statue of "two giant hands (God's hands)" and angels, doves, eagles, and hearts. The mayor of Oklahoma City, Ronald Norick, appointed a local lawyer, Robert Johnson, to head a task force to figure out what an appropriate memorial would be. Johnson was sensitive to the fact that people wanted to be heard, and he understood that the memorial had numerous constituencies—relatives of the people who were killed, those who escaped but were traumatized by the event, rescuers, and the general public. They had different priorities, different ways of mourning, and different aesthetic sensibilities.

The most important decision Johnson's task force made was to articu-   7
late the intentions of the memorial before thinking about any kind of physical design. The group struggled for months to create what it called a mission statement. The preamble to the final document declared that "we come here to remember those who were killed, those who survived and those changed forever. May all who leave here know the impact of violence. May this

memorial offer comfort, strength, peace, hope and serenity." The task force had fought over every word. "Killed" won out over the soft-sounding "lost" and the harsher "murdered" (which would have excluded a rescue worker whose death was not a direct result of the explosion). The language of the mission statement was too sophisticated for angels and praying hands. The memorial was not to include a representation of any known person, "living or dead," which was a way of indicating that statues of firemen carrying babies were not particularly welcome.

8   An open architectural competition was held. The model was the competition for the design of the Vietnam Veterans Memorial in Washington, which yielded the best American memorial of modern times, a design by an unknown twenty-one-year-old architecture student, Maya Lin. The Oklahoma City task force asked Paul Spreiregen, the architect who managed the Vietnam-memorial competition, to oversee the process. Spreiregen felt strongly that he and other professionals should be the ones to choose the best design, and he made it clear that survivors and members of victim's families were to have no more than an advisory role. The families refused to accept that. Although Spreiregen complained that permitting nonprofessionals to make the design decision was akin to going "to an accountant to have my appendix removed," the families had their way, and Sprieregen was off the job before he had ever really started.

9   By almost every professional standard, Spreiregen was right. Victims' families can't be expected to make a knowing judgment about what constitutes the best public memorial. Giving them control would seem to be a concession to a kind of victims' culture, elevating sentiment over any other value. In the end, however, Johnson's gamble that he could trust the families proved to be right, in large part because the mission statement set forth a program for the memorial that made the kitsch that Spreiregen feared almost impossible. The competition eventually received six hundred and twenty-four entries, which were narrowed down to five finalists.

10   Not many big-name architects felt like putting their fate in the hands of a mostly nonprofessional jury, but the level of the finalists was at least decent. The winner, as in the Vietnam-memorial competition, turned out to be relatively young and unknown: a married couple, Hans and Torrey Butzer, Americans who at the time worked in Berlin. The centerpiece of the Butzers' design, which they prepared with the help of a German colleague, Sven Berg, was the rows of empty chairs. In this sense, it was not altogether unlike Maya Lin's Vietnam memorial, where the V-shaped wall of black granite is an abstract object and the names carved on it create a realistic counterpoint.

11   The Butzers are sophisticated but not as subtle as Maya Lin. The chairs are semi-abstract, with open bronze backs and bases made out of glass cubes that are lit from within (which makes the place look like a glowing field of votive candles at night), but they still resemble tombstones. They are arranged in nine rows, each of which represents one floor of the Murrah Building. The chairs commemorating the children who were killed are miniature versions of the adult ones.

12   The Oklahoma City memorial is most effective, I find, when it is viewed as a series of abstract shapes—the monumental gateways, the glowing cubes

at night—although for a lot of people it is the very chair-ness of the chairs that is powerful. Great memorials use abstraction to engender feelings of peace and awe. The obelisk of the Washington Monument suggests George Washington's primacy in the history of this country in a way that no statue of him on horseback possibly could. The strength of the Lincoln Memorial comes at least as much from the rhythmic power of Henry Bacon's austere box of columns as from Daniel Chester French's seated figure of Lincoln, which it both encloses and ennobles. When you visit the Vietnam Veterans Memorial, you descend gently into the ground, on an axis with both the Lincoln Memorial and the Washington Monument, and you are uplifted by their grandeur while being drawn into a private, contemplative realm. The Butzers haven't achieved this in Oklahoma City, but they have made a place that is earnest and dignified, with architectural details on a high level.

Ever since Maya Lin inscribed the names of the Vietnam War dead on those black granite walls, it has been considered inappropriate to memorialize the dead as a mass, as they are at Gettysburg, for instance. The Oklahoma City mission statement stipulated that the memorial contain a hundred and sixty-eight pieces of something—it was left up to the architect to decide what. In addition to the field of chairs, the memorial has a section that lists survivors of the bombing on a granite plaque, and it also has a kind of children's garden, and the survivor tree. There is a lot going on, but in downtown Oklahoma City it is a welcome change to have a lot going on. The memorial is the most active piece of open public space in town, and the most elegant. 13

The adjacent museum is a mixture of conscientious history, special effects, and sentimentality. There is background material on the Murrah Building and testimony from people affected by the bombing, and one area is devoted to memorabilia and photographs of the people who were killed. Another section is a re-creation of the hearing room of the Oklahoma Water Resources Board, which was across the street from the Murrah Building. You enter, and the door closes behind you as a tape plays the first two minutes of a meeting, and then you hear the blast and the room goes dark. The museum provides a much more American experience, really, than the outdoor memorial, since it is grounded in the belief that almost anything, including the most horrendous events imaginable, can be made entertaining. 14

Rhetorical Considerations

1. Why does Goldberger consider the Oklahoma City memorial to be the best example for comparison with the site of the World Trade Center? (*Hodges'* 32b/*Writer's* 2a)
2. What is important about the context of this essay in terms of when it was written and where it was published? (*Hodges'* 32a/*Writer's* 1e)
3. List the differences Goldberger cites between the site of the Oklahoma City bombing and that of the World Trade Center attacks. (*Hodges'* 32e/*Writer's* 2e)
4. Does Goldberger focus more on similarities or on differences? Does he seem to think that similarities or differences are more important? (*Hodges'* 32e/*Writer's* 2e)

5. What other memorials does Goldberger include in his comparison? Why? (*Hodges'* 31c/*Writer's* 2d)
6. What is Goldberger's ultimate purpose in this essay? (*Hodges'* 32a/*Writer's* 1e)

Language and Style

1. Look up the following words in your dictionary: *homogenous* and *commemorate* (paragraph 1); *footprint* (paragraph 2); *concedes, ire,* and *hallowed* (paragraph 3); *defile, prefigures, catastrophe, icons, evocative, pilgrimage,* and *voyeurs* (paragraph 4); *deluged, obelisks, constituencies, aesthetic,* and *sensibilities* (paragraph 6); *articulate* and *preamble* (paragraph 7); *concession* and *kitsch* (paragraph 9); *abstract* and *counterpoint* (paragraph 10); *subtle* and *votive* (paragraph 11); *engender, austere,* and *earnest* (paragraph 12); *conscientious* and *sentimentality* (paragraph 14). (*Hodges'* 18e/*Writer's* 28e)
2. Find examples of descriptive detail in Goldberger's essay. How does this make his essay more effective? (*Hodges'* 31c/*Writer's* 2d)
3. What is wrong with "statues of firemen carrying babies" (paragraph 7)? Does Goldberger explain this explicitly?
4. While he is obviously concerned about excessive sentimentality, how does Goldberger use language to present himself as a sensitive person? (*Hodges'* 19/*Writer's* 28)
5. Do the verbs agree in number with their subjects in the third sentence of paragraph 5? Why or why not? (*Hodges'* 6a/*Writer's* 22e)

Writing Suggestions

1. The original designs for the World Trade Center memorials were scrapped because many New Yorkers didn't like them. Do you agree with Goldberger that "[v]ictims' families can't be expected to make a knowing judgment about what constitutes the best public memorial"? (284) Write an essay that compares that view to the view that people immediately affected by a tragedy should be involved in deciding how the tragedy is memorialized.
2. Examine a piece of public art in your community (a memorial, mural, sculpture, etc.). What is its purpose? Write an essay that examines how—and whether—it works to fulfill that purpose. How does it make you feel, and what about it makes you feel that way? Does its specific location add to its significance, or is it not relevant?

SMALL IS STILL BEAUTIFUL

David Morris

David Morris is vice president of the Minneapolis- and Washington,
D.C.-based Institute for Local Self-Reliance. He also directs the Institute's New Rules Project: "designing rules as if community matters."
This article was adapted from an address to the Place Matters Conference in St. Paul, Minnesota, on November 12, 1998.

"The real voyage of discovery," wrote Marcel Proust, "lies not in seeking new 1
lands but in seeing with new eyes." Seeing with new eyes requires challenging the conventional wisdom that bigger is better, that separating the producer from the consumer, the banker from the depositor, the worker from
the owner, the government from its citizens is a necessary requirement for
achieving a prosperous economy and a healthy society.

Seeing with new eyes means rediscovering the importance of place. 2
Perhaps the finest empirical analysis of the relationship between local institutions and community life was conducted 50 years ago by Walter
Goldschmidt, then a researcher for the U.S. Department of Agriculture.
Goldschmidt examined two remarkable similar farm communities in California's San Joaquin Valley. Dinuba and Arvin had the same volume of crop
production, comparable soil quality, and similar climate. The communities
were equidistant from major urban areas and were similarly served by highways and rail lines. They differed in only one major respect: the Dinuba
economy was based on many small family farms, while the town of Arvin
depended on a few large-scale agribusiness operations. Goldschmidt discovered that Dinuba's family farm economy provided its residents with a substantially higher median income and standard of living. Moreover, the
citizens of Dinuba, to a far greater extent than their counterparts in Arvin,
were involved in building a strong community.

For example, the quality and quantity of projects that benefited the en- 3
tire community, like paved streets and sidewalks and garbage and sewage
disposal, were far superior in Dinuba. The agribusiness town had no high
school and only one elementary school. Dinuba provided its citizens with
four elementary schools in addition to a high school. The family farm town
had three public parks. The corporate farm town had a single playground,
donated by a corporation.

Dinuba's residents not only invested their money in expanding their 4
community's physical infrastructure, they also invested their time in building its civic infrastructure. Dinuba had more than twice the number of civic
associations as Arvin. In Dinuba, there were various governmental bodies

that enabled residents to make decisions about the public welfare through direct popular vote. No such bodies existed in Arvin.

5   You would think that the government would have been delighted by Goldschmidt's findings, for he had empirically validated the uniquely American belief that the key to a healthy society is the broadest possible ownership of productive assets. You would be wrong.

6   For 30 years the USDA suppressed the report. Indeed, under pressure from industry, it abolished Goldschmidt's position and, later, the entire office that studied agriculture's impact on communities.

7   Hearing the story of Dinuba 50 years later, it seems Goldschmidt must have been describing a mythical town—or a scenario long since relegated to the dustbins of history. After all, that's what reading the daily headlines and watching the evening news would lead us to conclude.

8   The statistics are indeed sobering. A thousand farms a week have gone out of business since 1950. Community pharmacies have been closing their doors at a rate of about 1,000 per year for the past five years. In 1972, independent booksellers claimed 58 percent of all book sales. By 1997 their share had fallen to 17 percent. Almost 5 percent of all retail spending today is captured by a single company, Wal-Mart.

9   It's getting scary out there. Last September, the federal government gave its stamp of approval to the merger of Travelers Group and Citicorp, giving birth to Citigroup, a financial enterprise with $700 billion in assets that serves 100 million customers in 100 countries. In November, Cargill announced that it would purchase the grain operations of Continental Grain, reportedly allowing Cargill to control as much as 70 percent of the world's grain market.

10   These figures cannot be ignored. But they should not be overstated. The independent sector is under attack and has ceased to be the dominant organizational form, but it isn't dead.

11   Consider the following statistics from Minnesota, a state with a population (4.5 million) less than half that of Los Angeles, and typical of most U.S. states:

- More than 500 independent community pharmacies still exist.
- Almost 40 percent of all electricity customers own their own electric company, in the form of either a municipally owned or a cooperatively owned utility.
- Some 400 community banks and credit unions control more than 25 percent of all bank assets.
- More than 20,000 independent farmers dot the countryside.
- More than 30,000 second-generation family-owned businesses and 13,000 third-generation enterprises continue to compete successfully.

12   Place-based enterprises need not simply tap into our nostalgic yearning for a simpler and more rooted yesteryear. They can make a powerful case that humanly scaled institutions are the most effective way to go. In every sector of the economy, the evidence yields the same conclusion: Small is efficient, dynamic, democratic, and cost effective.

Consider education. Exhaustive studies have found that small schools 13
have less absenteeism, lower dropout rates, fewer disciplinary problems,
higher teacher satisfaction, and higher test scores than big schools. The
evidence is so compelling that big cities like Chicago and Philadelphia and
New York literally have begun down-sizing their schools by subdividing
existing school buildings into two or three or even four completely independent schools. And the most impressive results have occurred when
the school district not only shrinks the size of the school but also shrinks
the distance between authority and responsibility by delegating decision-
making power to the individual school.

The same scale of institution that best cares for our children best cares 14
for our money. In 1990, 92 percent of the nation's 12,165 banks had assets
under $300 million, and two-thirds had assets under $100 million. Happily,
the Federal Reserve has found that there are no efficiencies to be gained by
banks any larger than this. In the 1980s, researchers found that savings and
loans that stuck to their knitting and lent close to home did not, on average, require a federal bailout.

Community banks also serve their communities best. A 1996 Federal 15
Reserve study found that small banks made 82 percent of all commercial
loans to very small business borrowers. And fees for checking accounts and
other basic services were, on average, 15 percent lower at small banks than
at large, multistate institutions, according to a 1997 study by the U.S. Public
Interest Research Group.

In manufacturing, too, small scale pertains. Small manufacturers consti- 16
tute more than 98 percent of the 360,000 U.S. manufacturing enterprises.
Two-thirds have fewer than 20 employees. From 1979 to 1989, small- and
medium-sized manufacturing businesses created more than 20 million new
jobs while the Fortune 500 lost almost 4 million jobs.

Place-based enterprises are not only efficient, they are also wildly popu- 17
lar. Poll after poll concludes that the vast majority of the population supports community team policing, home-based health care, community
banks, neighborhood schools, and local businesses.

In brief, community-based enterprises and institutions still command 18
considerable resources and even more considerable respect and admiration.
Today, individually and collectively, these enterprises are building on this
foundation to survive in the age of planetary corporations and electronic
commerce.

Meanwhile, communities around the country are looking for ways to 19
encourage local ownership without interfering with the dynamism and en-
trepreneurialism of the private sector. Kent County in Maryland, Cape Cod
towns in Massachussetts, and other communities have adopted comprehensive plans that explicitly call for planning bodies to support "locally owned
business." On the West Coast, five cities, including Carmel, California, have
adopted bans on the "formula restaurant" (defined as a restaurant "required
by contractual or other arrangements to offer standardized menus, ingredients, food preparation, employee uniforms, interior decor, signage, or exte-
rior design" or "adopt a name, appearance, or food presentation format

which causes it to be substantially identical to another restaurant"). Carmel is not prohibiting McDonald's from setting up shop; it just can't look like a McDonald's. In essence, Carmel is outlawing uniformity—and therby encouraging local ownership.

20   Since the 1970s, Congress has provided handsome tax incentives to companies that give stock to their employees. More than a thousand companies are now majority-owned by their workers. These firms must operate in the same competitive marketplace as investor-owned firms, but they tend to have a different decision-making calculus. Absentee owners might well decide to close a profitable operation if they can make more money in another location. Such a decision would be unlikely at an employee-owned firm.

21   And Congress last year debated a bill that would have abolished the inheritance tax on family-owned farms and businesses bequeathed to family members who continued to operate them.

22   We live in an era of great change. But change is not necessarily progress. As Bertrand Russell said, change is inevitable, while progress is problematic. Change is scientific while progress is ethical. We will have change, whether we will it or not. But we will have progress only if we develop strategies that channel investment capital and entrepreneurial energies and scientific genius in directions compatible with our dearly held values. This means strategies that defend and nurture place-based enterprises as the building blocks and lifeblood of dynamic, self-conscious, and healthy communities.

Rhetorical Considerations

1. Does this essay focus primarily on comparison or on contrast? Support your answer with examples. (*Hodges'* 32b/*Writer's* 2a)
2. What is the central aim of this essay? (*Hodges'* 32c/*Writer's* 2b)
3. The major study on which Morris bases his argument is 50 years old. Does that fact present any problems for his credibility? (*Hodges'* 31c/*Writer's* 2d)
4. Does Morris use point-by-point or subject-by-subject organization? (*Hodges'* 32d/*Writer's* 2c)
5. Does Morris provide a variety of examples? Can you think of any major issues he might have used to strengthen his argument? (*Hodges'* 33c/*Writer's* 3a)

Language and Style

1. How does Morris distinguish between *change* and *progress?* (*Hodges'* 23e/*Writer's* 29e)
2. Find words in the essay that depict the environment Morris favors. (*Hodges'* 19/*Writer's* 28)
3. What kind of word is *seeing* (first sentence of paragraph 2)? How does the phrase "Seeing with new eyes" function in that sentence? (*Hodges'* 1/*Writer's* 16)
4. Is the first sentence of paragraph 13 a complete sentence? Why or why not? (*Hodges'* 1/*Writer's* 16)
5. Comment on Morris's use of *less* and *fewer* in paragraph 13. (*Hodges'* 19/*Writer's* 28)

Writing Suggestions

1. Write an essay comparing the advantages (or disadvantages) of a small town to a large city.
2. Morris argues against the cliché that "bigger is better." Choose a different cliché and argue that it is not true, using concrete examples to back up your argument.

IMAGES

Comparison and Contrast

Since evaluation is commonly at the heart of consumerism, comparison and contrast are frequently used in advertising. After all, companies must force you as a consumer to evaluate their product against the competition. Or, as you saw with the ads in chapter 5, companies try to convince you that your life will be significantly better if you use their product or service.

Examine the following ads and consider what two things are being compared in each. How is the comparison relevant to the quality of the product

Translation (above): "The same feeling, but in the shape of a car."
Translation (below): "New Corolla '03: Totally renovated. More powerful. More cool. More fun. Feel the freedom. Toyota: The journey of your life."

Toyota

or service being marketed? Look at the details of the ads. The Toyota ad shows two beautiful natural scenes—one of the ocean, the other of the desert. The woman in the upper portion of the ad is young, attractive, scantily dressed, and her pose suggests the "feeling" the ad is striving to evoke. The Working Assets ad is equivocating on the word *values* by recalling its intended audience's idealistic past, represented by the tie-dyed shirt and the peace symbol, and by stressing the company's philanthropic concerns as well as its offer of a good deal.

Working Assets

✦

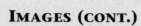

IMAGES (CONT.)

Comparison and Contrast

Rhetorical Considerations

1. What audience are these ads aimed at? Consider not only the product being advertised, but also the appeal of the ad. (*Hodges'* 32a/*Writer's* 1e)
2. What are the two things being compared in the Toyota ad? In the Working Assets ad? In each case, what is the purpose of the comparison? Are the ads making explicit or implicit assertions about the comparison and its relevance to their products? (*Hodges'* 32e/*Writer's* 2e)
3. Is one ad more effective than the other? If so, explain why. (*Hodges'* 32b/*Writer's* 2a)
4. Find a particular magazine that caters to a specific audience (teenagers, Asian Americans, or comic book collectors, for example) and consider how you would adapt these ads to this new market. (*Hodges'* 32b/*Writer's* 2a)

Writing Suggestions

1. Collect advertisements for the same type of product (toothpastes or shampoos, for example) from different types of magazines. Write an essay in which you explore how that product is marketed differently to different audiences.
2. Similarly, look at a group of magazines that targets a particular group (men's magazines, for example, or fitness magazines) and, by comparing the ads, discuss in an essay what assumptions about that audience are evident from the ads.

CHAPTER 7

Classification and Division

When you group ideas or objects into categories, you are classifying. When you separate ideas or objects into parts, you are dividing. Classifying and dividing are complementary. They are both important strategies in writing, but they are far more than that; they are fundamental to understanding and organizing information. For instance, if you have to buy grapes, hamburger, cheese, tomatoes, milk, chicken thighs, and butter at the supermarket, you'll proceed most efficiently through the store if you consider the categories into which the management has classified those items: produce, meats, and dairy products. But in the dairy section you will also want to consider how the milk has been divided—whether to buy whole, low-fat, or skimmed milk.

Understanding Classification and Division

Classification is important in every field, especially in science, which often progresses by refining categories and establishing new ones. Think of the great classification systems that enable botanists and zoologists to find order in and write intelligibly about the staggering diversity of living things on earth. Or consider, for that matter, how astronomers classify the Earth itself: as a *planet,* one of several classes of heavenly bodies that make up our solar system, which in turn belongs to a larger star system we call a *galaxy;* galaxies themselves are classified in four categories on the basis of their form: elliptical, spiral (ours is spiral, as is Andromeda), barred spiral, and irregular. Classification is a mode of thought—and of writing—that sorts individual ideas or things into groups with other similar ideas or things. (See *Hodges'* 32e(6)/*Writer's* 2e(6) for more information.) In "Which Stooge Are You?" Ron Geraci classifies individual men into three types according to which of the Three Stooges they represent—Moe, Larry, or Curly. Desmond Morris classifies kinds of territorial behavior; Martin Luther King, Jr., classifies three ways to resist oppression; and William Saletan identifies four classes of error and then analyzes each class into its various parts.

Division (also called *analysis*) breaks things down into their parts for a purpose, usually in order to understand them better, and often in preparation for putting the elements together again in new ways (called *synthesis*).

In division, the writer determines the various parts of a single item. In "The Qualities of Good Writing," Jacqueline Berke divides a single act, good writing, into three parts—writing that is economical, writing that is simple, and writing that is clear. Ellen McGrath examines recovery from a traumatic experience, breaking the process down into four separate stages. As a user of this book, you have continually been engaged in division, analyzing elements of the essays printed here in order to understand what makes the essays successful. Having analyzed the many individual choices the various writers have made, you will be prepared to put this information together in a new synthesis: your own, unique writing. Division helps us understand almost any subject—objects, ideas, emotions, processes, texts, and more.

When you think about classification and division, if you feel your mind boggle at keeping straight which is which, don't feel alone. Most people have the same reaction. That is because classification and division are rather like the two sides of a coin. Looking from one side, you try to take all the instances of, say, territorial behavior or resistance to oppression or even kinds of individual men and make sense of them by grouping them into categories. The other side of the coin is that you take a particular act, such as good writing or physical reactions to trauma, and try to see what it is made up of, what its parts are. In the first case, you take some small things and group them with other, similar small things—classification. In the latter case, you take one large thing and break it up into several similar smaller things—division. Furthermore, the two methods are frequently used in tandem. To return to the grocery store example for a moment: When you shop, your list includes a variety of items—hamburger, chicken thighs, grapes, cheeses, tomatoes, milk, butter, coffee, sugar, soup, paper towels, and dishwasher detergent. When you look for each item at the store, you must first identify its classification. Is it meat? Produce? A shelf good? When you arrive at the meat counter, you will analyze the parts of the display—the poultry on one end, the beef on the other, pork in between, and fish in its own case off to the side. So to purchase that pound of hamburger and package of chicken thighs, you have to both classify and divide.

Using Classification and Division

Subject

Classification involves recognizing common characteristics that diverse things share (and therefore is closely related to comparison and contrast, discussed in Chapter 6). Galaxies are normally classified on the basis of shape. Stars, however, can be classified on many different bases, including size, composition, color, brightness, age, and distance; the choice of a basis depends on the classifier's immediate purpose. In writing an essay or other paper, you may be able to classify your subject in several different ways, some of which will serve your purpose better than others.

Using division in writing might include analyzing a poem into its parts for a literature course, considering the various parts that make up the structure of a bridge for an engineering course, or analyzing a business situation for a management course. Beyond the campus, analysis usually serves very immediate practical ends: nurses and doctors analyze patients; lawyers analyze briefs; politicians analyze voters; coaches analyze teams; businesspeople analyze products, competitors, and problems; and so forth. It should be stressed that analytical writing does not merely report the findings of finished investigations. Even when you begin your writing with the sense that you have already investigated your subject thoroughly, you are quite likely to make further discoveries as you write about it. That is the nature of good analysis and is the reason analytical writing is so often called for in college courses, where the objective is learning.

Purpose

Five of the seven essays reprinted in this chapter illustrate classification, and two illustrate analysis. One of the classification essays is by a scientist writing with a primarily informative aim: Desmond Morris's "Territorial Behavior" examines the ways in which human beings establish and protect three types of "territories"—tribal, familial, and personal. Martin Luther King, Jr., makes classification a powerful tool for persuasion in "Three Types of Resistance to Oppression," arguing that nonviolent resistance in the face of oppression is the only kind that will work. Ron Geraci, a humorist, demonstrates that classification can entertain as well as inform, while William Saletan's essay shows the effectiveness of classification in examining logical flaws.

You want to be able to tell your readers why you have chosen to classify or divide your subject. Do you want to teach them something—that is, do you want to explain and interpret information? Classification and division are powerful tools for clarifying, interpreting, and justifying, as well as for identifying basic elements. When you have chosen your subject, you must be sure you know which of these purposes you will use to focus your essay. (See *Hodges'* 32a/*Writer's* 1e for more information.) Jacqueline Berke and Ellen McGrath, a professional writer and a psychologist, analyze their respective fields for the purpose of explaining them to novices; they clarify them and also identify their basic elements. Desmond Morris interprets human behavior, and Martin Luther King, Jr., justifies it.

When you know both your subject and your purpose, you are ready to try on a *thesis statement* that will identify for your readers the exact point you are making, your central idea, and your reason for writing about it. (See *Hodges'* 32e/*Writer's* 2b for more information.) This single sentence will guide you through your classification or your analysis, and it will also guide your readers as they follow the points you are making. Look at the essays in this chapter to see how those writers have stated their intent. For instance, Ellen McGrath, in "Recovering from Trauma," informs us of two things in her thesis statement: how she knows what the parts are that she will explain and that there are four of them:

> Direct experience with disasters ranging from the Gulf War to massive fires and California earthquakes has taught me that there are four basic stages in recovering from a profound stress. (317)

Audience

For essays of classification and division, audiences may vary greatly. (See *Hodges'* 32a/*Writer's* 1e for information.) For instance, the audience might be exclusively oneself, as in a diary entry written to sort out the writer's feelings or ideas about some experience. Or it might be a group of people who are oppressed, such as those for whom King was writing. Desmond Morris wrote for people interested in understanding the roots of human behavior. Jacqueline Berke was writing for first-year students taking a writing course. These audiences are different in some important ways, and each writer takes advantage of that specialization by understanding what their readers know and predicting what they want (or need) to know. Consider, for example, "Recovering from Trauma" by Ellen McGrath. Although McGrath holds a PhD in psychology and certainly is capable of writing at an extremely high level of technical sophistication, notice how her purpose in this essay requires that she write in simple, nontechnical language that will be understood by readers who are not trained in psychology but who are interested in the subject.

Organization

Classification

Lay out your points in some kind of order—*logical, chronological,* or *emphatic.* (See *Hodges'* 31b/*Writers'* 3c(3).) If you use a logical organization, you might consider presenting your points as premises leading to a conclusion in a logical argument. Obviously, this is an excellent strategy for a persuasive essay developed by classification or analysis. For other purposes, you might consider a chronological organization, in which you order your points by time sequence, or an emphatic organization, which involves presenting the most important points either first, to give them prominence, or last, as Martin Luther King, Jr., does, to give them power. Each of your classification categories or parts in your division will probably be a major subdivision of your essay—a paragraph or more.

Before you can lay out your classification, however, you must choose the *basis of classification* that is best suited to your purpose. To return again to the supermarket example, the management (though it might not remain the management very long) could choose an alphabetical basis of classification and arrange everything on the shelves accordingly—the apples next to the antacids, the bread between the beans and the brooms, and so forth. Such an arrangement works fine, after all, in the telephone directory, where "your fingers do the walking." Or the merchandise could be classified according to type of packaging: bottled things in aisle 1, canned things in aisle 2, boxed things in aisle 3, bagged things in aisle 4, loose things in aisle 5, and so on. Obviously, not all bases of classification are equally valuable. To return from shopping to writing, if you were writing with the purpose of showing that certain types of folk legends are found over and over again in many different cultures, you might classify legends by their content: creation legends, flood legends, and so on. If you wanted to emphasize the distinctive qualities of legends from different cultures, you might classify legends according to where they originated: Greek legends, Native-American legends, Japanese legends, and so on. Whenever you classify, have a clear idea of your purpose and your basis for classifying.

Once you have a basis clearly in mind, make sure that all of your categories are

- consistent,
- exclusive, and
- complete.

Consistent means that each classification category is established on the same basis and that each one sticks to that basis. Do not fall into the trap of creating illogical categories, such as classifying dogs as large, medium, small, and unfriendly. The last is a category formed on a different basis from the others—degree of friendliness rather than size. (Friendliness could, of course, be the basis of a classification, for example, in an entertaining essay on the dogs you have known: friendly to a fault, affable but reserved, indifferent, and downright hostile.)

Exclusive means that none of the categories overlap. For instance, if you included another category in your discussion of the size of certain dogs— perhaps "breed"—your categories would overlap because most breeds are a certain size: Cairn Terriers are small, while Labrador Retrievers are large. All of this may seem too obvious—and indeed, if you were writing about newspapers, you probably would not fall into the error of classifying them as conservative, moderate, liberal, or weekly. But it's not hard to imagine a writer illogically grouping newspapers into two classes such as interested in promoting the good of the public and interested in making a profit for themselves, as if these two interests could not be combined.

Complete means that you have not omitted any important categories from your classification. This does not mean that you must give equal attention to every category as you write; that decision will depend on your purpose. However, your readers will notice if you have overlooked a category they regard as significant in the context of your discussion. For instance, Martin Luther King Jr. writes about the ways in which oppressed people respond to oppression and includes the possibility of people simply giving in to oppression and accepting their situation as hopeless. By doing this, readers who have given in and lost all hope are justified in feeling that King's essay is intended for them, that he understands and cares about them even though they do not resist.

Analysis

Many of the same considerations apply if you are writing an analysis—a division of a subject. If that subject is complex, you may need to give considerable thought to the *basis* of your analysis, your reason for dividing it in a particular way. For example, Jacqueline Berke's essay in this chapter seeks to discover the qualities of good writing. To proceed, however, Berke finds that she must first establish what she means by *good:* "pungent, vital, moving, memorable" (326). This definition, focusing on the writing's effect on the reader, provides the basis for an investigation that leads Berke to certain qualities in the writing itself: economy, simplicity, and clarity. However, the story editor of a television soap opera might define good writing quite differently: writing that will create a popular show so that sponsors will pay a high price to sell their products during the commercial breaks. An analysis on this basis might reveal the qualities of "good" writing to include a slow pace to draw out the story line as long as possible, farfetched coincidences, plenty of drama and romance, and enough unpredictability that viewers stay tuned, even during commercial breaks.

Language and Style

Essays developed using classification and division can, as we have shown, be very complicated, so it is important to give your readers a clear path to follow. You can do that by taking care to keep the sequence clear. Use transitional words and phrases between logically ordered points. Some useful connectives include: *first, second, third, in the first place, finally, at the same time, likewise, also, on the whole, for instance, in the case of, indeed,* and so on.

You'll also want to provide adequate detail to make your classifications or analyses interesting. It is the detail that makes the similarities among members of a class clear, and it is the details that show the differences among the parts into which something is analyzed. Look at the details Ron Geraci uses to explain men who are like Larry:

> Larry is the passive, agreeable fellow who scrapes through life by taking his licks and collecting his paycheck. "Generally, things happen *to* a Larry; he doesn't make them happen," says Alan Entin, Ph.D., a psychologist with the American Psychological Association. Larry is the ubiquitous "nice guy" who commutes to his mediocre job, congenially tries to cover Curly's ass, and spends his day trying to avoid getting whacked in the nose by Moe. (331–32)

Geraci's details let us "see" the Larrys of the world. Similarly, Martin Luther King Jr. draws a portrait of oppression when he tells us

> Some people are so worn down by the yoke of oppression that they give up. A few years ago in the slum areas of Atlanta, a Negro guitarist used to sing almost daily: "Ben down so long that down don't bother me." This is the type of negative freedom and resignation that often engulfs the life of the oppressed. (305)

Carefully used language, well-chosen details, and sharply focused examples will make your points clear and your classification or analysis interesting.

Images

Images can also be an important device in classification and division. Look, for instance, at the photographs in this chapter. How do they classify the people being depicted? Are the images also analyses of these classifications?

Student Essay

This student essay by Joaquin Campos illustrates the classification principles expressed in this chapter. Campos was given complete freedom of subject and developed his topic from several current events, a subject he could assume any reader would have some interest in. He describes the various classifications of military action and gives examples along the way, and assumes his reader knows virtually nothing about his subject. As you read the essay and the commentary that follows, consider how Campos attempted to adhere to the principles just explained.

U.S. Military Actions

Introduction

Background

    The terrorist attacks against the United States of America on September 11, 2001, brought to the American people's attention the difficulty of understanding the kinds of action available to the U.S. military for reacting to such attacks. Indeed, military actions by one country against another have historically been narrowly defined as "declarations of war" and these kinds of actions require ratification by Congress. However, in the twenty-first century, a sophisticated understanding of global relationships makes clear that countries use various types of military actions short of declarations of war in order to maintain world peace. As the leading power, *the* superpower, the United States has, by way of the largest defense budget and military force on earth, three categories of military action to ensure peace around the globe—acts of deterrence, counterinsurgency, and policing. These three categories may escalate into nuclear or conventional war, either limited or unlimited.

Purpose

Thesis

    In light of the growing threat of terrorism, deterrence policies against countries and organizations that pose a threat to world peace are of increasing importance. The most notable U.S. military act of deterrence

continued

First category— note use of examples

was the threat of mutually assured destruction—or MADD—against the Soviet Union. To prevent the Soviet Union from attacking the U.S. with nuclear weapons, the U.S. made it clear that it would retaliate after an initial attack and launch a second strike that would destroy Russia. U.S. forces deemed this military action "unlimited nuclear warfare." After the Cold War between the U.S. and Russia ended, the U.S. need to threaten unlimited nuclear warfare diminished, and thus a policy of "limited nuclear warfare" took its place. Through this deterrence policy, U.S. military action aims to prevent the spread of nuclear weapons to terrorist groups or countries with outlaw regimes. U.S. forces achieve the goal of deterring limited nuclear warfare by keeping a large military presence throughout the world in areas that have the potential for acquiring and using weapons of mass destruction. If such a potential threat occurs, the U.S. is equipped and ready to strike with limited conventional military action that is quick and decisive. An example of a limited conventional war carried out by the U.S. is the Persian Gulf War.

Second category— note use of examples

Differentiation

Contrary to public sentiment strongly supporting the Persian Gulf War, the majority of the U.S. public will often not back military actions that are performed to counterinsurgencies in unstable countries. For instance, the Vietnam conflict began as an insurgency and ended in a war in which the U.S. participated. The conflict turned war caused citizens to stage massive protests against U.S. involvement in Vietnam. Yet, even without public support, the U.S. military will act against uprisings from outlaw forces when those forces revolt against established governments, particularly governments that the U.S. has amiable relationships with. This type of military action is called *counterinsurgency.* It differs specifically from limited conventional warfare in that the third-world countries with which the U.S. gets involved have generally not been attacked, or have not attacked other countries; instead, the U.S. gets involved with a "civil war" going on within the third-world country. Often, though, other countries support the insurgency within a specific third-world country because the established government's demise would benefit them. In such a case, the U.S. has a great need to reestablish order to ensure world peace.

Third category— note use of examples

Similar to counterinsurgency actions, U.S. military acts of policing around the globe maintain balance among neighboring countries by keeping abreast of groups that are trying to create discord in any country. These military actions take the form of efforts to stop terrorism, drug trafficking, and political instability and to promote peace in hostile regions. For instance, the U.S. interest in keeping nuclear weapons and other weapons of mass destruction out of the hands of known terrorist groups such as Al Qaeda was a policing action. Because of the attacks against America on September 11, the policing action turned into a limited conventional war in order to restore peace throughout the world and end random acts of terror. In addition to maintaining a military presence around the globe to police illegal activities, the U.S. armed forces and officials often take part in peace-keeping missions as part of their actions. Often viewed as unconventional uses of U.S. troops, policing acts in the name of peace keeping have, because of September 11, become an increasingly important military action, particularly in the Middle East region. U.S. attempts to encourage peace between Israel and the Palestinian State exemplify an ongoing peace-keeping mission in which military forces have been involved.

Conclusion echoes thesis — Indeed, throughout history the U.S. has been a leader in keeping the world in harmony and will remain involved in this mission as long as conflict arises in our world. U.S. forces are trained to engage in three kinds of military action that do not require approval by Congress—actions of deterrence, actions of counterinsurgency, and police-type actions. Other kinds of military actions do require Congressional approval—including unlimited and limited nuclear warfare as well as unlimited and limited conventional warfare. These kinds of responses are the U.S. military's tools to ensure world peace.

Commentary

In his introduction, Campos comments briefly on why he wants to classify the different kinds of U.S. military action—to explain what kinds of responses are possible following a terrorist attack. He then lists the three categories of action he will discuss. This introductory paragraph provides some background for the reader, announces his purpose, and states his thesis.

Using types of military action as a basis of classification, Campos first identifies a class of deterrence policies against countries and organizations that pose a threat to world peace and explains what this class is and how it might be, and has been, used. The next category he describes includes counterinsurgency actions in unstable countries and gives background to show how these actions differ from deterrents. The final class Campos identifies is police actions, efforts to stop terrorism, drug trafficking, and political instability and to promote peace in hostile regions. His conclusion summarizes the various kinds of military response and recaps his thesis.

✦ CHECKLIST FOR WRITING ESSAYS DEVELOPED BY CLASSIFICATION AND DIVISION

- What are you *classifying* or *analyzing?* Have you identified a *basis of classification?* Can you state it in a single sentence? Are your categories *consistent, exclusive,* and *complete? (Hodges'* 32e(6)/*Writer's* 2e(6))
- Is your *purpose* to persuade? To inform? To entertain? A blend? Can you state your specific purpose in a single sentence? (*Hodges'* 32a (1)/ *Writer's* 1e(1))
- Does your classification have a *point?* What is it? Can you state it as a *thesis* and have you focused your classification or analysis around that statement? (*Hodges'* 32c/*Writer's* 2b)
- What can you expect your *readers* to know about this topic? Have you provided sufficient background information? Does each classification have enough detail to aid the readers' understanding? (*Hodges'* 31c/*Writer's* 2d)
- Have you presented your categories in a particular *order?* What is it, and why is it appropriate for this information and audience? (*Hodges'* 31b/*Writer's* 3c(3))
- Have you checked your essay to be sure you have not fallen into any *logical fallacies? (Hodges'* 35f/*Writer's* 7i)
- Do *transitional words and qualifiers* link the various parts of your essay?
- If you have used *visuals,* such as charts, graphs, photographs, maps, or drawings, are they fully integrated with the text? (*Hodges'* 8c/*Writer's* 6b)
- What kind of *conclusion* have you written? Does it have a purpose? (*Hodges'* 33b(2)/*Writer's* 3b)

◆

THREE TYPES OF RESISTANCE TO OPPRESSION

Martin Luther King Jr.

Martin Luther King Jr. was born in Atlanta, Georgia, in 1929, and as-
sassinated in Memphis, Tennessee, in 1968—four years after he was
awarded the Nobel Peace Prize. The son of a Baptist minister, he himself was ordained to the ministry at the age of 18 and subsequently graduated from Morehouse College and Crozer Theological Seminary. He
received a PhD in systematic philosophy from Boston University in
1954. King became nationally prominent as a result of his activities in
the Montgomery, Alabama, bus boycott in 1955, and for the rest of his
life was an advocate of nonviolent resistance to racial injustice and a
powerful voice for the Civil Rights Movement, both as president of the
Southern Christian Leadership Conference and as a charismatic and
persuasive speaker. Among his writings are *Why We Can't Wait* (1964)
and *Where Do We Go from Here?: Chaos or Community?* (1967). The following selection is from his first book, *Stride Toward Freedom* (1958).

Oppressed people deal with their oppression in three characteristic ways. 1
One way is acquiescence: the oppressed resign themselves to their doom.
They tacitly adjust themselves to oppression, and thereby become conditioned to it. In every movement toward freedom some of the oppressed
prefer to remain oppressed. Almost 2800 years ago Moses set out to lead the
children of Israel from the slavery of Egypt to the freedom of the promised land. He soon discovered that slaves do not always welcome their deliv-
erers. They become accustomed to being slaves. They would rather bear
those ills they have, has Shakespeare pointed out, than flee to others that
they know not of. They prefer the "fleshpots of Egypt" to the ordeals of
emancipation.

There is such a thing as the freedom of exhaustion. Some people are so 2
worn down by the yoke of oppression that they give up. A few years ago in
the slum areas of Atlanta, a Negro guitarist used to sing almost daily: "Ben
down so long that down don't bother me." This is the type of negative freedom and resignation that often engulfs the life of the oppressed.

But this is not the way out. To accept passively an unjust system is to 3
cooperate with that system; thereby the oppressed become as evil as the oppressor. Noncooperation with evil is as much a moral obligation as is cooperation with good. The oppressed must never allow the conscience of the
oppressor to slumber. Religion reminds every man that he is his brother's
keeper. To accept injustice or segregation passively is to say to the oppressor
that his actions are morally right. It is a way of allowing his conscience to
fall asleep. At this moment the oppressed fails to be his brother's keeper. So
acquiescence—while often the easier way—is not the moral way. It is the

way of the coward. The Negro cannot win the respect of his oppressor by acquiescing; he merely increases the oppressor's arrogance and contempt. Acquiescence is interpreted as proof of the Negro's inferiority. The Negro cannot win the respect of the white people of the South or the peoples of the world if he is willing to sell the future of his children for his personal and immediate comfort and safety.

4   A second way that oppressed people sometimes deal with oppression is to resort to physical violence and corroding hatred. Violence often brings about momentary results. Nations have frequently won their independence in battle. But in spite of temporary victories, violence never brings permanent peace. It solves no social problem; it merely creates new and more complicated ones.

5   Violence as a way of achieving racial justice is both impractical and immoral. It is impractical because it is a descending spiral ending in destruction for all. The old law of an eye for an eye leaves everybody blind. It is immoral because it seeks to humiliate the opponent rather than win his understanding; it seeks to annihilate rather than to convert. Violence is immoral because it thrives on hatred rather than love. It destroys community and makes brotherhood impossible. It leaves society in monologue rather than dialogue. Violence ends by defeating itself. It creates bitterness in the survivors and brutality in the destroyers. A voice echoes through time saying to every potential Peter, "Put up your sword." History is cluttered with the wreckage of nations that failed to follow this command.

6   If the American Negro and other victims of oppression succumb to the temptation of using violence in the struggle for freedom, future generations will be the recipients of a desolate night of bitterness, and our chief legacy to them will be an endless reign of meaningless chaos. Violence is not the way.

7   The third way open to oppressed people in their quest for freedom is the way of nonviolent resistance. Like the synthesis in Hegelian philosophy, the principle of nonviolent resistance seeks to reconcile the truths of two opposites—acquiescence and violence—while avoiding the extremes and immoralities of both. The nonviolent resister agrees with the person who acquiesces that one should not be physically aggressive toward his opponent; but he balances the equation by agreeing with the person of violence that evil must be resisted. He avoids the nonresistance of the former and the violent resistance of the latter. With nonviolent resistance, no individual or group need submit to any wrong, nor need anyone resort to violence in order to right a wrong.

8   It seems to me that this is the method that must guide the actions of the Negro in the present crisis in race relations. Through nonviolent resistance the Negro will be able to rise to the noble height of opposing the unjust system while loving the perpetrators of the system. The Negro must work passionately and unrelentingly for full stature as a citizen, but he must not use inferior methods to gain it. He must never come to terms with falsehood, malice, hate, or destruction.

9   Nonviolent resistance makes it possible for the Negro to remain in the South and struggle for his rights. The Negro's problem will not be solved by running away. He cannot listen to the glib suggestion of those who would

urge him to migrate en masse to other sections of the country. By grasping his great opportunity in the South he can make a lasting contribution to the moral strength of the nation and set a sublime example of courage for generations yet unborn.

By nonviolent resistance, the Negro can also enlist all men of good will 10 in his struggle for equality. The problem is not a purely racial one, with Negroes set against whites. In the end, it is not a struggle between people at all, but a tension between justice and injustice. Nonviolent resistance is not aimed against oppressors but against oppression. Under its banner consciences, not racial groups, are enlisted.

If the Negro is to achieve the goal of integration, he must organize him- 11 self into a militant and nonviolent mass movement. All three elements are indispensable. The movement for equality and justice can only be a success if it has both a mass and militant character, the barriers to be overcome require both. Nonviolence is an imperative in order to bring about ultimate community.

A mass movement of militant quality that is not at the same time com- 12 mitted to nonviolence tends to generate conflict, which in turns breeds anarchy. The support of the participants and the sympathy of the uncommitted are both inhibited by the threat that bloodshed will engulf the community. This reaction in turn encourages the opposition to threaten and resort to force. When, however, the mass movement repudiates violence while moving resolutely toward its goal, its opponents are revealed as the instigators and practitioners of violence if it occurs. Then public support is magnetically attracted to the advocates of nonviolence, while those who employ violence are literally disarmed by overwhelming sentiment against their stand.

Rhetorical Considerations

1. What categories does King establish? What is the basis of the classification? Has King omitted any categories that ought to appear in this particular classification? If so, what? If not, show how the classification is complete. (*Hodges'* 32e/*Writer's* 2e)
2. What is King's primary purpose in the essay? How does classification help him accomplish that purpose? (*Hodges'* 32a/*Writer's* 1e)
3. From evidence in the essay, try to describe the audience King was writing for. What kinds of language help you to identify that audience? What allusions does King make in the essay, and how do they contribute to your understanding of King's audience? You are now also part of King's audience. How successful are King's rhetorical strategies for you? Explain. (*Hodges'* 32a/*Writer's* 1e)
4. Paragraphs 1 and 2 are alike in two ways: both are arranged similarly and both are developed by examples. In each paragraph, what is the topic? How do the examples develop the ideas presented? (*Hodges'* 31c and 32d/*Writer's* 2c–d)
5. Comment on King's use of transitional devices to ensure coherence in paragraph 3. (*Hodges'* 31b/*Writer's* 3c–d)
6. King's skillful use of various devices to establish clear transitions between paragraphs makes the reader's task of following the essay almost effortless. Show how King achieves this coherence. (*Hodges'* 31b/*Writer's* 3c–d)

Language and Style

1. Look up the following words in your dictionary: *tacitly* and *acquiescence* (paragraph 1); *corroding* (paragraph 4); *desolate* and *legacy* (paragraph 6); *synthesis* (paragraph 7); *malice* (paragraph 8); *sublime* (paragraph 9); *imperative* (paragraph 11); *anarchy, inhibited,* and *repudiates* (paragraph 12). Explain how each word helps to make precise the meaning of the sentence in which it appears. In each instance, can you think of any other word that would have served as well? (*Hodges'* 18e/*Writer's* 28e)
2. Explain the effect of the figurative language King uses in the first sentence of paragraph 6. (*Hodges'* 20b/*Writer's* 29b)
3. In the third sentence of paragraph 2, what is the subject of the clause, "that down don't bother me"? What part of speech is that word usually? What does this use tell you about rigid classifications of parts of speech? In standard English, the verb here would be *doesn't* rather than *don't*. How can *don't* be justified in this context? Do the same considerations apply to the deliberate misspelling of *been?* (*Hodges'* 1/*Writer's* 16)
4. What is the mood of the verb in the last sentence of paragraph 7? What reason might King have had for choosing that mood? What is the grammatical function of *individual, group,* and *anyone?* (*Hodges'* 1/*Writer's* 16)
5. In the second sentence of paragraph 8, King uses a series of prepositional phrases to clarify what he means by "noble height." Show how each prepositional phrase contributes to this classification. What part of speech is the object of the preposition? (*Hodges'* 1/*Writer's* 16)

Writing Suggestions

1. Consider some obstacle, limiting circumstance, or other frustration with which you are or have been confronted in your life (at work, at school, or at home) and write an essay in which you classify the possible responses to such a challenge, arguing that one response is better than the others. If you prefer, write the same kind of essay about possible responses to a specific opportunity.
2. Write an essay classifying the kinds of actions that may be taken to accomplish a purpose (such as purchasing a car or a home, getting a raise in pay, or changing someone's attitude towards you).

✦

Territorial Behavior

Desmond Morris

Desmond Morris, a noted British zoologist, is the author of several widely acclaimed studies aimed at the general reader explaining human behavior from a zoological perspective: *The Naked Ape* (1967), *The Human Zoo* (1969), *Intimate Behaviour* (1971), and *Manwatching* (1977). A graduate of Oxford University, Morris has taught at Oxford and worked as a research fellow of the university. He has contributed to a number of journals, among them *Behavior, British Birds, New Scientist,* and *Zoo Life.* "Territorial Behavior," from *Manwatching,* describes man's behavior by classifying it according to the kinds of territory being defended.

A territory is a defended space. In the broadest sense, there are three kinds 1 of human territory: tribal, family, and personal.

It is rare for people to be driven to physical fighting in defense of these 2 "owned" spaces, but fight they will, if pushed to the limit. The invading army encroaching on national territory, the gang moving into a rival district, the trespasser climbing into an orchard, the burglar breaking into a house, the bully pushing to the front of a queue, the driver trying to steal a parking space, all of these intruders are liable to be met with resistance varying from the vigorous to the savagely violent. Even if the law is on the side of the intruder, the urge to protect a territory may be so strong that otherwise peaceful citizens abandon all their usual controls and inhibitions. Attempts to evict families from their homes, no matter how socially valid the reasons, can lead to siege conditions reminiscent of the defence of a medieval fortress.

The fact that these upheavals are so rare is a measure of the success of 3 Territorial Signals as a system of dispute prevention. It is sometimes cynically stated that "all property is theft," but in reality it is the opposite. Property, as owned space which is *displayed* as owned space, is a special kind of sharing system which reduces fighting much more than it causes it. Man is a cooperative species, but he is also competitive, and his struggle for dominance has to be structured in some way if chaos is to be avoided. The establishment of territorial rights is one such structure. It limits dominance geographically. I am dominant in my territory and you are dominant in yours. In other words, dominance is shared out spatially, and we all have some. Even if I am weak and unintelligent and you can dominate me when we meet on neutral ground, I can still enjoy a thoroughly dominant role as soon as I retreat to my private base. Be it ever so humble, there is no place like a home territory.

Of course, I can still be intimidated by a particularly dominant individ- 4 ual who enters my home base, but his encroachment will be dangerous for him and he will think twice about it, because he will know that here my urge to resist will be dramatically magnified and my usual subservience banished. Insulted at the heart of my own territory, I may easily explode into battle— either symbolic or real—with a result that may be damaging to both of us.

5   In order for this to work, each territory has to be plainly advertised as such. Just as a dog cocks its leg to deposit its personal scent on the trees in its locality, so the human animal cocks its leg symbolically all over his home base. But because we are predominantly visual animals we employ mostly visual signals, and it is worth asking how to do this at the three levels: tribal, family, and personal.

6   First: The Tribal Territory. We evolved as tribal animals, living in compara- tively small groups, probably of less than a hundred, and we existed like that for millions of years. It is our basic social unit, a group in which everyone knows everyone else. Essentially, the tribal territory consisted of a home base surrounded by extended hunting grounds. Any neighboring tribe intruding on our social space would be repelled and driven away. As these early tribes swelled into agricultural super-tribes, and eventually into industrial nations, their territorial defense systems became increasingly elaborate. The tiny, an- cient home base of the hunting tribe became the great capital city, the primi- tive warpaint became the flags, emblems, uniforms, and regalia of the specialized military, and the war-chants became national anthems, marching songs and bugle calls. Territorial boundary-lines hardened into fixed borders, often conspicuously patrolled and punctuated with defensive structures—forts and lookout posts, checkpoints and great walls, and, today, customs barriers.

7   Today each nation flies its own flag, a symbolic embodiment of its terri- torial status. But patriotism is not enough. The ancient tribal hunter lurking inside each citizen finds himself unsatisfied by membership in such a vast conglomeration of individuals, most of whom are totally unknown to him personally. He does his best to feel that he shares a common territorial de- fence with them all, but the scale of the operation has become inhuman. It is hard to feel a sense of belonging with a tribe of fifty million or more. His an- swer is to form sub-groups, nearer to his ancient pattern, smaller and more personally known to him—the local club, the teenage gang, the union, the specialist society, the sports association, the political party, the college frater- nity, the social clique, the protest group, and the rest. Rare indeed is the indi- vidual who does not belong to at least one of these splinter groups, and take from it a sense of tribal allegiance and brotherhood. Typical of all these groups is the development of Territorial Signals—badges, costumes, headquarters, banners, slogans, and all the other displays of group identity. This is where the action is, in terms of tribal territorialism, and only when a major war breaks out does the emphasis shift upward to the higher group level of the nation.

8   Each of these modern pseudo-tribes set up its own special kind of home base. In extreme cases non-members are totally excluded, in others they are allowed in as visitors with limited rights and under a control system of spe- cial rules. In many ways they are like miniature nations, with their own flags and emblems and their own border guards. The exclusive club has its own "customs barrier": the doorman who checks your "passport" (your member- ship card) and prevents strangers from passing in unchallenged. There is a

government: the club committee; and often special displays of the tribal elders: the photographs or portraits of previous officials on the walls. At the
heart of the specialized territories there is a powerful feeling of security and
importance, a sense of shared defence against the outside world. Much of
the club chatter, both serious and joking, directs itself against the rotten-
ness of everything outside the club boundaries—in that "other world" beyond the protected portals.

In social organizations which embody a strong class system, such as mil-   9
itary units and large business concerns, there are many territorial rules, often
unspoken, which interfere with the official hierarchy. High-status individuals, such as officers or managers, could in theory enter any of the regions
occupied by the lower levels in the peck order, but they limit this power in
a striking way. An officer seldom enters a sergeant's mess or a barrack room
unless it is for a formal inspection. He respects those regions as alien territories even though he has the power to go there by virtue of his dominant
role. And in businesses, part of the appeal of unions, over and above their
obvious functions, is that with their officials, headquarters, and meetings
they add a sense of territorial power for the staff workers. It is almost as if
each military organization and business concern consists of two warring
tribes: the officers versus the other ranks, and the management versus the
workers. Each has its special home base within the system, and the territorial defense pattern thrusts itself into what, on the surface, is a pure social
hierarchy. Negotiations between managements and unions are tribal battles
fought out over the neutral ground of a boardroom table, and are as much
concerned with territorial display as they are with resolving problems of
wages and conditions. Indeed, if one side gives in too quickly and accepts
the other's demands, the victors feel strangely cheated and deeply suspicious that it may be a trick. What they are missing is the protracted sequence
of ritual and counter-ritual that keeps alive their group territorial identity.

Likewise, many of the hostile displays of sports fans and teenage gangs   10
are primarily concerned with displaying their group image to rival fan-clubs
and gangs. Except in rare cases, they do not attack one another's headquarters, drive out the occupants, and reduce them to a submissive, subordinate condition. It is enough to have scuffles on the borderlands between
the two rival territories. This is particularly clear at football matches, where
the fan-club headquarters becomes temporarily shifted from the club-house
to a section of the stands, and where minor fighting breaks out at the unof-
ficial boundary line between the massed groups of rival supporters. Newspaper reports play up the few accidents and injuries which do occur on such
occasions, but when these are studied in relation to the total numbers of
displaying fans involved it is clear that the serious incidents represent only
a tiny fraction of the overall group behavior. For every actual punch or kick
there are a thousand war-cries, war-dances, chants, and gestures.

Second: The Family Territory. Essentially, the family is a breeding unit   11
and the family territory is a breeding ground. At the center of this space,
there is the nest—the bedroom—where, tucked up in bed, we feel at our
most territorially secure. In a typical house the bedroom is upstairs, where a

safe nest should be. This puts it farther away from the entrance hall, the area where contact is made, intermittently, with the outside world. The less private reception rooms, where intruders are allowed access, are the next line of defence. Beyond them, outside the walls of the building, there is often a symbolic remnant of the ancient feeding grounds—a garden. Its symbolism often extends to the plants and animals it contains, which cease to be nutritional and become merely decorative—flowers and pets. But like a true territorial space it has a conspicuously displayed boundary-line, the garden fence, wall, or railings. Often no more than a token barrier, this is the outer territorial demarcation, separating the private world of the family from the public world beyond. To cross it puts any visitor or intruder at an immediate disadvantage. As he crosses the threshold, his dominance wanes, slightly but unmistakably. He is entering an area where he senses that he must ask permission to do simple things that he would consider a right elsewhere. Without lifting a finger, the territorial owners exert their dominance. This is done all the hundreds of small ownership "markers" they have deposited on their family territory: the ornaments, the "possessed" objects positioned in the rooms and on the walls; the furnishings, the furniture, the colors, the patterns, all owner-chosen and all making this particular home base unique to them.

12   It is one of the tragedies of modern architecture that there has been standardization of these vital territorial living units. One of the most important aspects of a home is that it should be similar to other homes only in a general way, and that in detail it should have many differences, making it a *particular* home. Unfortunately, it is cheaper to build a row of houses, or a block of flats, so that all the family living-units are identical, but the territorial urge rebels against this trend and house-owners struggle as best they can to make their mark on their mass-produced properties. They do this with garden-design, with front-door colors, with curtain pattern, with wallpaper and all the other decorative elements that together create a unique and different family environment. Only when they have completed this nest-building do they feel truly "at home" and secure.

13   When they venture forth as a family unit they repeat the process in a minor way. On a day-trip to the seaside, they load the car with personal belongings and it becomes their temporary, portable territory. Arriving at the beach they stake out a small territorial claim, marking it with rugs, towels, baskets, and other belongings to which they can return from their seaboard wanderings. Even if they all leave it at once to bathe, it retains a characteristic territorial quality and other family groups arriving will recognize this by setting up their own "home" bases at a respectful distance. Only when the whole beach has filled up with these marked spaces will newcomers start to position themselves in such a way that the inter-base distance becomes reduced. Forced to pitch between several existing beach territories they will feel a momentary sensation of intrusion, and the established "owners" will feel a similar sensation of invasion, even though they are not being directly inconvenienced.

14   The same territorial scene is being played out in parks and fields and on riverbanks, wherever family groups gather in their clustered units. But if ri-

valry for spaces creates mild feelings of hostility, it is true to say that, without the territorial system of sharing and space-limited dominance, there would be chaotic disorder.

Third: The Personal Space. If a man enters a waiting-room and sits at one 15 end of a long row of empty chairs, it is possible to predict where the next man to enter will seat himself. He will not sit next to the first man, nor will he sit a the far end, right away from him. He will choose a position about halfway between these two points. The next man to enter will take the largest gap left, and sit roughly in the middle of that, and so on, until eventually the latest newcomer will be forced to select a seat that places him right next to one of the already seated men. Similar patterns can be observed in cinemas, public urinals, airplanes, trains, and buses. This is a reflection of the fact that we all carry with us, everywhere we go, a portable territory called a Personal Space. If people move inside this space, we feel threatened. If they keep too far outside it, we feel rejected. The result is a subtle series of spatial adjustments, usually operating quite unconsciously and producing ideal compromises as far as this is possible. If a situation becomes too crowded, then we adjust our reactions accordingly and allow our Personal Space to shrink. Jammed into an elevator, a rush-hour compartment, or a packed room, we give up altogether and allow body-to-body contact, but when we relinquish our Personal Space in this way, we adopt certain special techniques. In essence, what we do is to convert these other bodies into "nonpersons." We studiously ignore them, and they us. We try not to face them if we can possibly avoid it. We wipe all expressiveness from our faces, letting them go blank. We may look up at the ceiling or down at the floor, and we reduce body movements to a minimum. Packed together like sardines in a tin, we stand dumbly still, sending out as few social signals as possible.

Even if the crowding is less severe, we still tend to cut down our social 16 interactions in the presence of large numbers. Careful observations of children in play groups revealed that if they are high-density groupings there is less social interaction between the individual children, even though there is theoretically more opportunity for such contacts. At the same time, the high-density groups show a higher frequency of aggressive and destructive behavior patterns in their play. Personal Space—"elbow room"—is a vital commodity for the human animal, and one that cannot be ignored without risking serious trouble.

Of course, we all enjoy the excitement of being in a crowd, and this re- 17 action cannot be ignored. But there are crowds and crowds. It is pleasant enough to be in a "spectator crowd," but not so appealing to find yourself in the middle of a rush-hour crush. The difference between the two is that the spectator crowd is all facing in the same direction and concentrating on a distant point of interest. Attending a theatre, there are twinges of rising hostility toward the stranger who sits down immediately in front of you or the one who squeezes into the seat next to you. The shared armrest can become a polite, but distinct territorial boundary-dispute region. However, as soon as the show begins, these invasions of Personal Space are forgotten and the attention is focused beyond the small space where the crowding is taking place. Now, each member of the audience feels himself spatially related, not to his cramped neighbors, but to the actor on the stage, and this distance is, if anything, too great. In the rush-hour crowd, by contrast, each member of the pushing throng is competing with his neighbors all the time. There is no escape to a spatial relation with a distant actor, only the pushing, shoving bodies all around.

18   Those of us who have to spend a great deal of time in crowded conditions become gradually better able to adjust, but no one can ever become completely immune to invasions of Personal Space. This is because they remain forever associated with either powerful hostile or equally powerful loving feelings. All through our childhood we will have been held to be loved and held to be hurt, and anyone who invades our Personal Space when we are adults is, in effect, threatening to extend his behavior into one of these two highly charged areas of human interaction. Even if his motives are clearly neither hostile nor sexual, we still find it hard to suppress our reactions to his close approach. Unfortunately, different countries have different ideas about exactly how close is close. It is easy enough to test your own "space reaction": when you are talking to someone in the street or in any open space, reach out with your arm and see where the nearest point on his body comes. If you hail from western Europe, you will find that he is at roughly fingertip distance from you. In other words, as you reach out, your fingertips will just about make contact with his shoulder. If you come from eastern Europe you will find you are standing at "wrist distance." If you come from the Mediterranean region you will find that you are much closer to your companion, a little more than "elbow distance."

19   Trouble begins when a member of one of these cultures meets and talks to one from another. Say a British diplomat meets an Italian or an Arab diplomat at an embassy function. They start talking in a friendly way, but soon the fingertips man begins to feel uneasy. Without knowing quite why, he starts to back away gently from his companion. The companion edges forward again. Each tries in his way to set up a Personal Space relationship that suits his own background. But it is impossible to do. Every time the Mediterranean diplomat advances to a distance that feels comfortable for him, the British diplomat feels threatened. Every time the Briton moves back, the other feels rejected. Attempts to adjust this situation often lead to a talking pair shifting slowly across a room, and many an embassy reception is dotted with western-European fingertip-distance men pinned against the walls by eager elbow-distance men. Until such differences are fully understood and allowances made, these minor differences in "body territories" will continue to act as an alienation factor which may interfere in a subtle way with diplomatic harmony and other forms of international transaction.

20   If there are distance problems when engaged in conversation, then there are clearly going to be even bigger difficulties where people must work privately in a shared space. Close proximity of others, pressing against the invisible boundaries of our personal body-territory, makes it difficult to concentrate on non-social matters. Flat-mates, students sharing a study, sailors in the cramped quarters of a ship, and office staff in crowded work-

places, all have to face this problem. They solve it by "cocooning." They use a variety of devices to shut themselves off from the others present. The best possible cocoon, of course, is a small private room—a den, a private office, a study, or a studio—which physically obscures the presence of other nearby territory-owners. This is the ideal situation for non-social work, but the space-sharers cannot enjoy this luxury. Their cocooning must be symbolic. They may, in certain cases, be able to erect small physical barriers, such as screens and partitions, which give substance to their invisible Personal Space boundaries, but when this cannot be done, other means must be sought. One of these is the "favored object." Each space-sharer develops a preference, repeatedly expressed until it becomes a fixed pattern, for a particular chair, or table, or alcove. Others come to respect this, and friction is reduced. This system is often formally arranged (this is my desk, that is yours), but even where it is not, favored places soon develop. Professor Smith has a favorite chair in the library. It is not formally his, but he always uses it and others avoid it. Seats around a mess-room table, or a boardroom table, become almost personal property for specific individuals. Even in the home, father has his favorite chair for reading the newspaper or watching television. Another devise is the blinkers-posture. Just as a horse that over-reacts to other horses and the distractions of the noisy race-course is given a pair of blinkers to shield its eyes, so people studying privately in a public place put on pseudo-blinkers in the form of shielding hands. Resting their elbows on the table, they sit with their hands screening their eyes from the scene on either side.

A third method of reinforcing the body-territory is to use personal mark- 21 ers. Books, papers, and other personal belongings are scattered around the favored site to render it more privately owned in the eyes of companions. Spreading out one's belongings is a well-known trick in public-transport situations, where a traveler tries to give the impression that seats next to him are taken. In many contexts carefully arranged personal markers can act as an effective-territorial display, even in the absence of the territory owner. Experiments in a library revealed that placing a pile of magazines on the table in one seating position successfully reserved that place for an average of 77 minutes. If a sport-jacket was added, draped over the chair, then the "reservation effect" lasted for over two hours.

In these ways, we strengthen the defences of our Personal Spaces, keep- 22 ing out intruders with the minimum of open hostility. As with all territorial behavior, the object is to defend space with signals rather than with fists and at all three levels—the tribal, the family, and the personal—it is a remarkably efficient system of space-sharing. It does not always seem so, because newspapers and newscasts inevitably magnify the exceptions and dwell on those cases where the signals have failed and wars have broken out, gangs have fought, neighboring families have feuded, or colleagues have clashed, but for every territorial signal that has failed, there are millions of others that have not. They do not rate a mention in the news, but they nevertheless constitute a dominant feature of human society—the society of a remarkably territorial animal.

Rhetorical Considerations

1. What purpose is most evident in this essay? Explain, using evidence from the essay. What evidence of a secondary purpose, if any, does the essay contain? (*Hodges'* 32a/*Writer's* 1e)
2. What evidence in the essay indicates the audience for which Morris was writing? Describe that audience. (*Hodges'* 32a/*Writer's* 1e)
3. What is the tone of the essay? Does the tone influence the reader's perception of the information the essay provides? If so, how? (*Hodges'* 33a/*Writer's* 3a)
4. What basis for classification does Morris use? Where does he state it? What kinds of background information does he offer for his classification? (*Hodges'* 32e/*Writer's* 2e)
5. Explain how Morris introduces his subject and arouses the reader's interest in the first five paragraphs of the essay. (*Hodges'* 33b/*Writer's* 3b)
6. Morris develops paragraphs 11, 17, 18, and 20 in different ways. Comment on his use of these different patterns of development. (*Hodges'* 32e/*Writer's* 2e)

Language and Style

1. In Britain, the following words have meanings different from those they have in the United States: *bathe, football, cinema, flat, garden.* What are the American equivalents? (*Hodges'* 18e/*Writer's* 28e)
2. In the last sentence of paragraph 15, Morris uses the cliché "like sardines in a tin." Explain why this cliché is or is not effectively used. (*Hodges'* 20b/*Writer's* 29b)
3. What is the source of the word *fan* (paragraph 10) in its informal meaning? List at least two other words with the same source. (*Hodges'* 18e/*Writer's* 28e)
4. The phrase following *unit* in the second complete sentence of paragraph 6 is an appositive. Comment on what this appositive adds to *unit,* the noun it is in apposition to. Do the modifiers of *unit* need to be taken into consideration? (*Hodges'* 1/*Writer's* 16)
5. Justify the use of a comma to separate the independent clauses in the second sentence of paragraph 8. (*Hodges'* 12/*Writer's* 31)

Writing Suggestions

1. Classify and describe the kinds of territorial behavior you have observed at one or more events (for example, at basketball games, in classrooms, in elevators, at parties, in meetings, and so on).
2. Analyze the street or block you live on in terms of territorial markings. How does each house or building distinguish itself from the others? If they don't seem to, why do you think that is? If they do, is there a specific marker that they share? How does that in turn define your block or street as an extended territory?

Recovering from Trauma

Ellen McGrath

Ellen McGrath, PhD, can be seen as the psychology expert on *ABC News, Good Morning America,* and *FOX News.* A clinical psychologist, McGrath is the author of *When Feeling Bad Is Good* (1992) and co-author of *The Complete Idiot's Guide to Beating the Blues* (1998); she also co-edited *Women and Depression: Risk Factors and Treatment Issues* (1990) during her tenure as chair of the American Psychological Association (APA) National Task Force on Women and Depression. McGrath has also served on the faculty of the University of California Irvine Medical School, the University of Rochester School of Medicine, and New York University. This essay was originally published in *Psychology Today's* newsletter, *Bluesbuster.*

Not everyone who endures a traumatic experience is scarred by it; the human psyche has a tremendous capacity for recovery and even growth. Recovering from a traumatic experience requires that the painful emotions be thoroughly processed. Trauma feelings cannot be repressed or forgotten. If they are not dealt with directly, the distressing feelings and troubling events replay over and over in the course of a lifetime, creating a condition known as post-traumatic stress disorder.

Whatever inner resources people need to mobilize for recovery, they still cannot accomplish the task alone. Depression and trauma are disconnective disorders. They do not improve in isolation. To fix them you have to be connected to others.

Direct experience with disasters ranging from the Gulf War to massive fires and California earthquakes has taught me that there are four basic stages in recovering from a profound stress. Progression through all four stages is essential to recovery.

Stage One: Circuit-breaking

If you overload an electrical system with too much energy and too much stimulation, the circuit breaker activates and shuts everything down. The human nervous system is also an electrical system, and when it is overloaded with too much stimulation and too much danger, as in trauma, it also shuts down to just basics. People describe it as feeling numb, in shock or dead inside.

The juice turns off. Intellectually, you lose from 50% to 90% of brain capacity, which is why you should never make a decision when you're "in the trauma zone." Emotionally you don't feel anything. Spiritually you're disconnected, you have a spiritual crisis or it doesn't mean anything to you at all.

6   Physically all your systems shut down and you run on basics. What is so intriguing is that physical symptoms that were previously prominent often disappear during this time. Back pain, migraines, arthritis, even acne often clear up. Then when recovery from trauma is complete, the physical symptoms return.

7   When the system starts to recover and can handle a bit more stimulation and energy—and the human system is destined to try to recover, to seek equilibrium—feelings begin to return.

Stage Two: Return of Feelings

8 Most people have not experienced so much primary trauma that they must see a professional counselor; they can work through their feelings by involving the people they are close to. They do it by telling their story—a hundred times. They need to talk talk talk, recount the gory details. That is the means by which they begin to dispel the feelings of distress attached to their memories.

9   The more that feelings can be encouraged, the better. The more you feel the more you heal. The expression of feelings can take many forms. For most people it may be easiest to talk. But others may need to write. Or draw. However they tell their stories, the rest of us have an obligation to listen.

10   It is often helpful to actually revisit the scene of destruction. That allows someone who has been impacted directly to emotionally experience the event and grasp the reality of it. That direct experience can stimulate the return of feeling. Visiting the site is not for everybody, however. For some it is too disturbing. Others may need the support of loved ones to revisit the scene.

11   There are four broad patterns of expression of feelings that people employ in response to a crisis. Call them feeling styles. Some people consistently maintain one style; others exhibit all four styles at different times.

12   It is important to recognize which style of emotional expression is characteristic of your response, and which patterns your loved ones display. Each one demands a different approach.

13   • The Trickle Effect—Feelings flow in little trickles, slow but steady. Tricklers have feelings at a low or medium level most of the time.

14   • Hit and Run feelings—Some people hit an emotion, experience it intensely, then find it so scary they run away from it. They avoid it and may not talk about it for days, weeks or even months. Then they hit the feeling again, it blows up and they run away from it again. This might be a pattern characteristic of the firefighters.

15   • Roller coasters—Many people go up and down emotionally. They are in touch with their feelings but their feelings are all over the place. Like a roller coaster, however, they can go very quickly through the feeling stage.

- Tsunamis—Emotions come in tidal waves that are so big, comprehen- 16
sive and overwhelming that those who get them feel like they're
going to drown. They flail about, and then the wave recedes; they
discover that they're still alive and they feel better. Tsunamis usually
occur because people repress their feelings of pain.

Stage Three: Constructive Action

People need to take action and make a difference even in the smallest ways. 17
Taking action restores a sense of control and directly counteracts the sense
of powerlessness that is the identifying mark of trauma.

The ways of action are many. You can write a letter to the rescue work- 18
ers. You can give blood. You can make a card for those who lost loved ones.
You can hang a flag if that means something to you, or donate to the Red
Cross. You can feed rescue workers or collect needed supplies for them from
your community. You can take in children whose families can't reach them.
You can help a person who is out of control to get more grounded during
the crisis.

You do whatever you can and never assume that any gesture is too 19
small. In a situation that is overwhelming, you don't go for the big picture.
You go for what is closest to you and where you can make a difference. Constructive action might be writing about the catastrophe or creating some
work of art about it. It also encompasses getting back to work so that you
can contribute something.

Stage Two and Stage Three go hand in hand. To go forward you feel and 20
you act. You can't do one or the other. Acting and feeling become an engine
that propels you forward.

Stage Four: Reintegration

In the wake of crisis it is possible to learn and grow at rates 100 times faster 21
than at any other time, because there is a door of opportunity. Growth can
go at warp speed in every domain of life.

You can learn much that is deep and profound. You do this by interact- 22
ing and by working together on the meaning of the difficult experience.
Those who have the courage to become part of the trauma tribe, to experience and share their pain, or to help them overcome their pain, also have
the opportunity to share their growth.

Everyone who goes through this process ends up better, stronger, 23
smarter, deeper, and more connected. They would say so and everyone who
comes in contact with them recognizes the change. It is like having a broken bone. If it heals properly, it is stronger in the spot where it fractured
than it was before the injury.

Traumatic experiences are broken bones of the soul. If you engage in 24
the process of recovery, you get stronger. If you don't, the bones remain
porous, with permanent holes inside, and you are considerably weaker.

25   In this stage of recovery, you reintegrate your self and your values in a new way. You incorporate meaning in your life. You integrate deeper and more authentic ways of communicating.

26   People at this stage may experience a new sense of the preciousness of life, a clarification of goals and renewed commitment to them, and new understanding of the value of ties to others. But to get to stage four you have to go through the first three stages.

Rhetorical Considerations

1. Does McGrath's essay concern all people who experience trauma? If not, what specifically is her focus? (*Hodges'* 32b/*Writer's* 2a)
2. According to McGrath, why should someone who has experienced trauma make a conscious effort to deal with those feelings? (*Hodges'* 32e/*Writer's* 2e)
3. What other expository modes does McGrath employ in her essay? How much does this essay resemble a process essay? (*Hodges'* 32e/*Writer's* 2e)
4. What are the most effective examples McGrath uses? (*Hodges'* 31c/*Writer's* 2d)

Language and Style

1. Look up the origins of the following words: *psyche* and *trauma* (paragraph 1); *equilibrium* (paragraph 7); *catastrophe* (paragraph 19). (*Hodges'* 18e/*Writer's* 28e)
2. What does McGrath mean when she writes, "Depression and trauma are disconnective disorders" (paragraph 2)? (*Hodges'* 18e/*Writer's* 28e)
3. Explain the analogy McGrath uses in paragraph 4. (*Hodges'* 32e/*Writer's* 2e)
4. Does the verb agree with the subject in the first clause of the essay? Why or why not? (*Hodges'* 6a/*Writer's* 22e)
5. What is the antecedent to the pronoun *that* in the second sentence of paragraph 10? (*Hodges'* 5/*Writer's* 21)

Writing Suggestions

1. Write an essay analyzing the emotional stages of a different process (falling in love, for example, or adjusting to a new school).
2. Choose a physical process with which you are familiar (doing or making something). and write an essay analyzing the steps that are involved.

GET IT STRAIGHT

William Saletan

William Saletan is the author of the forthcoming book, *Bearing Right: How Conservatives Won the Abortion War,* and is the chief political correspondent for MSN's online publication, *Slate,* which can be found at http://slate.msn.com. Saletan has also contributed articles to *Mother Jones* and *The New Republic.*

The one thing everybody knows about the Roman Catholic Church is that 1
you're supposed to confess your sins. Everybody, that is, except the church's leaders. First they failed to come clean about sexual abuse by priests. Then they failed to come clean about having covered up the abuse. Every time they assured the public that nothing else would come out, something else came out.

Now the bishops, the cardinals, and conservative interest groups have a 2
new story. The problem, they say, is homosexuality. If the church gets rid of gay priests, everything will be fine. But the more questions you ask about this story, the more contradictions you find. The cardinals' problem isn't that they can't keep the priesthood straight. The problem is that once again, they can't keep their story straight. Here are four key points on which their new alibi doesn't add up.

1. Profiling. The Family Research Council, the Traditional Values Coalition, 3
the Catholic League for Religious and Civil Rights, Roman Catholic Faithful, and numerous priests and bishops suggest that the church should weed out gay priests because a disproportionate share of sexual abuse cases involving priests are male-on-male. Credible reports say 90 percent of the victims are boys. Conservatives don't care that most gay priests don't molest kids. Their view is that it's fair to presume that an individual is dangerous if he's part of a high-risk group.

Unless, of course, we're talking about priests as a whole. In that case, 4
conservatives point out the unfairness of judging the group on the basis of a few bad apples. Consider the FRC's April 5 statement, "Media Hides Homosexuality Connection in Sex Abuse Scandal." According to the FRC, the "connection" is that "most cases" of abuse by priests are male-on-male. The standard for blaming a crime on a group, in other words, is what percentage of the crime is committed by the group. But in the same statement, FRC scolds the media for besmirching the Catholic clergy, when in fact the abusers are "a very small number of priests." Suddenly, FRC's standard for blaming a crime on a group isn't what percentage of the crime is committed

by the group—that would be inconvenient, since 100 percent of sex abuse by priests is committed by priests—but what percentage of the group commits the crime.

5   How do gays measure up to that standard? What percentage of gay priests have sexually abused children? The FRC doesn't say. Why not? Well, according to last Friday's *New York Times,* there are 46,000 Catholic priests in the United States; 30 percent to 50 percent of Catholic seminarians are gay; and lawyers for victims "claim to have lists of more than 1,000 priests accused of abuse in the United States." If you assume the worst—that only 30 percent of priests are gay, that 2,000 priests will end up accused, and that all the accused priests are guilty, gay, and current rather than former priests— fewer than 15 percent of gay priests have committed sexual abuse. If the 2,000 cases are spread over a period of 80 percent turnover in the priesthood, or if the number of guilty priests is more like 1,100, or if the percentage of priests who are gay is more like 50 percent, then only about 8 percent of gay priests have committed sexual abuse. According to the Catholic League, that's the rate of pedophilia "in the general adult population."

6   If you want to use profiling to weed out pedophiles, there's a far more effective way. One hundred percent of sexual abuse by priests is committed by men. So is nearly all sexual abuse of children. While it's hard to tell who's gay, it's easy to tell who's male. The ideal solution would be to ban men from the priesthood. The modest alternative would be to admit women. If conservatives were serious about protecting kids, they'd begin with that step. Instead, they've rejected it.

7 **2. Deviance.** When pedophiles such as the notorious Rev. Paul Shanley dissent from the Catholic hierarchy, conservatives dismiss them as twisted heretics. When these same pedophiles dissent from gay rights groups, conservatives infer that the pedophiles, not the gay rights groups, represent gay thinking. Connie Marshner, the director of the Free Congress Foundation's Center for Governance, argues that sexual liberalism has infected Catholicism and that the church must return to its roots. Meanwhile, she quotes a "pederast theoretician" who recently denounced the gay rights movement for preaching "assimilation" and trying to "demonize cross-generational love." So the gay rights movement, like the Catholic Church, rejects pederasty, right? Well, no. According to Marshner, the church's rejection is genuine, while the movement's rejection is tactical.

8 **3. Alternate causality.** According to conservatives, sexual abuse by priests can't be blamed on celibacy, since many clergymen who molest minors are married. "The best evidence suggests that the rate of priest pedophilia is about the same as found among the clergy of other religions," Catholic League President Bill Donohue pointed out four weeks ago. "Indeed, the Anglican dioceses in British Columbia are going bankrupt because so many ministers can't keep their hands to themselves. And these men are married." Donohue's logic sounds pretty solid: Some sexual abusers in the clergy are married; married clergymen aren't subject to the celibacy rule; therefore,

some sexual abusers in the clergy aren't subject to the celibacy rule; therefore, sexual abuse in the clergy can't be blamed on the celibacy rule.

Let's try the same logic on homosexuality. Some sexual abusers in the 9 clergy are married; married clergymen generally aren't gay; therefore, some sexual abusers in the clergy aren't gay; therefore, sexual abuse in the clergy can't be blamed on homosexuality—right? Uh, not exactly. "It is intellectually outrageous and deceitful to pretend that we don't know what's going on here," Donohue said on Fox News this week. "Too many sexually active gays have been in the priesthood, and it's about time they were routed out."

4. Gray area. The old school of sexuality held that deviance was 10 continuous: Stray from the path of righteousness, and pretty soon you'll be lying with other men, children, and dogs. The new school separates these practices into distinct orientations or disorders. The old school had coherence; the new school has cachet. The gay-blamers can't figure out which way to go. If they say homosexuality is distinct from pedophilia, they can't blame the latter on the former. On the other hand, if they say homosexuality is just one manifestation of waywardness, they can't assure the public that getting rid of the former will get rid of the latter.

The result is precisely the kind of moral confusion conservatives claim 11 to oppose. To project coherence, they attribute abuse by priests to "sexual anarchy" and "moral chaos." At the same time, to make the blame-gays theory look scientific, they draw convenient distinctions. According to Traditional Values Coalition Chairman Lou Sheldon, "To describe these priests as 'pedophiles' is clearly inaccurate—unless their victims are under the age of 13. The truth is that these are homosexuals who are engaging in pederasty or so-called consensual 'boy-love.'" Similarly, Cardinal Adam Maida of Detroit said this week that "the behavioral scientists are telling us, the sociologists, it's not truly a pedophilia-type problem but a homosexual problem."

Maida, Sheldon, and other clerics and activists think they're safeguarding 12 morality. But by describing a sexual relationship with a child between the ages of 13 and 17, unlike sex with a younger child, as a matter of hetero- or homosexual orientation, they are, in a strange way, normalizing such relationships. They're framing sex with teen-agers more like sex with adults and less like sex with children. They still believe it's wrong, but they're undermining the basis of that belief. And by insisting that the church has a gay problem, not a pedophile problem, they're letting pedophiles off the hook.

They're also letting men who have sex with teen-age girls off the hook. 13 Last Sunday, *National Review* editor Rich Lowry said of priestly abuse, "A lot of these cases don't involve the molestation of little boys, pedophilia. [They] involve having sex with teen-age boys, which is more sort of homosexual behavior. . . . I'm not justifying it. It's just not something heterosexual men do." Yesterday, Cardinal Francis George of Chicago added that the church should allow "wiggle room" in punishing abusive priests. "There is a difference between a moral monster like [homosexual molester Father John] Geoghan, who preys upon little children, and does so in a serial fashion, and someone who perhaps under the influence of alcohol engages in an action with a 17- or 16-year-old young woman who returns his affection," said George.

14   "Not something heterosexual men do"? "Wiggle room" for sex with a 16-year-old "young woman"? Look who's liberal now.

Rhetorical Considerations

1. How early in the essay does Saletan establish his tone and clarify his thesis? (*Hodges'* 32c/*Writer's* 2b)
2. Besides classification and division, what other expository modes does Saletan use to support his thesis? (*Hodges'* 32e/*Writer's* 2e)
3. Does Saletan use adequate examples? Why or why not? (*Hodges'* 31c/*Writer's* 2d)
4. Examine the logic and use of statistics in paragraphs 5 and 6. (*Hodges'* 35f/*Writer's* 7i)
5. Can you discern any reason for Saletan's choice to present his four major points in this particular order? Would another organizational pattern have been as effective? More effective? (*Hodges'* 32d/*Writer's* 2c)

Language and Style

1. Look up the following words in your dictionary: *pedophilia* (paragraph 5); *heretics* and *pederasty* (paragraph 7); *cachet* (paragraph 10). (*Hodges'* 18e/ *Writer's* 28e)
2. Explain the equivocation of the word *straight* in paragraph 2. (*Hodges'* 18e/*Writer's* 28e)
3. Examine Saletan's use of sentence fragments. Correct them. (*Hodges'* 2/*Writer's* 18)
4. What is the antecedent to the pronoun *they* in paragraph 1? Does it agree in number with its antecedent? (*Hodges'* 5 and 6b/*Writer's* 21a and 21d)
5. Does the verb agree with its subject in the second sentence of paragraph 5? Why or why not? (*Hodges'* 6a/*Writer's* 22e)

Writing Suggestions

1. Write an essay responding to Saletan's, either supporting or disagreeing with his thesis.
2. Find another group of people about whom there are false assumptions (you may even be a member of that group, but it is not necessary). Write an essay in which you logically explain why those assumptions are unfair or incorrect.

◆

The Qualities of Good Writing

Jacqueline Berke

Jacqueline Berke is Professor of English Emerita at Drew University, where she has taught both introductory and advanced writing courses and various courses in literature. A widely published writer herself, she has contributed to many journals and magazines, has been a fellow of the MacDowell Colony for artists and writers, and is the author of a widely used writing textbook, *Twenty Questions for the Writer* (1972). "The Qualities of Good Writing" is reprinted here from that book.

Even before you set out, you come prepared by instinct and intuition to make 1 certain judgments about what is "good." Take the following familiar sentence, for example: "I know not what course others may take, but as for me, give me liberty or give me death." Do you suppose this thought of Patrick Henry's would have come ringing down through the centuries if he had expressed this sentiment not in one tight, rhythmical sentence but as follows:

> It would be difficult, if not impossible, to predict on the basis of my limited information as to the predilections of the public, what the citizenry at large will regard as action commensurate with the present provocation, but after arduous consideration I personally feel so intensely and irrevocably committed to the position of social, political, and economic independence, that rather than submit to foreign and despotic control which is anathema to me, I will make the ultimate sacrifice of which humanity is capable—under the aegis of personal honor, ideological conviction, and existential commitment, I will sacrifice my own mortal existence.

How does this rambling, "high-flown" paraphrase measure up to the 2 bold "Give me liberty or give me death"? Who will deny that something is "happening" in Patrick Henry's rousing challenge that not only fails to happen in the paraphrase but is actually negated there? Would you bear with this long-winded, pompous speaker to the end? If you were to judge this statement strictly on its rhetoric (its choice and arrangement of words), you might aptly call it more boring than brave. Perhaps a plainer version will work better:

> Liberty is a very important thing for a person to have. Most people—at least the people I've talked to or that other people have told me about—know this and therefore are very anxious to preserve their liberty. Of course I can't be absolutely sure about what other folks are going to do in this present crisis, what with all these threats and everything, but I've made up my mind that I'm going to fight because liberty is really a very important thing to me; at least that's the way I feel about it.

3   This flat, "homely" prose, weighted down with what Flaubert called "fatty deposits," is grammatical enough. As in the pompous paraphrase, every verb agrees with its subject, every comma is in its proper place; nonetheless it lacks the qualities that make a statement—of one sentence or one hundred pages—pungent, vital, moving, memorable.

4   Let us isolate these qualities and describe them briefly. . . . The first quality of good writing is *economy.* In an appropriately slender volume entitled *The Elements of Style,* authors William Strunk and E. B. White stated concisely the case for economy: "A sentence should contain no unnecessary words, a paragraph no unnecessary sentences, for the same reason that a drawing should have no unnecessary lines and a machine no unnecessary parts. This requires not that the writer make all his sentences short or that he avoid all detail . . . but that every word tell." In other words, economical writing is *efficient* and *aesthetically satisfying.* While it makes a minimum demand on the energy and patience of readers, it returns to them a maximum of sharply compressed meaning. You should accept this as your basic responsibility as a writer: that you inflict no unnecessary words on your readers—just as a dentist inflicts no unnecessary pain, a lawyer no unnecessary risk. Economical writing avoids strain and at the same time promotes pleasure by producing a sense of form and right proportion, a sense of words that fit the ideas that they embody—with not a line of "deadwood" to dull the reader's attention, not an extra, useless phrase to clog the free flow of ideas, one following swiftly and clearly upon another.

5   Another basic quality of good writing is *simplicity.* Here again this does not require that you make all your sentences primerlike or that you reduce complexities to bare bone, but rather that you avoid embellishment or embroidery. The natural, unpretentious style is best. But, paradoxically, simplicity or naturalness does not come naturally. By the time we are old enough to write, most of us have grown so self-conscious that we stiffen, sometimes to the point of rigidity, when we are called upon to make a statement in speech or in writing. It is easy to offer the kindly advice "Be yourself," but many people do not feel like themselves when they take a pencil in hand or sit down at a typewriter. Thus during the early days of the Second World War, when air raids were feared in New York City and blackouts were instituted, an anonymous writer—probably a young civil service worker at City Hall—produced and distributed to stores throughout the city the following poster:

Illumination
is Required
to be
Extinguished
on These Premises
After Nightfall

6   What this meant, of course, was simply "Lights Out After Dark"; but apparently that direct imperative—clear and to the point—did not sound "official" enough; so the writer resorted to long Latinate words and involved

syntax (note the awkward passives "*is* Required" and "*to be* Extinguished") to establish a tone of dignity and authority. In contrast, how beautifully simple are the words of the translators of the King James version of the Bible, who felt no need for flourish, flamboyance, or grandiloquence. The Lord did not loftily or bombastically proclaim that universal illumination was required to be instantaneously installed. Simply but majestically "God said, Let there be light: and there was light. . . . And God called the light Day, and the darkness he called Night."

Most memorable declarations have been spare and direct. Abraham Lincoln and John Kennedy seemed to "speak to each other across the span of a century," notes French author André Maurois, for both men embodied noble themes in eloquently simple terms. Said Lincoln in his second Inaugural Address: "With malice towards none, with charity for all, with firmness in the right as God gives us the right, let us strive on to finish the work we are in. . . ." One hundred years later President Kennedy made his Inaugural dedication: "With a good conscience our only sure reward, with history the final judge of our deeds, let us go forth to lead the land we love. . . ." 7

A third fundamental element of good writing is *clarity*. Some people question whether it is always possible to be clear; after all, certain ideas are inherently complicated and inescapably difficult. True enough. But the responsible writer recognizes that writing should not add to the complications nor increase the difficulty; it should not set up an additional roadblock to understanding. Indeed, the German philosopher Wittgenstein went so far as to say that "whatever can be said can be said clearly." If you understand your own idea and want to convey it to others, you are obliged to render it in clear, orderly, readable, understandable prose—else why bother writing in the first place? Actually, obscure writers are usually confused, uncertain of what they want to say or what they mean; they have not yet completed that process of thinking through and reasoning into the heart of the subject. 8

Suffice it to say here that whatever the topic, whatever the occasion, expository writing should be readable, informative, and, wherever possible, engaging. At its best it may even be poetic, as Nikos Kazantzakis suggests in *Zorba the Greek,* where he draws an analogy between good prose and a beautiful landscape: 9

> To my mind the Cretan countryside resembled good prose, carefully ordered, sober, free from superfluous ornament, powerful and restrained. It expressed all that was necessary with the greatest economy. It had no flippancy nor artifice about it. It said what it had to say with a manly austerity. But between the severe lines one could discern an unexpected sensitiveness and tenderness; in the sheltered hollows the lemon and orange trees perfumed the air, and from the vastness of the sea emanated an inexhaustible poetry.

Even in technical writing, where the range of styles is necessarily limited (and poetry is neither possible nor appropriate), you must always be aware of "the reader over your shoulder." Take such topics as how to follow postal regulations for overseas mail, how to change oil in an engine, how to produce aspirin from salicylic acid. Here are technical expository descriptions that 10 defy a memorable turn of phrase; here is writing that is of necessity cut and dried, dispassionate, and bloodless. But it need not be difficult, tedious, confusing, or dull to those who want to find out about mailing letters, changing oil, or making aspirin. Those who seek such information should have reasonably easy access to it, which means that written instruction should be clear, simple, spare, direct, and most of all, *human:* for no matter how technical a subject, all writing is done *for* human beings *by* human beings. Writing, in other words, like language itself, is a strictly human enterprise. Machines may stamp letters, measure oil, and convert acids, but only human beings talk and write about these procedures so that other human beings may better understand them. It is always appropriate, therefore, to be human in one's statement.

11   Part of this humanity must stem from your sense of who your readers are. You must assume a "rhetorical stance." Indeed this is a fundamental principle of rhetoric: *nothing should ever be written in a vacuum.* You should identify your audience, hypothetical or real, so that you may speak to them in an appropriate voice. A student, for example, should never "just write," without visualizing a definite group of readers—fellow students, perhaps, or the educated community at large (intelligent nonspecialists). Without such definite readers in mind, you cannot assume a suitable and appropriate relationship to your material, your purpose, and your audience. A proper rhetorical stance, in other words, requires that you have an active sense of the following:

1. Who you are as a writer.
2. Who your readers are.
3. Why you are addressing them and on what occasion.
4. Your relationship to your subject matter.
5. How you want your readers to relate to the subject matter.

Rhetorical Considerations

1. Would you say that Berke's primary purpose in this essay is expressive, informative, or persuasive? Does knowing that the selection comes from a textbook on writing influence your judgment? Why or why not? What evidence can you find of purposes other than the one you named as primary? (*Hodges'* 32a/*Writer's* 1e)
2. Reread Berke's final paragraph, which concludes with a list of five things the writer must have actively in mind in order to have a "rhetorical stance." What do you suppose Berke's own answers to these five points were as she wrote "The Qualities of Good Writing"? (*Hodges'* 32a/*Writer's* 1e)
3. Analyze Berke's essay for its use of examples. Are any important points made that are not illustrated? (*Hodges'* 31c/*Writer's* 2d)
4. Consider the first two paragraphs and describe Berke's attitude toward her reader and the kind of relationship she wishes to establish with the reader. (*Hodges'* 33b/*Writer's* 3b)
5. Analyze the use of transitional devices in paragraph 8. (*Hodges'* 31b/*Writer's* 3c–d)

6. Find and discuss examples in Berke's own writing of the qualities of good writing she identifies: economy, simplicity, and clarity.

Language and Style

1. What is the usual meaning of the word *homely* (paragraph 3)? What word do we generally use to mean "having the qualities of home"? (*Hodges'* 18e/ *Writer's* 28e)
2. Look up the meaning of the prefix *para-*. Find three words in Berke's essay that begin with this prefix. What is the meaning of each? (*Hodges'* 18e/*Writer's* 28e)
3. The third sentence of paragraph 8 is actually an intentional sentence fragment. How might Berke justify using the fragment? (*Hodges'* 2/*Writer's* 18)
4. The first sentence of paragraph 9 is a complex sentence, comprising of a main clause and a subordinate clause. What is the verb of the main clause? Comment on the verb's number, tense, voice, and mood. (*Hodges'* 1e/*Writer's* 16d)

Writing Suggestions

1. Analyze some academic field of study, perhaps the one you expect to choose as your major, and divide it into its main parts or subfields. Then write an essay explaining it for a reader (such as a friend or relative) who knows little about it. Unless your instructor prefers otherwise, this could be in the form of a letter, which you might actually wish to send (thus getting a double benefit) after it has served its purpose in your writing course.
2. Write an essay analyzing in detail the wordiness and other weaknesses in Berke's long, windy paraphrase in paragraph 1 of Patrick Henry's statement, "give me liberty or give me death."

♦

WHICH STOOGE ARE YOU?

Ron Geraci

Ron Geraci is a senior editor for *Men's Health* magazine, for which he writes the monthly columns "Malegrams' and "This Dating Life," and where this essay was published (although it was originally published in the "Lifestyles" section of the *Seattle Times* in 1999). Geraci has especially received attention for a column in which he recounted his and three other editors' testing of treatments for baldness.

1 Men spend millions of dollars on psychotherapy trying to figure out why they're unhappy, why their kids don't respect them, why women treat them like idiots. Perhaps shrinks help some men, but for many others, it's money that would have been better spent on popcorn and videotapes. To solve many of life's problems, all you really need to do is watch the *Three Stooges*.

2 **Call it Stooge Therapy.** We're all variations of Moe, Larry, or Curly, and our lives are often short subjects filled with cosmic slapstick. When Moe (your boss) hits Curly (your buddy) with a corporate board and then blindsides you when you try to make it all nice, you're living a Stooge moment. Here you'll find the personality type each Stooge represents. Once you determine which Stooge you are, you'll better understand the problems you bring on yourself—and how you can be a generally happier, more successful knucklehead.

3 **Are You a Moe?** Everyone knows more than one Moe. These men are the insufferable know-it-alls who become driving instructors, gym teachers, and divorce attorneys. The coach who had you do pushups in front of the team? He was a Moe. So was that boss who made you carry his golf bag.

4 In short, Moes are hot-tempered men who intimidate people with verbal slaps and managerial eye pokes, according to Stuart Fischoff, Ph.D., a psychologist at California State University. "Moe has a paternalistic personality, which is pretty common among men," Fischoff says. "He treats everyone like a child and bullies people to keep them off balance." Being a temperamental loudmouth also helps Moe scare off critics who might expose his little secret: He's no smarter than the saps he terrorizes. Moe himself proved that point. Although he served up most of the nose gnashings and belly bonks in 190 shorts, he always ended up back in the mud with Larry and Curly.

5 Even if you've never actually threatened to tear somebody's tonsils out, there are a few other clues that can tag you as a Moe. First, naturally, Moes are explosive hotheads who storm through life constantly infuriated by other people. "These men suffer from classic low frustration tolerance," says

Allen Elkin, Ph.D., a psychologist in New York. "This not only makes them difficult to work with, but it also gives them high blood pressure, high cholesterol, and a much greater risk of heart attack." In fact, Moes often end up seeking counseling to control their anger, usually after it costs them a job, a marriage, or a couple of good pals. "I tell them to just get away from infuriating situations quickly," says Elkin. "Remember, you don't *have* to poke Curly in the eye because he destroyed the plumbing."

Second, in the likely event that a Moe manages to foul things up himself, 6 he'll find a way to blame his mistakes on other people, says Fischoff. In *Healthy, Wealthy, and Dumb* (1938), for example, Moe breaks a $5,000 vase with a 2-by-4 and screams at Larry, "Why didn't you bring me a softer board?!"

Your habits on the job are the most telling signs. If you're a Moe, you're 7 probably the hardest-driving wise guy at work. "High-strung, bossy men with Moe personalities tend to live at their jobs," says Elkin. To help stop overloading themselves with work they can't possibly finish (a common Moe peccadillo), workaholic Moes should make a list of projects they *won't* do each day—and then make sure they keep their hands off those folders.

Moe Howard (1897–1975) had a classic Moe personality. Even offscreen, 8 he was the fiery, short-fused leader of the trio who made all the decisions. Of course, this put a lot of worries on Moe's shoulders. "My father was an anxiety-ridden, nervous man," says Paul Howard, Moe's son. "He didn't have much patience. He always worried about his kid brother Curly, and if Larry flubbed a line, my father could become upset and criticize him almost like a director." Larry probably shaped up fast; Moe could always put some English into the next eye gouge.

Now, in fairness to all men with bowl cuts and bad attitudes, there are 9 some big advantages to having a Moe personality. "If I could choose my Stooge, I'd sure as hell be a Moe," says Fischoff. Because they're usually so domineering and assertive, Moes are often able to bark their way into leadership positions quickly. (Kennedy and Nixon were Moes; Carter was a Larry.) If you crammed all the *Fortune*-100 CEOs into one Bennigan's, you'd have Moe Central with a wet bar.

Another Moe perk: Women flock to you like geeks to a *Star Trek* pre- 10 miere. Moe is an aggressive, tenacious SOB, and women are genetically programmed to find those traits sexually attractive, says Barbara Keesling, Ph.D., a Southern California sex therapist. That's because prehistoric Moes used their superior eye-poking abilities to scare off those wise-guy tigers. It's why that Moe who gave you noogies in high school went through skirts faster than J. Edgar Hoover—and why he's probably divorced now.

"Moes are control freaks," says Keesling. "That can be sexually exciting at 11 first, but women get tired of it very quickly. I know—I've dated examples of all three Stooges. I'm thankful they didn't all try to sleep in my bed at once."

The Classic Larry Personality. Larry is the passive, agreeable fellow who 12 scrapes through life by taking his licks and collecting his paycheck. "Generally, things happen *to* a Larry; he doesn't make them happen," says Alan Entin, Ph.D., a psychologist with the American Psychological

Association. Larry is the ubiquitous "nice guy" who commutes to his mediocre job, congenially tries to cover Curly's ass, and spends his day trying to avoid getting whacked in the nose by Moe.

13   That's right: John Q. Taxpayer is a Larry.

14   A subtle testosterone shift, though, can make all the difference in what kind of life this lovable sap leads. Give the classic Larry a little more testicularity, and you have a good-natured man who isn't a biological doormat. He'll kick a wino off your lawn but won't fink on your free cable. That makes him a perfect coworker, neighbor, and pal.

15   But subtract a little gonad power, and a Larry can be an indecisive wimp whose greatest ambition in life is to watch *Everybody Loves Raymond*. These pitiful, wishy-washy slobs constantly get clobbered for being—as Larry would put it—"a victim of soicumstance," and that typically makes them passive-aggressive, says Fischoff.

16   "A Larry doesn't have the nerve to be assertive, so he protests by not doing something," Fischoff says: not securing the ladder on the triple-bunk bed, or not mentioning that the coffee is actually rat poison. Consequently, Larrys are rarely promoted. If a Larry actually does work up the courage to ask for a raise, the Moe he works for will usually give him a meaningless title upgrade—or say, "Get outta here before I murder ya."

17   To determine if you're an overly passive Larry, answer these three questions.

18   *What's new?* If you're a classic Larry, nothing is new. Your answer will be the latest yarn about the office Curly who once photocopied his own butt. "Larrys live vicariously through Moes and Curlys," says Fischoff. "They don't really have a strong identity of their own.

19   *Still dream about writing a screenplay?* "Larrys don't have a life plan," says Fischoff. They bumble from one opportunity to the next while awaiting their "break"; a Moe plots his life like a war and a Curly flatly avoids challenges.

20   *Do you weasel out of big projects?* Larrys become good at deflecting responsibility. This lets them avoid the risk of failure (and success) without looking like a bum. In *Idiots Deluxe* (1945), as Curly is being attacked by a giant bear, Moe screams, "Go out there and help him!" "The bear don't need no help!" Larry yells back.

21   The chief bonus in being a Larry, of course, is that almost everyone thinks you're a swell chum. The dames eventually warm up to you, too, although it might take a few decades. Women reeling from years of turbulent relationships with Moes and Curlys often settle down with a Larry, says Keesling, because he's a stable, predictable, okedokey guy who won't mind heading to the 7-Eleven for tampons. That makes him husband material. "I'd date Moe and Curley, but I'd marry Larry," confided several women we asked.

22   Like most Larrys, Larry Fine (1902–1975) spent his career following Moe and his free time ducking him. "Larry and Moe weren't friends," says Lyla Budnick, Larry's sister. "Their dealings were all business." Like any good Larry, he found passive-aggressive ways to make Moe fume. "My father would be at an airport hours early," says Joan Maurer, Moe's daughter, "but

Larry would show up 5 minutes before the plane took off. This made my dad very upset." For Larry, making Moe sweat in a crowded airport terminal was probably a tiny payback for the daily humiliations.

The Curly Syndrome. In *The Sweet Pie and Pie* (1941), Curly tries to throw 23 a pie at the usual gang of rich idiots but gets nailed with a pastry each time he cocks his arm. Finally he bashes himself with the pie to deprive others of the satisfaction. This illustrates Curly's strategy for life. "These men laugh at themselves so other people can't ridicule them first," says Elkin. "It comes across as funny, but this kind of defense mechanism really stems from a large reservoir of anger and resentment."

Curly had what's called an oral personality, and a particularly self- 24 destructive one. Boisterous, attention-seeking men, especially those who are secretly ashamed of something, like a beer gut or a bald head, often feel that they must perform in order to be liked, says Keesling. "These guys always come in for counseling, because they experience mood swings and addiction problems. It's what killed Curly and his modernday version, Chris Farley."

Men with Curly personalities are almost always fat, says Fischoff, because 25 they live to binge. They overdose on food, booze, gambling, drugs, or sex—and sometimes on all five in one badly soiled hotel bed. Curly, a consummate binger, even out-lined his plans for a utopian life in *Healthy, Wealthy, and Dumb:* "Oh boy! Pie á la mode with beer chasers three times a day!"

On the job, Curlys pride themselves on providing comedic relief. "A 26 curly senses he's no leader, so he garners attention by being a fool," says Fischoff. This nets him no respect, but it does defuse criticism. Who can fire a guy when he's down on the carpet running in circles?

Just like his two nitwit cohorts, Curly Howard's offscreen personality 27 was pretty similar to that of the Stooge he portrayed. He drank heavily, over-ate, and smoked several cigars a day. "He would always be out carousing and drinking, and playing the spoons in nightclubs," remembers Paul Howard, his nephew.

"I've heard stories that my father sometimes had to pay for the damage 28 Curly caused while drinking," says Joan Maurer, Moe's daughter. If woo-wooing was enough to get Curly belted onscreen, can you imagine what Moe dished out over a real-life antic like this?

Curly's lifestyle apparently made him foggy at work, too. When he 29 barked at women or said, "nyuk-nyuk-nyuk!" it was often because he had forgotten his lines. After having a series of obvious mini-strokes (he could barely grumble out his woos in 1945's *If a Body Meets a Body*), Curly had a career-ending stroke in 1946 and died in 1952 at age 48.

He had a hoot along the way, of course. Everybody loves a clown, so 30 Curlys get plenty of party invites—and nightcaps with attractive women. "If each of the Stooges were to flirt with a woman, Curly would probably take her home, because his humor radiates confidence," Keesling says. (And what woman could resist an opener like "Hiya, Toots"?) But a Curly's neuroses usually shine through within a few dates, which explains why Curlys tend to have few long-term sex partners, says Keesling.

31   Curly Howard was married four times. "With the exception of his fourth marriage, his best relationship was with his dogs," says Paul Howard. Curly expressed his marital outlook pretty clearly in 1941's *An Ache in Every Stake,* as he shaved a lathered block of ice with a razor: "Are you married or happy?"

Rhetorical Considerations

1. This article was published in *Men's Health* magazine. Who is Geraci's audience? What is his relationship to that audience? (*Hodges'* 32a/*Writer's* 1e(2))
2. How does Geraci establish tone in his essay? (*Hodges'* 33a/*Writer's* 3a(3))
3. Consider the order in which Geraci presents his three classifications. Would another order have been as effective? Why? (*Hodges'* 31b/*Writer's* 3c(3))
4. Find evidence of Geraci's use of other expository techniques (such as definition, comparison and contrast, for example). (*Hodges'* 31c and 32e/*Writer's* 2d–e)
5. Are there any weaknesses in his classification system? (*Hodges'* 33/*Writer's* 3)
6. Can you find an explicit thesis statement in the essay? If not, express the thesis in your own words. (*Hodges'* 32c/*Writer's* 2b)

Language and Style

1. Look up the following words in your dictionary: *peccadillo* and *workaholic* (paragraph 7); *English* (paragraph 8); *ubiquitous* (paragraph 12). (*Hodges'* 18e/*Writer's* 28e)
2. What is accomplished by the figurative expression "like geeks to a *Star Trek* premiere" in paragraph 10? (*Hodges'* 20b/*Writer's* 29b)
3. Explain how the following words contribute to Geraci's tone: *shrinks* (paragraph 1); *knucklehead* (paragraph 2); *soicumstance* (paragraph 15); *dames* (paragraph 21). (*Hodges'* 19c/*Writer's* 28c)
4. In the second sentence of paragraph 8, what is the antecedent of the pronoun? (*Hodges'* 5/*Writer's* 21)
5. What does *this* refer to in the third sentence of paragraph 23? (*Hodges'* 5/*Writer's* 21)

Writing Suggestions

1. Write an essay in which you classify a large group of people according to their similarity to another popular group of characters, possibly the characters on a television show like *Friends,* or characters from a cartoon.
2. Write an essay (either serious or humorous) classifying the different varieties of an emotion or attitude, such as different kinds of frustration, anger, happiness, love, envy, or excitement.

✦

IMAGES

Classification and Division

We frequently categorize people, classifying them according to age, gender, ethnicity, levels of expertise, interests, and so on. Both photographs here depict women in important, though different, roles.

Elliott Erwitt, USA. New York. New Rochelle. 1955

✦

IMAGES (CONT.)

Classification and Division

Laurence Monneret, Elderly couple kissing under umbrella

Rhetorical Considerations

1. Which of these two images aligns with some common classifications, and which breaks from stereotype?
2. Do you have emotional responses to either of these images? If so, what are they? (*Hodges'* 35b/*Writer's* 1d)
3. The photograph of the woman in the kitchen was taken in 1955. Could a similar picture be taken today? If you were going to photograph a contemporary woman in a similar environment, what details would you change to reflect her more accurately? (*Hodges'* 32a/*Writer's* 1e)
4. The photograph of the couple kissing may gross you out at first. Try to look at the image with more sensitivity. What do you observe now? (*Hodges'* 35b/*Writer's* 1d)

Writing Suggestions

1. Find a half-dozen or so different images of women in current magazines and write an essay that discusses how the images illustrate the ways in which women are classified today.
2. Go to the library and look at magazines from several different decades. Examine the ads that depict men, women, children, the elderly, or any other group and write an essay about any changes you may or may not discern.

CHAPTER 8

Definition

When you say, "I mean . . . ," you are defining. A definition, whether it is a short dictionary definition or an entire essay, explains what something is. You use definition daily, whether to explain what you are talking about, to clarify a point you have made, to identify which of two things you are referring to, or to persuade someone to change his or her mind. Whenever you respond to such questions as "What do you mean by that?" you are defining.

You will also find that you often need to use definition in your writing, sometimes very briefly with a synonym, sometimes at considerable length with an extended definition. A definition essay may involve many of the strategies discussed in this book, as the essays in this chapter show. Both Lindsy Van Gelder, in "It's Not Nice to Mess with Mother Nature," and Barbara Ehrenreich, in "A Mystery of Misogyny," use examples to define *ecofeminism* and *misogyny,* respectively. In "The 'Perfect' Trap" Monica Ramirez Basco begins her definition of *perfectionism* with a short narrative; and Bhikshuni Thubten Chodron, in "Land of Identities," compares and contrasts Jewish and Buddhist identities in an effort to define her own.

Understanding Definition

As mentioned above, a definition can be as short as a synonym or as long as a multivolume study. Look, for instance, at how Margery Guest defines *stove* with a synonym in her process essay "Sugaring": "An enormous wood 'arch' (stove) . . ." Definitions longer than a sentence or two are called *extended definitions.* Most of the definitions you will read in this chapter are extended definitions. They may be *objective* definitions, which focus on the thing to be defined, or *subjective* definitions, which focus on the writer's responses to the thing being defined. Kimberly Kagan's essay "Hegemony, Not Empire," is an objective definition. Bhikshuni Thubten Chodron's definition of what it means to be Jewish and Buddhist is a subjective definition that focuses on her feelings and beliefs about both faiths. Also subjective is Ruben Navarrette, Jr.'s definition of reverse discrimination. Although there are a number of other kinds of definition, the following are some of the most useful for writing:

- *Formal*—Dictionary (lexical) definitions are usually formal definitions. They consist of a single, rigidly structured sentence that states the three elements of formal definition:
  - *Term*—what is to be defined;
  - *Classification*—a group of similar things to which the term belongs;
  - *Differentiation*—the feature that makes the term different from other items in its class.

  Formal definitions are useful when you want to express the exact meaning of a word or identify an object or an idea. Lindsy Van Gelder uses a formal definition when she explains that measures such as the Gross National Product ignore much of the work that is done in this country and abroad, work that "I call the Love Economy—all the cooperative, selfless work we do for each other in communities and families, where no cash is exchanged" (362). Formal definitions can be built upon synonyms or antonyms, grammatical use, genus and species, cause, or function.

- *Descriptive*—Descriptive definitions characterize a term by describing it. For instance, *Merriam-Webster's Collegiate Dictionary* defines *church key* as "an implement with a triangular pointed head at one end for piercing the tops of cans and often with a rounded head at the other end for opening bottles." (This descriptive definition is also a functional one. See below.) Monica Ramirez Basco defines *perfectionism* by describing some of its effects:

  > Perfectionists are more vulnerable to depression when stressful events occur, particularly those that leave them feeling as though they are not good enough. In many ways, perfectionistic beliefs set a person up to be disappointed, given that achieving perfection consistently is impossible. (370)

- *Derivational*—A derivational definition shows when and how a word was established. The historical form of a derivational definition traces the use of a word through time, chronicling any changes in meaning. For instance, consider the following derivational definition of the word *ecofeminism,* which discusses the word's historical roots:

  > First coined by the French writer Françoise d'Eaubonne in 1974, *ecofeminism* combines the affix *eco-* (Late Latin *oeco,* household, from Greek *oikos,* house) with the base word *feminism* to produce a word meaning "a doctrine applying the principles of feminism to ecology."
  > —1981 West Coast Ecofeminist Conference

- *Functional*—It is also possible to define something by the way it works or how it is used. *Merriam-Webster's Collegiate Dictionary* offers a functional definition of *faucet:*"a fixture for drawing or regulating the flow

---

of liquid, esp. from a pipe." Barbara Ehrenreich's definition of *misogyny* is also functional—she describes how misogyny works and why it is used. (See also the descriptive definition of *church key*.)

• *Negative*—A negative definition explains what something is not, rather than what it is. It begins by stating a term, and then identifying a class that the term does not belong to. It concludes by offering a category into which the term does fit. Kimberly Kagan uses the following negative definition in "Hegemony, Not Empire":

> As the United States is engaged neither in controlling the policies of other states, nor in administering them, to call it an empire is inaccurate, and also harmful to American interests. It invites the criticism that is justly made of states, like Rome from the late Republic onward, that have sought to impose their rule on others. . . . The pax Americana is different from the pax Romana. America does not directly control small states, such as Bosnia or Afghanistan. It does not send governors, impose its laws, levy taxes, conscript soldiers, or permanently garrison its military forces abroad. In its foreign policy, America is not an empire, but a hegemon. "Hegemon" is the Greek word meaning leader. (354)

Note how this negative definition is also historical in its discussion of the derivation of the word *hegemon*. Negative definitions are particularly effective in changing the reader's mind or persuading the reader to think about something in a new way. They are also useful in introducing or concluding a topic.

• *Stipulative*—A stipulative definition specifies how a word will be used. When you ask "Do you mean *funny* (peculiar) or *funny* (ha, ha)?" you have stated a stipulative definition. You have narrowed the possible meanings of the word *funny* to a specific context. A stipulative definition may also make the meaning of a vague term more precise. The Supreme Court, for instance, clarified the meaning and implications of the term *intellectual property* in the recent case against Napster. You should be careful, though, when using stipulative definition to explain such loaded terms as *feminist,* since the connotations associated with such words tend to overshadow any context you try to confine them to. In such cases, try one of the other strategies outlined above.

Using Definition

Subject

In theory, choosing something to define ought to be as simple as making a list of everything you can see from where you sit and then selecting one thing. But definition is such a powerful tool in aiding critical thinking that people sometimes want to define large, emotionally laden concepts such as *love* or *hatred,* or else define an abstraction that is important in their lives such as *democracy* or *freedom*. Such topics are too broad to develop fully in most books, let alone in an essay. If you do decide to focus your essay on a topic such as *love,* you would do well to stick to a very limited aspect of that vast and problematic emotion, perhaps discussing your love for a particular pet, or a fondness for a specific place. Remember to choose lots of details and examples that will help your readers understand your definition and recreate your experiences in their minds. Look carefully at the kinds of details and examples each writer in this chapter chooses to convey information or a feeling, to inform or persuade you.

Purpose and Audience

Since you write a definition to explain a particular concept or object to your reader, you must consider what your reader already knows before you can decide what kinds of details and examples you need to supply and what kind of vocabulary you should use, or even whether you need to define at all. For instance, if you were writing about a *rumble seat* for a general audience, you would have to explain what you mean for any reader under 70, since such open passenger seats were not used in cars manufactured shortly after World War II. Older readers, however, could be expected to know what a *rumble seat* is without explanation, very likely having sat in a rumble seat as a child or as a teenager out on a double date.

An awareness, not only of your readers' background and interests, but also of your purpose for writing, is crucial to the decisions you will make. Are you writing primarily to convey information to a reader who you can safely assume is interested in learning more about your subject? If so, you may have the luxury of taking time and space to explore your subject in considerable depth, as Lindsy Van Gelder does in "It's Not Nice to Mess with Mother Nature." On the other hand, you might be writing with a strongly persuasive aim, hoping to win over skeptical readers to your point of view. In that case, you might try to be as brief as possible, relying on a few striking examples and carefully chosen details so as not to exhaust your readers' patience while you make your case. Such is Barbara Ehrenreich's method in "A Mystery of Misogyny."

Organization

One effective way to begin a good definition essay is to state a formal definition—the term, the classification, and the differentiation (*Hodges'* 20e/ *Writer's* 29e). This information can usually be framed in a single sentence which can serve as a *thesis,* such as the one developed by student Tanisha Carter in this chapter: White-collar crimes are "economic crimes committed by employees, who do not wear work clothes, but instead who wear white shirts and ties" (344). Accompanied by the appropriate background information, a formal definition can provide an effective introduction. Sometimes you will want to dispel common misconceptions at the outset with your definition, and it is always a good idea to summarize the main points of your essay early on so your readers have some idea of where you are leading them. Carter does this by listing the questions she will answer: "So what is white-collar crime? Whom does it affect? What kind of damage does it produce? How does the judicial system punish it?" (344).

You can develop the body of a definition essay by using one or more strategies (see *Hodges' 32e/Writer's 2e* for more information). Monica Ramirez Basco uses a combination of narration, example, cause and effect, description, and process analysis to develop "The 'Perfect' Trap." Ruben Navarrette Jr. combines chronology and example in "Is It Reverse Discrimination?" Alternatively, you might want to use a *spatial* or an *emphatic organization*. A spatial organization is particularly appropriate if you are defining an object by using description. In this kind of essay, you are transferring a visual perception into words. You will want to take up each point in an orderly manner, moving vertically or horizontally or even radially. (The definition of a cloverleaf in the Images section (see pages 376–377) lends itself to a radial description.) An emphatic organization is useful when your definition is persuasive and you take up your points in order of importance. Whatever plan you use, be sure to keep your definition focused on your thesis. It can be easy to stray from your topic and include irrelevant information or inadvertently leave out something important.

Definition essays often conclude with a restatement of the thesis or with a summary of the main points that you have addressed. By revisiting and expanding your controlling idea in the conclusion, you will encourage your readers to build upon what you have offered in the body of your essay, and your essay will ultimately be stronger.

Language and Style

As you write definitions, a few special cautions are worth bearing in mind. Be careful with your logic; one of the most frequent traps writers fall into with definition is circularity. You don't help your reader much when you define a Cistercian monk as a monk belonging to the Cistercian order. Also avoid the awkward and illogical use of *is when* or *is where* in definitions that do not involve time or place. For instance, do not write "Terrorism *is where* [or *is when*] violence and intimidation are used for some political purpose." Terrorism is neither a place (*is where*) nor a time (*is when*). Instead, write, "Terrorism is the use of violence and intimidation for some political purpose."

Also pay particular attention to the denotations and connotations of the words you use. Managing connotations is crucial to defining successfully for your readers. For example, there is a significant difference in connotation between *telescope* and *spyglass*. Aside from the suggestion of something antique, *spyglass* has some negative connotations: If you tell your neighbors you are getting a telescope, they will be much less nervous than if you tell them you are getting a spyglass. When you write definitions, use language that is accurate and that will draw the response you want from your readers.

Images

An image—a drawing, chart, or photograph—can help define a certain idea or object. Suppose you are defining a *cloverleaf*. You might say that it is a structure built at the intersection of two major highways that has four loops and four ramps to enable traffic to change from one highway to another without stopping. For a reader who has never seen such an interchange, this description would not be very helpful, but a drawing might be.

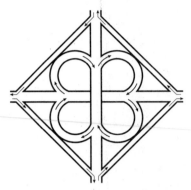

Diagram of a cloverleaf interchange

Look at the images in this chapter, each of which offers a different definition of *beauty*. What better way to define a visual concept such as this than to represent it graphically?

Student Essay

In the following essay, student Tanisha Carter uses definition to persuade her readers to be alert for white-collar crime. As you read her essay, notice the kinds of information Carter provides and the various development strategies she employs.

White-Collar Crime

Introduction

Formal definition

Background information

Foreshadowing main points

Did you know that the company who sold you the security system installed in your home to protect your family from violent crime might have already made you a victim? In fact, business entities perpetuate crimes that affect one in three American households every year. Consequently, in the 1930s, criminologist Edwin H. Sutherland coined the term "white-collar crime" to denote economic crimes committed by employees who do not wear work clothes, but instead who wear white shirts and ties. Still, many Americans understand much more easily such crimes as burglary, car theft, or robbery than the concept of *white-collar crime*. So what is white-collar crime? Whom does it affect? What kind of damage does it produce? How does the judicial system punish it? I believe answering the preceding questions will help us understand what white-collar crime is and support our fight against it.

Reasons for underreporting

First, we may be less apt to target a white-collar crime because of the "American Dream," the traditional belief that a person can build wealth by working hard. Many Americans assume that criminals are only those who, instead of working, use force and "steal" from other's homes and businesses. In contrast, the everyday processes of certain occupations mask white-collar crimes such as embezzlement, insurance fraud, insider trading, investment schemes, and forgery. In addition, some white-collar criminals engage in high-tech theft such as credit-card fraud, computer fraud, pyramid schemes, and counterfeiting. So, the perpetrators and even the crimes themselves often go undetected, making it difficult to bring widespread awareness of economic crimes and their victims to society's attention.

Those affected

However, from business owners, consumers, stockholders, and their family members to retirees and the unemployed, everyone is susceptible to economic crime. Most victims know just enough about economic crime that they will contact organizations such as the Better Business Bureau to report "bad business practices." But often, these people are unaware that what they perceive as "bad business practices" are really criminal activities. For them, it is much easier to report to the police the theft of personal property out of their garage than it is to report having invested in a "sure deal" and then never hearing again from the company that took their money. However, we need to report these types of crimes to law-enforcement agencies because these crimes produce the most detrimental costs to our society.

Evidence of damage— objective details

For instance, recent white-collar crime cases making big headlines in the media prove just how damaging these types of non-violent theft can be. Companies such as Enron and WorldCom have stolen billions of dollars from their employees in real and expected income from salaries and stock options. But these are not isolated cases. To be sure, according to a 1999 study, "The National Public Survey on White Collar Crime," conducted by the National White Collar Crime Center in Morgantown, West Virginia, economic crime costs Americans nearly twenty-one times the monetary amount that street crime costs. So, how are we dealing with these criminals whose crimes are so devastating?

Legal and judicial difficulties

Almost a year after Enron and WorldCom corporate personnel were arrested for white-collar crime, they have yet to be sentenced to prison time. America's judicial system, uncertain like society as a whole of what white-collar crime is and when an economic crime has happened, hesitates when charging and convicting perpetrators of economic crime. It seems to be much easier to charge and convict a street criminal who breaks into an innocent family's home, and, by use of force, physically

continued

injures a family member and steals family items. But, why do we not have the same ease in punishing the president of a company who allowed safety standards in his or her business to erode because of a desire for larger profits? What if the president's actions created an unsafe work-space in which an employee lost his or her life? What if, moreover, as a result of this crime, a family loses their primary source of income with the death of that employee? If the first criminal receives a sentence of twenty years in prison, what penalty should the "hard-working" company presi-dent receive? Perhaps that executive could be charged with involuntary manslaughter or reckless endangerment of life, but those are not white-collar crimes. What category can be applied to such stunning selfishness?

Conclusion— *solution to the* *problem and* *call to action*

In light of the damage white-collar crime causes, we should demand our law enforcement agencies deal effectively with these crimes by ar-resting, prosecuting, and sentencing white-collar criminals promptly and justly. Similar to statutes requiring certain lengths of incarceration time for violent criminal offenses, sentences for white-collar criminals should be consistent and reflect the scope of damage economic crimes create. But it is also up to all Americans to recognize and report white-collar crimes. Just as we are encouraged to be good citizens and report violent crimes, we need to be involved with stopping economic crimes.

Commentary

Carter introduces her essay with a question sure to get her reader's attention. She then provides some background information and a formal definition of white-collar crime. To extend her definition, she asks a series of questions and makes her readers aware that she wants to move them to action.

The body of her essay offers an analysis of why these crimes are under-prosecuted, points out how ordinary people are vulnerable, and suggests reasons that economic crimes are not reported when they occur. Her next point takes up the legal and judicial difficulties white-collar crime poses.

Her essay concludes with an appeal to readers to "be involved with stop-ping economic crimes" and with a solution for dealing with such criminals: "Similar to statutes requiring certain lengths of incarceration time for vio-lent criminal offenses, sentences for white-collar criminals should be consis-tent and reflect the scope of damage economic crimes create" (346).

Carter's strategy is interesting. Because the essay is an argument as well as a definition essay, Carter defers her strongest evidence. As she draws to a close, she points out some of the most egregious white-collar crimes and notes that a year after the perpetrators have been caught, no one has yet been convicted. Structuring the essay this way allows Carter to make her point strongly.

✦ CHECKLIST FOR WRITING ESSAYS DEVELOPED BY DEFINITION

- What are you *defining?* Can you state it in a single sentence? What kind of definition is it—*formal, descriptive, stipulative,* etc.? Is it *objective* or *subjective?*
- Are the *details* you use consistent with the kind of definition you have chosen to develop? (*Hodges'* 32e(7)/*Writer's* 2e(7))
- What is the *point* of your definition? Have you stated that point as a *thesis* and focused your analysis around that statement?
- Is your *purpose* to persuade? To inform? To entertain? A blend? Can you state your specific purpose in a single sentence? (*Hodges'* 32a(1)/ *Writer's* 1e(1))
- Have you presented the details and examples you have used to develop your definition in a particular *order?* What is it and why is it appropriate for this information and *audience?* (*Hodges'* 31c/*Writer's* 2d)
- Have you checked your essay to be sure you have not fallen into any *logical fallacies* such as *circularity?* (*Hodges'* 35f/*Writer's* 7i)
- Do *transitional words and phrases* link the parts of your essay? (*Hodges'* 31b/*Writer's* 3d)
- What kind of *conclusion* have you written? Does it reflect the point you have made? What effects do you anticipate your definition will have on your readers? (*Hodges'* 33b(2)/*Writer's* 3b(2))

◆

A Mystery of Misogyny

Barbara Ehrenreich

Barbara Ehrenreich is a political essayist and social critic who has contributed essays to *Time, Mother Jones, Harper, The Progressive,* and many other publications. She is the author or co-author of several books, including *Fear of Falling: The Inner Life of the Middle Class* (1989), *Blood Rites: Origins and History of the Passions of War* (1997), and *Nickel and Dimed: On (Not) Getting By in America* (2001). This essay was originally published in *Mother Jones* in 2002.

1 A feminist can take some dim comfort from the fact that the Taliban's egregious misogyny is finally considered newsworthy. It certainly wasn't high on Washington's agenda in May, for example, when President Bush congratulated the ruling Taliban for banning opium production and handed them a check for $43 million—never mind that their regime accords women a status somewhat below that of livestock.

2 In the weeks after September 11, however, you could find escaped Afghan women on *Oprah* and longtime anti-Taliban activist Mavis Leno doing the cable talk shows. CNN has shown the documentary *Beneath the Veil*, and even Bush has seen fit to mention the Taliban's hostility to women—although their hospitality to Osama bin Laden is still seen as the far greater crime. Women's rights may play no part in U.S. foreign policy, but we should perhaps be grateful that they have at least been important enough to deploy in the media mobilization for war.

3 On the analytical front, though, the neglect of Taliban misogyny—and beyond that, Islamic fundamentalist misogyny in general—remains almost total. If the extreme segregation and oppression of women does not stem from the Koran, as non-fundamentalist Muslims insist, if it is, in fact, something new, then why should it have emerged when it did, toward the end of the twentieth century? Liberal and leftwing commentators have done a thorough job of explaining why the fundamentalists hate America, but no one has bothered to figure out why they hate women.

4 And "hate" is the operative verb here. Fundamentalists may claim that the sequestration and covering of women serves to "protect" the weaker, more rape-prone sex. But the protection argument hardly applies to the fundamentalist groups in Pakistan and Kashmir that specialize in throwing acid in the faces of unveiled women. There's a difference between "protection" and a protection racket.

5 The mystery of fundamentalist misogyny deepens when you consider that the anti-imperialist and anti-colonialist Third World movements of forty or fifty years ago were, for the most part, at least officially committed

to women's rights. Women participated in Mao's Long March; they fought in the Algerian revolution and in the guerrilla armies of Mozambique, Angola, and El Salvador. The ideologies of these movements were inclusive of women and open, theoretically anyway, to the idea of equality. Osama bin Laden is, of course, hardly a suitable heir to the Third World liberation movements of the mid-twentieth century, but he does purport to speak for the downtrodden and against Western capitalism and militarism. Except that his movement has nothing to offer the most downtrodden sex but the veil and a life lived largely indoors.

Of those commentators who do bother with the subject, most explain   6 the misogyny as part of the fundamentalists' wholesale rejection of "modernity" or "the West." Hollywood culture is filled with images of strong or at least sexually assertive women, hence—the reasoning goes—the Islamic fundamentalist impulse is to respond by reducing women to chattel. The only trouble with this explanation is that the fundamentalists have been otherwise notably selective in their rejection of the "modern." The nineteen terrorists of September 11 studied aviation and communicated with each other by e-mail. Osama bin Laden and the Taliban favor Stingers and automatic weapons over scimitars. If you're going to accept Western technology, why throw out something else that has contributed to Western economic success—the participation of women in public life?

Perhaps—to venture a speculation—the answer lies in the ways that   7 globalization has posed a particular threat to men. Western industry has displaced traditional crafts—female as well as male—and large-scale, multinational-controlled agriculture has downgraded the independent farmer to the status of hired hand. From West Africa to Southeast Asia, these trends have resulted in massive male displacement and, frequently, unemployment. At the same time, globalization has offered new opportunities for Third World women—in export-oriented manufacturing, where women are favored for their presumed "nimble fingers," and, more recently, as migrant domestics working in wealthy countries.

These are not, of course, opportunities for brilliant careers, but for ex-   8 tremely low-paid work under frequently abusive conditions. Still, the demand for female labor on the "global assembly line" and in the homes of the affluent has been enough to generate a kind of global gender revolution. While males have lost their traditional status as farmers and breadwinners, women have been entering the market economy and gaining the marginal independence conferred even by a paltry wage.

Add to the economic dislocations engendered by globalization the on-   9 slaught of Western cultural imagery, and you have the makings of what sociologist Arlie Hochschild has called a "global masculinity crisis." The man who can no longer make a living, who has to depend on his wife's earnings, can watch Hollywood sexpots on pirated videos and begin to think the world has been turned upside down. This is *Stiffed*—Susan Faludi's 1999 book on the decline of traditional manhood in America—gone global.

Or maybe the global assembly line has played only a minor role in   10 generating Islamic fundamentalist misogyny. After all, the Taliban's home

country, Afghanistan, has not been a popular site for multinational manufacturing plants. There, we might look for an explanation involving the exigencies—and mythologies—of war. Afghans have fought each other and the
Soviets for much of the last twenty years, and, as Klaus Theweleit wrote in
his brilliant 1989 book, *Male Fantasies,* long-term warriors have a tendency
to see women as a corrupting and debilitating force. Hence, perhaps, the all-
male *madrassas* in Pakistan, where boys as young as six are trained for jihad,
far from the potentially softening influence of mothers and sisters. Or recall
terrorist Mohamed Atta's specification, in his will, that no woman handle
his corpse or approach his grave.

11   Then again, it could be a mistake to take Islamic fundamentalism out of
the context of other fundamentalisms—Christian and Orthodox Jewish. All
three aspire to restore women to the status they occupied—or are believed
to have occupied—in certain ancient nomadic Middle Eastern tribes.

12   Religious fundamentalism in general has been explained as a backlash
against the modern, capitalist world, and fundamentalism everywhere is no
friend to the female sex. To comprehend the full nature of the threats we
face since September 11, we need to figure out why. Assuming women matter, that is.

Rhetorical Considerations

1. Is Ehrenreich's primary purpose expressive, informative, or persuasive?
   (*Hodges'* 32a/*Writer's* 1e)
2. How much of the essay hinges on definitions of particular terms? What are
   those terms? (*Hodges'* 32e/*Writer's* 2e)
3. In what way could misogyny be a rejection of modernity?
4. According to Ehrenreich, what is the connection between misogyny and the
   global economy?
5. How effective are Ehrenreich's introduction and conclusion? (*Hodges'*
   33b/*Writer's* 3b)

Language and Style

1. Look up the following words in your dictionary: *egregious* and *misogyny* (paragraph 1); *deploy* (paragraph 2); *fundamentalist* (paragraph 3); *anti-imperialist*
   and *anti-colonialist* (paragraph 5); *chattel* (paragraph 6); *exigencies* (paragraph
   10). (*Hodges'* 18e/*Writer's* 28e)
2. Why is *madrassas* italicized (paragraph 10)? What does this word mean?
   (*Hodges'* 10/*Writer's* 38)
3. Find three sentence fragments in the essay. Rewrite them as complete sentences. (*Hodges'* 2/*Writer's* 18)
4. Does the pronoun *their* agree with its antecedent in the second sentence of
   paragraph 2? (*Hodges'* 6b/*Writer's* 21d)

Writing Suggestions

1. Ehrenreich writes, "Women's rights may play no role in U.S. foreign policy. . . ." Write an essay that defines "women's rights" and examines whether it should or should not be considered as part of U.S. foreign policy.
2. Write an essay examining the effect that cultural change and religion have had in transforming attitudes about a specific group of people.

HEGEMONY, NOT EMPIRE

Kimberly Kagan

> Kimberly Kagan received her BA and PhD from Yale University, and is an assistant professor at the United States Military Academy at West Point, where she teaches world civilizations, classical history, and the history of world religions. Her chief area of expertise is classical military history.

1   Critics of the United States have long called it imperialistic and compared its "empire" to those of the European colonial powers of the nineteenth and twentieth centuries. Now, however, some American thinkers lay proud (or reluctant) claim to the title of the empire. They compare the United States admiringly to ancient Rome, forger and protector of the rule of law, peace, and prosperity. Some of them say America already is such an empire, while others urge it to become one. But in fact, the United States is not an empire at all, and the analogy with Rome is deceptive and misleading.

2   Consider Rome at the height of the pax Romana, the reign of Trajan (A.D. 98–117), when no other state could challenge its military might. The great bulk of the empire had been conquered by force, destroying the independence and autonomy of the conquered lands. During Trajan's reign, the Roman state directly administered territories from Britain to Palestine, from Spain to Turkey. The emperor sent governors into every province. These governors collected taxes, administered justice, and conscripted provincials into the Roman army. The state could requisition goods and services from private individuals. The Roman army permanently occupied garrisons in every province.

3   These troops not only protected and expanded the borders of the empire, but also policed its residents. These people were not citizens of the Roman state, so they did not enjoy full legal rights or the opportunity to hold public office in the imperial administration. In contrast to provincials, Roman citizens paid no direct taxes. The peaceful conditions of the Roman Empire fostered economic prosperity and order, but these benefits came at a price: the highly intrusive presence of the Roman state in the life of the average provincial person.

4   The pax Americana differs fundamentally from the pax Romana. With the exception of three possessions, American Samoa, Guam, and the U.S. Virgin Islands, the United States treats no nations as protectorates, let alone incorporates them and places them directly under its power. However great its ability to project military force around the globe, the United States does not maintain garrisons in every foreign territory where its interests lie. Nor does it use its military power to establish American jurisdiction over those territories.

American policymakers have a fundamentally different goal from Roman 5
emperors. The United States seeks to maintain a peaceful world in which
conflict between or within states is settled without recourse to violence. The
Roman Empire in the time of Trajan had all but eliminated small states from
the Mediterranean world. There were no longer conflicts among states to settle by military or diplomatic means. Rome stood alone with the Parthian
(later the Persian) Empire, with which it fought occasionally for control over
territory. America, by contrast, works hard to preserve small states.

Another aspect of the pax Romana was Roman leaders' policy of export- 6
ing Roman culture—the Latin language, monumental architecture, and certain civic values—to the provinces in order to enhance the state's control
over those areas. Provincial elites often adopted and promoted outward symbols of Roman dominance in order to obtain favor, and ultimately power,
within the Roman administration. Today, American culture is pervasive, but
foreigners adopt its outward signs—speaking English, wearing blue jeans—
not to gain power within America, but to emulate and participate in our extraordinary economic and political success. Precisely because we do not
administer foreign territories, we do not engage in cultural imperialism in
the Roman sense.

Rome, of course, did not always directly control foreign states. Earlier, 7
during the Republic, the Romans constantly fought rival states, but without
at first annexing them as provinces. A few writers liken American power
after the Cold War to that of the Roman Republic at its height, after the defeat of Carthage in 201 B.C. or after the elimination of regional rivals in the
Eastern Mediterranean in 129 B.C. They suggest that the United States is on
the brink of establishing unrivalled control over the world as we know it,
and that, like the Romans, we are determined to conduct our foreign policy
so as to organize that world to suit our interests.

Yet the mechanism of republican Roman foreign policy was very differ- 8
ent from America's now. Rome declared war on states whose interests threatened its own. Once it had defeated them. Rome despoiled its enemies, levied
an annual tribute, enslaved captives, and compelled them to pursue Rome's
foreign policy goals. Even a "friend and ally" of the Roman people had no
scope for independent action in foreign affairs. The Romans actually took
land from one longtime ally that attempted to negotiate a peace between
Rome and a mutual enemy. (Imagine the United States punishing England
militarily for proposing peace negotiations!) During the Republic, the Romans sought to subordinate the foreign policies of all other states, enemies
and allies alike, to its own, so that no state could conduct an independent
foreign policy.

This is not true of America today. America seeks to prevent states from 9
attempting through violence to organize the world contrary to its interests,
but it does not prevent even its enemies from allying with one another to
pursue their interests, as long as those do not lead to conflict with the
United States. Nor does it control its allies' policies vis-à-vis each other.
Above all, the Romans were not merely willing, but usually eager, to use
their military power for conquest and domination, whereas America is

habitually reluctant to contemplate the use of force even in defense of its own interests.

10   As the United States is engaged neither in controlling the policies of other states, nor in administering them, to call it an empire is inaccurate, and also harmful to American interests. It invites the criticism that is justly made of states, like Rome from the late Republic onward, that have sought to impose their rule on others. Such domination was intended partly to achieve security, but also to accomplish the conquest of new lands, adding to the power, wealth, and glory of the imperial state.

11   The pax Americana is different from the pax Romana. America does not directly control small states, such as Bosnia or Afghanistan. It does not send governors, impose its laws, levy taxes, conscript soldiers, or permanently garrison its military forces abroad. In its foreign policy, America is not an empire, but a hegemon. "Hegemon" is the Greek word meaning leader. Most of the time America is a reluctant leader that needs to be persuaded to intervene, usually by the representatives of a troubled people. The difference is important. America—in Bosnia, in Korea, in Afghanistan—aims to secure its interests by preventing other states (or people protected by states) from overturning the international order by acts of violence. America is engaged in building infrastructures within independent states that will assist in the creation of peaceful, democratic, and independent regimes.

12   Hegemony is more complicated than empire. It is fairly easy for a state with overwhelming military resources to behave as Rome did: to fight its enemies without hesitation, impose peace terms, occupy lands with military forces, and ultimately establish its own administration to eliminate the treat of continued hostility. Rome's allies followed its policies without question for fear of being crushed. America's hegemonic role is much more difficult. The United States does not attack all of its potential enemies. It must persuade its allies to support its policies. It aims not to control disorderly regions, but to help those regions regain stability and then rule themselves. We must engage in military activities around the word to secure American interests, but we must also recognize the limits of American ambition and the unique position in world history that America now occupies.

13   The pax Americana is the peace established by a leader of free peoples, not the control of an empire of subjects. We should embrace our hegemony in all of its complexity and difficulty, precisely because it rests on the principles of democracy and sovereignty rather that on those of autocracy and subjugation.

Rhetorical Considerations

1. What is Kagan's primary purpose in this essay? Can you find an explicit thesis statement? If not, state the thesis in your own words. (*Hodges'* 32a and 32c/*Writer's* 1e(1) and 2b)
2. To what extent does Kagan use comparison and contrast in her essay? Why is this important in definition? (*Hodges'* 32e/*Writer's* 2e(5) and 2e(7))

3. What is the function of paragraph 11? (*Hodges'* 31/*Writer's* 2–3)
4. Does Kagan in any way assess empires and hegemonies? Which does she prefer? Why? (*Hodges'* 33/*Writer's* 3)
5. How would you characterize Kagan's perception of America's relationship to its protectorates?

Language and Style

1. Look up the following words in your dictionary: *autonomy* and *conscripted* (paragraph 2); *emulate* (paragraph 6); *vis-à-vis* (paragraph 9); *autocracy* and *subjugation* (paragraph 13). (*Hodges'* 18e/*Writer's* 28e)
2. Kagan identifies the pax Romana historically, but she doesn't really explain what it means. What is *pax*? (*Hodges'* 18e/*Writer's* 28e)
3. Identify the appositive in the third sentence of paragraph 1. (*Hodges'* 1f/*Writer's* 17f)
4. Find the passive construction in paragraph 2. Rewrite the sentence using the active voice. (*Hodges'* 7c/*Writer's* 22c)
5. Evaluate the parallelism in the second sentence of paragraph 4. (*Hodges'* 26/*Writer's* 25)

Writing Suggestions

1. Write an essay in which you examine how closely your campus community functions on a political basis. In other words, is it a true democracy? A republic? Totalitarian?
2. Kagan's essay clarifies the term *empire*. Choose a word that you think is frequently misused and write an essay defining how it should be used. (You might argue, for example, that *love* is used too carelessly, robbing it of its power, or examine how *patriotism* is used.)

◆

Is It Reverse Discrimination?

Ruben Navarrette Jr.

Born in 1967 in Fresno, California, Ruben Navarrette Jr. was valedictorian of his high school class in Sanger, California, the small town in the San Joaquin Valley where he has lived all his life except for the years he spent pursuing a bachelor's degree at Harvard University and graduate study at UCLA. Navarrette taught briefly at Fresno State University, and he has also taught kindergarten, an experience that provided him with what he calls the "most humbling experience of my life." Now a full-time writer, Navarrette is editor of *Hispanic Student*, a magazine for high school students. He writes regularly for the *Los Angeles Times*, the *Arizona Republic*, the *San Antonio Light*, and occasionally for the *San Francisco Chronicle*. He has also authored a book about a Mexican-American at Harvard, *The Darker Shade of Crimson: Reflections of a Harvard Chicano*, published in 1993 by Bantam.

1 Their young eyes stare at me with a hint of skepticism, and perhaps a bit of anger. I have come as a guest speaker to a government class at the high school in Sanger, California, I attended not long ago. Invited to defend an educational program that is continually under siege by those who want racial equity without sacrifice, I have come to confront an old friend—Allan Bakke.

2 It was six years ago, as a high-school senior, that I first met the spirit of the 33-year old NASA engineer who, a decade earlier, had decided to become a doctor. After being rejected by 12 medical schools, he had challenged the admissions policy at the University of California, Davis' medical school. Bakke charged that the school's special admissions program, which reserved 16 of 100 places for "economically and educationally disadvantaged" applicants, violated his 14th Amendment right to equal protection.

3 Though, in 1978, the U.S. Supreme Court, by 5–4, eventually ordered his admission to Davis, it also allowed—indeed encouraged—colleges and universities to consider the race and sex of its applicants in order to bring diversity and racial parity to U.S. higher education.

4 None of this seemed important to me at the beginning of my senior year in high school, when I was setting my sights on applying to some of the top colleges in the United States.

5 Not everyone shared my confidence. In the middle of the application process, my high school principal counseled me that it was "fine" that I was applying to schools like Harvard, Yale, and Princeton, but that I should also consider applying to Fresno State nearby "just in case." I thanked him for his concern and promptly disregarded his advice.

Rebuffed, he cast the first spear of a bitter attack that was to be taken 6
over by my Anglo classmates and maintained through spring. "You may be
right," He conceded with insincerity. "After all, your race should help you a
lot. . . ." In five minutes, he had dismissed four years of hard work and perfect grades.

My white classmates, many of them with grades not as good as mine 7
and reeling from rejections by the schools that were admitting me, were far
more direct. "Now, you know if you hadn't been Mexican. . . ." one of them
said. And it was then that I met Allan Bakke.

He was there in the eyes of my classmates, clutching in their fists letters 8
of rejection from Stanford. "It's not fair," I remember one of them saying.
"They turned me down because I was white."

I half-expected to find huge clusters of Mexican students at Harvard, 9
but I was one of only 35 Mexican-Americans in the school. Did this signify
the alleged "darkening" of higher education?

This is the legacy with which I entered the high school government class 10
and confronted Bakke. "Granted, racial discrimination was wrong back then
(presumably pre-civil rights movement)," a student conceded. "But now
that that's over with, shouldn't we get rid of affirmative action?"

The first time I'd heard this line was from Nathan Glazer, a professor of 11
mine at Harvard, who some say coined the phrase "reverse discrimination."
Once a society has liberated its employment and educational opportunities
and fully met the burden of its democratic principles, Glazer argues, any
further tampering with the laws of appropriation through race-preference
programs constitutes impermissible "reverse discrimination."

My dispute with my old professor is that U.S. society has not yet reached 12
Glazer's window of equal opportunity.

I suggested to the students that they needed only to look at their im- 13
mediate surroundings. Sanger is, I reminded them, 72.8 percent Mexican-
American. The fire chief, the police chief, the mayor, the city attorney, the
city manager, and the majority of the City Council are white. The dropout
rate of Latino students from the school system that produced me is consistent with the distressing national figure of 50 percent to 60 percent.

Clearly, no matter how slick and seductive the rhetoric about the suffer- 14
ing of "new victims," the reality of American society is that, as we enter the
year 2000, we have not yet ended the suffering of our old victims.

Rhetorical Considerations

1. Does the fact that this essay first appeared in a newspaper help you to explain
   why Navarrette's paragraphs are so short? How? (*Hodges'* 32a/*Writer's* 1e)
2. Is Navarrette's purpose in this essay predominantly expressive, informative,
   or persuasive? Explain how the essay reveals Navarrette's purpose. (*Hodges'*
   32a/*Writer's* 1e)
3. In paragraph 2 Navarrette explains the situation that motivated his definition
   of *reverse discrimination.* Does this explanation provide necessary information?

For example, would the essay have been as effective if it began with the information in paragraph 3? Why or why not? (*Hodges'* 32a/*Writer's* 1e)

4. To define *reverse discrimination,* Navarrette uses both functional and stipulative kinds of definition. From evidence in the essay, what part(s) of the definition is/are functional, and what part(s) stipulative?

5. Comment on how the rhetorical situation and the occasion influence the reader's understanding of Navarrette's essay. (*Hodges'* 32a/*Writer's* 1e)

Language and Style

1. In paragraph 11 Navarrette significantly changes tone. How does he accomplish this change? What do you think Navarrette's reason for the change was? (*Hodges'* 31d/*Writer's* 3d)

2. What is the "spear" that Navarrette says his principal "cast" (paragraph 6)? Comment on any other similes or metaphors used elsewhere in the essay. (*Hodges'* 20b/*Writer's* 29b)

3. Explain the time relationships among the verb tenses in the first sentence of paragraph 1. (*Hodges'* 7b/*Writer's* 22b)

4. What is the grammatical function of the clause "that U.S. society has not yet reached Glazer's window of equal opportunity" in paragraph 12? What are the implications of equating that clause with the subject of the sentence? (*Hodges'* 1/*Writer's* 16)

Writing Suggestions

1. Write a brief essay (500 to 700 words) defining a kind of behavior (procrastination, prevarication, exaggeration, and so on).

2. Define an object according to what it *does* (for example, a nuclear warhead, computer, or automobile).

◆

It's Not Nice to Mess with Mother Nature

Lindsy Van Gelder

Lindsy Van Gelder is the co-author of *Are You Two—Together?: A Gay and Lesbian Travel Guide to Europe* (1991) and *The Girls Next Door: Into the Heart of Lesbian America* (1996). This essay appeared in *Ms.* magazine in 1989 and was chosen to be featured in that magazine's recent thirtieth-anniversary issue.

I remember when the ecology movement first surfaced in the early seventies. 1
I was already active in the Women's Movement, and I wasn't exactly comfortable with all the rhetoric about the plight of Mother Earth—as if the entire planet were a damsel in distress. Nor did I want to be anybody's earth mother. In fact, a major focus of my life was to avoid drowning in fulltime motherhood. A guy from the ecology movement picked that moment to tell me I was Part of the Problem because I used disposable diapers. I would have cheerfully deposited the contents of same on his head.

Most of the ecology movement seemed to me to be a bunch of hetero 2
white boys who didn't have the Vietnam war to kick around anymore and were casting about for an issue. And on the scale of available issues, it was pretty puny. What were a few extra nondeposit bottles compared to, say, rape?

That was before Three Mile Island, Love Canal, Star Wars, the unravel- 3
ing ozone layer, and hospital syringes washing up on the beach. I now feel very differently—and so do a lot of other women. But it isn't just that the environment is turning into more of a hopeless sewer. One of the most interesting (and least reported on) developments of the last few years has been the integration of feminist and ecological concerns.

Mainstream peace and ecology groups like Greenpeace and the Sierra 4
Club now have feminists in leadership positions, and there's less of a sense that "their" issues are competing with "ours" According to Vickey Monrean, who is both development director for Greenpeace and a member of the national board of NOW, "Part of the consciousness that has to develop is an understanding [that] if you have a world that's falling apart and you achieve equality for women, what good is it? On the other hand, if you make the world safe and free of pollution and you don't have equality, then you really haven't created a world that's safe for everybody."

There's also a relatively small but growing movement of women who 5
are working for ecological concerns specifically as feminists. They organize demonstrations at missile bases and nuclear power plants, but what sets them apart is their theoretical work, collectively known as "ecofeminism," a philosophy that takes on not just the domination of the earth by polluters,

359

but domination *itself,* in all its forms—whites over people of color, men over women, adults over children, rich nations over the Third World, humans over animals and nature. Ecofeminists want an entirely new ethic.

6   In an ecofeminist society, no one would have power over anyone else, because there would be an understanding that we're all part of the interconnected web of life. Such a worldview requires some radical changes in perspective (not to mention behavior), since the whole world becomes part of one's self—not something Other to win, conquer, exploit, or get ahead of in the hierarchy.

7   But his new perspective is actually one that women have been edging toward for a long time. Harvard psychologist Carol Gilligan's ground-breaking work has amply demonstrated that as the traditional caretakers, women in this culture easily affiliate and identify with others, value people's feelings, and tend to base moral codes on the good of the entire group. Women do this, according to Gilligan, even though the culture at large doesn't recognize or respect those values. Ecofeminism in essence is saying that traditionally female values are our best shot at changing consciousness—and saving the world.

8   Feminists (like me, in my days as a Pampers ecocriminal) have historically resisted the equation of women and nature—and with good reason. Writers from Simone de Beauvoir to Ellen Willis have argued that the nurturing, more-naturally-peaceful stereotype is a fast ticket to keeping us barefoot and pregnant. But while it might have been crucial 20 years ago to say that no one is "naturally" anything, hasn't Margaret Thatcher now proved the point for us? Isn't it time to stop pushing our way into the boys' clubhouse—especially if it's about to fall off a cliff?

9   "We have to start saying that the problem isn't women's proximity to nature, but men's nonproximity—and the assigning by the culture of what it means to be perceived as closer to nature," explains women's studies professor Ynestra King.

10   Ecofeminists believe that the domination of women and of nature comes from the same impulse. "The oppression of women began with the separation of spirit and matter," says Susan Griffin, the author of *Woman and Nature.* "Once you have matter lacking spirit, it's a lowly substance, of its nature requiring domination and control." Women with all their messy childbearing faculties are associated with being more material and hence less valuable, according to Griffin. But the solution isn't to promote women to the exalted male realm. "The split itself needs to be healed."

11   Out of this desire to remerge matter and spirit comes much of the impetus for a new spirituality—one that understands that we need to clean up rivers not just because it's safer, but because we and the rivers are part of the same fabric; poisoning them is as crazy as cutting off one of your own fingers.

12   The ecofeminist movement has room for both atheists (like King) and nuns (one of the foremothers of the movement is the medieval abbess Hildegard of Bingen). But the most visible thread of spirituality, especially on the West Coast, is a resurgence of earth-based paganism, including Yoruba, Wicca, Native American religions, and Goddess-worship.

When Starhawk was a little girl growing up in Los Angeles in the sixties,   13
her name was Miriam, and she wanted to be a rabbi. "If I had grown up ten
years later, maybe I *would* have become a rabbi," she says now, "but it wasn't
a career option then for women. So I became a witch."

Starhawk's journey to becoming a serious practitioner of the craft of   14
Wicca took many years, but her initial attraction was based on the then-
radical notion that gods could be goddesses. Today the fuzzy-haired writer
(her latest book, *Truth or Dare: Encounters with Power, Authority and Mystery*),
and women's studies teacher is one of the most visible figures in ecofeminism. Her claim to fame is her ability to conduct spiritual rituals at demonstrations—like her "Political Despair Ritual" four years ago when Ronald
Reagan was reelected, in which participants danced around a caldron, going
up to the fiery pot in turn to light a candle and make a pledge for the future.

Spirituality has been something of a controversy in the worldwide ecol-   15
ogy movement (some West Germans in the Green political party, for instance, have charged that it smacks of the back-to-nature call of the Nazis).
But Starhawk's goal is to heal. "Rituals can be embarrassing to a lot of people, and I try to be sensitive to that," she explains, sitting in the San Francisco house she shares with a half dozen other pagans. "Instead of invoking
specific goddesses, I talk about the air, the water, the earth—things that
everyone can relate to."

"If people are happy without ritual in their lives," Starhawk adds, "I   16
don't think there's any need for them to change. But a lot of people do have
a hunger for experiences that connect people. Rituals can empower, and
they're a great healer of the burnout we so often feel. As a movement, we
shouldn't ignore that." The right wing, she adds, figured out the same thing
a long time ago.

Along with pagans, vegetarians and semi-vegetarians form a visible con-   17
tingent within ecofeminism. Some eat less meat because of limited global
resources—it takes the same amount of grain to feed 100 cattle *or* 2,000 people. Many ecofeminists avoid leather, recycle paper, ride bikes instead of
cars whenever possible, and otherwise put theory into everyday action—
although the actions vary with individuals. Living a purely ecofeminist life
in this culture is admittedly difficult. Some ecofeminists are expanding the
feminist examination of power relations to include other species. "There's a
principle involved," explains Ingrid Newkirk, national director of People for
the Ethical Treatment of Animals. "If you're against violence, domination,
slavery, and the abuse of the vulnerable, then you're for women's rights,
and you're not a racist, and you're for animal rights. If you only believe that
women should be treated with respect and not as chattel because *you're* a
woman, and you draw the line there, then you have a very narrow and selfish perspective, that has nothing to do with the fundamental principle."

The term "ecofeminism" was first coined by the French writer Françoise   18
d'Eaubonne in 1974, but it wasn't until 1980—partly in response to Three
Mile Island—that Ynestra King, peace activist writer Grace Paley, and others
organized "Women and Life on Earth: A Conference on Ecofeminism in the
'80s" at the University of Massachusetts at Amherst. The following year, the

first West Coast Ecofeminist Conference was held at Sonoma State University, organized largely by people who weren't at first aware of the Amherst meeting. Women from both coasts, including King and Starhawk, later formed Woman Earth Institute, the first national ecofeminist organization.

19   When I began researching this article, I was a member of Greenpeace and People for the Ethical Treatment of Animals, but I hadn't been exposed to ecofeminist theory. After the first "click," what struck me the most was the realization that it's a philosophy that could change everything—including oneself. For instance, when I first tried to wrap my brain around the idea of transcending the old he-who-dominates-wins ethic, I had some pleasurable fantasies about assorted gay-bashers, dolphin-killers, Republican yuppie realtors, and the rest of my personal hit list being deprived of their right to dominate. Then it dawned on me that I really was rooting for them to eat shit and die. Those who've been at it for longer say a more life-affirming consciousness comes with practice. "I think you have to phrase this very delicately," explains Susan Griffin, "because I wouldn't want to slop over into saying that Central Americans should be working to forgive Ronald Reagan. But I do think I've become less confrontational."

20   Los Angeles therapist Deena Metzger, who had a mastectomy several years ago, believes that an ecofeminist consciousness could transform medicine. Radiation and chemotherapy, she points out, are natural responses from a society that thinks in terms of chemical warfare and nuclear power; perhaps a mind-set less attuned to "conquering" cancer would have invented a different and better treatment. AIDS might be approached differently by a society that wasn't hysterical at the realization that its own defense system is becoming counterproductive.

21   Hazel Henderson, a Florida-based economic analyst, says that an ecofeminist analysis of the economy would realistically recognize that most of the "productivity" calculated in indexes like the Gross National Product is in fact only part of the work of the world. "I look at the economy not as a pie but as an upside-down layer cake," says Henderson. "The top two layers are the ones that economists notice: the private sector, and the public sector that it rests on—schools, roads, airports, and in our country, the military. But my cake has lower layers. First comes what I call the Love Economy—all the cooperative, selfless work we do for each other in communities and families, where no cash is exchanged. In Third World countries, this layer would include subsistence agriculture as well. The bottom layer is Mother Nature, which the whole thing rests on and which no one acknowledges."

22   Henderson believes that economists should junk the GNP as the sole indicator of reality, and instead augment it with measurements like "how well is the average person housed? What's the access to clean air? What about education and safe streets and political participation? We have to put money into trying to reverse the damage that's been done to the layers that no one was concerned with before. All the social and environmental bills are coming due, from drugs and crime to the hole in the ozone layer."

23   Ynestra King thinks that an ecofeminist consciousness will help women come to terms with their physical appearance. "Most of us will do anything

to our bodies to appear closer to norms of physical beauty which come naturally to about two percent of the female population," says King. "The rest of us struggle to be skinny, hairless, and lately muscular; we lie in the sun to get tan even when we know we're courting melanoma; we submit ourselves to extremely dangerous surgery. We primp, prune, douche, deodorize, and diet as if our natural bodies were our mortal enemies—and to the extent to which we make our own flesh an enemy, we are participating in the domination of nature."

But the real message for the future, King adds, is that anyone who still 24 thinks that ecofeminists are nice, harmless, ethereal earth mothers is crazy: "When you see what the roots of the ecological crisis are, you realize that you can't save the planet without radically transforming the economy and creating social liberation at every level. Feminism is absolutely central to that, since it's made the most advanced critique of social domination. The *only* solutions at this point ultimately are radical."

Rhetorical Considerations

1. What is the effect of Van Gelder's introduction? (*Hodges'* 33b/*Writer's* 3b)
2. What caused Van Gelder to finally make the connection between feminism and environmentalism? (*Hodges'* 32a/*Writer's* 1e)
3. How effectively does Van Gelder use examples? Find three of her best uses of examples. (*Hodges'* 31c/*Writer's* 2d)
4. According to Van Gelder, what is the spiritual aspect of ecofeminism?
5. Explain in your own words the analogy of the upside-down cake in paragraph 21. (*Hodges'* 32e/*Writer's* 2e)

Language and Style

1. Look up the following words in your dictionary: *ecology* and *rhetoric* (paragraph 1); *impetus* (paragraph 11); *hysterical* (paragraph 20); *augment* (paragraph 22). (*Hodges'* 18e/*Writer's* 28e)
2. In paragraph 3, which "Star Wars" is Van Gelder referring to? How can you tell? (*Hodges'* 18e/*Writer's* 28e)
3. Does the verb agree with its subject in the last sentence of paragraph 3? Why or why not? (*Hodges'* 6a/*Writer's* 22e)
4. What is the subject of the first sentence of paragraph 17? (*Hodges'* 1/*Writer's* 16)

Writing Suggestions

1. Write an essay in which you define *environmentalist* and discuss the extent to which you do or do not fit that definition in terms of your beliefs and behavior.
2. Find a label related to a belief that you often rejected until you came to some understanding of what it means. Describe how and why you came to accept that label.

♦

LAND OF IDENTITIES

Bhikshuni Thubten Chodron

Bhikshuni Thubten Chodron was raised as a Jew and named Hannah
Greene. After earning a degree in history from UCLA and teaching elementary school, she became a Buddhist in 1975 and was later ordained
as a nun in the Tibetan tradition, studying with the Dalai Lama. She
taught Buddhism at Dharma Friendship Foundation in Seattle and
moved in 2002 to the Midwest to start Sravasti Abbey. Her books include *Open Heart, Clear Mind* (1990), *What Color is Your Mind?* (1993),
Taming the Monkey Mind (1999), *Transforming the Heart: The Buddhist
Way to Joy and Courage* (1999), and *Modern Blossoms: Living as a Buddhist
Nun* (2000).

1 The headline of the article in the major Israeli newspaper read, "My Name
is Hannah Greene and I'm a Tibetan Nun." Interesting, I thought, those are
two labels I don't usually apply to myself. "Hannah" is my Jewish name,
not one many people know me by, and I'm not Tibetan. At least I was able
to answer when the journalists asked, "What is your Jewish name?" Their
second question stumped me. "Are you Jewish?"

2 What does being Jewish mean? I remember discussing it in Sunday
school, and when the rabbi asked that on a test, I managed to pass. Am I
Jewish because my ancestors were? Because I have dark curly hair (or at least
used to before it got shaved twenty-one years ago when I ordained as a Buddhist nun), brown eyes, a "noticeable nose" (as my brother politely puts it)?
Am I Jewish because I was confirmed and Rabbi Nateev no longer had to
face my persistent questions?

3 But now I was stumped. I hadn't thought about whether or not I was Jewish. I just am. Am what? The interviewer tried another tack, "You're American. What does being American mean to you?" I couldn't answer that
satisfactorily either. "I'm American because I have an American passport."
They looked at me quizzically. Am I American because I grew up with "Mickey
Mouse" and "I Love Lucy"? Because I protested the Vietnam War? (Some
would say that made me un-American.) Because I was born the grandchild of
immigrants who fled the pogroms, on a certain plot of land called Chicago?

4 How could I not know my identity? They were puzzled. As my fifteen
days in Israel unfolded, the issue of identity became a recurring theme. I realized how much my views had changed. I had been studying and practicing the Buddha's teaching and thus had spent years trying to deconstruct
my identity, to see it as something merely labeled, not as something fixed,
not something I truly was. So many of our problems—personal, national,

and international—come from clinging to these erroneous, solid identities. Thus in Buddhism, we are not trying to find out who we are but who we aren't. We work to free ourselves from all our erroneous and concrete conceptions about who we are.

My Israeli host understood what the journalists were getting at: "If there were another Holocaust and you were arrested for being Jewish, would you protest saying you're not Jewish, you're Buddhist?" I was baffled. "There is so much suffering in the world right now," I responded, "and I'd rather focus on doing something about that than on thinking up and solving future problems that may not even occur."

"Your mother is Jewish. You could go to the immigration office and within an hour be an Israeli," I was told. "Would you want to do that?" What does being an Israeli mean? I wondered.

Everywhere I went people wanted to know my identity; they cared deeply about the labels I attached to myself, thinking that if they knew all the labels, they'd know me. Israel is a land of identities. At the Ulpan Akiva, a unique language school in Natanya where Israelis can learn Arabic and Palestinians can learn Hebrew, some Palestinians said, "We're Muslims. We hope you can come to our new country, Palestine, someday." More identities. When they heard I follow Tibetan Buddhism, they said, "The Tibetans' situation is similar to ours. We sympathize with them." This startled me because in the Jewish-Tibetan dialogue I had been involved with until then, we had focused on the commonalities of two peoples in exile trying to maintain their unique religions and cultures. But the Palestinians were right: Their situation is like that of the Tibetans, for both live in occupied lands.

In a Reform synagogue in Jerusalem, I participated in a Jewish-Buddhist dialogue. A rabbi began to discuss meditation, but the subject changed when the moderator asked, "Can one be Jewish and Buddhist at the same time? Or must one be either a Jew or a Buddhist?" The Orthodox rabbi on my left said, "There are various Buddhist schools and yours may not be one of them, but in general, Buddhists are idolators." My eyes opened wide. Being an idolater was not an identity with which I associated myself. The Reform rabbi on my left, an American, said, "I agree; Buddhists worship idols." I was stunned. Calling someone an idol worshiper was about the worst insult a Jew could give someone, something tantamount to a Christian saying to a Jew, "You killed Christ." The Orthodox rabbi on my right added his view: "The various religions are like the colors of the rainbow. They all have their function. Many Jews are at the leading points of new religious movements, and it must be God's wish that there are many faiths." He turned to me smiling, and sincerely wishing me well, he said, "But remember, you're still Jewish."

By the time the moderator asked me to respond, I was so shocked that I was almost speechless. "To me, Jewish and Buddhist are merely labels. It is not important what we call ourselves. It is important how we live, how we treat others." Some people applauded.

I asked my Israeli Buddhist friends what they'd thought of the dialogue. "Oh, it was great," they responded. "We were afraid that the rabbis would be really judgmental and argumentative, but they were more open than we expected. It's remarkable that the two orthodox rabbis came to the Reform synagogue. Many won't, you know."

11   Some people who thought one could be a Jew and a Buddhist told me, "We have a Jewish soul, and we use Buddhist mindfulness meditation to bring out the best of it." Perplexed, because the Buddha refuted the idea of a permanent soul, let alone one that was inherently Jewish, I had asked what they meant. "We are part of the Jewish people. Our ancestors lived and thought in a particular way, and this culture and this way of looking at life are part of who we are." I wondered: Does their perspective mean that if you're born with "Jewish genes" in a Jewish family that you automatically have a certain identity?" That you cannot escape some fixed place in history as the descendant of everything that happened to your ancestors before you even existed?

12   As a child, I was aware of aspects of Jewish culture that I loved and respected, such as the emphasis on morality and treating all beings with equal respect. But I was also acutely aware of how the Jewish identity was shaped by persecution: "We are a unique group—look at how many times throughout history others have seen us as singular and have persecuted us even until death because of it." From early on, I had reflected on having an identity based on others' hate and injustice. I refused to be suspicious of people in the present simply because of experiences that my ancestors had in the past. Even as a child I wanted to have a positive view of humanity and not be shackled by keeping history's ghosts alive.

13   A ghost that haunts the Jews today is the Holocaust. They are a traumatized people, and the Holocaust seemed to permeate almost everything in Israel. As a child I'd read a lot about the Holocaust, and it had taught me compassion, morality, being fair, not discriminating against an entire group of people, sticking up for the persecuted and downtrodden, and living honestly and with a clear conscience. Learning about the Holocaust had shaped many of the positive attitudes that eventually led me to Buddhism.

14   But I could never—either as a child or now as an adult—think that Jews had the corner on suffering. In the Galilee, I led a weeklong meditation retreat. In one session, we had a spontaneous, heartfelt discussion about the Holocaust. One woman spoke about attending a gathering of second-generation Holocaust survivors and children of Nazis. When she listened to children of SS officers talk, she came to understand the deep guilt, suffering, and confusion they carry. How can you reconcile the memory of a loving father who cuddled you with the knowledge that he sanctioned the murder of millions of human beings? We talked about the parallels between the genocide of Jews and the more recent one of Tibetans by Chinese Communists. As Buddhists, how did the Tibetans view what happened to them? Why do we meet many Tibetans who experienced atrocities and do not seem to be emotionally scarred by the experience? Does forgiving mean forgetting? Shouldn't the world remember so that we can prevent genocide in the future?

15   Yes, we need to remember, but that remembering does not necessitate keeping pain, hurt, resentment, and anger alive in our hearts. We can re-

member with compassion, and that is more powerful. By forgiving, we let go of our anger, and by doing that, we cease our own suffering.

That night, as we did a meditation on Chenresig, the Buddha of Compassion, out of my mouth—rather, out of my heart—came the words, "When you visualize Chenresig, bring him into the concentration camps. Imagine him in the trains, prisons, gas chambers. Visualize Chenresig in Auschwitz, Dachau. And as we recite the compassion mantra, imagine the brilliant light of compassion radiating from Chenresig and permeating every atom of these places and the people who were in them. This light of lovingkindness purifies the suffering, hate, and misconceptions of all beings—Jews, political prisoners, gypsies, Nazis, ordinary Germans who turned a blind eye to save their own skin—and heals all that pain." We chanted the mantra together for over half an hour, and the room was charged. Very few times have I meditated with so concentrated a group.

The next day a young man asked, "Most of the people who operated or lived in the concentration camps died many years ago. How could our meditation purify all of them?" There was a pause, and I responded: "We are purifying the effect that their lives have on us. By doing this, we let go of our pain, anger, and paranoia, so that we can bring compassion to the world in the present and future. We are preventing ourselves from living in a deluded reaction to the past. We are stopping ourselves from creating a victim mentality that draws others' prejudice to us. We are ceasing the wish for revenge that makes us mistreat others. And although we cannot understand it intellectually, in a subtle way we do influence all the prisoners and Nazis in whatever form thay are currently born in. We have to heal."

One day I went to the Wailing Wall to pray. For a while I recited the mantra of Chenresig and visualized purifying light healing the centuries of suffering in the Middle East. From a Buddhist view, the cause of all suffering lies in our minds and the disturbing attitudes and emotions that motivate us to act in destructive ways, even though we all long to be happy. From my heart, I made strong prayers that all beings, and especially people in this part of the world, be able to generate three principal aspects of the path to enlightenment—the determination to be free from the cycle of constantly recurring problems, the altruistic intention to benefit all living beings, and the wisdom that realizes reality. I then put my head to the Wailing Wall in concentration. Suddenly I felt a "plop!" as something damp hit my cap. A bird was flying overheard. Recounting the episode to my friends, they informed me that it was said if a bird poops on one's head at the Wailing Wall, it indicates one's prayers will be actualized!

Rhetorical Considerations

1. What is Chodron trying to define in her essay? What is her primary purpose? (*Hodges'* 32a/*Writer's* 1e)
2. Who is her audience? How does she consider her audience in this essay? (*Hodges'* 32a/*Writer's* 1e)

3. What initiates Chodron's examination of the labels that are assigned to her? (*Hodges'* 32a/*Writer's* 1e)
4. How does Chodron define by exclusion? (*Hodges'* 32e/*Writer's* 2e)
5. How is her essay organized? In what order does she present her ideas? How is this effective? (*Hodges'* 32d/*Writer's* 2c)
6. What is Chodron's conclusion regarding the questions she has asked? (*Hodges'* 33b/*Writer's* 3b)

Language and Style

1. Look up the following words in your dictionary: *pogroms* (paragraph 3), *genocide* (paragraph 14); *mantra* (paragraph 16). (*Hodges'* 18e/*Writer's* 28e)
2. What is the exact definition of *Holocaust* (paragraph 13)? (*Hodges'* 18e/*Writer's* 28e)
3. What is the definition of *deconstruct* as Chodron uses it in paragraph 4? (*Hodges'* 18e/*Writer's* 28e)
4. Why is the verb *were* used instead of *was* in the first quotation in paragraph 5? (*Hodges'* 6a/*Writer's* 22e)
5. Justify the sentence fragment in paragraph 2. (*Hodges'* 2/*Writer's* 18)

Writing Suggestions

1. Is there a label that others tend to ascribe to you that you find limiting or otherwise uncomfortable? Write an essay in which you define this label, using yourself as the main example to clarify the limitations it engenders.
2. Write an essay in which you describe how you have redefined yourself through your travels, a significant experience, or someone you have met.

♦

THE "PERFECT" TRAP

Monica Ramirez Basco

Monica Ramirez Basco was a researcher and psychologist at the University of Texas Southwestern Medical Center at Dallas. Her book, *Never Good Enough: Freeing Yourself from the Chains of Perfectionism*, was published in 1999. She also co-authored *Cognitive-Behavioral Therapy for Bipolar Disorder* (1996) and *Getting Your Life Back: The Complete Guide to Recovery from Depression* (2001).

Susan, an interior designer, had been working frantically for the last month 1 trying to get her end-of-the-year books in order, keep the business running, and plan a New Year's Eve party for her friends and her clients. Susan's home is an advertisement of her talent as a designer, so she wanted to make some changes to the formal dining room before the party that would be particularly impressive. It all came together in time for the party and the evening seemed to be going well, until her assistant, Charles, asked her if Mrs. Beale, who owned a small antique shop and had referred Susan a lot of business, and Mr. Sandoval, a member of the local Chamber of Commerce and a supporter of Susan's had arrived.

Susan felt like her head was about to explode when she realized that she 2 had forgotten to invite them to the party. "Oh, no," she moaned. "How could I be so stupid? What am I going to do? They'll no doubt hear about it from someone and assume I omitted them on purpose. I may as well kiss the business good-bye." Though Charles suggested she might be overreacting a little, Susan spent the rest of the night agonizing over her mistake.

Susan is an inwardly focused perfectionist. Although it can help her in 3 her work, it also hurts her when she is hard on herself and finds error completely unacceptable. Like many people, she worries about what others will think of her and her business. However, in Susan's case her errors lead to humiliation, distress, sleepless nights and withdrawal from others. She has trouble letting go and forgiving herself because, in her mind, it is OK for others to make mistakes, but it is not OK for her to make mistakes.

Tom, on the other hand, is an outwardly focused perfectionist. He feels 4 OK about himself, but he is often disappointed in and frustrated with others who seem to always let him down. Quality control is his line of work, but he cannot always turn it off when he leaves the office.

Tom drove into his garage to find that there was still a mess on the work- 5 bench and floor that his son Tommy had left two days ago. Tom walked though the door and said to his wife in an annoyed tone of voice, "I told Tommy to clean up his mess in the garage before I got home." His wife defended their son, saying, "He just got home himself a few minutes ago." "Where is he now?" Tom demanded. "He better not be on the phone." Sure enough, though, Tommy was on the phone and Tom felt himself tensing up and ordering, "Get off the phone and go clean up that mess in the garage like I told you." "Yes, sir," said Tommy, knowing that a lecture was coming.

6   For Tom, it seems like every day there is something new to complain about. Tommy doesn't listen, his wife doesn't take care of things on time, and there is always an excuse. And even when they do their parts it usually isn't good enough, and they don't seem to care. It is so frustrating for Tom sometimes that he does the job himself rather than ask for help, just so he doesn't have to deal with their procrastination and excuses.

7   Tom's type of perfectionism causes him problems in his relationships with other because he is frequently frustrated by their failure to meet his ex-pectations. When he tries to point this out in a gentle way, it still seems to lead to tension, and sometimes to conflict. He has tried to train himself to expect nothing from others, but that strategy doesn't seem to work either.

8 **The Personal Pain of Perfectionists.** The reach for perfection can be painful because it is often driven by both a desire to do well and a fear of the consequences of not doing well. This is the double-edged sword of perfectionism.

9   It is a good thing to give the best effort, to go the extra mile, and to take pride in one's performance, whether it is keeping a home looking nice, writ-ing a report, repairing a car, or doing brain surgery. But when despite great efforts you feel as though you keep falling short, never seem to get things just right, never have enough time to do your best, are self-conscious, feel criticized by others, or cannot get others to cooperate in doing the job right the first time, you end up feeling bad.

10   The problem is not in having high standards or in working hard. Perfec-tionism becomes a problem when it causes emotional wear and tear or when it keeps you from succeeding or from being happy. The emotional conse-quences of perfectionism include fear of making mistakes, stress from the pressure to perform, and self-consciousness from feeling both self-confidence and self-doubt. It can also include tension, frustration, disappointment, sad-ness, anger or fear of humiliation. These are common experiences for in-wardly focused perfectionists.

11   The emotional stress caused by the pursuit of perfection and the failure to achieve this goal can evolve into more severe psychological difficulties. Perfectionists are more vulnerable to depression when stressful events occur, particularly those that leave them feeling as though they are not good enough. In many ways, perfectionistic beliefs set a person up to be disap-pointed, given that achieving perfection consistently is impossible. What's more, perfectionists who have a family history of depression and may there-fore be more biologically vulnerable to developing the psychological and physical symptoms of major depression may be particularly sensitive to events that stimulate their self-doubt and their fear of rejection or humiliation.

12   The same seems to be true for eating disorders, such as anorexia nervosa and bulimia. Several recent studies have found that even after treatment, where weight was restored in malnourished and underweight women with anorexia, their perfectionistic beliefs persisted and likely contributed to re-

lapse. Perfectionism also seems to be one of the strongest risk factors for developing an eating disorder.

Sometimes the pain of perfectionism is felt in relationships with others. 13 Perfectionists can sometimes put distance between themselves and others unintentionally by being intolerant of others' mistakes or by flaunting perfect behavior or accomplishments in front of those who are aware of being merely average. Although they feel justified in their beliefs about what is right and what is wrong, they still suffer the pain of loneliness. Research suggests that people who have more outwardly focused perfectionism are less likely than inwardly focused perfectionists to suffer from depression or anxiety when they are stressed. However, interpersonal difficulties at home or on the job may be more common.

How Did I Get This Way? There is considerable scientific evidence that 14 many personality traits are inherited genetically. Some people are probably born more perfectionistic than others. I saw this in my own children. My oldest son could sit in his high chair, happily playing with a mound of spaghetti, his face covered with sauce. My second son did not like being covered in goo. Instead, he would wipe his face and hands with a napkin as soon as he was old enough to figure out how to do it. As he got older, he kept his room cleaner than his brother. When he learned to write he would erase and rewrite his homework until it was "perfect."

Parental influences can influence the direction or shape that perfection- 15 ism takes. Many perfectionists, especially inwardly focused perfectionists, grew up with parents who either directly or indirectly communicated that they were not good enough. These were often confusing messages, where praise and criticism were given simultaneously. For example, "That was nice, but I bet you could do better." "Wow, six As and one B on your report card! You need to bring that B up to and A next time." "Your choice of performance was lovely, but that sound system is really poor. We could hardly hear you."

Unfortunately, with the intention of continuing to motivate their chil- 16 dren, these parents kept holding out the emotional carrot: "Just get it right this time and I will approve of you." Some psychological theories suggest over time the child's need to please her parents becomes internalized, so that she no longer needs to please her parents; she now demands perfection from herself.

Some perfectionists tell stories of chaotic childhoods where they never 17 seemed to have control over their lives. Marital breakups, relocations, financial crises, illnesses and other hardships created an environment of instability. One of the ways in which these people got some sense of order in their otherwise disordered lives was to try to fix things over which they had some control, such as keeping their rooms neat and tidy, working exceptionally hard on schoolwork, or attempting to control their younger brothers and sisters. As adults, however, when their lives were no longer in flux, they may have continued to work hard to maintain control.

Are You A Perfectionist? Perfectionists share some common characteristics. 18 They are usually neat in their appearance and are well organized. They seem to push themselves harder than most other people do. They also seem to push others as hard as they push themselves. On the outside, perfectionists usually appear to be very competent and confident individuals. They are often envied by others because they seem to "have it all together." Sometimes they seem perfect. On the inside they do not feel perfect, nor do they feel like they always have control over their own lives.

19   Let's look at some of these characteristics more closely and how they interfere with personal and professional life. Terry, 34, a divorced working mom of two, is a high achiever with high career ambitions. But she can sometimes get hung up on the details of her work. She is not good with figures, but does not trust her staff enough to use their figures without checking them herself. She gets frustrated with this mundane work and makes mistakes herself and then becomes angry with her subordinates for doing poor work.

20   Perfectionists also tend to think there is a right way and a wrong way to do things. When Joe, a retired Marine Corps drill sergeant, takes his boys fishing they have a routine for preparation, for fishing and for cleanup. It is time-efficient, neat, organized. The boys think the "fishing ritual" is overdone and they resent having to comply.

21   Expecting people to do their best is one thing. Expecting perfection from others often means setting goals that can be impossible to achieve. Brent, 32 and single, has been looking for Ms. Right for 12 years but cannot seem to find her. He does not have a well-defined set of characteristics in mind. He just has a general impression of an angel, a sexual goddess, a confident, independent, yet thoroughly devoted partner. Blond is preferable, but he's not that picky.

22   Perfectionists can have trouble making decisions. They are so worried about making the wrong one that they fail to reach any conclusion. If the person is lucky, someone else will make the decision for them, thereby assuming responsibility for the outcome. More often the decision is made by default. A simple example is not being able to choose whether to file income tax forms on time or apply for an extension. If you wait long enough, the only real alternative is to file for an extension.

23   Along with indecision, perfectionists are sometimes plagued by great difficulty in taking risks, particularly if their personal reputations are on the line. Brent is in a type of job were creativity can be an asset. But coming up with new ideas rather than relying on the tried and true ways of business means making yourself vulnerable to the criticism of others. Brent fears looking like an idiot should an idea he advances fail. And on the occasions when he has gone out on a limb with a new concept he has been overanxious. Brent's perfectionism illustrates several aspects of the way that many perfectionists think about themselves. There can be low self-confidence, fear of humiliation and rejection, and an inability to attribute success to their own efforts.

24 **Breaking Free.** To escape the tyranny of perfectionism, you need to understand and challenge the underlying beliefs that drive you to get things "just right."

25   Each of us has a set of central beliefs about ourselves, other people and the world in general and about the future. We use these beliefs or schemas

to interpret the experiences in our life, and they strongly influence our emotional reactions. Schemas can also have influence on our choice of actions.

Under every perfectionist schema is a hidden fantasy that some really good thing will come from being perfect. For example, "If I do it perfectly, then . . . I will finally be accepted . . . I can finally stop worrying . . . I will get what I have been working toward . . . I can finally relax." The flip side of this schema, also subscribed to by perfectionists, is that "If I make a mistake," there will be a catastrophic outcome ("I will be humiliated. . . . I am a failure . . . I am stupid . . . I am worthless"). 26

Changing these schemas means taking notice of the experiences you have that are inconsistent with, contrary to, or otherwise do not fit with them. June, who prides herself on being a "perfect" homemaker and mother, believed with 90 percent certainty that "If I do it perfectly, I will be rewarded." Yet she does a number of things perfectly that others do not even notice. June would tell herself that there would be a reward from her husband or her children for taking the extra time to iron their clothes perfectly. Her son did not even realize his shirts had been ironed. When Mother's Day came, she got the usual candy and flowers. No special treats or special recognition for her extra efforts. 27

When June begins to notice the inaccuracy of her schema, she begins to reevaluate how she spends her time. She decides that if it makes her feel good, then she will do it. If it is just extra work that no one will notice, then she may skip it. She is certain that there are some things she does, such as iron the bedsheets, which no one really cares about. As a matter of fact, June herself doesn't really care if the sheets are ironed. However, she does like the feel of a freshly ironed pillow cover, so she will continue that chore. June has modified her schema. Now she believes that "If you want a reward, find a quicker and more direct way to get it." 28

If your schema centers around more existential goals, like self-acceptance, fulfillment or inner peace , then you must employ a different strategy. If you believe that getting things just right in your life will lead to acceptance, then you must not be feeling accepted right now. What are the things you would like to change about yourself? What could you do differently that would make you feel better about who you are? If you can figure out what is missing or needs changing, you can focus your energies in that direction. 29

Or you may be motivated to take a different, less absolute, point of view. Instead of "I must have perfection before I can have peace of mind," consider "I need to give myself credit for what I do well, even if it is not perfect." Take inventory of your accomplishments or assets. Perhaps you are withholding approval from yourself, 30

If your schema is that other people's opinions of you is a mirror of your self-worth, you must ask yourself if you know when you have done something well, if you are able to tell the difference between a good performance and a poor performance. If you are capable of evaluating yourself, you do not really need approval from others to feel like you are a valuable worker or a good romantic partner. 31

In general, you must treat your perfectionistic shemas as hypotheses rather than facts. Maybe you are right or maybe you are wrong. Perhaps they 32 apply in some situations, but not in others (e.g., at work, but not at home), or with some people, such as your uptight boss, but not with others, such as your new boyfriend. Rather than stating your schema as a fact, restate it as a suggestion. Gather evidence from your experiences in the past, from your observations from others, or by talking to other people. Do things always happen in a way that your schemas would predict? If not, it is time to try on a new basic belief.

33   One of my patients described the process as taking out her old eight-track tape that played the old negative schemas about herself and replacing it with a new compact disc that played her updated self-view. This takes some practice, but it is well worth the effort.

Rhetorical Considerations

1. What is Basco's purpose in this essay? (*Hodges'* 32a/*Writer's* 1e)
2. Who is the intended audience? (*Hodges'* 32a/*Writer's* 1e)
3. Not only does Basco define *perfectionism* in her essay, she also uses comparison and contrast. Find evidence of the comparison-contrast expository mode in the essay. (*Hodges'* 32e/*Writer's* 2e)
4. Find examples of Basco's use of cause and effect. (*Hodges'* 32e/*Writer's* 2e)
5. How does the use of subtitles make the essay more effective? (*Hodges'* 32d/*Writer's* 2c)

Language and Style

1. Are clichés used excessively in Basco's essay? Find three examples of cliché. (*Hodges'* 19/*Writer's* 28)
2. Define the connotations of the following words: *goo* (paragraph 14); *tyranny* (paragraph 24). (*Hodges'* 20a/*Writer's* 29a (2))
3. What does *evolve* mean? Is it used correctly in paragraph 11? (*Hodges'* 20e/*Writer's* 29e)
4. Do the pronouns agree in number with their antecedent in the last sentence of paragraph 16? (*Hodges'* 6b/*Writer's* 21d)
5. Does the pronoun agree in number with its antecedent in the third sentence of paragraph 22? Why do you think Basco made this decision? (*Hodges'* 6b/*Writer's* 21d)

Writing Suggestions

1. Write an essay about either your tendencies or someone else's toward perfectionism or some other personality struggle.
2. Examine American society's emphasis on perfectionism as it is reflected in the media.

✦

IMAGES
Definition

Definitions of feminine beauty vary from culture to culture and from generation to generation. Both images here in some way comment on cultural ideas about beauty. The "full-figured" models featured in the paintings of Peter Paul Rubens were the epitome of beauty in their day, but later gave rise to the use of the adjective *Rubenesque* to describe a woman who is overweight. The photograph of the woman with neck bracelets—a stark contrast against the Ruben painting—represents the height of beauty in Karen culture.

Peter Paul Rubens, *Venus before a Mirror*, 1614–1615

✦

IMAGES (CONT.)

Definition

Kevin R. Morris, Karen woman

Rhetorical Considerations

1. What is your response to the Rubens painting? Would this woman be considered beautiful by today's standards in the United States? Why or why not? (*Hodges'* 35b/*Writer's* 1d)
2. What is your perception of the Karen woman? Can you think of any counterparts to her adornments in your own culture (that is, fashions that actually distort the human body)?
3. Viewing the two images together, can you make any generalizations about what beauty is, or about definitions of beauty held in common worldwide? If so, what are they?

Writing Suggestions

1. Gather a dozen or so images of women whom you consider beautiful. Write an essay in which you devise your own definition of beauty by referring to these images. How does it compare with society's definition?
2. Men have recently come under increasing pressure to be attractive. Find several recent images of men and compare them to images from 20 years ago. Write an essay examining how the standard of male attractiveness has changed. Which do you think is more realistic?

CHAPTER 9

Argument

By argument we do not mean quarreling or bickering, the meaning often given the term in everyday speech. Rather, argument is a method (or set of methods) for

- convincing readers of the rightness of an opinion or of a course of action through logical reasoning, or
- persuading readers to adopt a belief or a position through appeals to their emotions.

Generally speaking, any argument might use both reason and emotion to get readers to change their beliefs or act in a particular way, and both approaches can be used to move readers to a middle ground of cooperation and understanding rather than to achieve capitulation or victory. And writers use any or all of the other strategies discussed in this book—narration, description, classification, comparison, and so on—to develop arguments that will achieve these goals.

Argument can be difficult to write well. In fact, it may be the most difficult of the many kinds of writing considered in this book, in part because it can include all those other kinds. But, although difficult, argument is worth the effort; it is a kind of writing that very directly aims to make a difference, that gets things done.

Understanding Argument

An argument may rely on several different kinds of appeals (see *Hodges'* 36e/ *Writer's* 7e):

- appeals to the writer's own credibility or authority (sometimes called *ethical appeals*);
- appeals to reason (*logical appeals*);
- appeals to the reader's emotions, values, or attitudes (*pathetic* or *affective appeals*).

Writers appeal to their own credibility by demonstrating that they are knowledgeable about their subject and fair-minded in their argumentative approach,
and that they understand and respect the reader's viewpoint. They appeal to
reason by being logical—that is, by reasoning properly and supporting their
assertions with good evidence—and by using appropriate development strategies. They appeal to emotions, values, and attitudes by choosing examples
and raising issues about which the reader is likely to have strong feelings and
by using language appropriate in tone and with connotations that are favorable to their purpose (see *Hodges'* 24a(2)/*Writer's* 24a(2) for more information).

   As you plan an argument, consider how each kind of appeal can help you
achieve your purpose. Often it is useful to emphasize one kind over others.
For example, Aurora Levins Morales's "Liberation Genealogy" appeals to the
emotions and values of her audience as well as to reason. In contrast, Ralph
Nader, in "Blinded by Power," and Newt Gingrich, in "Follow the Light," rely
to a considerable extent upon their own authority, or at least upon the reader's
recognition of that authority (an ethical appeal). Nader expects liberal readers
to be well-disposed to his arguments, while Gingrich expects the same of his
conservative readers. Both expect their audience to grant that they know what
they're talking about. Even the author headnotes in this reader, and in many
others, are a sort of ethical appeal—a recitation of the authors' credentials so
you will be able to judge the validity of what they say. Remember, too, that a
photograph may emphasize the emotional appeal of your argument or bolster
your credibility; a chart or a graph can strengthen your logic. Both Picasso's
Guernica and the Forest Service poster in this chapter appeal to our emotions—
Picasso's to our feelings of empathy and the Forest Service's to our xenophobia
(fear and hatred of strangers or of anything foreign).

   Be careful not to rely on one appeal too heavily. Too great a reliance on
an appeal to your own credibility can give the impression that you are indifferent to your reader's values or that you have doubts about your reader's
ability to reason logically. Relying exclusively on logical appeals may make
you seem cold-blooded or heartless. Relying too much on appeals to the
reader's emotions may make you seem unreasonable or illogical.

Using Argument

Purpose

Arguments are mounted for three main purposes:

- to state an opinion or defend a position,
- to call some belief into question or criticize a course of action; or
- to seek to change what a reader thinks or intends to do.

All three intents are represented in this chapter. Aurora Levins Morales defends her belief that people should be rooted in their ancestral culture. In
"The Clone Wars," Gregory Stock and Francis Fukuyama state opinions and

defend their positions on cloning. Randall Kennedy calls the practice of racial profiling into question in "You Can't Judge a Crook by His Color." Nader and Gingrich both question the actions that led to the California energy crisis in the summer of 2001, although from different perspectives. Deborah Stone, in "Why We Need a Care Movement," seeks to change public policy in order to guarantee the right to health care.

Audience

Perhaps more than in any other kind of writing, the effectiveness of an argument depends on your consideration of the nature, needs, and interests of your intended audience. If you present too little evidence, the audience can justifiably dismiss your argument as weak. If you rely on evidence that the audience cannot understand or that is not pertinent to their own interests, they can dismiss your argument as irrelevant. If you make mistakes in logical reasoning, the audience can dismiss your argument as false. If you adopt or lapse into an inappropriate tone, your audience can dismiss your argument as tactless or insensitive. Try hard to put yourself in your reader's place and to see your argument from your audience's point of view. (See *Hodges'* 32a(2)/*Writer's* 1e(2) for more information.)

There are also a number of strategies you can employ to disarm any objections readers may have:

- *Identifying and acknowledging differences* shows that you can be objective and thus worthy of your readers' respect.
- *Finding common ground*—emphasizing similarities of experience and values—encourages cooperation.
- *Making open-mindedness a priority,* for writers as well as readers, helps bridge differences.
- *Characterizing opposing views responsibly* shows you are fair-minded and earns your readers' respect.
- *Anticipating the negative labels* hostile readers may apply to you and your ideas helps you counter them.
- *Using neutral language* keeps your statements about opposing views from being judgmental and alienating readers.

These techniques are useful for a wide spectrum of readers—from those who are well-disposed toward your arguments to those who are looking to be convinced that they should change what they think, and even to those who are hostile and determined to disagree.

Logic

The first thing you should do after you pick your topic is figure out why that topic is important to you. When you do that, state it as an affirmative sentence—that is, make a *claim,* which must have two or more sides; it must be arguable. (A *claim* is a conclusion drawn from accurate and sufficient evidence presented as a statement a reader should accept.) That claim is the foundation for your *thesis*. After you have made your claim, you will present evidence to support it and you must reason about that evidence in logical ways and draw logical conclusions.

The reasoning processes underlying an argument may be either *inductive* or *deductive;* more often they are both. Induction draws conclusions from amassed evidence; deduction applies a general truth to a particular case to reach a conclusion. Either method, if pursued carelessly, can lead the unwary writer into reasoning errors called *fallacies*. (See *Hodges'* 35c–f or *Writer's* 7h–i for more information.) Some of the most common fallacies are described below:

- *Ad hominem arguments* are personal attacks that deflect the reader's attention from the points at issue. "Widgets are not a good product because Joe thinks they are good, and Joe is not very smart and just likes anything he sees."
- The *bandwagon fallacy* argues that you should do things the same way everyone else is doing them. "Everyone else is getting a new car, so I should too."
- *Begging the question* assumes a point is true without proving it. "Obviously, Tiptop State University is the best university in the state, so you should enroll there."
- *False dilemmas* suppose that there are only two alternatives, whereas there are almost always more. "You have two choices: you can pay the bill in full or you can let the car be repossessed."
- *Hasty* or *sweeping generalizations* make claims based on insufficient or biased evidence. "The woman was arrested for shoplifting, so she must be guilty."
- *False authority* offers an expert in one field as a credible expert in another. "The winner of the best actor award testified that we must ban the use of fossil fuels."
- *False cause* (*post hoc, ergo propter hoc*) makes an assumption that because one event occurred before another, it is the cause of the other. "I got a big raise last month, and so then my significant other broke up with me."
- A *non sequitur* (*does not follow*) is an argument that draws an illogical conclusion from the evidence. "Peter loves to argue so he would make a good lawyer."
- A *red herring* seeks to distract attention from the real issue by dredging up an irrelevant one. "Why worry about a downturn in the economy when there are so many excellent movies being released?"

There are a number of other fallacies to be aware of, such as *equivocation* (proving your point by using two different meanings of a term), *straw man* (setting up an authority for the sole purpose of refuting it), *slippery slope* (if X happens, it will inevitably set off a specific chain of events); *appeal to tradition* (because something has always been done a certain way, it must be correct), and *guilt by association* (an economics student cheated on a test, so economics students are more likely to cheat than other students).

Organization

The basic formal elements of most arguments are

- the *thesis,* a statement of the position or proposition the reader is being urged to accept (see *Hodges'* 32c/*Writer's* 2b for more information);
- the presentation of *evidence* supporting the thesis;
- consideration of *opposing arguments* (if appropriate); and
- a *conclusion* emphasizing the thesis.

These elements can be organized in various ways, depending on the situation and the writer's purpose. One classic pattern begins by stating the thesis (and, if necessary, establishing the writer's credentials) in the introduction, goes on to present the evidence in favor of the thesis, next raises and refutes any likely objections, and concludes with a restatement of the thesis or perhaps with a recommendation or call to action based upon it. However, you may not always wish to open with a statement of your thesis. For example, if you are arguing in response to someone else's argument, it may be best to begin by summarizing the other person's position and then presenting your own. Or if you are arguing in favor of a policy or course of action that you believe will solve a problem, you may need to begin by showing that there is a problem before you go on to present and defend your solution. Sometimes—especially if your thesis is one your reader might find distasteful enough to dismiss without giving you a chance to defend it—you may be wise to postpone a direct statement of the thesis until the end of your essay, after you have presented your evidence. Wherever you decide to state the thesis itself, the case you build for it will usually be most effective if you present your specific supporting points in increasing order of importance, with your strongest points last. (However, note the word *usually;* there are exceptions.)

Language and Style

Language in argument is just as important as it is in any other method of development. The language you use must be tailored for your readers. Even if you think your audience is likely to disagree with you—perhaps especially then—you must pay attention to your tone. Do you sound authoritative, or patronizing? Objective, or emotional? Think about who your audience is and how you want them to react to your argument. An inappropriate tone can predispose your readers against you, no matter how good your points may be.

Also be sure that the connotations of the words you use are appropriate for your purpose. Stone, in "Why We Need a Care Movement," uses *care* rather than "provide health care or child care" to subtly appeal to her readers' emotions and reinforce the idea that affection should be present in a care-giving situation.

But it isn't enough to be careful with connotations and tone when you are writing arguments. You must also be aware of the effect of language on logic. For instance, one of the fallacies writers sometimes fall into is the fallacy of equivocation. That means the writer has used a word in two different senses to make a logical point: "He was right in his position on gun control—about as far right as possible." In this equivocation, the word *right* is used to mean both "correct" and "conservative." The statement might be amusing, but the humor is based on the violation of logic. Such statements might be useful under the right circumstances, but most of the time they represent a flaw in reasoning, and they are tricky to handle even under the best circumstances.

Student Essay

Not all arguments are concerned with issues of national and international policy. Argumentative writing can also be focused on personal concerns, as the following essay by student DeVon Freeman demonstrates by offering a number of good reasons for attending a community college.

Community College: Not Just for Dumb Kids

Introduction

Last year while my friends packed up their clothes, cleaned out their closets, and said goodbye to their parents and hometowns, I stayed behind. Excited and eager to be out on their own, my high school buddies sped away to their respective universities. Although I knew my goal was a career in physical therapy, and I had been accepted at several universi-

Context

ties, come August I was still undecided about which school to attend or how I was going to pay for it all. Money was going to be tight and time was running out. So, I enrolled in a nearby community college. For the entire school year I lived at home, obeyed Mom's rules, worked part time,

Anticipatory point and implied thesis

studied for my classes, and even managed to have a little fun. This experience changed my thinking about community college.

Initially, my mother was disappointed. I am the first member from either side of my family to be "college bound." Mom was secretly gearing up for family bragging rights. Her dream was one day to place the "My Son and My Money Go to X University" bumper sticker on the back of her station

Refutation of opposing view

wagon. Dad had the misguided notion that because I had worked so hard in high school, making mostly A's and B's, I would not be challenged at a community college nor be able to continue at a state university. A community college could not possibly offer me classes equal in rigor to that of any "real" college. My friends, like my parents, assumed that the teachers there were going to be lenient, classes were going to be simple, and my year would certainly be a waste of time.

First main point and evidence

Ethos

My freshman year at the community college was anything but a cinch. I soon discovered that, much like university professors, my teachers were experienced professors who were not in the business of handing out A's. They moved much more quickly through the material than I was used to in my high school honors classes, and they expected their lectures to be well-attended. In other words, attending class was not optional if I wanted to do well. I found that I had to spend several days studying for exams if I wanted to pass them, and it was necessary to turn in all of my homework assignments on time. By the end of the first semester, I was definitely ready for a study break!

Second main point and evidence

Cost, of course, helped me make my decision to stay at home and attend a community college. Living rent-free at my parents' house was a terrific savings that I am only now truly appreciating. Unlike my friends who went away to school, I was able to work and actually save money. Working and attending school full time also forced me to learn invaluable lessons in planning ahead, getting along with a variety of people, saving money, and not procrastinating. These, incidentally, are skills that cannot be taught inside the four walls of a classroom at any college.

Third main point and evidence

Many of my friends thought I was foolish to stay at home willingly for another year when I had the opportunity to experience life on my own. My high school friends had moved away and met new people. They came back at the semester break with countless stories about frat parties, late night Taco Bell runs, and both fun and tough times with their roommates. I was initially jealous of all the freedom and maturity that I thought they possessed and I lacked. But, now that I am attending a university this semester and living in a dormitory, I look back on last year and realize just how glad I am that I chose to attend a community college first.

Ethos

The problems students experience away at college for the first time can be overwhelming. Making good grades takes work and newfound freedom can be hard to handle. This year as a sophomore I found that I was academically prepared for more difficult classes and able to manage successfully the complete freedom that most freshmen struggle with. Knowing what to expect in the classroom relieved some of the anxiety of living in a new environment.

Conclusion

Statement of thesis

Not everyone needs to attend a community college before going away to a university, but there are good reasons to spend one's freshman year at home. By taking advantage of everything that one more year at home had to offer, I got exactly what I needed from my community collage experience to get my education off to a good start.

Commentary

DeVon Freeman takes up three main points in his argument in favor of community colleges. He begins by addressing the negative assumption he expects his readers to have—the assumption that community college is so easy that it is a waste of time. He discusses how his friends and family had the same expectation. Then he refutes that assumption by describing the rigor of his coursework.

Freeman's second point is cost. He points out how students at community colleges save housing costs by living at home and are able to save money for their final two or three years at a university by working full-time. An ancillary point is the lesson in time management he got from part-time work combined with full-time study. Freeman's final point is that living at home for the first year allowed him to mature enough to handle a heavy study load later at the university while enjoying the freedom of living away from home.

Clearly, Freeman's purpose is to persuade readers to change their opinion about community colleges. He uses several appeals to persuade his readers, but his strongest appeal is ethical. He was an honor student in high school; he was admitted to several good colleges; he works hard and takes his education seriously. Having validated his own experience, he presents evidence from it to help readers come to the same conclusion he did.

✦ CHECKLIST FOR WRITING ARGUMENTS

- What is your *point?* Is your argument intended to convince readers to change their behavior or to persuade them of the rightness of a point of view? Can you state your specific *purpose* in a single sentence? (*Hodges'* 36a/*Writer's* 7a)
- Have you stated your point as a *thesis* and focused your analysis around that statement? If your thesis is implied, do all of your main points contribute to it? (*Hodges'* 32c/*Writer's* 2b)
- What do you know about your *audience?* Are your readers disposed to agree with you or are they hostile? What constraints upon your writing does your audience's attitude impose? (*Hodges'* 32a(2)/*Writer's* 1e(2))
- What *appeals* are you using? If your appeal is to your own authority (*ethical*), how do you present yourself? If your appeal is to the reader's emotions (*pathetic*) have you exercised restraint? If your appeal is to reason (*logical*), have you been logical throughout? Have you checked your essay to be sure you have not fallen into any logical *fallacies?* (*Hodges'* 36e/*Writer's* 7f)
- Have you presented your points in a particular *order?* What is it and why is it appropriate for this information and audience?
- Have you countered any *potential objections?* (*Hodges'* 36d(2)/*Writer's* 7e(2))
- Do *transitional words and qualifiers* link the different parts of the essay? (*Hodges'* 31b/*Writer's* 3d)
- What does the *conclusion* do for your essay? (*Hodges'* 36g(6)/*Writer's* 7j(6))

LIBERATION GENEALOGY

Aurora Levins Morales

Aurora Levins Morales, poet, essayist, and historian, was raised in a politically radical family in the hills of Puerto Rico by her Jewish and
Puerto Rican parents. She is the author of *Getting Home Alive* (1986), a
multigenre work co-written with her mother, Rosario Morales, and
Remedios (1998), a prose-poetry retelling of the history of the Atlantic
world through the lives of Puerto Rican women. Her essays have appeared in *Ms., Woman's Review of Books,* and numerous anthologies. She
holds a doctorate in women's studies and history and lectures nationally. She lives in San Francisco and Minneapolis. This selection is from
Medicine Stories: History, Culture, and the Politics of Integrity (1998).

Raicism—from *raices* or roots—is the practice of rooting ourselves in the real, 1
concrete histories of our people: our families, our local communities, our
ethnic communities. It is radical genealogy, history made personal. It is a
keeping of accounts. Its intent is to pierce the immense, mind-deadening
denial that permeates daily life, that drowns our deepest grief and horror
about the founding and ongoing atrocities of racism, class, and patriarchy
in endless chatter about trivialities. Oppression buries the actual lives of real
and contradictory people in the crude generalizations of bigotry and pun-
ishes us for not matching the caricature, refusing all evidence of who we actually are in defiance of its tidy categories. It is a blunt instrument, used for
bashing not only our dangerous complexities, but also the ancient and permanent fact of our involvement with each other.

Raicism, or rootedness, is the choice to bear witness to our specific, con- 2
tradictory historical identities in relationship to one another. It is an accounting of the debts and assets we have inherited, and acknowledging the
precise nature of that inheritance is an act of spiritual and political integrity.

I grew up on stories of my mother's barrio childhood in Spanish Harlem 3
and the Bronx, of near starvation in the early years of the Depression, of my
grandmother's single dress. It was not until I went to the small Puerto Rican
town of Toa Alta and examined the parish registers that I discovered five
generations of slave-holding ancestors among the petty landed gentry of
northeast Puerto Rico. A handful of families held political and economic
power, married their children to each other, and consolidated their wealth
with the purchase of enslaved human beings. I remember the feelings, as
this reality dawned on me, of shame, but also of excitement. Over the years
I had found peasants, small farmers, revolutionaries in my family tree. This
was the thing I had not wanted to find. If I could figure out how to face it
and consciously carry it, how to transform shame and denial into whole-

387

ness, perhaps I could find a way out of the numbness of privilege, not only for myself, but also for the people I worked with in classes and workshops who came asking to learn.

4   So that day I wrote down the name of each and every slave held by my ancestors. I have used my own family history to break silence: to acknowledge publicly and repeatedly my family debt to their coerced labor, to expose and reject family mythology about our "kind" treatment of slaves as a step in challenging the generalized myth of kind slavery in Puerto Rico, and to decide that although none of these people had chosen me as a descendant, I owed them the respect one gives to ancestors because their labor had made it possible for my forebears to grow up and thrive. I have also made it my responsibility to make African people visible in every discussion of Puerto Rican history in which I participate.

5   Taking full responsibility for this legacy of relationships is empowering and radical. Guilt and denial and the defensive pull to avoid blame require immense amounts of energy and are profoundly immobilizing. Giving them up can be a great relief. Deciding that we are in fact accountable frees us to act. Acknowledging our ancestors' participation in the oppression of others (and this is ultimately true of everyone if you really dig) and deciding to balance the accounts on their behalf leads to greater integrity and less shame; less self-righteousness and more righteousness, humility, and compassion; and a sense of proportion.

6   At the same time, uncovering the credit side of the accounts, not the suffering but the solidarity, persistence, love, hard work, creativity, and soul of our forebears, is also an obligation. We are responsible for carrying that forward into our own time and for calling on our kin to do likewise. For people committed to liberation to claim descent from the perpetrators is a renewal of faith in human beings. If savers, invaders, committers of genocide, inquisitors can beget abolitionists, resistance fighters, healers, community builders, then any one can transform an inheritance of privilege or of victimization into something more fertile than either.

7   One of the rewards of discovering exactly who our people have been— and how and with whom they have lived—is the possibility of unimagined kinship. My Jewish ancestors were settled in the Ukraine as a buffer against Turkish invasion, alongside German Mennonites brought in to teach formerly landless Jews about farming. At a talk in Wichita, Kansas, I was able to thank their descendants and claim a relationship between us, as Eastern European Jew and German Christian, other than that of genocidal anti-Semitism.

8   Mapping the specificity of our ethnicity also revels hidden relationships. European Americans in this country need to find out in relationship to whom they became white. The answers will be very different for the descendants of a Scot from Iowa, an Irishwoman from Alabama, a New York Pole, a Louisiana French-Spanish Creole, a Texan with roots in 17th-century England and 19th-century Austria, and a Romanian Jew who settled in turn-of-the-century San Francisco. Questions about our place within the megastructures of racism become intimate and carry personality. It becomes possible to see the choices we make right now as extensions of those inherited ones, and to choose more courageously as a result.

Rhetorical Considerations

1. What is Morales's primary purpose in this essay? Is it expressive, informative, or persuasive? (*Hodges' 32a/Writer's* 1e)
2. What specifically is her thesis? (*Hodges' 32c/Writer's* 2b)
3. What type or types of argument does Morales use to develop her thesis (ethical, logical, or pathetic appeals)? (*Hodges' 36e/Writer's* 7f)
4. What is Morales's tone? Is she hostile or accusatory? Find evidence to support your answer. (*Hodges' 31c/Writer's* 2d)
5. Morales relies heavily on one personal example to support her argument. Is this one example sufficient for the purposes of her essay? (*Hodges' 32e/Writer's* 2e)
6. Does Morales end on a negative or a positive note? Explain. How does this affect your reading of the essay? (*Hodges' 33b/Writer's* 3b)

Language and Style

1. Look up the following words in your dictionary: *genealogy* (paragraph 1); *barrio* (paragraph 3); *genocide* (paragraph 6); *anti-Semitism* (paragraph 7). (*Hodges' 18e/Writer's* 28e)
2. Look up definitions for *radical* and *caricature* (paragraph 1). Do they mean what you thought they mean? (*Hodges' 18e/Writer's* 28e)
3. What is the effect of the words *chatter* and *trivialities* in the fourth sentence of the first paragraph? (*Hodges' 19/Writer's* 28)
4. What does Morales mean by *mapping* in the first sentence of paragraph 8? (*Hodges' 18e/Writer's* 28e)
5. Comment on the parallelism of the last sentence of paragraph 1. (*Hodges' 26/Writer's* 25)

Writing Suggestions

1. Write an essay in which you argue that the federal government should or should not make payments of restitution to the heirs of slaves.
2. Do some research into your own genealogy, and write an essay in which you examine the effects of your family history on your current quality of life.

◆

WHY WE NEED A CARE MOVEMENT

Deborah Stone

Deborah Stone is a fellow of the Open Society Institute and holds an investigator award in health policy from the Robert Wood Johnson Foundation. This essay was published in *The Nation,* in 2000.

1 We have the Bill of Rights and we have civil rights. Now we need a Right to Care, and it's going to take a movement to get it.

2   Care is as essential as the air we breathe. Two centuries of myth-making about rugged individualism will not yield easily to the painful fact that dependence is the human condition. In addition to the 38 million children under age 10 who need looking after, we now have somewhere between 30 million and 50 million people who need help with the basic tasks of daily life to be able to lead decent lives.

3   It took a movement to re-envision air and water so they didn't appear to be free and inexhaustible resources. By one recent estimate, 27 million people—more than 11 million of them men—are providing an average of eighteen hours a week of informal care to someone over 18. According to the National Alliance for Caregiving, caregivers to the elderly who also work in the paid labor force frequently turn down promotions, take leaves of absence or early retirement, or even give up their jobs to accommodate their caregiving. We need a movement to demonstrate that caring is not a free resource, that caring is hard and skilled work, that it takes time and devotion, and that people who do it are making sacrifices.

4   We need a movement because caregiving is a class issue and a labor issue as well as a social-welfare issue. Working alongside the informal-care brigade is an army of underpaid and overworked formal caregivers. While the rest of the economy is downsizing, caregiving jobs are booming. But these new jobs pay minimum wage or a little more, and usually lack any kind of security, benefits or possibility for advancement.

5   We need a care movement because this is how the left can and should reclaim family values from the right, which blames families for neglecting their responsibilities and castigates poor women for balking at below-subsistence wages in care work. The left must highlight all the ways society thwarts the primeval urge to care.

Three Rights to Care

6 Rights are not magic wands for curing social problems, but they are a splendid device for mobilizing a movement. By demanding the right to care, we can point out just how inhumane many current policies are.

A right to care means, first, that families are permitted and helped to care for 7
their members. Contrary to all the conservative rhetoric about families shirking their responsibilities, most families are making heroic efforts to care for themselves in the face of huge obstacles society puts in their way. The entire system of paid work is hostile to family responsibility. Rigid schedules, long hours, changing shifts, mandatory overtime, the near-universal lack of leave time to take care of sick relatives—all block workers from caring for their families.

The reformed welfare system won't tolerate (much less support) women 8
who choose to be full-time mothers. Such women are deemed irresponsible parasites, while—perversely—when they take care of other people's children for pay, as daycare workers or home health aides, for example, they are considered virtuous.

Most elders dread the nursing home and most families want desperately 9
to keep them out, but with the advent of sophisticated, high-tech home medical care, keeping a frail parent at home often requires outside help and the money to buy it. Yet in 1997 Congress slashed Medicare's home healthcare budget, forcing many families to put their elders in nursing homes.

A right to care means, second, the right of paid caregivers to give humane, 10
high-quality care without compromising their own well-being. As states and counties privatize social services, they are pushing care workers into shaky, independent-contractor status, where they have zero security and benefits. Most states subsidize childcare for low-income women, but they pay such low rates that many full-time childcare providers are themselves eligible for some public assistance. Home health aides and aides in mental health facilities are often similarly ill paid. With hourly wages of $6 to $9 per hour and usually no guarantees of full-time work, most are kept near or below the poverty level.

When health insurance plans pick up the tab for care, whether public 11
or private, they don't want to pay for non-essentials. In the name of efficiency, they're squeezing out the social time, the time it takes to treat a person with dignity and compassion instead of as a body with only physical needs. Caregivers often must disobey rules to provide decent care.

Last, a right to care must mean that people who need care can get it. Cultur- 12
ally, we are a nation that shudders at the very idea of dependence. We pretend that only the lazy and the poor need help, and that they get it. Meanwhile, people with the most utterly normal and ordinary dependencies cannot get the care they need. The litany is familiar: more than 44 million people without health insurance, a whopping shortage of daycare for children, thousands of children languishing in foster care, unaffordable and uncovered homecare, a shameful incapacity to treat the mentally ill.

The left should continue to champion this third right to care, the right 13
to receive care, but it's time to emphasize the first two rights, which are rights to give care rather than to receive it. One reason the right wing has been so successful on social issues is its one-sided portrayal of social aid as an entitlement, as all taking and no giving. We must show that the right to care is the right to be a decent person, to feel love and loyalty, and to act on

those feelings without being ground down or punished. The care movement must recapture the nobility of care.

What Kind of Movement?

14   It will take a movement to join the three corners of the care triangle: people who need care, families who care for and about their members, and people who give care for a living.

15   Each corner already has its grassroots beginnings, but they rarely make common cause. They are split by their relationship to the problem—whether they are users and buyers of care, or people who make a living at caregiving. Consumers want affordable, low-cost care, but people who care for a living must have livable wages and benefits. Care interests are split again by the sector of the service world they inhabit—childcare versus eldercare, chronic illness and disability versus acute illness, physical health versus mental health. Then, they are split yet again by the sector of the economy that presides over the resources they need—multiple levels of government; private agencies and firms that provide services and employ caregivers; and employers everywhere that control employees' time and may or may not provide fringe benefits crucial to meeting family care needs.

16   The way out of this impasse can be glimpsed in efforts like the disability-senior-labor coalition in California that is helping home health workers upgrade their pay and working conditions, while helping consumers get better-qualified and more reliable caregivers. A year ago, Service Employees (SEIU) Local 434B won the right to represent 74,000 homecare workers in Los Angeles County. It was the biggest influx of new union members in a single vote since 1941, and it was a long time coming. Home healthcare workers get paid from a mix of federal, state, county and private money, and when they first tried to organize, courts said they were independent contractors (who aren't allowed to organize) and that even if they were in a position to organize, they didn't have a single employer with whom to bargain.

17   To get around the courts, a coalition of labor, seniors, disability activists and other advocacy groups got state legislation authorizing counties to create Public Authorities to run the state's large In-Home Supportive Services (IHSS) program. The authorities serve as employers of record for homecare workers.

18   Many consumers were afraid of the new model. "We did not want to see IHSS become like an HMO, where companies come in and dictate the hours, what's to be done and for how long," says Lillibeth Navarro, a disability activist and consumer representative on the governing board of LA's Public Authority. "I myself had those misgivings," she admits, "but I also knew that we consumers were affected by the situation of our homecare workers. They had no health insurance, and we needed them for our survival. If they were sick or had a loss of health, we suffered." Verdia Daniels, president of 434B's executive board and a homecare worker for twenty-two years, adds that consumers became union allies "when they saw they couldn't keep their providers; the providers had to leave homecare and get other jobs because they couldn't support their families."

When homecare workers started to unionize in earnest, leaders of the dis- 19
ability community feared they would be out-organized. So they went into
low-income housing units where there were clusters of seniors and people
with disabilities. "A lot of seniors are fiercely independent," says Navarro,
"and they don't want to admit that they need help even though they might
be falling all over the kitchen and bathroom." The younger activists explained
the IHSS program and the dynamics of homecare. "They see us in wheelchairs,
and they see us functioning and they see there is life with disability—and it's
OK," says Navarro, explaining how she helped make alliances with seniors.

Since unionizing last spring, Los Angeles's homecare workers have got- 20
ten a modest 50-cent pay increase, bringing them up to $6.25 an hour. In
San Francisco, where the union (SEIU Local 250), the Public Authority and
consumer groups have been working together for much longer, and where
there are only about 5,500 homecare workers, the coalition has achieved a
$9 per hour rate, a comprehensive health insurance package and, just re-
cently, dental benefits. Donna Calame, executive director of the San Francisco Public Authority, says better compensation is having an impact on the
quality of care. "I do see a different kind of person coming in to be a healthcare worker. They seem more stable."

The Worthy Wage campaign for childcare workers is another place to 21
see the outlines of a care movement. The campaign is a loose coalition of
childcare advocacy groups in the states, inspired and supported by the Center for the Child Care Workforce. What moved the childcare crisis into the
public spotlight, says Marcy Whitebook of the University of California,
Berkeley, and founding director of the center, was a study that linked
preschool teachers' pay directly to quality of care. Low pay produces high
teacher turnover, which in turn makes for insecure kids who don't make
friends easily or engage with their environment. Interestingly enough, says
Whitebook, many teachers were more comfortable pressing for the interests
of children than for their own financial well-being.

"We knew that parents were our natural allies," says Lauren Tozzi, a Seat- 22
tle preschool teacher and Worthy Wage activist. In 1994 she helped organize Seattle's first Worthy Wage Day, a day on which childcare centers close
so teachers and parents can rally and lobby for more public resources. At
first, parents groused about losing their childcare. "We didn't want it to look
like a wildcat strike," says Tozzi, "so we did six months of preparation to get
teachers and parents to become advocates." Teachers asked parents to attend the rally, make calls and visit legislators, but if they couldn't do any of
that, to consider bringing their children to work. One father took his daughter and three other children. "It created complete havoc at his worksite,"
says Tozzi, and effectively told his co-workers, "*You* may not have children,
but if *I* don't have childcare, it impacts you."

Spurred by this kind of grassroots organizing, Seattle's thriving child- 23
care advocacy community has had a lot of successes. Last summer many
preschool teachers joined District 925 of the SEIU, and the union then negotiated a master contract that covers eleven childcare centers. A Business/
Child Care Partnership gets businesses to donate equipment, appliances and

services to childcare centers, which the centers promise to convert into bonuses and wages for their staff. In an innovative program to let teachers advance while continuing to work with kids (instead of having to go into administration, where there's more money), Governor Gary Locke has put up $4 million to reward teachers for education and experience. John Burbank, director of the Economic Opportunity Institute, hatched the idea in a graduate school paper in 1994. Now he's helping to implement the program in a way that pushes childcare centers by requiring them to meet wage and benefits standards in order to qualify for the state money.

24   Another route to a united care movement is being pursued in Massachusetts, through a focus on wage legislation. Rick Colbath-Hess, a social worker and father of two young children, told a Harvard Living Wage rally last year, "I had to stop the work I love because we couldn't afford to keep two children in daycare and keep my job in human services." Colbath-Hess founded Massachusetts Service Employees for Rights and Viable Employment (MASS SERVE), which is spearheading a living-wage bill in the state legislature. Most living-wage laws are local ordinances that set minimum wages for employees of firms and agencies that contract with a city or county. They are limited not only by their small jurisdiction but also by the types of jobs they cover. Most (there are now more than forty) apply to workers who take care of things, not people—janitors, security guards, construction workers and food-service workers.

25   MASS SERVE is unusual because it unites workers who care for many different kinds of vulnerable people. Like Colbath-Hess, they all want to help people as their life's work. The coalition's Human Service Workers Living Wage Bill would insure that workers paid by state funds earn at least 135 percent of the federal poverty line for a family of 4, or $10.50 an hour. Colbath-Hess sees the organization not only as a "bridge between providers and unions" but also as a partnership between care workers and people who need care. In addition to the usual labor organizations that would be expected to support such a movement—the National Association of Social Workers, the Massachusetts Nurses Association and SEIU Local 509—MASS SERVE has received endorsements from Empower, an organization of mentally ill care recipients; and also from the Alliance for the Mentally Ill and Mass ARC, organizations of families affected by mental illness and retardation, respectively.

26   These little seedling movements are inspiring models for a grand care movement. They demonstrate the breadth of care as a political issue and the power of coalitions to put care on the public agenda. Above all, they prove the force of caring as a motive for political action.

27   Caring for each other is the most basic form of civic participation. We learn to care in families, and we enlarge our communities of concern as we mature. Caring is the essential democratic act, the prerequisite to voting, joining associations, attending meetings, holding office and all the other ways we sustain democracy. Care, the noun, requires families and workers who care, the verb. Caring, the activity, breeds caring, the attitude, and caring, the attitude, seeds caring, the politics. That is why we need a care movement.

Rhetorical Considerations

1. Who is Stone's audience? Find evidence in the essay of her awareness of audience. (*Hodges'* 32a/*Writer's* 1e)
2. How many examples does Stone use? Why are several examples extended to multiple paragraphs? (*Hodges'* 31c/*Writer's* 2d)
3. Stone's major examples are from California, Washington, and Massachusetts. Might those examples present a challenge for some readers? Why or why not? (*Hodges'* 31c/*Writer's* 2d)
4. Is Stone arguing for better care for people who need it, or is she arguing for something more specific? (*Hodges'* 32c/*Writer's* 2b)
5. What are the "three rights to care"?

Language and Style

1. Look up the following words in your dictionary: *castigates* (paragraph 5); *rhetoric* (paragraph 7); *parasites* (paragraph 8); *advent* (paragraph 9); *litany* (paragraph 12). (*Hodges'* 18e/*Writer's* 28e)
2. Explain the metaphors used in paragraphs 4 and 6. (*Hodges'* 20b/*Writer's* 29b)
3. What is the subject of the second sentence of paragraph 2? (*Hodges'* 1/*Writer's* 16)
4. The first sentence of paragraph 19 is a complex sentence. What effect (if any) would result in reversing the order of the main clause and the subordinate clause? (*Hodges'* 1e/*Writer's* 16d)

Writing Suggestions

1. Write an essay about your own experience with caregiving (child care, care of a sick relative, etc.). Argue for certain social and/or political changes that would have made this time easier for you.
2. In paragraph 22, Stone recounts a story of a man who takes his children to work and explains to his co-workers, "*You* may not have children, but if *I* don't have childcare, it impacts you." Find another issue or problem you have observed that affects not just those directly involved, but also most or all of society at large. Write an essay in which you argue for all members of society to take action to resolve this problem.

♦

BLINDED BY POWER

Ralph Nader

Born in Winsted, Connecticut, in 1934, Ralph Nader is a consumer advocate, lawyer, and author. He graduated magna cum laude from Princeton University and received a law degree from Harvard University. During his career as a consumer advocate he founded many organizations, including the Center for Study of Responsive Law, Public Interest Research Group (PIRG), Center for Auto Safety, Public Citizen, Clean Water Action Project, Disability Rights Center, Pension Rights Center, and Project for Corporate Responsibility. He also established *The Multinational Monitor,* a monthly magazine. He was the Green Party candidate in the 2000 presidential election.

1   Here's the corporate party line: California's energy demand is soaring. Energy supplies are running low because environmental regulations have blocked new plants from being built. The disconnect between supply and demand is caused by a partial deregulation scheme that has artificially frozen consumer electricity rates below the free-market price. As a result, blackouts are unavoidable and California's utilities are teetering on the verge of bankruptcy.

2   That's the conventional wisdom concerning California's energy crisis, and reporters have adopted it as their thumbnail explanation. Every element of it is either wrong or misleading.

3   Myth No. 1: Energy demand in California is skyrocketing. Most news reports take this for granted. "Demand from ordinary consumers and energy-hungry commercial sectors like Silicon Valley has stretched California's energy resources to the breaking point," editorialized *The New York Times* in January. "One central fact in the current California energy crisis is not in dispute: Demand for electricity is outstripping supply," reported *The Washington Post* a month later.

4   In fact, California's energy demand is growing slowly, as a comprehensive *San Francisco Chronicle* study showed in March. Overall electricity usage in California rose approximately 2 percent a year in the nineties. Most importantly, peak use—the demand level that actually stressed the system—was lower at the end of 2000 than the year before, according to an analysis of statistics from the California Independent System Operator (CAISO) by Public Citizen [an organization founded by Ralph Nader in 1971].

5   Myth No. 2: Environmental rules have blocked construction of new generating plants. This is a favorite canard of the corporatist commentators. Lawrence Makovich and Daniel Yergin, partners at an energy consulting firm, complained in a *Washington Post* opinion piece about the "monumen-

tal obstacles to siting and granting permits to new facilities." *The American Spectator* devoted a full article to the idea that environmental regulations have plunged California into crisis. Environmental rules are in fact not blocking new plants: As California EPA secretary Winston Hickox wrote in a March Letter to *The New York Times*, "Since 1999, our Energy Commission has licensed 11 new power plants. Six are under construction." Generators did not invest in new electric plants because they did not think there would be sufficient demand.

Myth No. 3: A shortage of supply or spikes in demand are causing the 6 blackouts. The central narrative of most reports on the blackouts is that a surge in a particular day's demand exceeded California's "low reserves" of electricity. (For example: "The [CAISO], which runs the state's power grid, initiated the blackouts when reserves ran low," wrote *USA Today* reporter Scott Bowles in March.)

But the problem in California isn't a lack of supply. It's that the energy 7 producers have withheld supply from the utilities at strategic moments to protest the utilities' failure to pay debts, as *Los Angeles Times* reporter Julie Tamaki pointed out in March. The Foundation for Taxpayer and Consumer Rights points out that the blackouts have hit at just the moments when the suppliers wanted to extract new concessions and subsidies from the state, such as agreements to cover the utilities' debts to the suppliers. In total, California has 55,500 megawatts of power-generating capacity and 4,500 megawatts purchased through long-term contracts from out-of-state suppliers—approximately 15,000 megawatts more than peak demand, Public Citizen reports, citing statistics from CAISO.

Myth No. 4: The state-imposed cap on the rates that utilities can charge 8 consumers for electricity has irrationally placed the utilities in a vise; with expenses exceeding revenue, bankruptcy is unavoidable. Or, as *The New York Times* put it in a January editorial, "The wholesale prices [the utilities] pay for electricity vastly exceed the retail prices they can charge their consumers.

But the major news outlets regularly omit vital context: Legislation 9 deregulating electricity markets passed the California legislature unanimously in 1996. It was exactly what the private utilities wanted; certainly no bill would pass the legislature unanimously if PG&E or Southern California Edison was opposed in whole or part. The law was a remarkably lucrative deal for the utilities. They received $28 billion in ratepayer subsidies for what the utilities call "stranded costs"—previous plant investments gone bad—and were allowed for the first time to invest in unrelated businesses in the United States and abroad.

Press accounts regularly describe the utilities as "near bankruptcy" or 10 "failing—PG&E did file for bankruptcy in April—but most stories don't offer historical context or even identify the assets of the utilities' parent companies. The deregulation legislation passed in 1996 allowed the utilities to restructure themselves; their newly created holding companies have extracted billions of dollars from their utility subsidiaries and used the proceeds to buy back stock, pay out huge dividends to shareholders, and make out-of-state investments. The parent companies have also profited from the price increases in the wholesale electricity market, as one subsidiary (electricity generation) has sold at superinflated costs to another (utility provider). In a phrase, they gouged themselves. PG&E's creditors will surely point this out in bankruptcy court and go after the assets of its parent company.

11   Myth No. 5: The only solution to the crisis is to let consumer prices rise to free-market prices. In April, a *Washington Post* editorial called California governor Gray Davis a coward for his modest resistance to price hikes. In their op-ed in the same newspaper, Makovich and Yergin bemoaned "the political willingness to allow consumers to see real price signals." The free market, however, has nothing to do with the prices demanded by the power-generating cartel. According to CAISO, the wholesale suppliers have gouged Californians by at least 5.5 billion through market manipulation and artificially inflated prices. California's choice is not between free markets and regulation; it is between government price regulation and cartel price regulation.

12   Yet journalists have continued to repeat these errors, usually because of lazy reporting, an unwillingness to reassert the facts in the face of constant industry misrepresentations, or an ideological predisposition in favor of deregulation. One widespread, and typical, deficiency of the media is a failure to provide historical context—like the promises to lower prices the utilities made in exchange for supporting deregulation and the ways they exploited deregulation prior to the independent generators' recent profiteering. By March, news accounts suggested that price increases were inevitable. Many played off Governor Davis's public statements that rate increases could be avoided, noting that his staff quietly suggested the opposite. The media-generated crescendo of inevitablility helped create the conditions for a 46 percent rate increase by California's Public Utilities Commission in late March.

13   Largely lost in the process were viable alternatives that consumer advocates have proposed: requiring utility-holding companies to pay their subsidiaries' debts; regulating generators to lower cartel prices; enacting cost-based reregulation; buying out—not bailing out—the utilities; and expanding the role for public power, with an emphasis on energy efficiency and renewable energy.

14   Unfortunately, blackmailers frequently view ransom payments as an invitation to demand more. Even a huge rate increase and utility bailout may not satiate the greedy electric-power industry, which means that reporters may have a chance to repeat their errors—or report more critically on the manufactured California energy crisis.

Rhetorical Considerations

1. What is Nader's thesis? Does he state it explicitly? If so, where? If not, express it in your own words. (*Hodges'* 32c/*Writer's* 2b)
2. How does Nader's introduction set up his organization pattern for the rest of his essay? (*Hodges'* 33b/*Writer's* 3b)

3. What are Nader's most effective examples? (*Hodges'* 31c/*Writer's* 2d)
4. Whom does Nader blame for the energy crisis in California?
5. What kinds of argument does Nader use to support his thesis? (*Hodges'* 36/ *Writer's* 7)

Language and Style

1. Look up the following words in your dictionary: *deregulation* (paragraph 1); *crescendo* (paragraph 12); *viable* (paragraph 13). (*Hodges'* 18e/*Writer's* 28e)
2. Find descriptive words that reveal Nader's bias. (*Hodges'* 19/*Writer's* 28)
3. What is the antecedent of *this* in the second sentence of paragraph 5? (*Hodges'* 5/*Writer's* 21)
4. Identify all the main clauses in the last sentence of paragraph 9. (*Hodges'* 1g/ *Writer's* 17b)

Writing Suggestions

Because this essay and the following essay, "Follow the Light" by Newt Gingrich, are closely related, Writing Suggestions for both essays appear at the end of the Gingrich selection.

Follow the Light

Newt Gingrich

Newt Gingrich served as a member of Congress for twenty years and as Speaker of the U.S. House of Representatives from 1995–1999. He is considered to be the chief creator of the Republican Contract with America, as well as the major force behind the 1994 "Republican Sweep" (which resulted in the first GOP majority in Congress in 40 years). Gingrich has a bachelor's degree from Emory University and a master's and doctorate from Tulane University in modern European history. Currently CEO of The Gingrich Group, a consulting firm, Gingrich continues to provide political commentary on television and in print media.

1   Imagine a Third World leader who passed laws bankrupting two of his country's most important companies, depleted the government's cash reserves while refusing to share the books with the duly elected legislature, permitted hundreds of small local companies to be looted of their products without payment, sent his bureaucrats into the international market to buy essential goods at high prices at taxpayer expense, and, then, to the detriment of consumers and the economy, announced that he was going to "solve" the problem by allowing the politicians and the bureaucrats who created the mess in the first place actually to take over large parts of the private sector so the government could run them.

2   You might expect an onslaught of scathingly negative coverage of that leader and his government. Editorial writers would rightfully demand transparency and accountability in the expenditure of public funds. The responsible analysis would detail how the government's obsolete statist policies were ruining the economy, impoverishing citizens, and weakening the country's position in the world market. Just think of the scrutiny, for example, that journalists have applied to the International Monetary Fund and The World Bank.

3   That's what you might expect. But somehow the media have given California's political leaders, notably Governor Gray Davis, a free ride. What reporters don't seem to understand is that the crisis in California is not electrical in nature—it's political. Absent from the stories about stuck elevators, traffic-light mishaps, and office workers who lost their work on their computers because they didn't hit "save" was an examination of the political decisions that landed Californians in the dark. For example, a March *San Francisco Chronicle* story on a rate increase mentioned "bungled deregulation" but didn't bother to explain what failed. Instead, the story repeated anti-consumer tirades like this quote from the president of California's Public Utilities Commission: "Electricity hogs will need to pay more. If you

want to run your pool pump during peak hours this summer, you will pay for that."

First, there is enough electrical capacity to meet California's needs. It's just that consumers need to be charged the true market cost of electricity. You can bet that once that happens, people will not only learn to conserve energy, they will seek out low-cost solutions to high prices, creating the conditions necessary for the market-place to function. Supply and demand really does work. Instead we have Gray Davis following the example of President Jimmy Carter, who, in his efforts to outmaneuver the laws of supply and demand in gasoline prices, gave us the Department of Energy, long lines at gas stations, and a gas shortage. One of President Ronald Reagan's first acts after inauguration was to deregulate the petroleum market, and gas prices promptly dropped. We have not seen gas station lines since. Press accounts of the current crisis constantly repeat the conventional wisdom that the solution is to raise the rate caps for electricity consumers—the *Chicago Tribune* carried the headline "Californians' Power Bills May Skyrocket"; a *San Francisco Chronicle* headline read "PG&E Bills Set To Rise 40 Percent"—while ignoring the fact that no matter what the price of electricity is, any pricing mechanism other than a free market is bound to fail. Look for an article that mentions this lesson from the seventies gas crisis and you won't find it. 4

The press likes to point to deregulation as the problem. Take this March *Washington Post* article: "California's energy crisis has slowed or halted electricity deregulation in many of the two dozen states considering it." But the California energy market was *never* deregulated. The 1996 California legislation was a monstrosity of price controls at the retail level and free markets at the wholesale level. (I confess that the bill was crafted in part by Republican legislators and signed by a Republican governor.) The law guaranteed the worst of all worlds—the highest possible prices from the producers and no incentive for retail consumers to shop around for the best bargain. Why should they when they were feeling no pain? Yet the media couldn't grasp this simple concept. 5

Nor has the media held environmentalists accountable for their part in this mess. There are trillions of cubic feet of natural gas—a clean-burning source of power—in previously developed oil fields in Alaska, but there is no natural-gas pipeline parallel to the oil pipeline. Such a pipeline would clearly bring down the cost of the electricity, but California environmentalists have been the leading opponents of building it. Why haven't California newspapers held the Sierra Club accountable? Instead, reporters venerate the feel-good organizations. 6

Similarly, Mexico is currently producing surplus electricity (and has several more plants set to commence production soon with even more capacity). But the transmission lines north of San Diego aren't capable of carrying all of it. Why have the opponents of building new lines (again largely the environmentalists) not been held accountable for the current crisis? The lack of new production capacity in California is a direct result of environmentalist opposition, yet there are almost no stories on "the Sierra Club–driven California electricity crisis." 7

8   Instead of any of this analysis, the media have simply begun to accept the blackouts as if they were just a natural part of life rather than the result of politicians tinkering with a free market. "They raged, they shrugged, they got over it," read one March *Los Angeles Times* story, which detailed how a blackout "barely disturbed the members of the Orange County chapter of Daughters of the Confederacy, who went on with their lunch with a measure of Southern grace at the Split Rock Tavern in Laguna Hills."

9   Electricity has been a hallmark of civilization for nearly 125 years. Thomas Edison's invention of the electric light transformed our way of life. We are an electricity-dependent society. When blackouts have occurred in California, public safety has plummeted. Traffic lights have gone out at major intersections, causing car accidents. People have been trapped in high-rise buildings.

10   Journalists have been off the mark for three reasons. First, daily reporting is essentially a rip-and-write profession. Reporters need to turn in lots of copy quickly. They have no time to interview thoughtful experts and try to get at the larger story behind the press conference or the news release. Instead, they just insert quotes from the often uninformed "experts"—frequently of a liberal bent—whose phone numbers have been sitting in their Rolodexes for years. Second, the vast majority of California editorialists are even more liberal than the nation at large, and it would never occur to them to hold environmentalists, bureaucrats, or Gray Davis accountable. Third, the core analysis of free markets, supply and demand, and technological change is routinely covered in *The Economist* and *The Wall Street Journal*, but rarely in the dominant media in America.

11   The result is that journalists have covered a political crisis in California by writing "electricity lifestyle" stories that have been shallow, misleading, and ultimately harmful to California's future.

Rhetorical Considerations

1. How effective is Gingrich's introduction? How does it set up the development of the rest of the essay? (*Hodges'* 33b/*Writer's* 3b)
2. What are the fundamental political and economic principles of Gingrich's thesis?
3. How does Gingrich use examples and quotations from authorities? (*Hodges'* 31c/*Writer's* 2d)
4. Whom does Gingrich blame for the energy crisis in California?
5. Now that you've read the essays by Nader and Gingrich, do you see anything the two writers agree on? What?

Language and Style

1. Look up the following words in your dictionary: *scathingly* (paragraph 2); *venerate* (paragraph 6). (*Hodges'* 18e/*Writer's* 28e)
2. Find descriptive words that reveal Gingrich's bias. (*Hodges'* 19/*Writer's* 28)

3. The first paragraph consists of one long sentence. Assess parallelism in this sentence. (*Hodges'* 26/*Writer's* 25)
4. Comment on the sentence variety of paragraph 6. (*Hodges'* 30/*Writer's* 27)

Writing Suggestions

1. Write an essay in which you examine the essays by Nader and Gingrich, analyzing how effective their arguments are. How do the language, strategies, and appeals they use affect your willingness to agree with their points? Make your own argument for which essay is more effective.
2. Almost any topic can be argued from differing points of view. Choose a topic that is usually argued one way, and write an essay arguing that a different interpretation is more accurate. You might consider a local topic (a school policy or town ordinance, for example) or one on a larger scale.

◆

You Can't Judge a Crook by His Color

Randall Kennedy

A noted expert on black legal history and civil rights, Randall Kennedy is a professor at Harvard Law School. He received his undergraduate degree from Princeton and his law degree from Yale. He served as a clerk to Thurgood Marshall, Supreme Court Justice, and was a Rhodes Scholar. Kennedy is the author of *Race, Crime, and the Law* (1997) and *Nigger: The Strange Career of a Troublesome Word* (2002). This essay was first published in *The New Republic* in 1999.

1   In Kansas City, a drug Enforcement Administration officer stops and questions a young man who has just stepped off a flight from Los Angeles. The officer has focused on this man because intelligence reports indicate that black gangs in L.A. are flooding the Kansas City area with illegal drugs. Young, toughly dressed, and appearing nervous, he paid for his ticket in cash, checked no luggage, brought two carry-on bags, and made a beeline for a taxi when he arrived. Oh, and one other thing: The young man is black. When asked why he decided to question this man, the officer declares that he considered race, along with other factors, because doing so helps him allocate limited time and resources efficiently.

2   Should we applaud the officer's conduct? Permit it? Prohibit it? This is not a hypothetical example. Encounters like this take place every day, all over the country, as police battle street crime, drug trafficking, and illegal immigration. And this particular case study happens to be the real-life scenario presented in a federal lawsuit of the early '90s. *United States v. Weaver,* in which the 8th U.S. Circuit Court of Appeals upheld the constitutionality of the officer's action.

3   "Large groups of our citizens," the court declared, "should not be regarded by law enforcement officers as presumptively criminal based upon their race." The court went on to say, however, that "facts are not to be ignored simply because they may be unpleasant." According to the court, the circumstances were such that the young man's race, considered in conjunction with other signals, was a legitimate factor in the decision to approach and ultimately detain him. "We wish it were otherwise," the court maintained, "but we take the facts as they are presented to us, not as we would like them to be." Other courts have agreed that the Constitution does not prohibit police from considering race, as long as they do so for bona fide purposes of law enforcement (not racial harassment) and as long as it is only one of several factors.

4   These decisions have been welcome news to the many law enforcement officials who consider what has come to be known as racial profiling an es-

sential weapon in the war on crime. They maintain that, in areas where young African American males commit a disproportionate number of street crimes, the cops are justified in scrutinizing that sector of the population more closely than others—just as they are generally justified in scrutinizing men more closely than they do women.

As Bernard Parks, chief of the Los Angeles Police Department, explained 5 to Jeffrey Goldberg of *The New York Times Magazine:* "We have an issue of violent crime against jewelry salespeople. . . . The predominant suspects are Colombians. We don't find Mexican Americans, or blacks, or other immigrants. It's a collection of several hundred Colombians who commit this crime. If you see six in a car in front of the Jewelry Mart, and they're waiting and watching people with briefcases, should we play the percentages and follow them? It's common sense.

Cops like Parks say that racial profiling is a sensible, statistically based 6 tool. Profiling lowers the cost of obtaining and processing crime information, which in turn lowers the overall cost of doing the business of policing. And the fact that a number of cops who support racial profiling are black, including Parks, buttresses claims that the practice isn't motivated by bigotry. Indeed, these police officers note that racial profiling is race-*neutral* in that it can be applied to persons of all races, depending on the circumstances. In predominantly black neighborhoods in which white people stick out (as potential drug customers or racist hooligans, for example), whiteness can become part of a profile. In the southwestern United States, where Latinos often traffic in illegal immigrants, apparent Latin American ancestry can become part of a profile.

But the defenders of racial profiling are wrong. Ever since the Black and 7 Latino Caucus of the New Jersey Legislature held a series of hearings, complete with testimony from victims of what they claimed was the New Jersey state police force's overly aggressive racial profiling, the air has been thick with public denunciations of the practice. In June 1999, at a forum organized by the Justice Department on racial problems in law enforcement, President Clinton condemned racial profiling as a "morally indefensible, deeply corrosive practice." Vice President Al Gore has promised that, if he is elected president, he will see to it that the first civil rights act of the new century would end racial profiling. His rival for the Democratic nomination, Bill Bradley, has countered that Gore should prepare an executive order and ask the president to sign it *now.*

Unfortunately, though, many who condemn racial profiling do so without really thinking the issue through. One common complaint is that using 8 race (say blackness) as one factor in selecting surveillance targets is fundamentally racist. But selectivity of this sort can be defended on nonracist grounds. "There is nothing more painful to me at this stage in my life," Jesse Jackson said in 1993, "than to walk down the street and hear footsteps and start to think about robbery and then look around and see somebody white and feel relieved." Jackson was relieved not because he dislikes black people, but because he estimated that he stood a somewhat greater risk of being robbed by a black person than by a white person. Statistics confirm that

African Americans—particularly young black men—commit a dramatically disproportionate share of street crime in the United States. This is a sociological fact, not a figment of a racist media (or police) imagination. In recent years, victims report blacks as perpetrators of around 25 percent of violent crimes, although blacks constitute only about 12 percent of the nation's population.

9   So, if racial profiling isn't bigoted, and if the empirical claim upon which the practice rests is sound, why is it wrong?

10   Racial distinctions are and should be different from other lines of social stratification. That is why, since the civil rights revolution of the 1960s, courts have typically ruled—based on the 14th Amendment's equal protection clause—that mere reasonableness is an insufficient justification for officials to discriminate on racial grounds. In such cases, courts have generally insisted on applying "strict scrutiny"—the most intense level of judicial review—to government actions. Under this tough standard, the use of race in governmental decision making may be upheld only if it serves a compelling government objective and only if it is "narrowly tailored" to advance that objective.

11   A disturbing feature of this debate is that many people, including judges, are suggesting that decisions based on racial distinctions do not constitute unlawful racial discrimination—as long as race is not the only reason a person was treated objectionably. The court that upheld the DEA agent's action at the Kansas City airport, for instance, declined to describe it as racially discriminatory and thus evaded strict scrutiny.

12   But racially discriminatory decisions typically stem from mixed motives. For example, an employer who prefers white candidates to black candidates—except for those black candidates with superior experience and test scores—is engaging in racial discrimination, even though race is not the only factor he considers (since he selects black superstars). In some cases, race is a marginal factor; in others it is the only factor. The distinction may have a bearing on the moral or logical justification, but taking race into account at all means engaging in discrimination.

13   Because both law and morality discourage racial discrimination, proponents should persuade the public that racial profiling is justifiable. Instead, they frequently neglect its costs and minimize the extent to which it adds to the resentment blacks feel toward the law enforcement establishment. When O. J. Simpson was acquitted, many recognized the danger of a large sector of Americans feeling cynical and angry toward the system. Such alienation creates witnesses who fail to cooperate with police, citizens who view prosecutors as the enemy, lawyers who disdain the rules they have sworn to uphold, and jurors who yearn to get even with a system that has, in their eyes, consistently mistreated them. Racial profiling helps keep this pool of accumulated rage filled to the brim.

14   The courts have not been sufficiently mindful of this risk. In rejecting a 1976 constitutional challenge that accused U.S. Border Patrol officers in California of selecting cars for inspection partly on the basis of driver's apparent Mexican ancestry, the Supreme Court noted in part that, of the motorists passing the checkpoint, fewer than 1 percent were stopped. It also

noted that, of the 820 vehicles inspected during the period in question, roughly 20 percent contained illegal aliens.

Justice William J. Brennan dissented, however, saying the Court did not 15 indicate the ancestral makeup of *all* the persons the Border Patrol stopped. It is likely that many of the innocent people who were questioned were of apparent Mexican ancestry who then had to prove their obedience to the law just because others of the same ethnic background have broken laws in the past.

The practice of racial profiling undercuts a good idea that needs more 16 support from both society and the law: Individuals should be judged by public authorities on the basis of their own conduct and not on the basis of racial generalization. Race-dependant policing retards the development of bias-free thinking; indeed, it encourages the opposite.

What about the fact that in some communities people associated with a 17 given racial group commit a disproportionately large number of crimes? Our commitment to a just social order should prompt us to end racial profiling even if the generalizations on which the technique is based are supported by empirical evidence. This is not as risky as it may sound. There are actually many contexts in which law properly enjoins us to forswear playing racial odds even when doing so would advance legitimate goals.

For example, public opinion surveys have established that blacks distrust law enforcement more than whites. Thus, it would be rational—and 18 not necessarily racist—for a prosecutor to use ethnic origin as a factor in excluding black potential jurors. Fortunately, the Supreme Court has outlawed racial discrimination of this sort. And because demographics show that in the United States, whites tend to live longer than blacks, it would be perfectly rational for insurers to charge blacks higher life-insurance premiums. Fortunately, the law forbids that, too.

The point here is that racial equality. Like all good things in life, costs 19 something. Politicians suggest that all Americans need to do in order to attain racial justice is forswear bigotry. But they must also demand equal treatment before the law even when unequal treatment is defensible in the name of nonracist goals—and even when their efforts will be costly.

Since abandoning racial profiling would make policing more expensive 20 and perhaps less effective, those of us who oppose it must advocate a responsible alternative. Mine is simply to spend more money on other means of enforcement—and then spread the cost on some nonracial basis. One way to do that would be to hire more police officers. Another way would be to subject everyone to closer surveillance. A benefit of the second option would be to acquaint more whites with the burden of police intrusion, which might prompt more of them to insist on limiting police power. As it stands now, the burden is unfairly placed on minorities—imposing on Mexican Americans, blacks, and others a special kind of tax for the war against illegal immigration, drugs, and others a special kind of tax for the war against illegal immigration, drugs, and other crimes. The racial element of that tax should be repealed.

I'm not saying that police should never be able to use race as a guide- 21 line. If a young white man with blue hair robs me, the police should certainly be able to use a description of the perpetrator's race. In this situation, though, whiteness is a trait linked to a particular person with respect to a particular incident. It is not a free-floating accusation that hovers over young white men practically all the time—which is the predicament young black men currently face. Nor am I saying that race could never be legitimately relied upon as a signal of increased danger. In an extraordinary circumstance in which plausible alternatives appear to be absent, officials might need to resort to racial profiling. This is a far cry from routine profiling that is subjected to little scrutiny.

22   Now that racial profiling is a hot issue, the prospects for policy change have improved. President Clinton directed federal law enforcement agencies to determine the extent to which their officers focus on individuals on the basis of race. The Customs Service is rethinking its practice of using ethnicity or nationality as a basis for selecting subjects for investigation. The Federal Aviation Administration has been re-evaluating its recommended security procedures; it wants the airlines to combat terrorism with computer profiling, which is purportedly less race-based than random checks by airport personnel. Unfortunately, though, a minefield of complexity lies beneath these options. Unless we understand the complexities, this opportunity will be wasted.

23   To protect ourselves against race-based policing requires no real confrontation with the status quo, because hardly anyone defends police surveillance triggered *solely* by race. Much of the talk about police "targeting" suspects on the basis of race is, in this sense, misguided and harmful. It diverts attention to a side issue. Another danger is the threat of demagoguery through oversimplification. When politicians talk about "racial profiling," we must insist that they define precisely what they mean. Evasion—putting off hard decisions under the guise of needing more information—is also a danger.

24   Even if routine racial profiling is prohibited, the practice will not cease quickly. An officer who makes a given decision partly on a racial basis is unlikely to acknowledge having done so, and supervisors and judges are loath to reject officers' statements. Nevertheless, it would be helpful for President Clinton to initiate a strict anti-discrimination directive to send a signal to conscientious, law-abiding officers that there are certain criteria they ought not use.

25   To be sure, creating a norm that can't be fully enforced isn't ideal, but it might encourage us all to work toward closing the gap between our law and the conduct of public authorities. A new rule prohibiting racial profiling might be made to be broken, but it could set a new standard for legitimate government.

Rhetorical Considerations

1. Find Kennedy's thesis statement. (*Hodges'* 32c/*Writer's* 2b)
2. This essay was originally published in the *New Republic,* a political magazine. Does Kennedy consider his audience? Find evidence in the essay. (*Hodges'* 32a/*Writer's* 1e)

3. Why is cause and effect an important developmental tool for Kennedy's purpose? (*Hodges'* 32e/*Writer's* 2e)
4. Find evidence that Kennedy anticipates the arguments of those opposed to his thesis. (*Hodges'* 36d/*Writer's* 7e)
5. Does Kennedy attempt an argument that he cannot prove? Explain why or why not. (*Hodges'* 36b/*Writer's* 7b)

Language and Style

1. What is the origin of the word *hooligan* (paragraph 6)? Might this word be offensive to some readers? (*Hodges'* 18e/*Writer's* 28e)
2. Explain Kennedy's use of figurative language in the last sentence of paragraph 13. (*Hodges'* 20b/*Writer's* 29b)
3. Why does Kennedy use *fewer* instead of *less* in the second sentence of paragraph 14? (*Hodges'* 19/*Writer's* 28)
4. Explain Kennedy's use of figurative language in the sixth sentence of paragraph 20. (*Hodges'* 20b/*Writer's* 29b)
5. Justify the sentence fragments in paragraph 2. (*Hodges'* 2/*Writer's* 18)

Writing Suggestions

1. Write an argument in which you dispel the stereotype of a group of which you are a member.
2. Write an essay in which you explore how generalizations about a particular group of people have created hardship for that group.

THE CLONE WARS

Gregory Stock and Francis Fukuyama

Gregory Stock is the director of the Program of Medicine, Technology, and Society at the University of California at Los Angeles School of Medicine and is the author of several books, including *Redesigning Humans: Our Inevitable Genetic Future* (2002).

Francis Fukuyama is Bernard Schwartz Professor of international political economy at the Paul H. Nitze School of Advanced International Studies at Johns Hopkins University and author of several books, including *The End of History and the Last Man* (1992) and *Our Posthuman Future: Consequences of the Biotechnology Revolution* (2002). Dr. Fukuyama is a member of the President's Council on Bioethics.

The exchange here was conducted on *reason* magazine's Web site at http://www.reason.com over a period of several days, from March 18–22, 2002. It demonstrates how two acknowledged experts in a field can have disparate views, debate vigorously, and, for the most part, conduct themselves civilly.

Go Ahead and Clone: Don't Cause Real Damage to Assuage Phantom Fears

Gregory Stock

1   There has been a lot of hand wringing recently about cloning. Considering that not a single viable cloned human embryo has yet been created, that the arrival of a clinical procedure to do so seems quite distant, and that having a delayed identical twin (which is, after all, what a clone is) has limited appeal, why all the fuss?

2   The fuss arises because cloning has become a proxy for broader fears about the new technologies emerging from our unraveling of human biology. Critics like Francis Fukuyama imagine that if we can stop cloning we can head off possibilities like human enhancement, but they're dreaming. As we decipher our biology and learn to modify it, we are learning to modify ourselves—and we will do so. No laws will stop this.

3   Embryo selection, for example, is a mere spin-off from widely supported medical research of a sort that leaves no trail and is feasible in thousands of labs throughout the world. Any serious attempt to block such research will simply increase the potential dangers of upcoming technologies by driving the work out of sight, blinding us to early indications of any medical or social problems.

4   The best reason not to curb interventions that many people see as safe and beneficial, however, is not that such a ban would be dangerous but that it would be wrong. A ban would prevent people from making choices aimed

410

at improving their lives that would hurt no one. Such choices should be allowed. It is hard for me to see how a society that pushes us to stay healthy and vital could justify, for instance, trying to stop people from undergoing a genetic therapy or consuming a drug cocktail aimed at retarding aging. Imposing such a ban requires far more compelling logic than the assertion that we should not play God or that, as Fukuyama has suggested, it is wrong to try to transcend a "natural" human life span.

What's more, a serious effort to block beneficial technologies that might 5 change our natures would require policies so harsh and intrusive that they would cause far greater harm than is feared from the technologies themselves. If the War on Drugs, with its vast resources and sad results, has been unable to block people's access to deleterious substances, the government has no hope of withholding access to technologies that many regard as beneficial. It would be a huge mistake to start down this path, because even without aggressive enforcement, such bans would effectively reserve the technologies for the affluent and privileged. When abortion was illegal in various states, the rich did not suffer; they just traveled to more-permissive locales.

Restricting emerging technologies for screening embryos would feed 6 deep class divisions. Laboratories can now screen a six-cell human embryo by teasing out a single cell, reading its genes, and letting parents use the results to decide whether to implant or discard the embryo. In Germany such screening is criminal. But this doesn't deny the technology to affluent Germans who want it: They take a trip to Brussels or London, where it is legal. As such screenings become easier and more informative, genetic disease could be gradually relegated to society's disadvantaged. We need to start thinking about how to make the tests more, not less, accessible.

But let's cut to the chase. If parents can easily and safely choose em- 7 bryos, won't they pick ones with predispositions toward various talents and temperaments, or even enhanced performance? Of course. It is too intrusive to have the government second-guessing such decisions. British prohibitions of innocuous choices like the sex of a child are a good example of undesirable government intrusion. Letting parents who strongly desire a girl (or boy) be sure to have one neither injures the resulting child nor causes gender imbalances in Western countries.

Sure, a few interventions will arise that virtually everyone would find 8 troubling, but we can wait until actual problems appear before moving to control them. These coming reproductive technologies are not like nuclear weapons, which can suddenly vaporize large numbers of innocent bystanders. We have the luxury of feeling our way forward, seeing what problems develop, and carefully responding to them.

The real danger we face today is not that new biological technologies 9 will occasionally cause injury but that opponents will use vague, abstract threats to our values to justify unwarranted political incursions that delay the medical advances growing out of today's basic research. If, out of concern over cloning, the U.S. Congress succeeds in criminalizing embryonic stem cell research that might bring treatments for Alzheimer's disease or

diabetes—and Fukuyama lent his name to a petition supporting such laws—
there would be real victims: present and future sufferers from those diseases.

10   We should hasten medical research, not stop it. We are devoting massive resources to the life sciences not out of idle curiosity but in an effort to
penetrate our biology and learn to use this knowledge to better our lives.
We should press ahead. Of course, the resultant technologies will pose challenges: They stand to revolutionize health care and medicine, transform
great swaths of our economy, alter the way we conceive our children, change
the way we manage our moods, and even extend our life spans.

11   The possibilities now emerging will force us to confront the question of
what it means to be a human being. But however uneasy these new technologies make us, if we wish to continue to lead the way in shaping the
human future we must actively explore them. The challenging question facing us is: Do we have the courage to continue to embrace the possibilities
ahead, or will we succumb to our fears and draw back, leaving this exploration to braver souls in other regions of the world?

Sensible Restrictions: There Are Good Reasons
to Regulate Future Biotechnologies

Francis Fukuyama

12 Gregory Stock offers two sets of arguments against restricting future biotech-
nologies: first, that such rules are unnecessary as long as reproductive
choices are being made by individual parents rather than states, and second, that they cannot be enforced and will be ineffective even if they were
to be enacted. Let me respond to each in turn.

13   While genetic choices made by parents (either in the short run, via pre-
implantation genetic diagnosis, or in the more distant future, through
germline engineering) are on the whole likely to be better than those made
by coercive states, there are several grounds for not letting individuals have
complete freedom of choice in this regard.

14   The first two are utilitarian. When we get into human germline engineering, in which modifications will be passed on to successive generations,
safety problems will multiply exponentially over what we today experience
with drug approval. Genetic causation is highly complex, with multiple
genes interacting to create one outcome or behavior and single genes having multiple effects. When a long-term genetic effect may not show up for
decades after the procedure is administered, parents will risk a multitude of
unintended and largely irreversible consequences for their children. This
would seem to be a situation calling for strict regulation.

15   A second utilitarian concern has to do with possible negative externalities, which is the classic ground for state regulation, accepted by even the
most orthodox free market economists. An example is sex selection. Today
in Asia, as a result of cheap sonograms and abortion, cohorts are being born
with extremely lopsided sex ratios—117 boys for every 100 girls in China
and at one point 122 boys for every 100 girls in Korea. Sex selection is rational from the standpoint of individual parents, but it imposes costs on soci-

ety as a whole in terms of the social disruption that a large number of unattached and unmarriageable young males can produce. Similar negative externalities can arise from individual choices to, for example, prolong life at the cost of a lower level of cognitive and physical functioning.

A further set of concerns about the ability to "design" our children has to do with the ambiguity of what constitutes improvement of a human being, particularly when we get into personality traits and emotional makeup. We are the product of a highly complex evolutionary adaptation to our physical and social environment, which has created an equally complex whole human being. Genetic interventions made out of faddishness, political correctness, or simple whim might upset that balance in ways that we scarcely understand—in the interest, for example, of making boys less violent and aggressive, girls more assertive, people more or less competitive, etc. Would an African American's child be "improved" if we could genetically eliminate his or her skin pigmentation? 16

The final issue concerns human nature itself. Human rights are ultimately derived from human nature. That is, we assign political rights to ourselves based on our understanding of the ways members of our species are similar to one another and different from other species. We are fortunate to be a relatively homogenous species. Earlier views that blacks were not intelligent enough to vote, or that women were too emotional to be granted equal political rights, proved to be empirically false. The final chapter of Greg Stock's book opens up the prospect of a future world in which this human homogeneity splinters, under the impact of genetic engineering, into competing human biological kinds. What kind of politics do we imagine such a splintering will produce? The idea that our present-day tolerant, liberal, democratic order will survive such changes is farfetched: Nietzsche, not John Stuart Mill or John Rawls, should be your guide to the politics of such a future. 17

Stock's second set of arguments is based on his belief that no one can stop this technology. He is certainly right that if some future biotechnology proves safe, cheap, effective, and highly desirable, government would not be able to stop it and probably should not try. What I am calling for, however, is not a ban on wide swaths of future technology but rather their strict regulation in light of the dangers outlined above. 18

Today we regulate biomedical technology all the time. People can argue whether that technology is properly regulated and where exactly to draw various regulatory lines. But the argument that procedures that will be as potentially unsafe and ethically questionable as, say, germline engineering for enhancement purposes cannot in principle be regulated has no basis in past experience. 19

We slow the progress of science today for all sorts of ethical reasons. Biomedicine could advance much faster if we abolished our rules on human experimentation in clinical trials, as Nazi researchers did, and allowed doctors to deliberately inject infectious substances into their subjects. Today we enforce rules permitting the therapeutic use of drugs like Ritalin, while prohibiting their use for enhancement or entertainment. 20

21   The argument that these technologies will simply move to more favorable jurisdictions if they are banned in any one country may or may not
carry weight; it all depends on what they are and what the purpose of the
regulation is. I regard a ban on reproductive cloning to be analogous to current legislation banning incest, which is based on a similar mix of safety and
ethical considerations. The purpose of such a ban would not be undermined
if a few rich people could get themselves cloned outside the country. In any
event, the world seems to be moving rather rapidly toward a global ban on
reproductive cloning. The fact that the Chinese may not be on board should-
n't carry much weight; the Chinese also involuntarily harvest organs from
executed prisoners and are hardly an example we would want to emulate.

22   I don't think that a set of regulations designed to focus future biomedicine on therapeutic rather than enhancement purposes constitutes oppres-
sive state intervention or goes so far beyond the realm of what is done today
that we can declare its final failure in advance. By Greg Stock's reasoning,
since rules against doping in athletic competitions don't work 100 percent
of the time, we should throw them out altogether and have our athletes
compete not on the basis of their natural abilities but on the basis of who
has the best pharmacologist. I'd rather watch and participate in competitions of the old-fashioned kind.

Biotech Tyranny: Banning Enhancement
Would Be Massively Invasive

Gregory Stock

23 I have no problem with attempts to address serious externalities that arise
from otherwise harmless personal activities. But if government does not
bear a heavy burden of proof when justifying such intrusions into our lives,
it can employ vague arguments about social harm to take away our basic
freedoms. Francis Fukuyama would push us toward just such intrusions by
erecting a powerful regulatory structure charged with ensuring the ethical
and social desirability of future technologies.

24   Fukuyama is so suspicious of change in general and new technology in
particular that he won't even acknowledge the desirability of allowing people to use safe and beneficial interventions that would almost certainly improve their lives. He will admit only that if a technology is "safe, cheap,
effective, and highly desirable," government "*probably* [my emphasis]
should not try" to stop it. If he won't even embrace technologies that meet
this high threshold, he would never allow the far more problematic possibilities of the real world. But facing such possibilities is precisely what has
improved our health and raised our standard of living so greatly during the
last century.

25   Fukuyama speaks of safety, but his reluctance about even safe and
highly desirable technologies suggests that his major concern is neither
safety nor aberrant misuse. Moreover, he admits that these dangers are well
covered by existing agencies and institutions. He makes his primary focus
explicit in his book when he complains that the Food and Drug Administra-

tion is charged only with establishing "safety and efficacy," while we need institutions that can look at ethical consequences.

For the most part, Fukuyama is vague when it comes to precisely what 26 we should prevent. This may be good strategy, because notions of safety, caution, and minimized externalities are so appealing. But it is deceptive because it is in the details that the rubber meets the road.

In fairness, Fukuyama is specific about banning human cloning, which 27 in today's climate is about as risky as coming out for motherhood. His reasoning here is faulty, however. To liken a blanket ban on reproductive cloning to a ban on incest is not even fathomable if one considers the cloning of a deceased child or someone other than the parent. But as I said, cloning is a sideshow.

A more interesting situation is sex selection. I argued that in the U.S. 28 such selection—which can be done by sorting sperm, so that no embryos are destroyed—is innocuous. Sex selection does not harm children; indeed, it likely benefits them when a child of the "wrong" sex would seriously disappoint his or her parents. Fukuyama brings up the lopsided sex ratio in China, but this does not justify regulating the practice here, where such imbalances do not arise from the practice. Moreover, the problem in China is hardly an argument for government regulation, since sex selection there has long been illegal. Indeed, government regulation in China—namely, its one-child policy—exacerbates the problem of gender balance by pushing parents who want a boy toward aborting a girl, since they can't try again. Fukuyama opposes sex selection here and has proposed the formation of a review board like the one in Britain that has barred this procedure. But does he have anything better to offer than a fear that the practice would be a step down a slippery slope? If he sees a serious externality to sex selection in the U.S., it would be worth hearing about.

In response to my comments about the obvious appeal and benefit of 29 future anti-aging medications, Fukuyama points out that "negative externalities can arise from individual choices to . . . prolong life at the cost of a lower level of cognitive and physical functioning." This is true, but it is a frightening basis for legislation (as opposed to decisions regarding government funding). I shudder to think about regulatory boards tasked with balancing the additional years that an individual seeks against the social cost of those years. To see the peril, we need only apply Fukuyama's logic to medicine generally.

If he does not want to allow interventions to slow the onset of aging 30 and bring longer lives of relative health (though presumably not matching the vitality of youth), then why not block all treatments for the aged and debilitated? Their extra years are a net cost, and withholding medical treatment for those over 65 would work wonders for our ailing Social Security system. It isn't much of a step to go even further and block medical interventions that save accident victims who suffer crippling injuries.

Fukuyama no doubt feels that a sharp line between therapy and en- 31 hancement will avoid such perversions, but this distinction does not stand up to scrutiny. This line will increasingly blur in the years ahead. Anti-aging

interventions, for example, fall in a large realm that is best labeled therapeutic enhancement. If we could gain an extra decade by strengthening our
immune system or our anti-oxidation and cellular repair mechanisms, this
would clearly be a human enhancement. But it would also be a preventive
therapy, because it would delay cardiovascular disease, senile dementia, cancer, and other illnesses of aging, which we spend billions trying to treat.

32   Banning enhancement from sports competitions can obviously be justified as a way of enforcing the agreed-upon rules of the game. But neither
Fukuyama nor our democratic political institutions have a recognized right
to set the rules of life. Outlawing a whole realm of benefits that are not injur-
ing others is not just impractical; it is tyranny. Enhancement is not wrong,
and when such possibilities become safe and reliable large numbers of people will seek them. Fukuyama is right about the ambiguities of "improvement," but I have not suggested some grandiose government project that
seeks human perfection. I have spoken only of freely made parental choices,
and I argue that such choices are likely to lead toward great diversity.

33   I do not argue that parents need no oversight in the use of advanced
technology for the conception of children, just that it should be minimal,
should address real rather than imagined problems, and should be concerned
with the child's safety rather than the social order or the personhood of embryos. When it comes to children, I trust the judgment of individual parents
more than that of political or judicial panels. Most parents are deeply concerned about the welfare of their own children, whereas such panels are composed of individuals who are more oriented toward larger social and
philosophical concerns than the well-being of particular individuals.

Upholding Norms: Our Laws Should Be Updated to Take Account of Technological Advances

Francis Fukuyama

34 I think Greg Stock has misunderstood a couple of the points I was trying to
make in my initial response. The issue with regard to sex selection is not that
it would be a serious problem in this country; it's possible now, after all, but
not widely practiced. The point is that individual choice coupled with the
spread of cheap biomedical technologies can quickly produce population-
level effects with serious social consequences. In other words, the problem
with eugenics is not simply that it is state-sponsored and coercive; if practiced by enough individuals, it can also have negative consequences for the
broader society.

35   I suspect that if the U.S. ever gets into something like this in the future,
it will have to do with potential "enhancement" targets other than sex. One
I speculate about in my book is sexual preference: It seems pretty clear to
me that if parents, including ones who are perfectly accepting of gays today,
had the choice, they would select against their children being gay, if for no
other reason than their desire to have grandchildren. (Contrary to Stock, by
the way, gays can't reproduce, so I'm not quite sure how they'd do germ-

line intervention to produce gay children.) The proportion of gays in the population could drop quite dramatically, and I'm not at all sure that society as a whole (let alone gays as a persecuted minority) would be enhanced as a result.

Governments can intervene successfully to correct individual choices 36 like these. The severe sex-ratio imbalance in Korea that emerged in the early 1990s was noticed, and the government took measures to enforce existing laws against sex selection so that today the ratio is much closer to 50-50. If the government of a young democracy like Korea can do this, I don't see why we can't.

The reason I noted that life extension coupled with diminished capabil- 37 ity can create negative externalities was not to suggest that we should ban or regulate such procedures. Stock is perfectly right that we already have adopted a lot of medical innovations that produce this tradeoff, and that we can't stop future advances for this reason. The reason this is an important issue is that in contemporary debates over stem cells and cloning there is an unquestioned assumption that anything that will prolong life or cure disease is obviously desirable and automatically trumps other ethical concerns.

This is not obvious to me. Anyone who has walked around a nursing 38 home recently (as I have) can see that past advances in biomedicine have created a horrible situation for many elderly people who can't function at anything close to the levels they'd like but who also can't die. Of course, new advances in biotechnology may provide cures for degenerative, age-related diseases such as Alzheimer's or Parkinson's, but the research community is in effect just cleaning up the mess it created. So when we are balancing near-term rights and wrongs, the argument that more medical advance is necessarily good needs to be treated with some skepticism. At the hearing on Florida Republican Dave Weldon's bill banning cloning last summer, a representative of a patients advocacy group said the baby boomers were getting older and desperately needed cures for a variety of diseases with which they would soon be afflicted—as if research cloning would prevent them from ever having to die. If you want a real nightmare scenario, consider one in which we double life spans but increase periods of debility by a few decades.

Stock is correct in saying that much of my interest in having new regu- 39 latory institutions in place has to do with ethical and social consequences of new technology and not simply safety. States intervene all the time to shape norms and produce certain social outcomes. Incest is an example, and it seems to me a very apt analogy to reproductive cloning. Of course, you can find sympathetic situations where an individual might want to clone, say, a dead child. But you can also find sympathetic situations where you might want a brother and sister to marry and have children (e.g., they have grown up apart, have no dangerous recessive genes, etc.).

But the fact that there are certain sympathetic cases does not mean that 40 society would be better off without a ban on incest. The possible benefits of cloning need to be balanced against social harms. Consider the following scenario: A wife decides to clone herself because a couple cannot otherwise have children. As their daughter grows up to be a teenager, the husband will find his wife growing older and less sexually attractive. In the meantime, his daughter, who will be a physical duplicate of her mother, will blossom into sexual maturity and increasingly come to resemble the younger woman the husband fell in love with and married. It is hard to see how this situation would not produce an extremely unhealthy situation within the family; in a certain number of cases, it would lead to incest.

41   Stock is using a rhetorical ploy in suggesting that I am recommending new, tyrannical government intrusion into private lives. Rather, I am recommending an extension of existing institutions to take account of the new possibilities that will be put before us as a result of technological advance. This may result in regulation irksome to industry and to certain individuals, but it will be no more tyrannical than existing rules banning incest or, in the case of the Koreans, banning sex selection. All societies control social behavior through a complex web of norms, economic incentives, and laws. All I am suggesting is that the law part of the mix will need to be updated and strengthened in light of what is to come.

Clones, Gays, and the Elderly: Overestimating the Threats Posed by Technology—and Underestimating the Threats Posed by Regulation

Gregory Stock

42   I'm glad Francis Fukuyama agrees that sex selection here poses no serious threat. To me, this means it should not be regulated. Moreover, we should also hold off on passing legislative protections against other such technologies until actual problems show up. Fukuyama may worry about rapid "population-level effects with serious social consequences," but his example of Korea's success at handling the sex-ratio imbalances that arose there is not an invitation to regulate, but evidence that we can afford to wait.

43   Outlawing a whole realm of benefits not injurious to others—namely enhancements—would be tyranny. Potent regulatory structures that pass judgment on the morality and social cost of *future* technologies would move us in this direction. Judging from the composition of President Bush's Bioethics Advisory Commission, many potential regulators would be less moderate than Fukuyama and quite willing to abridge people's choices.

44   Consider Fukuyama's argument about cloning. It is one thing to worry about the obvious medical dangers of so unproven a technology, another to justify a complete ban with stories about a future father's possible sexual attraction for his wife's budding clone-daughter. Kids hardly need to resemble a parent to inspire incest, as many adoptees and stepchildren can no doubt confirm. If we start regulating families on the basis of hypothetical sexual attractions and perversions—and we can conjure ones more lurid and likely than Fukuyama's clone love—we will ultimately damage rather than protect the family. We have laws governing child abuse; let's content ourselves with enforcing them.

As to gays, if there are fewer in the future because of people's choices 45 about the genetics or rearing of their kids, so be it. But I am not at all convinced it would play out that way. Fukuyama asserts that gays can't reproduce, but they do so all the time using donor eggs or sperm, surrogate mothers, and partners of the opposite sex. Moreover, such reproduction will get ever easier. If we want to be sure to maintain our gay population, additional AIDS research would accomplish more than bans on embryo screening.

I'm glad to hear that Fukuyama doesn't oppose anti-aging interventions; 46 I've previously heard him say only that government would be unable to block such enhancements. He is right, of course, that advances in health care bring many challenges, and that the needless prolongation of a dying loved one's pain and decrepitude is nothing to boast about. But my reaction is not to deny the value of the good added years that modern medicine has brought so many of us, but to recognize that we must find better ways for individuals to reach death with dignity when it draws near. Why must so many of our elderly try to squirrel away a stash of lethal drugs in case they might be captured by a medical system that would torture them for their final few weeks or months? The issue of cloning pales alongside this cruelty.

Fukuyama says he is urging only a harmless extension of existing insti- 47 tutions. I disagree. The relegation of decisions about human reproduction to a political process typically driven by impassioned zealots on either side would invite disaster. New agencies with the power to project abstract philosophy, social theory, and even religious dogma into family life would be a frightening development. And when lawmakers on Capital Hill start telling medical researchers not to do certain types of embryonic stem cell research because adult stem cells will work just as well, something is very wrong. These legislators are micromanaging a realm they do not understand, assaulting our freedom of inquiry, and ignoring the entreaties of those afflicted with serious diseases. These steps are not small.

Nietzschean Endgame: Self-enhancement and "Immense Wars of the Spirit"

Francis Fukuyama

I think that one of the great virtues of Greg Stock's book is that he is willing 48 to take some risks in predicting what kinds of changes might be in store in the long-run future in terms of enhancement technology. Most people in the scientific community are not willing to speculate out beyond the next five to 10 years. I urge people to read the last chapter of *Redesigning Humans* if you want to understand why I'm worried about biotechnology.

There, Stock suggests a number of things that might happen in a future 49 world in which various forms of enhancement become safe, effective, and inexpensive. Among other things, he suggests that reproduction via sex may disappear altogether as a result of the difficulties of handling artificial chromosomes in vivo. Reproduction could not happen outside a lab. We could freely alter our personalities and moods through a combination of drugs and genetics.

50   But most importantly, the human race disappears. He suggests that there will be differentiation within our species, and, in effect, new speciation. Some groups of people may decide to enhance their children for musical ability, some for athletic prowess, others for math or literary ability. There will be a basic social divide between the enhanced and the unenhanced, and in the competitive situation that will emerge, it will be difficult for people not to join into this genetic arms race. Moreover, genetic differentiation will become a cornerstone of international politics. If we and the Germans decide not to take part, the Chinese will charge ahead with self-enhancement, and then we as a nation will be challenged to follow suit.

51   What I don't understand is why anyone thinks that in this kind of world—one in which the existing genetic homogeneity of the human race is being undermined—we will be able to continue to live within the nice, liberal democratic framework that we currently enjoy. Stock argues as if we can presume the continuity of that political world and fully enjoy the technological paradise opening before us, and that the biggest arguments we will have will concern whether we have a little more regulation and less progress, or the reverse.

52   But as I noted earlier, in this kind of world Nietzsche is the best guide to what politics will be like. What is going to happen to equality of opportunity when a non-musically enhanced child aspires to be a musician, which has become not just the territory of a guild of musicians, but of a subspecies of musicians whose total genetic identity is tied up in that form of life? Why shouldn't the enhanced start demanding superior political rights for themselves, and seek to dominate the unenhanced, since they will in fact be superior not just as a result of acquired social status and education, but of genetic enhancements as well? What is going to happen to international conflict, when other, hostile societies are not just culturally different, but not fully human either?

53   The fact is that there will be no theoretical or practical reason at that point not to abandon the principle of universal human equality (i.e., the one enshrined in the Declaration of Independence). It is strongly believed in today in part as a matter of faith, but also in part because it is empirically supported. When the principle was enunciated in 1776, blacks and women were not granted political rights in North America because it was believed that they were too stupid, or too emotional, or otherwise lacking in some essential human characteristic to be granted equal rights. This view resurfaced as scientific racism in the early 20th century, and one of the great achievements of our time is that both the empirical doctrine and the politics built on it have been discredited.

54   So if we are going to embrace this technology and the prospect of human self-enhancement, we ought to do it with our eyes open. We should say, with Nietzsche, that this is a wonderful opportunity because we can finally transcend liberal democracy, and reestablish the possibility of natural aristocracy, of social hierarchy, of the pathos of distance (i.e., the inability to empathize with the suffering of others), and otherwise usher in an era of "immense wars of the spirit."

55   As I said, I'm grateful that Greg Stock has clarified all of these issues for us.

Rhetorical Considerations

1. In your own words, state as clearly as you can the positions of Stock and Fukuyama on cloning and biomedical research. (*Hodges'* 32c/*Writer's* 2b)
2. How would you generalize Stock's philosophy? Fukuyama's?
3. Examine transitional devices used in any six pairs of paragraphs. (*Hodges'* 31d/*Writer's* 3d)
4. Trace shifts in tone from one entry to the next. Are there any examples of humor? Do the participants ever appear to be angry? Do they resort to any personal attacks? (*Hodges'* 27d/*Writer's* 3d)
5. Cause and effect is an important expository tool in a topic like this. Examine the causes and effects outlined by both Stock and Fukuyama. (*Hodges'* 32e/*Writer's* 2e)
6. Look for examples of the writers responding specifically to comments made in previous posts. How do they handle the ideas raised? Do they always refute them effectively? (*Hodges'* 36c/*Writer's* 7c)
7. Can you find any examples of one writer mischaracterizing or misunderstanding the other? Can you find any examples of one writer deliberately distorting the words of the other?

Language and Style

1. Look up the following words in your dictionary: *viable* (paragraph 1); *proxy* (paragraph 2); *deleterious* (paragraph 5); *relegated* (paragraph 6); *innocuous* (paragraphs 7 and 28); *utilitarian* (paragraph 14); *eugenics* and *coercive* (paragraph 34). (*Hodges'* 18e/*Writer's* 28e)
2. Find examples of descriptive words that reveal Stock's and Fukuyama's biases.
3. There are certain words that both writers pay considerable attention to in terms of their meanings and implications. Find three of those words and compare the two interpretations.
4. Why is *has* used instead of *have* in the first sentence of paragraph 1? (*Hodges'* 6a/*Writer's* 22e)
5. Explain Fukuyama's use of the colon in paragraph 12. (*Hodges'* 17d/*Writer's* 35d)
6. Are the correlatives parallel in the first sentence of paragraph 25? (*Hodges'* 26/*Writer's* 25)

Writing Suggestions

1. Write a response to the exchange between Stock and Fukuyama, offering your own analysis of the cloning controversy.
2. Choose a partner in class, then each of you choose a stance on a relatively controversial topic. Conduct a similar exchange over the period of a week online (via email or a discussion forum that may be provided in your class).

◆

IMAGES

Argument

The images here in some way concern war. The first, *Guernica* by Pablo Picasso (1881–1973), is widely considered to be one of the most powerful anti-war images. Picasso completed his now-famous painting in 1937 in response to a particularly brutal attack on a small civilian town by Generalissimo Francisco Franco during the Spanish civil war. When photographs of the massacre were published in Parisian newspapers, Picasso responded with this painting. The second image is a poster from the early days of the Forest Fire Prevention campaign. In 1942, a Japanese submarine that surfaced near the coast of southern California fired at an oil field near Los Padres National Forest. The campaign was then able to link the war effort to the prevention of wildfires.

Pablo Picasso, *Guernica*, 1937

Rhetorical Considerations

1. In *Guernica*, what effect does Picasso's choice of black, white and grey rather than color have on the spectator?
2. Look closely at the images that make up *Guernica* to see how many objects, people, and creatures you can identify. When you observe these details, does the painting have a different effect on you than it did when you first glanced at it? Why or why not? (*Hodges'* 3c/*Writer's* 2d)

U.S. Dept. of Agriculture Forest Service, 1942

3. Who are the people in the fire prevention poster? Can you identify their nationalities? Why are these particular images portrayed here?
4. How much of each image's argument relies on logic and how much on emotional responses? (*Hodges'* 35/*Writer's* 1d)
5. How much textual explanation of these images is required for a full understanding of their significance?

✦

IMAGES (CONT.)

Argument

Writing Suggestions

1. Look for similar images linked to the concepts of going to war or avoiding war. You may want to look at current publications, or you may wish to research publications from the time of a previous war. Write an essay in which you explore how the images communicate their ideas.
2. Find images that argue on different sides of an issue (for example, a billboard by Mothers Against Drunk Driving and an advertisement for beer) and write an essay examining how they make their point. Which one is more successful? How could the less successful one become more appealing?

CHAPTER 10

For Further Reading: Classic Essays and Images

◆

THE ALLEGORY OF THE CAVE

Plato

Born in Athens, Greece, c. 428 B.C.E., Plato was a philosopher during the pinnacle of classical Greek civilization. He was a follower of Socrates and taught Aristotle. Plato's work is preserved in his *Dialogues,* which use the persona of Socrates as the main character in each argument. *The Republic,* from which this excerpt derives, is one of his most famous writings and discusses the construction of an ideal state.

SOCRATES, GLAUCON. The den, the prisoners: the light at a distance;

And now, I said, let me show in a figure how far our nature is enlightened or unenlightened:—Behold! Human beings living in an underground den, which has a mouth open towards the light and reaching all along the den; here they have been from their childhood, and have their legs and necks chained so that they cannot move, and can only see before them, being prevented by the chains from turning round their heads. Above and behind them a fire is blazing at a distance, and between the fire and the prisoners there is a raised way; and you will see, if you look, a low wall built along the way, like the screen which marionette players have in front of them, over which they show the puppets. 1

I see. 2

the low wall, and the moving figures of which the shadows are seen on the opposite wall of the den.

And do you see, I said, men passing along the wall carrying all sorts of vessels, and statues and figures of animals made of wood and stone and various materials, which appear over the wall? Some of them are talking, others silent. 3

You have shown me a strange image, and they are strange prisoners. 4

5   Like ourselves, I replied; and they see only their own shadows, or the shadows of one another, which the fire throws on the opposite wall of the cave?

6   True, he said: how could they see anything but the shadows if they were never allowed to move their heads?

7   And of the objects which are being carried in like manner they would only see the shadows?

8   Yes, he said.

9   And if they were able to converse with one another, would they not suppose that they were naming what was actually before them?

10   Very true.

11   And suppose further that the prison had an echo which came from the other side, would they not be sure to fancy when one of the passers-by spoke that the voice which they heard came from the passing shadow?   The prisoners would mistake the shadows for realities.

12   No question, he replied.

13   To them, I said, the truth would be literally nothing but the shadows of the images.

14   That is certain.

15   And now look again, and see what will naturally follow if the prisoners are released and disabused of their error. At first, when any of them is liberated and compelled suddenly to stand up and turn his neck round and walk and look towards the light, he will suffer sharp pains; the glare will distress him, and he will be unable to see the realities of which in his former state he had seen the shadows; and then conceive some one saying to him, that what he saw before was an illusion, but that now, when he is approaching nearer to being and his eye is turned towards more real existence, he has a clearer vision—what will be his reply? And you may further imagine that his instructor is pointing to the objects as they pass and requiring him to name them,—will he not be perplexed? Will he not fancy that the shadows which he formerly saw are truer than the objects which are now shown to him?   And when released, they would still persist in maintaining the superior truth of the shadows.

16   Far truer.

17   And if he is compelled to look straight at the light, will he not have a pain in his eyes which will make him turn away to take refuge in the objects of vision which he can see, and which he will conceive to be in reality clearer than the things which are now being shown to him?

18   True, he said.

19   And suppose once more, that he is reluctantly dragged up a steep and rugged ascent, and held fast until he is forced into the presence of the sun himself, is he not likely to be pained and irritated? When he approaches the light his eyes will be   When dragged upwards, they would be dazzled by excess of light.

dazzled, and he will not be able to see anything at all of what are now called realities.

Not all in a moment, he said.   20

He will require to grow accustomed to the sight of the upper 21 world. And first he will see the shadows best, next the reflections of men and other objects in the water, and then the objects themselves; then he will gaze upon the light of the moon and the stars and the spangled heaven; and he will see the sky and the stars by night better than the sun or the light of the sun by day?

Certainly.   22

At length they will see the sun and understand his nature.

Last of all he will be able to see the sun, and not mere re- 23 flections of him in the water, but he will see him in his own proper place, and not in another, and he will contemplate him as he is.

Certainly.   24

He will then proceed to argue that this is he who gives the 25 season and the years, and is the guardian of all that is in the visible world, and in a certain way the cause of all things which he and his fellows have been accustomed to behold?

Clearly, he said, he would first see the sun and then reason 26 about him.

They would then pity their old companions of the den.

And when he remembered his old habitation, and the wis- 27 dom of the den and his fellow prisoners, do you not suppose that he would felicitate himself on the change, and pity them?

Certainly, he would.   28

And if they were in the habit of conferring honors among 29 themselves on those who were quickest to observe the passing shadows and to remark which of them went before, and which followed after, and which were together; and who were therefore best able to draw conclusions as to the future, do you think that he would care for such honors and glories, or envy the possessors of them? Would he not say with Homer,

> Better to be the poor servant of a poor master,

and to endure anything, rather than think as they do and live after their manner?

Yes, he said, I think that he would rather suffer anything 30 than entertain these false notions and live in this miserable manner.

Imagine once more, I said, such a one coming suddenly out 31 of the sun to be replaced in his old situation; would he not be certain to have his eyes full of darkness?

To be sure, he said.   32

And if there were a contest, and he had to compete in mea- 33 suring the shadows with the prisoners who had never moved

out of the den, while his sight was still weak, and before his
eyes had become steady (and the time which would be needed
to acquire this new habit of sight might be very considerable),
would he not be ridiculous? Men would say of him that up he
went and down he came without his eyes; and that it was better not even to think of ascending; and if any one tried to
loose another and lead him up to the light, let them only catch
the offender, and they would put him to death.

But when they
returned to the
den they would
see much worse
than those who
had never left it.

34   No question, he said.

35   This entire allegory, I said, you may now append, dear Glaucon, to the previous argument; the prison house is the world of
sight, the light of the fire is the sun, and you will not misappre-
hend me if you interpret the journey upwards to be the ascent
of the soul into the intellectual world according to my poor belief, which, at your desire, I have expressed—whether rightly or
wrongly God knows. But, whether true or false, my opinion is
that in the world of knowledge the idea of good appears last of
all, and is seen only with an effort; and, when seen, is also inferred to be the universal author of all things beautiful and
right, parent of light and of the lord of light in this visible world,
and the immediate source of reason and truth in the intellectual; and that this is the power upon which he who would act
rationally either in public or private life must have his eye fixed.

The prison is the
world of sight, the
light of the fire is
the sun.

36   I agree, he said, as far as I am able to understand you.

37   Moreover, I said, you must not wonder that those who attain to this beatific vision are unwilling to descend to human
affairs; for their souls are ever hastening into the upper world
where they desire to dwell; which desire of theirs is very natural, if our allegory may be trusted.

38   Yes, very natural.

39   And is there anything surprising in one who passes from
divine contemplations to the evil state of man, misbehaving
himself in a ridiculous manner; if, while his eyes are blinking
and before he has become accustomed to the surrounding
darkness, he is compelled to fight in courts of law, or in other
places, about the images or the shadows of images of justice,
and is endeavoring to meet the conceptions of those who have
never yet seen absolute justice?

Nothing
extraordinary in
the philosopher
being unable to see
in the dark.

40   Anything but surprising, he replied.

41   Anyone who has common sense will remember that the be-
wilderments of the eyes are of two kinds, and arise from two
causes, either from coming out of the light or from going into
the light, which is true of the mind's eye, quite as much as of
the bodily eye; and he who remembers this when he sees anyone whose vision is perplexed and weak, will not be too ready
to laugh; he will first ask whether that soul of man has come out
of the brighter life, and is unable to see because unaccustomed

The eyes may be
blinded in two
ways, by excess or
by defect of light.

to the dark, or having turned from darkness to the day is dazzled by excess of light. And he will count the one happy in his
condition and state of being, and he will pity the other; or, if
he have a mind to laugh at the soul which comes from below
into the light, there will be more reason in this than in the
laugh which greets him who returns from above out of the
light into the den.

That, he said, is a very just distinction.   42

But then, if I am right, certain professors of education must   43
be wrong when they say that they can put a knowledge into
the soul which was not there before, like sight into blind eyes.

The conversion of the soul is the turning round the eye from darkness to light.

They undoubtedly say this, he replied.   44

Whereas, our argument shows that the power and capacity   45
of learning exists in the soul already; and that just as the eye
was unable to turn from darkness to light without the whole
body, so too the instrument of knowledge can only by the
movement of the whole soul be turned from the world of becoming into that of being, and learn by degrees to endure the
sight of being, and of the brightest and best of being, or in
other words, of the good.

Very true.   46

And must there not be some art which will effect conver-   47
sion in the easiest and quickest manner; not implanting the
faculty of sight, for that exists already, but has been turned in
the wrong direction, and is looking away from the truth?

Yes, he said, such an art may be presumed.   48

The virtue of wisdom has a divine power which may be turned either towards good or towards evil.

And whereas the other so-called virtues of the soul seem to   49
be akin to bodily qualities, for even when they are not originally innate they can be implanted later by habit and exercise,
the virtue of wisdom more than anything else contains a divine element which always remains, and by this conversion is
rendered useful and profitable; or, on the other hand, hurtful
and useless. Did you never observe the narrow intelligence
flashing from the keen eye of a clever rogue—how eager he is,
how clearly his paltry soul sees the way to his end; he is the reverse of blind, but his keen eyesight is forced into the service
of evil, and he is mischievous in proportion to his cleverness?

Very true, he said.   50

But what if there had been a circumcision of such natures   51
in the days of their youth; and they had been severed from
those sensual pleasures, such as eating and drinking, which,
like leaden weights, were attached to them at their birth, and
which drag them down and turn the vision of their souls upon
the things that are below—if, I say, they had been released
from these impediments and turned in the opposite direction,
the very same faculty in them would have seen the truth as
keenly as they see what their eyes are turned to now.

52   Very likely.

53   Yes, I said; and there is another thing which is likely, or rather a necessary inference from what has preceded, that neither the uneducated and uninformed of the truth, nor yet those who never make an end of their education, will be able ministers of State; not the former, because they have no single aim of duty which is the rule of all their actions, private as well as public; nor the latter, because they will not act at all except upon compulsion, fancying that they are already dwelling apart in the islands of the blessed.

Neither the uneducated nor the overeducated will be good servants of the State.

54   Very true, he replied.

55   Then, I said, the business of us who are the founders of the State will be to compel the best minds to attain that knowledge which we have already shown to be the greatest of all—they must continue to ascend until they arrive at the good; but when they have ascended and seen enough we must not allow them to do as they do now.

56   What do you mean?

57   I mean that they remain in the upper world: but this must not be allowed; they must be made to descend again among the prisoners in the den, to partake of their labors and honors, whether they are worth having or not.

Men should ascend to the upper world, but they should also return to the lower.

58   But is not this unjust? he said; ought we to give them a worse life, when they might have a better?

59   You have again forgotten, my friend, I said, the intention of the legislator, who did not aim at making any one class in the State happy above the rest; the happiness was to be in the whole State, and he held the citizens together by persuasion and necessity, making them benefactors of the State, and therefore benefactors of one another; to this end he created them, not to please themselves, but to be his instruments in binding up the State,

60   True, he said, I had forgotten.

61   Observe, Glaucon, that there will be no more injustice in compelling our philosophers to have a care and providence of others; we shall explain to them that in other States, men of their class are not obliged to share in the toils of politics: and this is reasonable, for they grow up at their own sweet will, and the government would rather not have them. Being self-taught, they cannot be expected to show any gratitude for a culture which they have never received. But we have brought you into the world to be rulers of the hive, kings of yourselves and of the other citizens, and have educated you far better and more perfectly than they have been educated, and you are better able to share in the double duty. Wherefore each of you, when his turn comes, must go down to the general underground abode, and get the habit of seeing in the dark. When

The duties of the philosophers.

Their obligations to their country will induce them to take part in her government.

you have acquired the habit, you will see ten thousand times better than the inhabitants of the den, and you will know what the several images are, and what they represent, because you have seen the beautiful and just and good in their truth. And thus our State, which is also yours, will be a reality, and not a dream only, and will be administered in a spirit unlike that of other States, in which men fight with one another about shadows only and are distracted in the struggle for power, which in their eyes is a great good. Whereas the truth is that the State in which the rulers are most reluctant to govern is always the best and most quietly governed, and State in which they are most eager, the worst.

Quite true, he replied. 62

And will our pupils, when they hear this, refuse to take their 63 turn at the toils of State, when they are allowed to spend the greater part of their time with one another in the heavenly light?

They will be willing but not anxious to rule.

Impossible, he answered; for they are just men, and the 64 commands which we impose upon them are just; there can be no doubt that every one of them will take office as a stern necessity, and not after the fashion of our present rulers of State.

The statesman must be provided with a better life than that of a ruler; and then he will not covet office.

Yes, my friend, I said; and there lies the point. You must 65 contrive for your future rulers another and a better life than that of a ruler, and then you may have a well-ordered State; for only in the State which offers this, will they rule who are truly rich, not in silver and gold, but in virtue and wisdom, which are the true blessings of life. Whereas if they go to the administration of public affairs, poor and hungering after their own private advantage, thinking that hence they are to snatch the chief good, order there can never be; for they will be fighting about office, and the civil and domestic broils which thus arise will be the ruin of the rulers themselves and of the whole State.

Most true, he replied. 66

And the only life which looks down upon the life of politi- 67 cal ambition is that of true philosophy. Do you know of any other?

Indeed, I do not, he said. 68

◆

A MODEST PROPOSAL

Jonathan Swift

Clergyman, Irish patriot, critic, poet, Jonathan Swift (1667–1745) is considered by many to be the greatest satirist in the English language. Born in Ireland to English parents who had settled there, Swift spent much of his early career in London, where he wrote his first important satires, *A Tale of a Tub* and *The Battle of the Books* (both published in 1704). He became a leading writer for the Tory party and as a reward for his services was appointed Dean of St. Patrick's Cathedral in Dublin. He spent the rest of his life in that post, involving himself deeply in Irish politics. His masterpiece, *Gulliver's Travels* (1726), embodies Swift's increasing disgust with his fellow human beings. "A Modest Proposal," written in 1729, reflects his mordant view of callous British administrators and absentee landowners whose indifference to the sufferings of the Irish poor during a time of famine filled him with indignation.

For Preventing the Children of Poor People in Ireland from Being a Burden to Their Parents or Country, and for Making Them Benefecial to the Public

1 It is melancholy object to those who walk through this great town or travel in the country, when they see the streets, the roads, and cabin doors, crowded with beggars of the female-sex, followed by three, four, or six children, all in rags and importuning every passenger for an alms. These mothers, instead of being able to work for their honest livelihood, are forced to employ all their time in strolling to beg for sustenance for their helpless infants, who, as they grow up, either turn thieves for want of work, or leave their dear native country to fight for the Pretender in Spain, or sell themselves to the Barbadoes.

2   I think it is agreed by all parties that this prodigious number of children in the arms, or on the backs, or at the heels of their mothers, and frequently of their fathers, is in the present deplorable state of the kingdom a very great additional grievance; and therefore whoever could find out a fair, cheap, and easy method of making these children sound, useful members of the commonwealth would deserve so well of the public as to have his statue set up for a preserver of the nation.

3   But my intention is very far from being confined to provide only for the children of professed beggars; it is of a much greater extent, and shall take in the whole number of infants at a certain age who are born of parents in effects as little able to support them as those who demand our charity in the streets.

       As to my own part, having turned my thoughts for many years upon
4 this important subject, and maturely weighed the several schemes of other

projectors, I always found them grossly mistaken in their computation. It is true, a child just dropped from its dam may be supported by her milk for a solar year, with little other nourishment; at most not above the value of two shillings, which the mother may certainly get, or the value in scraps, by her lawful occupation of begging; and it is exactly at one year old that I propose to provide for them in such a manner as instead of being a charge upon their parents or a parish, or wanting food and raiment for the rest of their lives, they shall on the contrary contribute to the feeding, and partly to the clothing, of many thousands.

There is likewise another great advantage in my scheme, that it will pre- 5 vent those voluntary abortions, and that horrid practice of women murdering their bastard children, alas, too frequent among us, sacrificing the poor innocent babes, I doubt, more to avoid the expense than the shame, which would move tears and pity in the most savage and inhuman breast.

The number of souls in this kingdom being usually reckoned one mil- 6 lion and a half, of these I calculate there may be about two hundred thousand couple whose wives are breeders; from which number I subtract thirty thousand couple who are able to maintain their own children, although I apprehend there cannot be so many under the present distresses of the kingdom; but this being granted, there will remain an hundred and seventy thousand breeders. I again subtract fifty thousand for those women who miscarry, or whose children die by accident or disease within the year. There only remain an hundred and twenty thousand children of poor parents annually born. The question therefore is, how this number shall be reared and provided for, which, as I have already said, under the present situation of affairs, is utterly impossible by all the methods hitherto proposed. For we can neither employ them in handicraft or agriculture; we neither build houses (I mean in the country) nor cultivate land. They can very seldom pick up a livelihood by stealing till they arrive at six years old, except where they are of towardly parts; although I confess they learn the rudiments much earlier, during which time they can however be looked upon only as probationers, as I have been informed by a principal gentleman in the county of Cavan, who protested to me that he never knew above one or two instances under the age of six, even in a part of the kingdom so renowned for the quickest proficiency in that art.

I am assured by our merchants that a boy or a girl before twelve years 7 old is no salable commodity; and even when they come to this age they will not yield above three pounds, or three pounds and half a crown at most on the Exchange; which cannot turn to account either to the parents or the kingdom, the charge of nutriment and rags having been at least four times that value.

I shall now therefore humbly propose my own thoughts, which I hope 8 will not be liable to the least objection.

I have been assured by a very knowing American of my acquaintance in 9 London, that a young healthy child well nursed is at a year old a most delicious, nourishing, and wholesome food, whether stewed, roasted, baked, or boiled; and I make no doubt that it will equally serve in a fricasse or a ragout.

10   I do therefore humbly offer it to public consideration that of the hundred and twenty thousand children, already computed, twenty thousand may be reserved for breed, whereof only one fourth part to be males, which is more than we allow to sheep, black cattle, or swine; and my reason is that these children are seldom the fruits of marriage, a circumstance not much regarded by our savages, therefore one male will be sufficient to serve four females. That the remaining hundred thousand may at a year old be offered in sale to the persons of quality and fortune through the kingdom, always advising the mother to let them suck plentifully in the last month, so as to render them plump and fat for a good table. A child will make two dishes at an entertainment for friends; and when the family dines alone, the fore or hind quarters will make a reasonable dish, and seasoned with a little pepper or salt will be very good boiled on the fourth day, especially in winter.

11   I have reckoned upon a medium that a child just born will weigh twelve pounds, and in a solar year if tolerably nursed increased to twenty-eight pounds.

12   I grant this food will be somewhat dear, and therefore very proper for landlords, who, as they have already devoured most of the parents, seem to have the best title to the children.

13   Infant's flesh will be in season throughout the year, but more plentiful in March, and a little before and after. For we are told by a grave author, an eminent French physician, that fish being a prolific diet, there are more children born in Roman Catholic countries about nine months after Lent than at any other season; therefore, reckoning a year after Lent, the markets will be more glutted than usual, because the number of popish infants is at least three to one in this kingdom; and therefore it will have one other collateral advantage, by lessening the number of Papists among us.

14   I have already computed the charge of nursing a beggar's child (in which list I reckon all cottagers, laborers, and four fifths of the farmers) to be about two shillings per annum, rags included; and I believe no gentleman would repine to give ten shillings for the carcass of a good fat child, which, as I have said, will make four dishes of excellent nutritive meat, when he hath only some particular friend or his own family to dine with him. Thus the squire will learn to be a good landlord, and grow popular among the tenants; the mother will have eight shillings net profit, and be fit for work till she produces another child.

15   Those who are more thrifty (as I must confess the times require) may flay the carcass; the skin of which artificially dressed will make admirable gloves for ladies, and summer boots for fine gentlemen.

16   As to our city of Dublin, shambles may be appointed for this purpose in the most convenient parts of it, and butchers we may be assured will not be wanting; although I rather recommend buying the children alive, and dressing them hot from the knife as we do roasting pigs.

17   A very worthy person, a true lover of his country, and whose virtues I highly esteem, was lately pleased in discoursing on this matter to offer a refinement upon my scheme. He said that many gentlemen of this kingdom,

having of late destroyed their deer, he conceived that the want of venison might be well supplied by the bodies of young lads and maidens, not exceeding fourteen years of age nor under twelve, so great a number of both sexes in every county being now ready to starve for want of work and service; and these to be disposed of by their parents, if alive, or otherwise by their nearest relations. But with due deference to so excellent a friend and so deserving a patriot, I cannot be altogether in his sentiments; for as to the males, my American acquaintance assured me from frequent experiences that their flesh was generally tough and lean, like that of our schoolboys, by continual exercise, and their taste disagreeable; and to fatten them would not answer the charge. Then as to the females, it would, I think with humble submission, be a loss to the public, because they soon would become breeders themselves: and besides, it is not improbable that some scrupulous people might be apt to censure such a practice (although indeed very unjustly) as a little bordering upon cruelty; which, I confess, hath always been with me the strongest objection against any project, how well soever intended.

But in order to justify my friend, he confessed that this expedient was 18 put into his head by the famous Psalmanazar, a native of the island Formosa, who came from thence to London above twenty years ago, and in conversation told my friend that in his country when any young person happened to be put to death, the executioner sold the carcass to persons of quality as a prime dainty; and that in his time the body of a plump girl of fifteen, who was crucified for an attempt to poison the emperor, was sold to his Imperial Majesty's prime minister of state , and other great mandarins of the court, in joints from the gibbet, at four hundred crowns. Neither indeed can I deny that if the same use were made of several plump young girls in this town, who without one single groat to their fortunes cannot stir abroad without a chair, and appear at the playhouse and assemblies in foreign fineries which they never will pay for, the kingdom would not be the worse.

Some persons of a desponding spirit are in great concern about that vast 19 number of poor people who are aged, diseased, or maimed, and I have been desired to employ my thoughts what course may be taken to ease the nation of so grievous an encumbrance. But I am not in the least pain upon that matter, because it is very well known that they are every day dying and rotting by cold and famine, and filth and vermin, as fast as can be reasonably expected. And as to the younger laborers, they are now in almost as hopeful a condition. They cannot get work, and consequently pine away for want of nourishment to a degree that if at any time they are accidentally hired to common labor, they have not strength to perform it; and thus the country and themselves are happily delivered from the evils to come.

I have too long disgressed, and therefore shall return to my subject. I 20 think the advantages by the proposal which I have made are obvious and many, as well as of the highest importance.

For first, as I have already observed, it would greatly lessen the number 21 of Papists, with whom we are yearly overrun, being the principal breeders of the nation as well as our most dangerous enemies; and who stay at home on purpose to deliver the kingdom to the Pretender, hoping to take their advantage by the absence of so many good Protestants, who have chosen rather to leave their country than to stay at home and pay tithes against their conscience to an Episcopal curate.

22   Secondly, the poorer tenants will have something valuable of their own, which by law may be made liable to distress, and help to pay their landlord's rent, their corn and cattle being already seized and money a thing unknown.

23   Thirdly, whereas the maintenance of an hundred thousand children, from two years old and upwards, cannot be computed at less than ten shillings a piece per annum, the nation's stock will be thereby increased fifty thousand pounds per annum, besides the profit of a new dish introduced to the tables of all gentlemen of fortune in the kingdom who have any refinement in taste. And the money will circulate among ourselves, the goods being entirely of our own growth and manufacture.

24   Fourthly, the constant breeders, besides the gain of eight shillings sterling per annum by the sale of their children, will be rid of the charge of maintaining them after the first year.

25   Fifthly, this food would likewise bring great custom to taverns, where the vintners will certainly be so prudent as to procure the best receipts for dressing it to perfection, and consequently have their houses frequented by all the fine gentlemen, who justly value themselves upon their knowledge in good eating; and a skillful cook, who understands how to oblige his guests, will contrive to make it as expensive as they please.

26   Sixthly, this would be a great inducement to marriage, which all wise nations have either encouraged by rewards or enforced by laws and penalties. It would increase the care and tenderness of mothers toward their children, when they were sure of a settlement for life to the poor babes, provided in some sort by the public, to their annual profit instead of expense. We should see an honest emulation among the married women, which of them could bring the fattest child to the market. Men would become as fond of their wives during the time of pregnancy as they are now of their mares in foal, their cows in calf, or sows when they are ready to farrow; nor offer to beat or kick them (as is too frequent a practice) for fear of a miscarriage.

27   Many other advantages might be enumerated. For instance, the addition of some thousand carcasses in our exportation of barreled beef, the propagation of swine's flesh, and improvement in the art of making good bacon, so much wanted among us by the great destruction of pigs, too frequent at our tables, which are no way comparable in taste or magnificence to a well-grown, fat, yearling child, which roasted whole will make a considerable figure at a lord mayor's feast or any other public entertainment. But this and many others I omit, being studious of brevity.

28   Supposing that one thousand families in this city would be constant customers for infants' flesh, besides others who might have it at merry meetings, particularly weddings and christenings, I compute that Dublin would take off annually about twenty thousand carcasses, and the rest of the king-

dom (where probably they will be sold somewhat cheaper) the remaining eighty thousand.

I can think of no one objection that will possibly be raised against this   29 proposal, unless it should be urged that the number of people will be thereby much lessened in the kingdom. This I freely own, and it was indeed one principal design in offering it to the world. I desire the reader will observe, that I calculate my remedy for this one individual kingdom of Ireland and for no other than that ever was, is, or I think ever can be upon earth. Therefore let no man talk to me of other expedients: of taxing our absentees at five shillings a pound: of using neither clothes nor household furniture except what is of our own growth and manufacture: of utterly rejecting the materials and instruments that promote foreign luxury: of curing the expensiveness of pride, vanity, idleness, and gaming in our women: of introducing a vein of parsimony, prudence, and temperance: of learning to love our country, in the want of which we differ even from Laplanders and the inhabitants of Topinamboo: of quitting our animosities and factions, nor acting any longer like the Jews, who were murdering one another at the very moment their city was taken: of being a little cautious not to sell our country and conscience for nothing: of teaching landlords to have at least one degree of mercy toward their tenants: lastly, of putting a spirit of honesty, industry, and skill into our shopkeepers; who, if a resolution could now be taken to buy only our native goods, would immediately unite to cheat and exact upon us the price, the measure, and the goodness, nor could ever yet be brought to make one fair proposal of just dealing, though often and earnestly invited to it.

Therefore I repeat, let no man talk to me of these and the like expedi-   30 ents, till he hath at least some glimpse of hope that there will ever be some hearty and sincere attempt to put them in practice.

But as to myself, having been wearied out for many years with offering   31 vain, idle, visionary thoughts, and at length utterly despairing of success, I fortunately fell upon this proposal, which, as it is wholly new, so it hath something solid and real, of no expense and little trouble, full in our own power, and whereby we can incur no danger in disobliging England. For this kind of commodity will not bear exportation, the flesh being of too tender a consistence to admit a long continuance in salt, although perhaps I could name a country which would be glad to eat up our whole nation without it.

After all, I am not so violently bent upon my own opinion as to reject   32 any offer proposed by wise men, which shall be found equally innocent, cheap, easy, and effectual. But before something of that kind shall be advanced in contradiction to my scheme, and offering a better, I desire the author or authors will be pleased maturely to consider two points. First, as things now stand, how they will be able to find food and raiment for an hundred thousand useless mouths and backs. And secondly, there being a round million of creatures in human figure throughout this kingdom, whose sole subsistence put into a common stock would leave them in debt two millions of pounds sterling, adding those who are beggars by profession to the bulk of farmers, cottagers, and laborers, with their wives and children who are beggars in effect; I desire those politicians who dislike my overture, and may perhaps be so bold to attempt an answer, that they will first ask the parents of these mortals whether they would not at this day think it a great happiness to have been sold for food at a year old in the manner I prescribe, and thereby have avoided such a perpetual scene of misfortunes as they have since gone through by the oppression of landlords, the impossibility of paying rent without money or trade, the want of common sustenance, with neither house nor clothes to cover them from the inclemencies of the weather, and the most inevitable prospect of entailing the like or greater miseries upon their breed forever.

33   I profess, in the sincerity of my heart, that I have not the least personal interest in endeavoring to promote this necessary work, having no other motive than the public good of my country, by advancing our trade, providing for infants, relieving the poor, and giving some pleasure to the rich. I have no children by which I can propose to get a single penny; the youngest being nine years old, and my wife is past childbearing.

◆

THE DECLARATION OF INDEPENDENCE

Thomas Jefferson

A man with an astonishing range of talents, Thomas Jefferson (1743–1826) served as a member of the Virginia House of Burgesses, as a delegate to the Continental Congress (where he drafted the Declaration of Independence), as governor of Virginia, as ambassador to France, and then as our first secretary of state (under George Washington), our second vice president (under John Adams), and, from 1801 to 1809, our third president. He was also a scientist, an inventor, an architect, a farmer, a historian, and one of the most original political and social philosophers of his day, becoming president of the American Philosophical Society in 1797. Retiring to his beloved Monticello in 1809, he went on to found the University of Virginia, whose campus and buildings he designed. It was only logical that Jefferson's colleagues in the Second Continental Congress of 1775–1776 should choose him to draft the Declaration of Independence, for he was already one of the most articulate men of his—or any—time. Jefferson's complete draft is reproduced here as Garry Wills has reconstructed it from Jefferson's published papers. Brackets and underlining indicate the parts of Jefferson's original draft were struck out by the Congress (one member of which was Benjamin Franklin). Revisions that were inserted appear either in the margin or in a parallel column.

A Declaration by the representatives of the United states of 1
America, in [General] Congress assembled.

When in the course of human events it becomes necessary 2
for one people to dissolve the political bands which have connected them with another, and to assume among the powers
of the earth the separate & equal station to which the laws of
nature and the nature's god entitle them, a decent respect to
the opinions of mankind requires that they should declare the
causes which impel them to the separation.

We hold these truths to be self evident: that all men are cre- 3
ated equal; that they are endowed by their creator with ∧ [in-
herent and] inalienable rights; that among these are life,
liberty & the pursuit of happiness: that to secure these rights,
governments are instituted among men, deriving their just
powers from the consent of the governed; that whenever any
form of government becomes destructive of these ends; it is
the right of the people to alter or to abolish it, & to institute
new government, laying it's foundation on such principles, &
organising it's power in such form, as to them shall seem most

certain

439

likely to effect their safety & happiness. Prudence indeed will dictate that governments long established should not be changed for light & transient causes; and accordingly all experience hath shewn that mankind are more disposed to suffer while evils are sufferable than to right themselves by abolishing the forms to which they are accustomed. But when a long train of abuses & usurpations [begun at a distinguished period and] pursuing invariably by the same object, evinces a design to reduce them under absolute despotism it is their right, it is their duty to throw off such government, & to provide new guards for their future security. Such has been the patient sufferance of these colonies; & such is now the necessity which constrains them to ∧ [expunge] their former systems of government. The history of the present king of Great Britain is a history of ∧ [unremitting] injuries & usurpations, [among which appears no solitary fact to contradict the uniform tenor of the rest but all have] ∧ in direct object the establishment of an absolute tyranny over these states. To prove this let facts be submitted to a candid world [for the truth of which we pledge a faith yet unsullied by falsehood].

alter

repeated

all having

4   He has refused his assent to laws the most wholesome & necessary for a public good.

5   He has forbidden his governors to pass laws of immediate & pressing importance, unless suspended in their operation till his assent should be obtained; & when so suspended, he has utterly neglected to attend to them.

6   He has refused to pass other laws for the accommodation of large districts of people, unless those people would relinquish the right of representation in the legislature, a right inestimable to them & formidable to tyrants only.

7   He has called together legislative bodies at places unusual, uncomfortable, and distant from the depository of their public records, for the sole purpose of fatiguing them into compliance with his measures.

8   He has dissolved representative houses repeatedly [& continually] for opposing with manly firmness his invasions on the rights of the people.

9   He has refused for a long time after such dissolutions to cause others to be elected, whereby the legislative powers, incapable of annihilation, have returned to the people at large for their exercise, the state remaining in the mean time exposed to all the dangers of invasion from without & convulsions within.

10   He has endeavored to prevent the population of these states; for that purpose obstructing the laws for naturalization of foreigners, refusing to pass others to encourage their migrations hither, & raising the conditions of new appropriations of lands.

obstructed
by

He has ∧ [suffered] the administration of justice [totally to 11 cease in some of these states] ∧ refusing his assent to laws for establishing judiciary powers.

He has made [our] judges dependant on his will alone, for 12 the tenure of their offices, & the amount & payment of their salaries.

He has erected a multitude of new offices [by a self assumed 13 power] and sent hither swarms of new officers to harrass our people and eat out of their substance.

He has kept among us in times of peace standing armies 14 [and ships of war] without the consent of our legislatures.

He has affected to render the military independent of, & su- 15 perior to the civil power.

He has combined with others to subject us to a jurisdiction 16 foreign to our constitutions & unacknowleged by our laws, giving his assent to their acts of pretended legislation for quartering large bodies of armed troops among us; for protecting them by a mock-trial from punishment for any murders which they should commit on the inhabitants of these states; for cutting off our trade with all parts of the world; for imposing taxes

in many cases

on us without our consent; for depriving us ∧ of the benefits of trial by jury; for transporting us beyond seas to be tried for pretended offences; for abolishing the free system of English laws in a neighboring province, establishing therein an arbitrary government, and enlarging its boundaries, so as to render it at once an example and fit instrument for introducing

colonies

the same absolute rule and these ∧ [states]; for taking away our charters, abolishing our most valuable laws, and altering fundamentally the forms of our governments; for suspending our own legislatures, & declaring themselves invested with power to legislate for us in all cases whatsoever.

by declaring us out
of his protection &
waging war
against us

He has abdicated government here ∧ [withdrawing his gov- 17 ernors, and declaring us out of his allegience & protection].

He has plundered our seas, ravaged our coasts, burnt our 18 towns, & destroyed the lives of our people

He is at this time transporting large armies of foreign, mer- 19 cenaries to compleat the works of death, desolation & tyranny

scarcely paralleled
in the most
barbarous ages, &
totally

already begun with circumstances of cruelty and perfidy ∧ unworthy the head of a civilized nation.

He has constrained our fellow citizens taken captive on the 20 high seas to bear arms against their country, to become the executioners of their friends & brethren, or to fall themselves by their hands,

excited domestic
insurrections
amongst us, & has

He has ∧ endeavored to bring on the inhabitants of our 21 frontiers the merciless Indian savages, whose known rule of warfare is an undistinguished destruction of all ages, sexes, & conditions [of existence].

22   [He has incited treasonable insurrections of our fellow citizens, with the allurements of forfeiture & confiscation of our
property.

23   He has waged cruel war against human nature itself, violating it's most sacred rights of life and liberty in the persons
of a distant people who never offended him, captivating & carrying them into slavery in another hemisphere or to incur miserable death in their transportation thither. This piratical
warfare, the opprobrium of *infidel* powers, is the warfare of the
Christian king of Great Britain. Determined to keep open a
market where *Men* should be bought & sold, he has prostituted
his negative for suppressing every legislative attempt to prohibit or to restrain this execrable commerce. And that this as-
semblage of horrors might want no fact of distinguished die,
he is now exciting those very people to rise in arms among us,
and to purchase that liberty of which he has deprived them,
by murdering the people on whom he also obtruded them:
thus paying off former crimes committed against the *Liberties*
of one people, with crimes which he urges them to commit
against the *lives* of another.]

24   In every stage of these oppressions we have petitioned for
redress in the most humble terms: our repeated petitions have
been answered only by repeated injuries. A prince whose character is thus marked by every act which may define a tyrant is
unfit to be a ruler of a ∧ people [who mean to be free. Future   free
ages will scarcely believe that the hardiness of one man adven-
tured, within the short compass of twelve years only, to lay a
foundation so broad & so undisguised for tyranny over a people fostered & fixed in principles of freedom].

25   Nor have we been wanting in attentions to our British
brethren. We have warned them from time to time of attempts
by their legislature to extend ∧ [a] jurisdiction over ∧ [these our   an unwarrantable
states]. We have reminded them of the circumstances of our em-   us
igration & settlement here, [no one of which could warrant so
strange a pretension; that these were effected at the expense of
our own blood & treasure, unassisted by the wealth or the
strength of Great Britain; that in constituting indeed our several
forms of government, we had adopted one common king,
thereby laying a foundation for perpetual league & amity with
them: but that submission to their parliament was no part of our
constitution, nor ever in idea, if history may be credited: and,]
we ∧ appealed to their native justice and magnanimity ∧ [as well   have
as to] the ties of our common kindred to disavow these usurpa-   and we have
tions which ∧ [were likely to] interrupt our connection and cor-   conjured them by
respondence. They too have been deaf to the voice of justice &   would inevitably
of consanguinity, [and when occasions have been given them,
by the regular course of their laws, of removing from their coun-

cils the disturbers of our harmony, they have, by their free election, re-established them in power. At this very time too they are permitting their chief magistrate to send over not only soldiers of our common blood, but Scotch & foreign mercenaries to invade & destroy us. These facts have given the last stab to agonizing affection, and manly spirit bids us to renounce for ever these unfeeling brethren. We must endeavor to forget our former love for them, and to hold them as we hold the rest of mankind enemies in war, in peace friends. We might have been a free and a great people together; but a communication of grandeur & freedom it seems is below their dignity. Be it so, since they will have it. The road to happiness & to glory is open to us too. We will tread it apart from them, and] ∧ acquiesce in the necessity which denounces our [eternal] separation. ∧ !

we must therefore and hold them as we hold the rest of mankind, enemies in war, in peace friends

We therefore the representatives of the United States of America in General Congress assembled do in the name, & by the authority of the good people of these [states reject & renounce all allegiance & subjection to the kings of Great Britain & all others who may hereafter claim by, through or under them: we utterly dissolve all political connection which may theretofore have subsisted between us & the people or parliament of Great Britain: & finally we do assert & declare these colonies to be free & independent states,] & that as free & independent states, they have full power to levy war, conclude peace, contract alliances, establish commerce, & to do all other acts & things which independent states may of right do. And for the support of this declaration we mutually pledge to each other our lives, our fortunes & our sacred honour.

We therefore the representatives of the United States of America in General Congress assembled, appealing to the supreme judge of the world for the rectitude of our intentions, do in the name, & by the authority of the good people of these colonies, solemnly publish & declare that these United colonies are & of right ought to be free & independent states; that they are absolved from all allegiance to the British crown, and that all political connection between them & the state of Great Britain is, & ought to be, totally dissolved; & that as free & independent states they have full power to levy war, conclude peace, contract alliances, establish commerce & to do all other acts & things which independent states may of right do. 26

And for the support of this declaration, with a firm reliance on the protection of divine providence we mutually pledge to each other our lives, our fortunes & our sacred honour. 27

♦

THE PREVAILING OPINION OF A SEXUAL CHARACTER DISCUSSED

Mary Wollstonecraft

Mary Wollstonecraft (1759–1797), a major figure in the history of the struggle for women's rights, was well known in her own time not only as an advocate of women's rights but as a political thinker on a more comprehensive scale. In an age when it was notoriously difficult for a woman to support herself financially, Wollstonecraft (whose father's drinking had ruined the family) supported herself first as a governess, the traditional occupation for single women, and then by working for a London publisher, James Johnson. After spending several years in France observing the French Revolution at first hand, she returned to London and again worked for Johnson, becoming part of the group of influential radicals he gathered about himself, of which William Blake, William Wordsworth, and William Godwin were also members. Eventually she married Godwin, and not long afterward she died giving birth to a daughter, Mary (who later became the wife of the poet Percy Bysshe Shelley and wrote the novel *Frankenstein*). *A Vindication of the Rights of Woman* (1792), from which the following selection is taken, argues mainly for intellectual rather than social or political rights for women.

1   To account for, and excuse the tyranny of man, many ingenious arguments have been brought forward to prove, that the two sexes, in the acquirement of virtue, ought to aim at attaining a very different character: or, to speak explicitly, women are not allowed to have sufficient strength of mind to acquire what really deserves the name of virtue. Yet it should seem, allowing them to have souls, that there is but one way appointed by Providence to lead *mankind* to either virtue or happiness.

2   If then women are not a swarm of ephemeron triflers, why should they be kept in ignorance under the specious name of innocence? Men complain, and with reason, of the follies and caprices of our sex, when they do not keenly satirize our headstrong passions and groveling voices.—Behold, I should answer, the natural effect of ignorance? The mind will ever be unstable that has only prejudices to rest on, and the current will run with destructive fury when there are no barriers to break its force. Women are told from their infancy, and taught by the example of their mothers, that a little knowledge of human weakness, justly termed cunning, softness of temper, *outward* obedience, and a scrupulous attention to a puerile kind of propriety, will obtain for them protection of man; and should they be beautiful, every thing else is needless, for, at least, twenty years of their lives.

3   Thus Milton describes our first frail mother; though when he tells us that women are formed for softness and sweet attractive grace, I cannot

comprehend his meaning, unless, in the true Mahometan strain, he meant to deprive us of souls, and insinuate that we are beings only designed by sweet attractive grace, and docile blind obedience, to gratify the senses of man when he can no longer soar on the wing of contemplation.

How grossly do they insult us who thus advise us only to render our- 4 selves gentle, domestic brutes? For instance, the winning softness so warmly, and frequently, recommended, that governs by obeying. What childish expressions, and how insignificant is the being—can it be an immortal one? who will condescend to govern by such sinister methods! "Certainly," says Lord Bacon, "man is of kin to the beasts by his body; and if he be not of kin to God by his spirit, he is a base and ignoble creature!" Men, indeed, appear to me to act in a very unphilosophical manner when they try to secure the good conduct of women by attempting to keep them always in a state of childhood. Rousseau [whom Wollstonecraft argues against earlier, in a passage omitted here] was more consistent when he wished to stop the progress of reason in both sexes, for if men eat of the tree of knowledge, women will come in for a taste; but, from the imperfect cultivation which their understandings now receive, they only attain a knowledge of evil.

Children, I grant, should be innocent; but when the epithet is applied 5 to men or women, it is but a civil term for weakness. For if it be allowed that women were destined by Providence to acquire human virtues, and by the exercise of their understandings, that stability of character which is the firmest ground to rest our future hopes upon, they must be permitted to turn to the fountain of light, and not forced to shape their course by the twinkling of a mere satellite. Milton, I grant, was of very different opinion; for he only bends to the indefeasible right of beauty, though it would be difficult to render two passages which I now mean to contrast, consistent. But into similar inconsistencies are great men often led by their senses.

> To whom thus Eve with *perfect beauty* adorn'd
> "My Author and Disposer, what thou bidst
> *Unargued* I obey; So God ordains;
> God is *thy law, thou mine:* to know no more
> Is Woman's *happiest* knowledge and her *praise.*

These are exactly the arguments that I have used to children; but I have 6 added, your reason is now gaining strength, and, till it arrives at some degree of maturity, you must look up to me for advice—then you ought to *think,* and only rely on God.

Yet in the following lines Milton seems to coincide with me; when he 7 makes Adam thus expostulate with his Maker.

> Hast thou not made me hear thy substitute,
> And these inferior far beneath me set?
> Among *unequals* what society
> Can sort, what harmony or true delight?
> Which must be mutual, in proportion due
> Giv'n and receiv'd; but in *disparity*
> The one intense, the other still remiss

Cannot well suit with either, but soon prove
Tedious alike: of *fellowship* I speak
Such as I seek, fit to participate
All rational delight—

8   In treating, therefore, of the manners of women, let us, disregarding sensual arguments, trace what we should endeavour to make them in order to cooperate, if the expression be not too bold, with the supreme Being.

9   By individual education, I mean, for the sense of the word is not precisely defined, such an attention to a child as will slowly sharpen the senses, form the temper, regulate the passions as they begin to ferment, and set the understanding to work before the body arrives at maturity; so that the man may only have to proceed, not to begin, the important task of learning to think and reason.

10   To prevent any misconstruction, I must add, that I do not believe that a private education can work the wonders which some sanguine writers have attributed to it. Men and women must be educated, in a great degree, by the opinions and manners of the society they live in. In every age there has been a stream of popular opinion that has carried all before it, and given a family character, as it were, to the century. It may then fairly be inferred, that, till society be differently constituted, much cannot be expected from education. It is, however, sufficient for my present purpose to assert, that, whatever effect circumstances have on the abilities, every being may become virtuous by the exercise of its own reason; for if but one being was created with vicious inclinations, that is positively bad, what can save us from atheism? Or if we worship a God, is not that God a devil?

11   Consequently, the most perfect education, in my opinion, is such an exercise of the understanding as is best calculated to strengthen the body and form the heart. Or, in other words, to enable the individual to attain such habits of virtue as will render it independent. In fact, it is a farce to call any being virtuous whose virtues do not result from the exercise of its own reason. This was Rousseau's opinion respecting men: I extend it to women, and confidently assert that they have been drawn out of their sphere by false refinement, and not by an endeavour to acquire masculine qualities. Still the regal homage which they receive is so intoxicating, that till the manners of the times are changed, and formed on more reasonable principles, it may be impossible to convince them that the illegitimate power, which they obtain, by degrading themselves, is a curse, and that they must return to nature and equality, if they wish to secure the placid satisfaction that unsophisticated affections impart. But for this epoch we must wait—wait, perhaps, till kings and nobles, enlightened by reason, and, preferring the real dignity of man to childish state, throw off their gaudy hereditary trappings: and if then women do not resign the arbitrary power of beauty—they will prove that they have *less* mind than man.

◆

WHERE I LIVED, AND WHAT I LIVED FOR

Henry David Thoreau

Henry David Thoreau (1817–1862) remains for many Americans the most appealing of those nineteenth-century writers and thinkers known as the Transcendentalists (of whom Thoreau's friend Ralph Waldo Emerson was the most eminent). Well educated in the Greek and Latin classics and also in the modern languages, Thoreau briefly taught school and then worked as a tutor in his hometown of Concord, Massachusetts. In 1845 he built his now-famous cabin on some property belonging to the Emerson family near Walden Pond and began his experiment in simplifying his life to understand its real values. *Walden*, from which the following selection is taken, records and reflects upon that experience. Begun in 1846, *Walden* was not published until 1854, seven years after Thoreau had left the cabin. During those years he published his first book, *A Week on the Concord and Merrimack Rivers*, based on his journal of a trip with his brother John, and his famous essay "Civil Disobedience," whose doctrine of nonviolent resistance was later to influence both Mahatma Ghandi in his struggle for an independent India and the Reverend Martin Luther King, Jr., in his struggle for civil rights for black Americans.

I went to the woods because I wished to live deliberately, to front only the essential facts of life, and see if I could not learn what it had to teach, and not, when I came to die, discover that I had not lived. I did not wish to live what was not life, living is so dear, nor did I wish to practice resignation, unless it was quite necessary. I wanted to live deep and suck out all the marrow of life, to live so sturdily and Spartan-like as to put to rout all that was not life, to cut a broad swath and shave close, to drive life into a corner, and reduce it to its lowest terms, and, if it proved to be mean, why then to get the whole and genuine meanness of it, and publish its meanness to the world; or if it were sublime, to know it by experience, and be able to give a true account of it in my next excursion. For most men, it appears to me, are in a strange uncertainty about it, whether it is of the devil or of God and have *somewhat hastily* concluded that it is the chief end of man here to "glorify God and enjoy him forever." 1

Still we live meanly, like ants; though the fable tells us that we were long ago changed into men; like pygmies we fight with cranes; it is error upon error, and clout upon clout, and our best virtue has been for its occasion a superfluous and inevitable wretchedness. Our life is frittered away by detail. An honest man has hardly need to count more than his ten fingers, or in extreme cases he may add his ten toes, and lump the rest. Simplicity, simplicity, simplicity! I say, let your affairs be as two or three, and not a hundred 2

or a thousand; instead of a million count half a dozen, and keep your accounts on your thumb-nail. In the midst of this chopping sea of civilized
life, such are the clouds and storms and quicksands and thousand-and-one
items to be allowed for, that a man has to live, if he would not founder and
go to the bottom and not make his port at all, by dead reckoning, and he
must be a great calculator indeed who succeeds. Simplify, simplify. Instead
of three meals a day, if it be necessary eat but one; instead of a hundred
dishes, five; and reduce other things in proportion. Our life is like a German
Confederacy, made up of petty states, with its boundary forever fluctuating,
so that even a German cannot tell you how it is bounded at any moment.
The nation itself, with all its so-called internal improvements, which, by
the way, are all external and superficial, is just such an unwieldy and over-
grown establishment, cluttered with furniture and tripped up by its own
traps, ruined by luxury and heedless expense, by want of calculation and a
worthy aim, as the million households in the land; and the only cure for it,
as for them, is in a rigid economy, a stern and more than Spartan simplicity
of life and elevation of purpose. It lives too fast. Men think that it is essential that the *Nation* have commerce, and export ice, and talk through a tele-
graph, and ride thirty miles an hour, without a doubt, whether *they* do or
not; but whether we should live like baboons or like men, is a little uncertain. If we do not get out sleepers, and forge rails, and devote days and
nights to the work, but go to tinkering upon our *lives* to improve *them,* who
will build railroads? And if railroads are not built, how shall we get to
Heaven in season? But if we stay at home and mind our business, who will
want railroads? We do not ride on the railroad; it rides upon us. Did you
ever think what those sleepers are that underlie the railroad? Each one is a
man, an Irishman, or a Yankee man. The rails are laid on them, and they are
covered with sand, and the cars run smoothly over them. They are sound
sleepers, I assure you. And every few years a new lot is laid down and run
over; so that, if some have the pleasure of riding on a rail, others have the
misfortune to be ridden upon. And when they run over a man that is walking in his sleep, a supernumerary sleeper in the wrong position, and wake
him up, they suddenly stop the cars, and make a hue and cry about it, as if
this were an exception. I am glad to know that it takes a gang of men for
every five miles to keep the sleepers down and level in their beds as it is, for
this is a sign that they may sometime get up again.

3   Why should we live with such hurry and waste of life? We are determined to be starved before we are hungry. Men say that a stitch in time saves
nine, and so they take a thousand stitches to-day to save nine tomorrow. As
for *work,* we haven't any of any consequence. We have the Saint Vitus'
dance, and cannot possibly keep our heads still. If I should only give a few
pulls at the parish bell-rope, as for a fire, that is, without setting the bell,
there is hardly a man on his farm in the outskirts of Concord, notwith-
standing that press of engagements which was his excuse so many times
this morning, nor a boy, nor a woman, I might almost say, but would for-
sake all and follow that sound, not mainly to save property from the flames,
but, if we will confess the truth, much more to see it burn, since burn it

must, and we, be it known, did not set it on fire,—or to see it put out, and have a hand in it, if that is done handsomely; yes, even if it were the parish church itself. Hardly a man takes a half-hour's nap after dinner, but when he wakes he holds his head and asks, "What's the news?" as if the rest of mankind had stood his sentinels. Some give directions to be waked every half-hour, doubtless for no other purpose; and then, to pay for it, they tell what they have dreamed. After a night's sleep the news is as indispensable as the breakfast. "Pray tell me anything new that has happened to a man anywhere on this globe,"—and he reads it over his coffee and rolls, that a man has had his eyes gouged out this morning on the Wachito River, never dreaming the while that he lives in the dark unfathomed mammoth cave of this world, and has but the rudiment of an eye himself.

For my part, I could easily do without the post-office. I think that there are very few important communications made through it. To speak critically, I never received more than one or two letters in my life—I wrote this some years ago—that were worth the postage. The penny-post is, commonly, an institution through which you seriously offer a man that penny for his thoughts which is so often safely offered in jest. And I am sure that I never read any memorable news in a newspaper. If we read of one man robbed, or murdered, or killed by accident, or one house burned, or one vessel wrecked, or one steamboat blown up, or one cow run over on the Western Railroad, or one mad dog killed, or one lot of grasshoppers in the winter—we never need read of another. One is enough. If you are acquainted with the principle, what do you care for a myriad instances and applications? To a philosopher all *news*, as it is called, is gossip and they who edit and read it are old women over their tea. Yet not a few are greedy after this gossip. There was such a rush, as I hear, the other day at one of the offices to learn the foreign news by the last arrival, that several large squares of plate glass belonging to the establishment were broken by the pressure—news which I seriously think a ready wit might write a twelvemonth, or twelve years, beforehand with sufficient accuracy. As for Spain, for instance, if you know how to throw in Don Carlos and the Infanta, and Don Pedro and Seville and Granada, from time to time in the right proportions,—they may have changed the names a little since I saw the papers,—and serve up a bull-fight when other entertainments fail, it will be true to the letter, and give us as good an idea of the exact state or ruin of things in Spain as the most succinct and lucid reports under this head in the newspapers: and as for England, almost the last significant scrap of news from that quarter was the revolution of 1649, and if you have learned the history of her crops for an average year, you never need attend to that thing again, unless your speculations are of a merely pecuniary character. If one may judge who rarely looks into the newspapers, nothing new does ever happen in foreign parts, a French revolution not excepted.

What news! how much more important to know what that is which was never old! "Kieou-he-yu (great dignitary of the state of Wei) sent a man to Khoung-tseu to know his news. Khoung-tseu caused the messenger to be seated near him, and questioned him in these terms: What is your master doing? The messenger answered with respect: My master desires to diminish the number of his faults, but he cannot come to the end of them. The messenger being gone, the philosopher remarked: What a worthy messenger! What a worthy messenger!" The preacher, instead of vexing the ears of drowsy farmers on their days of rest at the end of the week,—for Sunday is the fit conclusion of an ill-spent week, and not the fresh and brave beginning of a new one,—with this one other draggle-tail of a sermon, should shout with thundering voice, "Pause! Avast! Why so seeming fast, but deadly slow?"

6   Shams and delusions are esteemed for soundest truths, while reality is fabulous. If men would steadily observe realities only, and not allow themselves to be deluded, life, to compare it with such things as we know, would be like a fairy tale and the Arabian Nights' Entertainments. If we respected only what is inevitable and has a right to be, music and poetry would resound along the streets. When we are unhurried and wise, we perceive that only great and worthy things have any permanent and absolute existence, that petty fears and petty pleasures are but a shadow of the reality. This is always exhilarating and sublime. By closing the eyes and slumbering, and consenting to be deceived by shows, men establish and confirm their daily life of routine and habit everywhere, which still is built on purely illusory foundations. Children, who play life, discern its true law and relations more clearly than men, who fail to live it worthily, but who think they are wiser by experience, that is, by failure. I have read in a Hindoo book, that "there was a king's son, who, being expelled in infancy from his native city, was brought up by a forester, and growing up to maturity in that state, imagined himself to belong to the barbarous race with which he lived. One of his father's ministers having discovered him, revealed to him what he was, and the misconception of his character was removed, and he knew himself to be a prince. So soul," continues the Hindoo philosopher, "from the circumstances from which it is placed, mistakes its own character, until the truth is revealed to it by some holy teacher, and then it knows itself to be *Brahma*." I perceive that we inhabitants of New England live this mean life that we do because our vision does not penetrate the surface of things. We think that this *is* which *appears* to be. If a man should walk through this town and see only the reality, where, think you, would the "Mill-dam" go to? If he should give us an account of the realities he beheld there, we should not recognize the place in his description. Look at a meeting-house, or a court-house, or a jail, or a shop, or a dwelling-house, and say what that thing really is before a true gaze, and they would all go to pieces in your account of them. Men esteem truth remote, in the outskirts of the system, behind the farthest star, before Adam and after the last man. In eternity there is indeed something true and sublime. But all these times and places and occasions are now and here. God himself culminates in the present moment, and will never be more divine in the lapse of all the ages. And we are enabled to apprehend at all what is sublime and noble only by the perpetual instilling and drenching of the reality that surrounds us. The universe constantly and obediently answers to our conceptions; whether we travel fast or slow, the track is laid

for us. Let us spend our lives in conceiving then. The pet or the artist never yet had so fair and noble a design but some of his posterity at least could accomplish it.

Let us spend one day as deliberately as Nature, and not be thrown off 7 the track by every nutshell and mosquito's wing that falls on the rails. Let us rise early and fast, or break fast, gently and without perturbation; let company come and let company go, let the bells ring and the children cry,— determined to make a day of it. Why should we knock under and go with the stream? Let us not be upset and overwhelmed in that terrible rapid and whirlpool called a dinner, situated in the meridian shallows. Weather this danger and you are safe, for the rest of the way is down hill. With unrelaxed nerves, with morning vigor, sail by it, looking the other way, tied to the mast like Ulysses. If the engine whistles, let it whistle till it is hoarse for its pains. If the bell rings, why should we run? We will consider what kind of music they are like. Let us settle ourselves, and work and wedge our feet downward through the mud and slush of opinion, and prejudice, and tradition, and delusion, and appearance, that alluvion which covers the globe, through Paris and London, through New York and Boston and Concord, through Church and State, through poetry and philosophy and religion, till we come to a hard bottom and rocks in place, which we can call *reality,* and say, This is, and no mistake; and then you begin, having a *point d'appui,* below freshet and frost and fire, a place where you might found a wall or a state, or set a lamppost safely, or perhaps a gauge, not a Nilometer, but a Realometer that future ages might know how deep the freshet of shams and appearances had gathered from time to time. If you stand right fronting and face to face to a fact, you will see the sun glimmer on both its surfaces, as if it were a cimeter, and feel its sweet edge dividing you through the heart and marrow, and so you will happily conclude your mortal career. Be it life or death, we crave only reality. If we are really dying, let us hear the rattle in our throats and feel cold in the extremities; if we are alive, let us go about our business.

Time is but the stream I go a-fishing in. I drink at it; but while I drink I 8 see the sandy bottom and detect how shallow it is. Its thin current slides away, but eternity remains. I would drink deeper; fish in the sky, whose bottom is pebbly with stars. I cannot count one. I know not the first letter of the alphabet. I have always been regretting that I was not as wise as the day I was born. The intellect is a cleaver; it discerns and rifts its way into the secret of things. I do not wish to be any more busy with my hands than is necessary. My head is hands and feet. I feel all my best faculties concentrated in it. My instinct tells me that my head is an organ for burrowing, as some creatures use their snout and fore paws, and with it I would mine and burrow my way through these hills. I think that the richest vein is somewhere hereabouts; so by the divining-rod and thin rising vapors I judge; and I will begin to mine.

◆

THE DEATH OF THE MOTH

Virginia Woolf

Virgina Woolf (1882–1941) is best known for experimental novels such as *Mrs. Dalloway* (1925), *To the Lighthouse* (1927), and *The Waves* (1931), but she was also influential as a critic and essayist. Born in London, the daughter of the eminent scholar Sir Leslie Stephen, Woolf was educated at home and read voraciously in her father's large library. She married journalist Leonard Woolf in 1912 and with him founded the Hogarth Press, which published works by several prominent artists, intellectuals, and writers known as the Bloomsbury group. Introspective and prone to depression, Woolf drowned herself in 1941. "The Death of the Moth," published posthumously in 1942, reveals her powers of observation and echoes a recurrent theme in her fiction, the interaction of time and consciousness.

1   Moths that fly by day are not properly to be called moths; they do not excite that pleasant sense of dark autumn nights and ivy-blossom which the commonest yellow-underwing asleep in the shadow of the curtain never fails to rouse in us. They are hybrid creatures, neither gay like butterflies nor sombre like their own species. Nevertheless the present specimen, with his narrow hay-coloured wings, fringed with a tassel of the same colour, seemed to be content with life. It was a pleasant morning, mid-September, mild, benignant, yet with a keener breath than that of the summer months. The plough was already scoring the field opposite the window, and where the share had been, the earth was pressed flat and gleamed with moisture. Such vigour came rolling in from the fields and then down beyond that it was difficult to keep the eyes strictly turned upon the book. The rooks too were keeping one of their annual festivities; soaring round the tree tops until it looked as if a vast net with thousands of black knots in it had been cast up into the air; which, after a few moments sank slowly down upon the trees until every twig seemed to have a knot at the end of it. Then, suddenly, the net would be thrown into the air again in a wider circle this time, with the utmost clamour and vociferation, as though to be thrown into the air and settle slowly down upon the tree tops were a tremendously exciting experience.

2   The same energy which inspired the rooks, the ploughmen, the horses, and even, it seemed, the lean bare-backed downs, sent the moth fluttering from side to side of his square of the window pane. One could not help watching him. One was, indeed, conscious of a queer feeling of pity for him. The possibilities of pleasure seemed that morning so enormous and so various that to have only a moth's part in life, and a day moth's at that, ap-

peared a hard fate, and his zest in enjoying his meagre opportunities to the full, pathetic. He flew vigorously to one corner of his compartment, and, after waiting there a second, flew across to the other. What remained for him but to fly to a third corner and then to a fourth? That was all he could do, in spite of the size of the downs, the width of the sky, the far-off smoke houses, and the romantic voice, now and then, of a steamer out at sea. What he could do he did. Watching him, it seemed as if a fibre, very thin but pure, of the enormous energy of the world had been thrust into his frail and diminutive body. As often as he crossed the pane, I could fancy that a thread of vital light became visible. He was little or nothing but life.

Yet, because he was so small, and so simple a form of the energy that 3 was rolling in at the open window and driving its way through so many narrow and intricate corridors in my own brain and in those of other human beings, there was something marvelous as well as pathetic about him. It was as if someone had taken a tiny bead of pure life and decking it as lightly as possible with down and feathers, had set it dancing and zigzagging to show us the true nature of life. Thus displayed one could not get over the strangeness of it. One is apt to forget all about life, seeing it humped and bossed and garnished and cumbered so that it has to move with the greatest circumspection and dignity. Again, the thought of all that life might have been he been born in any other shape caused one to view his simple activities with a kind of pity.

After a time, tired by his dancing apparently, he settled on the window 4 ledge in the sun, and, the queer spectacle being at an end, I forgot about him. Then, looking up, my eye was caught by him. He was trying to resume his dancing, but seemed either so stiff or so awkward that he could only flutter to the bottom of the windowpane; and when he tried to fly across it he failed. Being intent on other matters I watched these futile attempts for a time without thinking, unconsciously waiting for him to resume his flight, as one waits for a machine, that has stopped momentarily, to start again without considering the reason of its failure. After perhaps a seventh attempt he slipped from the wooden ledge and fell, fluttering his wings, on to his back on the window sill. The helplessness of his attitude roused me. It flashed upon me that he was in difficulties; he could no longer raise himself; his legs struggled vainly. But, as I stretched out a pencil, meaning to help him to right himself, it came over me that the failure and awkwardness were the approach of death. I laid the pencil down again.

The legs agitate themselves once more. I looked as if for the enemy 5 against which he struggled. I looked out of doors. What had happened there? Presumably it was midday, and work in the fields had stopped. Stillness and quiet had replaced the previous animation. The birds had taken themselves off to feed in the brooks. The horses stood still. Yet the power was there all the same, massed outside indifferent, impersonal, not attending to anything in particular. Somehow it was opposed to the little haycoloured moth. It was useless to try to do anything. One could only watch the extraordinary efforts made by those tiny legs against an oncoming doom which could, had it chosen, have submerged an entire city, not merely a city, but masses of human beings; nothing, I knew, had any chance against death. Nevertheless after a pause of exhaustion the legs fluttered again. It was superb this last protest, and so frantic that he succeeded at last in righting himself. One's sympathies, of course, were all on the side of life. Also, when there was nobody to care or to know, this gigantic effort on the part of an insignificant little moth, against a power of such magnitude, to retain what no one else valued or desired to keep, moved one strangely. Again, somehow, one saw life, a pure bead. I lifted the pencil again, useless though I knew it to be. But even as I did so, the unmistakable tokens of death showed themselves. The body relaxed, and instantly grew stiff. The struggle was over. The insignificant little creature now knew death. As I looked at the death moth, this minute wayside triumph of so great a force over so mean an antagonist filled me with wonder. Just as life had been strange a few minutes before, so death was now as strange. The moth having righted himself now lay most decently and uncomplainingly composed. O yes, he seemed to say, death is stronger than I am.

I Want a Wife

Judy Brady

Born in 1937 in San Francisco, Judy Brady received a BFA in painting from the University of Iowa. In the early 1960s, Brady was discouraged from pursuing graduate study and a university career because of her gender. She married, raised two children, and began a career as a politi-cal activist and writer.

This essay was published in the first issue of *Ms.* magazine in 1972 (under her married name of Syfers), becoming a classic and frequently anthologized example of feminist satire. A survivor of breast cancer, Brady has edited books about women and cancer, including *Women and Cancer* (1980) and *One in Three: Women and Cancer Confront an Epidemic* (1991).

I belong to that classification of people known as wives. I am a Wife. And, not altogether incidentally, I am a mother. 1

Not too long ago a male friend of mine appeared on the scene fresh from a recent divorce. He had one child, who is, of course, with his ex-wife. He is obviously looking for another wife. As I thought about him while I was iron-ing one evening, it suddenly occurred to me that I, too, would like to have a wife. Why do I want a wife? 2

I would like to go back to school so that I can become economically in-dependent, support myself, and, if need be, support those dependent on me. I want a wife who will work and send me to school. And while I am going to school I want a wife to take care of my children. I want a wife to keep track of the children's doctor and dentist appointments. And to keep track of mine, too. I want a wife to make sure that my children eat properly and are kept clean. I want a wife who will wash the children's clothes and keep them mended. I want a wife who is a good nurturant attendant to my children, who arranges for their schooling, makes sure they have an ade-quate social life with their peers, takes them to the park, the zoo, etc. I want a wife who takes care of the children when they are sick, a wife who arranges to be around when the children need special care, because, of course, I can-not miss classes at school. My wife must arrange to lose time at work and not lose the job. It may mean a small cut in my wife's income from time to time, but I guess I can tolerate that. Needless to say, my wife will arrange and pay for the care of the children while my wife is working. 3

I want a wife who will take care of *my* physical needs. I want a wife who will keep the house clean. I want a wife who will pick up after me. I want a wife who will keep my clothes clean, ironed, mended, replaced when need be, and who will see to it that my personal things will be kept in their proper 4 place so that I can find what I need the minute I need it. I want a wife who cooks the meals, a wife who is a *good* cook. I want a wife who will plan the menus, do the necessary shopping, prepare the meals, serve them pleasantly, and then do the cleaning up while I do my studying. I want a wife who will care for me when I am sick and sympathize with my pain and loss of time from school. I want a wife to go along when our family takes a vacation so that someone can continue to care for me and my children when I need a rest and change of scene.

5   I want a wife who will not bother me with rambling complaints about a wife's duties. But I want a wife who will listen to me when I feel the need to explain a rather difficult point I have come across in my course of studies. And I want a wife who will type my papers for me when I have written them.

6   I want a wife who will take care of the details of my social life. When my wife and I are invited out by my friends, I want a wife who will take care of the babysitting arrangements. When I meet people at school that I like and want to entertain, I want a wife who will have the house clean, prepare a special meal, serve it to me and my friends, and not interrupt when I talk about the things that interest me and my friends. I want a wife who will have arranged that the children are fed and ready for bed before my guests arrive so that the children do not bother us. I want a wife who takes care of the needs of my guests so that they feel comfortable, who makes sure that they have an ashtray, that they are passed the hors d'oeuvres, that they are offered a second helping of the food, that their wine glasses are replenished when necessary, that their coffee is served to them as they like it.

7   And I want a wife who knows that sometimes I need a night out by myself.

8   I want a wife who is sensitive to my sexual needs, a wife who makes love passionately and eagerly when I feel like it, a wife who makes sure that I am satisfied. And, of course, I want a wife who will not demand sexual attention when I am not in the mood for it. I want a wife who assumes the complete responsibility for birth control, because I do not want more children. I want a wife who will remain sexually faithful to me so that I do not have to clutter up my intellectual life with jealousies. And I want a wife who understands that *my* sexual needs may entail more than strict adherence to monogamy. I must, after all, be able to relate to people as fully as possible.

9   If, by chance, I find another person more suitable as a wife than the wife I already have, I want the liberty to replace my present wife with another one. Naturally, I will expect a fresh, new life; my wife will take the children and be solely responsible for them so that I am left free.

10   When I am through with school and have a job, I want my wife to quit working and remain at home so that my wife can more fully and completely take care of a wife's duties.

11   *My God, who wouldn't want a wife?*

✦

CLASSIC IMAGES

Leonardo da Vinci, *La Gioconda (Mona Lisa)*, 1503–1505

✦

Classic Images (cont.)

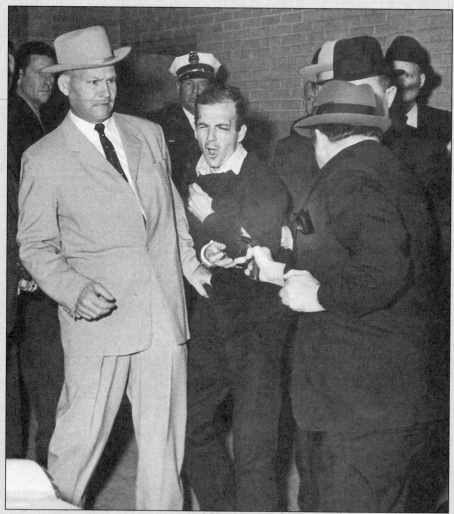

Bob Jackson, Lee Harvey Oswald being shot by Jack Ruby, 1963

Matty Zimmerman, Marilyn Monroe, 1954

✦

CLASSIC IMAGES (CONT.)

Coca-Cola

Credits

Chapter 1

Page 23: Alice Green, "Chick with the Stick." Reprinted by permission of the author.

27: Brent Staples, "Just Walk on By: A Black Man Ponders His Power to Alter Public Space" from *Ms.* magazine, 1986. Reprinted by permission of the author.

32: Lara Kate Cohen, "High School Confidential" from *Brill's Content,* June 2001. Reprinted by permission.

37: Sue Halpern, "Recipe for Change" from *Mother Jones* magazine, 2001. © 2001 by Foundation for National Progress.

42: Jack Hitt, "The Hidden Life of SUVs" from *Mother Jones* magazine, 1999. © 1999 by Foundation for National Progress.

46: Julia Cass, "The Moses Factor" from www.motherjones.com. Copyright © 2002 by Foundation for National Progress.

55: Brian Doherty, "John Ashcroft's Power Grab" from *Reason* magazine, June 2002. Copyright © 2003 by Reason Foundation, 3415 S. Sepulveda Blvd, Ste. 400, Los Angeles, CA 90034, www.reason.com. Reprinted by permission.

67: Courtesy of Texas Woman's University (photograph).

68: Ford Motor Company (advertisement), courtesy Ford Motor Co.

Chapter 2

75: Roy Fowler, "Roadblocks." Reprinted by permission of the author.

79: Maria Said, "Half-Walls between Us" from *re:generation quarterly,* Sept.–Oct. 1999. Reprinted by permission of the author.

82: John Hockenberry, "The Hockenberry File" by John Hockenberry from *We* magazine. Reprinted by permission.

85: Patricia Reynoso, "Loving Papi" from *Latina,* June 2002. Reprinted by permission.

89: Assaf Oron, "A Letter to American Jews (and Other Friends of Israel)." Reprinted by permission of the author.

95: Maya Angelou, "Momma, the Dentist, and Me" from *I Know Why the Caged Bird Sings.* Copyright © 1969 and renewed 1997 by Maya Angelou. Used by permission of Random House, Inc.

101: Cecilia Ballí, "Return to Padre." Reprinted with permission from the January 2001 issue of *Texas Monthly.*

114: *The Arnolfini Portrait,* 1434. Jan van Eyck © Archivo Iconografico, S.A./ CORBIS (painting).

115: Chevy Malibu (advertisement), used with the permission of General Motors Corp.

Chapter 3

Page 122: Marta Salazar, "Welcome to Wilderness!" Reprinted by permission of the author.

125: Patricia Brady, "The Blobs." Reprinted by permission of the author.

128: Mary Pipher, excerpt from *The Middle of Everywhere.* Copyright © 2002 by Mary Pipher. Reprinted by permission of Harcourt, Inc.

132: Aaron McCarroll Gallegos, "Singing with All the Saints" by Aaron McCarroll Gallegos. Aaron McCarroll Gallegos is a freelance writer in Toronto. This article originally appeared in *The Other Side* (300 W. Apsley, Philadelphia, PA 19144). Reprinted by permission.

136: Greg Smith, "The Body Farm" originally published in *The Oxford American.* From *Ms.* magazine, 1986. Reprinted by permission of the author.

140: Smita Madan Paul and Kiran Desai, "Sari Story" originally published in *Civilization,* October/November 1999. Reprinted by permission of West Media.

145: Bruce Barcott, "Beyond the Valley of the Dammed" reprinted from *Utne Reader,* May/June 1999. To subscribe, call 800-736-UTNE or visit www.utne.com. Reprinted by permission.

155: © Lorenzo Ciniglio/Corbis Sygma (photograph).

156: © Jennifer Brown/Corbis Sygma (photograph).

Chapter 4

163: Veronica Ashida, "Paper Mountains, Paper Valleys." Reprinted by permission of the author.

166: Leonard Felder, "Developing a Mindful Way of Eating" from *Tikkun,* vol. 17, no. 3, 2002. Used with permission.

170: Anamary Pelayo, "Hot Tempered?" from *Latina,* June 2002. Reprinted by permission.

174: Garrison Keillor, "How to Write a Personal Letter" excerpted from International Paper's *How to Use the Power of the Printed Word,* copyright © 1985. Reprinted by permission.

178: Margery Guest, "Sugaring" from *Lands' End* catalog. Reprinted by permission.

183: Michael Kernan, "Zoo Medicine" from the column "Around the Mall and Beyond" by Michael Kernan from *Smithsonian,* 1997. Reprinted by permission.

187: Jane O'Reilly, "Click! The Housewife's Moment of Truth" from *Ms.* magazine, 2002, originally 1972. Reprinted by permission.

194: © AP Photo/Tennessean, Eric Parsons (photograph).

195: Gaseous diffusion uranium enrichment process (diagram). Source: NRC. Public domain.

Chapter 5

203: Timothy Davis, "World Trade or World Charade?" Reprinted by permission of the author.

206: John M. Williams, "And Here's the Pitch" by John M. Williams from *We* magazine. Reprinted by permission.

Chapter 6

Chapter 7

Page 375: *Venus before a Mirror,* 1614–1615. Peter Paul Rubens © Erich Lessing/Art Resource NY (painting).

376: © Kevin R. Morris/CORBIS (photograph).

Chapter 9

384: DeVon Freeman, "Community College: Not Just for Dumb Kids." Reprinted by permission of the author.

387: Aurora Levins Morales, "Liberation Genealogy" from *Medicine Stories: History, Culture, and the Politics of Integrity,* 1998. Reprinted by permission of South End Press.

390: Deborah Stone, "Why We Need a Care Movement" reprinted with permission from the February 25, 2000, issue of *The Nation.*

396: Ralph Nader, "Blinded by Power" originally published in *Brill's Content,* June 2001. Reprinted by permission.

400: Newt Gingrich, "Follow the Light" originally published in *Brill's Content,* June 2001. Reprinted by permission.

404: Randall Kennedy, "You Can't Judge a Crook by His Color" by Randall Kennedy from *The New Republic,* 1999. Reprinted by permission of The New Republic (© 1999, The New Republic, Inc.).

410: Gregory Stock and Francis Fukuyama, "The Clone Wars" from *Reason Online.* Copyright © 2003 by Reason Foundation, 3415 S. Sepulveda Blvd, Ste. 400, Los Angeles, CA 90034, www.reason.com. Reprinted by permission.

422: *Guernica,* 1937. Pablo Picasso. © Superstock (painting).

423: U.S. Dept. of Agriculture Forest Service, 1942 (poster).

Chapter 10

425: Plato, "The Allegory of the Cave." Public domain.

432: Jonathan Swift, "A Modest Proposal." Public domain.

439: Thomas Jefferson, "The Declaration of Independence." Public domain.

444: Mary Wollstonecraft, "The Prevailing Opinion of a Sexual Character Discussed." Public domain.

447: Henry David Thoreau, "Where I Lived, and What I Lived For." Public domain.

452: Virginia Woolf, "The Death of the Moth" from *The Death of the Moth, and Other Essays, by Virginia Woolf.* Copyright © 1942 by Harcourt, Inc., and renewed 1970 by Marjorie T. Parsons, Executrix. Reprinted by permission of the publisher.

455: Judy Brady, "I Want a Wife" from *Ms.* magazine, 1972. Reprinted by permission.

457: *Mona Lisa,* 1503–1505. Leonardo da Vinci. © Gianni Dagli Orti/CORBIS (painting).

458: © Bob Jackson, 1963 (photograph).

459: © AP Photo/Matty Zimmerman, 1954 (photograph).

460: Coca-Cola (logo), used by permission of The Coca-Cola Company.

Index